| | HO.
| | ^S'

GW00683398

EDMOND:
OCCUPATION OF THE RHINELAND
1918-1929 .
943.4085 EDMO   23-536650

30130501637654

STAGES
OF THE
ADVANCE TO THE RHINE

HOLLAND

ESSEN

DUISBURG

DÜSSELDORF

ANTWERP

COLOGNE

BRITISH

BRUSSELS Louvain Maastricht

Audenarde

Courtrai

Ath

Hal Enghien Wavre Liège Aachen Bonn

AMERICAN FRENCH

LILLE Tournai

Orchies

St. Venceignes Charleroi Namur Meuse Spa Malmedy Montjoie Coblence

Wiesbaden FRANKFURT

Maubeuge Dinant Trois Ponts Mayence

Cambrai Aulnoye Marche Darmstadt

Busigny

R. Moselle Mannheim

Sedan LUXEMBURG

Saarbrücken

Verdun AMERICAN LORRAINE FRENCH

Metz

Toul R. Rhine Strassburg

ALSACE

R. Moselle

REFERENCE.

Frontiers	....
Armistice line	....
Line Nº 1	1
„ „ 2	2
„ „ 3	3
„ „ 4	4
„ „ 5	5
„ „ 6	the Rhine
Railways allotted to British.	

Bâle

SWITZERLAND

SCALE OF MILES.
10 5 0 10 20 30 40 50 60 70 80

Compiled in the Historical Section (Military Branch).

Ordnance Survey 1943.

Imperial War Museum

The Occupation of The Rhineland

1918-1929

Facsimile Edition with
Introduction by Dr G M Bayliss

London   Her Majesty's Stationery Office

© *Crown Copyright 1987*
First Published 1987

ISBN 0 11 290454 8

INTRODUCTION

It is rather surprising that, although the British official history of the First World War was started in 1922 and eventually finished in 1949, no accurate listing of the volumes produced is available to the historian. Her Majesty's Stationery Office's own guides have always been incomplete. For example, Sectional List no. 60 (revised 1 September 1976) did not mention the two volumes on the Gallipoli campaign but it does list *The Blockade of the Central Empires* by A C Bell (restricted at the time of its publication in 1937 and only released for general sale in 1961).[1] When the American historian Jay Luvaas contributed a chapter on 'The First British Official Historians' to Robin Higham's invaluable guide *Official Histories* the appended list of published works, supplied by the Cabinet Office Historical Section, included the Gallipoli volumes and Professor Bell's work.[2] However, like HMSO's sectional list, it missed the twelve volume history of the Ministry of Munitions and two other 'mysterious' official histories which were never put on public sale. Finally, even S S Wilson in his resumé of the work of the Cabinet Office Historical Section, while mentioning the Ministry of Munitions history, still did not refer to the two mystery volumes.[3] Although Wilson's list was yet again provided by the Cabinet Office Historical Section itself, he did have access to the relevant files at the Public Record Office which should have revealed a more comprehensive picture.[4] HMSO had actually printed (but were not allowed to publish) a detailed history of the campaign in Persia and a shorter account of the post-war occupation of the Rhineland.

Brigadier-General James Edmonds, as editor of the British official history series,[5] first proposed in 1930 that an account of the British Army on the Rhine should be published but the Treasury was not prepared to sanction it. It was hoped at this stage that the War Office could be persuaded to finance it. Nevertheless, Edmonds began to gather information from the various officers who had been in command of the British Army on the Rhine and their staffs. He also took steps to ensure that all relevant official records were safely collected and stored. However. Treasury economy was to continue to hamper the activities of the Historical Section and, in its inter-war reports, Edmonds complained bitterly about his small poorly paid staff and the comparative affluence of the French Service Historique and the German Reicharchiv. By the outbreak of the Second World War, Edmonds was sadly demoralised on account of poor accommodation, lack of staff promotions and a general feeling that research had to be undertaken on a shoestring, unworthy of what he always saw as 'a National Memorial'.[6]

Just before the outbreak of the Second World War, Edmonds was forced to become the Secretary as well as the Head of the Historical Section when Colonel E Y Daniel resigned. On 15 November 1939, the Section was moved to St. Anne's-on-Sea in Lancashire. From there it subsequently transferred to the National Library of Wales at Aberystwyth in April 1942.[7] In February 1942 the War Cabinet Committee for the Control of Official Histories decided that Edmonds should be allowed to proceed with the history of the Rhineland occupation. The President of the Board of Education, R A Butler, in the chair, believed that: 'When the Armistice and disarmament terms came to be considered such a study would have great value as an historical background, and would certainly be demanded.'[8] The usual utility criterion clearly applied but, doubtless, a secondary reason was to keep Edmonds himself happy and gainfully employed since he had been excluded from the writing of the Second World War histories. The Brigadier-General was personally very keen to compile what he regarded as the final volume of his Western Front campaign history. On 26 September 1942, he wrote to Sir Charles Fergusson: 'It has been decided to have an account of the occupation of the Rhineland· (I hope for use as a precedent),' adding that the long delay since 1930 in starting was due to 'Treasury parsimony.'[9]

Edmonds felt particularly well-qualified to write this narrative since he had visited the Rhineland during the occupation period and had special knowledge of the legal aspects of a military government from his earlier collaboration with Professor L Oppenheim on *The Laws and Usages of War*. His other great advantage was that he was on friendly terms with many of the British army personnel involved. On the negative side, however, he was handicapped by the fact that many of the official records had recently been destroyed in a Blitz fire at Walworth in 1942. Although at Aberystwyth he had 'plenty of food, a perfect library . . . a good billet, sea air and no complaints',[10] he was undoubtedly hindered by his remoteness from

London and its relevant libraries and a lack of research staff. His difficulties are evidenced in correspondence he conducted with the Director of the Imperial War Museum at the time pleading for bibliographical assistance. The Museum was unable to be of much help; many of its books were inaccessible having been moved to Barnstaple in Devon where they were 'being cared for by strangers' and its coverage of the occupation and of the inter-war period generally was 'not very strong' because of lack of funds.[11] Anyway, Edmonds proceeded in his usual diligent manner to approach leading participants in the British military administration of the Rhineland. It is worth quoting from some of the replies he received to show how discreet Edmonds continued to be with the confidences so freely bestowed upon him. Sir Charles Fergusson readily admitted that although he got on well with Plumer, he 'did not hit it off with "Willie" and that was how I came to resign,'[12] Field Marshal Sir Archibald Montgomery Massingberd accused Fergusson of being 'pro-German', of 'protecting the underdog . . . a not uncommon British trait'. The Field Marshal recalled telling Plumer at the time that Fergusson was 'too much of a gentleman for that job'. Plumer's response was to ask Massingberd if it was possible to be 'too much of a gentleman', to which the non-plussed Massingberd replied in the negative. In retrospect, he wished he had responded with the following statement:

> Yes, you can when you are fighting against animals like the Boche and the Japs [real hindsight!] . . . When you are fighting for your life against that kind of wild animal it is no good sticking to Queensberry Rules. You have to fight him as if he was a man eating Tiger or hunting Bull Elephant.

Massingberd also felt that Field Marshal William Robertson was not the man he had been and had become too 'fussy'.[13]

In his background research, Edmonds was hampered by his lack of access to German source material which he had used so extensively in earlier volumes of the campaign histories. The prevailing financial stringency also dictated that he was only allowed one galley proof and one page proof. In October 1943, he complained that 'speed and economy' were his orders and that 'the respect for military history in this country seems small.' He hoped that his work would have an educational value lest British forces again be called upon to occupy foreign territory. His conclusion was that 'the quick change of the German attitude from one of humble subservience to pre-war arrogance, and the call for the strictest economy regardless of the military

situation may be said to be the keynotes of the story of the occupation.'[14] Clearly, it was expecting a lot of a man of Edmonds's
background to produce an impartial history of an essentially political
event like the military occupation of the Rhineland at a time when
Britain was engaged in a life and death struggle with the same
enemy. The result was perhaps inevitable: the completed manuscript
was not good history. Even his friend Sir Alexander Godley advised
Edmonds: 'This is all right I think on the whole, though it doesn't
all read quite as easily or charmingly as most of what you have
produced.'[15] Others were to be far less kind in their judgements.

Edmonds's draft version was submitted to both the War Office
and the Foreign Office for comment. Brigadier W L Van Cutsen, on
behalf of the War Office, felt that the history should have 'been
conceived on a broader basis, at the expense of omitting possibly
various administrative and other minor details which are included
at some length.' Nevertheless, he did concede that the chapter on
the operations of the British Upper Silesia Force (ie Chapter XIV)
was particularly useful.[16] However, it was from the Foreign Office
that the most severe condemnation was forthcoming. Their official
response came in a memorandum, dated 3 January 1944, written on
behalf of the Secretary of State for Foreign Affairs, Anthony Eden.
It addressed itself to 'the incidental political references which are
the primary concern of the Foreign Office'. It concluded that:

> The present text is often misleading and in any case could not be
> complete without the introduction of a great deal of controversial
> material which would hamper rather than improve the military nar-
> rative. Mr Eden inclines to the view that the practical usefulness of the
> work would be increased if the political references could be reduced
> merely to the mention of facts and dates.

Detailed examples of Edmonds's bluntness were provided.
Schleicher should not be described as 'murdered by Hitler' but more
diplomatically as 'murdered in the purge of the 30th June, 1934'
(see page 35). Unemployment pay should not be referred to in an
official publication as 'the dole', thus implying that the British Army
of 1914 was composed of men 'who had enlisted as an alternative to
starvation' (see page 168). It was pointed out that Lloyd George
might be offended by being described as 'less well disposed' to
Germany than Bonar Law. The references to the former British
Ambassador Viscount D'Abernon as being 'pro-German' had to be
cut out. Other Foreign Office sensitivities included Edmonds's dismissal of the Dawes and Young reparation plans and the Locarno

Pact; it was 'most improper for an official historian to describe a treaty concluded by His Majesty's Government as "verbiage".'[17]

Confronted by this welter of criticism, Sir James rejoined that: 'The FO remarks are trifling or silly and I propose to ignore them,' except for the D'Abernon request. He emphasised that the views expressed were his own and were not 'official'. He pleaded that 'the war histories should be written from an unbiased standpoint and not from the point of view of the Admiralty, War Office or Foreign Office.' His volume was 'based on official documents' and he was prepared to stand by his personal interpretation of events such as his comment (page 245) that the fall of the mark was 'a great time for the British Army', adding that:

> The hired commentator does not like it because many Germans were ruined. I propose to leave it.[18]

In this specific defence of his text he was to be successful; nevertheless, the 'hired commentator' at the Foreign Office was in all other respects to be victorious. In May 1944 Edmonds wrote that he saw no point in 'trying to conceal our sometimes high-handed, sometimes over-kind ways' because the Germans had ready access to 'all the Allied decrees and actions, and the strange behaviour of the Rhineland High Commission carefully recorded'. He concluded his letter with a warning:

> I hope that the aesthetic pro-German at the Foreign Office who looked over the proofs is not meddling again. I have found out who it was.[19]

The 'aesthete' or 'hired commentator' in question was actually Charles Webster, later to be knighted, a distinguished diplomatic historian destined to be joint author of the British official history of the strategic bombing of Germany during the Second World War.[20] At the time Webster was employed in the Economic and Reconstruction Department of the Foreign Office. As part of the forward planning for another occupation of Germany, Webster had submitted several secret memoranda analysing the German Armistice period and the subsequent military occupation. When one of these papers was given to Edmonds for comment he was understandably highly critical and, in a letter to Webster, he defended his old commander Haig once more. In a double-edged conclusion, he added 'I see as ever that it is nearly impossible for the peace trained civilian (eg Curzon, Milner, Balfour, Lloyd George and Co.) to see the stark facts as soldiers who have seen war can do – and so we have more wars.'[21] It is evident from the contemporary records that Edmonds did not have much opportunity to confront his critics directly because there were too many official buffers in the way, anxious to avoid bruising his feelings. Although he was unaware of it, he had two critics at the Foreign Office: Webster was aided by another reputable diplomatic historian Llewellyn Woodward. They were united in their belief that it was a poor history. Webster thought it was 'too episodic', that the chronology of events was 'slurred over', that 'the feeding of the occupied territory, a highly controversial question', was 'misleading' and that the critique of the civilian authorities was 'not supported by the evidence' and was 'dogmatic and prejudiced'. Woodward was less severe than Webster and he pleaded with him to be more compassionate:

> I'm inclined to say now that if Edmonds has set his heart on it – we might give our *Nihil Obstat* to publication. The 'feel' of the book is hopelessly amateur. The bibliography would plough an MA thesis. [22]

Llewellyn Woodward had a kindly disposition, admitting that he was moved by the fact that 'Edmonds is old, eminent and charming – Well there it is'. [23] Charles Webster was temperamentally more severe; the book was not analytical and he refused to spend more time on it even if Edmonds was 'sorely hurt'. In the end it was left to R A Butler, as Chairman of the Committee on the Control of Official Histories, to turn it down for publication. Webster had pointed out that it was sometimes 'rude' to the French and he warned that at the end of the present war 'it was most important that German propaganda should not have at its disposal an Official History of this kind.' Indeed, when the question of publication was revived in 1949, it was felt that the fact that Germany was occupied again only raised 'further objections'. [24]

In spite of Edmonds's resistance, the decision was taken at the end of July 1944 that only a hundred copies of the official history should be printed for 'Office use' only. Many of the Foreign Office demands had to be met even to achieve this modest result. Amongst his Pyrrhic victories was the retention in a footnote (*see* page 114) of Emil Ludwig's quotation on the German character, his use of which Webster constantly cited as proof in 'itself' that the general's 'political judgement' was 'inadequate to his task'. Even the compiler's preface was to be drastically amended despite his simple protest that 'I had never had anyone's approval of my Prefaces.'

In summary, the compilation of the Rhineland history was started back in 1930, resumed in September 1942 and had its first draft completed in July 1943. A final version was prepared for press in

October 1943 and it was ready to print in May 1944. The order to print was not given until 31 July 1944 and eventually it was published in a limited official edition in December of that year.[26] HMSO undertook the printing since there was clearly no opportunity for the commercial firm of Macmillan, who had published earlier volumes, to profit from its production. Only one hundred copies were printed and distributed.[27] Amongst the fortunate recipients was the Director of the Imperial War Museum who had requested a copy on 28 March 1945. Subsequently, Edmonds tried unsuccessfully to have this small edition made public but in November 1947 HMSO were authorised to destroy the type of the book.[28] It was not until the relaxation of the Thirty Year rule on access to public records that the general public were allowed to scrutinise the surviving copies, several more of which have now found their way to the library of the Imperial War Museum.

The production of the Rhineland volume inevitably raised grave doubts about Edmonds's suitability to edit the remaining volumes of the official history. However, in view of the fact that it was considered 'a little outside of his normal beat', he was allowed to continue. He later produced a short multigraphed draft account of the occupation of Constantinople, saw the concluding volumes of the Western Front history through to publication and, finally, he retired as Head of the Historical Section in July 1949 just before a separate volume on the Italian campaign was printed, thus terminating a task begun thirty years earlier. To his chagrin, Edmonds saw the War Office order more than 800 copies of Brigadier-General J H Morgan's story of the occupation period entitled *Assize of Arms*, when it was published in 1946, and which he judged to be 'far more outspoken' than his own official work. He was also embittered by the publicity given to W K Hancock's and Margaret Gowlings's official account of the British economy in the Second World War 'an expense never permitted to the Military History 1914–1918!'[29]

Endnotes

1) *Histories of the First and Second World War and Peacetime Series* (London: HMSO, 1976) (Sectional List 60). The London firm of Heinemann actually published the Gallipoli volumes which accounts for their omission.

2) Robin Higham (ed.), *Official Histories: Essays and Bibliographies from Around the World* (Manhattan, Kansas: Kansas State University Press, 1970), pp 488–502.

3) S S Wilson, *The Cabinet Office to 1945* (London: HMSO, 1975).

4) This detailed account of the suppression of *The Occupation of the Rhineland* is based essentially on documents held at the Public Record Office and the private papers of Sir James Edmonds deposited in the Liddell Hart Centre for Military Archives, King's College, London. Edmonds's restricted volume did not remain totally obscure, for instance it was cited by J Gaston in an article on the Rhineland occupation in *History Today*, vol. XI, no. 7, July 1961, pp 479–489.

5) Brigadier-General Sir James Edward Edmonds CB CMG D Litt was born on 25 December 1861 and after a long career in the army became Head of the Historical Section of the Committee of Imperial Defence in 1919. Before he retired from that position in 1949 he edited all, and personally compiled several of the British official histories of the Great War. For biographical information on Edmonds, see *The Times*, 9 August 1956; *The Dictionary of National Biography 1951–1960*. (London: Oxford University Press, 1971); and the *Royal Engineers Journal*, vol. LXX, no. 4, December 1956, pp 395–398. For his editorship of the official histories, see his article in the *Army Quarterly*, vol. 64, no. 2, July 1952, pp 196–205; see also David French, 'Official but not History? : Sir James Edmonds and the Official History of the Great War' in the *Journal of the RUSI*, vol. 131, no. 1, March 1986, pp 58–63, and Tim Travers, 'The Hidden Army : Structural Problems in the British Officer Corps 1900–1918' in the *Journal of Contemporary History*, vol. 17, 1982, pp 523–544.

6) PRO CAB 15/52, Minutes and memoranda of the Committee of the Historical Section 1923–1939, particularly the Secretary's annual reports on the work of the Section.

7) This account is based on CAB 98/7–12, Minutes and memoranda of the Committee of the Historical Section 1940–1945; CAB 45/81–82, Comments and correspondence 1930, 1942–1944, 1943–1957; CAB 103/1–148, Progress reports, estimates and correspondence of the Historical Section.

8) CAB 98/9, 20th Meeting of the War Cabinet Committee for the Control of Official Histories, 26/2/1942.

9) CAB 45/81, Edmonds to Sir Charles Fergusson, 26/9/1942.

10) *Ibid*, Edmonds to General Sir Richard Hankey, 10/3/1943.

11) Imperial War Museum, Department of Printed Books files. Correspondence between Edmonds and L R Bradley, then Director, January 1943.

OCCUPATION OF THE RHINELAND

12) CAB 45/81, Fergusson to Edmonds, 3/10/1942.

13) *Ibid*, Massingberd to Edmonds, 23/1/1943.

14) CAB 45/82, Draft preface to *The Occupation of the Rhineland*, dated September 1943. The original preface was considerably censored because of Edmonds's complaints about the ill-treatment of the Historical Section.

15) CAB 45/81, Godley to Edmonds, 25/7/1943.

16) CAB 45/82, Van Cutsen to Charles Webster, 6/12/1943.

17) CAB 45/81, J F French to Edmonds, 3/1/1944.

18) *Ibid*, Edmonds to Sir Edward Bridges, 24/7/1944. Bridges was the Permanent Secretary of the Cabinet Office and Secretary of the War Cabinet.

19) *Ibid*, Edmonds to Bridges, 19/5/1944.

20) For Webster, see P A Reynolds and E J Hughes, *The Historian as Diplomat : Charles Kingsley Webster and the United Nations 1939–1946* (London: Martin Robertson, 1976).

21) CAB 45/82, memorandum by Edmonds, 22/9/1943 and his letter to Webster 22/9/1943 in CAB 45/81.

22) CAB 45/82, Woodward to Webster, 29/3/1944. There are helpful bibliographies on the Rhineland occupation period in Keith L Nelson, *Victors Divided : America and the Allies in Germany, 1918–1923* (Berkeley, California: University of California Press, 1975) and in Ernst Fraenkel, *Military Occupation and the Rule of Law : Occupation Government in the Rhineland, 1918–1923* (London: Oxford University Press, 1944).

23) *Ibid*, Woodward to Bridges, 10/5/1944.

24) *Ibid*, A B Acheson to J W Nicholls [Foreign Office], 9/3/1949 and Webster's minute dated 19/7/1944.

25) *Ibid*, Edmonds to Bridges, 28/10/1943.

26) CAB 98/12, Committee for the Control of Official Histories, C O H (45) 3, 13/3/1945. Report by Edmonds on work of the Historical Section for 1944.

27) A copy of the distribution list is in CAB 45/82; it shows that many of the recipients were involved in the post-war Allied occupation of Germany. It is worth observing that the appointed publishers of the British official history of the First World War, the firm of Macmillan, had to be heavily subsidised in order to make a profit out of the operation. The cost of the expensive map volumes was borne by HMSO and the limited circulation volumes were always printed by them. In the inter-war period several attempts were made to take the contract away from Macmillan so that the price per volume for young officers could be reduced. Macmillan, doubtless for prestige reasons, resisted this pressure. Harold Macmillan even wrote a personal letter to Edmonds on 8 September 1939 pleading that his company should be allowed to publish any official history of the war that had just broken out, adding, 'I wish that one could hope for it to be limited to a single volume and not have to record the sacrifices of several years' [CAB 103/53, Edmonds's personal

correspondence 1939–1946]. In his memoirs, Edmonds complained that the printing of the official histories was delayed still further when HMSO took over from Macmillan in 1942; the 'nationalised' volumes being considerably more expensive than the privatised (albeit subsidised) version. See Edmonds Papers, File 111/16, Memoirs, chapter XXXII and File VII/II, Experiences gained in compiling the official histories of 1914–1918.

28) CAB 45/81, Edmonds to Sir Gilbert Laithwaite, 25/8/1945. Edmonds complained that it was to protect the historians from interference by departments such as the Admiralty, War Office and Foreign Office that the Historical Section had been placed under the Committee of Imperial Defence.

29) CAB 103/111, Official History 1914–1918, Progress reports. The book referred to by J H Morgan was published by Methuen in London in 1945. Morgan's introduction, pp XIV–XV, contains an interesting reference to Edmonds 'the greatest military historian of our time'.

iii

PREFACE

This volume contains a military account of the 11-year occupation of the Rhineland by British forces and of matters which affected their sojourn and well-being. It continues the history of the War of 1914–18 on the Western Front,[1] taking up the narrative at 11 a.m. on the eleventh day of the eleventh month, the moment at which the Armistice of Réthondes became effective on land, and concludes with the withdrawal of the British Army of Occupation in December, 1929. Any opinions expressed in it are those of the Compiler and are not official.

The task of compiling a history of the occupation did not turn out to be as simple an affair as had been expected. The General Staff of the Army of the Rhine ceased to keep a diary after September, 1922, and for some months before that date the entries had been meagre. Worse than this, nearly all the office files of the Army of the Rhine, including all the reports of the Military Governor of the Cologne area, had been burnt in a fire caused by enemy action in a building in the outskirts of London, where these and other records had been sent from the War Office for safety. Most of the financial records were similarly destroyed in a northern town. The War Office copies of the correspondence with the Army of the Rhine had to be found and searched ; fortunately the places where they were stored had not been interfered with.

I had the advantage of having visited both Cologne and Wiesbaden towards the beginning and end of the occupation, and having written earlier on the subject of military occupation[2] had followed the events of the occupation with interest.

Fortunately, too, in 1930 I had appealed to the officers who had been Commanders-in-Chief of the Army of the Rhine, all of whom except Sir Thomas Morland were then alive, and to others who had served in it, and obtained a good deal of information. Nor was this, as will be seen, the only help which they gave. Many printed official documents were available : the State Papers containing the various armistices, treaties,

---

[1] The volumes dealing with the operations on the Western Front, 8th August to 11th November, 1918, have been written, but will not be published until the end of the present war.

[2] In the official pamphlet " The Laws and Usages of War," reprinted in the " Manual of Military Law " 1914, by Colonel J. E. Edmonds and the late Professor L. Oppenheim, Whewell Professor of International Law in the University of Cambridge.

agreements, reports and correspondence, including some letters of the Conference of Ambassadors in Paris ; the " *Rapport Final. État-Major*-1re *Section* " of the Inter-Allied Military Mission of Control in Germany, of over 500 pages ; the Official Gazette in four volumes of the Inter-Allied Rhineland High Commission ; and the German documents in relation to the Armistice and its prolongation in three volumes. A list of the principal non-official books on the subject including some German accounts is given separately ; the most notable of them are by Monsieur Paul Tirard, the President of the Inter-Allied Rhineland High Commission, and Major General H. T. Allen, commanding the American Army of Occupation. Among typewritten official records must be mentioned the despatches of the Chief of Mission (General Sir Richard Haking) of the Inter-Allied Armistice Commission, in 33 volumes, a most complete account of the work of that body ; and four volumes of official reports made by the General Staff of the American Army of Occupation.[1]

I have specially to thank Sir Henry MacGeagh, K.C., Judge-Advocate-General, for a paper on legal matters and crime ; Mr. S. D. Waley, Under-Secretary of the Treasury, as regards the financial side of the occupation ; and Captain A. S. Dewar, R.N., and Commander J. H. Lhoyd-Owen, R.N. of the Admiralty for details about the Rhine Flotilla.

For loan of papers and for revising, criticising and making additions to my T.S. chapters, I have to thank many officers, in particular General Sir Aylmer Haldane, commander of the VI Corps in the occupation of the Rhineland ; the three surviving Commanders-in-Chief of the British Army of the Rhine, in order of command, Generals Sir Alexander Godley, Sir John Du Cane and Sir William Thwaites ; Major-General Sir Evan Gibb, who served with the " Clearing Up Army " and was the last commander of the British Forces in France and Belgium ; General Sir Richard Haking and Major-General G. H. Addison, who served on the Armistice Commission ; Major-General Sir Neil Malcolm of the British Military Mission in Berlin ; Major-General Sir Sydney Clive, Military Governor ; of Cologne, after being Staff Officer to the first Military Governor; and some of the Staff Officers of the Army of the Rhine, particularly Major-General C. G. Fuller, Brigadier General E. D. Young and Colonel A. H. Hutton-Wilson. For contributions to the chapters on the Silesian excursion I have to thank

---

[1] See " List of Books."

Mr. F. B. Bourdillon of the Foreign Office, Major-General G. I. Gartlan, Brigadier General H. B. P. L. Kennedy and Colonel Sir Harold Percival (the British Commissioner). Mr. W. Y. Baldry (Librarian and Archivist) and Mr. W. H. Davison of the War Office have kindly helped me in clearing up various points.

In dealing with the huge mass of written and printed material I have had the assistance of Lieut.-Colonel R. Maxwell-Hyslop, who investigated the earlier war diaries up to the formation of the Army of the Rhine and the papers at the Foreign Office and made suitable extracts; and of Captain Wilfrid Miles who tackled two War Office document dumps and extracted relevant matter. As we have worked together for many years both these officers knew exactly what I wanted and saved me an immense amount of time.

I owe much to Major C. M. Kohan and to Mr. W. B. Wood, who read the whole of the text and made a large number of useful suggestions; to my old assistant Mr. H. Burge, who drew the sketch maps from my rough drafts; and last but not least to Mr. A. W. Tarsey, who has helped me with every volume of the Official History which I have written, watched each chapter, kept up to date a second copy of the T.S., which it was judged advisable to make, by inserting additions and corrections, and checked the many details in the text before it went to Press.

In this as in other volumes many actors have been consulted, but all officers interested may not have seen the draft or proofs. I beg, therefore, that any corrections or additions and criticisms thought necessary may be sent to the Secretary of the Historical Section, c/o Secretary of the War Cabinet, Great George Street, S.W.1.

September, 1943.

J. E. E.

NOTE

The word " Allies " is used throughout to mean the Allies during the War of 1914–18, including the U.S.A., although officially the Americans were only an " associated " Power, and the Alliance came to an end on the ratification of the Peace Treaty.

The spellings Cologne, Mayence and Coblence have been used instead of the German Köln, Mainz and Koblenz ; but Aachen (Aix la Chapelle) is employed because the British Army called it by that name.

The usual abbreviations of regimental names have been used : for example 8/Somerset L.I. for the 8th Battalion The Somerset Light Infantry (Prince Albert's) ; K.O.Y.L.I. for the " King's Own Yorkshire Light Infantry," and " Royal " has been usually written " R."

The abbreviations employed are " B.A.R." for " British Army of the Rhine," a shortening, alternatively with " B.A.O.R.", actually used by the Army ; and " G.H.Q." for " General Head-Quarters."

The exact title of the Commander of the B.A.R. was " General Officer Commanding-in-Chief," officially abbreviated to " G.O.C.-in-C.", but " C.-in-C.", the name by which he was called by the troops, is used in the text.

The End Paper, though entitled " British Occupied Area of the Rhineland 1918," is intended to be used as a general map.

Owing to printing restrictions, the usual marginal references to the sketch maps had to be omitted, and have been replaced by footnotes.

The chapter contents are given at the beginning of the volume and not at the head of each chapter.

CONTENTS

CONTENTS

CONTENTS

CONTENTS

CONTENTS

CHAPTER XIX

LIEUT.-GENERAL SIR J. DU CANE'S COMMAND (*concluded*)
1926

THE PRELIMINARIES OF THE MOVE TO WIESBADEN

CHAPTER XX

LIEUT.-GENERAL SIR WILLIAM THWAITES'S COMMAND
1927–1929 TO THE EVACUATION

CHAPTER XXI

THE FINAL EVACUATION

TABLE OF APPENDICES

TABLE OF APPENDICES

SKETCHES

(Bound in Volume)

LIST OF BOOKS, Etc.,

TO WHICH MOST FREQUENT REFERENCE IS MADE

ALLEN I : " The Rhineland Occupation." By Major-General H. T. Allen, U.S. Army. (Indianapolis : The Bobbs-Merrill Co.)

General Allen commanded the American Army of Occupation from 8th July, 1919, until that Army left the Rhine, and from 21st May, 1920, was American observer on the Rhineland High Commission. His book is a popular account of the early days of the Occupation.

ALLEN II : " My Rhineland Journal." By Major-General H. T. Allen. (Hutchinson.)

A very full diary from 27th June, 1919, to 19th February, 1923. Useful for the dates of occurrences. Contains a photograph of the last session of the High Commission in which the American observer participated, with 15 members seated.

AMERICAN OCCUPATION : " American Military Government of Occupied Germany, 1918–20. Report of the Office in Charge of Civil Affairs, Third Army and American Forces in Germany."

This multigraphed report is in the Library, U.S. Office of War Information, American Embassy, London, England.

AMERICAN SUMMARY : " American Representation in Occupied Germany." Three volumes. Compiled by the Assistant Chief of Staff (G.2), American Forces in Germany.

This multigraphed report is in the Library, U.S. Office of War Information, American Embassy, London, England.

APEX : " Uneasy Triangle. Four Years of the Occupation." By " Apex." (John Murray.)

A good account of the period 1923–27 of Army life on the Rhine, particularly as regards relations with the Germans, by an anonymous officer who was a regimental officer in Cologne and a member of the Civil Affairs Branch of the General Staff at Wiesbaden.

BROCKHAUS : " Der grosse Brockhaus." (Brockhaus, Leipzig.) In 20 volumes.

This is the *Encyclopædia Germanica*, an expansion of the well-known " *Konversationslexikon*." It was found useful for statistics and administrative, legal, historical and biographical matters. [Note the Germans write " *Das* Haus " (neuter), but " *Der* grosse Brockhaus " (masculine).]

DAWES : " A Journal of Reparations." By Charles G. Dawes. (Macmillan.)

The author, known to us as General Dawes, was Chairman, First Committee of Experts, Reparations Commission. A personal account of the meetings which led to the " Dawes Plan," with text of the report.

D'ABERNON : " An Ambassador of Peace." By Viscount d'Abernon. (Hodder & Stoughton.)

This is a diary of the author's life as first British Ambassador in Berlin after the War, from 1920 to 1926. Footnotes on the personalities mentioned are useful.

GUHR : " Sieben Jahre Interalliierte Militär-Kontrolle." By General-major Hans Guhr. (Breslau : G. Korn.)

The author was head, in Breslau, of the German liaison staff of the Commission of Control. An unashamed account of how the Germans tricked the representatives of the Commission.

KRIEGSBRAUCH : " Kriegsbrauch im Landkriege " [1902].

A German General Staff manual on the Laws and Usages of War. Translated as " The German War Book." (John Murray.)

M.W.B. : The military journal *Militär Wochenblatt*, defunct since 1st January, 1943.

PLUMER : " Plumer of Messines." By General Sir C. Harington. (John Murray.)

It gives an account of his period of command on the Rhine.

PURLITZ : " Vom Waffenstillstand zum Frieden von Versailles. Oktober 1918—Juni 1919." Edited by Dr. Friedrich Purlitz. (Leipzig : Meiner.)

A valuable collection of 700 pages of documents, mostly German, many not available elsewhere.

ROBERTSON : " From Private to Field-Marshal." By Field-Marshal Sir William Robertson. (Constable.)

It gives an account of his period of command on the Rhine.

ROQUES : " Le Contrôle Militaire Interallié en Allemagne. Septembre 1919—Janvier 1927." By Paul Roques. (Paris : Berger-Levrault.)

The author was a member of the Commission of Control in Berlin for six years, and his book is a good summary of the operations and difficulties of the Commission with more atmosphere than the official report.

STRESEMANN : " Stresemann. Vermächtnis." Edited by H. Barnhard. (Berlin : Ullstein.)

Material for Stresemann's autobiography from 1923 to the end, with many documents, in 3 volumes.

TIRARD : " La France sur le Rhin." By Paul Tirard. (Paris : Plon.)

The author was president of the Rhineland High Commission. His book gives a full account of the occupation, mainly from the political, economic and juridical points of view, laying stress on the efforts made to introduce French culture.

TUOHY : " Occupied 1918–30. A Postcript to the Western Front." By Ferdinand Tuohy. (Thornton, Butterworth.)

An excellent account of Army life on the Rhine by a journalist.

WOCHENDORF : " Zehn Jahre Fremdherrschaft am deutschen Rhein." By Karl Wochendorf-Berlin. (Berlin : Hobbing.)

This is a partisan history of the Rhineland Occupation, holding up the action of the Allies, and particularly that of the Rhineland High Commission, to the approbrium of the German people, but useful for the documents it quotes and its lengthy bibliography.

CALENDAR OF PRINCIPAL EVENTS

1918
November
11th	Armistice Signed.
15th	Inter-Allied Armistice Commission assembles at Spa.
17th	Second and Fourth Armies begin march to the German frontier.
24th	Leading troops reach German frontier.

December
1st	Second Army under General Sir Herbert Plumer enters Germany.
5th	Spartacist troubles in Berlin. Guard Corps arrest Executive Council. President Ebert refuses to be dictator.
9th	Cavalry reaches the Rhine.
11th	Lieut.-General Sir Charles Fergusson, Military Governor, reaches Cologne and hoists Union Jack.
12th	Cavalry cross Rhine and begin occupation of the Cologne Bridgehead.
	German Government sanction creation of civil guards.
13th	Infantry complete occupation of Cologne Bridgehead.
18th	First Prolongation of the Armistice.
22nd	Civil commission to advise the Generalissimo on the administration of the Rhineland assembles at Luxembourg.

1919
January
15th	Liebknecht and Rosa Luxemburg (Spartacists) murdered in Berlin.
16th	Second Prolongation of the Armistice.
18th	Peace Conference meets in Paris.
19th	Election of German National Assembly.

February
13th	Scheidemann becomes Chancellor.
17th	Third, and final, Prolongation of the Armistice.
21st	Bavarian President, Eisner, shot.

March
6th	German Imperial Army dissolved. Provisional *Reichsheer* (about 400,000) decreed.
13th	Allies agree to supply Germany with 300,000 tons of cereals and 70,000 tons of fat per month.
18th	Allied Commission for regulation of Rhine traffic appointed.

April
2nd	Second Army redesignated Rhine Army of Occupation.
12th–14th	Spartacist rising in Düsseldorf suppressed.
22nd	General Sir H. Plumer hands over command to General Sir W. Robertson.

June

1st   First proclamation of the Rhineland Republic posted in the French Zone.

21st   Bauer becomes Chancellor.

23rd   German warships scuppered at Scapa Flow.

28th   Peace terms signed by Germany.

July

12th   Naval blockade of Germany relaxed.

18th   Work of British Section of the Armistice Commission reported complete.

August

Reichstreuhandgesellschaft takes over sale of German military material belonging to the Allies.

October

1st   General von Seeckt becomes chief of the Army Directorate (see 8th October, 1926). *Wehrkreise* formed.

December

1st   Supreme War Council invites Germany to cut down police.

1920

January

10th   Ratification of Peace Treaty signed by the Allies (not by U.S.A.).
Inter-Allied Rhineland High Commission inaugurated.
League of Nations comes into legal existence.

19th   M. Millerand succeeds M. Clemenceau as *Président du Conseil*.

24th   Armistice Commission dissolved.

26th   Inter-Allied Rhineland High Commission demands suppression of civil guards.

February

26th   Governing Commission of the Saar Territory inaugurated.

March

3rd   Lieut.-General Sir T. Morland succeeds General Sir W. Robertson in command of the British Army of the Rhine.

13th   Kapp putsch reaches Berlin. Strikes begin.

19th   Kapp putsch fails.
Revolutionary movement in the Ruhr.

27th   Müller becomes Chancellor.

April

1st   *Reichswehr* (now reduced to about 200,000) troops enter the Ruhr to restore order.

4th   The French occupy Frankfort, Darmstadt and Hanau.

10th   Red Army in Ruhr dispersed.

18th–26th   San Remo Conference of Supreme War Council.

May

17th   The French evacuate Frankfort and the other occupied towns.

June
  6th   General Election in Germany. Democratic vote sinks.
  11th   Allenstein plebiscite.
  21st   Fehrenbach becomes Chancellor.
  22nd   Boulogne Note consents to the increase of local police,
             but " *Sipo* " to be dissolved.

July
  5th   Spa Conference on the German failure to disarm.
  9th   Germans sign the disarmament conditions of Spa
             Conference.
  31st   German law fixes *Reichsheer* at 100,000.

September
  7th   Conference of Ambassadors forbids militia in East
             Prussia.
  24th   M. Leyges becomes *Président du Conseil*.

October
  12th   Inter-Allied Rhineland High Commission demands strict
             suppression of any remaining civil guards.

November
  2nd   Harding (Republican) elected to succeed President
             Wilson (Democrat). He is opposed to a League of
             Nations.

December
  31st   *Reichsheer* reported to be reduced to 100,000.
             Maréchal Foch reports Germany is evading disarmament.
             The mark at 200 to the £.

1921
January
  16th   M. Briand becomes *Président du Conseil*.
  24th   Paris Conference formulates plan for German reparation
             payment.
  29th   Paris Note demands reduction of police, suppression of
             civil guard and imposes disarmament conditions.

February
  21st   London Conference on Upper Silesia plebiscite.

March
  1st   Warren Gamaliel Harding succeeds Woodrow Wilson as
             President, U.S.A.
             London Conference rejects Germany's counter-proposals
             on disarmament and gives four days' grace.
  8th   Düsseldorf, Duisburg and Ruhrort occupied by the
             Allies as sanction.
  20th   Upper Silesia plebiscite.
             Customs barrier imposed on Rhineland as sanction.
  22nd   German Government order suppression of civil guards—
             without effect.
  23rd   German law (*Reichswehrgesetz*) abolishes obligatory
             service and settles organization of New Army.

May

5th   Supreme Council's London Ultimatum presented to Germany, giving her until 12th to fulfil Peace Treaty, with threat of occupation of Ruhr.

Bavarian " Orgesch " disarmed and disbanded.

10th   Wirth becomes Chancellor.

Reichstag accepts Allies' terms, with reservations.

24th   *Reichstag* decree approves of military associations.

27th   British troops arrive in Upper Silesia to restore order.

June

Trial of War Criminals at Leipzig.

August

25th   United States of America sign separate peace with Germany.

Erzberger murdered.

31st   Germany pay first milliard gold marks.

November

11th   U.S.A. ratify separate peace treaty with Germany.

December

31st   Mark at 1/45th par value.

1922

January

13th   Reparation Commission grants Germany temporary moratorium.

15th   M. Poincaré becomes *Président du Conseil*.

March

8th   Lieut.-General Sir A. Godley succeeds Lieut.-General Sir T. Morland in command of the British Army of the Rhine.

April

16th   Germany makes political and economic agreement with Soviet.

June

24th   Herr Rathenau (Foreign Affairs) murdered.

July

17th   Part of Silesia transferred to Poland.

August

7th   London Conference grants Germany virtual moratorium.

October

24th   Mr. Bonar Law's Ministry takes office.

November

22nd   Cuno becomes Chancellor.

December

Germany declared a voluntary defaulter.

1923

January
8th	French troops enter the *Ruhr*.
24th	American troops leave the Rhineland.

March
1st	French and Belgian Railway *Régie* begins.
18th	Existence of Black *Reichswehr* revealed by Saxon Premier.

August
13th	Stresemann becomes Chancellor.

October
21st	Separatists proclaim Rhine Republic.

November
8th–9th	Hitler and Ludendorff putsch at Munich.
15th	*Rentenmark* issued.
30th	Marx becomes Chancellor.

1924

January
14th	Dawes Committee begin sitting.
22nd	Mr. R. J. MacDonald's Ministry takes office.

March
19th	German Law passed abolishing power of requisitioning in war time.
23rd	Dr. Stresemann in speech gives the patriotic associations Government authority.

May
11th	Dawes Committee present Report to Reparation Commission.

June
4th	Allied Governments demand dissolution of military societies and the prohibition of instruction of reserves.
15th	M. Herriot becomes *Président du Conseil*.
17th	Lieut.-General Sir J. Du Cane succeeds Lieut.-General Sir A. Godley in command of the British Army of the Rhine.

August
30th	London agreement with Germany to put Dawes Plan in action.

October
2nd	Geneva Protocol for settlement of international disputes adopted by the League of Nations.

November
7th	Mr. S. Baldwin's Second Ministry takes office.

1925

January
5th	German Government informed that Cologne area would not be evacuated.
15th	Luther becomes Chancellor.

February
28th	President Ebert dies.

March

Council of the League of Nations informed that Great Britain declined to accept Geneva protocol.

April

17th M. Poincaré again becomes *Président du Conseil.*

26th Hindenburg elected German President.

June

4th Allied Governments, in a collective Note, state failure of disarmament and demand suppression of the Railway Section of the *Heeresleitung.*

July

13th French begin evacuation of Ruhr.

September

12th Germany invited to Locarno.

October

5th Locarno Conference.

16th Locarno Treaty initialled.

November

29th M. Briand again becomes *Président du Conseil.*

December

1st British begin evacuation of Cologne.

5th Locarno Treaty signed.
Luther resigns.

30th Wiesbaden taken over from the French.

31st Evacuation of Cologne completed.

1926

January

17th Luther becomes Chancellor again.

30th British move to Wiesbaden completed.

May

17th Marx becomes Chancellor.

June

23rd M. Poincaré becomes *Président du Conseil* for the third time.

September

8th Germany enters the League of Nations.

15th Thoiry Conference (Briand and Stresemann).

October

8th General von Seeckt removed from the head of the Army.

December

16th Scheidemann reveals to the *Reichstag* that the *Reichsheer* is training the Patriotic Associations.

1927

January

31st Inter-Allied Military Commission of Control abolished.

March

13th Council of the League of Nations decide that all regular French troops shall be withdrawn from Saar territory.
French and British Delegations submit draft of disarmament convention to the League of Nations.

April
30th   Lieut.-General Sir W. Thwaites succeeds Lieut.-General Sir J. Du Cane in command of the British Army of the Rhine.

July
12th   International Force takes place of French in the Saar territory.

August
27th   Agreement between France and Great Britain as to the reduction of Allied Troops in the Rhineland.

1928

January
30th   Stresemann claims evacuation of Rhineland as consequence of Locarno.

February
20th   Earl of Erroll (Rhineland High Commission) dies and is succeeded by Mr. W. Seeds.

July
29th   Müller becomes Chancellor.

August
27th   Briand-Kellogg pact of Paris signed.

September
11th   Geneva Conference to discuss evacuation of Rhineland.

December
22nd   Allies and Germany reach agreement concerning constitution of Committee of Experts to deal with Reparation problems.

1929

June
7th   Reparation Experts report signed : Young Plan.
8th   Mr. J. R. MacDonald's Second Ministry takes office.
23rd   M. Briand again becomes *Président du Conseil*.

August
29th   Agreement reached at the Hague by which the evacuation of the Rhineland will begin in September and be completed by 30th June, 1930.

September
4th   British guard of Rhineland Commission withdrawn from Coblence.

14th   First detachments of British Rhine Army leave.

October
3rd   Dr. Stresemann dies.

November
3rd   M. Tardieu becomes *Président du Conseil*.

December
12th   Last British troops leave the Rhineland.

1930

June
30th   The last French and Belgian troops leave the Rhineland.

1

CHAPTER I
THE ARMISTICE TERMS
(Frontispiece)

The terms of the Armistice concluded at 5 a.m. on the 11th November, 1918, between the Allied and Associated Powers[1] and a German delegation presided over by Herr Erzberger, a Secretary of State, are contained in a " Convention d'Armistice " and two " Notes Annexes ", which must be read together.[2] All hostilities at sea were to cease immediately, and on land and in the air on the Western Front, with which alone this volume is concerned, six hours later, that is 11 a.m. (noon, Central European time).

THE STAGES OF THE EVACUATION

The articles provided for " the immediate evacuation of the " invaded countries : Belgium, France and Luxembourg, as " well as Alsace-Lorraine . . . to be completed within 15 days " of the signature of the Armistice ". They also provided for the evacuation of all German territory on the left (western) bank of the Rhine, so that the Rhine from Switzerland to, Holland would become the temporary frontier. In addition, three bridgeheads of 30 kilometres (say 19 miles) around Mayence, Coblence and Cologne, on the right bank, were to be evacuated within a further period of 16 days, and their occupation by the Allies was authorized.[3] A neutral zone on the right bank of 10 kilometres (say 6¼ miles) was also fixed, and, to prevent any collision during the movements of evacuation and occupation, these were regulated by conditions laid down in Note Annexe No. 1. On a map attached to this[4] five lines

---

[1] Represented by Maréchal Foch, as Commander-in-Chief of the Allied Armies, in conjunction with Admiral Sir Rosslyn Wemyss, First Sea Lord of the Admiralty. The United States of America were an Associated, not an Allied Power. In order to save space, this distinction will not be observed in the text. How the Armistice came about will be found in " 1918 ", Vol. V (to be published later).

[2] A translation of the French text, including all the articles (the Eastern and Western Fronts, East Africa and the Naval conditions) and the Annexes, as presented to Parliament and issued by H.M. Stationery Office, is given in Appendix I. It is by no means perfect, and the quotations which follow in the text vary slightly from this official translation.

[3] These bridgeheads were in the French, American and British Zones, respectively. A fourth bridgehead in the Belgian area was, it is said, " overlooked " and not obtained until 1923, when the French and Belgians entered the Ruhr (see Chapter XVI).

[4] See the Frontispiece.

were marked : the area up to Line No. 1, about 20 miles from the existing battle front, was to be clear of the German Armies in five days ; that up to Line No. 2, corresponding on the south with the eastern frontiers (the Rhine for the most part) of Alsace-Lorraine and Luxembourg with Germany, in four more days. The area up to Line No. 3, which existed in the north only, corresponding with the Belgian-German frontier and abutting on the Maastricht " Appendix ", was to be clear in six further days. Thus at the end of the 15th day the Germans would be out of Alsace-Lorraine, and northward of these provinces back across the frontier of 1914.

The Allied Armies in following up might cross the German front line held on the 11th November at 5 a.m. on the sixth day after the signature of the Armistice—that is at the hour the Germans had to be east of Line No. 1 ; Line No. 1 might be crossed on the tenth day, and Line No. 2 on the sixteenth.

The evacuation of other territory west of the Rhine was also to be carried out by the German Armies in three stages of four days each, which would bring them in succession behind Lines No. 4, No. 5 and No. 6, the last being the course of the Rhine from near Mayence to the Dutch frontier. Then, in another four days, the evacuation of the bridgeheads and of the neutral zone of the right bank of the Rhine was to be completed, the Allies following up at a fixed minimum distance as before.

Prohibition of Damage

It was particularly stipulated in Article 6 that no injury or damage was to be done to person or property of the inhabitants during the evacuation : " no kind of destruction of any sort " to be committed ; military establishments of every nature " shall be handed over intact, as well as military stores, " munitions and equipment not removed during the periods " fixed for evacuation ; the stores of food of all kinds for the " civil population, cattle, etc., shall be left where they are ".

Article 7 laid down that none of the means of communication, railways, roads, bridges, telegraphs, etc., should be deliberately damaged, that all military and civil personnel then employed on them and on the telegraph and telephone systems should be ordered to remain, the Commander-in-Chief of the Allied Armies retaining the power to change or replace any of them as he might think fit.

The Surrender of Rolling Stock and Lorries

In the matter of rolling stock : 5,000 locomotives and 150,000 coaches and trucks in good running order and provided with all the necessary spare parts and fittings were to be handed over to the Allies within the period fixed by Note Annexe No. 2, " which shall not exceed 31 days ". Similarly, 5,000 motor lorries were to be delivered within 36 days.

Note Annexe No. 2 stated that all the rolling stock above-mentioned should be handed over between the existing front (11th November) and Line No. 3, that is in Belgium,[1] but the detailed conditions were reserved for a Permanent Inter-Allied Armistice Commission (called in these pages, " The Spa Commission ") to settle. In order to prevent blocking of the lines, any rolling stock left on the western bank of the Rhine, as well as in the bridgeheads, had to be shunted so as to allow normal traffic to be maintained. During the period of the Armistice the German Government had to supply fuel and stores for upkeep to the depôts normally serving the railways on the western bank of the Rhine, and all the material required to restore the damaged railway lines eastward of the existing front.

PRISONERS OF WAR

Allied prisoners of war (including any under trial or sentence) were to be " repatriated immediately ", without reciprocity, in accordance with detailed conditions to be settled—when, where and by whom were not mentioned.

German prisoners in the hands of the Allies were not to be liberated : their repatriation was to be discussed in the peace negotiations : German sick and wounded who could not be removed from evacuated territory were to be cared for by German personnel and, like any other soldiers found in areas that should have been cleared, became prisoners.

DISCLOSURE OF DELAY-ACTION MINES

The German Command, under Article 8, was to disclose within 48 hours of the signature of the Armistice the positions of all mines and delay-action charges in the territory evacuated by the German troops, and thus facilitate their discovery and destruction.[2] It was also to disclose where wells, springs, etc., had been poisoned or polluted. In this article occurred the words " all the foregoing under penalty of reprisals ".

---

[1] Separate arrangements were made as regards rolling-stock in Alsace and Lorraine.

[2] Here the authorized translation renders " faciliter ", which *Littré* defines as " render less difficult ", by " assist in ". Actually, the Germans did hand over sketch-plans of the positions of the mines and charges, but by no means of all, and those received were far from accurate.

Surrender of Arms and Aircraft

The following material, in proportions to be fixed by the Spa Commission, was to be handed over to each of the Allied Armies by each tactical " groupement " of the German Army (this would mean each Army, Army Detachment, or Group of Armies), viz., 5,000 guns (2,500 heavy, 2,500 light), 25,000 machine guns, 3,000 trench mortars, 1,700 fighter and bomber aircraft (in the first place, all D.7's[1] and all night bombers). Half had to be handed over before the tenth day, and the rest before the twentieth day.

Naval Conditions

In regard to the Naval conditions, it is pertinent to mention that all German submarine craft were to be surrendered, the bulk of the surface vessels interned and the rest concentrated in German ports and disarmed ; and the existing blockade conditions remained unchanged.

Duration of the Armistice

The duration of the Armistice was fixed at 36 days, with option of extension, and the Spa Commission was to ensure the execution of the Convention under " the best conditions ". Whether, and if so with what status, Germany might be represented at the meetings of this international body was not mentioned.

Object of the Armistice Terms

It will be observed that the terms as regards the Western Front, submitted by the Commander-in-Chief of the Allied Armies and approved by the Governments concerned, had the undisguised purpose first of clearing the Germans out of the occupied territories and of recovering Alsace-Lorraine ; secondly, of setting the Rhine as at least a temporary frontier, with its passages if not all in Allied possession, at least not under German control ; and, thirdly, by forcing the surrender of such a quantity of arms, transport and railway material as to reduce the German Armies to impotence, and to make it impossible for them—at least for a long time—to renew offensive operations. The only security taken was the occupation of the Rhineland.[2] Should the Germans fail to carry out any of

---

[1] Fokker biplanes, the best German machines.

[2] Maréchal Foch wished to occupy Germany at least up to the Elbe. (*L'Armistice du 11 novembre 1918*, p. 194, by General Mordacq, who was Chief of the Military Cabinet of Monsieur Clemenceau.)

their obligations, the only remedy was to apply effective "sanctions" or bring the Armistice to a close and reopen hostilities.

It has sometimes been said that there were no precedents applicable to the situation : quick decisions had to be taken on questions requiring forethought and preparation, with the result that there were omissions and mistakes which led to complications later. As regards hurry, the files of the Supreme War Council (British Section), Versailles, show that the General Staff, War Office, early took up the question and submitted a memorandum on the 10th August, 1918. The file itself is labelled : "Armistice and Peace Papers 10th August 1918 to 11th March 1919". Three months were therefore available, and Germany's own terms to her adversaries in 1866, 1871 and, more recently, those granted to Russia and Rumania provided a valuable and exhaustive guide.

COMPARISON WITH GERMAN TERMS ON OTHER OCCASIONS

The terms of armistice, compared with those which Prussia and Germany had granted in recent times, were weak, incomplete and insufficiently defined, except as regards the successive lines of demarcation.[1] In 1866 Prussia insisted on Austria's acceptance of her peace conditions before granting any armistice, and amongst those conditions were surrenders of territory to Prussia and her Ally, Italy, and the payment of a war indemnity, the Prussians to remain in occupation of Austrian territory until this was paid.

Similarly, the Armistice terms between France and Germany in 1871 provided for the payment of a contribution of 200 million francs in 15 days ; as guarantee, besides the territory already occupied, the Paris forts had to be surrendered. As regards prisoners of war, the Convention read : "the German "prisoners will be set at liberty at the nearest point to the "frontier" ; and a later special Convention arranged that prisoners in Germany should be sent by fixed railway routes to fixed destinations, or by sea from Hamburg and Bremerhafen to French ports. A feature of the Armistice of Brest-Litovsk of the 15th December, 1917, between the Central Powers and Russia, was the "greatest feasible amelioration of the condition "of the prisoners of war of both sides", which was to be one of the principal tasks of the Governments concerned.

---

[1] The gist of the various armistices and peace treaties made by Germany is given in Appendix II.

Between Rumania and the Central Powers, a short preliminary treaty of peace (5th March, 1918) took the place of an armistice. By it, Rumania ceded territory vital for her future safety, made complete economic surrender, and agreed to begin demobilization forthwith. It was a "dictated peace" if there ever was one.

OMISSIONS AS REGARDS PRISONERS OF WAR

The Armistice failed in particular in making fully defined provision for the return of Allied prisoners of war, and, as will be seen, the Germans were not slow to take advantage of this in order to evade handing over railway locomotives and wagons, and to obtain certain ameliorations.[1]

DUTIES OF THE ARMISTICE COMMISSION

One thing the terms did make clear : the supervision of and the detailed arrangements for the execution of the armistice were made the business, under the Commander-in-Chief of the Allied Armies, of the Spa Commission ; but this body did not hold its first meeting until the 16th November. The Allied Armies were responsible only for leaving and reaching the various lines at and by the appointed dates, and they began their advance ordered on the 17th November, before the Spa Commission could get to work. The dilemma which thus arose was partly overcome by assembling certain subsidiary commissions, mentioned below, on the 15th and 16th ; they, however, were forbidden to take over any material, whether arms or rolling stock, from the Germans ; but this absolute prohibition, as will be seen, had to be considerably watered down.

OTHER COMMISSIONS

In bringing the Armistice terms officially to the notice of the Commanders-in-Chief on the 12th November, Maréchal Foch ordered the continuation or the formation of a number of commissions and sub-commissions, on which the British were to be represented, to control the Inter-Allied communications. These were :

the existing Calais Commission, for the control of the Belgian railway system ;

the Field Railway Commission (to assemble at the Maréchal's headquarters at 3 p.m. on the 14th), for the control of the Luxembourg railways, the German systems west of the Rhine and

---

[1] The omission seems to have been a piece of forgetfulness on the part of Maréchal Foch, who in the terms he submitted to the French Prime Minister said : "prisoners of war will be the subject of further agreements, aiming "at their return at the earliest possible date in view of transport conditions."

in the bridgeheads, with a British sub-commission to direct operations of all railways inside the area allotted to the British Army ;

the Calais International Commission of Navigable Waterways, for the control of all Belgian navigable waterways ;

the Brussels Inter-Allied Reception Commission, to examine and supervise the taking over of locomotives and wagons from the German Army (a duty eventually to be performed under the authority of the Spa Commission) ;

the Field Navigation Commission, to deal with the Rhine between Alsace-Lorraine and the Dutch frontier, the Moselle from Alsace-Lorraine to its junction with the Rhine, and the Saar from Alsace-Lorraine to its junction with the Moselle ;

the existing Road Sub-Commission, dealing with the French roads in the British area up to Armistice Lines Nos. 2 and 3 ;

the Inter-Allied Road Commission, to apportion the main forward lateral roads in the common interest ; and the

Inter-Allied Signal Commission, to control all Signals in the area between Line No. 3 and the Rhine.[1]

It was further notified by Maréchal Foch that at 2 p.m. on the 15th November accredited representatives of the German Army were to meet the Calais Commission and receive through the Commission the instructions of H.M. the King of the Belgians regarding the Belgian railways in German occupation. The Germans were to bring with them all documents relative to the condition of the Belgian railways and full information as to the personnel and material employed on those lines. At 2 p.m. on the 16th November accredited representatives of the German Army were to meet the president of the Field Railway Commission at Nancy to receive instructions regarding the railways in Luxembourg and German territory up to the Rhine and inside the bridgeheads, excluding the railways normally operated by the Alsace-Lorraine group. Two reception committees, with German representatives on each, were to sit, the one at Metz and the other at Brussels, the former for the railways connecting Alsace-Lorraine and France and the latter for the lines crossing into Belgium, to carry out the examination and transfer of the rolling stock. The number of locomotives and wagons to be delivered in the two areas in the first ten days, the next four days and in the following eleven days was stated. The German representatives were to have power to carry out the instructions of the Commission.

---

[1] Other Commissions which came later into existence were : The Coal Distribution Commission, the Postal Control Commission and the Shipping Commission (to deal with the handing over by the Germans of shipping, including river-craft). The food and economic commissions are dealt with below.

For the Navigable Waters, at 2 p.m. on the 15th November accredited German delegates of the Navigation Service dealing with the Belgian territory still in occupation were to arrive at Bruges station to receive the instructions of H.M. the King of the Belgians ; and at 2 p.m. on the following day German delegates representing the Navigation Service of the Rhine, Moselle and Saar were to meet the president of the Field Navigation Commission at Nancy station to receive his instructions.

For Signals and Roads, German delegates were to meet British representatives at Mons station at 2 p.m. on the 15th in the one case, and at a date to be fixed in the other, to arrange for the taking over of material and assuring the arrival of the personnel required for maintenance. As regards lorries four places were named where specified numbers were to be handed over before certain dates.

The details as regards the handing over were given in three. Annexes.

ARMY AREAS
DECEMBER 1918

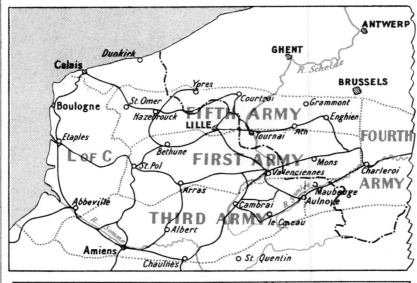

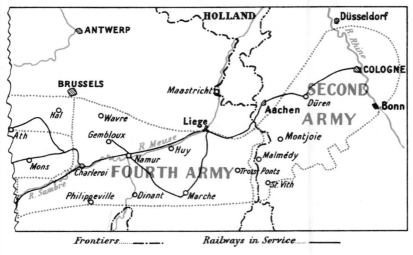

Frontiers............_._._.   Railways in Service............

SCALE OF MILES.

10   5   0   10   20   30

Compiled in the Historical Section (Military Branch).

Ordnance Survey 1943.

CHAPTER II

THE ADVANCE TO THE GERMAN FRONTIER
(Frontispiece and Sketch 1)

THE ORDER OF BATTLE

At 11 a.m. on the 11th November when the Armistice came into force the five Armies of the British array under Field-Marshal Sir Douglas Haig were in pursuit in line covered by general advanced guards of all arms of varying strength. The front of the Fourth Army (General Sir Henry Rawlinson) of two corps, the IX and XIII, on the right, was covered by an advanced guard consisting of the 66th Division and the 5th Cavalry Brigade under the command of Major-General H. K. Bethell (66th Division). The Third Army (General Hon. Sir Julian Byng), next on the left, containing the V, VI and XVII Corps, was similarly preceded by an advanced guard of the Guards and 63rd Divisions and the 4th Cavalry Brigade, under the command of Lieut.-General Sir Aylmer Haldane (VI Corps). All the three corps of the First Army (General Sir Henry Horne), the XXII, Canadian and VIII, were represented at the front, respectively by one, two and three brigades, with regiments of the 3rd Cavalry Brigade attached. The Fifth Army (General Sir William Birdwood) also had all its three corps, the I, III and XI, in the line, each with a regiment of the 2nd Cavalry Brigade attached, and led by two, one and two divisions, respectively, each covered by a brigade group of all arms. The Second Army (General Sir Herbert Plumer), led by the 3rd Cavalry Division, had only two of its four corps, the XIX and X, in the line, on frontages of two and three divisions, respectively, and similarly led by advanced guards, with portions of the 7th Cavalry Brigade attached. Behind the line of advanced guards the rest of the Armies were spread out in depth in order to ease the supply situation, the Second Army having the XV and II Corps in second line.

THE STAND-FAST ORDER :

BAN ON COMMUNICATIONS WITH THE ENEMY

The " stand-fast " order, telephoned from G.H.Q. at 6.50 a.m., directed that defensive precautions should be maintained and that intercourse of any kind with the enemy was forbidden. Further instructions followed by telegraph between 9 and 10 a.m. The ban on intercourse and fraternization with the enemy was reiterated in stronger form : attempts by Germans to approach the British lines were to be stopped, if necessary by fire ; parties coming over under a white flag were to be made prisoner ; no enemy aircraft were to be permitted to cross the front line ; our own aircraft were to keep not less than a mile behind the front line except for the purpose of driving back enemy machines ; and until further instructions, no civilians were to be permitted to pass in either direction. On the 14th, however, the last part of the order was modified to read that " repatriated Allied prisoners and civilians will " be allowed to pass through the lines from east to west, and " will be accommodated [segregated, by a later instruction] in " divisional areas until corps are in a position to arrange for " their reception at certain centres, pending orders to proceed " to their destinations, and as regards civilians in co-operation " with the French and Belgian Missions. No person to proceed " through lines from west to east ". On the 20th, even this last ban was removed.

The commanders of the German Armies and Groups of Armies soon began by wireless to invite the commanders of the Allied Armies opposite them to enter into negotiations on the subjects of the release of prisoners and the handing over of material but without response, until the orders totally forbidding communication with the enemy were gradually relaxed by Maréchal Foch. On the 13th he limited intercourse to the subjects of " the location of delay-action mines, the " repair of roads immediately in front of the present lines, " and meetings for which special orders had been given " ; but he still prohibited any entry into negotiations for handing over prisoners of war or war material, the following telegram being sent out on the 14th :

> " In view of continued proposals by German Army commanders to Allied commanders opposite them to hand over war material or prisoners, Maréchal Foch has forbidden Allied Armies to take over material or prisoners before the Armistice Commission starts work, and has instructed German Command that if they wish to leave material or prisoners behind they must leave guards commanded by officers responsible for handing over, after which these guards will be liberated."

On the 15th the Maréchal issued the following order :

> " In order to maintain order in the territory evacuated by the enemy, the Allied Armies when requested by the inhabitants or the German Command, or in case of necessity, may after 5 a.m. on the 16th send small detachments into the zone between our present line and Line No. 1."

He suggested that some armoured cars and artillery should form part of these detachments ; but in no circumstances were they to cross Line No. 1, and there was to be no fraternization.

The order then continued :

> " These detachments may also from to-day accept war material which certain German Armies have notified as being actually in position, in order to prevent pillage ; accurate inventories of quantity and condition to be taken and sent to Allied head-quarters.
>
> " Detachments left by enemy to safeguard material should be set free immediately inventory has been taken."

On the 16th direct communication was authorized between Armies opposite each other, " so as to co-ordinate their move-" ments in such a manner as to avoid misunderstandings " ; but in no case was the pace of the advance laid down in the Armistice terms to be slackened.

At the suggestion of the Intelligence Section of the General Staff, what were known as " Evacuation Liaison Groups " were formed under corps arrangements on each of the principal roads and railways to keep G.H.Q. informed regarding the progress of the German retirement, the state of railways, roads, signal communications, food supplies and position of dumps, and to report localities safe from mines and booby traps. They were provided with the necessary means of transport and, in some cases, with wireless sets.

G.H.Q. also directed on the 11th that :

> "All commanders are to pay the strictest attention to discipline, smartness and well-being of their troops, so as to ensure the highest state of discipline. . . . Troops will be given every opportunity for rest, training, recreation and leave."

Next day it was ordered that during the whole period of the Armistice no musketry should take place within 4 kilometres ($2\frac{1}{2}$ miles) of the front line, and no artillery practice within 8 kilometres (5 miles).

Maréchal Foch's Directive of 11th November

The following executive orders in the form of a Directive were issued by Maréchal Foch on the 11th, reaching G.H.Q. in the evening[1] : On the 17th, starting at 5 a.m., all Armies were to advance in two marches " *au maximum* " to Line No. 1 and there halt, and on the dates 21st and 27th to Lines Nos. 2 and 3 : on reaching the German frontier, that is Line No. 2 continued in the north by Line No. 3, they were not to cross it

---

[1] The text is in the French Official Account, vii. (ii), Annexe 570.

without further orders : any Germans found on the wrong side of the lines would be made prisoner :

> " The strength of the troops in front line will depend naturally on the number and state of the roads and the possibility of supply ; what, however, is of importance is that the Armies should be so organized that, if necessary, they will be in a position to resume the offensive with a force capable of breaking any hostile resistance, should it be offered, in 48 hours at most."

He assigned the zones of march, lines of railway communications and regulating stations to the American, French, British and Belgian contingents.[1]

Five days later Maréchal Foch communicated a Note to the Allied Commanders-in-Chief in which he laid down that, in addition to the forces detailed for the occupation of the Rhineland, the troops held ready to intervene immediately should have an effective minimum of 20 French, 10 American, 20 British and 2 Belgian divisions, with the British disposed west of the line Maubeuge-Mons, that is the Armistice front line : the other divisions should be kept at rest and training, but some of them in areas from which they could at once be entrained.

G.H.Q. ORDERS FOR THE ADVANCE

At a conference of Army commanders held at Advanced G.H.Q. at Cambrai at 11 a.m. on the 11th November, Sir Douglas Haig had explained the intentions of the Generalissimo, and next day, after the copy of the Maréchal's written Directive had arrived, G.H.Q. issued formal instructions for carrying out his wishes.

In accordance with these instructions, only two Armies, the Second and Fourth, under the two senior Army commanders, Sir Herbert Plumer and Sir Henry Rawlinson, were to advance on the 17th. Each of these Armies would consist of 4 selected corps and 16 selected divisions, out of the total of 16 corps and 61 divisions, with sufficient cavalry and air forces.[2] In choosing the divisions, the Commander-in-Chief told the Army commanders, " man-power and recruiting had " been taken into consideration ". The other Armies, with the remaining corps and divisions, were to stand fast, but might send back behind railheads such divisions as could not be easily supplied.

---

[1] The boundaries and the railway line assigned to the British are shown on the Frontispiece. The railway from Brussels to Liége was to be shared with the Belgians.
[2] Appendix III gives the Order of Battle.

On the 18th the American II Corps (27th and 30th Divisions), which had formed part of the Fourth Army, was, by arrangement with General Pershing, sent back by rail to the American forces.

Suggestions for Training and Recreation

The following " Notes " also were issued to the Army commanders :

" (1) During the period following the cessation of hostilities the maintenance of discipline is of the highest importance. Breaches of discipline must be repressed firmly and at once.

" The necessity for avoiding irritating restrictions must be impressed on officers, as there are a number of officers with the Armies at present who lack experience. The reason why certain things are not permitted should be explained.

" (2) Regimental, Brigade R.A. and Battalion Messes should be instituted for officers. The necessary transport will be provided.

" (3) Leave to visit places of interest should be granted freely to all ranks, and the necessary transport arranged.

" Demonstrations should be arranged : observation balloons, sound ranging, flash spotting, anti-aircraft shooting, projectors, trench mortars, wireless telegraphy and telephony, etc.

" It is the duty of regimental and other officers to organize and direct amusements for their men ; trips to places of interest; competitions between units, companies, platoons, etc. ; brigade, divisional and corps staffs will assist.

" Visits should be arranged between detachments of the various arms.

" Funds to provide games, footballs, etc., will be provided on application to G.H.Q. if divisions are unable to do so. A pamphlet describing different games, home, colonial and foreign will be compiled at G.H.Q.[1]

" (4) Every cantonment should be provided with recreation rooms, and canteens supplied with writing paper and indoor games.

" (5) Ceremonial parades will be held when the weather is fine. Army commanders and the Field-Marshal Commanding-in-Chief will attend when possible.

" Thirty-yard ranges should be built and competitions held on them.

" (6) Lectures on ' After the War Problems ' should be arranged

" A pamphlet on demobilization will be issued to the Army very early.

" (7) The restrictions on the use of cameras are cancelled.

" Regulations as to censorship will be relaxed ; men will now be allowed to describe where they are and the nature of their surroundings."

---

[1] One game played was football between two battalions : goals, the Grandes Places of two villages three miles apart, no off-side, umpires mounted.

Redistribution of the British Armies[1]

These suggestions were gradually carried out ; but the first business after placing posts on the roads and elsewhere to prevent any movement through the line, was the re-arrangement of the divisions for the forward march under the Second and Fourth Armies, and after that for cantoning the other three Armies abreast, west of the line Maubeuge–Grammont, with their corps partly east and partly west of the " devastated " area."[2] They were to be concentrated—in view of possible continuation of hostilities—as far as was compatible with the comfort of the troops, and close enough to railway stations to enable supplies to be drawn by horse-transport.

The Quarter-Master-General's General Instructions

On the 13th, the Quarter-Master-General, Lieut.-General Sir Travers Clarke, issued a comprehensive order with effect as follows[3] :

(1) Railway reconstruction work would be concentrated on the Tournai–Ath, Valenciennes–Mons and Aulnoye–Maubeuge lines ;

(2) the Second and Fourth Armies would be responsible for the upkeep of roads forward from railheads, and in principle roads would be limited to two per Army ;

(3) extra transport including one auxiliary bus company per Army would be allotted, and defective vehicles were to be evacuated ;

(4) one day's reserve rations would be taken forward on wheels, and two trucks of foodstuffs per day per corps would be sent for distribution at need to the civilian population ;

(5) units were to be brought up to their horse establishment before the move ; wagons, but not field guns, would remain on the four-horse team basis ;

(6) the amount of gun and S.A. ammunition to be kept ready in existing dumps for issue at short notice to the Second and Fourth Armies was fixed (it had already been ordered that only such ammunition as was in the horsed echelons—except in the case of siege batteries—should be taken forward) ;

(7) and (8), sick animals and surplus stores were to be evacuated under specified conditions ;

(9) the leading corps were to have priority in the distribution of ordnance stores ;

---

[1] See Sketch 1.

[2] That is the scene of the Battles of the Somme, 1916, and the German devastation in 1917, a 20-mile belt, extending across the British area, bounded on the west by Albert–Arras and on the east by Cambrai (exclusive)– St. Quentin. Sketch 1 gives the final distribution in December.

[3] Given in full in Appendix IV.

(10) and (11), the mobile workshops were to be reduced to two per corps, with one medium ordnance workshop, and the Second and Fourth Armies were directed to hand over their gun parks to the other Armies ;

(12) canteen stores would come up by supply trains ;

(13) the immediate needs of released British prisoners of war were to be met, with priority in the matter of blankets and clothing, and they were to be sent to Calais (where camps had been provided) by the most expeditious means.[1]

(14) orders with regard to captured and ceded material would be issued in due course.

The other headings were of departmental interest only.

The orders under (14) were issued two days later : in the case of ammunition no receipts were to be given and no caretakers posted, only warning given to the local authorities ; otherwise, if material was handed over by German personnel, receipts would be given ; for guns and other arms British caretakers were to be posted and inventories made ; supply dumps were to be taken over by the officers of the Director of Supplies ; serviceable M.T. stores, lorries, workshops, machinery, wagons and similar material, if not in charge of German personnel, were to be treated as captured material, and inventories made ; unserviceable material which might be classed as salvage could be disregarded, its position for future clearance being noted ; any German personnel (other than lorry drivers who were to be retained) should be rationed and sent back.

In order to save transport, corps and divisions were directed to form, at some convenient place near a railway station, depôts of any equipment and stores which they did not require, and were informed that these would be administered by the rear corps.

Economy in the demands for rations had been encouraged for some time—thus in the month of October the Cavalry Corps had saved £213 by under-demanding tinned goods, biscuits and oatmeal—and units were now reminded of the necessity of saving not only rations but transport. The Armies were ordered to ascertain how far the numerous light railways of the country could be used for distribution.

The Administrative Difficulties of the Advance

The acceptance of the armistice terms had greatly changed the aspect of the situation from the administrative point of view. With the temporary cessation of hostilities and of

---

[1] Unfortunately the entire lack of ordered arrangements for the release and handing over of prisoners of war prevented the Q.M.G.'s arrangements from being carried out, and on 15th November (before the Spa Commission had assembled) G.H.Q. ordered that prisoners of war who entered the areas of the Second and Fourth Armies should be transferred, by bus or lorry until the railway could take them, to the First or Fifth Army, which would receive further orders about forwarding them to the bases.

movement the old problems had become easier of solution, but, on the other hand, many new problems, including the supply of winter clothing and blankets for all hands, had to be faced immediately and simultaneously. First and foremost came the arrangements for the supply of the formations which were about to move to the German frontier and to the Rhine ; then for the maintenance of an unspecified number of civilians who might be found in the evacuated areas ; and concurrently for the reception on a generous scale of the back-flowing streams of British prisoners of war whom the enemy was pledged to release. These problems were likely to be complicated by the beginnings of the " winding up " of the campaign : for instance the immediate curtailment of shippings to France on the ground of economy, and the reduction of supply and transport staff by demobilization. On the 11th November the railheads[1] were on the line Busigny–le Cateau–Valenciennes–Orchies–Lille– Courtrai–Vichte (five miles east of Courtrai), 20 to 35 miles west of the Armistice line, and it was the power of transportation which ruled the situation.

Shortage of Rolling Stock

To aggravate the difficulties of the repair and reconstruction of the permanent way required at once, there was a shortage of trucks. The Armistice brought little relief'; for every mile of railway progress towards the German frontier meant an increase in the length of haul, not only for supply, but also for reconstruction material, besides delaying the " turn-round ", and entailed an addition to the number of trucks for the same number of trains a day. These factors had produced a marked effect even before the Armistice, the number of trains per day having fallen steadily since the end of September, when it averaged 170 a day, down to about 80 ; and at this figure it remained until the end of November. The festivities which the Armistice now inspired for a time also interfered considerably with the efficiency of French and Belgian civilian labour.

It was reckoned that sufficient rolling stock was available for about 60,000 10-ton units, enough, on the basis of two trains a day per division, to maintain 40 divisions on the German frontier as a fighting force engaged in active warfare. Under armistice conditions, when the transport of ammunition would cease and that of road metal be greatly diminished, the normal requirements could be met by one train per division, made up of more trucks, demanding about 40,000 trucks a day, and leaving 20,000 (with 600 locomotives) for civilian purposes.

---

[1] See Frontispiece.

As a practical measure, in the advance to the German frontier, it was proposed to attach two supply trucks to each corps train of the eight corps of the Second and Fourth Armies for the benefit of the Belgian population.

The Germans left a number of trucks behind on the railways, generally loaded with military material or looted civilian property which they had been unable to move in time ; but strict injunctions were soon received from the Spa Commission that they were not to be used until duly taken over by its officers. Apart from this, as all the locomotives had been got away, the trucks could not at once be put into circulation, and so merely proved an obstruction. A number of barges, also, loaded with looted machinery, had been abandoned ; but these and their cargoes were claimed by Belgians, and ownership could not at once be determined.

GAP IN THE FORWARD RAILWAYS

It was obvious that there would be a gap in the railway tracks between the British advanced railheads and those of the Germans situated beyond the zone of the latest fighting. This amounted to about 20 miles on the Charleroi line, 30 miles on the Enghien line and less, but more difficult on account of broken bridges, on the Mons line. In this belt, too, the enemy would have done his best to destroy both railways and roads.

Before the Armistice terms were known, three courses seemed open :

(1) to continue feeding the Armies by road until the railway gap had been filled ; this meant at the moment, and for some little time, that the main bodies could not advance more than another forty miles ;

(2) to bridge the gap by road transport and rely on re-railing troops and supplies beyond the gap—if rolling stock had been left by the enemy [1];

(3) to check the advance at some line within comfortable reach of the existing railheads and not continue it until the "head of steel" had sufficiently progressed to make a bound forward worth while. This would prevent supply traffic interfering with construction traffic ; but it meant delay.

The terms of the Armistice necessitated a compromise : there could be no long waiting ; the forward movement must be commenced on the 17th and maintained as steadily as circumstances would permit, it being recognised that no risk must be

---

[1] This was actually done on 25th November and following days, when supplies for the 1st Cavalry Division were carried by lorries from Valenciennes to Mons and there put on a local Belgian train which took them to Namur.

taken of the advance exceeding the distance at which supplies could be brought forward with certainty by road from the railheads.

PROGRAMME OF STAGES

Accordingly a programme of stages for the progress of the Armies to the German frontier was prepared by the Q.M.G., and issued on the day after the signing of the Armistice.[1] The distance from railheads to the German frontier was about a hundred miles; this was divided into three stages of roughly 20, 50 and 30 miles respectively, and it was decided that railway reconstruction should be concentrated on the lines capable of being opened most quickly. Of the eight corps and 32 divisions selected for the advance, half would go forward on the dates fixed, the rest following at a convenient distance. This retardation of the rearward divisions would make it possible to find the additional motor lorries required for doubling and, if necessary, for trebling the echelons of vehicles for the supply of the leading divisions, including the cavalry which would always be the best part of a stage ahead. Six additional M.T. companies from G.H.Q. pool were accordingly allotted to each of the two leading Armies. It was then decided that no M.T. ammunition echelons, not even the divisional M.T. companies, except those of the siege batteries, were to carry ammunition. One H.T. company was allotted to each corps to carry blankets, also one road construction company and one water-tank company to each Army for distribution as required.

Fuel and reserves of boots would be sent by rail as required, and canteen stores forwarded with divisional supplies. All surplus stores of the Second and Fourth Armies were to be handed over to the First and Fifth Armies.

UNITS LEFT BEHIND

The following units and material were to be left behind by the Second and Fourth Armies:

All trench mortars (but the personnel of the companies to go forward); R.E. special (gas) companies; balance of tunnelling companies, R.E.; railway troops; balance of road construction companies; labour H.Q. and units; reception camps and rest stations; area commandants, employment companies and signal detachments; the balance of ordnance

---

[1] The Frontispiece shows the railway lines allotted by Maréchal Foch; Sketch 1 those actually used.

mobile workshops ; salvage, camouflage and veterinary units ; evacuation stations ; agricultural and tramway units ; and all attached officers.

The Quarter-Master-General's Forecast

On the 18th November the Q.M.G. was able to inform the Chief of the General Staff that :

(1) Up to Line No. 1 there would be no difficulty in maintaining the Armies as at present distributed.

(2) On the 24th, new railheads would be open which would admit of the maintenance of the Cavalry Corps in depth on Line No. 2, and the heads of six divisions of the Second and Fourth Armies as far as the general line Dinant–Namur–Wavre, a little short of Line No. 2.

(3) On the 28th, when a single line Valenciennes–Namur should be open and the gap in the railway bridged,[1] the troops (new Second Army) earmarked for the occupation of the Rhineland could be maintained at any distance along the main Namur–Liége line, but the remainder of the Second and Fourth Armies would still be compelled to draw from the railheads mentioned in (2), and must therefore remain halted. On the 27th the day on which movement beyond Line No. 2 was ordered, it might be necessary to consume one day's reserve supplies carried on wheels in front of railheads.[2]

(4) On or about 7th December the northern line would be open for single-line working and then the remainder of the troops mentioned in (3) could be moved anywhere desired as long as they remained, quartered as near as possible to the railheads, within road transport radius of the main Namur–Liége line or the Courtrai–Audenarde–Enghien line (temporarily in British use, as it turned out that Ath, on the direct Tournai–Enghien line, would not be ready to receive supplies until 6th December).

---

[1] The first through connection to the Belgian system was made east of Mons, beyond which place little damage had been done, though great preparations had been made for demolitions, and many delay-action charges had to be located and withdrawn.

[2] In a later forecast, on 20th November, the Q.M.G. had to ask that, until the 28th, most, if not all, of the divisions not destined to form part of the Second Army for the advance into Germany should be kept within single echelon distance of railheads, and to point out that, after that date, owing to the favourable lie of the roads, none of these divisions need be located at a greater distance.

(5) By 14th December the situation would be normal and troops could be disposed where required.

Actually, throughout the advance up to 25th November the supply situation was precarious. On that date the gap between Valenciennes and Mons was bridged, and railheads of the Second Army could be advanced east of the gap ; but as there were no loops on this section, trains could not pass each other, and watering at Mons had to be done by a Merryweather pump, taking one whole hour per engine. Thus the full capacity of the line was only nine trains a day, and from the very first trains were running late owing to the interference of civilian traffic and to the drivers not being acquainted with the line. Special engines to haul on the heavy gradients from Mons to Charleroi had to be sent up.

During the month of November 120 miles of broad gauge line were reconstructed and 2.51 miles of new line built, the corresponding quantities of light railway being 4.28 and .92 miles.

Inability to Conform to Programme

The damage done by the Germans proved more serious than was anticipated, but did not extend much farther east than the German Armistice Line. To give an instance, the line between Maubeuge and Charleroi crossed the Sambre no less than 16 times and the five bridges beyond the British Armistice Line, large ones of 100 to 150 feet span, had been completely destroyed.[1]

East of the German old front line, although the track itself had not been much damaged, the signalling and switching equipment to a large extent had been damaged or removed, undoubtedly after the Armistice. Checks were also caused by the explosion of delay-action mines which were not indicated on the sketches handed over by the German representatives, as has already been mentioned. The destruction of watering facilities, besides accidents and derailments on the restored lines, which were no better than single-line " field railways " requiring great care in working, also led to delays. Moreover, the very hilly country over which the lorries had to work and the troops to march—the western sections of the Ardennes— is broken and traversed by the deep valleys of the Meuse and the Ourthe, besides those of many smaller streams, and threw a heavy strain both on man and machinery.

---

[1] An account of railway reconstruction will be found in the Official History " Transportation on the Western Front ", p. 471–5.

Thus, on 21st November when the time arrived for the Armies to advance from Line No. 1, the contemplated extensions of the railways had not been effected, the railheads were very little east of where they had been on the 11th, the roads ahead were still under repair ; so, instead of marching to Line No. 2, the troops were halted, as suggested by the Q.M.G., on an intermediate line through Namur. Fortunately, a spell of fine weather, with frosts at night, interrupted only on 28th and 29th November by heavy showers, helped to keep the roads in condition ; but as they were generally narrow and often covered with marching troops, even short stages entailed long hours, and many vehicles were ditched or broke down through the fatigue of the drivers.

FRENCH ALLOTMENT AND CONTROL OF RAILWAYS

One other aspect of the railway question deserves notice. Concurrently with Maréchal Foch's orders for the advance to the Rhine, the *Direction générale des Communications et des Ravitaillements aux Armées*[1] provisionally fixed the lines of communication for each of the Allied Armies, the authorities by which the lines would be controlled, and the arrangements for taking over locomotives and rolling stock from the Germans.

The railway lines allotted to the British across Belgium were :[2]

(1) Romescamps (between Rouen and Amiens and in railway communication with Havre, Rouen and Dieppe)– Amiens–Cambrai–Charleroi–Namur–Malmédy ;

(2) Boulogne–St. Pol–Arras–Valenciennes–Mons–Liége ;

(3) Calais–Lille–Brussels–Louvain.

The operation of the various lines was controlled in reoccupied France by the commission of the system concerned, and in Belgium by the military staffs of the Army in whose area the lines happened to lie, subject to co-ordination by the Calais International Railway Commission ; but these military staffs were replaced by Belgian personnel under the Belgian Commission when possible. In the Rhineland the German lines were to come under a new Inter-Allied Railway Commission, with a separate sub-commission for each nation. The general organization for all communications (railways, roads, navigable waterways, river ports, telegraph and telephone lines) was laid down in instructions issued by Maréchal Foch on 15th November.[3]

---

[1] Corresponding to the British Inspectorate-General of the Lines of Communication.

[2] Frontispiece and Sketch 1.

[3] Appendix V.

For some time after the signing of the Armistice, despite the provisions described above, the railway situation was in a state of confusion and uncertainty. The amount of destruction done in Belgium and the condition of the lines were unknown even to the Belgian personnel, and all hope of taking over the railways as a going concern, intended under Clause VII of the Armistice, had soon to be abandoned.

NOTICE TO THE GERMAN RAILWAY PERSONNEL

On the 19th November Maréchal Foch issued the following notice, which was broadcast by posters and handbills :

> " By the terms of the Armistice, the entire personnel of the lines and means of communication (railways, navigable waterways telegraphs, telephones, etc.) of the territories recovered or occupied by the Allied Armies should remain at their posts and continue work.
>
> " The personnel which is thus retained may be certain of good treatment, of being paid as before, and of having their food assured.
>
> " On the other hand, anyone who abandons his post is liable to be tried by Court Martial.
>
> " Thus it is in everyone's interest to remain at his post ; it is also in the interest of the inhabitants, whose supply cannot be ensured unless transportation functions normally."

Nothing was said about a brassard or distinguishing mark for the protection of the employees who wished to remain.

Instead of handing over the railways and communications in Belgium as going concerns, the German working personnel, about 10,000 in number, fled, carrying off the charts of the signalling systems and key plans of the telephone switchboards. The excuse for this breach of the Armistice terms was that this personnel went in fear of their lives in Belgium owing to the attitude of the population, and in the Rhineland owing to the advance of the British troops. The directing staffs refused to remain, on the ground that they had no personnel to direct, and, when questioned later, asserted that they could not give any information, as they had left the archives behind. Steps were taken to collect some of the personnel ; but by the time this had been done the whole of Belgium had been reoccupied.

Nevertheless, by 8th December, the Q.M.G. was working trains right up to the German frontier, and in the middle of that month it was decided that, except for work in connection with the reception of rolling stock, no German personnel would be employed by the British outside the *Reich*.

Communication by telegraph or telephone across the devastated areas and in Belgium hardly existed ; practically the only way to obtain information and circulate instructions was by motor car and despatch rider, and in Belgium lack of petrol at times hindered, and even stopped, this. Yet the Armies had to continue their advance.

The urgency of military traffic, however, diminished after the Armistice in the eyes of the French and Belgian Governments, and the re-establishment of railway services essential to their populations, particularly in the liberated regions, became their first object. On 20th November Maréchal Foch issued an order to the effect that it was necessary to confine traffic on the Nord and Est Railways solely to coal and supplies for armies and for the civilian population of the reoccupied areas : all large troop movements were to be suspended. Permission to move British divisions by tactical train across the devastated areas—where no billeting accommodation existed if they marched—was refused. In practice, military trains did not always receive priority over civilian trains ; in fact they were sometimes shunted to allow faster travelling passenger trains to pass, and, as will be seen, the troops suffered in consequence well into January, 1919.

SIGNAL ARRANGEMENTS

The following order affecting signals was issued by G.H.Q. on 13th November :

> " The G.H.Q. Telegraph and Signal Construction Companies will concentrate on the construction of one main Signal route : Binche [between Mons and Charleroi]–Charleroi–Namur. The Fourth and Second Armies will select their successive headquarters in as close proximity to this route as possible."

It was added as a service direction that all Army headquarters should go to places where existing lines admitted of their being connected to the main signal routes : within Army areas, as the supply and transport of stores was extremely difficult, telegraph and telephone communication was to be as far as possible by existing telegraph and telephone circuits, supplemented when necessary by cable : teeing-in to, cutting or crossing existing main routes at places other than existing test points was forbidden : no instruments were to be removed either from post offices or private dwellings.

Armies were made responsible for guarding telegraph and telephone routes and Signal offices and exchanges.

Precautions were to be taken that no communication by telegraph or telephone took place between Signal offices in the British area and in that still occupied by the Germans ; for this purpose it was recommended that Signal parties should occupy the Signal offices in the towns and villages where they were billeted ; but telegraph and telephone routes which ran through the British front line into German occupied territory were not to be cut ; they were to be disconnected at the most forward test point by linesmen specially detailed for the purpose by the A.D. Signals of the leading corps.

The Second and Fourth Armies were provided with an efficient wireless service of 50 to 60 miles to their leading corps, but only of six to seven miles' range to their rear corps. Communication with the cavalry was by wireless and motorcyclist despatch riders ; but on the 19th a postal air service was organized between fixed centres in the cavalry zone and the leading corps and Army headquarters, with the proviso that the pilots must be able to return before dark. It was decided that messages might be sent in clear, but with the names of units in the 4-letter code and with references to two named maps.

FOCH'S SMARTNESS ORDER

On the 15th November, on which day the British forces attended Thanksgiving Services, Maréchal Foch addressed the following circular known as the " pomp and polish order ", by cipher telegram to Groups of Armies, Armies and Missions :

" (1) I attach the greatest importance to all movements when taking possession of territory being executed with rigorous precision and order. Commanders of Armies, corps and other formations will exercise close personal supervision. No slackness in turn-out or march discipline should be tolerated.

" (2) Before settling down in a town, possession will be taken of all the exits and public buildings, including the Post and Telegraph offices, and measures devised to control traffic. After all this has been done a formal entry into the town will, if judged desirable, be made.

" (3) The troops taking part in the formal entry will not be stationed in the town, but be billeted outside it.

" (4) All commanders of formations, divisions and above will remain at their posts until further orders. I may, however, grant them short leave for special reasons."

Actually, a formal entry into Mons was made by General Plumer on the 15th, and by General Rawlinson into Charleroi on the 20th ; there and in other towns civic receptions were organized by the *Maires*. On the 22nd November a composite

British battalion consisting of English (29th Division), Highland (9th Division), Irish (29th Division) and Newfoundland (9th Division) companies, commanded by Br.-General Freyburg, V.C., D.S.O. (New Zealand), and headed by the massed pipe bands of the 26th Brigade and the 9/Seaforth Highlanders (Pioneers), marched eight abreast with fixed bayonets in the procession of the King of the Belgians into Brussels.

The March to the German Frontier

For the advance from the Armistice Line on the 17th, the Fourth and Second Armies were both disposed in the same manner, with two corps in front line and two in second, the IX, VI, Canadian and II Corps leading. Their march orders were much the same : the leading divisions, the 66th, Guards, 29th and 41st were to get into position near the line on the 16th by 6 p.m., with the 2nd Cavalry Division covering the front of the Fourth Army and the 1st Cavalry Division that of the Second Army : on the 17th the cavalry was to be clear of the Armistice front line by 10 a.m. and east of Line No. 1 by 6 p.m. : the infantry was to start at 8 a.m. according to a march table.

To take the VI Corps as an example, its advance was to be carried out in two columns, Southern and Northern ; the former consisted of the 62nd Division, marching with its units at wide distances, followed a day later by the 3rd Division ; the Northern consisted of the Guards Division, followed a day later by the 2nd Division, and another day later by the corps heavy artillery and corps troops. To each division was attached an Army brigade R.F.A., and to each of the leading divisions were allotted two troops of the 13th Australian Light Horse, one company of a cyclist battalion, a cable section, an Army Troops company R.E. for major road repairs, and a section of a tunnelling company R.E. to deal with booby traps and delay-action charges.

Routes were suggested by the corps, but it was left to the leading divisional commanders to vary them after receipt of road reconnaissance reports, and " evacuation liaison groups " were sent forward with the cavalry divisions to collect the necessary information. Very often a division was able to make use of two roads for at least part of its route—one indeed, managed to find three for a few days. Road repair troops (field companies R.E., pioneers, etc.) were also sent ahead of the main bodies behind the cavalry, protected by small advanced guards ; for, until craters had been filled in, the main bodies

could not well proceed.   During the advance, all military
precautions against surprise were taken, any "enemy"
encountered was made prisoner, the air along the routes was
patrolled from dawn to dusk, and the roads were piqueted at
night.   The troops were distributed in sufficient depth to
facilitate supply ; but arrangements were made to ensure that
sufficient forces could be made available at 48 hours' notice to
overcome any resistance the enemy might attempt to oppose
the advance.

INTELLIGENCE DUTIES

The attention of Intelligence officers was directed to :

(i) the detection of enemy agents and soldiers ;

(ii) the detection of attempts to spread anti-Ally propaganda ;

(iii) the detection of German soldiers who had no wish to
return to Germany (a number had already been reported to
have disguised themselves in plain clothes) ;

(iv) the investigation among civilians as to the position of
delay-action mines ; and

(v) the collection of information of interest, such as the
state of enemy morale, atrocities committed, breaches of
Armistice terms.

POSSIBILITY OF DELAYS

Maréchal Foch was informed by G.H.Q. that difficulties
might arise to prevent any advance in force at the named
dates, and on the 20th he replied as follows :

" It is necessary as much for the maintenance of order in
evacuated territories as for the strict execution of the Armistice
that the Allied troops should follow the movement of the German
troops in accordance with the conditions laid down.

" If the state of the roads and railways does not allow of the
advance of the whole of the forces ordered with the rapidity
required, will it not be possible to push light detachments of all
arms along the roads, capable of holding the country, of picking up
enemy stragglers, of taking delivery of war material and prisoners,
and, in fact, able to cross the lines laid down on the dates fixed ?
If, however, the infantry advanced guards cannot reach the German
frontier until an indefinite date subsequent to the 1st December,
on which day they should cross the frontier, the occupation of the
Rhine territories by British troops will be considerably delayed, and
this may make it necessary to push forward troops of another
nationality for the purpose."

As a result, the leading Armies were informed that, provided
the heads of the advanced guards arrived on the frontier by

the date fixed (cavalry 30th November ; infantry 1st December), the number of marches and the distances covered might be varied.

The Generalissimo at this moment made an attempt to jockey French divisions into the lead of the Allied Armies. He ordered two of them into the American Zone and three into the British Zone, with instructions to go to the top of the bridgehead, and two others to the front of the Belgian sector. General Hunter-Liggett ordered the pair sent to the U.S. Army to stand fast on the German frontier ; whereupon Maréchal Foch reduced the front of the American sector. Sir Douglas Haig objected to the presence of any French divisions in his sector, as also did H.M. King Albert, and the affair ended with one French division sandwiched in a tiny space on the left bank of the Rhine between the British and Belgians, where it was handy to enter Düsseldorf, if required.

ADMINISTRATIVE ARRANGEMENTS

The administrative orders drawn up before the advance were very thorough.[1] Amongst other things, they dealt with uniformity in dress ; sanitation in billets (a clearing-up party under an officer was to be left behind in every locality to tidy up, so as to ensure all was clean for the troops who were following) ; the dumping of unrequired stores, e.g. tents, trench shelters, light trench mortars and surplus ammunition, whilst spare boots and underclothing were to be carried ; the formation of rest stations to save having to evacuate the sick ; care of sick animals left behind with inhabitants, for which forage for seven days was to be dumped ; the issue of rations to German personnel left in charge of sick and wounded.

INCIDENTS OF THE MARCH

Various changes of the original programme had to be made on the 16th : all moves except of the cavalry and the road-repair parties were, on account of supply difficulties, postponed 24 hours, and on the 17th the cavalry went little more than half-way to Line No. 1 ; but they went over it to the line Charleroi (inclusive)–Hal next day. The infantry advanced on the 18th, their blankets and kits carried on wagons ; but on the 19th the second-line divisions were ordered to stand fast. On the 21st, only the cavalry and the divisions of the Second Army marched ; on the 22nd and 23rd, owing to the railway

---

[1] Those of the Cavalry Corps are given as a specimen in Appendix VI.

situation and the greasy state of the roads, no moves were made except by the II Corps (on the 23rd), and the road-repair parties and their covering advanced guards ; on the 24th the cavalry went on ; on the 25th the Meuse south of Namur was reached by the Fourth Army, the Canadian Corps and II Corps of the Second Army being a little ahead, actually on Line No. 2, and the cavalry abreast of Huy.

After another halt of two days by the Fourth Army and of one day by the Second Army, ten miles were covered on the 28th by the Fourth Army, the cavalry being abreast of Liége on the 27th and, halting on the 28th ; the 1st Cavalry Division alone was to go on towards the frontier on the 29th, but had to halt on that day on account of supply difficulties. On the 28th, the 62nd Division (VI Corps) began side-slipping south-wards for transfer to the IX Corps, the 3rd Division marching up to the Meuse in its place, and on the evening of that day, by order from G.H.Q., the Fourth Army came to a halt about 40 miles from the German frontier ; but the leading divisions of the Second Army continued on. The IX and VI Corps of the Fourth Army, and the New Zealand Division (from the IV Corps) were now transferred to the Second Army for the march into Germany ; the two corps were to follow behind the Canadian Corps and the II Corps, and the New Zealanders were to join the II Corps by march, the Fourth Army receiving the III and XXII Corps in the second line of the Second Army in their place.[1] The cavalry advanced guards reached the German frontier on the 30th November ready to cross it on the 1st December according to plan, and the infantry advanced guards of the 2nd Canadian and 29th Divisions, which now covered the whole, much narrowed, front of the British array, arrived there on the evening of the latter day.

Signs of German Demoralization

Few incidents of note occurred during the march to the frontier except the meeting of streams of escaped prisoners of war, British, French and Belgian in starved and ragged condition, a subject dealt with below, and troubles due to the destruction of road and railway ; in some cases, craters blocked the way, which had blown after the reconnoitring officers had reported all clear. Many unguarded German dumps, including much ammunition, were found, and some explosions were

---

[1] See Appendix III for the Order of Battle.

heard.[1] The Fourth Army had no communication with the enemy ; but an officer of the German *Seventeenth Army* spent three days with the Second Army cavalry locating dumps, including one in the railway station at Gembloux of 306 trucks loaded with guns, aircraft and munitions, 18 ambulance wagons and 120 empty trucks, abandoned without a guard, and another large one of trucks, aircraft, artillery and machine guns at Nivelles (18 miles south of Brussels) ; but the number of guns and other material discovered in most cases did not correspond with his lists. The 1st Cavalry Division found a large un-guarded dump of rolling stock, guns and explosives at Manage station (ten miles north-west of Charleroi), and at Dinant took over 150 trench mortars and corresponding stores from a German guard. Sometimes the local Belgian officials pointed out dumps, stating that the German guards posted on them had fled. Many dead horses and broken-down lorries were seen. Inhabitants reported that the retreating enemy had carried off all the horses, cattle and supplies he could, taking even crockery and bedding from the better houses where officers had lodged, and that generally a great deal of straggling, pilllaging and plundering had taken place, the marching columns being followed by swarms of marauders in search of food and drink. The only place at which the cavalry ran into a body of Germans was at Regné, actually on Line No. 2 east of Marche, where a squadron of the 12th Lancers arrived at 1 p.m. on the 24th. The place should have been clear by the night of the 20th, but as the Germans were unarmed and ran into the houses, they were not interfered with. All the German Armies were over the frontier in the British sector by the 26th.

On the 15th, the French had asked that a detachment might be sent to Philippeville, where the Germans were no longer under control of their officers, and looting was taking place. The 12th Lancers, a section R.H.A. and two armoured cars were despatched ; but the Germans had left before they arrived, and one squadron then went on to Florennes (13 miles south-east of Charleroi) to find it clear also. On the 19th the Governor of Namur similarly asked for assistance and a cavalry regiment and two machine guns were sent, and next day a squadron went to Hal to stop a disturbance.

There is no doubt that the inhabitants had themselves done some looting of the German dumps. In one case, under the impression that the German explosive Perdite, which is packed

---

[1] Amongst others, it was verified that the Germans had blown up dumps at Jamioulx (four miles south of Namur) on 14th November, and at Beez, east of Namur, on the 18th.

in oiled paper, was soap, civilians had carried off a considerable quantity. It was clearly established by sounds heard, indications discovered, and on the evidence of inhabitants that the Germans had blown up ammunition trains and dumps after Armistice Day, doing much damage to the railways and private property ; returned prisoners of war stated that they had seen Germans disguised as British prisoners engaged on this work in the zone between the belligerents.

Reinforcements continued to arrive during the march at the rate of a hundred to two hundred a division, and the grant of leave continued, but divisions complained that the guarding of the numerous dumps depleted their fighting strength. The billets had at first been poor, but as the columns strung out and villages untouched by war were reached, they gradually improved. Exchange presented a problem, as German paper money was in use throughout Belgium and the rate was fixed at 70 centimes per mark, while the inhabitants wanted the pre-war rate of 1.25 francs. The general attitude of the Belgians, however, was one of rejoicing, and rioting was reported only in Wavre, where damage was done to the houses of " pro-Boches " ; but there were stories of fighting between parties of German troops, in which a number of officers had been killed and injured. British officers making for Spa reported that the march discipline of the fighting troops was good, but not that of the communication units and specialists : the horsed vehicles were overloaded, often with household goods : there was no petrol whatever, and cattle and horses were being driven off. The attitude of the men, they thought, was sullen : the soldiers' councils were in control of everything, including railways, telegraphs, telephones and wireless, and a few red flags were seen : selected officers were permitted to function in order to get the troops back, the delegates listening rather than taking charge : the officers otherwise had little control and were afraid of the men, and in some cases their badges of rank had been torn off, and their decorations, which were not popular, had been discarded.

RETURN OF PRISONERS OF WAR

The first parties of liberated prisoners of war and internees for whom the Quarter-Master-General was called upon to provide, about 3,600 (including 250 women and children) came not from Germany but from Bulgaria and Turkey. Landed at Taranto at the beginning of November, they passed through by rail to camps at the Channel ports and were disembarked at

Dover. In view of the doubtless early return of the 140,000 British prisoners of war in Germany, Lieut.-General Sir Travers Clarke took up the subject anew, and Dover having been designated as the port at which they should land, he selected Dunkirk as the principal port of embarkation. The governing principle of his policy as regards the prisoners was that whatever the resources of the Armies in France could provide should be employed without the ordinary considerations of economy, to feed, clothe, comfort and transport them home.

Orders were immediately given for the preparation of a reception camp at Dunkirk capable of accommodating 40,000 men, with a view to its use later on for demobilization ; the Q.M.A.A.C. Camp at Havre was likewise prepared, also with an eye to the demobilization of that corps.

With a view, too, to the orderly repatriation of the prisoners in accordance with a well-thought-out plan, the Q.M.G. made urgent representations through the Commander-in-Chief to the War Office, that when the terms of the Armistice were under consideration, his control should not be confined to the Army areas and the Bases, but should be extended to Germany itself, in order that the despatch of prisoners might be regulated in accordance with the facilities existing on the British side. His forethought was frustrated by events. Hardly was the Armistice signed before reports were received at G.H.Q. that large numbers of ex-prisoners of war, including Italians and Russians, were arriving in the Army areas. They were mostly men held and employed in the German areas west of the Rhine, whose guards had simply abandoned them, leaving them without food, money or medical attendance to find their way to the Allied lines as best they could. To cope with this situation, the accommodation at the existing camps at Calais and Boulogne was hastily extended ; but the foreigners were segregated near the front. At a conference in the Q.M.G.'s room at G.H.Q. on the 14th, however, it was announced that the War Office had made arrangements that 100,000 prisoners should be sent through Rotterdam, and that the 40,000 who were comparatively near the Swiss border should be taken across France and despatched from the French ports ; but meantime evacuation as arranged could continue. For the foreigners accommodation was ordered to be prepared at Rouen, where, at a pinch, prisoners-of-war " cages " could be utilized. Thus two authorities, the War Office and G.H.Q., had begun to deal with prisoners of war—and a third, the Spa Commission, was soon to take a hand.

The released prisoners were collected by the troops at the front, the Cavalry Corps forming a committee, of which the French and Belgian liaison officers were members, to send them back in empty lorries. Many of them being in a starved and feeble condition, motor buses, and later motor ambulance vans, were detailed from the Army pools to meet them, and, with the consent of the German commanders, supplies of food for them were sent ahead of the foremost troops. The prisoners were directed through the two leading Armies to reception stations organized by the Armies in second line, where they were refitted with boots and clothing and despatched by train to the base, five train loads being sent before 14th December.

The first two train loads, carrying nearly a thousand men, reached Calais early on 15th November, before the Spa Commission had even met. From that date the stream was continuous, and the strain on the motor services was not relaxed until the 27th, when the railway was through to Mons, which then became the main forward collecting station, ambulance trains being run to it ; but until 13th December, when the line was doubled, it was not practicable to provide a through service to the base.

Many prisoners found their way into the American and French areas, and it was judged advisable to send railway transport officers to certain points in these areas to advise when parties were being despatched, special arrangements being made to forward to Calais those which arrived in Paris. By the end of November over 16,000 prisoners had been returned to England, and 6,600 foreigners, chiefly Portuguese and Italians, had been entrained and sent into the zones of their own divisions. In the first month of the Armistice, at least in France, 75,000 British, or more than one-half, reached the Allied lines.[1]

---

[1] The subject of returned prisoners is further dealt with in Chapter III.

CHAPTER III

THE PERMANENT INTERNATIONAL ARMISTICE COMMISSION

The Formation of the Commission

On 12th November the Generalissimo invited Sir Douglas Haig to nominate the chief of a British delegation to a Permanent International Armistice Commission which was to assemble at Spa in Belgium : its task would be to ensure that the terms of the Armistice were carried out. The choice fell upon Lieut.-General Sir Richard Haking, the commander of the XI Corps, who had been at the Staff College in the same year as the Commander-in-Chief, and spoke French well. On the following day the names of the other senior members of the Commission were telephoned to G.H.Q. from the Maréchal's headquarters, with a bald outline of the duties required of them, as follows :

" In accordance with the enactments of Article 34 of the Armistice Convention of the 11th November, a Permanent International Armistice Commission has been formed.

" The Commission is charged with the study and preparations for the execution of Articles 3, 4, 6, 7, 10 and 18[1] in co-operation with members nominated by the German General Staff. It has no authority to modify the conditions laid down in the original text of those Articles, which remains unalterable ; it has authority, however, when it has examined matters and deems it necessary, to lay before the Maréchal, proposals as regards the practical execution of the Articles.

" The Commission will consist of a delegation from each of the Allied Armies, comprising : a general, chief of the delegation, assisted by officers and officials specially experienced in dealing with questions of war material, prisoners of war, military and civil internees, transport and supply.

" The heads of the delegations are : French Army : General de Division Nudant[2] ; British Army : Lieut.-General Sir R. Haking ; American Army : Major-General Rhoades ; Belgian Army : Major-General Delobbe.[3]

" The Head of the French Delegation is the representative of the Maréchal Commanding-in-Chief of the Allied Armies, and is charged with referring to him all proposals made by the Commission ".

---

[1] See Appendix I. The articles refer to the repatriation of inhabitants, prisoners of war and interned civilians, the surrender of arms and aircraft, the cessation of demolitions, and the handing over of rolling stock and lorries.

[2] In the first ten months of the war General Nudant had commanded an artillery regiment and an infantry brigade, and had been Chief of the Staff of the Fourth Army, and head of the Operations Section at G.Q.G. ; in June, 1915, he received command of a division ; he was promoted to a corps in March, 1916, a position held by him until the Armistice.

[3] Italy and Japan were not represented.

The Duties of the Commission

In a letter to Sir Douglas Haig which followed, the Maréchal wrote :

" The duties of this Commission will be to investigate and discover, in agreement with the other Allied delegates and the German staff, any details of principle in connection with the clauses of the Armistice which were not settled when that instrument was signed.

" The Commission will make proposals and recommendations : decisions will be taken by Maréchal Foch. The subjects with which it will deal will be as follows :

" (i) Repatriation of Prisoners of War, military and civil—Articles Nos. 3 and 18. [No. 10 is here omitted.]

" (ii) Handing over of material of war—Article 4.

" (iii) Taking over of depôts, stores, etc.—Article 6.

" (iv) Handing over of locomotives, wagons and lorries —Article 7."

The Commission was at first to be small, but to have power to add to its numbers. Until Sir Douglas Haig's G.H.Q. was dissolved, Lieut.-General Haking addressed reports and communications to him, and afterwards direct to the War Office.

The British Delegation

The British delegation[1] left for Spa by car on the 14th and passed en route a number of German columns consisting mainly of artillery and transport, the infantry having been carried by rail, and these columns continued to pass through Spa for several days.

The German Representatives

The German Government nominated Minister Plenipotentiary von Haniel and Major-General von Winterfeldt, a General Staff officer who had been chief of a section of the Great General Staff before and after August, 1914, and the military member of the delegation under Herr Erzberger which had negotiated

---

[1] Besides Lieut.-General Haking, the delegation consisted of Br.-General A. F. U. Green (D.A. & Q.M.G.), Lieut.-Colonel G. H. Addison (Assistant to Engineer-in-Chief), Major A. Pam (D.A.D.R.T. Transportation), Captain E. A. Baring-Gould (Intelligence Corps), Lieut. S. Bellhouse (Cipher Officer), Captain W. H. Mann (a.d.c.), with clerks, batmen and transport.

On the 16th the following were ordered to proceed next day, and they arrived at Spa on the 18th : Major-General Sir J. Adye, Lieut.-Colonel G. E. C. Rabagliati, R.A.F., Major G. W. Ware, R.A.M.C., and Captain W. H. Anderson.

They were followed, at Lieut.-General Haking's request, by Major Gurney (D.A. & Q.M.G.), to take charge of the office, and Major E. T. Hynes (Camp Commandant). A signal officer, with a wireless set, was subsequently added.

and signed the Armistice. Their principal assistants were Freiherr von Lersner of the Foreign Office and Major Papst (for prisoners of war).[1] It must be premised that while the Allies to all appearance were dealing with a republican government in Berlin, behind the Government and directing its policy was the composite brain of the old Great General Staff, with the next war always in mind. Under the direction of that Staff, the returned Army put down revolution and saved the new Government, circumstances which President Ebert was never permitted to forget. For his part, he well knew that at a favourable moment the Great General Staff might turn him and his associates out. Observers noted that the nominal rulers, who had had no experience in ruling, were just as obsequious to the old privileged military caste as before 1918, and exhibited their old inferiority complex.[2]

On 16th and 20th December, 1918, two meetings of General Staff officers, with General Schleicher (later murdered in the " purge " of the 30th June, 1934) in the chair,[3] were held in Berlin for the purpose of deciding on a national policy. It was proposed by Schleicher first to re-establish internal order, then to rebuild Germany's economic system, and finally to reconstitute her armed forces. General von Seeckt, who had posted home from Turkey where he had been the German nominated Chief of the General Staff, proposed that the order of the last two items should be reversed. This idea met with

---

[1] An unaccredited German representative who " hovered around in the corridor " was Herr Stinnes, the millionaire industrialist. He provided much useful information about the Rhineland, particularly its power and water supply, hoping, it was suspected, to obtain in return special treatment for the industrial magnates, and particularly for his own properties.

[2] The power of the General Staff was soon reasserted. It brought to an end the *Reichstag's* Commission of Enquiry into the causes of the loss of the war and who were responsible for it, and stopped the publication of the proceedings which was in hand.

Once President Ebert asked Seeckt, " *Wie steht die Reichswehr* [How is the " *Reichswehr* getting on] ? " The general replied instantly, " *Die Reichswehr* "*steht hinter mich* [The *Reichswehr* stands behind me] ". M.W.B. No. 26 of 1942, column 707.

From March, 1919 onwards, Colonel Bauer, who had been a General Staff officer at O.H.L. in 1914–18 both under Falkenhayn and under Ludendorff, came from Berlin very secretly, and paid the British Military Governor of Cologne a monthly visit, in order, no doubt, to find out the lie of the land. On his third visit he asked, " What would the Allied Govern-" ments' representatives in Paris think if the *Reichstag* had been driven out " like your Parliament was by Cromwell ? " He was told that our people had not forgotten enough to allow them to regard an action of that sort with equanimity. On the next and last visit Bauer said : " We had a meeting " after I got back and decided to postpone action *sine die*. There were other " reasons, but what you told me about the Allied views in Paris was the " thing that caused the decision."

[3] See " Seeckt. Aus seinem Leben " ii., by General von Rabenau.

general approval, and Seeckt at once became the foremost member of the Great General Staff, possibly aided by the factor that his service, except in the opening phase, had been in the East and his name was not connected in any way with the defeats on the Western Front.[1]

German Attempts to Obtain Modification of the Armistice Terms

To use the words of Colonel S. G. Shartle, an American member of the Spa Commission,[2]

> " The Germans, having gotten over their first dazed condition, became cocky. . . . They began to recover somewhat from their stupor and wanted to be considered the delegates of a first-class Power. The whole period covered by the deliveries [of material] was marked by protests and excuses on the part of the Germans for their failure to carry out the conditions to which they had agreed."

It must be emphasized that at first, as the British General Staff reported on 28th June, 1920, the obstruction to the execution of " Armistice and Treaty terms came from the " military party in spite of apparent honest intentions on the " part of the Government and the people as a whole ". The policy of resistance to the peace terms was, in fact, directed by one man, General von Seeckt, in whose hands the civilian

---

[1] The compiler had a conversation with Seeckt in 1935, about 18 months before his death. The general admitted that Winterfeldt and his successor Hammerstein acted on the orders of the General Staff, but the German commissioners were also under the orders of a large Commission of 13 Sections, the *Waffenstillstand Kommission* (known as " *Wako* "), sitting in Berlin. (*Waffenstillstand* iii., p. 412 *et seq.*)

Seeckt was nominated by President Ebert to take over the peace duties of the Chief of the General Staff until the nominal dissolution of that body under the terms of the Peace Treaty, and he accompanied Graf Brockdorf-Rantzau to the Peace Conference as military expert. On 1st October, 1919, under the new conditions of the reduced Army of the peace terms, he was appointed *Chef des Truppenamtes* (literally, Chief of the Army Directorate), and next year *Chef des Heeresleitung* (Chief of the Army High Command). Actually, he was invested with all the powers and duties not only of the old Chief of the General Staff, but also with command of the *Reichswehr*. By 1926 Seeckt was becoming too powerful and was working for a Hohenzollern restoration, so the *Reichspräsident*, influenced perhaps by knowledge of a military intrigue against the " Chef ", took an opportunity which Seeckt gave by allowing the eldest son of the ex-Crown Prince to attend Army training, to put him on the retired list.

The *Tägliche Rundschau* of 15th October, 1926 (quoted in Stresemann iii., p. 84) had a note, sent by Herr Stresemann, that " the retirement of General " von Seeckt was due entirely to a matter of military discipline, and was " decided solely and alone by the *Reichswehr* Minister and the *Reichs* " President, von Hindenburg, without any action on the part of the Cabinet."

[2] In his book, " Spa, Versailles, Munich ". The present tense of the verb in the first paragraph has been changed to the past.

Minister of War, Dr. Gessler[1], was more or less of a puppet, with all the underground military and civil machinery at his disposal[2], and from 1920 onwards the support of the Government and people as a whole, to carry it out.

While the French sought to use the Armistice Commission in such a way as to complete the defeat of Germany, the German representatives took advantage of it to search for a weak spot in the Allied political front in order to obtain more lenient terms and reduce if not imperil the value of the Armistice to the Allies.

At the first assembly of the Commission, Winterfeldt appealed for the modification of the Armistice terms, which he had himself signed as military member of the Delegation only five days earlier.   He insisted that the German Armies must be allowed more time to carry out their withdrawal, urging it was a technical impossibility that by the agreed dates the 60 divisions of the *Fourth* and *Sixth Armies* could be squeezed through the space between Spa and the Maastricht Appendix (Holland), that the 66 divisions of the *Seventeenth* and *Eighteenth Armies* could pass between Spa and Luxembourg, and that three million men could be marched through the bottle-neck of the Rhine bridges ; so that a catastrophe must ensue.   He held out as a threat that to avoid capture the men would break ranks and disperse, plundering and pillaging in search of food.[3]

Winterfeldt further maintained that the demand for rolling stock was based on pre-war conditions and failed to take into account the casualties and wear and tear of four years of war ; and that the handing over of so many locomotives and wagons would bring about the disruption of the economic life of Germany and prejudice the evacuation of prisoners—a strong

---

[1] Otto Gessler was a civil official who had been a *Bürgermeister* and *Oberbürgermeister*.   He succeeded Noske as Minister of War in March, 1920, and continued in the post, regardless of change of Ministry, until he retired on account of ill-health in January, 1928.   He was retained by desire of Seeckt and his successor as useful cover.

[2] The British agents quickly found out the ramifications of an extensive German secret service directed by Seeckt's staff, whose principal object was the promotion of Communism among the troops of occupation and of division between the Allies.

[3] A swarm of marauders did follow the troops, but they had not deserted on account of fear of capture.   So far from the time proving insufficient, intercepted German Army wireless messages reported on the 24th November and subsequent days that the German rear guards were a day ahead of time ; and they were never caught up.   Certainly a number of guns and vehicles and much plunder had to be abandoned ; but the only soldiers encountered, as will be seen later, were a few parties left to guard depôts, marauders, and men who, being inhabitants of the Rhineland, had fallen out and demobilized themselves.

card which time after time he did not neglect to exhibit. He continually raised the question of the feeding of the German population, which was entirely outside the province of the Armistice Commission and was being dealt with by the Supreme War Council.[1] Winterfeldt also protested against the continuance of the land blockade, claiming that Article 26 applied only to the sea. Admission of this interpretation would have given the Germans a right to pass at will through the Allied outpost lines, an untenable contention. He and the other German representatives insisted upon regarding the War as ended by the Armistice.[2] It was only too obvious to them that the Allied political leaders also regarded the War as ended and had no desire to recommence it. But, unless specifically stated otherwise, the termination of hostilities, except perhaps in the case of complete conquest, can be brought about only by ratification of the peace terms. The Hague Rules are perfectly clear on this point : Article 36 states that an armistice only " suspends " operations. When some of the Allies on entering Germany issued proclamations copied verbatim from German posters put up in France and Belgium in 1914–18, the German delegates were loud in protest, on the grounds that the War was over and the enactments therefore were no longer applicable.[3]

From first to last the attitude of the German representatives was obstructive, and did not " facilitate ", as the Armistice terms intended, the settlement of affairs. The rapid demobilization of all the Allied Armies naturally encouraged them to stiffen that attitude. It is recorded that even by 18th November the Germans had " become less humble, and as " time went on they became increasingly arrogant ". In spite of the knowledge of the complete collapse of Germany and the German Army, it was only by the threat of Maréchal Foch to occupy more German territory, and by the actual occupation of a bridgehead at Strassburg, that they were forced to comply with the easy terms which they had obtained on suspension of hostilities.

---

[1] See Chap. VII.

[2] As an argument, they said that the Armistice had been negotiated with the Government, not with the High Command of the Army.

[3] *Deutscher Geschichtskalender. Der Europäischer Krieg in Aktenmässiger Darstellung* gives dozens of formal protests made by the Germans which are unmentioned in English or French records. Of the first 64 items of the Contents, 24 are " protests ", the subjects varying from the employment of coloured troops in the Occupied Territories to the meaning attributed by the Allies to the words " cost of occupation ".

The behaviour of the French representatives to the Germans was severely " correct ", but no more ; and they resented anything in the nature of friendliness on the part of the British towards their adversaries.   It turned out to be unfortunate that Winterfeldt and his colleagues had been treated courteously, an attitude they attributed to weakness : they should have been informed bluntly and firmly at the beginning, before demobilization had been begun, that the business of the Commission was to see the terms executed, and that though representations might be made the final decision lay with the Allied Commander-in-Chief.   General Nudant does not seem to have sought special powers from Maréchal Foch to suppress the German representatives : in verbal cut and thrust he invariably had the better of his Prussian antagonists, and with this he was content.

DEPARTURE OF THE COMMISSION FROM THE ORIGINAL INSTRUCTIONS

The German representatives at Spa early suggested that a high German official should be nominated, with whom, and with whom alone, the Allied military authorities should communicate in all matters affecting the Occupation.   The acceptance of this proposal would have placed all the German official hierarchy in the Occupied Territory under one man, making him virtually the German ruler of the Occupied Territory.   Maréchal Foch who naturally preferred that the Allied generals should do the ruling rejected this proposal. It would have been convenient, however, not only to the Generalissimo, as commander of all the Allied Armies of Occupation, but also to the Allied Governments, since diplomatic relations with Germany were not resumed until the Peace Treaty had been ratified as they could have communicated direct with some highly placed German authority instead of through the cumbrous and time-absorbing channel of a neutral Power.   Thus the Spa Commission very soon became the agency for obtaining information on the military, political and economic condition of Germany during the whole of the Armistice period, the debating chamber and clearing house of a vast number of questions, including economic and financial questions,[1] referring not only to the Western but to the Eastern Front and other theatres, and particularly to Alsace-Lorraine, which were entirely outside and beyond its original competence. This was exactly what the German representatives desired, and directing them was the hidden hand of General von Seeckt : it was with him that the Allied representatives had to contend.

Eventually, on 10th July, 1919, the vicarious duties of the Commission were officially recognised and defined in this sense by the Allied political leaders in Paris :

" (1) The Inter-Allied Armistice Commission will remain the machinery of communication between the Allied Governments and the Germans until the coming into force of the Treaty of Peace.

" (2) As soon as the Treaty has been ratified, communications between the Allied Governments and the Germans will pass through the channel of diplomatic representatives appointed to the respective capitals ".

---

[1] To give an instance of the work of the Commission, the proceedings of 18th July are taken at random. The Commission dealt with an amendment regarding the raising of the blockade ; reports on present conditions in Germany and in the Ruhr district ; the occupation of Silesia ; the evacuation of Latvia ; the grant of trade credit to Germany ; the influence of the German press in exciting hostile manifestations, amounting to incitement to murder, against Allied troops in unoccupied territory ; a complaint of the Union of West German Trade Mills that its mills were idle and asking for freedom of intercourse with the rest of Germany ; a request that the house of Dr. Vogels, an expelled professor of Strassburg University, in Bonn might be evacuated ; the repatriation of Alsatians ; organized train robberies in the Neutral Zone by a gang from Germany ; the missing luggage belonging to German seamen returning from Spain ; requests for passes for a German analytic chemist and a notary, and for the Bavarian Prime Minister to visit his mother in occupied territory ; the release of confiscated furniture belonging to a German general, a colonel and a police officer ; the confiscation of the money of persons leaving Alsace-Lorraine for Germany ; arrest in Belgium of German industrials on the ground that they had in their possession in Germany machinery and material looted in France and Belgium ; the discovery in Cologne of a large quantity of spirits belonging to the German Army and falsely declared to be private property ; other illegal sales ; the whereabouts of a missing German furniture van ; the return of papers belonging to former students of Strassburg University ; a request for extracts from Mannheim prison register ; Major-General Carton de Wiart's mission to Warsaw ; Bolshevist propaganda from Nauen ; supply of stone from Germany for upkeep of roads in occupied territory ; pass for *The Times* correspondent to go to Berlin ; the German merchant ensign ; documents in Nurse Cavell case (executed by the Germans in Belgium) ; and a dozen minor questions about various arrests and sentences.

Daily the German representatives raised protests against Allied action not only in the Rhineland as to the occupation of buildings, arrests, expulsion and imprisonment of individuals and details of the execution of the Armistice terms, but also about Poland, the Baltic provinces, the Ukraine, Turkey, particularly as regards the repatriation of German troops and the expulsion of individuals, and appropriation of their alleged private property in the last-named country.

THE SUB-COMMISSIONS

The Commission at its first meeting formed three sub-commissions : " Prisoners of War," on which the British were represented by Major-General Sir J. Adye ; " Transportation " (Handing Over)," of which Major Pam was a member, and " War Material (Handing Over)," of which Lieut.-Colonel Addison was a member.[1] The duties of the Commission and its sub-commissions were from first to last directing, co-ordinating, advisory and consultative : their members never left Spa on duty ; the executive work was done by agents provided by the Armies, over whom they exercised no more than general control.

As regards ceded transportation and material, the reception of aircraft was undertaken by the R.A.F. ; of locomotives and railway wagons by the *Commission Interalliée de Réception de Matériel* (C.I.R.M.). By a request of Maréchal Foch, made on 18th December, 1918, to the Commanders-in-Chief that they should appoint commissions for the purpose, the reception of the remainder, that is war material and lorries, was taken over and accounted for by the " Q " Branches of the Armies. In the case of the British, the subordinate " Q " staffs reported each night to the Q.M.G. at G.H.Q. the amount ceded or found abandoned during the previous 24 hours. Each of the Allied Armies similarly reported to the Spa Commission as the representative of Maréchal Foch for this purpose. It was evident that the policy of the Germans was the evasion of the terms. They pretended that the numbers required did not exist, since much had been captured or abandoned, and that, living from hand to mouth, they had no reserve ; or they tried to deliver damaged or obsolete goods. The discovery, however, of an attempt to sell aircraft and 500 aero engines to a neutral Power gave the sub-commission a timely lever ; by its use, by the pressure already being exercised at the prolongation of the Armistice, by the occupation of a bridgehead at Strassburg, and by other means the German representatives to some extent were brought back to realities.[2]   In the end everything except the full number of locomotives and wagons was handed over, and a quantity of agricultural machinery was substituted for the missing quota.

---

[1] The rest of the delegation was divided among the following sections : Office Administration, R.A.F., Signals, Medical, Intelligence (cipher and interpreters, etc.), camp command, all under Lieut.-Colonel J. A. Cuffe.

[2] As a protest against the occupation of the Strassburg bridgehead, Major-General von Winterfeldt resigned as German representative on the Spa Commission, and was succeeded by General Freiherr von Hammerstein, who was commanding in Wesel.

PROLONGATIONS OF THE ARMISTICE

The necessity for successive prolongations of the time limit of the Armistice afforded opportunities to stiffen the terms, which it had become evident that the German Army meant to evade as far as possible.

The nature of the Articles in the Conventions for the three prolongations of the Armistice gives a good general idea of the way Germany failed to fulfil the conditions to which she had pledged the national honour.

On 13th December, the day on which the infantry crossed the Rhine, the Armistice, due to expire on 17th January, 1919, was renewed for a month, that is to 5 a.m. on 17th February, 1919. The convention was signed by the same delegates as on 11th November.

Before the meeting a statement of the infractions of the Armistice terms was handed to the German delegates.[1] To this Herr Erzberger answered by a long series of excuses alleging in general the powerlessness of the German Government and the confusion reigning both in the country and in the Army. He received a formal reply signed on behalf of Maréchal Foch by General Weygand :

> " Taking into account, in particular, the bad treatment of and the cruelties (sévices) inflicted on the Allied prisoners, also the diminution of the financial guarantees given by Germany to the Allies, the Allied High Command continues from now onwards to reserve to itself the right to occupy, when it judges proper, as a fresh guarantee, the Neutral Zone of the right bank of the Rhine from the north of the Cologne bridgehead to the Dutch frontier "

This meant the occupation of the western part of the Ruhr almost up to Essen.

Two clauses were added to that formally extending the Armistice. Article II read :—

> " The execution of the clauses of the 11th November not yet completely carried out will be continued and completed during the prolongation of the Armistice in accordance with details settled by the Permanent International Armistice Commission under the instructions of the Allied High Command ".

Article III repeated the threat, already made in Maréchal Foch's letter, to occupy more German territory.

On 16th January, 1919, the Armistice was prolonged by a month for a second time. By its clauses, in lieu of the balance of a proportion of the locomotives and rolling stock which the

---

[1] This was embodied as Articles IV–XIX in the Convention prolonging the Armistice. See Note I at end of Chapter.

German Government professed their inability to furnish in accordance with the original Armistice terms, they were to hand over fixed quantities of agricultural machinery and instruments.[1] By another clause an International Commission, to sit in Berlin, was formed in order to care for the Russian prisoners of war in Germany. It was to be composed of officers of the Allied Armies already there to organize the evacuation of the prisoners of war belonging to the Armies of the Entente, and of the representatives of the various relief associations. After some additional naval clauses, provision was made for the immediate restitution of industrial and agricultural machinery and implements of all kinds carried off by the German Armies from France and Belgium. In order to secure the provisioning of Germany and the rest of Europe, the German merchant fleet was to be handed over to the Allies for the duration of the Armistice. As guarantee for the observance of the Convention, the Allied High Command reserved to itself the right to occupy the fortifications of Strassburg situated on the right (east) bank of the Rhine and a 10-kilometre Neutral Zone round them.

The Armistice was prolonged for the third, and last, time on 16th February, 1919.[2] The principal Article referred to Poland, and forbade Germany to continue offensive operations in that country ; the execution of the Articles of the earlier conventions, not fully accomplished, was to be proceeded with and concluded ; and the Armistice was prolonged indefinitely, the Allies reserving the right to terminate it by giving three days' notice.

DELIVERY OF AIRCRAFT

Two hundred bombing aircraft and 400 pursuit type were to be delivered within the British bridgeheads before 1st January, 1919. It was laid down that 1 in 20 of the aircraft handed over should, after a preliminary examination of all parts, be flown by a German pilot ; that any rejected on examination could be replaced by 20 horses, and any rejected after flight by 40 horses. The Germans were to provide the mechanics, the British the petrol ; the German delivery officer might make a prolonged stay, but the specialist personnel were to be sent home after satisfying the reception committees.

Reports showed that between 11th and 14th November, hundreds of aircraft had been flown back to Germany. Later reports indicated that many were in use on the

---

[1] See Appendix VII, for the text of the Convention.
[2] Appendix VIII.

Eastern frontier, where the Germans hoped by the retention of Courland, Lithuania, and Esthonia to enjoy compensation for the loss of Alsace-Lorraine. At first none were forthcoming. The excuse made was bad flying weather; then that the machines flown home had been dismantled; next that the revolutionaries had destroyed large numbers—actually in the Cologne area a number were destroyed by the German air troops, as they had not the pilots available to fly them home. The High Command of the Air Service stated that the numbers demanded did not exist, but was unable to produce any records to prove this, declaring that all documents referring to airfields had been destroyed at the beginning of the retreat. By 1st December, 1,700 aircraft should have been handed over, but by the 13th only 730 had been accepted. Of the first 1,500 aircraft delivered to the Allies, all sent back by rail, nearly a thousand were out of repair, and of these about 600 were hopelessly unserviceable. In the end, after very strong pressure and an extension of the time limit, more than the 1,700 of the Armistice terms were handed over; the original proportionate share of the British was 510, and they received 762.

RAILWAY MATERIAL

Maréchal Foch issued very detailed instructions in regard to taking over rolling stock and locomotives, and in May appointed Commissions to superintend the operation.[1]

The special "Reception of Material Commission" selected Metz as headquarters for the areas in France and in Alsace-Lorraine and adjacent territory, and Brussels for Belgium and adjacent territory. Delegates were despatched in the first instance to Saarbrücken, Aachen and Liége, and, at German request, were also sent to Crefeld, Neuse, Cologne, Coblence, Mayence and Ludwigshafen to safeguard the depôts of railway stores at those places. In the British area sub-commissions to take over the ceded vehicles, each consisting of a British officer with 30 Belgian railway officials, assembled at Mons, Charleroi, Braine le Comte, Ottignies, Namur, Revage, Trois Ponts and Walcourt. In order not to block the lines, only eight trains a day for handing-over were to cross the Armistice line.

It was known that Germany was in possession of at least 30,000 locomotives—and the Allies had official diagrams of the various types—besides what she had captured; many more

[1] See Note II at end of Chapter.

than half of these had been employed for military purposes, supplying and transferring troops ; so a demand for 5,000 could not be considered excessive. But the German representatives did their utmost to evade producing the agreed number. In the first place, they denied the accuracy of the Allied figures for German rolling stock and the existence of any inventory of the captured material ; they brought up engines which had been burnt out, and others which required considerable repairs ; similarly they produced unserviceable trucks which served only to block the lines, and the engine drivers refused to take orders from British officers to clear them. The reports furnished to the Spa Commission show that a very large percentage of the stock had to be rejected. Thus on 14th December, by which date the full number of 5,000 locomotives and 150,000 wagons should have been handed over, only 177 locomotives out of 1,286 offered, and 19,940 wagons out of 33,585 offered had been accepted. The delay was attributed by the German delegates to the difficulty in finding the numbers and types required, to ill-treatment of the railway personnel, and to rails being lifted by the revolutionaries—one instance of rail lifting did occur on 19th December at Siegburg, just inside the Cologne bridgehead, no doubt by order. In the official statement as regards delay made by Herr Erzberger to the Spa Commission on 15th January, he said :

" In the endeavour loyally to carry out the extraordinarily hard conditions, the German Government have made the greatest efforts imaginable to deliver the full quota regardless of the very urgent requirements of their own people. The German railway officials, the whole of the locomotive shops and carriage building establishments have for weeks worked solely for the Allies and their demands. Double shifts have been introduced, existing shops have been enlarged, new shops for locomotive and wagon erection added, and ordinary traffic reduced to the very lowest minimum. . . . At the conclusion of the Armistice 32 per cent. of the locomotives were under repair ; to-day it is 50 per cent."

Most of his speech was mere rhetoric and a perversion of the truth ; but at the prolongation of the Armistice next day (16th January) the Allies reduced the quota by 500 locomotives and 19,000 wagons, substituting agricultural machinery and apparatus.[1] By the end of April, 1919, the matter was virtually settled. On 18th July, 1919, Lieut.-General Haking reported that all had been handed over except 43 locomotives and 671 wagons, and that these were expected within a month, when the British representative at Brussels on the Railway Material Sub-Commission could be withdrawn.

[1] See Appendix VII, Article 3.

ARMAMENT

The Q.M.G., Lieut.-General Sir Travers Clarke, was prepared with a carefully thought-out scheme for the concentration, sorting and despatch to Calais, the base depôt selected, of all the German armament, including an immense quantity of engineer stores, captured or found abandoned ; accordingly his staff and its representatives in every formation were ready to take over the additional task of receiving and dealing with the ceded material. The dumps of stores were located in every case near railway communications, and the general idea was, after inventories had been made, to get guns also to the nearest railway station and despatch them on returning wagons and trucks. But the scheme could not be carried out with the desired speed owing to railway congestion.

Each of the German Groups of Armies had been ordered by O.H.L. to leave behind it a proportion of the total quota of 2,500 heavy guns, 2,500 field guns, 25,000 machine guns and 3,000 trench mortars, the conditions of the Armistice being that the first half should be delivered before 21st November and the second before 1st December, and " in good condition." The quantities left behind fell far short of the stipulated amount, and the weapons found were for the most part damaged and unserviceable ; nearly all the guards who should have been posted on the depôts of arms had deserted. The few officers who appeared in order to identify the position of the depôts could rarely do so, and most of the localities on their lists were inside the British lines on 11th November, 1918.

The reason for this failure to facilitate the execution of the terms soon became apparent. Having carried off the arms of the latest pattern, the Germans were trying to foist on the Allies weapons of the older types, obsolete guns from the fortress depôts, captured material, even " museum pieces " from the Eastern Front, and found trains to bring them across Germany, in spite of the alleged shortage of rolling stock. According to the records of the Spa Commission, the first deliveries were almost all of the older types. The German representatives argued that " en bon état " did not carry the meaning of the latest pattern. On 27th November it was reported to the Commission that, in spite of protest, only 40 per cent. of the guns were of modern pattern. The shortage on 13th December[1] amounted to 865 of the heavy guns alone. Pressure forced the Germans to give way, and by

---

[1] See Note I at end of Chapter, giving the Convention prolonging the Armistice.

the end of January, 1919, the matter was nearing solution, as the Germans had abundance of weapons. In the end the British received instead of their proportional quota of 1,500 guns, 2,467 ; instead of 7,500 machine guns, 10,430 ; instead of 900 trench mortars, 1,550. These figures probably included abandoned weapons. The three great engineer depôts abandoned by the enemy in his retreat contained stores valued at over £16,000,000.

LORRIES

In the first instance, Maréchal Foch directed that the 5,000 lorries to be handed over by the German Army should constitute an Inter-Allied automobile reserve at his own disposal, but organized into groups by the various contingents : four groups of 1,250 lorries by the American Army ; one of 300 lorries by the Belgian ; four of 1,250 by the British ; and six of 2,200 lorries by the French. Four places were named for their delivery before 13th December. This policy was not agreed to by the Commanders-in-Chief of the Armies allied to the French, and they took into use the lorries which were brought into their areas, eventually adjusting their share to the above totals.

The conditions of delivery were laid down in great detail.[1]

The staff of the Q.M.G. took charge of the reception of the lorries at six selected localities. Much the same delays and attempts at evasion of the terms were experienced as in the case of railway material. Of the first 350 lorries produced, only ten were fit to travel. The Germans at first refused to provide drivers, or the petrol for 100 kilometres, or spare parts, and did not bring the usual fittings ; but vehicles without equipment or spare parts were not accepted. Ultimately the lorries were produced, the British receiving ten more than their proportional share of 1,250. Delay occurred in the delivery of the spare parts, but by the beginning of July, 1919, 70 per cent. of them had been delivered. The British sub-commission then handed over its duties to the Mechanical Transport Inspection Office of the British Army of the Rhine, and was dissolved. The balance of the spare parts was handed over by the beginning of October.

---

[1] See Note III at end of Chapter.

C*

PRISONERS OF WAR

The Prisoners of War Sub-Commission had a difficult task before it. The return of the prisoners was the military item in the Armistice terms in which the British Government were the most interested.

Major Papst appeared at the Commission to deal with prisoner of war matters ; but he knew little about them, and could only act as an intermediary with Berlin. The selection of a junior officer for the job, was a clear indication to those who knew the German Army that trouble was expected, and that he was put up as a scapegoat.

The first difficulty was that during the War there was no central authority in Germany concerned with prisoners of war : they were divided among the 21 Army Corps Districts, whose officiating commanders dealt with them according to their will and pleasure. No consolidated nominal roll was kept, and it was impossible, or so the Germans pretended, to obtain lists of the men in the various camps, still less the names or even the number of the sick and wounded. Towards the end of December a nominal roll of officer prisoners, French and British, was handed in, but without the names of those who had been in the VIII Army Corps District. A list of prisoners undergoing punishment was demanded, but was never produced.

It was not until 29th December that Lieut.-General von Studnitz, a former General Staff officer, was appointed to deal with all questions connected with prisoners of war in a central office in Berlin. Here he was in daily communication with Major-General Sir Richard Ewart, sent from London for a similar purpose, with Mr. Abrahamson, of the Red Cross Society, who had done all that was possible to ameliorate the lot of the prisoners, and with Br.-General C. D. Bruce at the Hague. General Dupont, with a medical officer and supplies, was also sent to Berlin by Maréchal Foch, and General Sir Herbert Belfield, who had been in charge of prisoners in the United Kingdom, paid a visit to Spa for consultation. Finally, in March, 1919, to accelerate the repatriation of the prisoners of war, particularly of the Russian, an Inter-Allied Commission, of which Major-General Sir Neil Malcolm was the British member, was assembled in Berlin, and as he travelled all over Germany, he was able to gain a clear idea of the economic and political situation.

In the sequence, the larger aspects of the subject were dealt with in Paris by an Inter-Allied Commission, and the general disposal of the prisoners was settled in Berlin in consultation with Paris and London and communicated to Spa, where details as regards the transfer by land were worked out. G.H.Q. was kept informed of the assistance required from the British Army by the occasional attendance of one of its " Q " Staff officers at the meetings of the sub-commission in Spa.

Treatment in the different prison camps had varied considerably ; but there is no doubt that in the majority of them gross cruelty and brutality were either deliberately practised or allowed to obtain through indifference.[1] It will be sufficient here to state some of the conditions existing at the end of 1918. Everywhere there was shortage of food, clothing, blankets and medicine, little having been delivered since early November, and parcels sent to the prisoners were stolen. At one camp only one medical officer was provided for 13,000 prisoners ; at another, where about a thousand men were working, there was no medical officer at all ; prisoners were found after the Armistice working in salt mines and unloading ballast without being provided with sufficient food or clothing ; and after the Armistice prisoners were fired on by their guards without warning and 16 killed. During the reburial of prisoners who had died in captivity, a number were found with their skulls battered in.

The first meeting of the sub-commission was not held until 20th November, for the German delegate did not arrive until then, and by that time prisoners had been streaming through the British outposts for more than a week. The British prisoners, he said, fell into three categories : first, those immediately behind the Armistice line and working in the zone of the Armies. These, reckoned at about 32,000, had been freed by their guards and were already making their way back.[2]

Secondly, there were the prisoners in the German territory to be occupied on the western bank of the Rhine, reckoned at about 8,600. These, it was proposed, should remain in their

---

[1] This will be found recorded in " State Papers and Accounts, 1919 ", vol. liii. also in Reports Presented to Parliament on " The Treatment by " the Enemy of British Prisoners of War ", Miscellaneous : No. 10 (1916), No. 19 (1916), No. 3 (1918), No. 7 (1918), No. 19 (1918), No. 27 (1918), No. 28 (1918).

[2] It must be added, as best they could without money or food or guides. They should have been collected and marched back, preferably under officers freed for the purpose, with proper supply arrangements and medical attendance. How these men, haggard, footsore, starving and in rags, were dealt with is related later in the account of the advance of the British Armies. It must be placed on record that the inhabitants of Belgium and Holland near the front formed committees to feed and shelter the many Allied prisoners of war who were wandering about the country.

camps until the Allies arrived ; but on hearing of the Armistice, they had sought to escape. Thirdly, there were the men scattered all over Germany up to the Eastern border. It was agreed that this class, except men in the south who were to go to Switzerland and thence be sent by train, should be collected on the four rivers, the Oder, the Elbe, the Weser and the Rhine, and thence proceed by water to the ports where ships would be sent to receive them. In the outcome, the Rhine was made use of in this way, but the other rivers were not.

By a notice inserted in the German newspapers prisoners were requested to remain in their camps, as any attempt to make their way homewards would delay repatriation. It subsequently transpired that many prisoners working in the country on farms were not informed either of the Armistice or of the action they should take. Nothing was said in the German proposals as regards the sick and wounded ; but it was decided that these and infectious cases should be left, and lists of them and their whereabouts handed in—which was never done, except in bulk.

Winterfeldt was at once warned by Lieut.-General Haking that no amelioration of the terms could be expected if ill-treatment of the prisoners were continued. This did not prevent the Germans delaying the return of prisoners, on the ground that the Allied demands for engines and rolling stock were so heavy that few were available for the collection of prisoners at the proposed centres. So little was done that on 17th December Lieut.-General Haking again warned the German representatives that full reparation would be exacted for unnecessary suffering inflicted on the prisoners,[1] and that reprisals might become necessary. He demanded (1) the collection of the sick in properly equipped hospitals, from which they could be evacuated by hospital train ; (2) the collection of scattered prisoners into camps ; (3) the avoidance of over-crowding and the provision of proper food and clothing ; and (4) a steady transport of prisoners to the ports.

Special complaints were made that prisoners had been sent by train to the Swiss border without money or food ; that one train with 512 sick and wounded was sent to Cologne without a medical officer, and that 33 had died en route ; and that no notifications were made to the Spa Commission of the despatch of trainloads of prisoners.

---

[1] At the prolongation of the Armistice on 13th December, the occupation of the Ruhr was threatened if the ill-treatment was continued.

A series of excuses was put forward : that the ill-treatment and muddle were due to the rule of the Soldiers' and Workmen's Councils ; that too many Allied authorities were concerned, and the matter would be managed better by discussion in Berlin alone ; that transport by water in barges would interfere with the temporary bridges by which the German Armies were passing the rivers ; that train transport was impossible owing to shortage of rolling stock ; that only eight of the 88 German ambulance trains were serviceable, and for these locomotives must be provided by the Allies ; that empty trains of wagons which had brought back troops could not be used because they had no kitchens or conveniences, and stopping places for meals, etc., would take time to improvise. Passenger shipping, however, as demanded by Maréchal Foch was supplied.

The total numbers to be expected were put by the Germans : at Königsberg, total Allied 6,000 (British, 1,000) ; Danzig, 8,000 (750) ; Stettin, 100,000 (16,500) ; Lübeck, 28,000 (9,400) ; Hamburg, 90,000 (13,000) ; Bremerhaven, 65,000 (9,000) ; Rotterdam, 277,000 (46,000) ; Switzerland, 100,000 (4,500). British civilian prisoners, 3,800, would be released first and sent to Stettin or Hamburg.

On 9th January, 1919, the Commission reported a discrepancy of over 22,000 in the count of prisoners. By the British records there should have been about 36,000 still in the hands of the Germans, but they insisted that the total was only 13,579. A strongly worded letter was handed to Winterfeldt demanding that the name of every prisoner of war, living, sick or dead, should be furnished, but there is no record that the discrepancy was ever cleared up.[1]

The Western Allies declined to take over Russian, Serb, Rumanian and Italian prisoners who were on the left bank of the Rhine : they were to be sent eastwards for repatriation at the same time as the German troops retired. This refusal was repeated when it came to notice that the Germans were transferring Russian prisoners into the zone about to be occupied by the Allies in order to get rid of them, and again when the Russians were found in the Neutral Zone.

---

[1] Enquiries revealed that when any prisoner died the Germans did not trouble to notify the International Red Cross in Geneva, nor even to find out to what nationality he belonged ; they simply buried him. This may account for a good many missing not reported dead.

Many employed within shell-fire of the Allied Armies were killed by British guns and their deaths were not reported. The existence of many prisoners was concealed by holding up the postcards and letters which they wrote. (Report No. 7, 1918.)

Little could be done immediately by the Spa Commission except to request G.H.Q. to send transport and food to meet the parties tramping towards the British lines, and ask the good offices of the Red Cross Society to receive and forward food and comforts sent to the ports, as it was deemed impracticable to despatch them from the Armies by rail or lorry. A proposal to send a British officer to each of the camps to keep the prisoners quiet was never carried into effect ; but a medical party with equipment was despatched either by motor or train to each of the 21 corps districts, and ambulance trains, British and American, were sent into Germany. The evacuations were almost evenly divided between the German ports, Dutch ports, and Calais–Boulogne ; only 3,000 prisoners came through Switzerland.

Various Committees

In addition to its original three main sub-commissions and a subsidiary one, which dealt with transport material, arms, prisoners of war and aviation, the Spa Commission formed four others ; for finance, for the settlement of the costs of the occupation, for the recovery and restitution of industrial machinery and material carried off, and for the delivery of agricultural implements in lieu of rolling stock.

At the meetings of the Finance Sub-Commission on 1st and 13th December, 1918 (at the first prolongation of the Armistice) two protocols were signed by the German delegates by which they engaged their Government not to dispose of the metal reserve of the Treasury or of the *Reichsbank,* or effects or securities abroad belonging to the Government or banks, nor to allow securities or valuables possessed by private individuals or societies to be sent out of the country without previous permission of the Allies. On 29th January, 1919, the German Government were called on to furnish a complete list of their assets at home and abroad and they complied within a few days.

As regards the cost of occupation, Maréchal Foch, so that he might be in a position to inform the German Government of the total cost of the Allied occupation, called for the following information from each contingent :

(1) The total effectives of the Army of Occupation of the Rhineland (officers, men, horses) ;

(2) The daily average cost of the maintenance per officer (rank of captain), man (corporal) and horse.[1]

---

[1] The cost per head per day, gradually falling, varied from 36s. to 27s. per officer, 11s. 9d. to 7s. 8d. per man, and 4s. 9d. to 2s. 9d. per animal.

(3) The general expense of maintenance per thousand men, with corresponding establishment of horses, under the headings armament, vehicles and harness.[1]

(4) The general cost of transport per thousand men, with corresponding establishment of horses (*a*) by rail for rations and forage, clothing, material, leavemen, reinforcements ; (*b*) by motor lorry for the same.

He added that the French calculation would be made on the basis of 40 officers and 250 horses per thousand men.

On 2nd December, 1919, the Spa Commission handed to the German representatives the requirements in cash for the maintenance of the Armies of Occupation for one month, and requested that the following sums should be handed over :

For the British : 10 million marks at Düren on 5th December ; 30 million marks at Cologne on 12th December.

For the Americans : 10 million marks at Treves on 10th December ; 44 million marks later.

On 4th December, at the first meeting of the Finance Sub-Commission (it had one British, one American and one French member all belonging to the Commission, in the absence of financial advisers, who had been asked for), the German representatives made a number of requests, as follows : (*a*) the exact place of handing over, *e.g.*, pay office or bank ; (*b*) the name and description of the officers appointed to receive the money ; (*c*) the size of the notes required ; (*d*) an assurance of post or railway communication with the *Reichsbank* ; (*e*) ten days' notice, if possible ; (*f*) an assurance that all requirements for the month were included, so that increased demands would not be made later ; (*g*) an approximate sub-division of each Army's demands, *i.e.*, amounts allocated to pay, supplies, forage, transport, etc., etc.

It was agreed that a tariff of maximum prices for goods, where it did not already exist, should be fixed in each case in collaboration with the local authorities.

The question of the rate of exchange was left for higher authority to settle, and it was fixed every fortnight.

Two separate accounts were kept : one for the cost of the German civil administration, and the other for the cost of the military occupation. The former was refunded regularly each month, except in two crises in 1921 and 1923 ; the latter

---

[1] " Harnachement." Strictly this means the equipment of a cavalry horse.

was paid irregularly by cash advances and by deliveries of goods and supplies, less any sums that might be due for requisitions, etc.

The full cost of the occupation was never paid. The Parliamentary accounts show that the Rhine Army (not including the Army in France and Flanders) cost the British Treasury : in the year ended March, 1921, £3,050,594 ; March, 1922, £2,160,322 ; March, 1923, £1,428,087 ; March, 1924, £1,247,233. It rose in 1925 and 1926 to over £1,800,000, fell by 1929 to £1,152,672, and the last payment, in 1930, was £588,720.

The End of the Spa Commission

As early as 6th March, 1919, Lieut.-General Haking reported to G.H.Q. that affairs had reached a stage when political and economic questions were much more important than military ones, as four months' steady pressure by Maréchal Foch upon the Germans had completely broken down German military resistance, and Spartacism had weakened the German Government. He suggested that the Commission should now be composed of political, economic and military officials responsible to their Governments. Sir Douglas Haig, in forwarding the letter to the War Office, endorsed Lieut.-General Haking's opinion ; but the advisers of the Prime Minister in Paris preferred that matters should remain in the hands of Maréchal Foch rather than in those of some French civilian.

On the 18th July, Lieut.-General Haking reported direct to the War Office that " All questions regarding the repatriation " of British prisoners of war have now been wound up insofar " as they concern the Commission. The questions remaining " over refer to those who died and those reported or believed to " have been prisoners of war in Germany and not accounted " for." These might, he thought, be left to the British Military Mission in Berlin to investigate, whilst questions affecting German prisoners of war were being adjusted by the Prisoners of War Information Bureau in London. On 14th August the War Office concurred in this course. On the following day Lieut.-General Haking wrote to the Chief of the Imperial General Staff :

> " The original duties of the Commission which related to the terms of the Armistice are finished, and economic and similar questions with which we became engaged are now taken over by more suitable bodies. Our functions as a forwarding agency for the British Government are now only spasmodically and partially used, and, speaking generally, the only matters on which we take complete definite action are those requiring the presentation of a formal note to the Germans."

General Haking expressed the opinion that the British Section of the Armistice Commission might be reduced to two Staff officers and a small clerical staff, under Lieut.-Colonel A. G. M. Sharpe, to act as a forwarding agency. His suggestion was approved. The reduced Commission continued in being until 13th January, 1920, that is until three days after the ratification of the Treaty of Peace, when it was formally dissolved by order of Maréchal Foch. Its papers referring to general and political affairs were transferred to the Foreign Office ; questions of industrial, agricultural, *artistic and personal property to the Service of Industrial Restitution in Brussels ; and passports and circulation in Occupied Germany to a new High Commission for the Rhineland, whose formation and duties are described later in the volume.

In order to have specialist advice on the many economic, administrative and social problems certain to arise during the military occupation of the Rhineland, on 15th November, 1918, Maréchal Foch had called together a committee of three experts, under the chairmanship of M. Paul Tirard.[1] This committee met on 22nd November and despatched to the Commanders-in-Chief of the Allied Armies directions for the constitution of their civil affairs service and for the institution of a control of the German administration in the Occupied Territories. On 22nd December the committee established itself at Luxembourg, the Maréchal's advanced headquarters, as the *Contrôle général de l'Administration des Territoires Rhénans*. With a staff of diplomatic, administrative and financial officials and professors of international law, the committee followed events and gave advice on the solution of the problems.[2]

Alongside this committee an inter-allied economic committee was formed, composed of the delegates of the occupying Powers.[3] Both these committees received instructions on economic questions from the *Commission pour la rive gauche du Rhin*, formed on 8th January, 1919, in Paris, under the presidency of a high functionary of the French Foreign Office, M. Seydoux, and on other questions from the Inter-Allied Military Board (of the Supreme War Council), which continued to meet at the headquarters of Maréchal Foch.

By April, 1919, it was recognised that the results obtained by these committees were not altogether satisfactory. On 21st April, therefore, the Supreme Economic Council in Paris

[1] He had been a civil administrator in Morocco under Maréchal Lyautey.
[2] See Chap. VI.
[3] See Chap. VII : " Economic Committee."

brought into existence a sub-committee for Germany, entrusted with the direction of the most urgent economic questions. The local authority charged with the application of the directions of this sub-committee was to be the *Commission interalliée des Territoires Rhénans* (Inter-Allied Rhineland Commission). It held its first meeting at Luxembourg on 29th April and thus became known as the Luxembourg Commission, and the Luxembourg Economic Committee was then dissolved.

M. Tirard remained under Maréchal Foch as Controller-General of the Administration of the Rhineland, and became president of the new commission, as commissary of the French Republic ; Great Britain nominated as member, Sir Harold Stuart, of the Indian Civil Service ; the United States sent Mr. Pierrepont B. Noyes, an industrialist and friend of President Wilson, and Belgium sent M. Digneffe, a senator and governor of Liége, also an industrialist.[1]   The duties of the Commission were confined to economic matters, particularly exports and imports, and in order to set trade going again, it gave its first attention to the difficulties of the supply of the factories of the left bank of the Rhine with raw material.

NOTE I

CONVENTION PROLONGING THE ARMISTICE WITH GERMANY
13TH DECEMBER, 1918

INFRACTIONS OF THE ARMISTICE CLAUSES

Article IV[2]

Delivery of War Material

On the 9th December the following were delivered or abandoned in good condition :—

> *Heavy guns.*   1,635 guns instead of 2,500, which should have been delivered on 1st December.
>
> *Minenwerfer.*   2,000 instead of 3,000, which should have been delivered on 1st December.
>
> *Machine guns.*   18,000 instead of 25,000, which should have been delivered on 1st December, 1918.
>
> *Aircraft.*   A maximum of 730 fighting and bombing craft delivered, of which only 25 are bombing craft ; 1,700 should have been delivered on 1st December.

A total of 1,999 aircraft has certainly been either delivered or abandoned, of which more than 1,000 are in bad condition and 600 absolutely unfit for use ; and this number includes about 200 observation aircraft.

---

[1] More is said about these gentlemen in Chapter XI.

[2] Articles I, II and III are given on p. 42.   Articles V, IX and XII to XVIII are omitted in the British, French and German texts.

Article VI

Safeguarding of Inhabitants and Property

Numerous infractions have been reported which are at present under investigation and for which the question concerning reparation is reserved.

Two distinct infractions have been clearly proved :—

1. Region of Charleroi.—Explosions instigated by the Germans after 11th November. (Vouched for by a written statement from the Burgomaster of Charleroi.)
2. Outrages against persons and property in Belgium, verified by the Belgian Consulate in Maastricht.

Article VII

A. Delivery of Rolling Stock

1. *Rolling Stock to be delivered in Belgium and France.* Out of 5,000 locomotives to be delivered, 810 were given up, of which only 206 were accepted.

Out of 150,000 wagons, 15,720 were delivered and only 9,098 were accepted.

2. *Material on Alsace-Lorraine railways.* Out of 1,442 locomotives belonging to the Alsace-Lorraine railway system, 1,420 are on the track.

Out of 41,449 wagons belonging to this system, only 22,428 (accruing from all the German systems) are at present on the track.

B. Restoration of material of depôts and workshops

Machinery, tools and stocks of tools taken from certain depôts and workshops in France and Belgium have not yet been delivered.

C. Delivery of motor lorries

Out of 5,000 lorries, only 460 (in good condition) have been delivered.

Article VIII

Indication of position of delay-action fuzes

It has been officially reported that at Poix Terron (Ardennes) a delay-action fuze, placed in a German sawmill (the situation of which was not indicated by the Germans), exploded on 23rd November, killing a woman and causing serious material damage.

Article X

Repatriation of prisoners of war

Up to 9th December, 264,000 Allied prisoners (not including 23,000 Russians and 1,300 Poles) have been repatriated.

A very large number of these prisoners were set free *en masse* and sent across the Allied lines without means of obtaining shelter or food— thus rendering it most difficult for the Allies to receive them. A number of these prisoners died from exhaustion.

In spite of protests from the English and French Governments, this inhuman procedure was continued.

Moreover, repatriated civilians report that on 27th November, 16 prisoners (9 Frenchmen, 3 Englishmen, 2 Italians and 2 Russians) were killed and 24 others wounded in the Langensalza Camp. In the same camp there are a thousand prisoners in hospital without medicaments or medical attention.

Article XI
Care of sick and wounded unfit to be moved

An official report issued on 13th November by the Spanish Consul at Charleroi states that, when the German troops evacuated that town, French and English wounded were left uncared for and without food.

Article XIX
Financial Clauses

The Germans have permitted a large number of securities to leave German territory, thus diminishing the guarantees given to the Allies.

They have also substituted jewellery and valuables for the gold reserve in the *Reichsbank*, and at the same time greatly increased the issue of paper money.

They have not yet delivered any of the securities and documents confiscated by Germany, nor have they furnished the Allies with a list of such securities, etc.

NOTE II

Maréchal Foch's instructions regarding the rolling stock handed over by the German Army were as follows :

1. Rolling stock (handed over by the Germans) will be utilised for the common transport needs of the Allied Armies. Trucks will be turned into a general pool. Eighty thousand of the wagons will be allotted to the Belgian system, and will be repaired and maintained by the British and Belgian Armies. Forty thousand will be maintained by the Nord Railway Company and 30,000 by the Est. Locomotives will be divided between the Allied Armies in proportion to the demands of the railways operated by each.

In the first instance the allocation will be as follows :

Period	Number of locomotives to be handed over			
	On the Belgian Lines		On Alsace-Lorraine Lines	
	Belgian and French Armies	British Army	American Army	French Army
In the ten days following the signing of the Armistice.	400	500	100	500
In the ten subsequent days	400	500	100	500
In the 11 subsequent days..	400	300	300	1,000

Ceded locomotives used by the Allied Armies on the Belgian system will later be placed at the disposal of the Commission of that system as and when the operation of it is taken over by that Commission, up to a total of not less than the number of locomotives captured by the Germans on the Belgian system.

2. The Inter-Allied Commissions responsible for examining and taking over the stock in the name of the Maréchal commanding the Allied Armies will be composed of a military representative of each of the Allied Armies concerned. The latter will place at the disposal of their representatives such military and technical personnel as may be required to enable them to carry out their duty.

The representatives of the Allied Armies on the two Commissions will give all necessary instructions to the railway transport services of their respective Armies to ensure the rearward flow of the wagons after delivery and the taking over of the locomotives allotted to their Armies.

The 5,000 locomotives to be handed over should be capable of drawing a load of 900 tons without rushing on a grade of 1 in 100.

They will be delivered manned (three specialists per engine) and can be utilised under their own personnel or any other on any portion of the system controlled by the Allied Armies.

The wagons will contain the usual proportion of covered vehicles, cattle trucks, flats, and coaches, and will include 1,000 petrol tank wagons.

All this stock will be in good running repair and provided with all the usual spare parts and appliances.

Note III

Maréchal Foch's Instructions regarding the Delivery of Lorries

Lorries will be of a useful load of from 2½ to 5 tons, and will be in good repair, each with a driver and sufficient fuel for a run of 100 kilometres.

The drivers will eventually be returned to the German Armies, but in any case not before the end of the Armistice.

Tools and spare parts to be delivered with the lorries.

Each lorry shall be equipped with the necessary tool outfits and spare parts required for ordinary maintenance. In addition, with each group of fifty lorries of the same make, a set of spare parts and tools as laid down below will be provided :

(a) The necessary detachable parts for each vehicle required normally as replacements after 3,000 kilometres.

(b) Ten engines, 10 gearboxes, 10 radiators, 10 magnetos, 10 back axles or countershafts (for vehicles equipped with them), 2 steering gears complete, 2 water circulating pumps, 2 front axles, 10 front wheels, 10 back wheels, 1,000 kilogrammes of suspension springs (machined or in bars).

In addition for chain-driven vehicles 2 back axles and 30 pairs of chains.

(c) Six 5-ton screw jacks, 2 tackles, 2 portable forges equipped with the following outfit : 2 fitters' vices, 2 grindstones for sharpening tools, 2 bench drills, and 4 boxes of fitters' tools (each containing hammers, cold chisels, scribers, adjustable spanners, callipers, scales, files, pincers, taps and dies, etc.).

In the event of the German Army being unable to deliver the whole of the spare parts specified above immediately the following maximum periods may be granted within which to effect delivery :

One-fifth of the spare parts with the lorries ;

One-fifth of the spare parts one month after delivery of the lorries ;

The remaining three-fifths 60 days after delivery of the lorries.

The delivery of the spare parts will be made either at the points where the corresponding lorries are handed over or at such other points as may be decided by the Maréchal Commanding-in-Chief the Allied Armies.

CHAPTER IV

THE MARCH INTO GERMANY

THE PRELIMINARY PROCLAMATIONS AND INSTRUCTIONS

(Frontispiece and Sketch 2)

THE HAGUE RULES IN REGARD TO OCCUPIED TERRITORY

No special preparations had been made by the Allies to deal with the problems of occupation and control of enemy territory.

The general rules with regard to " Military Authority over " the Territory of the Hostile State," that is " Military " Occupation," had been laid down at the Hague Conference in 1907, in the " International Convention Concerning the Laws " and Customs of War on Land," and in its annex, " Regulations " respecting the Laws and Customs of War on Land," better known as " The Hague Rules."[1] The Convention of 1907 superseded an almost similar international agreement drawn up at the first Hague Conference in 1899. It will be seen that the Rules cover only general and major matters and are not a complete code : they contain none of the customary regulations which affect the daily life of the inhabitants, such as restriction of movement and of lighting and telephonic communication, passes, censorship of press and letters, and billeting. These were left to well-established usage.

By Article I the Contracting Parties[2] bound themselves to " issue instructions to their land forces which shall be " in conformity with the Regulations " annexed. Great Britain proceeded to do so in a pamphlet entitled " The Laws and " Usages of War on Land," later embodied as Chapter XIV of the " Manual of Military Law.[3]" This contained the text of all the Conventions and Declarations affecting war on land (among them the Geneva Convention regarding sick and wounded), and an explanation of them, illustrated by examples from military history.

---

[1] The Articles which refer to military occupation are printed in Appendix IX.

[2] The Convention was ratified by all the belligerents concerned : Great Britain, France, Belgium, United States and Germany, besides other States.

[3] The pamphlet was written by the late Professor L. Oppenheim of Cambridge and Colonel J. E. Edmonds, under the instructions of the Secretary of State for War, the late Lord Haldane.

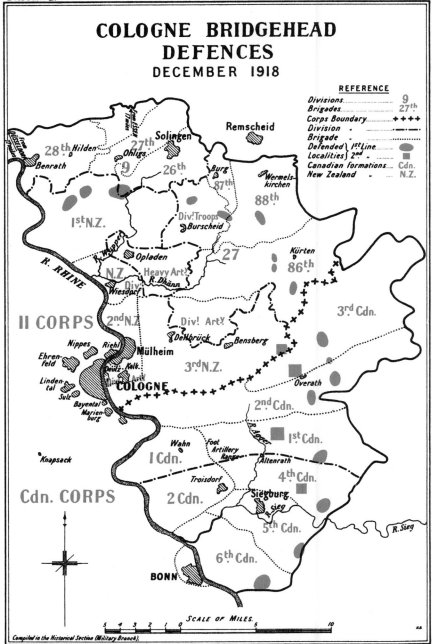

Sketch 2.

COLOGNE BRIDGEHEAD
DEFENCES
DECEMBER 1918

REFERENCE

Divisions	9
Brigades	27th
Corps Boundary	+ + + +
Division	
Brigade	
Defended } 1st Line	
Localities } 2nd	
Canadian formations	Cdn.
New Zealand	N.Z.

Remscheid

From DÜSSELDORF 7 miles

28th Hilden

Benrath

27th Solingen

Ohligs

9

26th

Burg

87th

Wermels-kirchen

Div! Troops
Burscheid

88th

1st N.Z.

Wupper

Opladen

27

Kürten

86th

N.Z. Div! Heavy Art?
R. Dhünn

Wiesdorf

II CORPS 2nd N.Z.

Div! Art?

3rd Cdn.

Dellbrück

Bensberg

Nippes Riehl

Mülheim

Ehren-feld Deutz Kalk

3rd N.Z.

Overath

Linden-tal Heavy Art?

Sulz COLOGNE

Bayental

Marien-burg

2nd Cdn.

R. Agger

1st Cdn.

Knapsack

Wahn Foot
Artillery
Range

I Cdn.

Altenrath

4th Cdn.

Troisdorf

Siegburg

Cdn. CORPS

2 Cdn.

R. Sieg

5th Cdn.

R. Sieg

6th Cdn.

BONN

SCALE OF MILES.

5 4 3 2 1 0   5   10

Compiled in the Historical Section (Military Branch).

Ordnance Survey 1943.

The German General Staff had already, in 1902, before the Second Hague Conference, issued a pamphlet entitled "*Kriegsbrauch im Landkriege*," more or less in accordance with the Hague Rules of 1899,[1] but not giving the text of the Rules and placing a somewhat harsher interpretation on them than they warranted. No further instructions on the subject were made public after the Conference of 1907. The principal differences between the German manual and the Hague Rules were that the former did not forbid " collective punishment " on account of the acts of individuals (Article 50 of the Rules), and it definitely sanctioned the taking of hostages, a matter entirely omitted in the Hague Rules. Germany in 1907 had formally declined to accept Article 44, which read :

> " A belligerent is forbidden to compel the inhabitants of a territory occupied by it to furnish information about the army of the other belligerent, or about its means of defence."

This rule, therefore, was not binding on her opponents, although they had accepted it.

As regards military occupation, it is desirable to quote a few principles from "*Kriegsbrauch*" to demonstrate that the inhabitants of the Rhineland had no cause for grievance or complaint against the Allied regulations.

> " To employ ruthlessly the necessary means of defence and intimidation is obviously not only a right but indeed a duty of the staff of the Army. . . . Martial Law and Courts-Martial must take the place of ordinary jurisdiction " (p. 120).[2]
>
> " The inhabitants of the occupied territory owe the same obedience to the Government and administration of the conqueror as they owed before the occupation to their own " (p. 139).
>
> " The conqueror can, as administrator of the country and its Government, depose or appoint officials. He can put on their oath the civil servants who continue to act, as regards the scrupulous discharge of their duties " (p. 140).

The German manual enumerated the following servitudes as those most frequently demanded (p. 116) :

> " (1) Restriction of freedom of movement within the country, and of railway and postal communication, or, indeed, total prohibition of the same.
>
> " (2) Limitation of freedom of movement within the country ; prohibition to frequent certain parts of the theatre of war, or specified places.
>
> " (3) Surrender of arms.

---

[1] Translated in 1915 as " The German War Book " (John Murray).
[2] The pages refer to " The German War Book ".

" (4) Obligation to billet enemy soldiers ; prohibition of illumination of windows at night and the like.

" (5) Performance of work on streets, bridges, drainage, railways, etc."[1]

MARÉCHAL FOCH'S INSTRUCTIONS FOR CIVIL ADMINISTRATION

The correct behaviour of the Allied troops in German territory was one of the special preoccupations of Maréchal Foch. The little manual on international law in relation to war issued to the French Army fully covered the accepted principles ; but as early as 15th November the Generalissimo sent a lengthy Note of instructions for the civil administration of the Occupied Territories to the Allied Commanders-in-Chief.[2] He requested them to nominate delegates to meet at his headquarters (about to move to Luxembourg) under the presidency of Colonel Payot, formerly his Assistant Chief of the Staff, and, since 8th October, Director-General of Communications and Supply, to settle upon the common instructions to be issued.[3]

As guiding idea, the Note enunciated :

" The Allied Armies should adhere to the principles laid down with regard to cases of occupation by the Hague Convention,"

and added

" The German officials will continue to perform the functions entrusted to them, and they are to carry out the administration of the occupied territories under the direction of the military authorities."

THE BRITISH POLICY DEFINED

A meeting of the delegates as requested by Maréchal Foch took place at Luxembourg, on 22nd November ; subsequently, on the 27th, the Adjutant-General, Lieut.-General Sir George

---

[1] Those interested in the subject of the behaviour of the German authorities in occupied France in 1914–18 will find a useful compendium in " Lille sous la Griffe Allemande," by André Fage. It contains all the municipal regulations and all the proclamations and posters of the German authorities from 24th August, 1914, to 1st December, 1915. It is a story of torture, mental and material, and financial extortion. Hostages were held ; the punishment for nearly every infringement was death ; if the offender could not be discovered heavy collective fines were inflicted ; the inhabitants were forced to provide meals for the officers and men quartered on them. The table of normal daily deaths indicates that they were virtually trebled even in the first year of German occupation.

[2] Appendix X. The official English translation was found in the records, and, the original French version not being available, it was thought best to leave the translation, in spite of its imperfections, as it stood.

[3] The draft instructions discussed at the meeting are given in Appendix XI.

Fowke, sent the following memorandum to General Plumer as commander of the Army of Occupation :

"The Second Army having been detailed as Army of Occupation of German territory under the terms of the Armistice, the whole of the German territory occupied by the British Forces will be included in your Command and the supreme control of the civil government in that area will be vested in you, subject to the general direction of the Commander-in-Chief.

" 1. *General Policy*.

" The general policy of the Allied Armies is that the life of the civilian population shall so far as possible continue uninterrupted and with the minimum of interference. All civilian institutions will continue to perform their functions under the supervision of and subject to the control of the military authorities.

" Order among the civilians themselves will be maintained through the German law courts and German police except when military action is rendered necessary. The German civil authorities will be held responsible in their own persons that the civil laws are enforced and that regulations promulgated by the military authority are complied with. The Commander-in-Chief Allied Armies has been requested to instruct the German Government to appoint an official as Chief of the Civil Administration in the Zone occupied by the British Army, so that you may hold him responsible for the civil administration of the whole of your area.

" For the purpose of punishing neglect or disobedience of the regulations published by the military authorities and acts prejudicial to the Army of Occupation or any members thereof a system of military courts will be instituted.

" Collective punishments must on principle be avoided but if the inhabitants of a particular locality are generally obstructive and offences cannot be brought home to specific individuals, the civil authorities should be warned of the possibility of levying a fine on the district, and such a fine should if necessary be imposed.

" Intercourse between the territory occupied by the Allied Armies and the remainder of Germany will be suspended except so far as is absolutely necessary for the maintenance of the industrial life and the provisioning of the population, and any other purpose which the Allied military authorities may find desirable.

" In pursuance of this policy :

" (1) No civilians will be allowed to pass from occupied to unoccupied German territory or vice versa.

" (2) No telephone conversation between occupied and unoccupied German territory will be allowed.

" (3) The extent of the postal and telegraph communications between occupied and unoccupied German territory will be generally governed by the requirements of normal business. All such communications will be censored.

" 2. *System of identification*

" The authority controlling local government will be the divisional commander except in respect of those districts which are retained immediately under the corps or Army commander.

Area commanders and officers to assist them will be appointed as may be necessary from your own resources. The chain of local government will coincide with the chain of military command.

" A British Military Governor of the German territory occupied by the British Army has been nominated. The Military Governor will act as your deputy in respect of all questions relating to the control of civil government in that area.

" 3. *Orders to inhabitants*

" In order to bring their liabilities by virtue of the military occupation to the knowledge of the civil population two proclamations are being published :

" (A) General proclamation issued by Maréchal Foch in the capacity of Commander-in-Chief of the Allied Armies. This will be printed when the German version is received. A copy of the English version is attached.[1]

" (B) Proclamation issued by the Commander-in-Chief of the British Armies warning the inhabitants of the liability to punishment which they will incur if they disobey the orders of the military authorities or do any acts to the prejudice of the military authorities.[1]

" Any general regulations which you may find it necessary to issue for the control of the civil population, in pursuance of the last paragraph of the Commander-in-Chief's proclamation, should be issued by you. Proclamations and regulations of general application will be posted in every locality throughout the Occupied Territory whether troops are actually stationed in the locality or not.

" Local military authorities should be authorised to issue regulations of purely local application, but they should not issue regulations on matters of general application without reference to you. If a question of policy arises in respect of which it is desirable that there should be a uniform practice throughout the territory occupied by the Allied Armies, it should be referred to G.H.Q.

" Notices issued by the German civil authorities should be countersigned by the local British authority.

" 4. *Courts*

" The following tribunals will be constituted for the purpose of trying offences committed by civilians in the nature of breaches of orders issued by the British military authorities, acts to the prejudice of the British Armies, or offences against the persons or property of British or Allied subjects :

" (1) In rural districts a Summary Court consisting of at least two officers, one of whom will be of field rank.

" (2) In urban districts, if found necessary a Summary Court Officer will be appointed who will be an officer of suitable standing and legal experience.

" Summary Courts will be convened by officers in control of districts to whom authority to do so is granted by division or corps commanders. Summary Court Officers will be appointed by G.H.Q. if sufficient cause for the appointment is shown.

---

[1] Given below.

" Summary Courts and Summary Court Officers will have the power of awarding sentences either jointly or severally of imprisonment not exceeding six months and of a fine not exceeding 5,000 francs. Whenever a fine is awarded there should be an alternative sentence of imprisonment to be undergone in default of payment.

" A record will be kept of the members of the Court, the name and address of the offender, particulars of the offence, names and addresses of witnesses, sentence awarded.

" There will be no appeal against the decision of a Summary Court or Summary Court Officer, but a convicted person will have the right of preferring a written petition within a week of his conviction, in which case the President of the Court or Summary Court Officer will be called upon for his remarks on the petition before it is forwarded. The petition will be forwarded to G.H.Q., through the usual channels with observations.

" When an offence has been committed of a character such that the Area Commandant considers that a heavier sentence than the above will be necessary, reference should be made to Army or corps or divisional headquarters, for a Military Court to be convened by order of the commander. A Military Court will consist of at least three officers, one of whom will be a court martial officer. The President will be of field rank. A record will be kept similar to that of a field general court martial, and a similar procedure and rules of evidence will be observed.

" Such court may award death, imprisonment or fine of any amount in addition to or without imprisonment.

" Findings and sentences of Military Courts will be confirmed by the convening officer.

" The confirmation of death sentences will be reserved for the decision of the Commander-in-Chief.

" All records of trials held by either a Summary Court, Summary Court Officer, or Military Court will be sent to Deputy Judge Advocate-General, General Headquarters.

" 5. *Sentences of imprisonment*

" These will be carried out in civil prisons, in such division of the prison as the convening officer may direct. A commitment order in writing in any suitable form will be made by the convening officer.

" It will be for consideration whether it may be desirable to institute a military prison in the field in German territory. If it were decided to do this it would be possible to set apart a section for such German prisoners as it might be desired to keep in exclusively military custody.

" 6. *Alcohol*

" The sale of spirits will be forbidden except on production of the written order of a competent British military authority. As regards facilities for the sale of wine and beer, it will probably be advisable that in each place certain cafés and restaurants should be set aside as exclusively available for officers and men respectively either during certain hours of the day or entirely. It may be found expedient to take over certain cafés regimentally as canteens.

" 7. *Brothels*

" It is desirable that the inmates of brothels should be registered at such brothels at the earliest possible moment after occupation of the town by British troops. In order to prevent the danger of the dispersion of the prostitutes before registration, it will be advisable that the local authorities should not be informed that brothels are out of bounds to British troops until after the registration has taken place.

" 8. *Money*

" The question of currency is under the consideration of the War Office.

" 9. *Food*

" In view of the shortage of food believed to exist, troops should not be allowed to purchase from inhabitants food other than vegetables until the situation in this respect becomes clearer.

" 10.

" The following annexures in addition to those before mentioned are sent herewith :—

" (C) Copy of regulations which have been drafted after consultation with representatives of the Allied Armies. A translation of these regulations is being prepared. Will you kindly let me know whether you consider them suitable for issue in their present form or whether you have any alterations or additions to make. I will then have them printed over your signature, and order supplies to be sent to you.[1]

" (D) Copy of instructions for handing to Burgermasters or corresponding civil officials when a particular district is taken over. Will you please say whether you think they will be useful in their present form.[1]

" (E) A copy of the form in which regulations for civilians should be promulgated.[2]

" (F) Copy of instructions for the Provost Branch."[2]

THE FRENCH AND BRITISH PROCLAMATIONS

The Generalissimo's proclamation for issue in Germany was brief :

PROCLAMATION

" The Allied military authorities are taking over the command of the country.

" They demand the fullest obedience from all.

" The rules and regulations in force at the time of the occupation will be guaranteed by us in so far as they do not prejudice our rights and our safety.

" The public services will operate under the supervision and control of the military authorities.

" The officials will have the duty and will be under the obligation to carry out conscientiously and honestly the functions entrusted to them. The tribunals will continue to administer justice.

---

[1] Given below.   [2] Not found in the records.

" The inhabitants must abstain both by words and acts from any hostility either direct or indirect towards the Allied authorities.

" They must comply with the requisitions made from them in accordance with the law.

" Any person found guilty of a crime or offence, whether he be the perpetrator or an accomplice, will immediately be put under arrest and tried by court-martial.

" Any infraction of orders brought to the notice of the population, and any act of refusal to obey the orders given, will be severely dealt with.

" The present proclamation establishes the occupation of the country by the Allied Armies ; it lays down the duties of all, which are to assist in the resumption of local life by work, order and discipline.

" Let all parties concerned spare no exertions to that effect."

Sir Douglas Haig's proclamation, published as a large wall poster in English and German in parallel columns, was as under :

PROCLAMATION

To All Persons in Places entered and occupied by the Forces of His Britannic Majesty :

I WARN ALL PERSONS in this place THAT THEY MUST NOT IMPERIL the safety of any officer or man in the service of HIS BRITANNIC MAJESTY OR the operations of HIS BRITANNIC MAJESTY'S FORCES. IT IS THE DUTY of all persons to help in the repression of any act which offends against my Orders and I CALL UPON all State and Municipal Officials to help in maintaining good behaviour.

I DECLARE THAT ALL INHABITANTS OF THIS PLACE WILL BE PROTECTED so long as they conduct themselves in an obedient and peaceable manner BUT WITHOUT PREJUDICE TO the right of HIS BRITANNIC MAJESTY and His Troops to exact such punishment as is recognised by International Law against any place in which this Proclamation is disregarded.

THE MORE READILY OBEDIENCE IS SHOWN TO MY ORDERS THE GREATER WILL BE THE SECURITY OF THE INHABITANTS.

AND I DECLARE THAT :

1. IF VIOLENCE is done to any Officer or Man under my Command or if any stores, supplies, equipment or other property of the Army under my command are stolen or injured, or
2. IF DAMAGE is done to any building, road, railway, canal, bridge, telegraph, telephone, water supply or other useful works, or to any supplies, or if any such works or supplies are in any way interfered with or rendered unsafe or unsuitable for use,

The persons directly responsible, whether as principals or accessories will, after due trial, be punished with DEATH or such other penalty as I may decree.

AND I ALSO DECLARE THAT THE SEVEREST PENALTIES WILL BE INFLICTED UPON :

1. Any person AIDING, HIDING or otherwise assisting any German or other enemy soldier or anyone who is or has been ACTING IN DISOBEDIENCE OF MY ORDERS.

2. Any person concealing or failing to disclose any MEANS OF COMMUNICATING WITH THE ENEMIES OF HIS BRITANNIC MAJESTY.

3. Any person who does not IMMEDIATELY OBEY EVERY ORDER affecting him or his property, movable and immovable.

4. Any person doing any act, whether specially prohibited by regulation or not which may be to the prejudice of good order or endanger the welfare or safety of any of the TROOPS OR SUBJECTS OF HIS BRITANNIC MAJESTY OR OF HIS MAJESTY'S ALLIES.

REGULATIONS will be published in due course for the proper ordering and control of the inhabitants of the districts occupied by the Troops of HIS BRITANNIC MAJESTY : AND I COMMAND ALL PERSONS well and truly TO OBEY THESE REGULATIONS AND ALL ORDERS GIVEN BY ME or by any person acting UNDER MY AUTHORITY.

Given under my hand this first day of December, 1918, at my General Headquarters,

D. HAIG, Field-Marshal,

Commanding-in-Chief, British Armies.

GOD SAVE THE KING

THE *ANORDNUNGEN*

Sir Herbert Plumer's proclamation announcing the regulations, in conformity with the Adjutant-General's instructions, which would be in force in Occupied Territory was dated 2nd December. As the regulations were known both to the British and the Germans as *Anordnungen*, that name is retained for them in this volume.[1]

A special *Anordnung* as regards Bounds was issued next day :

" On arrival of British troops in a town or village in occupied territory steps will at once be taken to select a certain number of public houses and restaurants for the use of the troops.

" These will be placed out of bounds for all civilians and will be for the use of troops only. The notice ' Out of Bounds to Civilians, to be Used by Troops Only ' will be posted in the windows of all houses selected.

" Houses selected may be used by the troops at any time during the day and until 2030 hours; but wine and beer may only be sold during the hours 1030 to 1330 and 1730 to 2030.

" All other public houses and restaurants will be out of bounds to all troops."

---

[1] They are printed in full, and followed by the notice on the duties of civil authorities in occupied localities, in Notes I and II at end of Chapter.

In continuation of the Adjutant-General's memorandum of 27th November instructions for taking over the telegraph and telephone systems and the censorship of civilian communications were sent to General Plumer by G.H.Q. on 3rd December.[2]

On the 5th December divisions were informed that all German soldiers found who were not duly demobilized—as their papers would show—were to be arrested ; that demobilized persons who had been resident in the Occupied Territory before the War might remain ; that the military services of the *Intendantur* (barracks, clothing, pay, supply), fortress works, medical department and record offices were to continue for the present to function under British control ; that on no account were the German railway personnel to be interfered with in their legitimate duties, under the Armistice terms, of working the lines. As few of this personnel encountered had either pass or armband (the passes for railwaymen are first mentioned in orders on 21st December and brassards on 6th January), a few unfortunate incidents occurred ; for there was no means of distinguishing genuine personnel from *saboteurs*. Wounded or sick German officers and men not fit to be moved were not to be made prisoner ; but they were to be evacuated eastward to Germany as soon as their state of health permitted. Finally, if the members of any Soldiers' and Workmen's Committees in existence attempted to distribute propaganda or issue memoranda or instructions for action in any way calculated to disturb the civilian population or to tamper with the loyalty of the British troops, they were to be at once arrested and brought to trial.

The Security Section

For the control of information in Occupied Territory a " Security Section " was formed by the General Staff. It consisted of three Sections : (1) Signal Security Section, which was concerned with the security, but not censorship, of telephone, telegraph and wireless communications, and the investigation of intercepted enemy wireless messages ; (2) Contre-Espionage Section, concerned with watching enemy political propaganda, enemy agents, sabotage and like matters, and with assisting the Provost-Marshal in any contre-espionage work ; and (3) Censorship (Postal and Press) Section, particularly concerned with the control of enemy postal services, the prevention of the private carrying of letters, telegraph and

---

[2] See Note III at end of chapter.

telephone censorship and the control of the Press. Censors and Intelligence Police were appointed gradually as required to a total of 44 officers and 209 other ranks, transferred from similar duties at G.H.Q. and elsewhere.[1]

The whole Army naturally gave attention and assistance at all times to watching and detecting hostile action ; it has been seen that the Signal Service was charged with taking over control of telegraph and telephone offices, and by a special order the troops were called on to help as regards railways and signals also :

> " The attention of advancing Armies is directed to the importance of guarding railway stations and important railway or signal installations from risk of sabotage. Temporary protection must be afforded by the first troops to arrive at important points, permanent protection being subsequently furnished by the garrison or anti-aircraft companies at the disposal of Armies. As additional garrison or anti-aircraft personnel cannot be provided, any guards required in excess of their numbers must be furnished from fighting troops."

The troops were specially warned against espionage :

> " The French authorities have information that German officers and soldiers have remained in the area of the Belgian Army in civilian clothes in order to spread revolutionary ideas amongst the troops and induce the formation of soldiers' councils. Careful watch should be kept for such persons in our area. Their presence in our area in plain clothes constitutes a War Crime. If such a person claims to be an Alsatian or Lorrainer it is essential that before trial he should be examined by a French officer and that a written report should be obtained from the latter to the effect that the man's claim is held unfounded. If the man's claim is upheld, he must be handed over to the French Mission."

Keeping Order in No Man's Land

As the time for the advance into the Rhineland drew near the German High Command became anxious as to what might happen in the interregnum between their troops leaving large centres of population and the arrival of the Allies. On 1st December they asked that their troops might be maintained in the larger towns until the Allies appeared ; they also asked that an Allied General Staff officer might be sent to Cologne at once to confer with the Governor. Maréchal Foch would not

---

[1] The official proposal to form a Security Section, actually already formed, sent to London on 10th December, was opposed by the War Office on the ground that the details furnished as given above, with exact tables of establishments, were " too vague for effective discussion," and it asked " what exactly is it proposed to censor ? " On 3rd January further explanations were required ; the establishments were approved on 16th January, after a delay of five weeks.

agree to the enemy remaining beyond the dates settled by the Armistice, and regretted that an advanced staff could not be sent in time. He was, however, prepared to send an advanced detachment (*détachement précurseur*) to make arrangements for the occupation of the bridgeheads. The Germans were due to leave Cologne by 5 a.m. on 4th December, and it seemed unlikely that the infantry advanced guards would have reached much farther than Line No. 4 on the evening of that day, or that the cavalry could reach Cologne before the 6th. The Germans were unable to supply trains to carry British troops, as suggested, and the matter was finally settled by their organizing " civil guards," of which more will be heard.

It was decided by Maréchal Foch that once German territory had been entered, the necessity for the shifting 10-kilometre No Man's Land between the belligerents no longer held good ; the Germans, however, had made such a speedy retreat that their columns were never caught up, and only stragglers, at times in large bodies, were encountered.

Administrative Arrangements

Over the signatures of the Adjutant-General and the Quarter-Master-General a printed memorandum entitled " Method of Administration and Maintenance of British troops " located in Germany." was issued on 26th November. It began by stating that an " Advanced Administrative G.H.Q. " would be established and opened at Spa [whither the Second " Army Advanced H.Q. moved from Namur on 1st December] " on 2nd December, under Br.-General A. A. McHardy, as " D.A. and Q.M.G.", with a staff on which officers of certain G.H.Q. directorates would serve.[1] The duties of the D.A. and Q.M.G. were laid down in detail : " his chief function is to " assist the Second Army by anticipating any administrative " difficulties which may arise from the G.H.Q. point of view, " and by adjusting them locally if possible " : he was to keep G.H.Q. informed of any difficulties which he might foresee before they arose : in emergency, he could settle major questions of policy ; otherwise, he was empowered only to act as deputy of the Adjutant-General and the Quarter-Master-General in administrative matters of a routine nature, and as their representative at all conferences and commissions at Maréchal Foch's headquarters, and to settle minor questions of policy or principle in the Second Army area.

---

[1] Spa, being a fashionable watering-place, contained a number of good hotels, and had been used as German G.H.Q.

D

He was specially directed to keep in touch with the Prisoners of War Sub-Commission of the Spa Commission, and to take such executive action as the means at his disposal would allow to assist in the return of prisoners of war. He was made responsible for co-ordinating the work at the Second Army (Railway) Regulating Station, which was fixed at Montignies (just east of Charleroi) in the Fourth Army area, and near which small depôts, to be ready by 15th December, were to be formed for transport (M.T. and horse), supply, ordnance stores, remounts and sick animals.

Among the subjects dealt with in the Memorandum were :

Ammunition. The amount in excess of that carried in field echelons was fixed : six trainloads of it were to be held ready, east of Liége ; the remainder was to be dumped.

Supply. Besides two days' reserve to be held at the Regulating Station, three days' forage and preserved rations were to be held in Germany ; otherwise supply was to be normal—from base direct to railhead, a journey estimated as taking four days.

Engineer Stores. An advanced engineer stores depôt was to be formed in the Second Army area.

Medical. Evacuation was to be on the normal system, two' ambulance trains being held ready. Seven casualty clearing stations were allotted to the Second Army.

Postal. Ordinary mail was to be carried by special through train ; parcel mail by supply train.

Salvage. The normal system of evacuation to be maintained.

The staffs for Spa and the Regulating Station, the number of motor cars for the pool, and the daily and weekly returns to be rendered, were enumerated, and it was settled at a conference that the northern ports (including Antwerp, if available) should be used for the maintenance of the British Army in Germany.

Routine Orders to the Troops

A number of instructions were issued to the troops regarding their behaviour in occupied Germany :

Dress

Officers and warrant officers entitled to do so, were always to carry revolvers ; others were to wear side arms. It was pointed out that for all ranks it was undesirable to walk about singly.

Billeting

" (1) Accommodation required for troops in Germany, whether land, billets or buildings, should be obtained by written demand delivered to the local civil authority of the town or district. This demand should be delivered through the British Town Major or Area Commandant, where such officer is available.

" The demand will be signed by the officer commanding troops concerned, and will state the time when the accommodation must be available, and, where necessary, the particular land or building required.

" (2) The demand will be made out on Army Form W.3856 in triplicate. The original will be retained by the German civil authority. The official demanding will, except in the case of public or government properties, keep a record of :

" (a) in the case of land, the location, area and period of occupation ;

" (b) in the case of buildings used as offices, the address of the building, the average number of rooms occupied per week, and the period of occupation ;

" (c) in the case of depôts used for stores, etc., the address of the building occupied, the floor space occupied, and the period of occupation ;

" (d) in the case of accommodation for officers, men and horses, the address of the buildings, the average weekly number accommodated and the period of occupation.

"*At the termination of the occupation* by the unit, a summary of this record, with a note of any damage caused in excess of fair wear and tear, will be endorsed by the officer commanding the unit on the remaining two copies of the demand notes and signed by him with the name of the unit. The duplicate will be forwarded to the Central Requisition Officer, Base, so that assessment may, if necessary, be made. The triplicate will be retained by the unit.

" (3) On no account will any promises as to payment be made, as this question will be settled by the Governments concerned.

" (4) When accommodation cannot be obtained through the German local civil authority, the procedure laid down in paragraphs (1) and (2) will be followed, the occupant being substituted for the local authority.

" (5) Officers commanding units will be responsible that unnecessary damage is avoided and that due care is taken of all property belonging to civilians.

" (6) Books of A.F. W.3856 are being printed and will be sent to units when received. [Specimen form was issued.]

"Authority is given to commanders of formations, as a temporary measure subject to confirmation later, to evacuate Germans completely from houses required for headquarters and offices.

" Billeting books for friendly countries must not be used in Germany, and pending the issue of A.F. W.3856, written demands should be made on the municipality. Records of the numbers billeted in private buildings should be sent to the branch requisition office, Second Army, for transmission to the Central Requisition Office. The fullest use must be made of vacant buildings.

"As to whether military requirements necessitate the evacuation of inhabitants from buildings is a matter for decision on the spot in conjunction with the local authorities.

" If occupied houses are used as billets, fraternization can be avoided by billeting officers in the same buildings as the men."

REQUISITION OF STORES AND SUPPLIES.

" (1) Until orders to the contrary are issued by G.H.Q., no local purchase of stores or supplies will be made in Germany. This does not apply to the purchase of milk and eggs.

" (2) Stores or supplies required for the needs of the Army which can be obtained locally, without unduly depleting supplies necessary for the civil inhabitants, will be obtained by issue of a requisition order.

" (3) Requisition orders (except in cases of emergency) will be issued only by brigade requisitioning officers.

" (4) Requisition orders will be served on the civil authority of the district. They will be served on civilians only when the civil authority fails, after due notice, to produce the stores or supplies, and these are known to be in the possession of an individual. When a British Town Major or Area Commandant is available, all requisitions will be made through this officer.

" (5) A draft General Routine Order giving the procedure to be adopted for the requisitioning of stores and supplies in Occupied Territory in Germany can be seen by brigade requisitioning officers at brigade headquarters. They will make a copy for guidance."

ISSUE OF FOOD TO GERMAN PERSONNEL

" Under Clause 11 of the Armistice, authority is given for the issue of food from British stocks to German personnel left behind to care for sick and wounded who cannot be moved, as well as to patients."

A number of additional administrative orders were issued day by day, notably with regard to fraternization, prices and requisitioning.[1] The censorship of officers' and soldiers' letters remained in force.

MILITARY COURTS

The following instructions as regards " war crimes " and the courts to try them were circulated by the Adjutant-General G.H.Q. under date 25th November :

" An enemy who violates the laws of war by treachery, looting or molesting inhabitants, commits a ' war crime.' Such a crime is not punishable under the Army Act or by a court-martial held under that Act, but under the general laws of war which permit such offenders to be tried and punished in accordance with civilized military custom. ' War crimes ' and their punishment are dealt with in Chapter XIV., paragraphs 441 to 451, on pp. 302–4 of the *Manual of Military Law*. See especially paragraphs 441, 442, 448, 449, 450.

" Offenders of this class, if any, with whom the Army may have to deal in its advance should be tried by what is technically called a ' military court ' (to distinguish it from a court-martial held under the Army Act).

---

[1] They are given for record in Note IV at end of Chapter.

" The procedure at the trial should be on the lines of that of a field general court-martial : e.g. witnesses should be sworn, the evidence recorded in writing, and the accused given an opportunity of asking them questions and making his defence.

" Army Form A.3 can be conveniently used, the necessary amendments being made thereon.

" It is desirable that trial should be ordered and the court itself convened by some responsible commander, e.g. a brigade commander, or if he is not available, the commanding officer of a regiment of cavalry or battalion of infantry.

" An A.F. A.3 should always be procurable, but, if not, a short written order convening the court and stating the charge will be sufficient, e.g. :

  ' I order a military court to assemble to try Fritz Johann
  Grimm for the war crime of looting the church at Nivelles '
followed by a detail of the members and signature, with rank and unit.

" A court of three members is desirable, and a court-martial officer should attend, if available ; but undue delay must be avoided.

" The court can award any civilized punishment, including death, but not corporal punishment, and a death penalty will not be carried out without the sanction of the Commander-in-Chief.

" These instructions will apply only until the occupation of German territory is completed. Further instructions will then be issued."

The detection and punishment of crime in the civil community remained the responsibility of the German police. The British Special Investigation Bureau was concerned principally with thefts of British Government property : clothing, blankets, stray horses and mules. The culprits were fined or imprisoned. In some cases plunder from France was recovered. The most common offences were supplying alcohol to the troops, being in possession of arms, and failing to display " Out of Bounds " notice boards on brothels and drinking shops.

Two British soldiers were tried by court martial and found guilty of the murder of German women of the prostitute class, with whom they had been consorting—in the second case the murderer, through jealousy, had at the same time killed a lance-corporal of his own regiment. According to German law, unpremeditated murder is not punishable by death and, this being so and it being considered unsuitable that they should die by the hand of firing parties, both men were reprieved and sentenced in the one case to 15 years' imprisonment and in the other to penal servitude for life.

NOTE I

ANORDNUNGEN

Issued by General Sir H. Plumer

WHEREAS by Proclamation dated the first day of December 1918, the Field-Marshal Commanding-in-Chief British Armies has commanded all persons well and truly to obey all Orders given by any person acting under his authority :

NOW I, General Officer Commanding Second British Army, acting under the authority of the said Commander-in-Chief, DO HEREBY ORDER as follows :

I. *Dwelling Houses*

There shall be fixed on the inside of the outer door of each inhabited building a list stating the name, nationality, sex, age and occupation of every person residing in such building.

The head of each household will be held responsible for fixing such a list of the members of his household, and for the accuracy of the list, and for making all alterations necessary owing to the departure or arrival of members of the household.

In the case of an inhabited building containing several flats or tenements, a separate list shall be made out for each flat or tenement and fixed on the inside both of the outer door of the flat or tenement and of the outer door of the main building. The head of each separate household will be responsible for the list of persons forming his household.

Any alterations in a list necessary owing to changes in the members of a household shall be made by the head of the household within three hours of the change occurring.

No person may change his residence without permission from the British military authorities.

II. *Identity Cards*

Every inhabitant over 12 years of age must be in possession of an identity card, bearing his address, photograph and signature, and the signature and stamp of the appropriate civil official.

Identity cards will be valid for 3 months, at the end of which they must be renewed. The old card must be handed in before a new one is issued.

Every inhabitant losing his identity card will at once report the loss to the appropriate civil official.

III. *Circulation*

1. Inhabitants may circulate freely within their town or *Gemeinde* provided that they are in possession of their identity cards.

2. Inhabitants may not circulate beyond their town or *Gemeinde* without the written permission of the British military authorities.

3. Circulation on horseback is forbidden.

4. Circulation by motor car, motor bicycle, or bicycle is forbidden, except in the case of persons such as clergymen, doctors or midwives, travelling in performance of their duties who must be in possession of a special pass, or special endorsement of their ordinary pass obtained from the British military authorities.

5. Circulation by night between the hours of 19 and 6 is forbidden, except in the case of persons travelling in performance of their duties, who must be in possession of a special pass or special endorsement of their ordinary pass obtained from the British military authorities.

6. Circulation of hawkers, musicians, pedlars, beggars and other itinerant persons is forbidden.

7. All persons arriving in a town or *Gemeinde* must report to the appropriate civil authorities within three hours of arrival.

8. No person will be permitted to enter or leave the territory occupied by the British Army without written permission from the British military authorities.

IV. *Passes*

1. Passes for circulation by night, or by day outside the town or *Gemeinde*, will be obtained from the civil authorities and must be signed by the British military authorities. All persons circulating with passes must carry their identity cards, without which passes are not valid.

2. The fees payable for passes will be :

For clergymen, doctors, midwives, labourers for the British Army, and persons working for the British Army, *e.g.* milkmen	*Nil*
To go outside the town or *Gemeinde*	1 franc
For renewal of lost Identity cards	4 francs. [1]

3. Passes for a single journey must be handed into the civil authorities on completion.

Passes valid for a limited period must be handed in at the end of the period.

No person to whom a pass has been issued will receive a further pass unless the previous pass has been handed in.

Persons failing to return passes on expiration to the civil authorities will be punished.

4. All passes and identity cards must be produced when required by any British Officer or other person acting on behalf of the British military authorities or of the German police authorities.

V. *Press, etc.*

No pamphlet or leaflet may be printed or distributed. No newspaper may be published or distributed without the written permission of the British military authorities.

VI. *Alcohol*

The sale or gift of alcoholic drink other than wine or beer either to any member of the British Army or to civilians is forbidden except by written order of the British military authorities. The transport of spirits by any means from one place to another is forbidden. A contravention of the order will render the offender liable, in addition to other punishment, to confiscation of his stocks.

---

[1] On 10th December a ruling was given : " Passes will be numbered consecutively. Money taken by the Provost Branch will be handed to the Field Cashier. Counterfoils of passes and Field Cashier's receipt will be sent to the Military Governor through the usual channels."

VII. *Public Meetings*

All assembling in crowds is forbidden.

No meeting or assembly of any kind is permitted without the written permission of the British military authorities. In making application for such permission a list of the matters to be discussed at the meeting must be produced, and if permission is granted no matter not included in such list, as approved by the British military authorities, shall be discussed at such meeting.

VIII. *Places of Entertainment*

No place of entertainment shall be open without written permission from the British military authorities. Permission, if granted, may be recalled at any time.

IX. *Arms and Ammunition*

The carrying of arms and ammunition of any kind is forbidden. Every person in possession of arms and ammunition of any kind must deposit them immediately in the hands of the British military authorities at such time and place as may be appointed.

Any person knowing of the existence of any arms not so deposited must inform the British military authorities.

X. *Requisitions*

Requisitions will be made according to British Regulations. Every person must comply with any requisition made upon him.

XI. *Telephones*

The use of telephones is forbidden, except with the permission of the British military authorities, which will only be given in very special cases. All persons in possession of a private telephone installation not connected with a public exchange must inform the British military authorities thereof.

XII. *Wireless Telegraphy*

The use of wireless telegraphy is forbidden. Any person possessing apparatus for wireless telegraphy must inform the British military authorities and hand it over at such time and place as may be appointed.

XIII. *Carrier Pigeons*

The use of carrier pigeons is forbidden. All persons possessing carrier pigeons must immediately inform the British military authorities thereof. Pigeon houses must be kept open day and night.

XIV. *Post and Telegraph*

Telegrams may be sent within the German territory occupied by the British Army subject to censorship and during fixed hours only.

Letters may be sent within the German territory occupied by the British Army but only by the ordinary civil post and subject to censorship.

Correspondence with parts of Germany not occupied by the British Army and with other countries by letter, or telegram, is forbidden, except for the purpose of important business or urgent private affairs, or for communicating with German prisoners of war.

All letters and telegrams addressed to such destinations must be deposited for censorship in open envelopes at such places as may be appointed.

XV. *Photography*

Taking of photographs out of doors by civilians is forbidden ; civilians are forbidden to carry photographic apparatus out of doors.

XVI. Whenever application has to be made to the British military authorities for any purpose, such application will be made to the appropriate civil official, who will decide whether to refuse such application or to submit it to the British military authorities.

XVII. The appropriate civil official will be in a *Stadtgemeinde* the *Stadtbürgermeister*, and in a *Landgemeinde* the *Gemeindevorsteher*. In any places in which neither of these officials exists, the appropriate civil official will be the civil head of the community.

XVIII. The British military authorities will have the right of search in cases of suspected concealment of arms or other irregularities.

XIX. All persons of the male sex will show proper respect for British officers and at the playing of the British National Anthen, in the case of civilians by raising their hats, in the case of persons in uniform by saluting.

AND I GIVE NOTICE THAT any act of disobedience to this order will be punished in manner set forth in the proclamation first above mentioned.

Herbert Plumer,
General.

2nd December, 1918.

NOTE II

THE INSTRUCTIONS TO BE HANDED TO THE CIVIL AUTHORITY OF A DISTRICT OR TOWN WHEN IT WAS OCCUPIED

By virtue of the authority delegated to me by the Field-Marshal, Commanding-in-Chief, British Armies, I, General Officer Commanding Second British Army, order the civil authority[1] to perform their duties herein assigned to him and any other duties which may from time to time be assigned to him by the British military authorities.

I. *General*

The Civil Authority will be personally responsible for the performance of the duties assigned to him in any regulations issued by the British military authorities and for the observance both of the civil laws and of military regulations on the part of the community administered by him.

II. *Identity Cards*

He will issue identity cards to all members of the community over the age of 12 years.

Identity Cards must bear :

    1. The description, address, photograph and signature of the person to whom issued.

    2. The stamp and signature of the Civil Authority.

    3. The date of issue and a serial number corresponding to the number of the person concerned in the register of inhabitants.

They will be valid for three months, at the end of which they must be handed in to the Civil Authority and replaced by new cards.

---

[1] *Note.*—The term "Civil Authority" will mean *Bürgermeister* or *Gemeindevorsteher*, or in places where there is no such official, the civil head of the community in that place. For an account of the German organisation of Civil Government see Chap. VII.

III. *Register of Inhabitants*

He will prepare and keep up to date a register of all inhabitants of the district administered by him, the names being serially numbered with numbers corresponding to those on Identity Cards issued.

IV. *Passes*

He will consider all applications from civilians for passes and will use his own discretion whether to refuse them or submit them to the British military authorities. All passes must be prepared on the prescribed forms which will be supplied to him by the British military authorities.

All passes must bear :

1. The name, Christian names and (in cases of married women, the maiden name), nationality, date and place of birth of the bearer.

2. The maximum amount of money to be carried by the bearer.

3. The amount or quantity of goods to be transported by him.

4. The destination and route to be followed.

He will collect and hand in to the British military authorities all expired passes. He will report in writing to the British military authorities the deaths of any holders of passes.

Passes for Circulation beyond the District Administered by the Civil Authority

Such passes will only be sparingly issued, and the Civil Authority must satisfy himself of the urgency of application.

Passes for visiting sick relations beyond the district will only be issued to parents, sons and daughters and brothers and sisters, and on production of a certificate from a doctor that the case is serious and not infectious.

No passes will be issued for the purpose of visiting the sick by the British military authorities except on production of the above certificates from a doctor and the Civil Authority.

Passes for Circulating within the District by Night

Such passes will be sparingly issued, and the Civil Authority will satisfy himself of the urgency of the application.

They will be valid for one month, when they will be returned to the Civil Authority. A new pass will not be issued until the expired pass has been returned.

They should only be necessary for doctors, midwives and exceptional cases, such as mill-hands working at night.

Passes for crossing the Lines of Examining Posts

The Civil Authority must satisfy himself of the absolute necessity of such a pass, and must write to that effect on the pass itself.

They should seldom be necessary except for doctors, midwives and persons travelling for revictualling purposes.

V. *Civilians of Allied Nationalities*

The Civil Authority will prepare and furnish to the British military authorities a list of all civilians of Allied nationality in the district administered by him.

VI. *New Arrivals*

The Civil Authority will without delay inform the British military authorities of all new arrivals in the district administered by him.

VII. *Prostitutes*

The Civil Authority will without delay prepare lists of :

1. All brothels in the district administered by him, with the names of the inmates.

2. The names and addresses of all known prostitutes outside brothels.

3. The names and addresses of all women known to be suffering from venereal disease.

VIII.

The Civil Authority will consider all applications for permits of any kind, or for exemptions from regulations issued by the British military authorities, and will decide whether to refuse such applications or to submit them to the British military authorities.

2nd December, 1918.   Herbert Plumer.

Note III

INSTRUCTIONS FOR TAKING OVER THE TELEGRAPH AND TELEPHONE SYSTEMS AND THE CENSORSHIP OF CIVILIAN COMMUNICATIONS

1. *Postal and telegraphic communications between German territory occupied by the British Army and German territory occupied by the Allies, or unoccupied German territory or other countries.*

No postal or telegraphic communications will be permitted in the first instance, except to German prisoners of war in Allied countries.

Communications with German territory occupied by the Allies, or unoccupied German territory, or other countries by letter or telegram may be permitted later for important business or urgent private affairs, but only when G.O.C. Army of Occupation, in the exercise of his discretion, thinks fit, and subject to such censorship regulations as may be imposed at a later date.

2. *Postal and telegraphic communications within occupied German territory.*

(a) *Postal Censorship.*—Civil post offices will be permitted to remain open under German civil post office authorities.

No restrictions will be made as regards the number of letters to be sent, or the contents of letters in the first instance, but censorship will be established and restrictions will be imposed as found necessary.

Central censorship stations will be established at suitable centres and travelling censors appointed to deal with periodical inspection at civil post offices.

Censorship regulations for occupied German territory, on the above lines, will be drawn up by the Deputy Chief Field Censor and printed.

Censorship personnel in occupied German territory will work under the Security Staff, which will be placed at the disposal of the Military Governor.

(b) *Telegraphic and telephonic communications. Use of Telegraphs.*— Telegraph lines not required for military purposes will be left at the disposal of the German telegraph service for the use of the civil population, and telegrams will be subject to censorship at central censorship stations under arrangements to be made between Censorship and Signal Services.

Further instructions will be issued after more information has been received from representatives of the German Signal Service, who have been instructed to attend at Spa to meet a representative of the British Signal Service.

(c) *Use of telephones.*—Telephone lines required for military purposes will be taken over by the British Signal Service. The remainder will be closed down and will not be re-opened until permission for use in special cases is given by the G.O.C., Army of Occupation, when the necessary censorship will be imposed.

3. *Press, etc.*

Printing presses will be controlled and only a selected number permitted to print subject to censorship. Newspapers, pamphlets, leaflets, programmes, etc., will be controlled in this way.

Note IV

Additional Routine Orders issued at Various Times

Billeting Parties. These were to march in rear of the advanced troops, and not in front of them.[1]

Night Piquets. In every village and town units were to detail piquets at night to patrol and ensure that the regulations regarding lights, circulation, etc., were carried out.

Meals at Hotels. On 14th December an instruction laid down that British officers and British civilians who wished to have meals at hotels must comply with the regulations as regards food cards, or arrange with the manager to cook their military rations. Food cards were obtainable at the Military Governor's office at the Dom Hotel, Cologne; meals were to be paid for at current prices, and any complaints made to the Military Governor's office.[2]

Requisitioning. On 15th December the requisitioning of milk, butter and eggs, and requisitioning or hiring of motor vehicles by units and formations was forbidden. On the 20th the channels for all requisitioning were defined : (a) supplies such as straw, coal, briquettes, through brigade supply officers ; (b) engineer material such as timber, iron, stoves, bricks, mortar, through an officer commanding a field squadron or company R.E. ; (c) buildings, other than the ordinary billets, through the divisional D.A.A. and Q.M.G. alone, and it was laid down that on no account were railway premises, station buildings, sheds or yards to be occupied as billets.

---

[1] It will be recalled that the fight at Landrecies on 25th August, 1914, was brought about by a German billeting party going ahead of its troops as night fell.

[2] The duties of this officer are dealt with in Chapter VII.

Fining of Localities. The infliction of fines on localities was forbidden except on the authority of the Military Governor.

Arms. All arms, including shot guns taken from civilians, were to be handed to the nearest provost officer.

Fraternization. On the 17th all ranks were warned against fraternization with the inhabitants. " Any man seen walking with a " German woman will be arrested." This order soon became a dead letter, and " to frat " acquired a special significance. The name of the principal shopping street in Cologne, the Hohe Strasse (but locally, perhaps to prevent mistakes, called Hoch Strasse) was pronounced by the troops as one syllable with a " W " in front of it.

Prices. An instruction on the 18th announced that the *Oberbürgermeister* had been ordered to arrange that all goods exposed for sale in shops were to be marked with the price, which was binding on both seller and buyer. Any cases of complaints of excessive prices were to be brought to the notice of the Military Governor.

CHAPTER V
THE MARCH INTO GERMANY (*continued*)
THE ADVANCE FROM THE FRONTIER TO THE RHINE
(Frontispiece and End Paper)

THE RHINELAND AND ITS POPULATION [1]

The territory which the British Army was about to enter
and over which General Sir Herbert Plumer was called upon to
rule, virtually the Department of Cologne, contained about a
million and a quarter inhabitants.[2] Of these, in normal times,
almost exactly one-half were wage earners, half of them in
industry, and one-sixth each in agriculture and in trade and
transport. Of the total, about 600,000 lived in Cologne,[3] the
metropolis of the Rhineland, the seat of the Government of a
Department, a fortress, a great manufacturing city, and
one of the most important railway centres in Germany. It had
very extensive suburbs, separated from the semi-circle of the
old city by a " green belt " : on the western bank of the
Rhine were Bayental, Sulz, Lindental, Ehrenfeld, Rickendorf,
Nippes, Riehl, Merheim and Niehl, all industrial, except
Lindental and the parts of Bayental and Niehl near the
Rhine ; and on the eastern bank, Poel, Deutz, Kalk, Mülheim
and Stammheim, all industrial. Each of these suburbs had its
own *Bürgermeister* and team of officials. The only other large
towns in the area were steel-manufacturing Solingen (in the
bridgehead) with 135,000 inhabitants ; the university of Bonn,
with about 100,000 inhabitants (5,000 students) ; and Düren,
a manufacturing centre containing cloth and paper mills and
glass works, with about 40,000. Not only railways, but the
Rhine and its tributaries and a good canal system also provided
for the distribution of its manufactures and the import of its
requirements. Owing to the small amount of its surface being
suitable for agriculture, the greater part of its food supplies
had to be brought from other parts of Germany.

Cologne itself contained a mass of industries : manufactories of machines of all sorts, of electrical plant, motors,
chemicals, explosives, textiles and paper, besides printing,
dyeing, food canning, and the adaptation of brown coal for
industrial purposes.

It must not be overlooked that the inhabitants of the
Rhineland, slightly built, lively, and wine drinkers, were
different in temperament as well as to some extent in physical

---

[1] See End Paper
[2] 1,434,827 in 1925. The Düsseldorf Department (Ruhr) contained about
four million, and that of Coblence only about 80,000.
[3] 643,000 in 1919.

build from the inhabitants of north and central Germany, and as much like the tall, over-drilled, Schnaps-drinking Lithuanian-Slavs of East Prussia, as, say, a Parisian is like an Hanoverian [1] ; also that more than four-fifths of the inhabitants were Catholics.[2] Of their sincere devotion to the Hohenzollern family there was no room for doubt.

Since the Rhineland, after being a collection of 72 prince-archbishoprics, princedoms, dukedoms, countships, free cities (of which Cologne was one), etc., came in 1815—with an addition in 1866—into the possession of Prussia, and the Prussian eagle had been placed in a label on its provincial shield of arms, it had been treated almost as a conquered province, and gradually and artificially but not completely Prussianized.

West of the Rhine and north of a line Bonn–Düren–Aachen, the area is a plain, traversed west of Cologne by the wooded Vorgebirge ridge ; south of this line are the mountainous outlyers of the Eifel and the Ardennes : the Schneeeifel, Ahrgebirge, Zitterwald and Hohe Venn, the last, as its name suggests, a high moorland. Black coal deposits (Ruhr, Aachen, Eschweiler, Saar) lie just outside the territory, but the Vorgebirge district is very rich in brown coal.

The peacetime garrison of the Rhineland had been the VIII Army Corps, with headquarters at Coblence ; the troops of the 15th Division (less five battalions) had been quartered, in what was now the British area, in Cologne (with Deutz), Bonn and Düren. A foot-artillery regiment and two engineer battalions of the VII Corps (Westphalia), were also quartered in Cologne. At Elsenborn, near the Belgian frontier, were permanent barracks for 25,000 men, built, to facilitate the invasion of Belgium, on a great, lonely, well-wooded upland, with airfields and artillery manœuvre grounds and ranges. At Wahn, in the bridgehead, was a foot-artillery range. Thus, the amount of barrack accommodation was considerable ; and for offices and the accommodation of officers in Cologne

---

[1] This difference was fully recognized in the old German Army, in which there was a saying : " The Pomeranian will march till he dies, the Branden-" burger until he drops, the Saxon until he is tired, and the Rhinelander as " long as he feels inclined."

The Rhinelanders—and other tribes of Germanic origin—did not regard the Prussian as a German, and among themselves spoke of him as the *Ost-Elbier*, " the fellow east of the Elbe," the barbarian beyond the border ; the southern tribes of mixed origin, like the Bavarians and Austrians, called him *Sau-Preuss*, " the Prussian swine," and, as a term of abuse, used " *Verdammter preussischer Schulmeister* (damned Prussian schoolmaster)."

[2] 1,133,143 to 263,745 Lutheran in 1925, and in the City of Cologne, 563,860 to 134,360.

alone 18 hotels, eight of them large and modern, were available ; the Excelsior and Dom hotels were requisitioned as the headquarters offices, and the Monopol as living quarters for the staff. Besides good public and scholastic buildings, there were 31 hospitals and 55 schools, an opera house, two theatres and three variety theatres, an exhibition hall, which accommodated on the first arrival all the horses of a cavalry regiment, a dancing hall used for the men, and a racecourse with the usual buildings—which were occupied by a cavalry regiment.

Crossing the Frontier

Only the Second Army, including the 1st Cavalry Division (Major-General R. L. Mullens), was to enter Germany. General Plumer's orders of 26th November for the advance, after giving the boundaries and stating that the American Army would be on the right and the French Sixth Army (later altered to the Belgian Army) on the left, directed that the Canadian and II Corps (Lieut.-Generals Sir A. Currie and Sir Claud Jacob) were to carry out the occupation. With cavalry attached, they were to cross the frontier on 1st December, reach Line No. 4 on the 4th, leave it on the 5th, reach the Rhine on the 8th, and cross it to occupy the bridgehead on the 13th. The VI and IX Corps (Lieut.-Generals Sir A. Haldane and Sir W. Braithwaite) were to cross the frontier and occupy reserve areas at a date to be notified later, and an order on the 28th instructed the VI Corps to begin its advance on 4th December so that the whole of it would be east of the frontier by 6 p.m. on the 10th December. The IX Corps was to follow the VI on 7th December, and all its troops were to be east of the frontier by 6 p.m. on 14th December. Thus in the occupation of the Rhineland the Dominions were represented by the Canadian Corps, by the New Zealand Division,[1] by the 13th Australian Light Horse (which for a little time was with the Guards and 62nd Divisions of the VI Corps), by the 50th (South African) Heavy Battery, and by the 1st Royal Newfoundland Regiment (in the 9th Division).

The advance at 5 a.m. on 1st December was headed by the 1st Cavalry Division, with the 17th Armoured Car Battalion attached, and the 5th Cavalry Brigade (2nd Cavalry Division), so that the front and outer flank of each of the two leading corps of the Second Army were covered by two cavalry brigades. As far as possible, men who had arrived in France in 1914— they were not many—were put in the advanced guard so as

---

[1] Which marched to Herbestal (four miles north-west of Eupen), where the infantry was entrained on 20th December for the bridgehead.

to be the first to cross the frontier. The rest of the cavalry was withdrawn and remained west of the frontier in the Fourth Army area. The advanced guards of the 2nd Canadian, 1st Canadian, 29th and 9th Divisions followed the cavalry at 9 a.m. At the end of the day's march the cavalry line ran through Montjoie, but the main bodies of the infantry were barely over the frontier. Railheads on 30th November had been[1] : for the 1st Cavalry Division, Marche ; for the Canadian Corps, Huy ; and for the II Corps, Amay (four miles E.N.E. of Huy), that is some 30 miles west of the German frontier, with reserve supply railheads farther back at Heule (close to Courtrai) and Audenarde.

HALT OWING TO RAILWAY DIFFICULTIES

Owing to an accident at La Louvière (a large junction between Mons and Charleroi), no supply trains arrived on 30th November, and in the afternoon of 1st December General Plumer, whose Advanced Headquarters were in Namur, informed G.H.Q., confirming his statement at 10.15 p.m., that, as there was little prospect of immediate improvement and petrol was short, he felt compelled to order all his forces to halt on the 2nd and the following day. The cavalry and advanced guards could probably have existed by requisitioning, but General Plumer did not wish to mark the entry of the British Army into Germany by such a demonstration of its rights. Oats and hay, which after local enquiry, the cavalry did requisition, were readily produced.

On the 2nd and 3rd, therefore, the Second Army remained halted ; the squadrons, batteries and battalions, being billeted with a village apiece, were fairly comfortable. A few cases of influenza were reported, but the epidemic was kept from spreading by scattering the troops in the various billets as far as possible, a few men only to each house, and by instituting gargling parades. Trains for the 1st Cavalry Division and II Corps reached railhead at daybreak on the 2nd some 40 hours late, and arrived at the other railheads during the day. On 3rd December the trains were only 24 hours late ; but at 10.30 p.m. General Plumer reported that the situation, after improving, was again disquieting—railway working was seriously delayed by five accidents in the back areas and by six in the forward areas in the first week of December—but the march would be continued on the 4th.

---

[1] See Frontispiece.

CONTINUATION OF THE MARCH

On that day the 1st Cavalry Division reached a line through Schleiden and Düren, roughly Line No. 4, and thence nearly due north and thus short of it ; the 5th Cavalry Brigade (2nd Cavalry Division) was on the right, holding a flank about Setz, to cover the Canadian right and keep touch with the Americans ; the infantry divisions gained Setz, Amel, Elsenborn and Rötgen, about ten miles east of the frontier.[1]   The march, over the hilly and wooded region of the Eifel and Hohe Venn, was by no means easy ; it had evidently been disastrous to the enemy, as he had left behind many lorries, vehicles and hundreds of foundered horses.   Photographs seen later showed that field guns were hauled into Cologne by man-power.   The cavalry met everywhere numbers of German soldiers without arms, about 5,000 in Düren on the 4th, some with discharge papers, some without.   They were ordered to remove all badges and insignia of rank and uniform buttons, and were left under observation of a few troopers for the main bodies to deal with. In handling them great inconvenience was felt from having very few interpreters.

Area Commandants and Town Majors were appointed in the various localities as the divisions came along to arrange billeting and to control the civil population and stragglers. The inhabitants at first stayed in their houses, but, finding that they were not molested or robbed as they had been by their own troops, gradually appeared.   All, particularly the children, looked well clothed and nourished, a striking difference from the people of the French villages which had been occupied by the Germans, just as the smug, food-and-drink-satisfied inhabitants of Cologne, Bonn and Düren offered a marked contrast to the haggard figures of the people of Lille, Roubaix and Tourcoing, with their clothes hanging loosely on them scarecrow fashion.[2]   Soap and rubber were certainly scarce—

---

[1] Their itinerary is shown on the End Paper.

[2] These are the compiler's own impressions confirmed by those of others. Thus a diary for December of H Battery R.H.A., attached to that of the VII Brigade, R.H.A. (in the 1st Cavalry Division), says : " Our impressions " of the German population are that they all look fat and well-fed, and there " is no scarcity or starvation ; but our returned prisoners of war as they " came through looked very different and had, obviously, been deliberately " starved."   The diary of the 15th Hussars notes " abundant supplies of " vegetables in the country, and even butter and cream were obtainable." A press correspondent wrote : " A smiling, prosperous countryside with most " ' folk ' looking mighty fit.   No starving hordes, no collapsing children, no " coughing.   Germans, and quite fat Germans, going about their business as " usual.   Restaurants filled.   Silk hats, furs." (Tuohy, p. 70).   That Germany was starved by the blockade is another lie " Made in Germany " ; the shortage *after* the Armistice, caused by strikes, muddle on the railways and breakdown of distribution, is discussed later in Chapter VII.

messenger boys rode bicycles with a circle of spiral springs instead of pneumatic tyres—and clothing seemed made of paper.

The attitude of the Germans may be described as one of indifference tempered with curiosity ; the officials were studiously polite, and the inhabitants, accustomed to billeting in peace time as well as in war, made few difficulties on that account. The few who did so were shown a German order on the subject issued in occupied France.[1]

The only " incidents " recorded are that on the 4th a mounted German civilian knocked down a sergeant of the 19th Hussars. He was tried by a military court and acquitted. A boy set a motor-bicycle on fire. What happened to him is not recorded. The local official clocks were put back one hour to accord with French time ; the police were disarmed, but allowed to keep their batons. The exchange troubles were got over by the issue of 50-mark notes (no smaller were at once available), and by arranging that the German Government should pay part of the first instalment of the indemnity due into the State Bank at Düren, where it was taken over.[2] The field cashiers were instructed to change any notes other than German in possession of the troops at the rate of 70 centimes to the mark, and issue pay at 5 marks per 2s. 4d. ; but they and the troops were warned to accept only the notes of three named German banking institutions. It was made an offence to take German notes into Belgium, and forbidden to cash cheques at German banks.

---

[1] (Translation)

Commandantur Order
13 Sept. 1918.

Etappen-Commandantur 146,
    Field Post 42.

I was able to convince myself personally to-day that in some places uncertainty prevails as to whether resting troops have full and complete right to the living rooms and beds of the inhabitants. The answer to this is, in the fullest sense, " Yes." As far as beds are available, they should be ruthlessly taken from the inhabitants for use in quarters. Similarly all the living rooms are at the disposal of the billeted troops, the inhabitants are to be relegated to the attics (auf die Boden zu verweisen). I beg all commanding officers and senior officers of detachments to instruct their subordinates in this sense.

Thilo,
Colonel and Commander
Et Commandantur, 146

This order is to be given by the area commanders to the leaders of every billeted party, against receipt, and the execution duly reported.

[2] The matter is dealt with in Chapter III.

On the 5th, the 1st Cavalry Division arrived at the line of the river Erft, 16 miles beyond Line No. 4 on the right and up to it on the left ; but the 5th Cavalry Brigade remained stationary until the 19th, when it was withdrawn to winter quarters in the Fourth Army area. The 2nd Canadian Division reached Kronenburg, the 1st did not move, for its supplies had failed owing to a derailment between Valenciennes and Mons ; the heads of the 29th and 9th Divisions reached Kesternich and Vassenack. The marches were only ten to twelve miles air line in length ; but on twisting, hilly roads through dense woods were tiresome and painful. A great many ammunition dumps were reported, and occasionally one exploded. The troops therefore were warned to keep away from them, as it was quite impossible to examine every shell and pick out those which had demolition fuzes, only distinguishable from gun fuzes by a tiny mark.

On the evening of 4th December the headquarters of the 1st Cavalry Division, then at Düren, heard from repatriated French prisoners that there were disturbances at Cologne. Major-General Mullens thereupon telephoned to the *Bürgermeister*, who confirmed that on 3rd and 4th December crowds had looted shops, and on the afternoon of the latter day had been fired on by order of the German commandant ; he added that the situation was not yet quiet, but quieter than on the night of the 3rd/4th. He was instructed to keep Düren informed, and at 1 a.m. (5th) a message was received from the German General Staff in Cologne, again asking that the British troops might be hastened to help the civil authorities, as the German troops were due to leave that day.

The Cavalry Reaches the Rhine

The 1st Cavalry Division, after reporting the situation to the II Corps, sent the 2nd Brigade, with two armoured cars, to Cologne. Its orders were (1) to occupy all the bridges in the Cologne area, including those at Mülheim, with strong parties of cavalry with machine guns, and prevent any attempt to destroy them ; (2) to assist the German civil authorities of Cologne in the event of disturbance. On the 6th the brigade occupied the perimeter of Cologne, marched into the city, and sent parties to the bridges and examining posts to the ferries ; the main body occupied the Artillery Barracks at the southern end of the city. By that time the civil guard, aided by the feeling of fear of what the British might do, had restored order in Cologne. At Bonn the town bridge was guarded by a squadron of the 1st Cavalry Brigade. General Plumer meanwhile had ordered the 28th Brigade Group (1/Royal Newfoundland Regiment, 9/Scottish Rifles, 2/R. Scots Fusiliers, a section 63rd Field Company R.E., a machine-gun company, a field ambulance and a R.A.S.C. company), of the 9th Division then at Düren, to move by rail to the western suburbs of Cologne, and directed the G.O.C. 9th Division (Major-General H. H. Tudor) to go forward and assume command at Cologne : he was to take no measures for policing the city, but hand copies of the Commander-in-Chief's proclamation to the authorities for distribution.

The rest of the cavalry halted on the 6th on the railway between Liblar and Modrath, and thence along the river Erft. The four leading infantry divisions, after another ten-mile march, reached Blankenheim, Hallenthal, Thum and Düren.

On the 7th the railway situation had so much improved that the supply trains were only 12 hours late ; the cavalry (less the 2nd Brigade in Cologne) remained halted except the 9th Cavalry Brigade and divisional troops, which moved into the north-western suburbs of Cologne ; the four divisions made short marches, in order to close up, to Effelsberg, Satzvey, Zulpich and Habbelrath, just short (except on the extreme left which was only eight miles from the Rhine) of the Vorgebirge, the line of low wooded heights overlooking Cologne. The 28th Brigade was sent by rail from Düren to Ehrenfeld, a western suburb of Cologne, outside the ceinture railway. The three columns (Guards, 2nd and 3rd Divisions) of the VI Corps were still about ten miles west of the German frontier.

On the 8th the 1st Cavalry Division moved to the Rhine and, according to orders, with the assistance of the 28th Brigade, secured all the river crossings, and put guards on the Mülheim wireless station and all public buildings. The four infantry divisions swung northwards towards Cologne, the right having much farther to go than the left, and reached Miel, Wichterich, Gymnich and Frechen, the last place being only seven miles from the Rhine at Cologne.

On 9th December the heads of the 2nd Canadian, 1st Canadian, 29th and 9th Divisions all reached the Rhine on the whole front of the British sector from Bonn (like Cologne on the left bank of the Rhine) nearly to Düsseldorf, relieving the cavalry, which concentrated in the Cologne suburbs, with one brigade in the Duisdorf area (four miles south-west of Bonn). Cologne City (which was made a special area), and

Bonn were put out of bounds for the troops, unless on duty or
provided with passes.   This restriction was removed on the
20th December, but all troops not on duty had to be out of
Cologne by 9 p.m.   The inhabitants were friendly and anxious
to make the troops comfortable, and on the whole the civil
authorities of Cologne appeared to be glad to see the British
troops, as they were in fear of more rioting.   The VI Corps
crossed the German frontier.

According to the Armistice terms, the Allies were not to
cross the Rhine until 13th December ; but, with German
consent, General Plumer was authorized to send reconnaissance
parties into the bridgehead before that day, and preparations
were made accordingly.[1]

In this period, on 11th December, the first notice with
regard to demobilization appeared in divisional orders.   The
advanced instructions on the subject had been received some
weeks before, and the classification of men under their pro-
fessions or trades begun.[2]   The notice announced the imminent
commencement of demobilization of the coal miners (excluding
shale workers).   On the 29th December the diaries mention
that long-service men, miners and policemen were being sent
to demobilization concentration camps.

NOTE

DEMOBILIZATION [3]

Demobilization, as it affected British Armies in France, was carried
out on the basis of the individual soldier as the unit, taking into account
the requirements of trade at home.   To put the substance of the
Demobilization Instructions as shortly as possible : in the first place,
every Command at home and abroad rendered a return showing the
composition of its forces by " Industrial Groups " (i.e. the main
categories into which the many trades and industries had been grouped
for the purpose).   The return also showed the number of men desirous
of repatriation into each of the various 19 Disposal Areas into which
the United Kingdom had been divided.   The number of men selected to
go home for demobilization was fixed periodically at a rate depending
on the transport available and the receptive capacity of the labour
market, and according to a " priority " order of Industrial Groups
which necessarily varied.   The allotment per category was eventually
communicated to unit commanders, by whom the actual selection
was made.

To give an example of allotment : the I. Corps, with other corps of
the First Army, was directed to find 800 men for Dispersal Area VA.,
Dispersal Station, Ripon, at the rate of 24 men a day, with priority

---

[1] *See* Chapter VI.
[2] A short summary of the instructions is given in Note I at end of
Chapter
[3] " Army Demobilization Instructions, France." Issued at G.H.Q.,
France, January, 1919, consisted of 180 printed foolscap pages.

for the trades notified. The men chosen were sent to a Corps (or Area) Concentration Camp, such camps having been opened at Düren and Cologne on 19th December, and even earlier elsewhere, and thence forwarded to an Embarkation Camp, and so to England and the dispersal station.

As units became smaller by the gradual demobilization of their officers and men—when not kept up to strength for the Rhineland garrison by drafts of young soldiers—they were either amalgamated with other units, or reduced to cadre establishment, that is, sufficient officers and men were retained, in accordance with definite establishments, for the care of the arms and transport animals of the units, and of any equipment not handed in to the Ordnance Department. Several cadres could be united to form a " Brigade Group " and so maintained until the cadres, with or without their belongings, were ordered to the United Kingdom.[1] A scheme for re-mobilization, in case of necessity, was always kept in hand.[2]

---

[1] See also Chapter IX, in which the organization of the Clearing Up Army is described.

[2] Appendix XII.

CHAPTER VI

THE OCCUPATION OF THE COLOGNE BRIDGEHEAD

(End Paper and Sketch 2)

PRINCIPLES LAID DOWN BY G.H.Q.

On 23rd November G.H.Q. informed General Plumer that he should be guided by the following principles in the organization of the Cologne bridgehead :

> " It will be organized defensively in such a way as to be capable of resisting a hostile attack should one be made on it. Tactical features will, therefore, be prepared for defence, trenches dug, wire entanglements erected, and such defensive measures taken as you may consider necessary. No more damage should be done to houses, trees, etc., than is absolutely necessary for military reasons.
>
> " The distance from Cologne of the defensive zones will be settled by you, but no defences must be constructed a greater distance than 30 kilometres from the city."

In transmitting these instructions to his corps commanders on 28th November, General Plumer added :

> " Until such a time as reconnaissance in detail can be made the preliminary dispositions for the defence of the Rhine bridgehead will be made by corps commanders within the limits of the areas allotted to them. Orders will then be issued by the Army giving the general line to be held permanently and the nature and extent of the defensive work which is to be carried out."

MARÉCHAL FOCH'S INSTRUCTIONS

On the following day Maréchal Foch sent two Notes to the Allied Commanders-in-Chief with regard to the bridgeheads and the Neutral Zone. The first of these ran[1] :

> " I. A space of 30 kilometre (say 19 miles) radius is reserved round each of the fortresses Cologne, Coblence and Mayence for the organization of a bridgehead.
>
> The object of this bridgehead is to open and hold assured a passage to the right bank of the Rhine.
>
> It will therefore be organized and occupied on the following principles :
>
> (1) As many passages as possible from the left to the right bank should be constructed.

---

[1] The Second Note is dealt with in Chapter VIII.

(2) The defensive organization should take acçount of the topographical features and of the defences of the neighbouring bridgeheads, and avoid damage to property.[1]

(*a*) the largest possible perimeter within the above radius should be taken as the outpost line ;

(*b*) behind this should be successive lines of defence (position of resistance, position of security, etc.).

(3) The troops should be distributed :

(*a*) so that in case of surprise-attacks they can occupy the principal position of resistance in force and to time ;

(*b*) so that they can maintain order, particularly in industrial centres, but without quartering large bodies of troops in these centres.

" II. The forward limit of each bridgehead will be formed by the arc of a circle of 30 kilometre radius, the centre of which is the easternmost abutment of the centre bridge of each fortress.

As exceptions to this rule, the great towns of Frankfort (cut by the circle) and Darmstadt (tangent) will be definitely left outside the territory to be occupied.

To avoid giving the enemy any cause for complaint, the forward limit of each bridgehead is to be exactly determined and will be brought to the notice of the troops and marked on the ground (boards, sentries). Members of the Allied Armies are on no pretext whatever to cross the line.

" III. A Neutral Zone, which is not to be entered by the troops of any nationality, will be reserved on the right bank of the Rhine between that river and a line traced at 10 kilometres (say 6 miles) distance parallel to the bridgeheads and the river, from the Swiss frontier to the Dutch frontier.

The maintenance of order in the Neutral Zone will be assured by a German police force, constitution and control of which is reserved to the Allied High Command.

The organization mentioned in Section I. will be at once studied by the advanced parties as defined in my Note [see next paragraph]. Their reports, of which a copy should be addressed to Allied G.Q.G., should be ready so that as soon as the troops complete occupation, the work of fortification can be begun.''

---

[1] A month later, on 31st December, 1918, Maréchal Foch, in a Note addressed to the commanders-in-chief, said :

" This phrase [avoid damage to property] must not be interpreted as forbidding the execution of defensive works, but as an invitation to avoid as far as possible all serious and lasting damage. Thus the putting into a state of defence of dwelling houses, boundary walls, orchards and gardens, should be avoided unless absolutely necessary. On the other hand, on the countryside (fields and woods) defences may be freely constructed.

" The assessment of the damage can with advantage be left to commissions on which both the occupying military command and the local public authorities are represented, it being made clear to the latter that the Allied Governments decline all responsibility for making good the damage.''

THE RECONNOITRING PARTIES

Maréchal Foch invited the commanders-in-chief to send as soon as possible advanced parties "composed at first of only a few staff officers," in order to make preparations for the occupation of the bridgeheads.

Accordingly, General Plumer detailed an advanced party for the bridgehead under Major-General Sir F. Glubb, his Chief Engineer, consisting of thirteen General Staff, artillery and engineer officers. He instructed them to be prepared to start from Cologne at some date not earlier than 7th December, and after a preliminary reconnaissance to submit an outline scheme. The local authorities, without demur, furnished all the required information about water, gas and electric power supplies, and their source both in the bridgehead and the Occupied Area west of the Rhine.

The following instructions were issued as a guide in disposing troops and preparing defences in the bridgehead :

" (i) The object of holding the bridgehead is to ensure that a zone is maintained east of the Rhine securing the crossings of that river, and available for the deployment of troops for operations to the east.

(ii) The approximate forces to be held east of the river will be :
Canadian Corps, 2 divisions (less 2 brigades) ;
II Corps, 2 divisions.

(iii) Plans and facilities for the rapid deployment of troops are to be perfected. Crossings from the left to the right bank of the Rhine are to be increased.

(iv) Taking into consideration topographical conditions, the situation in the neighbouring bridgeheads, and the necessity for doing as little damage as possible to the property of the inhabitants, the defences will be organized with :—

(a) An outpost zone, the front of which will be at approximately 30 kilometres from the eastern end of the Cologne bridge.

(b) In support of this outpost zone, defended localities covering the main lines of approach.

(c) Immediate defences of the river crossings.

(v) (a) A proportion of the troops will be disposed in such a manner as to be able to occupy rapidly the defensive positions allotted to them.

(b) Troops will also be disposed to ensure the maintenance of order throughout the area, especially in large industrial centres. They should, however, be billeted in the neighbourhood of, and not actually in, these centres.

(vi) The limits of the bridgehead (30-kilometre radius) are to be very clearly marked by notice boards, and sentries are to be posted to prevent any of the Allied troops crossing the line.

(vii) A 10-kilometre Neutral Zone is to be maintained under Marshal Foch's orders beyond the 30-kilometre bridgehead zone ; in the maintenance of this Neutral Zone corps are not at present concerned.''

INSTRUCTIONS FOR THE OCCUPATION

On 9th December the Second Army issued the following instructions for the crossing of the Rhine and the occupation of the bridgehead :

" 1. (a) The cavalry to cross the Rhine on the 12th December and advance to a general line about half-way between the river and the perimeter of the bridgehead. The head of the cavalry columns to pass the western end of Bonn and Cologne bridges simultaneously at 10.00 hours.

(b) The cavalry to push forward to the perimeter of the bridgehead on the 13th December.

(c) The infantry to cross the Rhine on the 13th December in four columns, each column strength of one division. The Canadian Corps columns to cross by the Bonn and southern Cologne bridge, and those of the II. Corps by the northern Cologne and Mülheim bridges. The heads of columns to pass the western end of bridges at 0930 hours.

" 2. The Advanced Reconnaissance Party under C.E., Second Army, will carry out its reconnaissance of the river on the 10th and 11th December, and will start work east of the river on the 12th December after the cavalry have crossed.

" 3. The dispositions of troops holding the bridgehead will be made with a view to offence rather than defence.

" 4. The defences will be organized so as to ensure the safety of the passages over the river for troops coming from the west.

" 5. The troops will be so disposed as to admit of an advance eastward at short notice should the necessity arise.

" 6. Owing to the densely populated nature of the bridgehead, the Army Commander has decided that it will be necessary to modify the previous proposals and to locate the II. and Canadian Corps east of the Rhine, with the exception of such portions of the Canadian Corps as the corps commander considers necessary to hold the left bank of the river south of Bonn. Bonn to remain in the Canadian Corps area.

" 7. This will necessitate modification of the provisional corps areas already allotted. The areas of the II. and Canadian Corps west of the Rhine will be reduced, the boundaries of the VI. and IX. Corps will be extended northwards and an area will be allotted to the 1st Cavalry Division. After reconnaissance, further instructions will be issued.''

It was subsequently added that until after 5 a.m. on 13th December the Second Army was not entitled to take prisoner any German soldiers in the bridgehead, or take possession of any war material found there.

ASSISTANCE OF GERMAN OFFICERS OFFERED

On the 10th a telegram was received from Maréchal Foch, which began :

> "The German High Command has asked that German officers should be allowed to remain in the bridgeheads so as to furnish the Allied Armies with all the information they may need for the occupation of the bridgeheads."

The offer was possibly designed to enable the strength of the occupying forces to be judged. The Generalissimo authorized the use of the German officers, but only on the express understanding that their stay did not exceed one week after the arrival of the troops of occupation, and Sir Douglas Haig informed General Plumer accordingly. It was, however, found convenient for a time to retain one German staff officer to deal with personnel matters.[1]

On the 11th, the Military Governor, Lieut.-General Sir Charles Fergusson, arrived in Cologne, and was met at the station by a travelling escort of the 8th Hussars, which accompanied him to his official residence, the Hotel Monopol-Metropol[2]; and on the 12th General Plumer also arrived, C Squadron, 8th Hussars providing a guard of honour.

TRAIN TRAFFIC ACROSS AND THE NAVIGATION OF THE RHINE

On the 13th the following order was issued by the Allied High Command :

> "No passenger, goods or empty trains will cross the Rhine from the moment the advanced posts of the Allied Army reach the river. As exception, the Rhine may be crossed by the following :
>
> "(a) Military trains of the Allied Armies—i.e., troops in the bridgeheads of Cologne, Coblence and Mayence—and their returning empty trains ;
>
> "(b) trains bringing raw material from the right bank of the Rhine destined for Alsace-Lorraine and for the Rhine Provinces on the left of the river, and by the returning empties used for this purpose ;
>
> "(c) trains of rolling stock, locomotives and wagons, to be delivered to the Allies by Germany under the terms of the Armistice.
>
> "By order of the Allied High Command, transport of supplies destined for the population of Germany will be carried out by water."

To control the navigation of the Rhine in occupied territory, an Inter-Allied Commission was formed, with headquarters in Cologne, with a sub-commission at Rotterdam.

---

[1] See Chapter VII.
[2] The duties of the Military Governor are dealt with in the next chapter.

THE OPERATIONS

On the morning of the 12th the 1st Cavalry Division (less its 1st Brigade) entered Cologne and crossed by the Hohenzollern bridge, General Plumer taking the salute at the western end. It was accompanied by Major-General Glubb's reconnoitring party, and advanced about half-way to the eastern perimeter of the bridgehead. The 1st Cavalry Brigade crossed at Bonn, Lieut.-General Currie, commanding the Canadian Corps, taking the salute. In the industrial suburbs on the east bank many red flags were seen, and the inhabitants were described as "friendly, curious and socialistic." The whole area of the bridgehead is densely wooded—the coloured 1 : 200,000 map of the area looks wholly green veined by brown roads and dashed with white spots of clearings—except for a 5-mile strip near the Rhine and a space around the Solingen-Ohligs industrial area. Up to a line about a third of the way to the eastern edge of the perimeter, the country was flat, but gradually became very hilly and split by many ravines ; but the roads were good. Soon after 11 a.m. rain began to fall and continued all day ; but the men were promptly housed in comfortable billets, although the horses could be only indifferently covered.

On the 13th the 1st Cavalry Division advanced to the perimeter, to find that the Germans had erected a number of signboards well inside the 30-kilometre limit ; of these no notice was taken. The 2nd Canadian, 1st Canadian, 29th and 9th Divisions crossed the Rhine by the Bonn, South Cologne, Hohenzollern and Mülheim bridges, and halted on a line of villages about ten miles from the river. The cavalry remained in position on the 14th, the divisions of the Canadian Corps swung to the right a little short of the perimeter ; those of the II. Corps did not move. The divisions of the VI. Corps reached a line through Düren in the centre of its area. From Düren the 2nd Guards Brigade was despatched by rail to Cologne, and was accommodated in the Pioneer Barracks, and by 23rd December the whole of the Guards Division (VI. Corps) was assembled in and around Cologne ; on that date the IX. Corps crossed the German frontier.

On the 15th the infantry divisions[1] in the bridgehead relieved the 1st Cavalry Division, which commenced concentrating on its right opposite Bonn, its final distribution being one

---

[1] The leading brigade of the New Zealand Division did not arrive until 20th December. It detrained at Ehrenfeld and marched through Cologne into the bridgehead. The other brigades followed on the two next days. The artillery remained at Rötgen.

brigade in the Artillery Barracks, Cologne, one brigade in the Cuirassier Barracks, and one brigade in Düren.

The construction of defences in the bridgehead, with a view to future offensive action rather than defence, was at once taken in hand[1]. The system adopted was a line of resistance formed of a number of largish defended areas, for a battalion or two companies, covered by an outpost system extending virtually to the perimeter. Later, a second line of defended areas was constructed. Work was hampered at first by lack of barbed wire and other engineer material ; for although wood and timber were in abundance for the cutting, very little else except pumping plant and roof felting could be found east of the Rhine—in particular no cement or corrugated iron was available—and, as will be seen in the next chapter, the carrying power of the railways was still limited. A forestry detachment was sent up for tree felling, and arrangements were made to obtain stone from quarries near Bonn.

The Defence Scheme

Defence schemes were taken in hand. That of the II Corps, of which the general principles are given here[2], contemplated an advance eastwards at short notice ; for this three good roads, with connections between them were available. As regards opposition :

" the most favourable direction for the development of any organized military effort by the enemy would be from the north. The mountainous nature of the country towards the east does not favour military operations on a large scale. At the first threat of an hostile operation in the north, advantage would undoubtedly be taken by the Allied Commander-in-Chief of the clauses lately added to the terms of the Armistice enabling him to occupy the Neutral Zone between the Cologne bridgehead and Holland.

" Such a threat would therefore be met by the occupation of Düsseldorf and Ratingen by the Belgian Army of Occupation, and of the Neutral Zone by the II. Corps as preparatory measures for a further advance eastwards."

Divisions were therefore to be prepared to move northwards.

Defensive measures were also considered :

" Although in the event of threatened hostile action by the German Armies, it is intended that the Allied Armies should advance eastwards, yet it is necessary to take precautionary measures to ensure the safety of the passages over the Rhine for troops crossing from the west. In the event of it being necessary

---

[1] See Sketch 2.

[2] The Canadian Corps scheme is given in Appendix XIII. The maps prepared by the two corps have been combined to form Sketch 2.

to adopt temporarily a defensive attitude, the present outpost line roughly along the boundary of the bridgehead area will be strongly reinforced and the enemy will be met as far forward as possible."

A line of works intermediate between the outposts and the defended areas was to be prepared. Finally :

" On account of the mountainous nature of the country in the southern portion of the area, and the number of towns and villages in the northern portion, no fixed defences consisting of isolated localities can be effective for long unless supported by the action of mobile reserves. The defence must be active and mobile. The garrisons allotted to the various sectors are those considered necessary for passive defence only. It would be necessary to depend on formations withdrawn from the front or on fresh units brought up to provide the necessary troops to carry out an active defence."

On the 16th the Commander-in-Chief, Sir Douglas Haig, coming by train with an escort, paid a visit to Cologne, and was received ·by the commander of the Second Army and the Military Governor. He gave the following instruction to General Plumer :

" The general policy to be followed by you is that, within the territory occupied by the British Army, industries are to be promoted and facilitated as far as compatible with military interest.

" To facilitate this policy, the line of blockade will be the perimeter of the bridgehead, and not the Rhine as at present. In carrying out this policy, you are authorized to issue such orders to the railway and navigation authorities as you consider necessary."

MINOR ALTERATIONS OF THE PERIMETER

The only useful result which accrued from the presence of German officers in the bridgehead was the adjustment of the 30-kilometre perimeter to the parish boundaries ; it then ran sometimes slightly outside, sometimes slightly inside the exact circular perimeter.[1] The boundary between the British and Belgians west of the Rhine was similarly adjusted to conform with the German civil boundaries.

At the end of February a proposal was made to advance the perimeter of the bridgehead slightly into the Neutral Zone. In the northern part this was solely for tactical reasons ; in the southern, it was at the suggestion of the German authorities, because the villages in the Neutral Zone immediately south of the bridgehead were much visited by the inhabitants of Cologne and Bonn, who would be barred from them if they remained in the Neutral Zone. The occupation of this area would have had the advantage of helping the Security Section to stop the illicit traffic in letters and parcels carried in workmen's trains from Bonn into the Neutral Zone. It was opposed by the German representatives on the Spa Commission

---

[1] As shown on the End Paper.

as going beyond the terms of the Armistice, and the proposal was dropped.

Maréchal Foch, on the other hand, gave permission for the cadet schools in the Coblence and Cologne bridgeheads, at Oranienstein and Bensberg, respectively, actually occupied by troops, to be reopened as soon as they could be evacuated, provided that the cadets did not wear military uniform and that the instructors were in civilian clothes.

Maréchal Foch also authorized the transmission of postal and telegraph matter connected with the preparations for the elections for the German National Assembly (19th January) and the elections themselves. In connection with them he also accorded liberty of the press and liberty of meetings in measure compatible with the maintenance of order and the current attitude of the population to the Allied Armies ; and permitted entry from Germany into and exit from Occupied Territory of persons furnished with a request of laissez-passer by the regular German administrative authorities.[1]

As appeals from the courts at Düsseldorf were normally carried to the Court of Appeal at Cologne, it was agreed to permit this procedure to continue provided the necessary passes were obtained by those concerned.

THE SAFEGUARDING OF THE BRIDGES AND FERRIES

The Rhine at Cologne is over four hundred yards wide, and for patrolling it at first six, and later twelve, motor boats, each armed with a 3-pdr. gun, under Commander Hon. P. G. E. C. Acheson, R.N., were sent up via the French canals to Nancy and thence to the Rhine, as they might not pass through neutral Dutch waters.[2] Maréchal Foch, not unnaturally,

---

[1] Before the elections, from 5th to 13th January, some desperate fighting took place in Berlin between the Spartacists (a new name which the German Communists took on 2nd January), who had attempted to seize the Government, and troops brought in from all the garrisons in Brandenburg. The outbreak was suppressed and the leaders, Liebknecht and Rosa Luxemburg, murdered after being taken prisoner. The result of the election was in favour of the Moderate Socialists. Herr Ebert (Chancellor) became President of the Republic with a Ministry of Moderate Socialists, Democrats and Centre under Herr Scheidemann as Chancellor. Further rioting and risings took place in March and were suppressed by armed force. In Bavaria, after the President, Herr Eisner, had been shot by a reactionary Army officer, the Soldiers' and Workmen's Councils gained possession of Munich and other towns, and the movement was not finally crushed until 9th May.

[2] In August, 1919, the flotilla was reduced to 6, and the Admiralty asked the War Office whether, for reasons of economy, it could not be dispensed with. The G.O.C.-in-C. decided it could not be. On 7th March, 1921, Commander A. R. A. Macdonald, R.N., took over command of the flotilla, and at the end of the year it was reduced to five boats. The suppression of the flotilla was again suggested from time to time, but it was decided to retain it for the sake of prestige, as it would have been replaced by French vessels, and it remained until the evacuation of Cologne, leaving for the United Kingdom on 27th January 1926.

was anxious about the safety of the bridges, and on 6th December he had sent the following Note to the Allied commanders-in-chief :

" In execution of Article 1 of Note Annexe No. 2 of the Armistice, the Allied troops, in their respective zones will ensure the guard, technical inspection and maintenance, or verification of the maintenance, of all the Rhine bridges and ferries from the Swiss frontier to the Dutch frontier.

" Outside the Mayence, Coblence and Cologne bridgeheads the action of the detachments detailed as guard will be limited by the eastern bank (exclusive). Notwithstanding this restriction, *technical* parties of the Allied troops necessary for the preservation, inspection and repair of the bridges and ferries will have the right to come alongside and land on the right bank, and even to establish themselves permanently in the *immediate* vicinity of the points of passage, so far as is strictly necessary for the performance of their duties. The *German civilian personnel* normally employed in the service and maintenance of the bridges and ferries may be retained at their duties, provided the local Allied commander has no objection.[1]

" But the *German military personnel* will be relieved as soon as possible by Allied military personnel.

" The above arrangements have just been notified by General Nudant, President of the Permanent Inter-Allied Armistice Commission to the German commissioners, who have been requested to inform the German military authorities concerned.

" The details of the reliefs will be settled between the commanders of the American, Belgian, British and French Zones and the commanders of the Groups of Armies opposite them.

" Reports of the arrangements made will be sent to the Maréchal Commander-in-Chief of the Allied Armies."

On 1st January, 1919, as the German representatives at Spa made protests, they were informed in writing that the police forces at the disposal of the Rhine Navigation Commission had the right to move on the river between the right and left banks, to land on the east bank at any point, and station themselves anywhere, particularly in the ports and at points of disembarkation, in order to ensure the control of the river traffic.

In the British sector there were in Cologne, besides the Hohenzollern Bridge, which carried both railway and roadway, the South Bridge, which did the same, the Hindenburg Suspension Bridge (built in 1913–15) between the two, carrying a tram line, and the Mülheim pontoon bridge [2] ; and in Bonn

---

[1] Footnote in the original : It is taken for granted that in execution of Article II of Note Annexe No. 2 the material necessary for the upkeep of the road and rail communications (bridges and ferries) will be furnished by the German Government.

[2] The suspension bridge at Mülheim was built during the occupation and opened in 1929.

a bridge carrying a tram line. Of ferries there were, beginning in the south, a train ferry, then a tram ferry just south of Bonn, two vehicle-carrying ferries at Bayental (the southern suburb of Cologne, one and a half miles below the Hohenzollern Bridge), and nine ferries between Bonn and Cologne. Those outside the bridgeheads had specially to be watched to prevent communication between occupied and unoccupied Germany.

The roads in the British Zone were kept up under British instructions by the local authorities, being classified for military purposes as first, second and third priority. The road metal came from quarries on the right bank of the Rhine. Many bridges on the road system had not been built to carry heavy artillery or tanks, and measures to strengthen those on the first priority list were taken in hand.

THE LUXEMBOURG COMMISSION

On 20th December a second meeting of the body known as the Luxembourg Commission[1] took place under the presidency of Colonel Payot, for the purpose of co-ordinating the economic measures to be taken in Occupied Territory. Colonel Payot stated that the Maréchal had decided to form a " service " with four sections—administrative, financial, legal and economic, the last to deal with the distribution of raw material and manufactured products, and to control production and permissions to export. He introduced Monsieur Tirard as Controller-General of the Administration of the Occupied Territories and Monsieur Polaillon as Controller-General of Finance, and stated that general and political questions would be handled by an Inter-Allied committee in Paris. The British representative on this committee, Mr. S. P. Waterlow of the Foreign Office, subsequently put himself in communication with the Q.M.G. and promised to send two experts to sit on the Luxembourg Economic Committee.

Monsieur Tirard then took the chair as Controller-General. The members at the meeting unanimously reported that the German officials had remained at duty, and were under the control of the respective Armies of Occupation, that only the regular officials were acknowledged and no communication had taken place with any new superior officials whom the German Government had sought to introduce. It was agreed to forbid any election meetings until the Berlin Government had duly notified Maréchal Foch.

---

[1] See p. 56.

A number of minor matters were then settled. As regards saluting it was agreed :

" The following are obliged to salute Allied officers :

(1) All police in uniform.

(2) All railwaymen in uniform.

(3) Uniformed civil employees (customs house officers, firemen, etc.).

Saluting is not obligatory for civilians."

Workmen's trains through the outpost line, strictly limited as to number and length of journey, were to be permitted ; but they were to be searched daily to ensure that every passenger had an identity card (and later a blue pass), and that no smuggling of goods or letters took place. It was agreed that the peace-time river passenger service should be re-established.

Earlier, on 21st December, 1918, Maréchal Foch had called the attention of the Allied commanders-in-chief to the necessity for re-establishing and maintaining the customs barrier between Holland—Belgium and Germany and between France—Belgium and Luxembourg. He had asked them to ensure that the German customs service was maintained on the frontiers. He suggested that the German posts should be combined with the French or Belgian posts opposite them, and that military posts also should be established in order to ensure that the frontiers were effectively closed. The posts, in addition, were to be instructed to prevent the smuggling of German money and Bolshevist tracts or proclamations. Monsieur Tirard had announced that the blockade line, hitherto the Rhine, would now be pushed forward to the perimeter of the bridgehead, and that the general question of trade permits was being dealt with by a committee in Paris. He also said that traffic over the border between Holland and Germany was being watched by the Belgian authorities ; that until further orders were issued, no telegraph or telephone communication across the blockade line would be permitted, except on railway service ; and that financial representatives would be sent to various places in occupied territory to investigate the local budgets.

WITHDRAWAL OF THE CANADIAN CORPS AND REPATRIATION OF THE DOMINIONS TROOPS

The withdrawal of the splendid troops of the Canadian Corps requires mention. On 16th December, just as the 1st and 2nd Canadian Divisions had established themselves in the bridgehead, Lieut.-General Sir A. Currie received the following telegram, from Canadian G.H.Q. London, asking his views :

> "War Office order G.H.Q. [to] despatch 400 men daily this month, 17,500 in January and 20,000 each succeeding month, and that two Canadian divisions be released for this purpose. G.H.Q. desire 3rd Division to go in January—this owing to railway situation—and 1st Division in February."

At the moment the 3rd and 4th Canadian Divisions were out of the line in the Fourth Army area.

Lieut.-General Currie would have preferred to send home the divisions in the order in which they had arrived, but it was impossible to have the 1st Division concentrated near the base in time to leave in January, and he arranged accordingly that the 3rd should go first. He pointed out, however, that when one Canadian division had been sent to the base the other divisions would want to follow as quickly as possible. He therefore suggested in a letter to the Chief of the General Staff that the Canadian Corps as a whole should be concentrated in some area not too far from the base, so that he could superintend demobilization without difficulty.

It was finally settled that the Canadian divisions in the bridgehead should be relieved by the X. Corps (32nd, 34th and 41st Divisions, all New Army), under Lieut.-General Sir R. Stephens, from the Fifth Army, and this was done by 28th December; that the 3rd Canadian Division, then at Wavre (south of Brussels), whither it had marched from Mons, should be moved to the Tournai area, and demobilized thence into concentration camps at Aubin St. Vaast (the Canadian Reinforcement Camp in the Canche valley, about 28 miles southeast of Boulogne), and at Etaples (14 miles south of Boulogne) which would be ready to receive men early in January. The other three divisions would be concentrated in the Fourth Army area between Brussels and Liége : on account of the railway situation it was not possible to place them nearer to the coast.

The policy adopted for repatriation and demobilization of the Canadians divided the operation into two parts : first the divisions and the cavalry brigade would be dealt with, and then the troops on the lines of communication and units such as railway and forestry, outside the corps framework, or in the British Isles. In this second class, priority was given to married men and widowers with children, according to length of service overseas. Otherwise the return to Canada was to be by units of each division, in order that the organization under which the men had been commanded and supplied, and had fought so contentedly, should remain in existence until the last possible moment. It was also decided that the troops should return via the United Kingdom, as the great majority of the men had either relatives or friends whom they wished to see before they returned to Canada. For this purpose each man could have eight days' leave. Lieut.-General Currie was made responsible for the demobilization of the troops in France, in co-operation with the General Staff of the Overseas Military Forces of Canada in England.

In England the divisions as they arrived were concentrated at Bramshott Camp (12 miles due south of Aldershot), and subsequently at Witley (9 miles south-east of Aldershot) as well. From these centres they were entrained for the ports of embarkation. The corps troops and other troops from France were concentrated at Kinmel Camp (30 miles from Liverpool), which by 2nd April, 1919, had dealt with over 90,000.

Up to that date the total number of Canadians returned to Canada from the United Kingdom was 110,384. The total included 5,400 patients sent in hospital ships and the troops of the 3rd Canadian Division, all of whom had sailed by 19th March, with the exception of divisional headquarters and a few details. The balance was made up by a few troops outside the corps from France ; but the majority consisted of long-service men and married men, already in England, who had seen service in the field.

It may be added here, as regards the Australians, that on 21st November Lieut.-General Sir John Monash, the corps commander, was appointed Director-General of Repatriation and Demobilization, and Major-General Sir John Talbot-Hobbs took over command. Lieut.-General Monash's scheme was as well thought out and as successful as had been his military plans.[1] He estimated that he had to send home 180,000 men and at least 7,000 dependents. Length of service and then family responsibilities, and assured employment, were made the criteria for priority. The corps was gradually assembled around Charleroi. Each division (troops outside the five divisions were counted as a sixth division) then classified its members into " quotas " of a thousand (plus 5 per cent, to allow for casualties), as the normal train, also ship, load. The quotas were organized as battalions, although drawn from all arms.; but the squadrons of the air force were shipped separately as units. The 40,000 convalescents went separately under medical

---

[1] Details will be found in the Australian Official History, vi.

control. All embarked at British ports. In December and January 20,000 convalescents and " Anzac leave " men sailed. In May the last 10,000 in France were brought to England, where the Australian camps still held 70,000 men owing to a shipping strike in February and to the supply of transports not quite keeping pace with the arrival of the troops. The number of dependents, owing to marriages, had risen to 15,386. At the end of September, 1919, only 10,000 Australian troops remained in England. On 1st April, 1921, the First Australian Imperial Force ceased officially to exist.

The New Zealand demobilization proceeded on the same lines, the last " quota " leaving the Rhineland and the division, whose place in the bridgehead was taken by the 62nd Division (VI Corps), being disbanded on 25th March, 1919.

CHAPTER VII

THE FIRST PERIOD OF THE OCCUPATION
FROM THE ARRIVAL OF THE SECOND ARMY UNTIL
THE FORMATION OF THE ARMY OF THE RHINE

(End Paper)

THE PRUSSIAN SYSTEM OF GOVERNMENT

The ease with which, on one side, the Rhineland was governed during the occupation and, on the other, the execution of the Armistice and the peace terms was systematically evaded and obstacles were placed in the way of the various Allied Commissions will be the more readily grasped if the Prussian form of civil government is considered. Its organization was eminently suited for war, either open or underground, and—to quote the words used on 16th June, 1919, by the President of the Peace Conference to the German delegation—it enabled the Central Authority to " dictate to and " tyrannize over a subservient Germany."

It soon became apparent that the word had gone forth from Berlin that the French Army of Occupation should be given as much trouble as possible and that all should go smoothly in the American and British areas, with the specific purpose of separating the English-speaking contingents from their Gallic ally and creating prejudice against her, if, as she did, she rose to the fly. This was a matter of common knowledge, and is not often referred to in the records ; but the following appears, under date of 29th October, 1920, in a letter from G.H.Q. of the British Army of the Rhine to the War Office :

> " Propaganda is working vigorously, and no opportunity is lost of preaching about the iniquities of the French to British listeners and extolling the correct behaviour of the British in comparison. It would seem more probable, however, that this flattery of the British is merely cupboard love, destined to separate them from their Alliance with France.[1] It may be mentioned that no improve-

---

[1] British experience is confirmed by American witnesses. General H. T. Allen, who commanded the American Army of Occupation, has written (see Allen I., p. 26) :

> " The population was desirous of creating a favourable impression. . . . It is probable that this mode of reception had been instigated by the German Government."

Mr. F. Tuohy, a war correspondent, writes (Tuohy, p. 71) :

> " As Marwitz's Army marched back, its officers, acting on instructions from Berlin, instructed the German population to smile on the Americans, to cultivate their good graces ' for the good of the Fatherland.' The

Continued at foot of next page

ment in the moral virtues of the average German is apparent as this office has to deal with him. He continues to deceive and lie when it suits his purpose, until he is found out."

The twelve provinces of Prussia, of which the Rhineland was one, were ruled over by a complete official hierarchy, whose primary duty was to carry out the orders of and issue the regulations received from its superiors. Local self-government in the form of councils and committees did exist ; but, except that the larger cities had considerable municipal independence, at best they were only consultative ; any wishes which the communities might venture to express were subject to the approval, generally the disapproval, of the representative of the central authority. And, notoriously, no people were more obedient to officialdom and the police than the Germans.

The organization was as follows : In each province, under the Ministry for Home Affairs, was an *Oberpräsident* (Senior President). In the Rhineland his seat was Coblence, and his province was divided into five *Regierungsbezirke* (Administrative Departments), Aachen, Coblence, Cologne, Düsseldorf and Treves, each under a *Regierungspräsident* (Departmental President). A *Bezirk* was divided into *Kreise* (Districts) of two kinds ; *Stadtkreise* (Urban Districts) and *Landkreise* (Rural Districts). The former were without sub-division, and under an officially appointed *Oberbürgermeister*, with such assistant *Bürgermeistern* as were required. Each Rural District was under an official *Landrat* (District Magistrate) and divided into *Gemeinde* (parishes), each under a *Vorsteher* (Headman), whose business it was to see that laws and regulations were obeyed. The German Civil Service has been described as the staff in plain clothes of an Army in plain clothes : its powers were certainly as autocratic as those of an Army in the field, and its orders of whatever nature, good or evil, and whether given by a *Präsident* or a policeman, were implicitly obeyed.[2]

Government in war time was further facilitated by a *Friedensleistungsgesetz* (Law concerning duties in Peace), which laid down, *inter alia*, the powers of the Army to billet troops

---

Continued from previous page

clergy and school teachers delivered homilies on the matter. Policy was to humour the Amerikaner in order to get Wilson sympathetic to Germany at the peace negotiations."

Another factor, however, must not be overlooked, which Germans of the Cologne area of all classes admitted in confidence when no fellow-countryman was listening. It is that the American-British occupation gave the Rhineland security against the violent disturbances with which the rest of Germany was plagued : it meant continued disciplined order, a thing very precious to the German mind.

[2] A note on the German police system will be found in Chapter VIII.

and requisition transport and labour. As these powers were exercised in peace time—in the manoeuvre period, for practice—when as a rule the troops bivouacked for one night only, the German population were quite accustomed to have soldiers billeted on them, to have their transport and produce taken and to suffer loss and damage—without much compensation.

THE MILITARY GOVERNOR

On 26th November Lieut.-General Sir Charles Fergusson, Bt., commander of the XVII Corps and previously of the 5th Division in the original B.E.F., and formerly in the Grenadier Guards, was, as already mentioned, appointed Military Governor, becoming General Plumer's deputy in all matters in connection with the control of the civil population.[1] Br.-General (later Major-General Sir Sidney) Clive, head of the Intelligence Branch at G.H.Q., was selected to be his chief of staff. This staff eventually included sections for Civil Government, Policy, Personnel, Circulation and War Material, Censorship, Economics, Labour, Motor Cars, Imports and Exports, and Publicity. Earlier in the month Br.-General Clive had selected what German-speaking officers he could spare from Intelligence for the Military Governor's purpose.

In the Adjutant-General's order nominating Lieut.-General Fergusson and his staff, it was stated that the " Security Section "[2] would be placed at his disposal, also the A.P.M. Amiens with his complete staff.

On their way to Cologne General Plumer and Lieut.-General Fergusson visited General Nudant at Spa, and it was arranged that Lieut.-General Haking, as being in touch with the German members of the Armistice Commission, should forward direct to the Second Army such representations or suggestions as he thought expedient regarding details of British administration of occupied territory.

By this time British cavalry and infantry were around Cologne on the western bank of the Rhine, and the 28th Brigade in the city ; and on 11th December General Fergusson made his formal entry as before mentioned.

---

[1] It was suggested later that Sir Charles Fergusson was " too much of a gentleman " for the job. When told of this General Plumer " just paused " and then said, ' Is that possible ? ' " (Plumer, p. 196). In 1924–30 he was a most popular and successful Governor of New Zealand.

[2] *See* p. 69.

The duties of the Military Governor and his staff were laid down as under :

" 1. The Military Governor's department is responsible for the control of the civil population.

" 2. Personnel at the disposal of the Military Governor for this purpose comprises :—

(i) Staffs of Area Commandants.

(ii) I (b) officers attached to corps and divisions with their Intelligence Police.

(iii) Security Officers in divisional areas or large towns under certain senior Security Officers, with their personnel.

(iv) Censorship staff.

These act under the orders of the Area Commandants as a permanent staff for the control of the inhabitants in the area. Officers of (ii), (iii), (iv) will receive instructions on technical or special Intelligence matters direct from the Military Governor's branch at Army headquarters ; but for all other purposes these will be sent through the Area Commandants.

Channels of Information.

" 3. Reports on technical or special Intelligence matters, as called for by the Military Governor's branch, will be forwarded direct to that branch at A.H.Q.

" 4. Other information, and all information affecting the civil population obtained by G.S. ' I ' of corps and divisions, will be forwarded through divisional and corps headquarters to Second Army G.S. ' I,' where it will be collated, and passed to the Military Governor's branch. The Military Governor's branch will collate reports on the political and economic situation for the information of G.H.Q.

" 5. General Staff officers, and officers of the Intelligence Corps in divisions and corps will have access at any time to the I (b), Security and Censorship offices in their areas, and should keep themselves and their commanders informed on all matters which affect the area ; but this does not relieve the staffs mentioned in paragraph 2 from the responsibility of keeping their Area Commandants informed on questions and events dealt with by them."

It must be emphasized that the Military Governor was merely the senior staff officer at General Plumer's headquarters for civil administrative work : he commanded no troops and could issue no orders to corps commanders except with the authority of the G.O.C. Second Army. The title often puzzled the Germans, who were used to the Military Commandant in his " *Kommandatur* " being supreme, and it certainly tended to create confusion in the minds of the corps commanders as to the authority it appeared to convey. When Field-Marshal Sir William Robertson succeeded General Plumer, he was minded to change the name ; but as it had been in existence since the British entered the country, he decided not to make any alteration, as it might cause further confusion. In instructions issued to corps commanders he did make it clear, however, that they were responsible to him for their respective areas, and that the Military Governor was not a commander but the staff officer through whom his instructions regarding civil administration were conveyed.[1]

For administrative purposes as regards the civil population, the Military Governor was empowered to correspond with the area commandants, that is : the four corps commanders, the G.O.C. 1st Cavalry Division, and the commandants of Cologne, Montjoie, Malmedy and Hollenthal, the last three of these dividing the Army Troops area between them.

On 1st January, 1919 [2] General Fergusson issued some new *Anordnungen* which, instead of adding to restrictions, reduced the severity of the rules for the circulation of Germans in the Occupied Territory ; relaxed the short-lived order about saluting officers so that male civilians did not need to remove their hats unless actually addressing officers or being addressed by them[3] ; and prevented the British troops from buying up certain articles of food.[4] This kind of treatment the Rhinelanders did not understand, and they attributed the British

---

[1] *See* Robertson, p. 359.

In the U.S. Army an " officer in charge of Civil Affairs in Occupied Territory " was appointed, and was " the direct representative of the Commander-in-Chief in such matters." American Occupation, p. 59.

One item of American practice deserves notice :

" As a general policy, American soldiers serving within the limits of the American Army of Occupation will not be employed on duties which will tend to belittle their dignity or lower their status in the opinion of the German population. This will apply particularly to such work as the construction and maintenance of roads. In such circumstances, whenever practicable, German labour will be employed under American supervision." American Occupation, p. 175.

[2] On 23rd December the weather broke with heavy showers of rain and sleet, but at Cologne on Christmas Day it cleared and became fine and frosty ; the first mention of snow occurs on the 24th at Spa, and next day in other places.

[3] The original order was not as severe as would appear. It must be recalled that the custom in Germany of men taking off their hats to each other in the street was by no means extinct. Clubs whose members pledged themselves to abandon the practice, called (in translation) " The-never-when-meeting-in-the-street-take-off-hats-to-greet-one-another " clubs, had been formed.

German officers and officials in uniform had still to salute British officers. General von Hammerstein protested to the Spa Commission against officers (of whom, of course, there were exceedingly few) having to salute, and said that if the ruling was maintained he would order them into plain clothes. To this Lieut.-General Haking replied pertinently that German officers found in the Occupied Area in plain clothes during the Armistice would be arrested as spies.

[4] *See* Note I. at end of Chapter.

attitude not to humanitarian motives but to weakness, or stupidity, or both, and presumed accordingly.[1]

On 6th January the Military Governor issued revised instructions as regards the circulation of civilians and the issue of passes.[2] They enumerated nine different kinds of passes : the identity card, the Brown (male) and Green (female) for circulation from British Occupied Territory into other territory ; the Blue (worker), the Pink (motor car or lorry), Yellow (bicycle), the White with bar (night circulation) and special cards for railway officials and "navigation" (for permanent members of the crews of all vessels on the river). The term " workers " and the interpretation of the phrase, " urgent private or business affairs " were defined. The former included professional men, officials and business staffs, and it was directed that considerable latitude should be allowed as regards the latter.

The Permit Office in Cologne at once became a very large affair, with an extensive " Black List," employing 25 German-speaking British and 150 Germans, and dealing with 2,500 applications a day, about one-fifth of which were refused. It was soon discovered that three " British Permit Offices " had been openly set up in unoccupied territory and were selling well-forged spurious passes ; but it was some time before the German Police could be persuaded to take action to stop the abuse.

Detailed instructions permitting but still controlling telephone and telegraph traffic, were posted up.[3]

On 8th January the Military Governor issued " Instruc-" tions for German Civil Officials Within the British Occupied " Area who are Deputed to Examine and Certify Letters " Addressed to Unoccupied Germany and Neutral Countries,"[4] and special detailed " Instructions to the *Oberpostdirektor* " and the Personnel under his Control in German Territory " Occupied by the British Army."[5]

---

[1] A German, Emil Ludwig, has remarked about his fellow-countrymen, that

> " a people inured to obedience admires even in its conquerors nothing but coldness and severity ; the nervous character of the German yields before threats, while it interprets a conciliatory attitude as a sign of weakness and cowardice."

[2] Appendix XIV.
[3] *See* Note II. at end of Chapter.
[4] Appendix XV.
[5] Appendix XVI.

The Military Governor as a rule corresponded with, or summoned to his office the *Ober-* or the *Regierungs-Präsident,* or the *Bürgermeistern,* reserving always the right to deal direct with their subordinates if he thought fit.

Railway traffic inside the occupied area was made free. Trains carrying foodstuffs, raw material, coal and certain licensed manufactured articles into the area from Germany might be admitted, but only empty trains might leave for Germany. In the bridgehead only the special Berlin-Spa train and the specially licensed workmen's trains were permitted. Up and down river traffic was allowed, but not transit from bank to bank.

On 13th February the following *Anordnung* was issued to the *Regierungspräsident* and other officials concerned :

" 1. The recruiting or calling up of men now resident in British Occupied Territory for service in the German Army or with any German volunteer corps or unit is forbidden.

The publication of notices in the press, the posting of notices, and the sending of letters and telegrams in this connection is forbidden.

" 2. The case of persons notified as deserters from the German Army who come into British occupied territory with false, or without, demobilization papers, will be investigated by the German General Staff Office, Cologne bridgehead. The latter will report the results of the investigation to the Military Governor for decision whether the person, or persons, are to be allowed to remain in the British Zone or deported to unoccupied Germany.

All telegrams and correspondence from unoccupied Germany dealing with deserters should be addressed to the German General Staff Officer, Cologne Bridgehead."

Bürgermeistern were ordered to prepare lists of the official personnel in their areas, and of all persons legally domiciled there, and furnish full particulars of military institutions, the system of communications and the manufactories. It was ruled that all demobilized soldiers must have passes, even when still in old uniform, which, on account of the shortage of clothing, they were permitted to wear, until the end of 1920. Former students of Bonn university domiciled outside the Rhineland were allowed to return to complete their studies.

In order to assist General Plumer in financial and commercial matters of a non-military character, on 9th January the Army Council appointed Mr. Frank C. Tiarks, of the Bank of England, as a consultant, with the title of " Civil Commissioner," in order to distinguish his duties from those of the Financial Adviser at G.H.Q., who was concerned with Army financial questions.

As regards requisitions, which in the British Zone were audited like any other form of expenditure before being allowed, it was settled that in the British Zone they would be paid by the German Government, and money thus advanced would be credited to that Government ; in other Zones requisitions would be paid for direct by the Armies with marks advanced by the German Government.

As regards loss or damage of German private property, only such as was caused by gross negligence, serious default or wilful act on the part of the troops would *not* be a charge against the German Government.

One of the troubles of the Occupying Army was the lack of German-speaking officers and men.   Until a number of linguists, including some women, were sent out from home, the Services, and particularly the provost police, were dependent to a dangerous degree on German interpreters.

GENERAL CONDITIONS OF THE OCCUPATION

The German officials of every grade whose business it was to arrange billets provided on demand, without demur, buildings which were suitable.   The general rule was that units were accommodated in barracks and factory premises, and officers and small parties such as signal personnel, police, staff clerks, in hotels and billets.   The only official complaint came from the daily-protesting Major-General von Winterfeldt at Spa, who objected to 10,000 men being quartered in Düren, with a population, he said, of only 33,000.   Actually two barracks provided accommodation for a battalion of infantry and a brigade of artillery ; and though the troops were somewhat close-packed the inhabitants were not.[1]   No local complaints were made, and one of Winterfeldt's subordinates on the same day handed in a petition from the *Burgermeister* of Düren begging for fuel, as otherwise 20,000 workmen would be unemployed, thus indicating a substantially larger population. Church property, including the houses of the clergy, was exempt from occupation ; but amicable arrangements were made for holding English services in the German churches.

Funds were obtained monthly for the Command Cashier by the Command Paymaster by requisition on the German Government in Berlin, and drawn through the *Reichsbank*, Cologne. Watch was kept on events in Germany, and at the time of the

---

[1] In 1871 the Germans in France refused to use barracks, and insisted that all their troops, even privates, should be accommodated in billets. Tirard, p. 108.

Kapp putsch in March, 1920, an indent for an extra supply of marks was made in case the transit might later be prevented. From the fragmentary figures available, it appears that in March, 1920, the required sum was 35 million marks a month ; in the summer of 1921, 30 million. Early in that year a German estimate of the yearly cost of the maintenance of the High Commission and the Armies of Occupation came up for consideration. The figure was nearly 16,000 million marks, of which 13,000 million represented accommodation and requisitions. The Financial Adviser stated to the War Office that no British records existed for checking these figures.

In 1926, under the Reparation Scheme,[1] the Agent-General for Reparations was making, on behalf of the British Army, a monthly advance to the Germans of 875,000 marks for requisitions and damage, plus 35,000 marks for railway services. This was reduced in April to a total of 700,000 marks. Up to December, 1924, Britain had received less than 60 per cent. of the cost of the British Army of the Rhine, while France and Belgium had obtained their full costs.

The Army, an island of British folk in an ocean of foreigners, settled down to the routine of an ordinary overseas garrison life, less its womenfolk who were not allowed to rejoin their husbands until after peace had been signed.[2] It enjoyed the advantage of the low exchange value of the mark, which about 21 to the £ before the War, had fallen to 5 for 2s. 8d., and continued to fall, the rate of exchange being fixed fortnightly ; by December the mark was worth only 1½d. Wine and beer were about a tenth and a sixth of the British prices ; tram fares were half-price for Army personnel not on duty ; and, all round, living was very cheap.[3]

The principal club in Cologne, with staff complete, was requisitioned as an officers' club ; the Ewige Lampe Hotel (better known as " The Earwig "), with 80 of its 100 bedrooms, as an officers' rest house. The latter in the course of time was given up, and in March, 1919, the " VI Corps Officers Club," a continuation of the club founded at Avesnes le Comte in August, 1916, was opened in the Augustiner Platz Casino. Cafés at first were allotted to the various categories of the Army, and others put out of bounds ; but all restrictions were soon

---

[1] *See* Chapters XV and XVII.
[2] For a time wives wore a special armband.
[3] The low value of the franc against the mark deprived the French of this advantage, and, combined with their small pay, prevented them, particularly the officers, from living up to the British standard. This made them somewhat envious, a feeling which the Germans did their best to encourage.

abandoned, with the exception that the hours were limited, being from 11.30 a.m. to 1 p.m. and 4 to 8.30 p.m., and hotel bars were reserved for officers.   One theatre in Cologne was taken over for the troops to organize their own performances, and at the opera blocks of seats, according to German custom, were reserved for officers and men at prices varying from the equivalent of 2s. to a few pence.   The G.O.C. entered the opera house box escorted by military police with revolvers in their hands, and no one was allowed to leave his seat until the general had left his box.   The Churches, the Y.M.C.A., the Church Army, the British Empire Leave Club, and similar societies, continued the good work which they had carried on with the Armies in the field[1] ; the Church Army took over the Zur Post Hotel in Cologne to lodge men arriving by train and individual soldiers on duty in the town.   Certain swimming baths were reserved for formations at fixed hours, and the men who used them had their linen exchanged for new.   The washing for the whole Army was done in the town.

Recreation and troop training grounds were available in plenty, with rifle and artillery ranges, and outside Cologne even a golf course.   Some football grounds already existed ; others, as well as hockey grounds, were soon prepared.   They were hard, as there was no grass ; this did not matter, but the severe winter conditions which prevailed restricted the length of the season.   The cricket pitches were limited in number. The Expeditionary Force Canteen produced 2,380 sets of boxing gloves ; 37,000 pairs of " gym " shoes ; 8,000 " gym " vests ; 224 football pumps ;   17,200 football jerseys ;   840 pairs of football hose ;   52,700 football boots ;   530 hockey sticks and 90 hockey balls ;   and daily shipments were received during January, representing in the aggregate very large quantities. Rhine steamers were put at the disposal of formations to arrange trips.   A musical society was formed, and two newspapers, the daily *Cologne Post*[2], which appeared throughout the occupation, and a weekly sports journal were set in circulation, while the II Corps had its own paper, the " *Wacht am Rhein* " at 1d.

---

[1] " 1916 ", Vol. I., pp. 134–44.

[2] When the first number of this was ready, the Military Governor went to the Commander-in-Chief to ask him to give the journal a name.   It was at a moment when there was much difficulty about the trains.   General Plumer replied, " Call it what you like, but for heaven's sake don't call it the *Cologne Express.*"   The successive manager-editors were Captain W. Rolston (who died in harness August, 1921) ; Lieut.-Colonel W. J. Cranston (a G.S.O. 3) ; and, in June, 1923, Captain J. H. Haygarth (the Amusements Officer).

The following Army colleges and schools were established : General and Commercial College in the *Handelsrealschule,* Cologne ; Science College in a house in Bonn ; Physical and Recreational Training School at the Engineer Training Ground at Riehl ; Technical College in a gun factory in Siegburg ; Correspondence College in a house in Cologne ; Rifle Training School at Hallenthal ; Reconnaissance School at Montjoie ; School of Musketry and Machine-Gun School at Drove ; and Signal, Tank Driving and Cookery schools in or near Cologne.

Education and technical courses were organized in each corps area for the subjects required for the 1st Class Army Certificates, for other subjects such as electricity, and for trades, and were well attended. In the II Corps area, for instance, the numbers were :

	January	February	March
1st Class Certificate	2,172	3,343	3,659
Other Subjects	1,538	3,167	3,313
Trades	710	559	311
	4,420	7,069	7,283

The difficulty was to keep instructors, who were constantly being demobilized, but this was got over by sending some out from home.

On 27th February the machinery of demobilization was improved by the inauguration of a second route via the Rhine, Rotterdam (where a small staff was maintained) and Harwich.

There were few signs of war in Cologne, and less in the other towns, except for the khaki and foreign uniforms in evidence, demobilized Germans in old military clothing with the shoulder-straps and badges cut off, many sentry posts and occasional machine-gun posts, the presence of many police and frequent " out of bounds " notices and lighting restrictions. Night life went on in cinemas, cafés and dancing halls. There was little mixing of the officers with the better classes, but other ranks gradually established good relations, even the forbidden " fraternization," with the general public after the order that every German male should take off his hat to officers had been rescinded.

Cinemas and theatres had soon been set going. No general censorship was exercised ; but it was laid down as a principle and guide for proprietors that no film or play might be staged which prejudiced the dignity or security of the Allied authorities or troops, or was in any way calculated to arouse hostility towards the Occupying Powers. Exhibitors and producers were informed that they could consult the General Staff (Civil Affairs) if in doubt, and they often gave preliminary shows of films. Performances were of course watched. Between February, 1926, and November, 1929, it is on record that 34 films were banned, 38 permitted after certain cuts and alterations, 10 permitted on a second application after alterations had been made, and 18 banned after a second application. Six plays were banned between April, 1928, and May, 1929, amongst them *Das Franktireurdorf*, performed outside the British area by the " Hitler Jugend," which was adjudged " slanderous and most prejudiced."

A gramophone record of a song *Der Fremdenlegionär* (the Foreign Legion Man) was ordered to be seized in March, 1929, and this was done by the German police.

A lecture on the raider " Wolf," which had been delivered by a retired naval officer in 1929 in a small town in French Occupied Territory, was prohibited.

In the early days of the occupation permission to British serving soldiers to marry German subjects was not granted ; but in July, 1919, Sir William Robertson asked the War Office if on ratification of the Peace Treaty such permission might be given. The formalities were arranged with the German Government and the Registrar-General of Marriages, Somerset House, and the procedure was published in orders in March, 1920. In November, 1920, General Robertson pointed out the danger of intermarriage from the point of view of security, and suggested that the husbands of German wives should be transferred from the Rhineland to other stations. This was adjudged to be unfeasible. Up to 15th November, 1923, about five hundred marriages had been celebrated ; but the number per annum subsequently decreased.

In spite of the registration of prostitutes, their number, with or without German encouragement, quickly increased— and venereal disease likewise. The worst brothels and low-class drinking shops were closed. The streets in the bad quarters of the towns were put out of bounds, and trouble between the soldiery and the local inhabitants, after one flare-up at Bonn, was rare.

Unfortunately some members of the criminal classes in the Army, who had given little trouble during hostilities, broke out or deserted, and, until suppressed, committed a series of burglaries, robberies and hold-ups, sometimes with German accomplices.

A matter which had to be carefully watched was the attempts of German agents in cafés and other public places to spread anarchist and Bolshevist propaganda amongst the troops. The records show that 43 such persons were arrested in one month in the bridgehead. The German representatives at Spa immediately demanded their release ; yet at the same time the German Government were begging to be allowed to retain troops and material to combat Bolshevism on the Eastern Frontier, and, regardless of Allied representations, were forcibly interfering with the efforts of the Poles and Letts to do so. Subversive ideas made in Germany, however, had no attraction for the fighting troops, anxious as they were to get home, and two divisions sent from the First and Third Armies dealt effectively with what had become a serious disturbance amongst the L. of C. personnel. They did so with the greater gusto as the commotion had resulted in derangement and stoppage of the leave trains.

The British authorities never interfered with the activities or free speech of the political parties in the Rhineland as long as these had no anti-Allied or Bolshevist tinge. Processions were permitted provided the route was approved, no flags were carried, and the meeting dispersed and went home as soon as the speeches were finished. No escorts were found necessary and no disturbance ever took place. Similarly, no discrimination between religions was allowed, and the law passed in Berlin towards the end of December 1918 closing church schools and seminaries was not applied in the British occupied area.

Rumours, with most circumstantial details, of coming Spartacist risings, spread during late February and March. Thus a rumoured meeting of 7,000 unemployed in the Stadtwald to march on Cologne and break open the civil prison turned out to be an orderly meeting of a few hundreds to discuss wages. Another *canard* was that five hundred thousand Russian prisoners were to unite with the German Spartacists in an attempt against the Army of Occupation, in sympathy with which a strike was to take place in Cologne. Nothing materialized in the British area. In Düren where the feeling against the local " capitalist " manufacturers was strong, seven agitators were arrested, but released with the exception of three found to have British stolen property in their possession;

the unarrested Spartacists were then attacked by the friends of the arrested men, who suspected them of treachery, and the two bands fought among themselves. At Opladen trouble which arose owing to the dislike by the railwaymen for the 10 hours' working day was prevented by the timely arrival of a guard of three hundred men of the New Zealand Division.

At Euskirchen and other places Spartacists, finding no opportunity for revolution, turned their activities to theft and robbery. Serious Spartacist risings occurred in Düsseldorf in the French and Belgian Neutral Zone at the end of February and early in April, and were only suppressed by the German Government sending troops there. In order to be fully prepared, the troops were given training in dealing with civil disturbances.

The local German press made attempts, which were punished by fine and suspension for a few days, to develop an anti-Entente tone by garbled and inflammatory accounts of the Peace Conference, the erection of Poland as a separate State, the revolution in Hungary, and the food question.

In general, the Germans in British Occupied Territory enjoyed greater liberty and quiet than did their fellow countrymen in the unoccupied *Reich*. They fully understood this, as letters read by the censors showed. Thus, in March, one German wrote :

> " Every Rhinelander would be sorry if the British left. Rhineland territory would then be exposed to Spartacism. To-day trade flourishes on the left bank of the Rhine. I cannot level a single reproach against the British. We Rhinelanders are very pleased to have them."

Another wrote :

> " The troops of occupation are behaving blamelessly, and the population are glad they are here. I am not exactly pleased at the 9 p.m. ' lights out ' ! "

From the bridgehead, one wrote :

> " Solingen is occupied by the British. Everything goes on as before except that the Reds dare not utter a sound.
>
> " As everywhere in Occupied Germany, the fair sex has exercised its blandishments, which in several instances have been rewarded with imprisonment. We are very pleased with the garrison for this."

Another wrote :

> " The British are very well-behaved. We have a lieutenant and three lads quartered on us, and they take care not to put us to inconvenience. If ' Tommy ' were not here things would be in a very, very bad way, as the towns around Solingen, Remscheid, etc., are full of the disciples of Liebknecht."

On the whole, the German police in the Occupied Territories behaved well; but they made no effort to prevent their comrades of the unoccupied *Reich* entering and kidnapping Germans, even in 1920. It may be added that the latter police were never, by their own account, able to put their hands on identifiable Germans who, after committing assassinations and other political crimes in Occupied Territory, had escaped into the *Reich*.

TRANSPORT TROUBLE

The difficulties of supply had been little diminished by the arrival of the Second Army on the Rhine and the cessation of forward movement. In a review of the situation at the end of December, the Q.M.G. attributed this to the " bottle-neck " at Liége, which still hampered railway operations; to the intensified demands of civilian traffic for repatriation and restoration in France and Belgium, to deal with which was beyond the diminished capacity of the Nord and Belgian State railways; to the shortage of trucks in the area, as the British had not received their proper share of the Allied pool; to the tracks, rolling stock and equipment generally being, after 4½ years of war, in a condition far below the normal standards of efficiency; and to the personnel having in consequence to work long hours, so that fatigue had become an additional source of accidents and confusion. " It had to be reckoned that any " military train would exceed by 150 per cent. its scheduled " allowance of time." During the hours of darkness a good deal of pilfering took place when the trucks were halted in sidings. On 20th December, owing to the slowness of the trains, 30,000 lbs. of meat on arrival at Cologne were found to have gone bad. Only the supply of essentials could be maintained. Luxuries, Christmas extras and canteen stores could not be sent up with any regularity and leave trains were continually delayed. In the Second Army area the Expeditionary Force canteen stores for the Christmas festivities were not expected to arrive in time. To prevent grumbling and discontent, Sir Douglas Haig ordered that the transport difficulties should be explained to the men; they continued to believe, however, that the non-combatants on the lines of communication had annexed the good things. The situation was saved by 37½ tons of canteen stores, including crackers, oranges, apples, sides of pork and 1,500 Union Jacks arriving at the last minute, and by sending lorries into France and Belgium to bring back any delicacies which were purchaseable.

" The only real hope of effecting an improvement seemed to be in the possibility, which was being actively explored, of developing the Rhine as the main line of communications for the Second Army, while trying to persuade the French Government to investigate the present working of the Nord Railway and possibly cut down the civilian traffic which so palpably overburdened it."

In January the scheduled length of journey by leave train from the Second Army was 35 hours, but the time actually taken often came to 4 days and the accommodation provided was indifferent. The Second Army had 3 " Noah's Ark " rakes, the Fourth Army the same and one " W.D." rake.[1]

In addition to the maintenance of two Armies in and close to Germany, the Q.M.G. Branch was responsible for the collection and removal of war material both captured and ceded ; for the collection and removal of salvage in the area of the battlefields ; for the collection of Army stores generally into central depôts as a preliminary to the disposal of them by local sale or shipment home ; and for the organization of trains, supplies and camp accommodation both for returned prisoners of war and the men selected for demobilization.[2]

On 4th January General Plumer brought to the notice of G.H.Q. that the whole of the railway system in the British Occupied Territory, including the bridgehead, was worked by German personnel numbering about twenty-five thousand men ; and that in case of the enemy suddenly resuming active operations the whole supply of the Army would be dependent on them, even should they decide not to join their countrymen.

---

[1] A " rake " is a complete train less locomotive. A " Noah's Ark " was an improvised passenger coach converted from an ordinary open truck by adding a framework to carry a roof and sides of light boarding ; it had windows of oiled silk, pegs for equipment and sometimes benches ; in winter a stove was provided. In the W.D. pattern, corrugated iron took the place of wood in the roof and sides. All leave trains had kitchen vans, for the arrival of trains at any given station was too irregular for the men to be fed at the *haltes repas* according to a time-table as originally intended. Reserve iron rations were always carried on the trains. The food was served three times a day, drawn in dixies and eaten either before the start or at one of the thirteen *haltes repas* on the route to Boulogne, which were provided with the necessary lavatory conveniences ; but it was early found desirable to attach trucks with ablution benches and latrines, and canteen stalls for the sale of light refreshments and cigarettes *en route*. The service proved unsatisfactory owing to delays, but was better than none at all.

From 20th December " the Cologne–Boulogne Express," as it was called, made up of ambulance stock no longer required, was run for the use of senior officers and the conveyance of mails. Light refreshments were served on the train, a stop being made at Charleroi for a meal.

During the Christmas season, when more leave was given, some extra rakes were organized, but as they had no kitchens or lavatories, this led to complaints and discontent. Later some rakes of German steam-heated coaches were organized, but they did not carry as many men as the Noah's Arks, and finally eight rakes of steam-heated coaches were sent over from the United Kingdom.

[2] See Chapter IX in which the disposal of material is dealt with.

The Q.M.G. pointed out that 25,000 men were required to work a complete " reseau " on a peace basis, and that many less would suffice if active operations were recommenced, and made arrangements accordingly. He reported on 21st January that two railway construction companies had been stationed close to the Belgian-German frontier ready in case of need to go forward immediately into Germany, with two more in the neighbourhood of Mons available at short notice to follow them : these 1,500 to 2,000 men would be sufficient in the first instance to open and maintain military traffic.

LINES OF COMMUNICATION

As soon as the Army settled down, Cologne–Aachen–Ostend–Dover became the usual route for the passenger service of the British Army of the Rhine, and Antwerp–Harwich for the mail. Drafts travelled by the ordinary Belgian mail service and the sea passage was made this way by whole battalions until October, 1922. The Belgian Maritime Service then stated that it could not guarantee space for more than 150 men and 10 tons of baggage per mail boat, and offered the use of a paddle steamer capable of carrying 600 men and 40 tons of baggage, at less cost, but taking 5 hours instead of the normal 4 hours of the mail boats. The War Office agreed to this plan being carried out when the number of men to be conveyed exceeded 300.

The bulk of the stores and supplies were shipped from England to Antwerp, or to Rotterdam, and thence, by rail or by barge, up the Rhine to Cologne[1]. At the end of 1920, however, the general officer commanding the British Army of the Rhine pointed out the disadvantages of Antwerp : it could only be reached from home by passing through the neutral Dutch waters of the Schelde, so could not be used as a base against Germany, and it required half a battalion for guard duties. This base was, therefore, closed in December, 1920, and the bulk of stores and supplies were then shipped direct from London to Cologne by War Department vessels, which could navigate the Rhine for six months of the year, or by ships and barges of the British Rhine Steam Navigation Company. In January, 1926, however, a relief of two battalions was carried out via Antwerp–Harwich, and in the trooping season of October-December, 1927, two cavalry regiments, two brigades R.F.A. and four battalions used this route.

---

[1] Barges and wagons containing arms and ammunition had their hatches or doors sealed before entering Dutch territory.

ECONOMIC COMMITTEE

The Luxembourg Economic Committee, which Mr. Tiarks, the British "Civil Commissioner," attended on behalf of General Plumer, met on 12th January, 1919, and received instructions, signed by General Weygand, for the forming of "Economic Sections" under the commanders of each Army, with a view to preventing a complete stoppage of commercial relations between occupied and unoccupied Germany, yet without their complete uncontrolled restoration. The section officers were given powers of inspection of factories, and authority to control the import and export of goods, with the proviso that supplies of foodstuffs and raw materials, also implements for industrial purposes, should be authorized without special formalities. The sections had to keep records so that the equable distribution of raw material and manufactured goods could be ensured by the Inter-Allied Committee. A provisional list of materials and produce whose export was forbidden until further orders was attached ; it included coal and fuel, metals and metal products, tools, cement, carpentering wood, leather, sugar and paper.[1]

THE FEEDING OF THE GERMAN INHABITANTS

The feeding of the inhabitants had early become a problem. On 30th December it was calculated that the Rhineland had only one month's supply in hand. The province, as already pointed out, was normally dependent on supplies from the unoccupied part of Germany, and, owing partly no doubt to the desire of the German General Staff to embarrass the Allies, after the signature of the Armistice, no food trains had been sent into Occupied Territory, although the trains which had conveyed the German infantry from the front back to their garrisons could have been used for the purpose, as also for returning prisoners.

According to disclosures made after the War, there was no real shortage of essential foodstuffs in Germany,[2] which in normal times produced nearly all the meat, including pork, and three-quarters of the corn required,[3] and in the pre-war days of prosperity the Germans ate in excess, so that half the

---

[1] *See* Appendix XVI.

[2] This controversial question cannot be treated at length here.

[3] These are German figures. The report of E. H. Startin, C.M.G., M.D., F.R.S., on "Food Conditions in Germany" 1919, printed in "State Papers. "Accounts and Papers," Vol. LIII., August, 1919, says (p. 441) : "Before "the war Germany produced 85 per cent. of the total food consumed by her "inhabitants."

peace-time consumption was an ample ration. The trouble was, first, bad distribution. For instance : eggs, potatoes, etc., were collected in great depôts, and considerable quantities of food went bad in them or on the long railway journeys from the depôts to the distributing centres. Anyone near the depôts could get food for the asking.[1] Secondly, the farmers

---

[1] Extracted from " *Das Schwarze Jahr* " (1929), by Dr. E. Gugenmeier, member of the *Reichstag*. An intendant official, P. Gesche, in " *Heeresverpflegung und Zusammenbruch* ", gives a mass of detail as reasons for the breakdown of the supply system : for instance, the rapacity of the Army ; the slowness of the trains, drawn by engines and rolling stock which had gradually become less efficient, so that food went bad *en route* ; profiteering— speculators bought up all the supplies they could and transported them to places where they commanded the best prices ; and pilfering—thousands of deserters and others lived on what they stole from trains and depôts.

The reports of British officers who went to Berlin in December, 1918, to January, 1919, printed in " State Papers, Accounts & Papers, 1919 ", Vol. LIII., clearly show that sufficient food was obtainable, even *paté de foie gras*, salmon, turkey, fish, poultry, tea, sugar and shortbread. Milk was limited owing to the low yield of the cows due to scarcity of forage. The poorer classes were being fed at communal kitchens (*Volksküchen*) on food which looked repulsive, but was exactly what they—and the soldiers—ate in peace time. Limited suffering there was, but small in comparison with what the French and Belgians had endured for four years in the occupied areas.

The report of the Officer in charge of Civil Affairs American Forces in Germany (printed in "American Military Government of Occupied Germany, 1918–20 "), page 18, reads :

" The revolution of November 9th, 1918, and the Armistice Terms, brought about the first really critical situation. When hostilities closed no real danger of actual starvation seems to have existed for Germany. . . . The revolution, however, lowered the public morale and the disordered state of the country prevented the enforcement of the food laws. Disorganization of the railways and surrender to the Allies of rolling stock [not the blockade] still further tended to destroy the intricate machinery of the Food Administration."

A good summing-up is provided by a neutral writer, J. van den Veer, London Editor of the Dutch newspaper *De Telegraaf*, printed in the *Sunday Times* of 13th July, 1919 :

" It is the fashion of certain neutrals and others, who plead for the ' poor starving German people', to call Britain's blockade applied to Germany the ' hunger blockade'. The phrase is used to evoke pity for the vanquished, who during the war never showed any pity, and scorn for the vanquisher.

" There can be no doubt that the British blockade, by crippling German trade and industry, has been very effective in aiding the German defeat on land. But it had not caused the German people to starve. It kept them short of many things ; but, on the other hand, it threw Germany largely on her own rich resources, and spurred her on to develop them. How she made use of her numerous prisoners of war is not yet fully, albeit fairly well known. In any case, it is playing to the gallery to say that the whole German people are or have been starving."

A mass of detail as regards the blockade can be found in " *The Blockade of Germany after the Armistice 1918–19* ", by Bane and Lutz (Stanford, California, University Press), which shows that there were famine conditions in Russia, Poland, Finland, Czecho-Slovakia, Yugo-Slavia and Armenia, but not in Germany ; and this was indeed the case.

in the occupied areas hid their food stores in order to carry on a black market with well-to-do Germans, a course which it proved difficult to prevent, even by taking inventories of all stocks of food, owing to the connivance of the German officials. The revolution upset all routine, and caused failure in everything appertaining to the railways.

So far from attempting to assist their countrymen in Occupied Territory, the German Government on 9th December made a protest—it was the first of the many hundreds of wordy protests—that Maréchal Foch had " forbidden the " export of foodstuffs from the left bank of the Rhine and " traffic into the Neutral Zone, and so with the rest of Germany." The absurdity of the protest was easily proved from German statistics ; the normal movement of foodstuffs was in the reverse direction.

On 22nd December the Luxembourg Commission held a meeting, which was attended by eight British members, to consider the feeding of the German inhabitants of the left bank of the Rhine, and it called for reports from each Army as to the number of inhabitants and their requirements. The German officials threatened that dangerous unrest would arise and Bolshevism spread if food were not provided ; but in occupied France and Belgium the Germans themselves had starved the inhabitants without such results, and none were observed in the British area.

The German railway employees who were performing duty were from the first rationed by the British Army, but not their families.

Acting from purely humanitarian motives, and being particularly moved by an impressive telegram from General Plumer which Mr. Lloyd George read aloud at once when it was put into his hand in the midst of a conference, the Supreme Economic Council, sitting in Paris, gave authority to the Allied Commands to assure the food supplies of the left bank of the Rhine. In his telegram, General Plumer had depicted the seriousness of the situation, and pointed out how bad was the effect upon the British Army of the sufferings of the German women and children, and the Prime Minister had concluded the reading of the message by remarking, " Gentlemen, you cannot say that General Plumer is a pro-German."[1] Arrangements were made to send the necessary foodstuffs by Rotterdam and Antwerp.

[1] Shortly after this a German conspiracy to assassinate General Plumer was discovered by the Security Section. The plotters were duly tried and convicted.

Fortunately, there was plenty of barge tonnage. Surplus Army stores, to the amount of 12,000 tons of preserved meat, 2,725 tons of pork and beans, 10,495 tons of meat and vegetable rations, 6,325 tons of biscuits, and 100,000 tons of potatoes were despatched from the United Kingdom to the Second Army. Finally, after sending officers into Germany to report on the economic conditions, which were rapidly deteriorating owing to muddling and strikes,[1] a general agreement was made (19th January, 1919) to supply Germany as a whole with bread-stuffs, cereals and pork, to be carried in German merchant ships released for the purpose. This service was to start as soon as the financial questions involved were settled. Payment by individual purchasers presented a difficulty in view of the falling value of the mark—by the end of the year it was $1\frac{1}{2}d$.—and payment in German currency was out of the question. The communities in the British Occupied Area therefore offered the whole of their property and taxes as guarantee for their share. After further representations by General Plumer, sanction was given as a temporary measure for the supply from British stocks to the poorer inhabitants of a sufficient amount of food each week against food cards, issued by the German administration, the price being fixed by the local committees.

It was not until well into March, 1919, that the financial question was finally settled, " the delay having been due to " the uncertainty of financial adjustment," and owing to the Paris authorities being desirous of differentiating between the supply of food to the left and right banks of the Rhine, the former being regarded as essential and the latter not so. The German Government later agreed to set aside customs duties to pay for food ; but after providing 60 per cent. of the sum required, they ceased payment.[2]

---

[1] The instructions given to these officers are in Appendix XVIII.

[2] A general relaxation of the blockade having been suggested, Maréchal Foch, in a special Note to the French Minister for Foreign Affairs, on 3rd February, 1919 (of which a copy was sent to the C.I.G.S.), agreed with him that the Blockade Regulations should be strictly maintained, saying :

" When the Allied Armies have been so far reduced in numbers as to make difficult the execution of any military operation, the blockade, which can be relaxed or tightened as circumstances may require, will remain the best and quickest means of securing respect for the Armistice Convention, and generally of imposing our will on Germany."

The matter was discussed by the War Cabinet, after the Admiralty had pointed out that the blockade organization was complicated and would be difficult to re-establish if once suspended, and on 9th May, 1919, it was agreed that it would be better to wait until it was known whether the Germans would sign the Preliminary Peace Terms. The blockade was relaxed on 12th July, 1919, after the signature of the Peace Treaty and automatically ceased on its ratification.

In recording the delays and difficulties of food supply, it should be noted that a number of authorities were interested in this problem. First, the American Relief Committee, and the American Commission for the Relief of Belgium, under Mr. (later President) H. D. Hoover, who in 1919 became the United States Food Administrator for Europe. Secondly, the newly-formed Food Section of the Supreme Economic Council, a member of which, Mr. Wise, dealt with British questions in connection with the provisioning of the left bank of the Rhine ; he was authorized to correspond direct with General Plumer, and urgent questions could be referred to the " Mission Anglaise de Ravitaillement " in Paris, which had a member in the Rhineland. Thirdly, there was the Luxembourg Commission, formed in April, 1919, as part of the " Inter-"Allied Commission for the Rhineland,"[1] under Monsieur Tirard, Maréchal Foch's deputy in the administration of the Rhineland. The newly formed " Paris Commission for the Rhenish Territories "[1] and the Spa Commission also took a hand.[2] As in S. Africa in 1902, after the peace, too great haste was exhibited in trying to switch over from military to civil administration. By means of the military machinery controlled by the Quartermaster-General, the German inhabitants could have been fed easily and without fuss or delay once the Supreme War Council decided that food should be supplied to them.

TRADE

In February, 1919, an international committee for the resumption of commercial relations with Germany was set up, and the Board of Trade authorized the resumption of trade with Occupied Germany, subject to a number of regulations and under the supervision of the Luxembourg Economic Committee. A temporary obstacle which arose was the inability of the mail trains to carry more than a limited number of letters, the Army post taking most of the space available. Some trouble occurred when French industrial experts insisted on entering factories, bent, the Germans averred, on commercial espionage and they protested that this was going beyond what was warranted by the Armistice terms. Accordingly instructions were issued to the effect that visits—applications for which were to be made

---

[1] See Chapter XI.

[2] Besides these an Inter-Allied Food Commission was created to distribute rations in the Rhineland supplementary to the amounts granted to Germany as a whole ; a Rotterdam Food Commission to settle commercial and other details arising from the sale of foodstuffs to Germany ; and, at Compiègne, a Finance Commission to manage financial transactions between the Allies and Germany.

to the Luxembourg Economic Committee—should be encouraged, but confined to such work, processes, etc., as the German owners were willing to show; no compulsion was to be used, and any information obtained made available for manufacturers and traders generally. The issue of permits was to be made in London for British subjects, the itinerary of the journey to Cologne being laid down; and it was left to the British member of the Luxembourg Economic Committee to arrange the visits. The full right to enter any building for military purposes and inspection, of course, remained, and it was found necessary to visit many factories to prevent the manufacture of war material, aircraft, engines, poison gas, etc., to control the consumption of coal, and to search for machinery stolen from France and Belgium.

On 14th February Maréchal Foch found it advisable to forbid the municipal elections ordered by the Prussian Government to fill all the seats of the councils, as good relations having been established with the existing councils, the results might have been contrary to the interests of the Armies of Occupation in the matters of billeting and requisitioning. On the other hand, from 12th February letter post, hitherto forbidden, was allowed, subject to censorship, between occupied and unoccupied Germany.

LABOUR TROUBLES

On 15th January the policy as regards labour troubles was laid down by General Plumer. The British military authorities would not interfere in the relations between employers and workmen unless intervention was demanded in the interests of law and order; the settlement of such questions would be regarded as primarily a matter for the local authorities. Should labour troubles, however, threaten a decrease in the production of an article essential to the welfare of the Army, or of the civil population as a whole, it might be necessary, after settlement by the civil authorities had failed, to take action. The civil authorities were informed that men out of work from preventable causes would be formed into labour gangs for work on the roads, and it was expected that this would act as a sufficient deterrent to any unemployed unrest.

Signs of both national and socialist, if not revolutionary, propaganda became evident towards the end of January, and on 27th January and 5th February General Plumer drew attention of G.H.Q. to the *Reichtag's* proposal to socialize the coal mines; for the first result of this might be a decrease in the output, and have serious consequences in the British Occupied Area, where a shortage already prevailed. The election of workmen's councils had already been ordered by the German Government ; but until socialization of the mines became law, General Plumer considered it inadvisable to allow any change to be made in the control of the mines in the British area. The Commander-in-Chief thought it best to inform Mr. Waterlow, as the question was mainly a commercial and political one, and request that a decision on the subject by the Inter-Allied Paris Commission might be communicated to him.

Copies of any memoranda on political and industrial matters drawn up at British Headquarters in Cologne had been regularly sent to Luxembourg, but the first effect of Sir Douglas Haig's request was that, on 21st February, Maréchal Foch asked through the Luxembourg Commission that, for the centralization of information, reports might be addressed to him on the 1st and 15th of each month on

　　　(1) The electoral situation—position of parties, political and constitutional programmes ;

　　　(2) economic programme of the industrials ;

　　　(3) social situation—number of unemployed, wages, food ;

　　　(4) tendencies of the local authorities and officials ;

　　　(5) press campaign.

As General Plumer had anticipated, although socialization did not take place, trouble in the mines arose. The Aachen and Ruhr coal-fields declared a strike on 21st February and then a general strike, but in spite of the efforts of the Spartacists, the latter soon collapsed into small local clashes. In the British Zone at least these strikes were tame affairs, without violence or sabotage, merely intended to frighten the managers and directors into compliance. A " citizen division " of 15,000 men was formed in the Ruhr, however, to keep order, and on the 28th strong *Reichswehr* forces entered the towns ; they met with no opposition and discovered large stocks of weapons. In the central German coal-fields, a general strike was called on 28th February, and the pits closed. All German industries were becoming increasingly hampered by coal shortage ; as regards Central Germany it was said that, unless the strike ended by 1st March, bakeries, food industries, waterworks and slaughter industries would close down on that date, and that on the Eastern frontier operations against the Bolshevists would have to cease. Considerable rioting took place, but by 16th March Government troops had more or less restored order. It was arranged to send 25,000 tons of coal a day from Rotterdam by way of the Rhine to the Occupied Territory.

By the beginning of April the industrial unrest in Germany had again become rampant, and well-justified fears arose that it might spread into Occupied Territory. After full consideration, General Plumer came to the conclusion that the time had arrived for action to prevent this, and on 15th April he issued a proclamation declaring strikes to be illegal, and therefore forbidden.[1] At the same time he pointed out that in the interest of the population itself the trouble raging in Germany proper should not be allowed to extend to the Occupied Territory, as it would inevitably lead to misery and starvation. The proclamation ordered that all industrial disputes were to be brought before Arbitration Courts composed of British officers, sitting with assessors representing the parties to the dispute, two from each side : the award of the Court was to be final, subject only to review by the Commander-in-Chief.

The proclamation was generally well received and, although at first some hesitation was shown in submitting disputes to the decision of the Courts, it was soon appreciated that their awards held both justice and good sense ; consequently the Courts became so much used that restrictions had to be placed on the nature of the cases submitted to them.

General Sir William Robertson, when he took over command, improved the arbitration machinery by directing that in the first instance disputes should be submitted to a German " Court of Conciliation " on which both sides were represented ; then, if agreement were not reached, the case could be laid before a British Court of Arbitration, whose decision was final and binding. No picketing was allowed. The general result attained was that during the 13 months of British military administration no great or prolonged strike occurred. In no German account of the occupation are the courts mentioned, a sufficient testimonial to their complete success.

Instructions as regards Financial Transactions, Circulation and Censorship

On 14th January Colonel Payot forwarded to G.H.Q. a copy of the long series of instructions with regard to financial control, the regulation of circulation, and the organization of

---

[1] *See* Note III at end of Chapter.

censorship. These were unanimously adopted by the representatives of the Allied countries at conferences held at Paris on 20th January and at Lamorlaye on 21st January. They are translated in full for record.[1] The financial instructions dealt with both private and public operations, and were designed, while giving the fullest liberty for the transfer of stocks and bonds, bills and specie within Occupied Territory, to prevent their escaping from the supervision of the finance committee of the Armistice Commission, and their transfer to non-occupied Germany or neutral countries ; and to ensure the due collection of rates and taxes and the proper use of the funds raised.

For the most part the rules respecting circulation were already in force : the new directions laid down that the bridgeheads were to be regarded as " Reserved Zones " to circulate in which a special authorization was necessary (this was cancelled by order of the Supreme War Council) ; and that subjects of the Neutral Powers who wished to enter or leave the Rhineland must obtain passes from the *Bureau Internationale de Circulation* in Paris, or the *Bureau de Circulation* in Brussels. Circulation between occupied and unoccupied Germany was absolutely forbidden, except in election times and for workmen living near the boundary line, as well as persons who left the Rhineland without intention of returning.

The censorship instructions were concerned solely with printed publications, newspapers, books, pamphlets, posters, drawings, photographs and cinematograph films, leaving trade and price catalogues and circulars free.

Summary and Military Courts

The special instructions as regards the trial and punishment of inhabitants for offences against the British Army during the march into Germany were withdrawn when. the occupation was complete.[2] To deal with infractions of the military proclamations, orders and instructions by the German civil population, and to conduct the preliminary investigations into more serious charges, area commandants were empowered to set up Summary Courts, similar to English police courts, consisting of two officers, with limited powers of punishment. A brief record was kept of each case, and the awards took effect at once, subject only to mitigation or remission by superior military authority.

---

[1] Appendix XIV.
[2] *See* p. 64.

The more serious offences were reserved for trial by Military Courts. These were specially convened in the same manner and followed the same procedure as a field general court martial, with similar wide powers of punishment. Their findings and sentences were subject to confirmation, the Military Governor being the reviewing authority for all Military and Summary Court proceedings, except in the case of a sentence of death, which required the confirmation of the Commander-in-Chief of the Army of Occupation.

The proceedings of the Military Courts were advised on and reviewed by the Deputy Judge-Advocate and his staff, and, under the Indemnity Act of 1920, a right of petition to the Judge-Advocate-General from the decisions of such courts was given.

Both tribunals exercised jurisdiction over all persons of whatever nationality in the Occupied Area, save those subject to the military law of one or other of the Allies.   In regard to civil affairs, the German courts of all degrees continued to function in the normal manner.

The Summary Court of two officers was found inconvenient and within a short period an Order was issued empowering any officer holding command of a battalion or equivalent unit to exercise the functions of such court.   In urban areas, such as Cologne or Bonn, summary jurisdiction was exercised by specially selected officers with legal qualifications, permanently detached for the duty, and styled Summary Court Officers.

The Provost-Marshal's Branch was responsible for the preparation and conduct of prosecutions before the Military Courts, and had under its supervision the German Civil Police, which could be called on to make arrests and assist in the suppression of offences against the Army and breaches of the *Anordnungen*.

Sentences of imprisonment were carried out in the civil prisons under military supervision, subject to the same conditions as sentences awarded by a German Court, with the exception that important political prisoners were held in British custody.

The behaviour of the inhabitants in general towards the troops was correct.   The incidence of requisitioning, and particularly billeting, occasionally caused friction, and from time to time, after any show of leniency on the part of the military authorities, wealthy property owners exhibited a somewhat truculent attitude.   In such cases an unexpected award of imprisonment " without the option " produced a salutary effect.

Thefts of military stores and horses on a large scale were prevalent at one period and became a serious problem, owing to the unwillingness of the German civil authorities to take steps for prevention and detection. In a few instances—after repeated warnings—financial compensation was exacted from the municipality concerned.

In only one other instance, it appears, was a money penalty fine inflicted, namely, when a soldier was murdered in broad daylight in a village street in the presence of a number of inhabitants, and the civil authorities professed inability to produce any evidence as to the identity of the assailants. In every case the decision to exact compensation was signed by the Military Governor; no subordinate commander was authorized to inflict a general fine on a locality. In very few cases was a sentence of death by a Military Court carried out.

Note I.
Anordnungen of 5th January, 1919.

By virtue of the authority delegated to me by the General Officer Commanding British Second Army, I, British Military Governor of Occupied German Territory do hereby order that :

1. S.S.776 *Anordnungen* dated 2nd December, 1918, be amended as follows[1] :

Para. III (1) and (2) and amendments are cancelled and the following substituted :—

" Inhabitants may circulate freely within the British Occupied Territory provided they are in possession of their identity cards." [Hitherto only in their own town or district.]

Para. III (5), line 2, for " 19 and 6 " [clock hours] read " 21 and 5." [That is, the " curfew " hours were reduced.]

Para. IV (1), line 2, the words " or by day outside the Kreis " will be erased. [That is, passes for internal circulation were no longer necessary.]

Para. XIX is cancelled and the following is substituted :

" All persons of the male sex will show proper respect to British officers and when addressing or being addressed by them will raise their hats.

" Uniformed officials will always salute them.

" When the British National Anthem is played, civilians will remove their hats and persons in uniform will salute." [That is, civilians were not required to salute officers in passing by raising their hats.]

2. *National Flag.*

The display of the German National Flag in the British Occupied Territory is forbidden both on land and by vessels on the waterways.

---

[1] See p. 76.

3. *Taxes.*

No luxury tax or wine tax will be charged to any member of the British Forces in the territory occupied by the British Army.

4. *British clothing and stores.*

German civilians are forbidden to acquire, or to be in possession of articles of British military equipment, rations, supplies or goods of any description, including goods supplied from military canteens or clothing stores, except such as may be shewn to have been officially supplied to them by duly authorised officers.

Such articles are supplied to British troops for their military duties or personal use only, and they are forbidden to sell or otherwise dispose of them to inhabitants.

All inhabitants found in possession of any such articles, whether acquired by purchase or any other means, will be severely punished.

5. *Sale of food.*

The sale of the following articles to British troops is forbidden :—

Bread	Cheese	Soap	Shoes
Flour	Jam	Methylated Spirits	Biscuits
Butter	Rice	Boots	Fat
Margarine	Sago	Barley	Oil
Eggs	Potatoes	Coffee substitute	Maccaroni
Milk	Artificial Honey	Lard	Petroleum
Sugar	Coffee	Oatmeal	Textile fabrics
Meat	Gingerbread	Soap powder	(rationed articles
Bacon	Sausages	Coal	only)

[A separate order notified that articles of wool and leather could be purchased only by means of tickets controlled and stamped by the German authorities who asked that such goods might not be bought at all by the troops of the Army of Occupation.]

6. *Regimental Colours.*

All persons of the male sex will pay respect to the Regimental Colours of the troops of the Allied Powers when carried uncased. Uniformed officials will salute and civilians will raise their hats as the Colours pass.

Charles Fergusson,
Lieut.-General.
British Military Governor.

Cologne, 5th January 1919.

Note II.
PROCLAMATION.
Telephone and Telegraph Traffic.

The proclamation " Telephone and Telegraph Traffic " dated 18th December, 1918, is cancelled and the following substituted :

Telephone :

1. Local telephone traffic in the British Occupied Area is permitted.

2. Trunk telephone traffic in the British Occupied Area and the use of certain trunk lines to the remainder of Germany are permitted only for urgent official, professional and business purposes.

3. All public call-offices are closed.

4. All owners of private telephone systems, not directly connected to public exchanges, must notify in writing the Area Commandant of each area through which the system passes.

5. The use of railway telephones is confined to the necessities of railway control.

Telegraph :

6. Only certain telegraph offices (*see* Appendix I) will be open for civil traffic, and only between hours which will be notified at the different offices.

7. Certain offices (*see* Appendix II.) will be open for messages connected with Navigation only.

8. All other offices are closed.

9. Telegrams may be sent within the Occupied Areas, but will be subject to censorship and must comply with the following regulations :—

(*a*) Every telegram must be written in clear English, French or German—in legible Latin hand.

(*b*) Every telegram must end with the Christian and surnames of the sender.

(*c*) The name and full address of the sender must be written legibly on every telegram.

The latter will only be forwarded when the sender so desires.

10. Telegraph traffic with the unoccupied part of Germany and with foreign countries is only permitted for communication with German prisoners of war or for important business or urgent private affairs. Telegrams of this nature must be stamped by the *Bürgermeister* on behalf of the competent local Authority as a guarantee of their urgency and in confirmation of the identity of the sender.

11. The use of railway telegraphs is confined to the necessities of railway control.

*　　　*　　　*　　　*

12. Breaches of these regulations in any locality will lead to curtailment of these concessions in the District concerned.

Charles Fergusson,

Lieut.-General.

British Military Governor of Occupied
German Territory.

Cologne, 1st February 1919.

APPENDIX I.

Telegraph Offices open for Civil Traffic :

[36 places]

APPENDIX II.

Telegraph Offices open for Navigation, etc., messages only :

[34 places]

NOTE.

Censorship Offices for telegrams directed to neutral countries, to unoccupied Germany or to German prisoners of war will be found as follows in Cologne :

(*a*) for telegrams to German prisoners of war : [1 place] ;

(*b*) for important business telegrams : [1 place] ;

(*c*) for urgent private telegrams : [7 places].

NOTE III.

PROCLAMATION AGAINST STRIKES.

The condition of affairs throughout Germany is becoming daily more serious owing to industrial unrest and to the prevalence of strikes.

So far, the inhabitants in the British Occupied Territory have been living under law and good order. There have been no scenes or rioting and bloodshed such as have convulsed other parts of Germany. It is in the interests of all inhabitants that this should continue. Increased supplies of food are now becoming available and their distribution will shortly be fully organized.

Strikes and disturbances will not improve the conditions of life ; on the contrary, they will only lead to increased misery and unhappiness and cannot be permitted to continue.

In the interests of all inhabitants of the British Occupied Territory, I therefore require all to co-operate with me in the maintenance of law and good order. Only in this way can the people be spared the misery which has arisen elsewhere.

In accordance with the Law, all disputes and differences are to be brought for settlement to the existing German Courts of Arbitration (*Organization, Schlichtungsausschuss Gewerbegericht*).

In the event of a settlement not being reached by these means, the case will be brought before the British military authorities, who, after hearing both sides with sympathy and impartiality, will make a decision which will be binding for both parties.

It is my firm intention to safeguard the rights of workers to the fullest degree.

I warn all that severe measures will be taken against any person who, in defiance of this proclamation, acts in any way contrary to these orders or subversive of their intention.

This Proclamation supersedes all previous proclamations issued on this subject.

HERBERT PLUMER,
General,
Commanding-in-Chief, British Army of the Rhine.

16th April 1919.

CHAPTER VIII
THE NEUTRAL ZONE
(End Paper)

THE NEUTRAL ZONE IN THE ARMISTICE TERMS

The Neutral Zone by the terms of the Armistice had a width of 10 kilometres (say 6 miles) round the bridgeheads and along the eastern bank of the Rhine. In the British area, at the suggestion of the local German authorities, the perimeter of the Cologne bridgehead had been adjusted to the communal boundaries, and the definite eastern boundary of the Neutral Zone was similarly agreed upon. Nothing more than its width was mentioned in the terms, but it was provided that the Zone must be evacuated by the German Armies in their withdrawal within thirty-one days of the signature of the Armistice. It seems to have been accepted that, according to precedent, the maintenance of order in the Neutral Zone was the duty of the defeated belligerent, it being his territory, but that the victors were entitled to exercise control there in order to ensure that no measures were taken within its boundaries which might serve as military preparations either for offence or defence.[1]

On 29th November, 1918 Maréchal Foch in a Note addressed to the Allied commanders-in-chief, deputed General Nudant, the president of the Spa Commission, to issue orders as regards the Neutral Zone, and asked that advanced parties of a few staff officers might be sent to Spa to meet General Nudant and advise him as to the strength and distribution of the German police to be permitted in the zone, and other matters. Each Army, French, American, British and Belgian, was made responsible for the section of the Zone opposite its front, and the Germans correspondingly divided the Zone into four sectors.

The advanced parties were duly sent, and on 22nd December the instructions relative to the exercise of control in the Neutral Zone, drawn up at Spa, were issued in Maréchal Foch's name to come into force on 1st January, 1919.

ARRANGEMENTS FOR CONTROL

It was recognized that in the disturbed condition of Germany, particularly in an area which contained the great industrial towns of Frankfort, Düsseldorf, Elberfeld, Duisburg, etc.,

---

[1] In 1871 during the German occupation of certain French Departments as security for the payment of the indemnity, according to the Peace Treaty, "in the interests of security of the German troops, they will have at their "disposal the neutral zone".

and large coal-fields, the regular police forces of the strength existing before August, 1914, which in times of emergency used to rely on the support of the local military garrison, would now be insufficient, and that civil guards might not be reliable. Permission was therefore accorded to Germany to send " security garrisons " into the Zone of a total strength of 10 battalions and 10 squadrons, distributed in conformity with a table, given below, and subject to certain rules. Further, in case of trouble or expected trouble, the German authorities might request permission to send additional armed forces into the Zone. Lieut.-General Haking, Chief of the British Mission with the Spa Commission, felt it necessary to warn General Plumer that in any industrial troubles the German soldier would probably go over to the strikers, and that it would be as well to be prepared to send troops into the Neutral Zone.

Maréchal Foch's Instructions for the Military Rule of the Neutral Zone

I. The strength and distribution of the security garrisons are given in the attached distribution table.

As regards the police force, every commander of a German sector will within 24 hours of the present instructions coming into effect, inform the corresponding Allied commander of the strength and stations of his force.

II. No modification of the strength and distribution of these forces (security garrison and police) will be made without the previous authority of the Allied commander concerned. The commanders of the German sectors will notify the Allied commanders concerned in good time of any reliefs they may order.

III. Russian prisoners may not be stationed in the Neutral Zone.

IV. The duty of the German troops in the Neutral Zone being purely that of police, they may not perform any military drill or manoeuvre whatsoever. In particular these troops may not fire even blank ammunition, nor practise throwing grenades, nor exercise with any weapons whatsoever.

V. No work which can be considered as likely to contribute, even in a purely indirect manner, to its offensive or defensive organization may be executed in the Neutral Zone, work done by civil labour not excepted. In particular, the railways will not be altered either by additions or reductions ; no modification of the existing systems, even the narrow gauge, may be made.

Should any work appear urgently necessary, authority may be requested from the local Allied commander.

VI. The sport of shooting in any form is forbidden. Should it become necessary to undertake the destruction of harmful animals, it may not be begun without the previous authority of the local Allied commander and under the conditions laid down by him.

Fireworks are forbidden.

VII. Supplies in the Neutral Zone susceptible of military use, of every nature, must within 48 hours of the present instructions coming into force be reported to the Allied commander concerned, who has the right, if he thinks fit, to require their removal.

VIII. The use of visual signals and all methods whatever of signalling is forbidden in the Neutral Zone. This prohibition applies to both members of the German Army and civilians.

No wireless station may be retained or established in the Neutral Zone without the authority of the local Allied commander. [The Karlsruhe station was closed.]

Pigeon lofts, both civil and military, are forbidden. Aircraft are forbidden to fly over the Neutral Zone.

No camouflage work may be carried out in the Neutral Zone, even by way of training, or by civilians.

Exercise of Control

I. In principle, the control officers in the execution of their duty will address themselves to the German officers commanding the police sectors and sub-sectors ; it is through the channel of these officers that they will deal, if occasion arises, with all other authorities and private persons.

II. The commanders of German police sectors or sub-sectors will correspond direct with the local Allied commanders. The Allied Army commanders will inform each of the commanders of police sectors or sub-sectors with which of the local Allied commanders he should correspond.

III. The control officers should be in possession of an authority signed by the Allied commander responsible for the control. These officers may be accompanied by any escort judged necessary for the execution of their duty. They should present themselves under a white flag ; the German military authority will give such orders as will ensure that they may move about freely on presentation of their signed authority, and that they may carry out their duties without hindrance from subordinate authorities.

IV. The control officers may require from the German authorities any written certificates they consider necessary. The signers of these certificates will be held personally responsible for their accuracy. The control officers may also insist on the communication of certain documents as mentioned below.

V. The commander of each sector must be in possession of a nominal roll, fully kept up to date, of the officers and men of all ranks (security garrisons and police) forming every garrison of his sector. The nominal roll must be handed to the Allied control officers on demand. These officers may also demand to see all ration requisitions, receipts and ration rolls, and other military administrative documents.

VI. Soldiers on leave in the Neutral Zone will be entered on a special list kept at the town hall of their commune. This list should give the rank and corps of the leaveman, his mobilization class and length of stay.

VII. Demobilized German soldiers may not be authorized to enter the Neutral Zone and come into residence unless they were domiciled there before 1st August, 1914.

Each district must keep a list of the men of the district who were mobilized, as well as a list of those demobilized who are domiciled in the district, with a record of the date of their return and their mobilization class.

VIII. The commander of each sector will inform in writing the corresponding Allied commander of the total of the civil population of each locality of his sector. Any increase of the population beyond one per cent.[1] will be reported at once, with the cause of the increase, to the Allied military authority concerned.

IX. Should it happen that part of a district is situated in the Neutral Zone but the chief town of the district is outside it, the control officers may summon the civil or military authority under whom the district is placed to any point of the district in the Neutral Zone as they may indicate.

The German security garrisons were to be distributed as under :

Sector	Name and Residence of the Commander		Troops	Garrison
I.	Colonel X.		1 bn.	Weser
			1 bn.	Düsseldorf
		Weser	1 sq.	Weser
II.	Colonel v. B.		1 bn.	Remscheid
			1 sq.	Wipperfurth
		Wipperfurth	1 sq.	Eitorf
III.	Major S.		1 bn.	Hachenburg
			1 bn.	Limburg
		Westerburg	1 sq.	Westerburg
IV.	Major-General U.		1 sq.	Homburg
			1 bn.	Frankfort
			1 bn.	Darmstadt
			1 sq.	do.
			1 bn.	Mannheim
		Karlsruhe	1 sq.	Schwetzingen
			1 bn.	Karlsruhe
			1 sq.	do.
	1 sq.	Mülheim	1 bn.	Lahr
	1 coy.[2]	Weil	1 sq.	do.

Liaison officers were sent to each of the four German sectors, but Maréchal Foch refused to sanction the presence of German liaison officers at the various Allied headquarters.

---

[1] This was altered a week later to one-tenth. It was the duty of the German police in peace time to maintain the "National Registration of Inhabitants" (Einwohnermeldewesen). This included a record of all arrivals, departures and changes of residence of inhabitants, notification of children liable to vaccination, compilation of annual local directories, and trade and residential address books. One special branch, Hotel and Lodging House Police (Gasthofpolizei), watched the movements of travellers and the temporary and floating population in lower-class hotels, boarding houses and common lodging houses. Another branch, the Aliens Police (Fremden-polizei), supervised foreigners, strangers and suspects, passports, expulsions, changes of name. Finally the Political Police dealt, amongst other things, with censorship, press offences, the supervision of clubs, associations, meetings and public processions. The police therefore had complete control of a district.

[2] Company detailed to furnish guards for the trains carrying supplies to prisoners of war.

F*

The Zone in 1919

In view of the large and turbulent working population of Frankfort, in 1918 about half a million souls, on 8th August, 1919, permission was given to the Germans on their request to form a fifth, Frankfort, sector and increase and vary the total garrison from 10 battalions and 10 squadrons to 15 battalions, 8 squadrons and 2 batteries. The number finally sanctioned was 20 battalions, 10 squadrons, 2 batteries, a total, including headquarters, of 17,765 men.

During 1919 the British section of the Neutral Zone gave no trouble : this came later, as will be narrated.[1]

---

[1] See Chapter XII.

CHAPTER IX

THE END OF G.H.Q. THE FORMATION OF THE
BRITISH ARMY OF THE RHINE AND OF THE
CLEARING UP ARMY. THE DISPOSAL OF MILITARY
STORES

(Sketch 1)

THE FORMATION OF THE ARMY OF THE RHINE

On the reconstruction of Mr. Lloyd George's Ministry,
announced on 10th January, 1919, Mr. Winston S. Churchill,
from being Minister of Munitions became Secretary of State
for War in succession to Lord Milner. The due and proper
occupation of the Rhineland required about a quarter of a
million troops—more than the strength of the original
Expeditionary Force. The French were already complaining
that we were dispersing our trained units too quickly, while
the British press was publishing more than grumbles that we
were not demobilizing quickly enough. Mr. Churchill set about
speeding up demobilization and freeing the fighting men. The
calls on the British Army were many : in addition to providing
its share of the Armies of Occupation of the Rhineland and of
the Dardanelles and, very soon, Constantinople, Bulgaria,
two divisions for Trans-Caucasia, and Irish, Indian and
Colonial garrisons, about a hundred thousand men were required
in Mesopotamia during the period of transition from Turkish
rule to independence, and about a division in Palestine.
Higher pay would not induce many conscripted men to remain
in the Army ; the gradual building up of a new voluntary
service Army of some 220,000 on the Rhine would certainly
take up the greater part of the current year. Mr. Churchill
therefore decided to send to Germany battalions of conscripted
18-year-olds.[1] Thirty-eight Young Soldiers and Graduated
Battalions were used intact to replace battalions of the Second
Army, and 22 others were broken up and distributed amongst
the old battalions.[2]

---

[1] Mr. Churchill's explanatory Note is given in Note I at end of Chapter.
[2] The change-over was reported as completed on 15th April.
The Young Soldiers Battalions of the Training Reserve received recruits,
gave them their initial training, and passed them, company by company, to
two affiliated Graduated Battalions, so called because they were organized
in four companies (originally five) according to age, thus : one company for
recruits between 18 and $18\frac{1}{4}$; one between $18\frac{1}{4}$ and $18\frac{1}{2}$, etc. During the
War the senior company was drafted to France as a whole. At the end of
1917 all Young Soldiers Battalions became the 53rd Battalions and all
Graduated Battalions either 51st or 52nd Battalions of the Regiments to
which they were affiliated.

It had been settled on 10th January to repatriate 1,200 men a day from the Rhineland up to the 20th, and thenceforward 2,400 a day, and in the course of the month of February, as demobilization proceeded more or less according to plan, it was further decided by the Government that at the beginning of April the General Headquarters of Sir Douglas Haig should come to an end. At the same time, on his advice, the four Armies quartered in France and Belgium were to be replaced by a single Army, while the Second Army under General Sir Herbert Plumer in Germany, reduced by one division (Guards),[1] was to be made independent, reporting direct to the War Office, and renamed the British Army of the Rhine (" B.A.R.").[2]

The ten divisions remaining in Germany were, contrary to Sir Douglas Haig's advice, given new names, and organized in five corps, the II, IV, VI, IX and X, respectively under Lieut.-Generals Sir Claud Jacob, Sir Alexander Godley,[3] Sir Aylmer Haldane, Sir Walter Braithwaite and Sir Thomas Morland.

The new names for the divisions, their commanders and corps, were :

Title	Commander	Corps
Western (late 1st) Regular ..	Major-General Sir P. Strickland ..	IX
Light (late 2nd) Regular ..	Major-General G. D. Jeffreys ..	II
Northern (late 3rd) Regular..	Major-General A. A. Kennedy ..	VI
Midland (late 6th) Regular..	Major-General G. F. Boyd	IX
Lowland (late 9th) (New Army).	Major-General H. H. Tudor ..	IV
Southern (late 29th) Regular	Major-General Sir W. Heneker ..	II
Lancashire (late 32nd) (New Army).	Major-General Sir H. Jeudwine ..	X
Eastern (late 34th)(New Army)	Major-General Sir L. Nicholson ..	X
London (late 41st) (New Army)	Major-General Sir S. Lawford ..	VI
Highland (late 62nd, 2nd West Riding) (Territorial Force)[4]	Major-General Sir D. Campbell ..	IV

Within the division the brigades were numbered 1st, 2nd and 3rd, thus, 1st Western Brigade, 2nd Western Brigade, etc.

The regiments of the Cavalry Division (Major-General Sir W. E. Peyton) were regrouped, so that its three brigades could

[1] The Guards Division handed over its area to the 3rd Division and on 20th February commenced leaving for the United Kingdom by train to Dunkirk, the last units going on 29th April.

[2] Sometimes called " B.A.O.R." For the American Army of Occupation see Note II at end of Chapter.

[3] *Vice* Lieut.-General Sir Montagu Harper, who returned to the United Kingdom to take over the Southern Command.

[4] The 62nd Division from the IX. Corps relieved the New Zealand Division on 2nd February.

be called the Dragoon Brigade (6th Dragoon Guards, 1st Dragoons, 6th Dragoons), Lancer Brigade (9th, 12th and 17th Lancers), and Hussar Brigade (3rd, 10th and 15th Hussars).

Of the extra-divisional artillery, under Major-General C. R. Buckle, 11 Brigades R.G.A., with 20 batteries of 60-pdr. guns, 20 batteries of howitzers of various calibres, and 5 anti-aircraft batteries, were to remain with the British Army of the Rhine.

The extra-divisional engineer units, under the Chief Engineer, Major-General Sir R. Buckland, included 7 Army Troops companies, 1 Siege company (= 2 Army Troops companies), a field survey battalion, 5 sound ranging sections, 5 observation groups, 20 searchlight sections, 1 electrical and mechanical company, 1 Army workshops company, 1 pontoon park, 1 base park, 2 advanced R.E. parks, and a meteorological section.

Two brigades of the R.A.F. under Major-General Sir J. Salmond, were allotted to the British Army of the Rhine, with six wings (24 squadrons) and a balloon wing ; also two brigades of the Tank Corps, with seven battalions under Br.-General E. B. Hankey.

A cyclist battalion was left with each corps, and a proportion of the usual ancillary services. The Transportation units were reduced to 3 Railway Traffic sections, 1 Survey section, 2 Docks headquarters, 1 Port Construction company, and 1 Inland Water Transport detachment ; thus the railway operating companies and the road units disappeared, and, with other superfluous units, were at once demobilized.

The total of the numbers remaining in Germany was put at 10,882 officers and 263,660 other ranks.

For maintenance, a reserve of 75,000 tons of ammunition was to be held, 15,000 tons in the Rhineland, and the remainder in depôts in Western France, together with 30 days' reserve of supplies, besides engineer and ordnance stores. Of transport, reserves of 10 per cent. of the cars on the establishment, 5 per cent. of lorries, 4 per cent. of ambulance vehicles, 3 per cent. (1,800 horses) of animals, were allowed. Reserves of transportation stores were to be kept in France ; timber was to be procured locally and all salvage sent direct to the United Kingdom via the Rhine. The Base Post Office was to remain at Boulogne (or Calais) until a mail service could be organized through Antwerp or Rotterdam, when the Base Post Office would move to Cologne.

The official date of all these changes was made 2nd April, 1919.

On 1st August, 1919, after the signing of the Peace Treaty, when Maréchal Foch ceased to be Generalissimo, it was decided by the Supreme Council of the Allied and Associated Governments, which became the name of the Supreme War Council, that the Commander of the French Army of the Rhine should exercise supreme command of the troops of occupation. On 16th October General Degoutte succeeded General Mangin in this appointment.

The Clearing Up Army

For some months before the Armistice the problem of winding up the affairs of the British Armies in France and Belgium, and the disposal of the vast quantity of warlike stores, hutments, transport and animals in the theatre of war, part War Department property and part captured, which were not likely to be required when peace should ensue, had been studied at G.H.Q. and discussed with visitors from the War Office and Ministry of Munitions. No organization for the purpose existed, even as a nucleus ; for the ephemeral and improvised divisional and corps machinery for the collection of " salvage " (that is abandoned stores, repairable articles and " scrap " left on the field), and for the removal of captured material could not be so regarded. The disposals organization was clearly the responsibility of the Home authorities, and must cover all Services, civil and military, in all theatres of war and on the home front. As soon as hostilities ceased, G.H.Q. pressed the War Office for instructions, and put forward a scheme, only to be told from London that the whole subject was under consideration, and instructions would be issued. In February a civilian representative of the Ministry of Munitions, who had already visited France several times, appeared at G.H.Q., but after attending a few of the Q.M.G. conferences, disappeared. It was not until 8th March that authority was received for the Q.M.G. to carry out his own scheme. The delay of more than two months, in one way, was not of great importance, for the Army had been employed on the vast task of collecting, sorting, listing and guarding the masses of material scattered over the war and Occupied Areas, and the men had worked like navvies. There had been some loss due to deterioration and looting ; but this was of much less importance than the loss of markets, and the passage of time which had seriously and adversely affected the personnel situation :[1] the staffs and troops on whom reliance had been placed to do the work had been reduced by demobilization to such an extent that little further assistance could be expected from them.   For instance, all the tunnellers and experts in removing timber from dug-outs had been demobilized.   The liquidation would obviously take time, especially as the French and Belgian railways were already being worked beyond their carrying power.   Some small part of the vast accumulation was required by the Ministry of Munitions for issue at home or in the Colonies ; the rest was ordered to be sold.   Meantime, in order to release the remaining men of the four Armies in France and Belgium it had been decided that the new Army, known as " The Clearing Up Army," should consist of about 120,000 including labour and transport.   On this Army would fall the duties of the custody and care of the goods and the animals in the old theatre of war, the guarding of prisoners of war, the maintenance of discipline in the various coloured labour detachments and the continuation of the demobilization of troops in France, Belgium, the British Army of the Rhine and many thousands from India, Salonika, the Black Sea, Egypt and Italy.

The four areas of the First, Third, Fourth and Fifth Armies, and the Lines of Communication area were maintained, slightly adjusted in places in order to fit in with the civil boundaries ; a major-general was put in charge of each ; and the four divisions (30th, 33rd, 59th and 61st),[2] then on the Lines of Communication, were allotted to them and moved to the areas as required.

On 22nd March G.H.Q. issued an order which began as follows :

" (1) The First, Third, Fourth and Fifth Armies will cease to exist as such on the dates mentioned below, and their areas will

---

[1] On 29th November, 1918 G.H.Q. pointed out to the War Office by telegram that a good market for hutments and reconstruction material would be lost if powers of disposal were not given and a policy laid down.   Provisional authority to make discretionary disposals was given on 7th, 9th and 11th December, but the total value of disposals was limited to £1,000,000 for France, £500,000 for Belgium and £250,000 for Italy.   No authority for an adequate staff and organization being received, sanction to inaugurate preliminary measures was requested on 5th January, and reminders sent on 13th January, 5th February and 25th February.   Approval of the Q.M.G.'s scheme was given on 8th March.

[2] The 30th and 33rd (New Army) Divisions landed in France in November, 1915.   The 59th and 61st were 2nd Line Territorial Force divisions, and had landed in France in January, 1917, and May, 1916, respectively.

then come respectively under the orders of general officers as follows :

First Army Area : Major-General H. R. Davies [late 11th Division], 1st April, 1919, Headquarters, Valenciennes.

Third Army Area : Major-General P. R. Robertson [late 17th Division], 1st April, 1919, Headquarters, Flixecourt.

Fourth Army Area : Major-General H. Bruce-Williams [late 37th Division], 24th March, 1919. Headquarters, Namur.

Fifth Army Area : Major-General C. E. Pereira [late 2nd Division], 28th March, 1919. Headquarters, Lille.

" (2) The L. of C. area will come under the orders of Major-General Sir D. G. M. Campbell [late 21st Division] on 2nd April, 1919, when Lieut.-General Sir J. J. Asser [commanding L. of C.] will take over his new duties as G.O.C. British Troops in France and Belgium."

Lieut.-General Asser was to move to G.H.Q., and, after taking over from the Field-Marshal Commanding-in-Chief, supervise and control the clearing up and the disposal of the surplus stores ; he was to demobilize the G.H.Q. Staff, including the 3rd Echelon at Rouen, retaining a G.H.Q. Staff in miniature with all the old directorates represented. On 12th April Lieut.-General Asser moved his headquarters to Wimereux. The Claims Commission and the Directorate of Hirings and Requisitions, which were settling up with French and Belgian creditors of the Army, were to continue their work. The Effects Branch was sent home ; the Central Registry, except as regards outstanding correspondence, closed down on 1st May, a portion of the staff proceeding to the United Kingdom. A small portion of the Records Section was sent to the head-quarters of the Clearing Up Army.

The various staffs engaged on demobilization duty in each area were not in the first instance disturbed ; but pending the issue of definite tables of establishment by the War Office, the major-generals in charge of areas were instructed to ensure that as demobilization proceeded redundant staffs were eliminated and every effort was made to amalgamate offices and reduce the personnel to a minimum.

It was arranged with the French and Belgian authorities that from 2nd April the control of billeting, and the normal maintenance services, e.g., upkeep of roads except those specially used for military traffic in the various areas, passed to the French and Belgian military authorities ; that these authorities would make no change without the consent of the G.O.C. British Troops in France and Belgium ; and that should it become necessary at any time to alter the existing dispositions of troops or the areas, facilities to do so would be granted. The British would maintain the railway services required for operating their own traffic ; and this they did until the end was nearing, when the French provided what was required for final closing down.

Each of the five areas was divided into sub-areas under lieut.-colonels, the number being 10 in the Lines of Communication area and 6 or 7 in each of the others. The various services and departments were represented on the staffs in each area.

As regards demobilization, in the transition period the infantry brigades, each with a proportion of divisional troops, had already shrunk to " brigade groups " : the brigade groups of each division had been placed under a brigadier-general ; brigade groups of Army and corps troops were attached to these divisional " packets." Then the divisional " packets " of each corps or part of a corps had been collected under the command of a major-general, with a nucleus staff from corps headquarters. Corps and divisional headquarters then disappeared, only such individual members being retained as were required to administer and demobilize the " packets." On the arrival of the four Army area commanders about the end of March, the Army headquarters disappeared, only such members remaining as might be required.

The ports were not evacuated, the docks being worked and ships loaded until demobilization, including the embarkation of cadres, had been completed, when their staffs were closed down, first at the five southern ports and then, beginning in the south, in the order : Havre, Rouen, Boulogne, Calais, and Dunkirk.

The Expeditionary Forces Canteen continued to do business until 1st July, when the Navy and Army ,Canteen Board took over its work. The Graves Registration remained under the Army, and was maintained from Army resources, until June, 1921, when it became a civilian organization.

The total number of troops in the area of the Clearing Up Army at the beginning of April, 1919, was 20,184 officers and 638,673 other ranks, excluding women of the Q.M. A.A.C., prisoners of war, and labour, who brought the total ration strength to over a million (not counting the Portuguese Corps and its base depôts), organized in over 5,000 units, with about

75,000 animals.[1] Of the million total, 7,724 were Q.M. A.A.C., and 420 women of the Women's Legion of Motor Drivers, who came to relieve men for demobilization, about 100,000 Indians (13,800 for care of horses), West Indians, Chinese (80,000) and Fijians ; and 193,000 German prisoners of war,[2] besides some Russians, Rumanians and Poles who had escaped from Germany. The Germans were in about 364 camps and required 23,000 men to guard them.

DISPOSAL OF WAR MATERIAL AND STORES

The immense mass of material to be cleared up, sorted, listed, guarded against looters and disposed of, lay mainly in an area some 200 miles long and varying from 35 to 75 miles in width around the Lines of Communication, but was also scattered over a considerable part of France and in the French ports in use by the British Army.

To give some idea of the immense quantities to be dealt with, besides captured and surrendered material, there were :

Rolling stock : 1,000 standard gauge locomotives and 55,000 wagons, 30 ambulance trains, 1,500 60-cm. locomotives and tractors, 5,000 carriages and wagons.

1,800 miles of standard railway *in situ*, 1,700 miles of 60-cm. railway *in situ*.

Six railway workshops and four transportation stores (holding about 150,000 tons each), containing stores and spare parts of the estimated value of several millions.

Dock plant and equipment : floating power plants, grain elevators, cranes, excavators, piling plant, machinery and timber.

Inland Water Transport : 940 barges and tugs, besides other craft and plant.

Road Directorate plant : quarry plant, road rollers and repair equipment on a very large scale.

Ammunition : about 500,000 tons of British ammunition, of which about 150,000 remained to be collected and despatched from Army areas to the Base, besides about 200,000 tons of German ammunition either in dumps or collected, with an unknown quantity scattered all over the forward areas.

---

[1] The final numbers of the personnel of the Services, fixed on 26th March, were : mechanical transport, 18,500 (including 9 ambulance coys. and convoy, and 33 M.T. coys.) ; horse transport, 5,500 (22 auxiliary horse coys.) ; supply, 2,400 (including bakeries and butcheries) ; remounts, 1,778 ; veterinary, 3,970 ; ordnance, 11,118 ; engineer stores, 4,000 ; works, 9,000 ; salvage, 3,000 ; pay, 500 ; post, 500 ; hirings and requisition services, 463 , labour (including labour coys. : 82 British, 5 Alien, 3 Conscientious Objector, 3 Russian), 37,010, or, including exhumation and cemetery work, 40,818.

[2] Of 2,415 who escaped between April and October, 1919, 2,218 were recaptured.

Tanks : 1,350, with large workshops, and 13,000 tons of tank stores.

Mechanical transport : 41,759 vehicles and 14,892 motor cycles.

Horse transport : 25,000 vehicles and workshops.

Ordnance Stores : huge warehouses, workshops and factories, with a vast accumulation of equipment recently returned to store.

Hospitals : accommodation for over 70,000 patients (reduced by October, 1919, to 25,000) [1].

Signal stores : an incalculable length of line and great quantities of stores.

Engineer stores : several immense depôts, extending over many square miles, and innumerable small depôts, very extensive shops, cement factories and brickworks.

Supplies : large depôts covering scores of acres and innumerable small ones, bakeries, petrol canning installations, etc.

Huts and camps : with water and electric light installations, capable of accommodating over a million men ; in one Army area alone were 100 water installations, with tanks, pumps and miles of piping.

Laundries : capable of washing for hundreds of thousands.

Veterinary hospitals and stables.

Salvage dumps : already 28 main dumps and 38 intermediate ; the map of No. 1 Area alone shows 116 small dumps.

The collection, concentration and movement of all material and stores (Government property and that captured or ceded, with the exception of aircraft and stores appertaining thereto, which were the concern of the R.A.F., and of locomotives and railway wagons, which devolved on a special commission)[2] were regarded throughout as a purely military function for which the Army organization was solely responsible. The disposal of surplus Government property, on the other hand, was recognized from the moment of the Armistice as a matter which would ultimately devolve on a civil department.

The problem to be faced by the Army varied according to areas, which for this purpose may be classed into three districts : first, the easternmost, No. 4 Area ; the centre, that of Nos. 1, 3

---

[1] From 1st April to 30th September, 1918, 62,500 patients were carried in hospital trains ; 45,000 returned to the United Kingdom by hospital ships, together with 14,500 from the East and 10,500 sent to China, India, etc.

[2] See Chapter III. Railway material, at least in part, was dealt with by the British Railway Financial Commission appointed in December, 1916, to consider the financial aspects of British railway construction and working in France, and to negotiate terms for the transfer of rolling stock and other railway material and works to the French. In 1919 the scope of this Commission was extended to include, amongst other matters, the bases of payment for railway installations and lines, docks and the like, constructed in whole or part by the British in France.

Further, in April, 1919, the British Transport Liquidation Commission was formed to value railway installations, material and equipment and treat with the French and Belgian Governments for their sale.

and 5 Areas ; and thirdly the rest of France. The first district was almost entirely in Belgium and the question of ownership of material found in it arose. A decision was given by an Allied Conference in Paris on 29th March, 1919, that all property seized or requisitioned by the Germans and subsequently captured should not be regarded as prize, but restored to its original owners. No. 4 Area contained many German munition and repair installations organized in the huge factories of Namur, Charleroi and the Borinage (coal mining district), full of machinery and electrical plant either collected or made in France and Belgium, or brought from Germany. The question of ownership had to be determined as quickly as possible, since the factory owners wanted to resume work, at least with what was at hand, regardless of ownership. There was too a vast conglomeration of material and loot which the Germans had been unable to remove, part of it loaded on over 15,000 railway wagons[1] and over 800 barges ; some part of this had been re-looted by the inhabitants. The district was also cumbered with booty in the shape of guns, ammunition, vehicles and horses left behind, the two last sometimes sold to inhabitants by the enemy in the final stage of his hurried marches for home. Such transfers were not recognized. The local authorities did their best to help the recovery of animals and goods by posting notices that pilfered stores and anything purchased from the enemy must be returned under penalty of heavy fine. The true ownership in nearly all cases was, it may be said, satisfactorily thrashed out, thanks largely to the energy and tact of Lieut.-General Asser and Major-General Bruce-Williams, commanding No. 4 Area. All German stock was marked " P.G.A." (*Prise de Guerre Anglaise*).

The second district, in the Mons and Avesnes neighbourhood, also contained factories with gear of doubtful ownership ; but the eastern part was a region of small towns and villages used for billeting, with the usual flotsam and jetsam left by the passing tide of war. Behind lay the " devastated area " dotted with material worth salving and strewn with ammunition and débris of all kinds. Farther back came a belt of camps and hutments covered with a network of light railways and sidings and telegraph lines, with dumps and depôts, cemeteries and isolated graves.

---

[1] In order to clear the lines, these trucks were sent to the Regulating Station at Monceau near Charleroi, there sorted and sent back to appropriate depôts. Thus, guns, machine guns and technical artillery vehicles and spare parts to Le Cateau ; engineer stores to the great dump at Les Attaques near Calais ; motor transport to the M.T. Depôt, Rouen ; civilian furniture to Liége. Some material was sold locally in the Charleroi area.

In rear of all were the great installations on the Lines of Communication and at the bases, towns in themselves, containing hospitals, reinforcement depôts, storehouses, refrigerating plant, repair shops, bakeries, butcheries, washing establishments, petrol and fuel dumps. Under War Office authority of 8th March, " Disposals and Accounting Officers," a colonel and 8 to 10 subordinate officers to each of the five areas, were appointed to deal, under the supervision of the Q Branch of the area staff, with the disposal of all surplus property ; also to act as liaison officers between the area staffs and the French and Belgian Missions at Army headquarters, and the governors and *préfets* of the provinces and departments concerned. The Salvage offices at Calais and Havre were absorbed into the disposal organization of the Lines of Communication area.

" Administrative Liaison Bureaux " were opened in Paris and Brussels as centres of information regarding possible buyers and dealers, market prices and the financial standing of prospective purchasers. The question of taxes incurred and customs duties involved by sale and movement had to be investigated.

The system of dealing with Government property and booty was as follows :[1]

After providing for the reserves required for the British Army of the Rhine, catalogues were prepared by the Army ; those which concerned military stores were sent to the War Office in order to ascertain whether any items were required at home or elsewhere, or whether they should be considered surplus; if surplus, the lists were passed to the Disposals Officers. Unfortunately tedious and expensive delays occurred, owing to the long retention of the lists in London. After many conferences, on 1st July, 1919, Br.-General J. M. Young (a regular officer of the R.A.S.C.), who had been appointed Commissioner for France of the Surplus Government Property Disposals Board of the Ministry of Munitions, and had arrived, with a small staff, on 1st April, took over charge of disposals. Although Lieut.-General Asser was thus relieved of this service and of the major accounting, he continued to be responsible for the custody, sorting, listing, handling and movement of the goods until the purchasers took them over. He was also charged with the despatch to the ports and the shipment of the stores and animals marked for retention.

---

[1] A detailed description will be found in the printed G.H.Q. " Report on Progress in Collection and Disposal of Government Stores and Salvage Material in France and Belgium from November, 1918, to June, 1919 " (Army Press, 12/19 9886S.)

The general policy of disposal was to effect " mass deals." Surplus huts, rails, iron bridges and scrap were disposed of in that way : *e.g.*, the South African Government took 300 miles of normal gauge track for £500,000 ; the French and Belgian railways purchased many locomotives and wagons and barges ; the French Government acquired all the 60-cm. rolling stock, workshops and track. As the French permitted only a limited sale of M.T. vehicles in France, the greater part of them were shipped home.

As early as May it was found necessary to confine salvage to such material as would obviously repay the cost of labour and transport, and to ensure that only usable British ammunition should be collected. The French Government agreed to take over all German ammunition in France. The levelling of trenches and defences and the removal of wire in the fighting areas were left to the French and Belgian authorities concerned, whilst the British tidied up camping and training grounds in the rear areas.

The signing of the Peace Treaty, with the consequent reduction of the Army of the Rhine, to be described later on, markedly diminished the importance of purely military requirements ; what remained to be done mainly concerned the Disposals Board and the Graves Registration Commission, for which the Army provided the labour. Two officers, Major-General Sir Gerald Ellison and Br.-General A. A. McHardy, sent over by the War Office, recommended that, in view of the serious railway situation in France and Belgium, the volume of material to be consigned to the United Kingdom should be reduced to a minimum ; that on a definite date, say 31st December, 1919, the direct responsibility of the War Office should cease ; and that control of all expenditure on administrative services carried out by the Army at the instance and on behalf of the Disposals Board (Ministry of Munitions) and Graves Registration Commission should be transferred to those departments.

Thanks to the protracted peace negotiations, German prisoners were held until the end of August, when they were repatriated by rail and by road, all being sent away by early October. By that time the heavier work of collection on which they were employed had been completed nearly three months.

As clearing up progressed the maintenance services, labour and guards were cut down ; but the reduction and disbandments required careful watching, to ensure that, in spite of constant changes of personnel, the machinery did not check or break down. By October it was possible to dispense with the services of the five major-generals commanding areas and to withdraw three of the four divisions. The areas were reduced to districts under a G.O.C. Forward Districts (excluding Lines of Communication). The Chief Engineer took over " Roads ", and the Director of Engineer Stores took over railway stores from the Director-General of Transportation ; the Director of Inland Water Transport absorbed " Docks," and the Director-General of Transportation, who had ruled over nine Directorates and Departments, was replaced by two Controllers (Movement and Maintenance).

By the end of 1919, when Lieut.-General Asser handed over command to Br.-General Evan Gibb, the number of British troops in France and Belgium was down to 38,000. Of these about 10,000 were in charge of installations, stores and vehicles, and about 18,000 were engaged on exhumation and cemetery work.[1] The remainder were employed on the staffs, on demobilization and at the rest camps, in charge of Chinese and on maintenance services. Of the Chinese, 25,000 remained, but 15,000 were to embark in January, and the balance in February. Some 7,000 Indians were awaiting repatriation. The repatriation of the Portuguese and the removal of their stores was just about to be completed.

About 480,000 tons, dead weight of material, had been shipped home, largely by the Channel ferry. As regards Army stores, the work was virtually finished. In all, 250,000 animals, including those from Egypt, Salonika and the Black Sea landed at Marseilles, had been disposed of ; 205,000 were sold and the others shipped home, but 2,000 still remained to be looked after.

On 13th May, 1920, nearly all the work had been completed, but no less than 270 letters, mostly dealing with writing off losses, were still awaiting answers from the War Office, as the Finance Branch would not delegate powers for writing off losses of more than £50. Eventually, however, it appears to have given way.

Br.-General Gibb then completed the clearing up, and after the Claims Commission and the Directorate of Hirings and Requisitions had been transferred to Paris, at the end of July, 1920, his headquarters were moved to London, leaving only about 4,000 British personnel of the units under the

---

[1] As the cemeteries were completed they were handed over to the Imperial War Graves Commission.

Director of Graves Registration and Enquiries, Br.-General L. J. Wyatt. In London the office of the G.O.C. British Troops in France and Flanders, its work done, gradually faded out.

Some tables attached to Br.-General Gibb's report of 9th September, 1920, giving the figures in francs, here converted at 28 to the £, the exchange ruling during the War, show that stores and animals had been sold on the Continent to the amount of £152,820,920 and shipped home to the value of £141,730,000.

NOTE I

THE ARMIES OF OCCUPATION

Explanatory Note by the Secretary of State for War
(the Right Hon. Winston S. Churchill), 28th January, 1919

1. On the 11th November, when the Armistice was signed, there were about 3,500,000 Imperial British officers and soldiers on the pay and ration strength of the British Army. During the two months that have passed since then, rather more than three quarters of a million have been demobilized or discharged. The system of demobilization which has been adopted aims at reviving national industry by bringing the men home in the order of urgency according to trades. There is no doubt that this is the wisest course, and it will continue to be followed in the large majority·of cases. The time has now come, however, when military needs must be considered as well as industrial needs.

2. Unless we are to be defrauded of the fruits of victory, ar.d, without considering our Allies, to throw away all that we have won with so much cost and trouble, we must provide for a good many months to come Armies of Occupation for the enemy's territory. These Armies must be strong enough to exact from the Germans, Turks and others the just terms which the Allies demand, and we must bear our share with France, America and Italy in providing them. The better trained and disciplined these Armies are, the fewer men will be needed to do the job. We have, therefore, to create, in order to wind up the war satisfactorily, a strong, compact, contented, well-disciplined Army which will maintain the high reputation of the British Service and make sure we are not tricked of what we have rightfully won. It will be an Army far smaller than our present Army. In fact, it will be about one-quarter of the great Armies we have been using in the war.

3. Our Military Commanders, who know what Marshal Foch's wishes are, say that in their opinion not more than 900,000 men of all ranks and arms will be sufficient to guard our interests in this transition period. Therefore, when this new Army has been organized and while it is being organized, over two and a half million men who were held to military service when the fighting stopped will be released to their homes and to industry as fast as the trains and ships can carry them and the Pay Offices settle their accounts. In other words, out of 3,500,000 it is proposed to keep for the present about 900,000 and release all the others as fast as possible.

4. How ought we to choose the 900,000 who are to remain to finish up the work ? When men are marked for release they obviously ought to go home in the order which will most quickly restart our

industries, for otherwise they would leave their means of livelihood in the Army and relinquish their rations and their separation allowance only to become unemployed in great numbers. But, when men are kept back in the Service to form the Armies of Occupation a choice cannot be made simply on trade grounds. It must be made on grounds which appeal broadly to a sense of justice and fairplay. Length of service, age and wounds must be the main considerations entitling a man to release. The new Army will, therefore, be composed in the first instance only from those who did not enlist before the 1st January, 1916, who are not over 37 years of age, and have not more than two wound stripes. If anyone has to stay, it must be those who are not the oldest, not those who came the earliest, not those who have suffered the most.

5. We, therefore, take these broad rules as our main guide. According to the best calculations which are possible they should give us about 1,300,000 men, out of which it is intended to form the Army of 900,000. If we find, as we shall do in all probability, that we have in the classes chosen more men than we actually require after dealing with a certain number of pivotal and compassionate cases, we shall proceed to reduce down to the figure of 900,000 first by reducing the age of retention to 36, to 35, next releasing the men with two wound stripes and then on to 34.

As the time goes on we shall not require to keep so large an Army as 900,000 in the field, and it will be possible to continue making reductions on the principle of releasing the oldest men by the years of their age. When, however, the results of the war are finally achieved, the divisions which have remained to the end will be brought home as units and make their entry into the principal cities of Great Britain with which they are territorially associated.

Volunteers for one year's service at a time for the Armies of Occupation will be accepted from men who would otherwise be entitled to release if they are physically fit and otherwise suitable ; and young soldiers now serving will be sent from home to take their turn and do their share. All these will be in relief of the older men. They will enable the age limit to be further reduced and the older men to be sent home. In particular the 69 battalions of young soldiers of 18 years of age and upwards who are now at home will be sent at once to help guard the Rhine Bridgeheads. They will thus enable an equal number of men, old enough to be their fathers, to come home, and they themselves will have a chance to see the German provinces which are now in our keeping and the battlefields where the British Army won immortal fame.

6. The new Armies of Occupation will begin forming from 1st February and it is hoped that in three months they may be completely organized. There will then be two classes of men in khaki, viz., those who form the Armies of Occupation, and those who are to be demobilized. Everything possible will be done to send home or disperse the two and a half million men who are no longer required. But they must wait their turn patiently and meanwhile do their duty in an exemplary manner. Any of these men who are marked for home who are guilty of any form of insubordination will, apart from any other punishment, be put back to the bottom of the list. There are no means of getting these great numbers of men home quickly unless everyone does his duty in the strictest possible way. It is recognized, however, that service in the Armies of Occupation is an extra demand which

the State makes in its need upon certain classes of its citizens.   The
emoluments of the Armies of Occupation will, therefore, be substantially
augmented, and every man will draw bonuses from the date of his
posting to these Armies with arrears from 1st February.

The bonuses will be as follows :—

	Per week.
	s. d.
Private soldier	10 6
Paid lance-corporal	12 3
Corporals	12 3
Serjeants	14 0
Colour-serjeants, company-serjeant-majors, company-quartermaster-serjeants, and quartermaster-serjeants	17 6
Warrant officers, Class I	21 0
2nd Lieutenants	24 6
Lieutenants	28 0
Captains	31 6
Majors	35 0
Lieut.-Colonels	38 6
Higher ranks..	42 0

These graduated bonuses will be paid as a special addition to the
pay of the Army during the period of occupation in recognition of the
fact that the service is compulsory.   The total cost of these additions
in one year for an army of 900,000 will be about 29,000,000l. ; of this
26,000,000l. will go to the rank and file.

8. Leave will be granted to men of the Armies of Occupation, Home
and Overseas Garrisons, on as generous a scale as possible.   No leave
will be given to men marked for home and waiting their turn for
demobilization, as it is desirable that all the facilities should be concentrated for the benefit of those who have to stay (except in cases of
special urgency).

9. The Armies of Occupation will be as follows :—

Home Army.
Army of the Rhine.
Army of the Middle East.
Detachment of the Far North.
Garrisons of the Crown Colonies and India.

These forces will be varied as circumstances may require, but no
young soldier under 20 will serve elsewhere than at Home or in the
Army of the Rhine.

10. Besides the men of the classes mentioned who will be held to
form the Armies of Occupation, and the Home and Overseas Garrisons
(who include the Regular Army and such Special Reserve and Territorial
Force officers and men as must be retained), there are a certain number
of special services on the Lines of Communication, at the Bases, and
here at home in which all men must be retained whatever their class,
because like the Railwaymen, the necessary Royal Army Service Corps
units and the Pay and Record Office staff, they are vitally necessary for
demobilizing and paying off all the others.   These, not exceeding the
numbers required, will therefore be deemed to be included in the
Armies of Occupation as indispensables and will participate in the

increased rates of pay. They will, however, be demobilized as soon as the great bulk of the two and a half million men, who are to be dispersed, have passed through their agencies back into civil life. At the rate at which demobilization is now proceeding, *viz.*, over 35,000 a day, this should not take many weeks.

11. There remains the British Army in India. Many of the Territorial and garrison battalions who left England in the autumn of 1914 to guard our Indian Empire or our Overseas possessions have served four hot weathers in the East without either relief or the excitement of battle. Up to the present hardly any volunteers have come forward to take their places or those of the Home garrisons, as part of the permanent after-war army of the British Empire. It is, therefore, necessary while this " after-war " or " Old British Army " is being reconstituted that these men should remain abroad for another hot season. It is felt that in all the circumstances they ought to participate in the bonuses which apply to the Armies of Occupation.

12. The above arrangements seem to be the best that can be devised for the year 1919. During this year, however, we must remake the Old British Regular Army so as to provide on a voluntary basis the Overseas Garrisons of India, Egypt, the Mediterranean Fortresses and other foreign stations.

It is believed that volunteering for the Regular Army will improve, as soon as the great mass of those who volunteered for the war against Germany in the early days have come back to the freedom of civil life, and have had a chance to look round. It is upon the steady rebuilding of this Army that the relief of the Territorial battalions in India and various detachments in distant theatres now depends. Every effort will therefore be made to hasten its formation both by recruiting and by re-engagement.

13. It is not necessary at this stage to settle the conditions on which the National Home Defence Army for after the war will be formed. There are many more urgent problems which should be solved first.

14. The entire scheme of the War Office for dealing with the many difficulties of the present situation and for safeguarding British interests is thus published to the Army and the Nation at large ; it has been agreed upon between all the authorities and departments concerned. The consent of Parliament, where necessary, will be asked for at the earliest possible moment. It remains for all ranks and all classes to work together with the utmost comradeship and energy to put it into force, and thereby to safeguard the best interests of each one of us and the final victory of our cause.

NOTE II

THE AMERICAN ARMY OF OCCUPATION

By decision of President Wilson, the American Army of Occupation was to consist of what was practically a small reinforced brigade of approximately 7,500 men. Its establishment was an infantry regiment of three battalions, a field artillery battalion, a machine-gun battalion, a cavalry squadron, an engineer company, a signal company, etc. A provisional battalion sent to guard surplus stores belonged to it until absorbed in February, 1921. A provisional infantry brigade arrived in

November, 1919, for plebiscite duty ; but, as the U.S.A. did not ratify the Peace Treaty, it remained with the Army of Occupation until the end of 1921, when it was disbanded.   In September, 1920, an air-service detachment of 13 officers and 88 men arrived.   After December, 1920, no replacements were received, but from lack of ships repatriation was slow.   On 31st December, 1919, the total strength was 842 officers and 17,986 men ; on 31st December, 1920, 622 and 15,887 ; on 31st December, 1921, 465 and 8,245.   (Allen i., pp. 128–36.)

On 22nd March, 1922, the decision of President Harding (who in 1921 had succeeded Woodrow Wilson) to withdraw all troops by 1st July, was cabled ; but three days later Major-General Allen, the American Commander-in-Chief, was told to make preparations only.   The American Ambassador was opposed to total withdrawal, and Major-General Allen himself suggested that a whole division was required.   He was nevertheless ordered to demobilize the 1st Brigade on 9th April, and its regiments sailed, one battalion being detained until 20th July on account of quartering complications at home.   To make up for this loss of men, the French put the 4th Dragoon Brigade under Major-General Allen's orders.   On 3rd June he was informed that a force not exceeding 1,200 officers and men would remain indefinitely on the Rhine, and this reduction was effected.   On 4th July he was further told that no more replacements would be sent.   On 1st January, 1923, the American strength was 106 officers, 10 warrant officers, 4 nurses and 1,079 other ranks.   (Allen i., pp. 251, 256, 263 ; American Summary iii., pp. 21, 54, 55, 301.)

Sketch 3

BRITISH OCCUPIED AREA
OF THE RHINELAND
MARCH 1920

BELGIAN AREA

RUHRORT
DUISBURG
MÜLHEIM
ESSEN   BOCHUM   Witten
R. Ruhr

RATINGEN
BARMEN
DÜSSELDORF   EBERFELD
REMSCHEID
NEUSS
SOLINGEN
Hilden
Benrath   OHLIGS
R. Wupper   Wermelskirchen
Opladen
Wiesdorf   R. Thünn
Bergheim   Riehl   Mülheim   Bensberg
Ehrenfeld
R. Erft   COLOGNE   Kalk   AREA
Deutz   Rösrath   HANDED
DAS VORGEBIRGE   Marienburg   TO THE
DÜREN   Wahn   Siegburg
R. Sieg
AACHEN
Drove   FRENCH
Zülpich   Duisdorf   BONN
Euskirchen   12th Feb 1920
Eupen   Rötgen
AREA HANDED
Montjoie
TO THE FRENCH
Schleiden
3rd Nov. 1919
AREA
Elsenborn
HANDED
Malmedy   AMERICAN AREA
TO THE
Amel
BELGIANS
St. Vith
12th Aug. 1919

R. Rhine

SCALE OF MILES
5   0   5   10   15   20   25

Compiled in the Historical Section (Military Branch).

Ordnance Survey 1943.

CHAPTER X

THE REDUCTION OF THE BRITISH ARMY OF THE RHINE

GENERAL SIR WILLIAM ROBERTSON'S COMMAND

SIGNING OF THE PEACE TREATY

22nd April, 1919—2nd March, 1920

(Sketch 3)

TRAINING OF THE YOUNG ARMY

On 21st April, 1919, General Sir Herbert Plumer relinquished the command of the B.A.R. on appointment as Governor and Commander-in-Chief of Malta.[1] He was succeeded on the Rhine by General Sir William Robertson.

The first task to which the new Commander-in-Chief and his Chief of the General Staff, Major-General Sir A. A. Montgomery[2] had to give attention was to complete the conversion of the Second Army into the Army of the Rhine and train its new units. The old divisions and brigades had been renamed, their infantry dislocated by the inclusion of Young Soldiers and Graduated Battalions, and their other arms similarly diluted by the recruits who had replaced demobilized soldiers. The numbers available for the other arms did not prove sufficient, and in May, owing to shortage of personnel, 39 batteries of artillery, and 11 field ambulances had to be disbanded. In the moral sphere regimental traditions and reputations were in danger of disappearance ; on the material side the Army was lacking, among other things, in two important classes of men—commanding officers and cooks. Few of the young battalions had received trained cooks before leaving the United Kingdom, and most of those in the Army had been demobilized, so that the cooking for the young battalions was done by Germans. Complaints about the messing reached the House of Commons ; but enquiry showed that the real trouble was not the inadequacy of the ration but the low standard of interior economy in some units, and

---

[1] He was promoted Field-Marshal on the following 31st July.

[2] Later Field-Marshal Sir A. Montgomery-Massingberd. He was succeeded in August by Major-General Sir H. Jeudwine, who was followed in November by Br.-General C. G. Fuller. Major-General A. F. Sillem was Adjutant-General and Major-General Sir A. Chichester was Quarter-Master-General until August, when they were succeeded by Colonel Sir R. Hutchinson as D.A. & Q.M.G.

the insufficient instruction of the officers in catering matters. Of the 90 battalions in the Army, 30 had not yet received permanent commanding officers, and in most of the remainder the commanders had been but recently posted, knew little or nothing about their officers or men, and in some cases, having been in " soft jobs " at home during the War, proved unsuitable. Many of the junior regimental officers had been but lately " brought in " from disbanded battalions ; they were mainly drawn from the temporary officer class, the Regular officers having been sent home to join the Regular units now in the process of remaking.   These young officers knew little about training or administration ; their military experience and their own training had been limited to the methods of position warfare.   Thus they were somewhat indifferently qualified, as a rule, to undertake the new duties required of them.

Most of the Regular N.C.Os. had also been recalled to the United Kingdom to join the Regular units, and those who remained on the Rhine had gained their stripes during the War, were young both in age and service, had none of the old authority over the men, and little experience in maintaining order.

The young soldiers received from home were not fully trained : some of the infantry had never fired a rifle, some of the artillerymen did not know the work of either gunner or driver ; some of the cavalry regiments were so weak in numbers that they could not move from one station to another without borrowing men from other regiments to lead their spare horses.

On 10th April the Royal Army Medical Corps of the Army was reported by the incoming Director of Medical Services, Major-General H. N. Thompson, to be more than 200 officers and 1,700 other ranks under establishment.

The corps, divisional and brigade commanders, however, were all men of the old Army.   More than half of the generals of the corps and divisions had well-established reputations in 1914 for training brigades and battalions, and the facilities for training in the Rhineland were of a nature never obtainable in the United Kingdom even under the Manœuvre Act.   The Army commander had therefore only to explain to his corps commanders that his aim was to have his troops ready, if necessary, for the active operations of an advance into Germany, and leave the details to them, ensuring uniformity and getting to know his units by constant visits and inspection.   Although an idea was prevalent in the ranks that, the War being over, strenuous training was a thing of the past, he soon found that all were responding to his call, and in a couple of months a reasonable standard of general efficiency was reached. Plenty of leave continued to be granted. On 1st May trains to Calais, taking 16 hours, were substituted for those to Boulogne taking 22 hours.

PREPARATIONS FOR ADVANCE INTO GERMANY

No long period for training was vouchsafed. On 20th May, only four weeks after he had assumed command, Sir William Robertson received a telegram from the Chief of the Imperial General Staff ordering him to make all necessary preparations for an advance into Germany at the earliest possible moment in order to bring pressure upon Germany to sign the peace treaty.[1] By later telegrams the date of the probable advance was given as the 23rd, and then the 27th ; on 3rd June the British Mission at Maréchal Foch's headquarters telegraphed that no advance would take place before 15th June.

In the old Fourth Army style, the headquarters of the Army of the Rhine issued a series of " Instructions," which are given in brief as an example of the nature of Army operation orders just after the War of 1914–18 :

No. 1, dated 21st May, stated shortly the situation, and notified that the Army would have 72 hours' warning of an advance being necessary, as that amount of notice had to be given to Germany of the termination of the Armistice. Preliminary steps were therefore to be taken to enable formations to complete the arrangements necessary on J—3, J—2 and J—1 days, " J " being the day of the advance.

" The first stage of an Allied advance would have as its objective the occupation of the Ruhr Valley and the complete control of the German railway systems considered essential [which were named in the next Instruction] for any advance after the first stage."

As much rolling stock as possible was to be captured. The advance was to be carried out by the X, VI and II Corps, the IV Corps taking over the areas of the II and VI Corps, and the IX Corps the areas of the X Corps, of the Corps Troops and of the Highland Division of the IV Corps, with the civil control involved. A composite cavalry regiment was to be formed by the Cavalry Division, with a battery R.H.A., to accompany the VI Corps, and Tanks and Squadrons R.A.F. were allotted. A table showed the fighting troops to be taken forward or left behind during the first stage.

---

[1] See Chapter XI.

The first stage of the movement, according to Instruction No. 2, also issued on 21st May, was to be completed by the evening of J + 4. The several corps, having formed up inside the perimeter of the bridgehead on J Day, were to push forward detachments, the X Corps eastwards, the VI north-eastwards, capable, with the assistance of motor lorries and buses, of advancing 30 to 40 miles a day. Each column was to consist of cyclists, a brigade of infantry, a machine-gun company, and a battery of tractor-drawn 6-inch howitzers, and be accompanied by aircraft. The II Corps, moving northwards, was to occupy the group of towns Remscheid–Barmen–Elberfeld–Düsseldorf. A forecast of the movements of the next three days was given.

Instruction No. 3 dealt with reliefs and preparatory movements.

Instruction No. 4, issued on 22nd May, gave the code word for the notification of J Day, and ordered some minor attachments. No. 5, of 26th May, dealt with the establishment of control over the German railways. No. 6, also of the 26th, directed the strict observance of the orders with regard to circulation, the outposts being reinforced if necessary. Until an intention to resist became apparent, aircraft were only to reconnoitre and were not to use their machine guns against personnel on the ground; in no case were they to begin bombing without orders from G.H.Q.

Instruction No. 7, of 26th May, moved a battalion of tanks to the Solingen area and notified some minor amendments as to movements and allotment of roads.

Instruction No. 8, of 27th May, gave information as to the operations of the American and Belgian Armies, with French reinforcements, on the flanks of the British Army of the Rhine.

Instruction No. 9, of 28th May, gave directions for the complete control of civil telegraphic and telephonic communications by the Signal Service and Security Section.

Instruction No. 10, of 29th May, laid down the signal (red Very lights) to indicate that the advance was being resisted, and gave directions for the disposal and examination of the prisoners and captured documents.

Instruction No. 11 of 4th June merely notified that Düsseldorf, previously given as an objective to the II Corps, had been transferred to the Belgians, and readjusted boundaries accordingly.

On 15th June a warning was received from Maréchal Foch that J Day would be 20th June, and pending its confirmation all necessary preliminary precautions were ordered.   Maréchal Foch also gave warning that a considerable number of Russian prisoners of war were in the German territory which the Allied Armies might reach, and it was to be expected that the Germans would attempt, as they did after the signature of the Armistice, to be rid of them by releasing and sending them into the Allied lines.

On 17th, 18th and 19th June the movements laid down for J—3 and J—2 and J—1 days were carried out ; but on the 19th the commanders were informed that the time allowed for the Germans to sign had been extended to 7 p.m. on 23rd June, and that in the event of their not signing, hostilities would begin at that hour.   On the 20th the preliminary concentration of troops in readiness to cross the perimeter was completed, with the Western and Light Divisions in second line near the Rhine, and the Midland Division in reserve between Cologne and Düren.

At the last moment on the 23rd the Germans agreed to the peace terms without reserve ; but the troops were ordered to remain in positions of readiness until the Treaty was signed.   On the 28th orders were issued for the return of the troops to their normal stations, and movement was begun on 30th June.

During this anxious period the German population had given no trouble, since no one wanted the War to recommence ; but, on 27th May, there was a strike in Cologne as a manifestation against the formation of a Rhine Republic ; elsewhere in the British area public meetings about this matter were held.[1] On the 28th an industrial strike occurred at Benrath (in the bridgehead, five miles south-east of Düsseldorf) where, as the strikers refused to accept the ruling of the British Arbitration Court, the leaders were expelled into unoccupied territory, and everything became normal again.

New defence schemes for the reduced numbers were prepared against disturbances, rather than an attack by Germany now considered unlikely.   These disturbances, it was thought, might take the form of a local strike, a general strike, a railway strike, or a Spartacist rising against the Government.   In the event of serious trouble the first essential must be to protect

---

[1] The so-called " Separatist Movement " is dealt with in Chapter XVI. The first mention of it occurs in December, 1918 ; some proclamations were posted by its adherents in June, 1919, in the French area ; it did not become troublesome until 1923.

life and property, and the preliminary steps must be to assemble headquarters, including civil officials, at their offices, guard food depôts, ammunition depôts, railway stations and tunnels, bridges, telephone exchanges, prisons, and power stations. Code words were arranged as warnings for the various situations, and everything was foreseen down to substitutes if the telephone system and electric lighting failed. It was found necessary to order that " all ranks must know what the ' alarm ' on the " bugle sounds like."

REDUCTION OF FOUR DIVISIONS

During the months of July and August a number of distinguished soldiers, including H.R.H. the Duke of Connaught, Maréchal Foch, Maréchal Joffre, Major-General Allen, now commanding the American Army, General Michel, the Belgian Chief of the Staff, and the Army Council as a corporate body, visited the British Army of the Rhine. In consequence of the signature of the peace terms, drastic reduction of numbers was under consideration.[1] The War Office did not know how to find the troops for the many Empire commitments ; men could not be retained in peacetime under the powers of the Military Service Acts ; voluntary recruiting was not producing the numbers required, for the " dole " had removed one reason for enlistment, the compulsion of hunger.[2]

On 6th August orders were received at Cologne for four of the ten divisions, the Highland, Eastern, Western and Midland, and the IX Corps troops, to proceed to the United Kingdom in the order named. The civil administration of the IX Corps area passed to the Military Governor, and the military command to the X Corps. On the 8th came orders for the reduction of the R.A.F. by one squadron, and on the 11th for the return of the Cavalry Division. The liabilities of the British Army of the Rhine were only slightly reduced by the handing over to the Belgians of the Malmédy area, now part of their national territory.[3] On the 14th the entrainment of the Highland Division was completed ; on the 21st, that of the Eastern Division ; and, next day, the entrainment of the

---

[1] To quote the words of the *Cologne Post* : " With the signing of the Peace Treaty in June, 1919, came the new regulations. Mr. Winston Churchill, then Secretary of State for War, and ever an economist, visited the garrison and started his campaign for retrenchment. Then followed ' The Geddes Axe,' bonuses ceased and all temporary and Young Soldiers were replaced by the regular battalions."

[2] Field-Marshal Sir William Robertson, once a private, said at a General Staff conference before 1914 : " We have always had compulsory service, the compulsion of hunger."

[3] See Sketch 3.

Western Division was begun. This was completed on the 28th ; and on the 29th the move of the Midland Division was begun and was completed on 5th September. But on 30th August the War Office, by telegram, suspended further departures of all units reduced to disbandment level by demobilization on the ground of a possible change of policy.

On 1st September, however, the break-up of the Lowland Division, already reduced in numbers, for its infantry brigades on 31st May averaged only 1,030 officers and men, was taken in hand, two battalions (3rd Brigade) being sent to the United Kingdom. On the 15th the War Office ordered home by name three more battalions, one from each brigade, and reduced another (of the 1st Brigade) to cadre. The headquarters of the 1st and 3rd Brigades were then broken up, the division was transferred to the II Corps, and the IV Corps, having no troops, now disappeared : its last corporate act had been to stage a magnificent moonlight tattoo in which, among other items, infantry battalions trickled down the hillsides as rivulets of light to form themselves into their regimental crests, and all useless star shells and rockets were expended. All the anti-aircraft batteries were next ordered home, and other units of the Lowland Division followed ; but it was not until 24th October that its divisional headquarters was disbanded, command of the remaining units passing to the 2nd Lowland Brigade. The order of battle of this brigade became 3 battalions (total strength 28 officers and 622 other ranks), 2 brigades R.F.A., 1 machine-gun company.

One of the effects of the signing of the Peace Treaty was that the British Military Missions with the different Allied Armies were broken up, and their place was taken by liaison officers, who were posted to Coblence, Aachen and Mayence, the American, Belgian and French headquarters.

Provisioning of the Rhine Army

In August, when the new harvest was becoming available, the question of the provisioning of the Allied Armies of the Rhine was raised by the French and Belgians. They wished to " live on the country," doing so by simple requisition as the Germans had done in occupied areas, and thus saving their own supplies and transport. Sir William Robertson replied that the British troops did not desire to obtain from German sources any foodstuffs except potatoes, green vegetables, hay and oats. General Allen, commanding the U.S.A. force, formally refused any arrangement which would make his troops dependent upon supplies delivered by the German Government.

After negotiations, it was finally approved by the Luxembourg Commission in October that foodstuffs obtained by each Army should be divided into three categories : (1) imported ; (2) acquired by purchase in its own zone ; and (3) requisitioned from the German authorities (chiefly coal). In cases of urgency recourse could be had to direct requisitioning, but every such case must be reported by the Army concerned to the Luxembourg Commission.

PREPARATIONS TO OCCUPY ELBERFELD

On 9th September, in the midst of the break-up of the Lowland Division, directions were received from the Generalissimo that in the event of the German Government refusing within 15 days to modify their constitution to conform, with the stipulations of the Peace Treaty, especially as regards the abolition of Universal Service, it might be necessary to carry out an advance east of the Rhine. The general idea was to occupy, in succession so as to exert graduated pressure, the large towns situated in the Neutral Zone, Frankfort, Mannheim, Elberfeld and Düsseldorf. The occupation of Elberfeld was allotted to the British Army of the Rhine, and Sir William Robertson ordered the II Corps to organize a mobile column comprising an infantry brigade, field artillery, a company of tanks, and cyclists, no cavalry being available, to undertake the military occupation of the town. Eight days later notice was received that there was little probability that the British force would be required until after the 15th October when the French Army would move ; the British would not be called upon to take action until after the result of the French occupation of Frankfort and Mannheim had been observed.

MEASURES IN CASE OF CIVIL DISTURBANCES

The reduction of the strength of the British Army of the Rhine was already increasing the burden of the units which remained. Official warning had been given on 2nd September that a Spartacist rising in Berlin was expected and would " probably be accompanied by attempts to foment trouble " in Düsseldorf, Elberfeld and other industrial centres on the " perimeter [of the bridgehead] and might induce disturbances " in the area occupied by our troops." Besides ordinary guard duty, the Rhine garrison was responsible for carrying into effect the local defence schemes ; for preparations for instant action, including the holding in readiness of a " flying column "

in lorries, in case of civil disturbances in their own and neighbouring areas ;[1] for the control of the railways ; and for the
protection of vulnerable points (bridges, power stations and
certain factories). The duty which weighed most heavily,
however, was that of finding troops for the various control of
circulation posts in the bridgehead area. Until the Peace Treaty
was definitely ratified, it was not considered desirable to remove
the restrictions on the movement of the civil population, or
to abolish the pass system. To meet the conflicting conditions,
the number and the size of the posts had to be reduced, and in
some cases occasional patrols were substituted for permanent
posts.

FURTHER REDUCTION OF THE BRITISH ARMY OF THE RHINE

Worse was to come. On 15th September the War Office
sent definite instructions that the establishment of the
permanent Rhine garrison would be 451 officers and 11,770
other ranks with 2,605 horses, comprising one cavalry regiment—
the 6th (Inniskilling) Dragoons was selected—one brigade
R.F.A. (four batteries), one 60-pdr. battery, one field company
R.E., one divisional signal company, one machine-gun battalion,
six infantry battalions organized in two brigades, one pioneer
battalion, and two light trench-mortar batteries, with the usual
ancillary troops.

On the 20th, however, a further communication was
received from the War Office to the effect that for the present
the British Army of the Rhine would not be so greatly reduced,
and would be organized in three divisional groups as a corps
command :

I. The Rhine garrison of the strength and composition notified five days earlier, with headquarters troops.[2]

II. An " Independent Division " of the establishment of
a division at full war strength " or as near to it as our resources
" in personnel will admit," with three brigades R.F.A. instead
of two.

---

[1] The general instructions were : (1) no large crowd will be allowed
to assemble in the vicinity of troops or of military establishments ; (2) civilians
carrying arms will be arrested ; (3) civilians making use of firearms or
explosives will be shot ; (4) looting, damage to property or communications,
and acts of incendiarism will be prevented, by shooting if necessary ; (5) fire
on crowds will not be opened unless they assume a threatening attitude, and
then only by order of the senior officer on the spot ; fire when opened must be
effective ; firing over the heads of a crowd with a view to intimidating it is
absolutely forbidden.

[2] See Appendix XIX. At the end of November the two brigades numbered
respectively 73 officers and 1,460 other ranks, and 76 and 1,855, and the cavalry
regiment 19 officers and 343 other ranks.

III. The " Residual Force," amounting probably to 12 battalions, organized in three brigades, and possibly other arms, with the necessary services.

Group I would probably be stationed in the Cologne area ; Group II in the Bonn and Wahn area ; Group III in and around Solingen and possibly Düren. " It is probable that the greater " part of the present British occupied area will be available." No aircraft or tanks were included in the War Office forecast, but one squadron R.A.F. and one battalion of tanks were eventually added.

On 5th October orders were issued to carry the reorganization into effect, " after the demobilization at present in progress is completed."   Simultaneously orders were received from another department of the War Office to send two divisions home at short notice in view of a railway strike. Next day the contingent was reduced to eight battalions. In the end the troops were not required. but demobilization was held up for a fortnight, and then the Residual Force, from lack of troops, dropped out. On the 17th orders were received to send the 52/King's of the Independent Division, to entrain at Bonn on 6th November and embark at Havre for Flensburg to maintain order during the plebiscite on the 30th in Schleswig-Holstein, and on the 27th for the Independent Division to be ready to move to other plebiscite areas in unoccupied Germany, *viz.*, Danzig, Memel, Upper Silesia, Marienwerder and Allenstein. The move home of the 51/Hampshire was cancelled, and it was attached as an extra battalion to the Independent Division. The disbandment of the 11/Royal Scots was suspended. Much relief was brought to the British Army of the Rhine by the French Army on 3rd November taking over a large area from Malmédy almost to the Vorgebirge, thus leaving it only the bridgehead and an area of similar size west of the Rhine.[1]

Towards the end of October German railway strikes appeared likely, and on the 30th the following instructions were circulated :

> " German civil authorities are responsible for the safeguarding and protection of all railway property including buildings, tracks, lines, signal apparatus, rolling stock, etc., throughout their area.
>
> " In the event of a strike, corps will take measures to protect railway bridges, junctions, etc., of military importance [a list of these was given].
>
> " Corps will also be prepared to assist the civil authorities in suppressing sabotage, and local commanders should normally

---

[1] See Sketch 3.

refer the question to corps for decision unless the urgency of the situation demands immediate action."

The reduction according to the War Office orders of the British Army of the Rhine from five divisions and an infantry brigade, containing 48 infantry battalions, to five brigades, containing 15 battalions, involved selection and rearrangement of the infantry units, and much the same steps in the other arms and the services. For the new force five battalions, including one complete brigade, were taken from the Light Division, three from the London, three from the Southern, two from the Lancashire, and one each from the Northern Division and the 2nd Lowland Brigade. The infantry brigades were again renamed : 1st and 2nd Infantry Brigades of the Rhine Garrison, and the 1st, 2nd and 3rd Infantry Brigades of the Independent Division. The London Divisional Signal Company formed the nucleus of the signal company of the Rhine Garrison, the Southern Divisional Signal Company that of the Independent Division.

A printed pamphlet of 31 foolscap pages was necessary to contain all the information and instructions with regard to the units to be sent home (nine battalions), reduced to cadre (three 1st Line Territorial Force battalions), or disbanded (of Signal units alone there were 41 to be broken up) ; to the disposal of equipment and stores ; and to the cross-posting of officers and other ranks, which was to be complete by 31st October.

To give instances of cross-posting of the rank and file, premising that Class A contained soldiers of 20 and under, and Class B other retainable men : the 17/Royal Fusiliers, which was to be disbanded, was to send all Class A men to the 23/Royal Fusiliers (detailed to the Rhine Garrison) and all Class B to the 26/Royal Fusiliers (of the Residual Force) ; the 53/R. Warwickshire, which was disbanded, was to send 330 of Class A to the 51/R. Warwickshire, the remainder of Class A, about 320, to the 52nd Battalion, and Class B to the 51st Battalion. Men of the disbanded battalions not retained were sent to the demobilization camps. Equipment guards were to be left behind by disbanded units, and 12 railway stations were named in the vicinity of which equipment and stores were to be parked.

Among the directions were :

" No infantry officer is to be compulsorily retained " ;

" officers other than Regulars who become surplus will be demobilized—compulsorily if necessary " ;

" care should be taken to ensure that a fair proportion of

n.c.os. should be included on each draft, and that experienced
n.c.os. and specialists should be evenly distributed ";
    " warrant officers and n.c.os. and men who have volunteered
for six months or more and also all young soldiers of 20 years or
under, will be posted, first to units of the Rhine Garrison, and
secondly to those of the Independent Division ".

The cross-posting, a matter more intricate and delicate than
any jig-saw puzzle, was carried out with the usual heart-
burnings and grumblings at the break-up of cherished units,
arbitrary transfers, and the separation of " pals."

In October 74,269 officers and men were demobilized, in
November 66,366, and in December 24,038. The " Q " diaries
contain long lists of changes and new instructions as regards
demobilization, e.g., in November, 1919, such mercantile
marine officers, as are bona fide " candidates for Board of Trade
" certificates are to be demobilized at once " ; " Soldiers who are
" surplus may volunteer for a further period in another arm of
" the Service ; " and give directions for treatment of demobilized
men under suspended sentence, and other minute details.

THE NEW ORGANIZATION

On 3rd November Lieut.-General Sir A. Haldane handed
over the command and the area of the VI Corps to Lieut.-
General Sir T. Morland, and on the 8th Lieut.-General Sir
C. Jacob similarly handed over the II Corps. On 14th
November it was announced that the territory occupied by
the British Army of the Rhine would be divided into two
areas : that of the VI Corps under Lieut.-General Morland and
that of the Independent Division, under Major-General Sir
W. Heneker (formerly commanding the 8th and then the
Southern Division).[1] The Rhine Garrison, under Major-
General Sir S. Lawford (formerly commanding the 41st and
then the London Division) with some attached units, were
included in Lieut.-General Morland's command.

The new nomenclature was as follows :[2]

The London Division became The Rhine Garrison.
    3rd London Brigade became 1st Rhine Garrison Brigade.
    3rd Light Brigade became 2nd Rhine Garrison Brigade.

The Southern Division became Independent Division :
    1st Southern Brigade remained 1st Southern Brigade.

---

[1] The VI. Corps area is that shown on Sketch 3 as being handed to the
French on 12th February, 1920 ; the Independent Division held the area
retained after that date.

[2] For Order of Battle, see Appendix XIX.

2nd Lancashire Brigade became 2nd Northern Brigade.
1st Light Brigade became 3rd Light Brigade.
The Base of the B.A.R. was now Antwerp.

In December rumours of Spartacist risings again became prevalent. Special instructions were issued,[1] and the two area commanders directed to revise and rehearse their schemes.

Contrary to expectation, the return of the many thousands of German prisoners of war in the latter half of 1919 caused no disturbance, hardly a ripple, it was said, on the prevailing calm.

PREPARATIONS FOR DESPATCH OF A PLEBISCITE DIVISION

The administrative troubles of the Staff of the British Army of the Rhine were not yet over. On 20th December, 1919, a War Office letter informed Sir William Robertson that,

" In view of the delay which has occurred in the ratification of the Peace Treaty with Germany and the uncertainty existing as to the date when the Independent Division will be required to proceed to the areas allotted to it, it has been decided that the temporary units now comprising that division will not be used for the purpose mentioned [plebiscite duty in Germany], and that they will be replaced by Regular units as detailed in Schedule A attached."[2]

The letter continued that the Regular units would not be despatched to the Rhine before 15th January, 1920, where they would take over animals and equipment from the temporary units which they were replacing ; that the battalion and the medical unit for Schleswig would proceed direct ; that in no case would temporary units of Rhine Army personnel be sent with the division " except possibly in certain cases, e.g., signal service, " R.A.M.C., R.A.O.C., in which difficulty may be experienced in " obtaining sufficient Regular personnel " ; and that advanced parties (their strength and arm of the Service were given in detail) should be held in readiness to move, also " Canteen " Stores, Bakery and Casualty Clearing Station," escorts for stores and a garrison for the regulating station. The commander of the division, now called the " Plebiscite Division," was to be under the orders of Lieut.-General Sir Richard Haking (of the Spa Commission), who would administer the troops in East

---

[1] Appendix XX.

[2] It enumerated : 3 battalions for Upper Silesia ; 7 for East Prussia ; 1 battalion and 1 Detention Hospital, in lieu of a Casualty Clearing Hospital, for Schleswig ; and the Guards Machine Gun Battalion and the XXXV. Brigade R.F.A., without destination.

Prussia. Finally, the temporary units freed by the Regulars were to proceed to the United Kingdom as units, but no non-demobilizable personnel were to accompany them ; such personnel should be sent first and separately as drafts to report to their respective depôts ; on arrival home the units would be treated in the same way as demobilizable drafts.

The month of January, 1920, was signalized by the ratification, except by the U.S.A., of the Peace Treaty, by the coming into power of the Inter-Allied Rhineland High Commission, dealt with in the next chapter, by a series of strikes all over Germany, including the British Occupied Area, brought about by economic conditions and the prospect of unemployment, and by the demobilization of the Independent Division.

The strikes, which were " sympathetic " and not directed against the British occupation, began on the 5th, when some of the brown-coal miners came out, and by the 10th 9,000 were working and 10,000 absent ; the movement then spread to the municipal transport workers at Solingen and Opladen, to electrical power stations, and to the railwaymen, who undertook, however, not to interfere with British transport. Guards were sent to various places, including all stations in Cologne, for their protection and to prevent picketing ; and, after warning, some of the leaders were arrested. By the middle of the month most of the strikes had died down, and Sir William Robertson had given orders that no more arrests should be made for the offence of striking. In the midst of the trouble, on the 13th the Inter-Allied Rhineland High Commission now sitting at Coblence, anxious to take charge of the situation and unaware that the Military Governor was only a Staff officer, telegraphed that his post was abolished.

By the 13th January preparations for the despatch of the Plebiscite Division were in full swing ; a table of the grouping of the battalions was received from the War Office, which gave orders that the staff of the Independent Division should be responsible for the reception, administration and equipping of the advanced parties proceeding to the Plebiscite Areas, and instructed the Commander-in-Chief as to various details. For instance, it laid down that " these parties should take with " them five days' rations (including 3 days' fresh meat) and a " reserve of 30 days' forage, fuel and canteen stores ; truck " kitchens should be attached to the trains, with sufficient fuel " and water." On the 15th the War Office notified Sir William Robertson that the advanced parties would embark at Dover for Cologne on the 19th and 21st; next day it telegraphed that the first main body would embark on the 28th, and two days later cancelled the move of one battalion. On the 19th Sir William Robertson, hurt by continued interference, felt it necessary to ask that his responsibilities towards the troops for the Plebiscite Area might be defined. He was informed next day that no British troops excepting those for Flensburg would now proceed to the Plebiscite Areas. On the following day an order was received from Maréchal Foch postponing the move of the Allied contingents to the Plebiscite Areas for five days, and simultaneously the War Office telegraphed that three battalions (including the one for Flensburg) would proceed to the areas.

Accordingly, on 25th January the British Army of the Rhine issued operation orders for the move to the Plebiscite Areas as follow: one battalion (1/Sherwood Foresters) to go direct from England to Flensburg, the 3/Royal Fusiliers to Danzig, and the 1/Royal Irish to Allenstein (in East Prussia), with ancillary details, in trains provided by Germany, the main bodies of the two latter battalions arriving in Cologne on 29th January and 1st February.[1] The move of the remaining troops previously destined for the Plebiscite Areas was definitely cancelled, and on 31st January the demobilization, and on 3rd February, the disbandment, in the Rhineland, of the Independent Division was ordered; the men were to be sent home by parties of 450 men daily, Fridays excepted.[2] As demobilization proceeded the Bonn and Siegburg areas were handed over to the French; their advanced parties arrived on 6th February, and the formal handing over took place on the 12th. The headquarters of the Independent Division was closed on 29th February, and that of the VI Corps on 3rd March; both formations left a small staff with the headquarters of the British Army of the Rhine to clear up outstanding questions.

Thus the British Army of the Rhine was reduced to seven battalions, with other arms in proportion, a force, according to a General Staff Memorandum of 27th July, 1920, prepared for the Committee of Imperial Defence, "which bears no relation "to the possible requirements of any situation in which it may "become involved."

---

[1] The Upper Silesia plebiscite was not taken until 20th March, 1921. See Chapter XIII.

[2] Seventeen returns had to be rendered by disbanded battalions.

THE ALLENSTEIN PLEBISCITE

The taking of the Allenstein plebiscite affords an example of the duties required of British troops in the execution of the Peace Treaty. The greater part of the Allenstein department (the town of that name being 20 miles north-east of the battlefield of Tannenberg) and the Oletzko district, on the southern border of East Prussia, containing about 600,000 inhabitants, had been claimed as Polish territory, and Article 94 of the Treaty prescribed a plebiscite. Pending the ratification of the Treaty, an Inter-Allied Commission was formed in September, 1919, with Mr. (later Sir) Ernest Rennie of the Diplomatic Service as president, and French, Italian and Japanese members. It was considered necessary to support the authority of this Commission (and other similar commissions) by military force, and on 5th February the 1/R. Irish (500 strong, but later raised to 800) under Major E. C. Lloyd, with the details mentioned in the text, reached Allenstein ahead of the Commission, which arrived on the 11th. Both were received without any sign of hostility by the local officials and inhabitants. The recollection of survivors is that they were comfortably housed and spent most days of their sojourn in route marching. An Italian battalion also arrived, and was quartered at Lyck, with one company at Allenstein.

On 14th February the Commission, with a German and a Polish delegate attached, took over the administration. In order to supervise the local German authorities, Allied officers (five British, three French and three Italian) were sent to 11 of the more important centres, and the local police (about 3,000 *Sicherheitspolizei* and 120 *Grenzschutz*)[1] were placed under the supervision of two British officers, the *Grenzschutz* being directed to form a cordon along the southern border of the plebiscite area. With the co-operation of the German authorities a system of passports was inaugurated to control persons wishing to leave or enter the area.

In March the *Einwohnerwehr* (Home Guard), formed in March, 1919, to combat Spartacist activity, was disarmed without any special friction, and the arms handed in were stored under Allied guard. The State police, numbering roughly 3,800, were found to be armed with howitzers and machine guns, and during April and May they also were disarmed, by stages, their howitzers and machine guns, and subsequently their rifles, being handed over to the Allied troops ; and they were given a normal police equipment. Both State

---

[1] See Chapter XII.

and local police were maintained, as it was obviously undesirable that Allied troops should become involved in the suppression of local trouble except in the last extremity. Additional Allied officers arrived to assist the 11 district officers in the control of the police, and in June Br.-General C. J. Hawker, who had experience of gendarmerie duties, was appointed to control the whole of the police forces as Inspector-General. He completed the disarmament of the police by destroying three aircraft found in their possession. The German police commandant having protested and refusing to assist, he was superseded. Polish complaints that the police was entirely a German force were met by dismissing 420 men and offering to enrol Polish recruits—but, owing to intimidation, none presented themselves. This is the more understandable when it is remembered that a Bolshevik invasion was in progress, and in a few weeks' time Poland might have ceased to exist as a State.

After restoring order, including order in the railway, telegraphic and telephone services, which were found entirely disorganized, the Commission reported on 10th March that the taking over of the Administration had been completed, and was then instructed that, in spite of Polish requests for delay on account of the Bolshevik advance, the vote should be taken before 15th July. But it was not until 5th June that Mr. Rennie was able to notify that 11th July had been fixed as the date of the plebiscite, when he was satisfied that everything feasible in the circumstances had been done to guarantee the freedom of vote and to reform the police.

Little had been required of the troops except to demonstrate the authority of the Commission to the rural population, for which purpose several companies of the Royal Irish toured the area by special trains and paraded in selected places. Officers were employed as presidents of Mixed Courts, assisted by German and Polish judges, to hold enquiries into alleged disturbances at political meetings. Escorts were found for trains bringing in voters across the border, and on the voting day troops were posted in certain towns and danger areas (but otherwise they were confined to barracks). In August, in the face of the Bolshevik invasion of Poland, a Polish regiment crossed into the plebiscite area, where it was disarmed and interned.

The plebiscite was taken without incident, and military intervention was found unnecessary. The voting went overwhelmingly in favour of Germany, 1,694 districts voting for East Prussia and only 8 for Poland, with 363,370 votes against

7,858 ; about 80 per cent. voted. The result, however, gives an exaggerated picture of German preponderance, in view of the fact that the voting lists were made up and revised by Germans, that there were many Polish absentees who were serving against the Bolshevists, and that many Polish-minded citizens voted German for fear of having local officials, police, clergy, etc., against them for life.

In spite of a somewhat tense situation owing to the proximity of the Bolshevik forces, it was decided, in order to avoid complications, to withdraw the Allied troops, whose conduct had been admirable, as soon as possible. The Italian battalion entrained on 12th August, the Royal Irish on the 15th, leaving one platoon as escort to the Commission. On the 16th, with due ceremony, the Commission handed back the Administration to the Germans and left for Paris and Berlin without incident. Before they had departed, however, the police were observed to be patrolling Allenstein equipped as they were before they had been disarmed.

Exchange of Temporary for Regular Units

On 22nd February the War Office issued orders for the relief of the 7 (temporary) infantry battalions, including the Lines of Communication battalion, of the Rhine Army by Regular battalions from the United Kingdom, and the return home of one brigade R.F.A. and one battery R.G.A. ; the 41st Machine Gun Battalion was replaced by a single company of the 4th Machine Gun Battalion. Here, again, elaborate orders were necessary : some of the items will be quoted. On the day before the arrival of the relieving unit, demobilizable personnel were to proceed to a concentration camp, leaving a rear party to hand over barracks and equipment to the incoming unit. The rear party was to include the commanding officer (or second in command) and all transport personnel. Non-demobilizable personnel (all ranks) were to be sent to the B.A.R. Reception Camp at Deutz for disposal. A senior officer of each incoming unit was to accompany the advanced party for the purpose of purchasing regimental property, etc., and was to take over the equipment (less personal equipment) and horses of the unit relieved. Band instruments of disbanded units, properly packed, might be despatched via Antwerp to regimental depôts by the trains provided for equipment, and were to be marked " in transit through C.O.O. Didcot." Regimental baggage, but in no circumstances privately owned property, might similarly be sent home in reasonable quantities.

The infantry brigades were now to be named, constituted and stationed as under :

1st Rhine Brigade	2nd L. North Lancashire.	Mülheim (north-eastern suburb of Cologne on east bank of Rhine).
	2nd R. West Kent ..	Solingen.
	3rd Middlesex ..	Kalk Barracks (eastern suburb of Cologne on east bank).
2nd Rhine Brigade	4th Worcestershire ..	Riehl Infantry Barracks (northern suburb of Cologne, on west bank).
	2nd Black Watch ..	Marienburg (southern suburb of west bank).
	1st Durham L.I. ..	Riehl Pioneer Barracks.
L. of C.	1st. R. Sussex ..	Zugweg Barracks, Cologne (near the southern goods station).

Thus six of the seven battalions were in the suburbs of Cologne.

The strength of the Rhine Garrison on 28th February was : infantry, 2,032 ; cavalry, 379 ; artillery, 649 ; engineers, 252 ; with a grand total of 6,676 instead of the establishment of about 11,000.

On 29th January the commander of the 1st Rhine Brigade, then only 62 officers and 953 other ranks on ration strength, reported that " the greater part of the brigade has been employed on guards," and five days later that the brigade was reorganized " on a two-platoon per company basis." The 2nd Rhine Brigade was slightly stronger, but it also had to report, " owing to the number of officers and other ranks employed on guard, training was cut down to a minimum and was restricted to individual training."

With the reduction of the garrison the original l defence scheme could not be carried out and the defended ocalities were abandoned. The B.A.R., too small even as a police force and quite unequal to deal with the camouflaged German forces in the Neutral Zone and provinces adjacent, was dependent for its security on prestige and on the presence of the Allied Armies around it.[1]

---

[1] The figures approximately for 1st January of each year, including the Clearing Up Army were :—

			British	French	Belgian
1920	..	..	40,594	79,324	14,663
1921	..	..	12,421	68,488	—
1922	..	..	4,630	81,563	33,961
1923	..	..	8,730	87,991	30,704
1924	..	..	8,873	99,305	21,251
1925	..	..	8,118	77,800	16,176

The strength of the American contingent has been given in the previous chapter.

DEPARTURE OF SIR WILLIAM ROBERTSON

These changes were carried out during March, 1920. In consequence of the reduction of the Army and the change in the system of civil Government brought about by the formation of the Inter-Allied Rhineland High Commission, General Sir William Robertson suggested to the Army Council that he might hand over the command of the British Army of the Rhine to an officer of less rank, and on 3rd March Lieut.-General Sir T. Morland (VI Corps) took over. General Degoutte and General Michel, commanding the French and Belgian Armies of Occupation, came to Cologne to bid General Robertson farewell. He had previously been entertained at dinner by General Allen, commanding the American contingent. On his return home he was promoted to Field-Marshal and appointed Colonel of The Royal Horse Guards (The Blues).

CHAPTER XI

THE TREATY OF VERSAILLES AND THE FORMATION OF THE INTER-ALLIED RHINELAND HIGH COMMISSION AND THE INTER-ALLIED COMMISSION OF CONTROL

THE CONTENTS OF THE PEACE TREATY

The Treaty of Peace between the Allied and Associated Powers and Germany was signed at Versailles on 28th June, 1919, after six months' discussion between the representatives of those Powers. It comprised 15 Parts, divided into Sections, sometimes subdivided into chapters, with 440 Articles, and covered 231 foolscap printed pages. The fifteen parts had the headings : I. The Covenant of the League of Nations ; II. Boundaries of Germany. III. Political Clauses for Europe (including a section on the Saar Basin) ; IV. German Rights and Interests outside Germany ; V. Military, Naval and Air Clauses ; VI. Prisoners of War and Graves ; VII. Penalties ; VIII. Reparation ; IX. Financial Clauses ; X. Economic Clauses ; XI. Aerial Navigation ; XII. Ports, Waterways and Railways ; XIII. Labour ; XIV. Guarantees ; XV. Miscellaneous Provisions.

In territory, besides her Colonial possessions, Germany lost Alsace-Lorraine (acquired in 1871) to France, parts of West Prussia, Posen and Silesia (acquired by conquest or the partitions of Poland) to the new Polish State, and the *Kreise* of Eupen and Malmédy to Belgium. In certain border cases, notably Upper Silesia, a plebiscite was to be taken to ascertain to which State the inhabitants wished to belong.

Future security was provided for first by Section iii. of Part III. " Left Bank of the Rhine " (Articles 42 to 44), which forbade Germany to maintain or construct fortifications on the left bank or on certain parts of the right bank, or to maintain or assemble troops or hold manœuvres in these areas. Secondly, by the Military Clauses, in four chapters (Articles 159–180) [1] :

(i) The effectives and cadres of the German Army were limited to 7 divisions of infantry and 3 divisions of cavalry, with a total of 100,000 men, of whom not more than 4,000 might be officers. Within three months of the coming into force of the Treaty, the total number of effectives was to be reduced to 200,000, and the total of 100,000 reached by 31st March, 1920.

(ii) The maximum of armaments, munitions and material which might be held was fixed ; quantities in excess were to be handed

[1] Printed in full in Appendix XXI.

over ; the number of armament factories was restricted ; the manufacture of poison gas was forbidden ; and the importation of arms, munitions and war material was prohibited.

(iii) Universal military service was abolished, and the German Army was to be recruited by voluntary enlistment, the rank and file engaging for twelve consecutive years. The military schools were reduced to one each for the officers of the four arms. Societies and associations of all descriptions, including educational establishments, sporting clubs, societies of ex-soldiers, were not to occupy themselves with any military matters, in particular not to allow military instruction or exercises, and they were to have no connection with the Ministry of War or any other military authority. All measures of mobilization were forbidden.

(iv) All fortresses, forts and field works in Germany west of a line drawn 50 kilometres east of the Rhine were to be disarmed and dismantled, and no new fortifications erected in this area. The Neutral Zone became 50 kilometres (say 30 miles), instead of 10 (say 16).

The "Air Clauses", by Article 198, forbade Germany to possess any naval or military air forces.

Clauses in Part XII., Chapter IV (Articles 354–362), provided for the free navigation of the Rhine and for the assembly of a Central Commission to revise the Convention of Mannheim, which governed the navigation of the Rhine.

Part XIV. Section i. (Articles 428–32) provided as a guarantee of the execution of the Treaty by Germany that the Rhineland west of the Rhine and the bridgeheads should be occupied for 15 years ; but if the conditions were faithfully carried out by Germany, a certain portion would be given up in five years, and another portion in ten years, and the remainder in fifteen years. In the case of unprovoked aggression by Germany the evacuation might be delayed, and if during the occupation or after the expiration of 15 years the Reparation Commission found that Germany refused to observe the whole or part of her obligations with regard to reparations, the whole or part of the areas would be reoccupied by the Allied and Associated forces.

By the Financial Clauses (Part IX), the German Government were obliged to pay in gold marks, as a prior charge, the total cost of all Armies of the Allied and Associated Powers in Occupied German Territory from the date of the signature of the Armistice of 11th November, 1918, including pay and allowances, "keep of men and beasts," and lodging, transport, training and maintenance.

Many matters in the Treaty were of permanent military importance, such as : the inclusion of the Covenant of the League of Nations ; the changed status of Belgium ; the break-up of the Austro-Hungarian Empire and the emergence of Poland, Czechoslovakia and a new, much reduced, Austria ; the creation of the free city of Danzig ; the demilitarization of Heligoland and the Kiel rectangle ; and the renunciation of German colonies.

To ensure the execution of the Armament clauses of the Treaty (Articles 203–8), three Inter-Allied commissions of control, military, naval and air, were to be formed and to establish themselves at the seat of the central German Government in Berlin. These commissions would take their instructions from the Versailles Allied Military Committee, over which Maréchal Foch presided, whose duty it was to advise the Allied Governments on military questions regarding the execution of the Peace Treaty.

The Germans never intended to carry out, and did not carry out, either the letter or the spirit of the Treaty. On 13th December, 1919, the Minister of War, Noske, said to a member of the Military Inter-Allied Commissions of Control :

> " We signed the Peace Treaty knowing we could never fulfil the terms and believing no nation would ever expect us to do so."[1]

On 7th July, 1920, at the Spa Conference of the Supreme Council, convened to settle certain details of the execution of the Peace Treaty, when Mr. Lloyd George was pressing the German delegates to carry out disarmament, particularly of the irregular corps, Dr. Fehrenbach, the then *Reichs* Chancellor, " exclaimed with apparent sincerity "

> " ' I am an old man who will soon be appearing before the Great Judge ; believe me, therefore, I beg of you, when I say I am perfectly honest in my desire and in my undertaking to execute the Treaty, but I cannot achieve the impossible.' "[2]

THE RHINELAND DECLARATION

On 16th June, twelve days before the signature of the Treaty, the Governments of the U.S.A., Great Britain and France had made a curious Declaration, a subject of considerable controversy later on, with regard to the Occupation of the Rhine Provinces.[3] It announced that the three Powers did not insist on making the occupation last until the reparation clauses had been completely executed, on the assumption

---

[1] *Memoirs of Sir Almeric Fitzroy* [Clerk of the Privy Council], ii., p. 717.
[2] D'Abernon, i., p. 63.
[3] Appendix XXII, partly summarized here.

that Germany would be obliged to give every proof of her good will and every necessary guarantee before the fifteen years were up.

The Rhineland Agreement

Further, on the same day as the signature of the Peace Treaty took place, a special Agreement (known as " The " Rhineland Agreement ") with regard to the Military Occupation of the Territories of the Rhine was reached between the U.S.A., Belgium, the British Empire and France.[1] This document brought into existence a civilian body, styled " The " Inter-Allied Rhineland High Commission," which was to be " the supreme representative of the Allied and Associated " Powers within the Occupied Territory," that is, it was to supersede the military authority as ruler. It thus brought about the second period of the occupation. The powers of the High Commission were to come into effect on the ratification of the Peace Treaty, which, owing to lack of unanimity among the Allies, did not happen until 10th January, 1920,[2] thus giving the Great General Staff time to marshal voters and organize intimidation in the plebiscite areas already mentioned.[3]

In the discussions on the terms of peace, the organization of the Occupation of the Rhineland, under the conditions which would obtain after the ratification of the peace treaty, had taken an important place. On 29th May, 1919, the Supreme War Council had decided to create an " Inter-Allied Commission for the Left Bank of the Rhine," and by its terms of reference this body was to prepare the draft of a convention respecting the Occupation of the Rhineland Provinces The president of the Commission was M. Loucheur (lately Minister of Munitions), with Lord Robert Cecil (Great Britain), Mr. John Davis (U.S.A.), Baron de Gaiffier d'Hestroy (Belgium) and Marchese Imperiali (Italy) as members. Maréchal Foch and other soldiers were associated with the Commission only as expert witnesses.

---

[1] Appendix XXIII. It should be read at this stage, as it goes into detail, particularly Article 8, as to the rights of the troops of occupation.

[2] The U.S.A. did not ratify, but on 25th August signed a separate Peace Treaty with Germany, ratified on 11th November. It was the same as the Treaty of Versailles, except that the U.S.A. were not bound by the Articles relating to the Covenant of the League of Nations, or to those parts of that Treaty relating to " Boundaries of Germany," " Political Clauses for Europe " (including the section on the Saar Basin), and " German Rights and Interests outside Germany " (e.g. in China, Liberia and Egypt, but the Section on the German Colonies held good).

[3] Chapter X.

The great question on which the Commission had to adjudicate was whether the occupation should be a military occupation under the military authority, maintaining the state of siege (as the Germans had done in the occupation of the eastern provinces of France in 1871), or—for the first time in the history of occupations—a civil one, under a High Commission composed of the representatives of the Occupying Powers, which could if necessary, re-establish a state of siege. The power of the High Commission would be sovereign, and it would govern not only the local German civil authorities (who would retain their administrative functions) and the inhabitants, but also the Allied generals and the troops of occupation, that is the occupying military force would become the instrument of a civil organization.

A scheme for civil control had been put forward by Mr. P. B. Noyes, an American industrialist friend and counsellor of President Wilson, in a letter in which he suggested that the civil régime should be based on the general principles :

I. As few troops as possible, concentrated in barracks or special areas, with no billeting on the inhabitants, except, perhaps, in the case of officers.

II. Complete autonomy of the Occupied Territory, with certain exceptions ;

III. A civil commission, having the necessary powers :

(a) to issue regulations or change existing German regulations in every case when German law or German action either imperilled the execution of the enactments of the Peace Treaty or the well-being or the security of the troops of occupation ;

(b) to authorize the Army to resume power under a state of siege, either at vital points or over the whole territory, at any time that the Commission judged that the situation rendered this measure necessary.

The proposal for civil control prevailed, and the recommendations of the Commission were embodied in the Agreement already mentioned.

THE BIRTH OF THE INTER-ALLIED RHINELAND HIGH COMMISSION

It has been mentioned that in November, 1918, Maréchal Foch had called into existence a body, under the presidency of M. Paul Tirard, known as the Luxembourg Commission, to co-ordinate in his name the administrative measures to be taken in occupied territory,[1] M. Tirard subsequently receiving the title of " *Controleur général de l'administration des territoires occupés* ". The authority of this Commission was very small " as a result of certain Governments failing to give their Armies " instructions, and there was no uniformity, particularly in " economic matters, either in method or in practice."[2] In April, 1919, therefore, the Supreme Economic Council in Paris formed a sub-committee to deal with the most urgent economic questions in Occupied Territory, and deputed to a local authority, to be called the " *Commission interalliée des territoires rhénans* " the duty of carrying out the directives of the sub-committee. This Commission met on 29th April, 1919.

It was the Luxembourg Commission in a stronger form. M. Tirard, renamed " *commissaire de la République française*," remained the president, but was primarily a member of Maréchal Foch's staff ; he was not an appointed official of an Inter-Allied body ; the British member was Sir Harold Stuart, an Indian civil servant,[3] the American, Mr. P. B. Noyes, industrialist, and the Belgian, M. Digneffe, senator and industrialist. The rôle of the Commission was solely economic, and, with the assistance of the existing economic section in each Army, it set about continuing the task of providing food, fuel and raw material in Occupied Territory, and promoting trade between the territory and the various Allied countries. At the request of the German Government, after some hesitation, the Allied Governments permitted Herr von Starck to join the Commission as a co-opted member to represent the *Reich*.[4]

When three months later, on 28th June, the question of the constitution of the High Commission under the special Agreement had to be settled,[5] the Allied Governments had already decided that M. Tirard's commission sitting at Luxembourg, which now had some experience of Rhineland affairs, should be transformed into the High Commission, and take charge not only of economic matters, but also of the due co-

---

[1] See p. 55–6.

[2] Tirard, p. 100. This unfortunately was the case. The administrative difficulties due to the occupation of the Rhineland by four different Armies with different administrative systems and occupying areas which did not conform to German administrative districts, must be borne in mind.

[3] He had specialized in police and C.I.D. investigation ; had been Home Secretary in India ; during 1916–18 he was in the Ministry of Food, London.

[4] He was a Prussian civil servant who had been *Regierungspräsident* at Cologne, and therefore had special knowledge of the government of the Rhineland.

[5] See Appendix XXIII.

ordination of administration. Herr von Starck continued duty with the new Commission as *Reichskommissar*.

The American Government declined to appoint Mr. Noyes to any function other than observer. The Belgian delegate always supported M. Tirard, so that the President commanded a majority without having to use the casting vote assigned to him, and he became the Autocrat of the Occupied Territory. M. Tirard's policy has been thus summarized[1] :

" Maximum diminishing of German influence. Forcing of French culture. Fashioning of Separatism. Industrial and commercial exploitation of the Occupied Territory. Sanctions. Linking of the Ruhr with the Left Bank. Grande Finale : Determining coup when the left bank had become sufficiently demoralized, dependent and ripe to succumb to the ' Join France ' lure."

THE HIGH COMMISSION ORDINANCES AND INSTRUCTIONS

The High Commission at once set to work to make preparations for its task, and drafted a Proclamation of its policy[2] and eleven Ordinances (77 Articles), which had the force of law in relation to persons in Occupied Territory who were not subject (in the British Area) to the Army Act. These, with five Instructions,[3] it issued from Luxembourg on the very day and at the very hour, 10th January, 1920, 4.15 p.m., Peace was ratified, an event which deeply affected and radically changed the position of the Armies of Occupation and the status of their commanders. A preliminary article of the Ordinances laid down that

" the Inter-Allied High Command, the Army commands and the competent German authorities shall be responsible, in so far as they are severally concerned, for the execution of the Ordinances of the High Commission."

The Ordinances contained a number of legal articles, but otherwise consolidated and legalized under the new conditions the various *Anordnungen* issued over the name of the Military Governor, whose office, it has been seen, the High Commission immediately abolished. They dealt with the operation of German laws and regulations in the Occupied Territories ; criminal and civil law ; civil jurisdiction ; offences relating to the occupation ; immunity from proceedings for acts under authority of the Commission ; movement of persons ; postal,

---

[1] Tuohy, p. 179.
[2] See Note at end of Chapter.
[3] Appendix XXIV.

telegraphic and telephonic communications ; the press ; public meetings ; the possession of and trade in arms and ammunition ; sport ; the administration of the Kehl bridgehead ; and the safety and requirements of the Allied forces in case of industrial disputes.

The five Instructions referred to the use of the Allied forces in the Occupied Territories for the maintenance of public order ; the duties of the German authorities in matters of Security and Police ; the appointment and dismissal of German public officials ; the notification of disease ; and certain exemptions from the jurisdiction of all courts in occupied German territory.   The original Ordinances were followed in the course of the occupation by 376 others, making a total of 387, besides dozens of instructions and decisions, which will be dealt with later.

MOVE OF THE HIGH COMMISSION TO COBLENCE

A few days later the High Commission migrated to Coblence. For the residence of M. Tirard and its offices it took possession, much to the annoyance of the German civil hierarchy, of the Palace of the *Oberpräsidium* of the Rhineland Provinces, a huge block of modern buildings containing a vice-regal residence with reception and ball rooms and magnificent offices.   The military authorities had been content with hotels. The ousted Germans were informed that they could move to the less imposing private mansion which the *Oberpräsidium* had selected for the High Commission.   A huge staff was collected, and delegates were stationed in the various *Kreise*. These for the most part were officers of the Armies of Occupation who were already acting in a similar capacity as representatives of the Military Governor.[1]   The military machinery for liaison and information was also retained.

An Inter-Allied guard was provided for the High Commission consisting of a company of French chasseurs for the President, and for the British and Belgian High Commissioners a platoon of British troops (Highlanders when possible) and a platoon of Belgian grenadiers.

Mr. Noyes soon left the Commission and was succeeded in the capacity of observer by Major-General Allen, the commander of the American contingent.   The U.S.A., not being a party to the High Commission, the Ordinances and other

---

[1] Tirard, p. 116.

pronouncements of that body were without validity in the American area ; Major-General Allen tactfully got over this difficulty by issuing them, as supreme authority, over his own signature.[1] Sir Harold Stuart resigned in October, 1920,[2] Mr. Arnold Robertson taking his place until the arrival of Lord Kilmarnock (of the Diplomatic Service) to succeed him.[3]

Herr von Starck proved quite incapable of combating the skill and brains of M. Tirard either at the council table or in the Frenchman's subtle outside campaign of pressure and persuasion. He had at the very outset shown his native diplomatic clumsiness by refusing to dine with M. Tirard and forbidding his staff to have friendly relations with the Allied delegates. He proved so unhelpful a colleague that, on 6th May, 1921, the High Commission unanimously requested his removal, and he resigned on 30th May. His policy, no doubt dictated to him, had been to ignore German precedents and to attempt to limit to the minimum the rights and prerogatives of the occupying Armies by interpreting in their very narrowest sense the Articles of the Rhineland Agreement.[4]

After an interval of a month the German Government informed the Occupying Powers that they desired to nominate Prinz Hatzfeld-Wildenburg in Starck's place. Certain conditions, however, were now made : that the German representative should co-operate with the High Commission, that all secret societies should be dissolved, that indemnities should not be paid to persons punished by the Military Courts, and that Germans wanted by the military tribunals, who had fled into unoccupied territory should be given up. These conditions accepted, Hatzfeld-Wildenburg's nomination was formally approved, and in October, 1921 he entered on his duties. He gave the same trouble as his predecessor, and during the Ruhr occupation in 1923 left the High Commission. After Locarno the *Reich* proposed that Baron Langwerth von Simmern, German Ambassador at Madrid, should become Commissioner. He was accepted and though incidents occurred nothing seems to have troubled his good relations with the Allied representatives.

---

[1] American Summary i., p. 21.

[2] In 1921 he was sent as British Commissioner to the Inter-Allied Upper Silesian Commission. He died on 1st March, 1923.

[3] He succeeded as Earl of Erroll on 8th July, 1927, and died as High Commissioner on 20th February, 1928.

[4] For instance, he insisted that no Ordinance could be promulgated without his agreement, that a state of siege could not be proclaimed until he had been consulted. He tried to force the Allies to limit their rights of requisition, their control of the railways and their supervision of the police. Tirard, p. 107–8. American Summary, p. 186.

THE CHANGES INVOLVED BY THE ADVENT OF THE RHINELAND HIGH COMMISSION

By the advent of the Rhineland High Commission the authority of the Commander-in-Chief of the Occupying Armies was considerably restricted. The Army commanders under him were no longer responsible for the civil government, but they retained power to billet and requisition, to try by Military Court offenders against the person or property of their forces, and to take steps to restore order in an emergency, reporting their action at once to the High Commission. Their powers, however, derived sanction not from rights inherent in the commander of an Occupying Army as defined in and regulated by the Hague Rules, but from the express terms of the Rhineland Agreement. Conditions were practically the same, though technically different.

For the inhabitants the principal changes were that permits were no longer necessary for circulation, that the controls, except on the railways, were withdrawn, and that regulation of prices could not be enforced except by the Germans themselves.

To the troops the new régime brought alleviation in that they had far fewer controls and posts to find, but otherwise it made little difference.

The following notification of the existence of the High Commission was sent out from British Army headquarters on 15th January, 1920 :

> " The following instructions are issued in regard to the Ordinances and Instructions of the Inter-Allied Rhineland High Commission, copies of which were issued on the 13th instant.
>
> " 1. Troops will for the present remain in undisturbed possession of any premises, whether billets or buildings used for other purposes, now occupied by them, and any requests by the German authorities for their evacuation will be referred to these headquarters for instructions. (*See* Art. 7.)
>
> Billeting instructions for the billeting of civilians and military officers and their families will shortly be issued. (*See* Art. 8.)
>
> " 2. The arrangements at present in force regarding the transportation of and non-payment of duties on food supplies, etc., for the Army of Occupation will continue. (*See* Art. 9.)
>
> " 3. Private telegrams and telephones used for private purposes (with the exception detailed in G.R.O. 3736 of December 19th, 1919)[1] will continue to be paid for. (*See* Art. 11.)

---

[1] Not discovered.

" 4. It is the duty of members of the police force, whether Allied or German, to ensure the execution of the Ordinances of the High Commission. The military police are therefore empowered to arrest, with or without the assistance of the German police, any person, whether Allied or German, who contravenes these Ordinances, or commits any offence against the persons or property of the Armed Forces of the Allies. Normally, however, arrest should be carried out by the German police. (*See* Ordinance No. 2, Arts. 1–5.)[1]

" 5. The above offences are contained in Ordinance No. 2, Part III, Articles 24–30 inclusive, Ordinance No. 3, Part I, Articles 2 and 10, Part III, Article 15, Part IV, Article 18, Part V, Articles 20–22, and Part VI, Articles 24–26.

" 6. Circulation in the Occupied Rhineland Territories is unrestricted and permits are no longer required. With the exceptions noted below, every person over 14 years of age, of whatsoever nationality, having his legal domicile in the Occupied Rhineland Territories must, however, provide himself with an identity card, with a photograph attached, and endorsed under their responsibility by the competent German authorities. The exceptions are the armed forces of the Allies and persons accompanying them, to whom special passes have been issued by the General Officers Commanding the Armies of Occupation. In the British Area the persons accompanying the Army of Occupation (i.e., wives and families, members of the Church Army, Y.M.C.A., etc.) must be in possession of the white pass issued by the British military authorities. All civilians other than those accompanying the Armies of Occupation must be in possession of a passport issued by their national authorities and must obey the provisions of the German law on travellers. (Ordinance No. 3, Articles 1 to 7, and Ordinance No. 2, Article 1, and Article 2, clause 5.)

" 7. By the Peace Treaty the Neutral Zone is to extend for 50 kilometres east of the Rhine. The existing Neutral Zone and its extension according to the Peace Treaty, as well as unoccupied Germany are " out of bounds " to all troops, and permission to visit them must first be obtained from G.H.Q. The exact limits of the complete Neutral Zone will be notified later.

" 8. The Control of the Frontier of British Occupied Territory is cancelled, except as regards the Railway and Rhine Control Posts which will continue as heretofore. The instructions regarding the British Frontier Control in para. 4 (*a*), (*b*) and (*c*), Section III of O.A.98 dated May, 1919, are cancelled.

" 9. Instruction No. 1 of the Rhineland High Commission regarding the ' Use of the Allied Forces in the Occupied Territories for the Maintenance of public order ' (*vide* Article 2) is not quite clear in some respects and an explanation has been requested. Meanwhile it should not be interpreted to override the instructions

---

[1] The German police might arrest members of the Armies of Occupation caught in commission of serious crime such as murder, rape, arson, burglary, but had, without delay, to hand them over to the nearest Allied authority.
Germans held for offences against the Armies of Occupation were confined in a separate branch of the British Military Detention Barracks ; for if sent to German prisons in the Occupied Area they received preferential treatment.

contained in para. 4 (*d*) of S/2632 of the 2nd August, and normally the local military commander on receiving a request for the employment of troops will refer the question for approval to these headquarters. Should an emergency arise, it will be dealt with as in Clause 7 of Instruction No. 1.

C. G. Fuller,

Brigadier-General,

General Staff."

G.S. (O).,

General Headquarters.

15th January, 1920.

The following procedure in case of disturbances was laid down.

" The representative of the High Commission, known for short as the British Administrator, Cologne, will deal with all local disturbances in the town, and have at his disposal the A.P.M. Cologne and the Military Police.

" Should he consider that the police at his disposal are insufficient to deal with the situation, he will call on the 2nd Rhine Brigade (Riehl Barracks) for assistance up to one company of infantry.

" If this force is not sufficient, he then will consider a Civil Disturbance to have occurred and will report to the G.O.C. through the Staff Captain for Civil Affairs that he cannot cope with the situation. The G.O.C. will then order, if he thinks necessary, the G.O.C. Rhine Garrison to take over control.

" As soon as the military take over control all Military Police come under their orders.

" If a serious Civil Disturbance should break out suddenly, a maroon will be fired to warn all soldiers to return at once to their billets, and all British and Allied civilians to proceed to their allotted places for protection.

" This signal will be fired only on the orders of a Staff officer of field rank, of a brigadier or general officer of higher rank, or a commanding officer of a unit."

For the professed purpose of assisting the High Commission, but really to aid in obstructing it, in April, 1920, the German Government brought into existence a *Reichsvermögensverwaltung* (National Property Administration) to control all national property in the Occupied Territory. Its duties were to meet the requirements of the occupying forces with regard to funds, housing and military buildings and lands in general. Although it was obviously part of another attempt to divert into a single channel all dealings with the Allies, the new body was permitted by the High Commission to begin operations on the assurance that its object was to co-operate in supplying the needs of the Armies. Early in 1921, however, it started obstructive tactics, refusing, for instance, to repair certain military buildings and construct others. Under the powers of the High Commission, the head of the new organization and three other officials were removed, and direct negotiations with the ordinary civil authorities resumed.

THE MILITARY INTER-ALLIED COMMISSION OF CONTROL[1]

It was the task of this Committee of Control to superintend the execution of the military clauses (159–80) of the Peace Treaty. Besides the destruction of arms and armament factories, these included the modification of German military legislation (under Article 211) for the abolition of universal service and the reduction of the Army, and the prohibition to maintain or construct fortifications on the left bank of the Rhine, or within fifty kilometres of the right bank.

In September, after the signing of the Peace Treaty, at the suggestion of the German Government, an advanced Commission was sent to Berlin in order to give some idea as to what would be required and to make the preliminary arrangements.

The head of this advanced party was General Nollet (who had commanded the French I Corps), and he became president when, on the ratification of the Treaty, the full Commission assembled. Belgium, Great Britain, Italy and Japan (not the U.S.A.) were represented respectively by Major-General de Guffroy, Major-General Hon. F. R. Bingham (an artillery-man, who was followed later by Major-General A. G. Wauchope), General Calcagno and Colonel Furuya, with a British legal expert (Colonel J. H. Morgan, followed in 1923 by Lieut.-Colonel Norris).

Three sub-commissions were formed to deal respectively with armaments (presided over by Major-General Bingham), effectives (presided over by a French general), and fortifications (presided over in the absence of a U.S.A. delegate by a French colonel). Twenty-two district committees were assembled, 11 for armaments, 8 for effectives and 3 for fortifications. They had their headquarters in 13 towns, as two, even three, committees found it convenient to reside in the same place. The towns were Berlin, Königsberg, Breslau, Stettin, Dresden, Munich, Stuttgart, Cologne,[2] Hanover, Düsseldorf, Frankfort, Münster and Kiel.

---

[1] A printed French report of this Commission, 514 pages foolscap, *Commission Militaire interalliée de Contrôle. Rapport Final* (Imprimerie Nationale, Paris) is available.

[2] The Cologne Committee consisted of an artillery lieutenant-colonel as president, an average strength of 18 British officers (constantly changed), the majority of whom held temporary commissions in the R.A.O.C., several interpreters, one or two French delegates and one Belgian.

The Commission at its inception numbered 337 officers (109 British), with 573 other ranks. By July, 1921 the maximum of 383 officers and 737 other ranks had been attained. By September, 1924 the total had fallen to 174 officers and about 400 other ranks, and finally at its dissolution, after seven years, included no more than 35 and 89. All these officers and their clerical staffs were housed by the German Government at the principal hotels in the different towns, provided with transport facilities and given allowances for the cost of living.

By Article 206 of the Peace Treaty, qualified German liaison officers were to be attached to each of the three Commissions to act as intermediaries between the Commissioners and the German military and civil authorities. General von Seeckt made use of this loophole to form an opposing organization, called the *Heeresfriedenskommission* (Army Peace Commission), under General von Cramon.[1] It had a *Hauptverbindungsstelle* (Principal Liaison Office) in Berlin with a section for each of the three Sub-Commissions of Control, and a *Verbindungsstelle* for each of the inter-Allied district committees. Its business was to organize obstruction and resistance, not to assist ; to shadow the officers of the Commission ; and to give warning of the visits of these officers. Without the support of the smallest force, the Commission was to a great extent in the hands of the *Verbindungs* officers.[2] These, among other instructions, had one to the effect that " war material " was material whose sole use was for battle and was unusable in civil life : thus even flame-throwers were not instruments of war because these could be used to quell riots and spray vines. The *Verbindungs* officers had to permit a certain amount of destruction, but it was mostly of material not immediately required for the German reserve forces. Their word of honour was found worthless.[3]

The chief work of the Armament Sub-Commission was to receive the surrender of war material and supervise its destruction. The material was handed over to a German company (*Reichstreuhandgesellschaft*, the *Reichs* trust company), formed *ad hoc*, which set up about a thousand destruction centres. The schedule of articles for destruction contained 37 headings and

---

[1] German plenipotentiary with the Austro-Hungarian Army, 1914–18.

[2] When Napoleon disarmed Prussia after the battle of Jena, the search parties were supported by garrisons in the fortresses and principal towns.

[3] For instance : a liaison officer gave his word of honour, at the close of a day's inspection, that certain material should not be interfered with. By next morning it had disappeared. He explained that he meant that he would not personally move it.

included such items as tanks and armoured cars, all military harness, field bakeries, apparatus for military mining and military bridges, barbed wire specially prepared for war purposes, uniforms of every kind.[1] The totals of some of the most important articles said to have been destroyed were : guns, 33,556 ; machine guns, 87,946 ; gun ammunition, 39,254,827 rounds ; small arm ammunition, 497 million rounds.

Its next most important work was the attempt to carry out the destruction or conversion of machinery in the over 7,000 factories which had made war materials. Such success as was achieved was only temporary.

The Effectives Sub-Commission supervised the conversion of the German Army into the post-war Army of 100,000 men, the abolition of various educational establishments and schools for the training of officers, and the formation of a new police force.

At a special conference held at Spa in July, 1920, at which the French, British and German Prime Ministers were present, the German Minister of Defence, Herr Gessler, made a formal statement that an Army of only 100,000 men was too small a force to keep order. He had to admit the existence of the *Einwohnerwehr* (Home Guard) and *Sicherheitspolizei* (Security Police, known as " *Sipo* "), and large " Private Armies," probably about a million armed men.[2] The only concession he obtained was a delay of six months, until 1st January, 1921, in which to reduce the *Reichswehr* to 100,000, to withdraw the arms of the *Einwohnerwehr* and *Sipo*, and to secure the surrender of arms in the possession of the civil population.

The Fortifications Sub-Commission inspected the fortifications and gave the necessary orders, at Kiel in co-operation with the Naval Commission, for the destruction of the forts which were to be dismantled or destroyed. Owing to the militarily inexact wording of the Peace Treaty (Article 180), the Germans raised many quibbles, and little was done for six months. They said " a line drawn 50 kilometres to the east of the Rhine " meant a line obtained by tracing the course of the river on transparent paper which should then be shifted 50 kilometres eastward. This brought about curious results at the double right-angle bend of the Rhine near Mayence, and the line was not what the Treaty makers probably meant, a line at no point within 50 kilometres of the river. The

---

[1] The schedule was contained in a printed *Organization and Proposed Method of Procedure of Munitions, Armament and Material Sub-Commission of the Military Inter-Allied Commission of Control.*

[2] The irregular German forces are discussed in the next chapter.

Germans also contended that " the system of fortified works " of the southern and eastern frontiers " which might be maintained, did not mean only the defences near the national borders, but included all fortifications back to Berlin facing east or south. The Germans were of course justified ; it was the draftsmen of the Treaty who were at fault. Not until 1927 was a demarcation line fixed.[1]

The limit line of the fortifications was not the only point that the Peace Treaty offered as an opportunity for difference of interpretation. " Material of War " not being defined in the Treaty,[2] did it or did it not include motor cars (not armoured) and lorries of civilian pattern used by the Army ? In the former case were those supernumerary to the permitted establishment, though of general use, to be destroyed ?

Article 203 read :

> " All the military, naval and air clauses contained in the present Treaty, for the execution of which a *time-limit* is prescribed, shall be executed by Germans under the control of Inter-Allied Commissions specially appointed for the purpose."

The Germans argued that the abolition of universal compulsory service (Article 173) and other matters for which no time limit was fixed were not within the purview of the Commission of Control.

Article 168 directed that all establishments for the manufacture of arms and munitions, except a limited approved number, should, according to the French text, be " *supprimés* " (a verb whose meaning *Littré* defines as " *faire disparaître* ") ; the English text said " closed down." The Germans naturally claimed the latter interpretation.

On the last day of 1920 Maréchal Foch reported to the Allied Governments on the progress of disarmament. As regards the surrender of weapons and aircraft it was satisfactory but incomplete ; otherwise it was claimed that the stipulations of the Peace Treaty had not been fulfilled, the *Einwohnerwehr* in East Prussia and Bavaria had not been disbanded, and the system of fortifications on the southern and eastern frontiers had not been left, as covenanted, " in its existing state."

---

[1] The question of the fortifications in the Rhine Neutral Zone is dealt with in the next chapter.

[2] Not only was " Material of War " not defined in the Treaty, but it was not laid down who was to define it : it should have been the Commission of Control. Further, by Article 204, which was the cause of endless delays, the Principal Allied and Associated Powers reserved the right to themselves, instead of to the Commission of Control, to take decisions.

In spite of the exertions of the Commissions of Control, it is only too well known that Germany was never disarmed.

From first to last the Military Commission met with evasion and opposition, and General von Seeckt did his best to disembarrass himself of it and get on with rearmament unnoticed.[1]

Constant endeavour was made to intimidate the members of the Commission, passive resistance to them was usual, and in a few cases they were exposed to physical violence. In the closing months of 1922 there were incidents at Stettin, and at Passau and Ingolstadt mobs made attacks on them and stoned their cars. The Conference of Ambassadors[2] demanded an apology and a payment of 500,000 gold marks by each of the two latter towns, under threat that the revenues sent to Bavaria from the Palatinate would be stopped. The money was paid. At all three places the responsible police officers and military commander were dismissed.

Three times relations between the Commission and the German authorities were interrupted : first when the Allied Governments demanded the surrender of many high officers of the German Army as " war criminals " ; secondly, in March, 1920 when, during the Kapp putsch, a revolutionary Government was in power for a short time ; and thirdly, for twenty months, when, in January, 1923, the French and Belgians occupied the Ruhr.[3] These interruptions of the surveillance of

---

[1] Many illustrations of the German obstruction could be quoted—they were later boasted of. Guhr, who was one of the German representatives attached to the Commission, gives the following. The Commission demanded entrance to some locked cellars in a fort, where it was assured there was nothing. No key was forthcoming, so the doors had to be opened by a locksmith. The electric lighting had been cut off, but by the light of torches the Commissioners saw a number of chests. The German representative would not allow soldiers to open them : " Soldiers," he said, " don't enter into the question of working for the enemy." No civilians appearing for some hours, the younger members of the Commission broke open the chests and found them full of military apparatus. The German author himself says : " There was every appearance from the freshly opened and broken chests, that there had been more stuff in them which had been recently removed in great haste."

The official excuse was that these chests had been stolen and hidden by revolutionaries, and owing to the dissolution of the Army had been lost sight of.

[2] The Supreme Council of the Allied Powers formally came to an end as such on 21st January, 1920, after the ratification of the Peace Treaty. It was succeeded in Paris by the Conference of Ambassadors, consisting of the American, British, Italian and Japanese Ambassadors and a French representative. The business of the Conference was to settle the technical details of the Treaty, under instructions from their Governments. For all important decisions, such as " sanctions," the Supreme Council was revived, meeting at various places.

[3] An interesting lecture on " Work with the Allied Commission of Control in Germany 1919–24," was delivered by Major-General Hon. Sir Francis Bingham at the Royal United Service Institution (see *Journal*, Vol. LXIX, pp. 747–63).

the Commissioners gave the German liaison officers opportunity to conceal stores of arms more thoroughly ; and when inspections were resumed after the long third cessation they were no more than an attempt to save-face. Organized obstruction was offered even to this, not only by the armed forces, but also by the police and, to some extent, by public and private authorities.

The German Government continued to ask for many relaxations of the Treaty terms, including permission to keep, provisionally, a number of supernumerary officers and n.c.os., all of which were refused. Certain, however, that hostilities would not be resumed, they, or rather General von Seeckt with their connivance, continued to raise and train camouflaged forces and reserves under the guise of police,[1] of patriotic societies and of Sports and Social Clubs, really " Private Armies."[2] The *Reichsheer* was only for a short period reduced to 100,000 ; the condition of 12 years' service was ignored, and large numbers were passed through its ranks to form a reserve. Both officers and other ranks were picked men, calculated to form a corps of instructors ; in the choice of officers, those with the Staff College certificate were taken first.[3] Other officers of the old Army were hidden in the police, the universities and the railway service. The abolished Staff College course of three years in Berlin was carried on by three courses of one year, called *Wehrkreis* classes (an authorized form of training), at three different towns ; the work of the General Staff was performed by a large so-called Historical Section ; the duties in connection with registration for service and mobilization, by the Pensions offices.

Arms too were not lacking. The Commission in reporting that a number of arms factories had been closed down, said that " the restoration of the factories to war purposes remains, " nevertheless, a possible eventuality," and that, although considerable quantities of material had been destroyed or put out of use, " these do not include great quantities in excess of the " authorized establishments."

In the original census of arms the local authorities had admitted the possession of a total of **988,523** rifles and **8,528**

---

[1] See next chapter.   [2] See Chapter XVIII.

[3] Seeckt said to his staff : " Direction of my endeavours : out of the small army to create the army of leaders of the future." In order to train the staff the *Reichswehr* Ministry was filled with supernumerary officers, so that, in joke, it was called *Wasserkopf*" (that is " a person with swollen head "). (M.W.B. No. 26 of 25th December, 1942, columns 707–8.)

machine guns ; it was claimed by the German Government that 816,916 and 7,419, respectively, had been given up ; actually only 702,350 and 6,402 had been surrendered. Everywhere over the *Reich* were secret depôts of arms, large and small, not only of rifles, pistols and ammunition, but also tanks, guns, trench mortars, military vehicles, and other war material. The position of some of these was revealed to the Commission of Control by informers. They were found in barracks, forts, police and municipal buildings, factories and business premises, farms, restaurants, schools and private houses.[1] When 10,000 rifles were discovered at Königsberg in July, 1920, the German authorities merely said that they knew of this depôt and were just about to declare it. For fear of " incidents," the Conference of Ambassadors virtually forbade the Commission of Control to make unexpected visits in search of arms, and at the time of " Locarno " the Commission reported that " arms, forbidden by Treaty, in quantities impossible to cal- " culate, but certainly far from negligible, still exist in Germany, " arms which, owing to the restrictions imposed, can only be " revealed by the German Government itself." A nation which does not want to be disarmed cannot be made to deliver up its weapons except by force, and it must be done at once before the people and the government have recovered from the shock of defeat. But by the end of 1920 it may be said that Germany was for the moment quite powerless to fight a war with any fully organized military power ; part of the armament and material requisite for an Army in a European war had been surrendered and destroyed and, so many factories had been temporarily put out of action that guns and war material could not be replaced in sufficient quantity for a considerable time. The old Army had been broken up and the new Army reduced to small numbers, but the old cadres were available and large numbers of reserves were already under training.[2] There seemed, however, no fear of an organized aggressive military operation on the part of Germany in the near future unless all the Armies of Occupation were reduced to small dimensions. It is known now that General von Seeckt and his successors did not intend to move until they could regard the result as an absolute certainty.

---

[1] A long list is given in the Final Report of the Inter-Allied Military Commission of Control (French text), pp. 388–93.

[2] See Chapter XII for Germany's camouflaged forces and Chapter XVIII for the " private armies."

NOTE

THE INITIAL PROCLAMATION OF THE INTER-ALLIED RHINELAND HIGH COMMISSION

" Inspired by the instructions of the Allied Governments, the High Commission desires to render as light as possible the burdens of the occupation to the Rhineland population, on the sole condition that the German Government set themselves to carry out the reparation due to the nations which were victims of the War.

" The High Commission guarantees to the Rhineland population, both in letter and in spirit, the Statute of Occupation, and the regulations it contains are not only exceptionally liberal, but also without precedent in history for their mildness.

" The High Commission, on its part, in co-operation with the High Command of the Allied Troops, will watch that nothing is done to endanger the security of the occupying troops. It will repress, without unnecessary severity, also without hesitation, any attempt against the security of those troops. Let it not be forgotten that they in 1918 crossed the frontier with their blood still hot with the excitement of battle, deeply stirred at the sight of their devastated homes and filled with horror at the treatment which had been meted out to their wives, their children and their relatives. These troops, having achieved the greatest of all victories—over themselves—have for more than twelve months brought to the Rhineland the blessings of good order, the benefits of a restored food supply, and the example of discipline.

" The Inter-Allied High Commission desires to count upon the co-operation of the German officials and magistrates in complete harmony with it to ensure to the population of the occupied territories work, peace and the rule of order. Responsible for public order, the assurance of which falls in the last resort on the Armies of Occupation, the Commission intends to guarantee to the Rhineland justice, the exercise of public and individual liberty, the development of legitimate aspirations, and prosperity.

" The High Commission expresses the hope that contact between the troops of the Allied nations and the Rhineland population will not be a source of friction but a means of their learning to know each other better, and, brought together by work, good order and peace, a means of progress towards a higher humanity."

In order to exchange information and to ensure uniformity of action towards the inhabitants of the Occupied Territory and solidarity in bringing matters to the notice of the High Commission, an Inter-Allied Military Commission was formed, and representatives of the American, Belgian, British and French Armies met at Wiesbaden whilst it was in French occupation. Some of the questions discussed were the high prices and inferior quality of the food and forage supplied by German contractors, so that it was cheaper to import comestibles ; the measures to be taken for the supply of food to the civil population in the event of disorders ; the preference given by the German authorities to the population of unoccupied Germany in the distribution of coal ; the illegal sale of craft of the German Rhine flotilla to a Dutch company ; theft of telephones and telephone wire. The majority of subjects discussed concerned small matters such as validity of passes, transportation, navigation and telegraphic facilities in the occupied areas.

CHAPTER XII

LIEUT.-GENERAL SIR T. MORLAND'S COMMAND

3RD MARCH 1920–16TH MARCH 1922

INTERNAL TROUBLES IN THE *REICH* : GERMAN RESISTANCE TO DISARMAMENT AND TO THE REDUCTION OF THE ARMED FORCES

(Sketches 2 and 3)

THE CHIEF OF THE GENERAL STAFF ON THE SITUATION IN THE RHINELAND

At the beginning of March, the C.I.G.S. Field-Marshal Sir Henry Wilson, paid a ten-day visit to the Rhineland, and on the 17th, on his return to London, he submitted a memorandum to the Secretary of State for War. In this he reported, first, that Maréchal Foch a few days before had conducted a war game at Mayence, which was attended by about two hundred generals and staff officers of the Allied Armies. The outcome showed that the Allies were not strong enough to hold the line of the Rhine against a comparatively small force. Secondly, he was of opinion that the Germans no longer feared the Armies of the Rhine ; for the Americans were shortly to be withdrawn ; the Belgians were of poor quality and inefficient ; the British were small in numbers and wholly untrained ; and the French contingent contained 60 per cent. coloured troops.[1] Thirdly,

---

[1] This was a mistake. At the time the Senegalese and Moroccan troops numbered about 15,000 out of 72,000 (see Chapter XIII), and this proportion was normal. In the early days of occupation, when the French Army had been stronger, the total of coloured troops had reached a maximum of 40,000. Many gross exaggerations concerning the numbers and the conduct of the French coloured troops were circulated in the German press (and spread by a portion of the British press). In this connection, it is pertinent to quote the American General Allen's report on the colour question, dated 2nd July, 1921 (American Summary i., p. 95), which had been called for by the War Department :

"The allegations in the German press have been for the most part so indefinite as to time, place and circumstances, as to leave it impracticable to verify the alleged facts, or to disprove them. Their simultaneous appearance was probably an adroit political move which would tend to sow antipathy to France in other lands. The allegations have been refuted by responsible German officials and citizens of the Rhineland. . . . The attitude of certain classes of German women towards the coloured troops has been such as to invite trouble. German women have openly made advances to coloured soldiers, as evidenced by letters and photographs now on file in this office records."

British reports are to the same effect, one of them concluding :

"the immorality and shamelessness of large numbers of German women in the Occupied Territories and in unoccupied Germany was notorious."

Clara Viebig's " *Töchter der Hekuba* " and novels by less distinguished authors confirm this as regards the unoccupied *Reich*.

the neutrality of Holland, in view of the routes of the lines of communication with the United Kingdom, constituted a grave danger. Fourthly, our troops in the plebiscite areas would run considerable risk and danger if they were forced to withdraw under pressure.

Sir Henry Wilson then suggested that a decision should be taken in the near future either to strengthen our force or to withdraw it altogether : if, he said, it was decided to remain, a firm defensive alliance with France and Belgium should be concluded, in which case Holland should be requested to define her situation and intentions ; in any case, the Supreme Council should be pressed to agree to the withdrawal of our forces from Danzig and East Prussia. No action was taken on this advice, except to remove these small garrisons as soon as possible.

THE KAPP PUTSCH

In the early hours of 13th March the marchers of the Kapp putsch, headed by Ehrhardt's *Marine Brigade*, entered Berlin. Their purpose, though it was concealed at the time, was to restore the Hohenzollern régime. Herr Wolfgang Kapp was no corner-boy, but a high Prussian official, a *Generallandschaftsdirektor*, founder of the Fatherland Party, and his movement had the support of General Baron von Lüttwitz, commanding the Berlin garrison (*1st Reichswehr Division*), General Ludendorff and most of the generals. General von Seeckt, commanding the Army, did not send troops to oppose the entry of Kapp and his partisans, saying, officially, that the police could deal with them ; and he then departed on leave. The Republican Government, too, one member only remaining in the capital, decamped to Dresden, and, that city proving unquiet, went on to Stuttgart. Kapp declared himself Chancellor and appointed Lüttwitz as Minister of Defence. The old Imperial colours were hoisted. For four days the Kappites held the capital. The population, however, were against any change from the recently acquired Republic ; a call for a general strike made by President Ebert met with an almost universal response, and this opposition, combined with want of funds and divided councils, killed the putsch. Kapp and Lüttwitz fled to Sweden on the evening of the 17th, and on the 19th their agitation collapsed ; but for a time the Spartacists, taking advantage of the strikes, continued to stand out against the Government.

SPARTACIST INSURRECTION IN THE RUHR[1]

The Kapp movement had immediate repercussions in the provinces. Both Socialists and Spartacists in the Ruhr and Rhineland and adjoining Westphalia openly manifested opposition to the Kapp ideas ; an opportunity for a Spartacist rising seemed to have come ; workmen's mass meetings were held and some looting took place. As early as 13th March Lieut.-General Morland had felt it necessary to order precautionary measures. On the 15th, Opladen[1] and Wiesdorf (2 miles south of Opladen), in the bridgehead, set up a Workers' and Soldiers' Council, and evicted the *Bürgermeister*. The British troops were confined to barracks ; tanks paraded Cologne ; an infantry company was railed to Opladen ; cavalry and police patrols were sent to the scene of reported looting ; motor transport for moving infantry was assembled, and next day aircraft were sent to fly over Benrath, Opladen and Solingen, from which last place workers were marching via Elberfeld on Remscheid. Soon news was received that Barmen[2], Dortmund and Remscheid were in the hands of the Spartacists. One British battalion was already stationed at Solingen, and orders were given for the move of another battalion from Mülheim to Ohligs,[3] both battalions being placed under the orders of Lieut.-Colonel C. E. Kitson (2/R. West Kent). Two motor launches of the Rhine Flotilla were despatched to guard the petrol dump at Benrath.

On the 19th, 110 officers and 1,450 other ranks of the *Reichswehr* were driven into occupied territory near Solingen by the Spartacists and, caught on a railway viaduct, surrendered to Kitson's forces, now reinforced by a squadron of the Inniskilling Dragoons and a tank detachment. The prisoners were sent to a camp at Dellbrück (north-east of Cologne), and then to two of the old German forts on the western bank of the Rhine, where they were less comfortable. On the 20th, Düsseldorf and Duisburg were reported to be in the hands of the Spartacists and on the 22nd they held the entire Ruhr district.[4]

The German Government requested permission to send additional troops into the Ruhr, now in the 50 kilometre Neutral

---

[1] See Sketch 2.

[2] See End Paper.

[3] Two miles west of Solingen and since 1929 combined with it into one township. It had 30,000 inhabitants ; Solingen 50,000.

[4] The accumulating of arms in the Ruhr had come to notice in a curious way. The perimeter post on the Opladen–Düsseldorf road reported the frequent passing of funerals from the bridgehead to a cemetery in the Neutral Zone. It was decided to open a coffin : it was found to contain rifles, revolvers and ammunition.

Zone, as the police and authorized garrison (due to be removed under the Peace Treaty) were insufficient to deal with the emergency. This was refused by Maréchal Foch, who did not care to run the risk of the presence of a large German force in the proximity of the small Armies of Occupation. Notwithstanding this refusal, General von Watter, commanding the *6th Division* of the new *Reichswehr*, was sent nominally with a brigade, actually as his biography states, " with his little Freecorps of 120,000 men."[1]   During 2nd to 6th April, Watter put down the revolution with a high hand, shooting many of the Spartacists.[2]   On the 4th fugitives of the rising began crossing into British Occupied Territory and handing in arms at Benrath, Hilden and Solingen. They were sent to the camp at Dellbrück, where a post was maintained to keep order, but no guard, and released on the 28th ; for it was the policy of the British not to interfere in any way with German internal politics in the occupied territories—our late adversaries could have any form of government they desired.   On the 10th the *Reichswehr* prisoners were, by Maréchal Foch's orders, sent back to Germany by train via Siegburg, under military escort, and handed over to the German authorities at the frontier.

The French Occupation of Five Cities in the Neutral Zone

The great display of force by the Germans in the new Neutral Zone, in which Essen and the Ruhr were situated, and its despatch there without permission contrary to the provisions of the Peace Treaty, had considerably alarmed Maréchal Foch.   Four days later, on 6th April, in order to secure a gage for their removal, he ordered the occupation by French troops of Darmstadt, Hanau, Homburg, Frankfort and Duisburg, all in the Neutral Zone.   After the trouble in the Ruhr had died down, the German Government satisfied the Allies by reducing the total number of troops in the Neutral

---

[1] " *General Oskar Freiherr von Watter*," a memorial volume published after his death in 1939.   He was one of our principal adversaries at Cambrai in 1917.   The Security Branch reported the presence of large numbers of " Freecorps " formations, actually the most reliable units of the old Army, nominally not in Government pay.   This was of course denied by the German Government.

[2] This slaughter did not please President Ebert, and on 12th July Watter was put on the retired list, whereupon the Old Army proceeded to honour him by electing him President of the Old Comrades of the Field Artillery.

Zone to the 17,500 previously allowed,[1] and the French were withdrawn from the occupied cities. By 23rd April all the British troops had been recalled from the frontier of the bridgehead to their normal garrisons.

During the year a difference of opinion arose as to the dismantlement of the fortifications in the Rhine area. According to the Peace Treaty, Article 180, all fortified works west of the line drawn 50 kilometres east of the Rhine were to be disarmed and dismantled. The Germans protested against the demands of the Inter-Allied Military Commission of Control that this should be carried out to the letter on the ground that they did not want to incur the expense involved. The Army Council were in favour of meeting the German objection on some points, particularly as regards the razing of the ramparts of old works. The Committee of Control, with its French president, was not disposed to give way, and ordered the dismantlement to be completed in six months.

It then appeared that the Armies of Occupation wished certain fortifications maintained, notably all forts on the right bank, as they formed an inner line of defence to the bridgeheads, also certain forts close to the Rhine on the left bank; the destruction of the others on this bank was being proceeded with.[2]

Maréchal Foch then called for a classification of the works into those to be dismantled forthwith and those to be used by the Armies of Occupation until dismantled prior to evacuation. Both Generals Degoutte and Morland then furnished detailed reports. The gist of these was that the minor (all modern) works on the right bank should be retained ; that as far as the British Zone was concerned, they could be demolished by 300 men in $2\frac{1}{2}$ months. This recommendation was approved by the Conference of Ambassadors in February, 1922.

The matter assumed a different aspect in December, 1924, when it appeared that the Dawes Reparation Plan[3] would throw all future expenses of demolition upon the Allies. The complete levelling of the old works was then abandoned, and it was agreed merely to blow up the concrete and brickwork of the others before evacuation, leaving the débris on the spot.

---

[1] See p. 144.

[2] No map showing the forts is available, but from the reports it appears that in the Cologne bridgehead there were 4 main forts, 9 intermediate works, 7 infantry redoubts, and 25 minor infantry and artillery works and magazines, and about three times as many in the Cologne fortifications on the left bank.

[3] See Chapter XVIII.

Events in the Army of the Rhine

At the turn of April and May some fighting between the Spartacists and the *Reichswehr* took place in Düsseldorf ; but, beyond occasioning precautionary measures, this did not affect the Allies.   The rest of the year 1920 passed quietly, except in August, when, by order of the High Commission, a battalion, accompanied by a representative of the Commission, was sent to the Rhineland—Westphalia Electrical Works at Knapsack (8 miles south-west of the Cologne *Dom*), in consequence of a strike.   Its instructions were to maintain law and order, to prevent sabotage, to protect the workmen who wanted to work, and to assist in the arrest of such persons as might be designated by the *Kreis* officials.   On the arrest of a few ringleaders, the strike collapsed.

Field firing and artillery practice were carried out on the Wahn ranges, by arrangement with the French, in whose area these ranges now were.   In August the 1/Royal Irish returned from the Allenstein plebiscite area.   On 24th and 25th October, after being warned on the 19th, in consequence of a coal strike which began on the 16th, the 1/R. Sussex and 3/Middlesex proceeded to the United Kingdom.   They returned on 10th and 11th November.   Armistice Day was duly observed in Cologne.   In December, the 14th (King's) Hussars took the place of the 6th (Inniskilling) Dragoons.   In August the war privilege of free postage for soldiers' letters was withdrawn.

The military portion of the *Südfriedhof* (South Cemetery), Cologne, was acquired by purchase, the Imperial War Graves Commission assuming responsibility for general maintenance, but not for providing headstones.   Later, the military cemetery at Wiesbaden was taken over.

In August, 1920 the air troops with the British Army of the Rhine, No. 12 Squadron R.A.F., had been reduced to one flight (6 machines), and in June, 1921 the Air Ministry, faced with demands elsewhere and having little to meet them, pressed for the withdrawal of even this small contingent.   The permission of Maréchal Foch had to be obtained, and he consented. But he imposed three conditions : that the withdrawal should not take place until the British troops had returned to the Rhine from Silesia ; that one squadron R.A.F. should be held in readiness to reinforce the British Army of the Rhine in case of need ; and that the Bickendorf airfield, north of Cologne, near Ehrenfeld, should be maintained, and French and Allied aircraft authorized to make use of it.   Lieut.-General Morland very naturally desired to retain a few aircraft for combined training ; but he could obtain no satisfaction except a promise that when Ireland was settled with a reallotment of a squadron to the British Army of the Rhine might be considered. The one flight remaining was withdrawn in May, 1922, two months before Maréchal Foch's first condition had been fulfilled. A request of the Army Council to the Air Ministry in 1923 for the loan of some aircraft for co-operative training on the Rhine was refused.

In July, 1924, the War Office proposed to withdraw the tank company from the British Army of the Rhine, offering an armoured car company in exchange. The G.O.C., then Lieut.-General Sir J. Du Cane, objected, and the authorities in London gave way.

By 1921 venereal disease was reported to be well under control in the British Zone. In this matter the British Military Police worked in co-operation with the German. Women could be arrested and sent to German hospitals for examination, and, if necessary, detained. 'They could be deported from the Occupied Zone. In consequence of an agitation at home, Mrs. Corbett Ashby was given permission to visit Cologne in December, 1922. She suggested that British and German women police should be employed to deal with women in the streets. The German authorities were not enamoured of the idea ; but on 1st July, 1923, six British policewomen began duty with three German women attached. As they cost £1,200 per annum without any noticeable result, and were ridiculed by the German press, they were abolished on 31st March, 1925.

At the close of 1921 it was discovered that the German Censorship Office in Cologne had detained and secretly opened letters forwarded through the German Post, addressed to British officers. The High Commission therefore proposed to the commanders of Armies that the German Postal Censorship should be subject to Allied control, and in December found the necessary officials for the purpose in the British sector.

THE POLICE IN THE NEUTRAL ZONE

The number of police to be maintained in the Neutral Zone was a subject of long discussion. The Peace Treaty was scarcely ratified before the High Commission received two memoranda from the Germans. One, dated 11th January, 1920, from the Ministry of the Interior, estimated at 14,000 men the establishment of the extra police necessary in the Neutral Zone after the departure of the troops, and indicated as their armament heavy machine guns, flame-throwers, trench mortars, field howitzers, etc. The second, dated 23rd January, emanated from the military authorities. This claimed that the extra police could not be less in number than the troops, 17,000 to 18,000, previously allowed, adding that this figure was indeed insufficient. In the end, on 2nd September, 1920, a total police force of 20,000 men was permitted, as part of the total of 150,000 police allowed to the *Reich*, and its armament was limited to that of the police in general : sword, hand-grenades, ordinary pistol, a rifle per 3 men, and one machine gun per thousand. For a time, however, there remained in the Neutral Zone, in addition to the 17,000 troops, the greater part of 18,300 police, in possession of a number of all the arms forbidden them, all in close proximity to the small British garrison, and it was only very gradually that the soldiers were withdrawn. A new force was soon to appear in the Neutral Zone.

The *Sipo*

The whole question of police was a thorny one. The German Administration, accustomed to maintain order by fear and brute force, the Army reinforcing the police as required, could not conceive that it could govern without large armed forces, and the Great General Staff was fully prepared to play up to the idea of a highly armed police as a nursery for officers and soldiers. By Article 162 of the Peace Treaty, the *Reich* was allowed the same total of police as before the War, with an addition proportional to any increase of the population since 1913. Deduction made in consequence of lost territory brought this total to about 80,000 men. Directly, however, the Inter-Allied Commission of Control settled down to work, it found in existence in the large towns, in large centres of population and in the Neutral Zone, a new and additional category of police already mentioned, called *Sicherheitspolizei* (Security Police), usually spoken of as " *Sipo*." It had been organized in August, 1919 by the *Reichswehr* Ministry as " Militarized Police," with the name of " *Sicherheitswehr*," nominally to perform duties previously undertaken by the Army at times of strikes and rioting. To avoid Allied attention and objection, " *Wehr* " (guard) had been changed into " *Polizei* " ; but the green colour of the uniform, that of the *Garde Jäger*, had been retained. There was no doubt whatever, that the " Green Police " as the *Sipo* was sometimes called, was a military body ; it was recruited from the Freecorps ; its officers and n.c.os. came from the Old Army ; it possessed a military hierarchy, staffs, and administrative services analogous to those of the Army, and an armament of artillery, tanks and aircraft ; and it received military training.

On 1st December, 1919 the Peace Conference invited the *Reich* to reduce the police to the number mentioned in the Treaty, and restore its former local and municipal character. The German Government replied on 14th February arguing that political and economic circumstances demanded a different sort of police, and that, as to numbers, in consequence of the 8 hours' working day introduced by Article 427 of the Treaty, an augmentation of 75 per cent. over the pre-war establishment was required. The latter reason could not of course stand, as the number of police allowed, and the 8-hour day, formed part of one and the same Treaty.

The Commission of Control, acting on instructions, demanded that the number should be cut down by 10th April, 1920, and pointed out that the police might not possess the prohibited arms (tanks, flame-throwers, gas and aircraft), nor a war armament (artillery, trench mortars, heavy and light machine guns). The German Government did not reply until the very day fixed as the time limit, and then to the effect that the principles on which the police was organized in 1913 had not been changed, and, as regards the *Sipo*, they had nothing to add to their letter of 14th February.

After further correspondence, on 22nd June, 1920, the Allied Governments in the " Boulogne Note " specified that the *Sipo* must be totally dissolved within three months, but consented to the total of the ordinary police being raised to 150,000, armed as the Commission of Control should determine, and retaining its local and municipal character. The Commission authorized some armoured cars, each with two heavy machine guns, in the proportion of one per thousand men. It was not until 4th October, after the expiration of the three months' notice, that Prussia issued the necessary decree, the other States following suit ; but no action was taken, except to change the name of *Sipo* to " Schupo " (*Schutzpolizei*, protective police), and to increase its numbers.

Another intervention by the Allied Governments, the " Paris Note " (29th January, 1921), had no effect, the *Reich* Government merely replying that the police had not the essential characteristics of a military force ; that the numbers in excess of 150,000 were in plain clothes, and therefore not intended by Article 162 to be counted as police.

The London Ultimatum of 5th May, 1921, which will be dealt with later, demanded, as regards the police, that the *Sipo* should cease to be a mobile military force ; that short service in the police should be abolished ; that interchange of personnel between Army and police should be stopped ; that the number of police schools should be reduced to the pre-war figure and their pre-war character resumed ; that the police aircraft formations should be suppressed ; and that the total personnel, uniformed and plain clothes, should be limited to 150,000. On 4th June the *Reich* Government declared its firm intention of conforming to the demands, and it issued circulars ; but nothing was done. In March, 1922, by separate letters addressed to the various Governments, the *Reich* Government openly objected to the idea of the police resuming its local as opposed to its centralized character, on the ground that by " atomizing " it lost its value. Further intervention by the Conference of Ambassadors and the Allied Governments followed, and a " Collective Note " was sent on 4th June, 1925, but the *Reich* took no action except to increase the police by new auxiliaries, called *Hilfspolizei*, *Notpolizei* (Auxiliary and Emergency Police), etc.

Nazi boastings since 1933 have fully demonstrated that the *Sipo* was simply a branch of the *Reichswehr* and that it played its part in the creation of the new German Army. [1]

Other uniformed Government services : the Customs, the Forestry, the prison warders and the penitentiary guards were increased in numbers, although Germany was smaller, and the new services of *Reichwasserschutz* (Waterway Guards) and *Bahnpolizei* (Railway Police for guard of the permanent way, bridges and establishments) were created. All were armed, and all contributed their quota in training soldiers and forming reserves outside the 100,000 men settled by the Peace Treaty.

There were also other scarcely hidden sources of armed strength.

---

[1] The following appeared in *The.Times* of 12th January, 1943, translated from an article in *Deutsche Verwaltung* :

" In 1935, 56,000 police officers were transferred to the *Wehrmacht* in corresponding positions. [The transfer was begun secretly before conscription was re-introduced in March, 1935.] This gave the Army a cadre of commanders with experience of the Four Years' War and schooled in street fighting, who acquired with surprising speed what they lacked in knowledge of tactics and modern arms. Of these police officers, six have been promoted full generals, 40 lieutenant-generals and 89 major-generals."

GERMAN CAMOUFLAGED ARMED FORCES

Under the aegis of the Great General Staff, which scented the coming diminution of the Army, a number of new armed forces sprang into existence as soon as the defeated German troops reached the Homeland. The so-called Freecorps were simply bands of nominally demobilized soldiers, under professional officers, often re-formed into their old units ; they were mostly evident on the Eastern Frontier, although it has been seen that 120,000 appeared in the Ruhr under General von Watter in March, 1920, and others were known to be lurking near the Neutral Zone. A fair proportion of Germany's eight million trained men appeared to be only too eager to remain in arms, in order to avoid " unemployment," but many did so purely from patriotic motives.

The *Einwohnerwehren* (Home Guards, literally Inhabitant Guards), or *Volkswehren* (Civic Guards, literally People's Guards), and other organizations of the same nature, grouped together under the common name of *Selbstschutz* (Self Protection), appeared immediately after the Armistice, nominally to reinforce the police in keeping order, or to strengthen frontier defences, often to ensure the domination of a particular political party in a district. They were recognized by the *Reich* Government as early as 12th December, 1918, armed from military depôts, organized into units by civil and municipal machinery under the direction of high civil officials, administered by a special department of the Ministry of the Interior, called the *Reichzentralstelle* (Reich Central Office), and supported by State subsidies and the subscriptions of wealthy industrialists. The total number of members could never be ascertained, but was undoubtedly well over a million, with sufficient rifles and machine guns.

When the Imperial Army was abolished by the law of 6th March, 1919 and the provisional *Reichswehr* came into existence, it was at first more than 400,000 men strong instead of the 200,000 temporarily permitted. On 5th August, 1919, by order of the *Reichswehr* Ministry under Allied pressure, it was reduced to 250,000 ; but at least 50,000 more remained as *Zeitfreiwillige* (Temporary Volunteers). On the 1st January, 1920, the strength of the Army was, according to the report of the Military Commission of Control, between 400,000 and 500,000. Allied pressure, as will be related in dealing with the events of 1921, again forced a temporary reduction to 100,000 men as laid down in the Peace Treaty ; but the 12-years' term of service was evaded, and a larger number of recruits was trained, vacancies being created by discharging men as sick and unfit, and by giving indefinite leave. During 1919 the Freecorps tended to disappear, some men being absorbed into the *Reichswehr*, others transferred to the Police, others converted nominally into labour corps (*Arbeitskommandos*).[1]

A well-equipped " Volunteer East Army " of considerable strength actually carried out an offensive campaign of conquest in the old Russian Baltic provinces, and it was December, 1919 before the Inter-Allied Commission of Baltic Evacuation and military pressure from the Letts and Poles compelled the Germans to recross their frontier.[2]

The suppression of the *Einwohnerwehren* was demanded by the Allied Governments on 1st December, 1919 as their existence was contrary to the Articles of the Peace Treaty, which limited the number of weapons and forbade associations of a military character. The German Great General Staff made a determined effort to retain them, and its representatives on the Spa Commission put forward various arguments : that the *Selbstschutz* was not a military force ; that it was required to guard Russian prisoners ; that in the existing political situation the population should be able to protect themselves ; and that, if the *Wehren* were officially dissolved, the inhabitants would form secret societies. In an attempt to hoodwink the Allies, the Minister of the Interior addressed a secret circular to the various German States, in which, instead of ordering them to dissolve the *Einwohnerwehren*, he informed them of the Allied demand. He told them to prepare to carry it out without delay, adding that they were free to create some other protective organization and thus evade the Articles of the Peace Treaty. Bavaria and Bremen declined openly to abolish their forces : the other States converted the banned levies into auxiliary

---

[1] They were commanded by ex-officers and administered by the *Wehrkreise*, and seem, among other things, to have played the part of a *Gestapo*, spying on and terrorizing the inhabitants, and to have been in charge of the hidden depôts of arms ; but it was difficult to say where they left off and the " Black *Reichswehr*," a definitely secret terrorist organization, began.

[2] German official publications from 1937 onwards (*Der Feldzug im Baltikum*—to May 1919, and *Die Kampfe im Baltikum* after that date) have revealed that amongst the troops were the so-called *2nd Guard Reserve Division*, " a miniature Army " of 32,000 men with aircraft and other forbidden armament ; the " *Iron Division*," with tanks and armoured cars ; the *45th Reserve Division* ; " *Brigade Schaulen* " ; the Baltic *Landeswehr* (of German Balts), with 28 machine-gun companies, aircraft and armoured cars, and a number of Free Corps composed of old soldiers, since officially admitted to be *Reichdeutsche Truppen* (Reich-German Troops), numbering about 50,000, besides White Russians and reinforcements resulting from the spontaneous march of single units to the Baltic provinces from the [frontier] *XVII. Corps* Area. These troops were based for supplies and reinforcements on the *I.* and *XX. Army Corps Districts.*

police (*Hilfspolizei*) or voluntary local police. All evaded even the pretence of giving up their arms. In July the German Government, after calling up all reserves of trained men in East Prussia, made a direct request to the Allied Governments to authorize a volunteer force (*Freiwillige Schutzwehr*) to protect the eastern frontier of Prussia, and, without waiting permission, the local authorities set about organizing a militia under new names, such as *Ortswehren* (Local Guards) and *Grenzwehren* (Frontier Guards). The Conference of Ambassadors in Paris, on 7th September, 1920, refused the German request, and ordered the Commission of Control to ensure that the militia disappeared. The German Government soon gave assurances that this had been done ; but only a portion of the arms were given up, and the various names of the formations were replaced by a new one, *Grenzschutz* (Frontier Protective Force).

The imminence of an inroad of Bolshevists was urged as a good and sufficient reason for the retention of illegal armed forces. But the invasion never developed ; the forces, in fact, were to be used against the Poles in Silesia and elsewhere. The continued existence of the *Einwohnerwehren* was proved by the discovery of an official clandestine organization known as " *Orgesch* ", a title formed from the beginning of the word " organization " and of the name of its prime mover, Herr Escherich, an official of the Woods and Forests. Already at the head of the Bavarian *Einwohnerwehren*, nominally abolished in April, 1920, but continuing to flourish as a recognized secret society, smaller but more combative, Escherich from a Government office in Munich, and in direct communication with *Wehrkreiskommando VII* (the *Ersatz* for an Army Corps District) was engaged in extending his scheme to include the whole of Germany in one vast federation, like the *Tugendbund* of 1812.

On 12th October, 1920 the Commission of Control demanded the communication of the measures proposed for the complete suppression of what remained of the *Selbstschutz*. A controversy ensued, during which it emerged that Bavaria was keeping up armed forces in order to resist payment of her share of reparation. On 29th January, 1921 the Allied Governments gave the *Reich* until 30th June to dissolve all the forbidden armed forces, and on 28th June the German Government, momentarily scared by the Ultimatum of London (5th May, 1921), with regard to reparation and the delivery of arms (which will be discussed later), sent to the Commission of Control copies of three decrees, dated 24th June, which dissolved *Orgesch* and the remaining *Wehren*. Legally, therefore, they ceased to be, and even Bavaria gave up a portion of their arms ; but the *Reich* refused to communicate lists of the organizations abolished.

They continued to exist openly as *Arbeitskommandos* (Labour Corps), and more or less openly as *Wehrverbände* (Defence Unions). Events in Upper Silesia and other plebiscite areas, where they reappeared as Freecorps, showed that they were still very much alive. In the next stage of evasion they took the names of sports and artistic clubs and social societies, and formed various secret organizations, notably the " Black *Reichswehr.*"

In May, 1920 a considerable number of Germans in uniform entered the occupied territory, alleging that they were on leave and had no civilian clothes. The practice was forbidden by the High Commission. A formal application made by the German delegate to allow uniformed men to enter under the same conditions as civilians was refused. Men in uniform were required to have an individual Allied permit, and without one were liable to arrest. An exception was made in favour of the *Sipo* ; but this general permission was withdrawn in June, 1921 on the ground of the unauthorized increase in the number of the police.

CHAPTER XIII

LIEUT.-GENERAL SIR T. MORLAND'S COMMAND

(concluded)

1921—EARLY 1922

REDUCTION OF THE ARMY OF THE RHINE BY THE DESPATCH OF TROOPS TO THE UNITED KINGDOM AND SILESIA

(End Paper)

THE FIRST SANCTIONS

The routine life of the Army of the Rhine[1] was seriously affected in 1921 by events outside the occupied area, where it was a year of discontent and disorder. At the end of February instructions were received to send four of its eight battalions to keep order during the Upper Silesia plebiscite ; and at the very time these units were leaving the Cologne area Allied sanctions were imposed on Germany, so that the British Empire could only send a token force with the French and Belgian divisions which occupied the selected Neutral Zone cities.

The occasion for drastic action had not arisen suddenly. The total sum to be paid by Germany as reparation for war damage and loss had not been fixed in the Peace Treaty. That instrument determined in Articles 231–243 that Germany should pay on account during 1919, 1920 and the first four months of 1921, that is before 30th April, 1921, the equivalent of 20,000 million gold marks (£1,000,000,000), either in gold, commodities, ships, securities or otherwise, and that an Inter-Allied Commission, to be called the " Reparation

---

[1] The Order of Battle was now :

    1st Rhine Brigade (Colonel-Commandant* C. J. Steavenson) : 1/R. Sussex, 2/R. West Kent, 1/Middlesex.
    2nd Rhine Brigade (Colonel-Commandant* H. B. P. L. Kennedy) : 2/Black Watch, 3/Middlesex, 1/Durham L.I.
    L. of C. Battalions : 4/Worcestershire, 1/Royal Irish.
    14th (King's) Hussars.
    III. Brigade R.F.A. (18th, 62nd, 75th and 147th [How.] Batteries).
    29th Battery R.G.A.
    7th Field Company R.E.
    X. Machine-Gun Company.
    B Company, 5th Tank Battalion.
    Nos. 365, 498 and 585 (M.T.) Companies R.A.S.C.
    Detachments of Nos. 8, 13, 14 and 17 Companies R.A.O.C.
with a Headquarters staff of 80 officers (Army List of January, 1921).

    * From 1st January, 1921, until 31st May, 1928, Colonel-Commandant was the temporary rank of a brigade commander.

Commission," should by 1st May, 1921, assess the total amount of damage and decide as to the manner in which it should be paid.[1] The Commission, on 27th April, fixed Germany's liability at 132,000 million gold marks (£6,600,000,000).

A conference of Ministers in Paris at the end of January had considered the plan of the Reparation Commission, and also fixed dates for the fulfilment of all disarmament demands :

> 28th February for the delivery of the remaining war material ;
> 15th March for the repeal of a new *Reichswehr* law, which did not absolutely forbid universal service ;
> 31st March for the surrender of all guns, and two-thirds of the rifles and machine guns of all *Selbstschutz* organizations ;
> 30th April for the disarmament of all ships in reserve ;
> 30th June for the complete disbandment of all *Selbstschutz* organizations and surrender of the rest of their arms ;
> 31st July for the destruction of warships in course of construction.

How the military demands were being evaded has been narrated in the previous chapter ; on this account and because the preliminary reparation payments had not been made, it was decided by the Allied Governments that " sanctions " must be applied. Germany was therefore informed that Duisburg, Ruhrort and Düsseldorf, on the right bank of the Rhine, in the Neutral Zone, would be occupied by the Allied troops, that tribute would be raised from the sale price of German goods in the Allied countries, and that a Customs frontier on the Rhine would be erected under Allied supervision. It was not easy to find even a small British force to co-operate in the proposed occupation.

Four Battalions Recalled to the United Kingdom

One cause of strain on the military forces of the Crown was due to Ireland being in a serious phase of unrest with 50,000 British troops in the country.[2] As if this were not enough to employ the small military forces in the United Kingdom, in March–April came threats of a " Triple Alliance " strike in

---

[1] Most Germans were well aware that they would be called on for reparation : it was uppermost in their minds from an early date. When, on the night of 9th September 1914, General-Colonel von Moltke, Chief of the German General Staff, realized that the Battle of the Marne was a defeat, he wrote to his wife : " Things are going badly . . . and we shall have to pay for all the destruction we have done." (*Erinnerungen*, p. 385.)

[2] Another strain on the forces was the Army of the Black Sea, under Lieut.-General Sir Charles Harington, consisting of the 28th Division, a cavalry regiment and L. of C. troops. The last of the B.E.F. in France and Belgium, except for some administrative and technical staff, had been withdrawn in July, 1920. See Chapter IX.

England, Scotland and Wales of coal, railway and transport workers, and a coal strike actually took place from 14th April to 4th July. In consequence of these troubles, Lieut.-General Morland was informed by the War Office on 4th April that the Government had decided to concentrate all available troops in England, and ordered him to send home four battalions (amended to three, a provisional brigade), withdrawing for the purpose the four battalions in Silesia.[1]

THE SILESIAN PLEBISCITE

To take the movements of the Army of the Rhine in order :

Instructions to send four battalions, with engineers, signal detachment, etc., to Upper Silesia to keep order during the plebiscite were received from the War Office on 23rd February. Someone seems to have forgotten that since February, 1918, an infantry brigade contained three, not four, battalions. The French had already sent a division and the Italians a large contingent.[2] The administrative orders for the move, which ran to 5½ typewritten pages, were a model for an operation of this kind ; nothing was forgotten, not even an officer responsible for seeing that cooking utensils were put on board the kitchen vans to be attached to the trains.[3] The " Silesian Plebiscite Force," as the British contingent was called, was to proceed by train, and be maintained in personnel, stores, supplies, etc., by means of " maintenance trains " run weekly ; headquarters would be at Lublinetz, where a depôt with 30 days' supplies, sent under special guard, would be established ; 5 days' rations (including 2 days' fresh meat, 3 days' fresh bread and fuel for five days), augmented for each man by 4 oz. bread, ½ oz. milk and ½ oz. cocoa, were to be taken on the train. *Bona fide* rum-drinkers might be given a daily issue. The following extra clothing was to be issued : 2 blankets (making 6 per man), a leather jerkin, a pair of fingerless lined gloves (except to M.T. drivers), sheepskin-lined coats for use of sentries for 10 per cent. of the force, one balaclava cap, one muffler and two woollen vests. Battalion interpreters were to accompany their units " if willing."

---

[1] At home a " Defence Force " of 75,000 volunteers was organized for service in England, Scotland and Wales.

[2] An American brigade available (see Chapter IX, Note II) was not sent as the U.S.A. had not ratified the Peace Treaty.

[3] Appendix XXV.

The 1/R. Sussex, 2/R. West Kent, 1/Middlesex of the 1st Rhine Brigade, and 2/Black Watch of the 2nd, were detailed.

The advanced party under Colonel A. G. Wauchope of the Black Watch left on 28th February in trains arranged by German officials under orders of the Inter-Allied Railway Commission, and arrived in Silesia on 6th March, instead of the 2nd as was expected. The main body, under Colonel-Commandant C. J. Steavenson, left on 3rd March, arrived on the 8th, and was distributed to five centres.

An Inter-Allied Commission to take over the government with a view to the plebiscite, consisting of General le Rond (France), Colonel H. F. P. (later Sir Harold) Percival (British), with Mr. F. B. Bourdillon sent by the Foreign Office as his Deputy, and an Italian officer, had arrived in Upper Silesia a year earlier.[1] With it had come 12 French and 3 Italian battalions, some 13,000 men in all, under General Gratier (French)—the British being at that time unable to supply a contingent.

The new State of Poland had claimed the whole of Upper Silesia ; Germany had naturally protested against any such cession, and on 2nd June, 1919, Mr. Lloyd George had proposed that a plebiscite should be held. This was decided on after considerable hesitation on the part of President Wilson and opposition by Monsieur Clemenceau. In the Peace Treaty it was stipulated that the plebiscite should not be held earlier than six months or later than eighteen months after the ratification of the Treaty (10th January, 1920).

In the year intervening a good deal of unrest and lawlessness had occurred in Upper Silesia, but the plebiscite was carried out on 20th March, 1921, in a manner similar to that already described for Allenstein, under conditions of " exemplary quiet," as the regulations in Upper Silesia contained more adequate provisions against impersonation and intimidation. Owing to the careful preparation of the German plebiscite organizations, backed by all the resources of the German Government, it resulted as a whole in a majority of votes for Germany, five of the nine polling areas voting for the Reich. This, however, did not settle the matter, as will be seen later in this chapter.

---

[1] It had a staff of 128 officials (69 French, 33 British, 26 Italian) and employees. At the end of May, 1922 the staff numbered 274 officials (122 French, 82 British and 70 Italian), with 293 employees (including 30 to 40 prison warders).

THE OCCUPATION OF DÜSSELDORF

Meanwhile on 6th March, the War Office concurring, Maréchal Foch had ordered the occupation of Düsseldorf, Duisburg and Ruhrort, all lying on the right bank of the Rhine. An Inter-Allied force, under General Gaucher (French 77th Division) was formed in two columns :—

No. 1 Column for Düsseldorf :

French, a cavalry regiment, an infantry regiment, a group of motor machine guns, an engineer company ;

Belgian, an infantry regiment ;

British, two squadrons cavalry, four tanks, Rhine flotilla.

No. 2 Column for Duisburg–Ruhrort :

French, an infantry regiment, a chasseur battalion, two engineer companies, flotilla ;

Belgian, two cavalry squadrons, an infantry battalion, a group of field artillery, a cyclist company, a section armoured cars, flotilla.

Air Force, two French reconnoitring and two French bomber squadrons, and what the British and Belgians could spare.

To ensure surprise, postal, telegraph, telephone and press censorship was imposed and the columns then rendezvoused, the British close on the perimeter, during the night of the 7th/8th. They moved at dawn, the two squadrons of the 14th Hussars, under Lieut.-Colonel J. G. Browne, which left Cologne by road half an hour after midnight, moving into Düsseldorf at 7 a.m., followed by the tanks brought up by train, without waiting for the French infantry, which was delayed owing to motor transport difficulties. By midday the occupation was completed without any resistance being offered. A state of siege was declared by proclamation in the newly occupied areas with the usual prohibitions and penalties. At Düsseldorf the British took possession of the southern portion of the city, the French the centre, and the Belgians the northern part. The 12th Squadron R.A.F. was employed in carrying out demonstration flights over Düsseldorf. During the day a line about four to five miles out was reconnoitred by Generals Degoutte and Morland and occupied by posts. All remained quiet, so that some of the troops could be withdrawn, and on the 21st one squadron of the 14th Hussars returned to Cologne. On the 30th, however, to help the German police maintain order, by desire of the local commissioner a company of the 1/Royal Irish was sent to Ohligs, where an outbreak had occurred in sympathy with a serious Spartacist rising in Central Germany. This rising was easily suppressed, and its leaders sentenced to long terms of imprisonment. In Remscheid, just outside the bridgehead, the rioting amounted almost to a battle, and hundreds of the defeated rioters fled into the British Zone. In Solingen British troops had to intervene to keep order. In Cologne itself shop windows were smashed as a protest against food profiteering, but a single tank exhibited in the Domplatz at once restored order.

The British High Commissioner asked for troops—about two battalions each about 400 strong were required—to occupy posts on the perimeter of the British bridgehead pending a customs reorganization. As most of his infantry was in Silesia, Lieut.-General Morland requested reinforcements from home. None, however, were available, and he was told to do the best he could with the men he had.

Withdrawal of Troops from Silesia and their Despatch to the United Kingdom

By War Office orders, the machine-gun company and the Rhine Army Musketry and Lewis Gun Schools were disbanded at the end of March ; but Lieut.-General Morland was allowed to retain 106 machine-gunners until 30th June, 1921.[1]

In obedience to another War Office order, the detachment in Upper Silesia was withdrawn, arriving in Cologne between 10th and 14th April, and three of the four battalions entrained for the United Kingdom via Ostend on 12th, 13th and 14th, the 2/Black Watch being left behind with the 1st Rhine Brigade staff. Meantime, by a third War Office order, 200 M.T. drivers, R.A.S.C., and a strong detachment of the 4/Worcestershire (18 officers and 500 other ranks) had left for home on the 8th. All the battalions left their transport behind, but on 6th June the transport personnel was ordered to join them in the United Kingdom.

Preparations to Occupy the Ruhr Valley

The reduced British Army of the Rhine had only a short interval of rest. Arrangements had to be made in view of possible civil disturbances on May Day. One infantry company, with 7 lorries, was kept in readiness at the orders of the Deputy Provost Marshal to assist the German police, and all units had outlying piquets on duty ; but the day passed off quietly.

---

[1] When X. Company Machine-Gun Battalion was disbanded a temporary Machine Gun School was organized at Riehl Barracks (Cologne) with a range near by. Besides the normal courses, 5 officers and 10 n.c.os. were trained as instructors. As a result each battalion was provided with a minimum of 24 trained machine-gunners (4 full teams).

The occupation of Düsseldorf not having had any effect, on 5th May the Allied Powers issued another ultimatum. The German Government had shown no sign of accepting the findings of the Reparation Committee and the method of payment spread out over 42 years. They were still in default as regards (1) disarmament ; (2) the reparation payment due on 1st May ; (3) the trial of war criminals ;[1] and (4) certain other important matters, notably trade, navigation, transit and transmigration obligations. The Allies had therefore decided to proceed forthwith with the preliminary measures for the occupation of the Ruhr valley, and gave Germany six days to accept the terms and declare that she would carry out her obligations.

In accordance with Maréchal Foch's instructions, orders were issued by the British Army of the Rhine on 6th May for preliminary moves to be made for the occupation of the Ruhr. The French were about to concentrate the XXXIII. Corps (one cavalry and two infantry divisions) on the northern side of the British bridgehead in the area Wermelskirchen-Solingen-Ohligs on or after the 9th, the head arriving at Bergheim (15 miles west of Cologne) on or after the 7th, and it was the task of the British Army of the Rhine to cover the detrainment of the French force, to guard all vulnerable points on the railways in the British area in rear of the deployment area, and to be prepared, in the event of a strike of German railwaymen, to protect the French technical personnel who would work the lines.

The 3/Middlesex (at Solingen), with the squadron of the 14th Hussars from Düsseldorf, all under Lieut.-Colonel H. Goodwin of the Middlesex, was ready in position on the night

---

[1] Articles 227–30 of the Peace Treaty provided for the trial of the ex-Kaiser " for a supreme offence against international morality and the sanctity of peace treaties," and of persons " accused of having committed acts in violation of the laws and customs of war." The offenders were not handed over, but certain " persons " underwent what the American Summary (i., p. 114) calls a " farcical trial " before the German Supreme Court at Leipzig in June, 1921. From the list of 900 cases prepared for the Supreme Council the Allies put up 45 as a test. Of these only 12 were tried and 6 were acquitted. The others received sentences, " to our estimate, far too light " (said by Sir Ernest Pollock, K.C., M.P., who as Solicitor-General, led the British Mission at the Leipzig trials, in the Introduction (p. 10) to *The Leipzig Trials*, by Claud Mullins). An Inter-Allied Commission which investigated the trials rejected the findings and recommended the extradition of the offenders. Chancellor Wirth, in a speech, said such a demand would never be complied with.

" War crimes," according to the *Manual of Military Law* (1914 Edition, p. 302), include " violations of the recognized rules of warfare by members of the armed forces," but nothing is said about offences against international morality and reversion to methods of barbarism in occupied territory, where the rule of the invader is sovereign.

of the 8th/9th. It held the three detraining stations Wermels-kirchen, Solingen and Ohligs, and reconnoitred to the north and east to the limit of the occupied zone. Opladen junction and three railway bridges over the Dhünn south of it were specially guarded, and 22 other posts were found requiring 301 men ; aircraft look-outs with Lewis guns to form a line of observation along the Rhine were organized with special care for the airfield, and the petrol and supply depôts.

For the occupation of the Ruhr the British contingent detailed to come under the orders of the G.O.C. French 77th Division consisted of 2 squadrons of the 14th Hussars (one in Düsseldorf), one 18-pdr. battery and the four tanks (from Cologne, still leaving four in Düsseldorf), and they were ordered to be concentrated at Solingen by 5 p.m. on the 13th under Lieut.-Colonel J. G. Browne (14th Hussars). On the 11th, however, Maréchal Foch notified the postponement of the occupation, as the German Government had made the necessary declaration, and the concentration was cancelled. The French relieved the covering force from midnight 12th/13th, and it was withdrawn ; on the 14th the railway guards were also withdrawn. Such training as was possible was resumed. The French corps, numbering about 25,000 men, with 9,000 horses, remained in the British Zone for several weeks.

Despatch of the Remaining Infantry Battalions to Upper Silesia

Some days later, on the 23rd, a telegram was received from the War Office ordering all four remaining battalions to be held in readiness for despatch to Silesia : their place on the Rhine would be taken temporarily by French units which would come under Lieut.-Genéral Morland's command.

The reason for the despatch of a British force was that an insurrection had taken place against the authority of the Inter-Allied Commission, followed by fighting between the rival races in Silesia. The Polish insurgents, under Korfanty, the leader of the Polish political and propaganda organization, fearing that by the plebiscite the " Industrial Triangle "[1]

---

[1] See Sketch 4. The triangle, which contains the coalfields, is marked by Gleiwitz, Beuthen and Kattowitz. Roughly, the northern part of Upper Silesia is a country of vast estates, agricultural, with many forests, wheat and timber being its products, and the southern part, industrial. In both parts, ownership and management, even of shops, were in the hands of Germans. The Poles, men and women, provided the labour, often being driven to it by whip and big stick.

might be lost to them, had taken forcible possession of the territory claimed by Poland, including the triangle. The Germans, who held the Upper Silesian *Selbstschutz* already organized against such an event, reinforced it by Freecorps from other parts of the *Reich*, under a German general, Hoefer, thereupon attacked the Poles, and after a fight at the Annaberg (7 miles south-west of Gross Strehlitz) on 21st May, stopped their further progress. An Inter-Allied force was required to expel both parties.

The British contingent selected to go, under Colonel A. G. Wauchope of the Black Watch, was to be known as " The British Upper Silesian Force," which was generally shortened to " Upsi." It consisted of the four battalions remaining in the Rhineland, but it was reinforced by the 2/Connaught Rangers and 2/Leinster from home. These two battalions arrived in Cologne on 31st May and 1st June respectively. The six battalions were then organized under Major-General Sir W. C. G. Heneker (lately commanding the Independent Division on the Rhine), with a staff made up in Cologne, into two brigades under Colonel-Commandant H. B. P. L. Kennedy (2nd Rhine Brigade) and Colonel Wauchope.[1]

The first train left at 11 p.m. on the 26th and was followed by two trains daily to make 18 in all. The administrative orders were similar to those issued for the earlier move to Silesia, but as the weather was now warm, tents and camp kit were taken instead of winter clothing, and arrangements made for " *haltes repas* " and frequent watering of the horses. Copies of orders for the British Upper Silesian Force had to be sent, in addition to the usual recipients, to the Cologne Commissioner, the French, Belgian and American Missions, the British liaison officers at Mayence (French), Bonn (French), Aachen (Belgian) and Coblence (American), the Secretary of the British Section Inter-Allied Military Committee Versailles, and the Military Attachés, Paris and Warsaw.[2]

---

[1] Order of Battle :
    1st British Silesian Brigade : 2/Black Watch, 1/Durham L.I., 2/Leinster.
    2nd British Silesian Brigade : 1/Royal Irish, 3/Middlesex, 2/Connaught Rangers.
    62nd and 65th Batteries R.F.A. (one 18-pdr. ; one howitzer).
    7th Field Company R.E.
    Four Tanks
and the usual detachments and Services, including an M.T. Company and a Bakery Section R.A.S.C., and a field hospital (150 beds).

[2] For the action of the British Upper Silesian Force, see next chapter.

The Residual Force Reinforced by a French Brigade

The command of the residue of the British Army of the Rhine, called officially the " Composite Rhine Brigade," now amounting to only two squadrons, two batteries R.F.A., one battery R.G.A., one section of the tank company, and the " details " of the infantry battalions, was taken over by Colonel-Commandant C. J. Steavenson (1st Rhine Brigade). He had to find 11 detachments and guards over ammunition and petrol dumps, detention and military police barracks, besides official residences, offices and hospitals. On 28th June, at the request of Major-General Heneker, one squadron of the 14th Hussars was railed to Upper Silesia.

General Degoutte sent the Brigade Bessens of the 13th Division (headquarters Wiesdorf, near Opladen) to replace the British battalions. The three battalions of the 21st Regiment arrived to take over the duties in Cologne on 28th, 30th and 31st May, and were stationed in the barracks at Kalk, Mülheim and Riehl. The other regiment of the brigade (headquarters at Ohligs) relieved the detachment in Solingen, and provided most of the Customs and railway posts.

For some months the German representatives with the High Commission had been trying to find out the strength of the Armies of Occupation, with a view to protesting against it, but ostensibly for budget purposes. The Army Council, in November, 1920, had objected to the Germans being told more than they could gather, in arrear, from the claims for cost of occupation—or, it might have been said, from the order of battle in the monthly Army List. It then transpired that the figures had been promised to them by the Allied Military Committee in Versailles, and the Army Council, for this purpose, said that the British strength might be taken at 15,000, reserving the right to increase or diminish it.

The protests were duly made, and a fresh assault was launched after the British contingent had left for Silesia. The British representative on the High Commission, taking the German view, on 3rd August, 1921, wrote to London suggesting the urgent consideration of the strength of the Allied forces on the ground that the occupation of buildings and farmland was inflicting unnecessary hardships on the inhabitants, and since—as he thought—Germany was practically disarmed, a serious reduction of the forces was indicated.

The strength of the Armies of Occupation at the time was given as :

> French, 72,000 effectives (excluding one division on the Saar).
> American, 14,000.
> Belgian, 15,000.
> British, 5,000 (ration strength and excluding the division in Silesia).

On being consulted, the Army Council gave the opinion, on 4th August, that the British forces on the Rhine could not be reduced below eight battalions, with a proportion of other arms and services, and that the strength of the troops of other nations should be based on this hypothesis.

On 27th August the Germans made fresh protests against the simultaneous quartering of French and Belgian troops in the towns bordering on the Ruhr, including Opladen in the British area. It transpired at a meeting of the High Commission on 9th September, 1921, that the French would shortly withdraw one division from the Belgian Zone and one from the British ; the total French ration strength in the Rhineland, 119,000, would thus be reduced to about 100,000. No steps were taken to comply with the German protests in view of the large total of armed forces, *Reichswehr*, supernumerary *Reichswehr*, *Einwohnerwehr*, *Sicherheitspolizei* and Freecorps, which General von Seeckt had at his disposal.

QUIET TIMES ON THE RHINE

During the rest of the term of service of Lieut.-General Morland, who left on 8th March, 1922, to assume command at Aldershot, and was succeeded by Lieut.-General Sir Alexander Godley, nothing of importance happened. An instalment of the Reparation was paid by Germany on 1st August, but the unpunished murder on 25th August of Herr Erzberger, who had signed the Armistice as the leader of the German delegation, tended to show how the situation was changing in the *Reich*. The French provided two more infantry companies from Bonn for the relief of British Customs and control posts ; two more battalions from the United Kingdom, the 1/R. Munster Fusiliers and 2/R Inniskilling Fusiliers, passed through on the way to reinforce the British Upper Silesian Force ; reinforcement drafts for this force and parties of time-expired men from it were also dealt with in transit. The only cause for anxiety was a short railway strike from 6th to 11th February, 1922. The fall by the end of the year of the German exchange to nearly 1,000 marks to the £ and its continued fall was all to the advantage of the British garrison, who were paid in sterling. Protected by French troops, the small remnant of the British Army of the Rhine was left in peace, and the diaries it sent home do not seem to have been examined, for the duplicates were still undetached from the originals in 1943.

The most important of the Ordinances of the High Commission promulgated in 1921 were three in number. No. 69 provided that if the accommodation (buildings, land or moveable property) required by the Armies under Article 8 of the Rhineland Agreement[1] was not handed over by the time appointed it might be seized ; and that if work or repairs required were not executed as demanded they might be carried out at the expense of the responsible German authorities. No. 71 tightened the regulations with regard to espionage, particularly the possession and use of photographic and wireless apparatus, and any tampering with passports.[2] No. 90 protected Germans who rendered service to, or had relations with the Allied authorities of Occupation, and gave power to the High Commission to adjudicate on or review any proceedings against them.

MARRIED QUARTERS

On all occasions when troops were sent on special duty either in Germany or to the United Kingdom, wives and families were left on the Rhine, but were allowed to return home if so wishing. As a rule they remained, for the " married quarters " were good. Early in 1921 the German local authorities, on their own initiative, began building rows of smallish houses for their own people, who would thus be enabled to leave their old houses as billets for British families, and an attempt was made to put the cost upon the British Army of the Rhine. Married quarters were required at Mülheim and Halfeshof, but to the erection of these the local authorities raised objection, saying that they had " voluntarily " (that is without reference to the British Army of the Rhine) built extra quarters. All amounts spent on the Armies of Occupation being deductible from Reparation, the policy of the Germans was to run up a big bill in carrying out their own plans of improvement, and charge the cost to the British, while preventing the British Army of the Rhine from having

---

[1] See Chapter XI and Appendix XXIII.
[2] Being a useful model, the Ordinance is given in Appendix XXVI.

definite control of money alleged to have been expended on its behalf. In this case they were told that if they did not build the quarters where they were required under Article 8 of the Rhineland Agreement, suitable billets would be requisitioned. This gave occasion for another formal protest against the " hardships inflicted on the civil population." Actually, to avert inflicting inconvenience on the Germans, some of the British troops were accommodated in hutments. The rows of new small houses were, however, taken over, and the accommodation found so good that certain of them were occupied by officers and their families.

CHAPTER XIV

THE OPERATIONS OF THE BRITISH UPPER SILESIA FORCE

MAY, 1921—JULY, 1922

(Sketch 4)

THE TASK OF HENEKER'S DIVISION

The task in Upper Silesia of the Inter-Allied Force under the command of General Gratier (succeeded in September, 1921, by General Naulin), of which Major-General Heneker's division formed part, was an unusual one, and for that reason alone deserves notice. It was to ensure that the two contending parties should cease fighting, that the Polish " insurgents," as they are called throughout the British records, under Korfanty, from outside the area, and the Freecorps from other parts of Germany, under General Hoefer, should both evacuate Upper Silesia, and that the rest, the local inhabitants, should be disbanded and go home. As in the Rhineland, where the (French) General-in-Command of the troops received orders as to the use of force from the High Commission, General Gratier took his instructions from the Upper Silesia Commission. Of this the French General le Rond was still president, but Sir Harold Stuart of the Rhineland High Commission was at the end of May appointed the British member in succession to Colonel Percival, who had fallen sick.

The presence of a British force at once brought serious fighting to an end, and such " scrapping " as occurred from time to time usually ceased on the appearance of an Allied patrol, or even on the arrival of a motor car flying the Union Jack.

The British contingent arrived between 29th May and 6th June and was assembled without incident. It made Oppeln, in Germany to the north of the disputed territory, its headquarters ; but on 14th June they were shifted forward south-eastwards to Gross Strehlitz, and on 6th July to Tarnowitz, on the northern edge of the industrial area. Beuthen then was the southernmost town held by the British, with the French division on that flank, with headquarters at Gleiwitz, and an Italian force to the west.

UPPER SILESIA

REFERENCE.

Frontier in 1914	▬ ▬ ▬
„ Fixed in 1920	++++
Railways	▬▬▬

British dispositions 6th/7th July 1921

Headquarters and divisional troops	✳
Brigade headquarters	▼
Cavalry	◪
Infantry companies	■
less than a company	●

From Öls

From BRESLAU

To POSEN

To CZENSTOCHAU

R. Stober

R. Prosna

R. Warte

R. Malapan

R. Klodnitz

R. Oder

R. Oppa

R. Przna

R. Vistula

Kreuzburg

Rosenberg

Turawa

Guttentag

Kochtschütz

Lublinitz

OPPELN

Wessowska

Kruppemühle

Gross Strehlitz

Blottnitz

Brynnek

Krappitz

CHELM HILLS

Annaberg

Tarnowitz

Peiskretscham

XBEUTHEN

Ober Glogau

Bobrek

Königshütte

Kosel

Laband

GLEIWITZ

Lipine

KATTOWITZ

Antonienhütte

Rybnik

RATIBOR

Pless

POLAND

AUSTRIA

SCALE OF MILES.

| 10 | 5 | 0 | 10 | 20 | 30 |

THE GENERAL POLICY

The general policy of the British contingent was, in combination with the French, to drive the Polish insurgents eastwards, following the railways and occupying the larger towns one by one. At first battalions and later single companies were sent forward, either in lorries or by train, and before they could advance bridges had often to be repaired and mines removed.

The first order, dated 5th June, issued by Major-General Heneker, was :

> " British troops are not to interfere with either German **or** Polish armed forces. If, however, either German or Polish forces attack British troops, the latter will reply with fire in co-operation with neighbouring Allied forces."

Every endeavour was made to exhibit that any action taken was an Inter-Allied affair, not the whim of a single nation. For this purpose, battalions were interchanged, a French chasseur à pied battalion being with the 1st Rhine Brigade, and an Italian battalion with the 2nd Rhine Brigade, in exchange for British battalions. When a party was sent in lorries, the order was given that " British and French troops will be mixed, there being representatives of each nationality on each vehicle." In every case a summons was issued or warning given, and persuasion tried before force was used.

THE FIRST OPERATIONS

At the outset neither the Poles nor the Germans proved easy to deal with. The first endeavour to separate them was made on 5th June at the Annaberg in the Chelm hills, the only high ground in Upper Silesia. Here the *Selbstschutz* staff officers were inclined to allow the British to relieve their troops ; but when they found that the 2nd Rhine Brigade did not intend to fight the Poles, but merely to hold a line to keep the two forces apart, they refused to budge. The next attempt was made on 7th June, 30 miles to the north, at Rosenberg. Here, after a certain amount of discussion, the Poles agreed to move eastwards at 4 p.m. When, however, Lieut.-Colonel Orpen-Palmer of the 2/Leinster and his adjutant went forward at that hour under a flag of truce to take over the town, the Poles, having in the interval cheered themselves with drink, refused to hand over. They were threatened with an artillery bombardment—although no guns were available—and left in haste. On the 14th it is recorded that three companies of the

Leinster (leaving one in Rosenberg) " had some difficulty in turning Poles out of Guttentag " ; but the insurgents, after fining the town 90,000 marks " for showing pleasure at the British occupation," departed eastwards. Both sides soon became reasonable, the Germans probably because they felt sure of the result of the plebiscite, the Poles because they felt sure of French support. Very few regrettable incidents occurred, and these were due to gangs of marauders, not to organized resistance. On 9th June on a route march, a sergeant of the Black Watch who, contrary to orders, had wandered off the road—which was actually the " battle-front " —into a field with tall standing crops, was fired on and killed. Which side fired the shot was never discovered, but, after some talk, the Germans paid compensation. On 4th July a French colonel was mortally wounded in Beuthen by a German of sub-normal intelligence, on the occasion of the entry of French troops accompanied by a company of the 3/Middlesex. By order of General Gratier, nine influential men of the town were held as hostages, but released on the 8th ; the *Bürgermeister*, who was in the custody of the British, was handed over to the French police " at 2030 hours on the same date, and a receipt obtained ". On the 12th a sergeant of the Durham L.I. was mortally wounded, and there was a clash at Kreuzburg, without casualties, between French soldiers and German police. Near the same place a detachment was ordered to collect a dump of arms ; it did so without taking proper military precautions, and was surrounded by armed Germans and forced to surrender the arms, which had already been loaded on a lorry. This incident was the cause of a diplomatic commotion, and was eventually settled by the Conference of Ambassadors, which decided that the Germans must hand over the arms, apologize and pay compensation. Some later instances are mentioned below.

German aircraft occasionally flew over dropping leaflets, and the Allies had no aircraft to chase them off. An incident nearly occurred when the pipers of the Leinster, who wore brown kilts unpleated, were reported as Germans trying to masquerade as Highlanders.

Organization of Local Constabulary

By order of the Commission, " Parish Constabulary " (*Gemeindewachen*), to reinforce the police, were set up in the districts as fast as they were evacuated by the insurgents, and six delegations of control, each with one British officer, selected for his knowledge of the German language rather than representative qualities, as a member, were appointed by the Commission. They were to make certain that all military organizations of the insurrection period were effectively dissolved ; to bring about the dissolution of all small armed parties still existing ; to make sure that all non-Upper-Silesians belonging to insurrectionary formations had actually left the country ; to enforce the departure of all non-Upper-Silesians not in possession of a correct passport ; and to report on the organization and working of the Parish Constabulary. A party of about 200 " Inter-Allied Police of Upper Silesia," half Germans, half Upper Silesian Police, sworn to neutrality, were placed at the disposal of each control officer.[1]

The conditions for recruits of the Constabulary were :

(1) to have turned 21 ;

(2) to have been born in Upper Silesia, or to have lived there since 1904 ;

(3) to be able to produce a certificate of good behaviour issued by a municipality, dated after 29th May. Men who had been convicted or who being in the Upper Silesia Police had disappeared, or who had taken part in the insurrection, were ineligible.

The effective of the Parish Constabulary was fixed as :

5 policemen in Districts of less than 500 inhabitants
10 ,, ,, ,, ,, from 500–1,000 inhabitants
15 ,, ,, ,, ,, ,, 1,000–2,000 inhabitants
20 ,, ,, ,, ,, ,, 2,000–5,000 inhabitants
30 ,, ,, ,, ,, ,, 5,000–10,000 inhabitants

For guards numbering from 5 to 30 men there was to be one n.c.o. *Wachtmeister* or *Oberwachtmeister*.

For guards numbering over 30 men there was to be an officer and one or more n.c.os.

The uniform was plain clothes with police shoulder straps sewn on, a uniform cap and a lettered brassard. The arms were a revolver or pistol with 40 cartridges. The pay was the same as that of the Upper Silesia Police.

Until the Parish Constabularies were formed the Allied troops policed the country ; after they had come into existence the troops only acted in aid of the civil power as in normal times.

IMMEDIATE IMPROVEMENT IN THE SITUATION

By 14th June conditions had so far improved that an exchange of prisoners was carried out. The trains conveying them were provided with an Allied escort.

---

[1] A large number of the Poles were ex-insurgents. A vivid account of the work and difficulties of the Inter-Allied Upper Silesian Police will be found in Chapter XVII of *Bandit Hunting or More Reminiscences of an Old Bohemian*, by Major Fitzroy Gardner, who was Control Officer at Tarnowitz and Nikolai.

On 24th June the Polish Commander-in-Chief, General Warwus, gave a written undertaking to the Commission that the non-resident insurgents would be withdrawn from Upper Silesia in accordance with a programme by which they would retire behind certain fixed lines by fixed dates, completing the evacuation by 5th July.

The 28th June was the first day, and on that day General Hoefer signed an agreement that the German irregular forces would similarly retire and be dissolved. The Allied forces did not make any bound forward until the delegates of the Commission had reported that the insurgents had retired according to programme. No need to follow the Germans existed, except to verify that they had gone. Evacuation being completed, the state of siege was raised and, as in the Rhineland, the Commission continued to rule until the partition of Upper Silesia was announced and carried out.

An Inter-Allied flying column, consisting of a British company, an Italian company, a French machine-gun company and a French Hussar squadron, was organized to patrol the Neutral Zone which had been created between the Germans and Poles. Its duties were to make sure that this Zone was clear, to receive complaints and claims from inhabitants, to establish the functioning of the police and to tranquillize the inhabitants by its presence.

The roads were very good, but the distances were long, and the British troops got very bored. Those in the three big towns of Oppeln, Beuthen and Tarnowitz found a certain amount of distraction, but those in the villages had little chance of any amusement, except football. Cinemas did not exist, the inns were very small and poor, and the womenfolk were most unattractive. Both nationalities were friendly ; but there was very little contact with the Polish population, as its social status was a low one.

SEARCH FOR UNDESIRABLES AND HIDDEN ARMS

On 6th July Upper Silesia was reported free of both organized Polish insurgents and the German *Selbstschutz*. There remained, however, considerable numbers of armed undesirables engaged in looting. It was also certain that large quantities of arms had been hidden by both sides. The brigades were therefore ordered to organize search parties, which, as the country contained large tracts of forest, had no easy task. Special instruction in clearing such country, by the use of wide-flung flanking parties, was given to the troops. By visiting simultaneously all the public establishments in the towns a number of armed men, without identity cards or passports were secured. At Krappitz on 16th July, a column consisting of a French Hussar squadron, a section of French armoured cars, a company of the Durham L.I. and an Italian company, under Chef d'Escadron Horment, which had been sent to capture an important depôt of arms, forbidden emblems and documents, was opposed by an excited and hostile armed population, who tried to intimidate the officers sent forward to parley and actually pointed rifles at them. Energetic action was at once taken, and 25 suspects, known to be ringleaders, were arrested, without bloodshed. It was subsequently decided by the Commission that the clearing operations should be conducted in agreement with the administrative authorities and the police, so that secrecy and sudden pounces became out of the question. It was also decreed that the actual searching should be done by the police, the troops " forming a reserve to help them if necessary and to block the roads and stop the exits." The flying column was not to participate in the clearing operations except at the request of the Allied district controllers : its business was to " show the flag."

These instructions being obviously incompatible with the safety of the troops, General Gratier added a " *Note de service* " to the effect that commanders of troops must not hesitate to search suspected individuals and houses, and take steps to gain possession of large " *caches* " of arms ; but house-to-house searches by the troops were forbidden.

As there were not sufficient troops to guard the frontier effectively, infantry posts were placed at the points where the railways crossed it in order to search incoming trains for arms in co-operation with the railway and customs authorities ; mounted troops kept watch on the frontier roads and searched incoming vehicles for arms.

PREPARATIONS AGAINST TROUBLE WHEN THE PARTITION WAS ANNOUNCED

To decide how Upper Silesia was to be divided was a matter for the Allied Supreme Council. In view of the probability that disturbances might take place when the decision was announced, various contingencies were considered by the Allied commanders in order to be prepared for either a German insurrection, a Polish insurrection with help from Poland, or a rising of inhabitants who were supporters of the Polish political party. The last was considered the most likely. It was decided that the frontier must be watched, but more thoroughly, and that the remaining forces should be concentrated as rapidly as possible. Two areas were selected by Major-General Heneker : one near Oppeln (the seat of Government), where all the British troops, with an Italian battalion, could be concentrated in twelve hours, and the other north-west of Beuthen in the industrial area, for which only six hours were required. In the event of Polish troops crossing the frontier in the British Zone and an immediate concentration not being ordered, the general policy laid down was that the troops should hold their positions, only retiring when forced to do so, and always with a view to concentrating in the Beuthen area. The railways were to be destroyed as the troops retired, and immediate steps were taken to prepare them for demolition at the frontier crossings, and to select places for blocking the main roads into Upper Silesia.

From the middle of July, a short pause in the unrest ensued, for the harvest had to be gathered, and on 6th, 7th and 8th August Inter-Allied Sports were held at Oppeln, and there was " nothing else to report ". But as the middle of the month, and the date of the expected decision of the Supreme Council, approached, preparatory orders were issued : on the 12th for the concentration of the British and the French force in the industrial area Beuthen–Tarnowitz, with single British battalions at the railway junctions of Lublinitz, Vassowska (advanced railhead) on the way to Oppeln, and Rosenberg and Kreuzburg on the route northwards. The French were to attend to the Gross Strehlitz line. These precautions were cancelled on the 15th, as " the question of the future of Upper Silesia has been referred to the League of Nations ".

Winter Quarters and Minor Troubles

In view of the possible delay, on 26th August orders were issued to make preparations to go into winter quarters. There were a good number of barracks : for two battalions and a cavalry regiment at Gleiwitz ; for one artillery regiment and one cavalry regiment at Tarnowitz ; for three battalions at Beuthen ; for three at Oppeln ; for three at Ratibor ; and for one at Lublinitz. As most of the small posts were to be withdrawn, no great inconvenience was inflicted on the inhabitants by billeting.

A number of small troubles soon arose. On 27th August the British Military Police had to go to the assistance of the civil police to deal with Poles who had defied them.

On that day the German *Bürgermeister* of Lipine, a mining town of 17,000 inhabitants three miles south of Beuthen, had been murdered at the door of his house. On the 29th, 700 bayonets, 89 rifles and 22 boxes of ammunition were discovered in a kiln. It was decided therefore to resume raiding, for which special instructions were issued, and to send two companies to Lipine.[1]

By decision of the Supreme Council in view of the onerous and dangerous nature of the work,[2] two more battalions were added to each contingent. The 2/R. Munster Fusiliers and the 2/R. Inniskilling Fusiliers were, in consequence, sent from the United Kingdom, arriving on 5th and 7th September, and two small armoured trains were organized and kept at Oppeln.

On 9th October, in view of possible trouble, all the troops in Beuthen and Tarnowitz were held in readiness to send detachments to Kattowitz (nine miles south-west of Beuthen). Rumours of a putsch were in the air as the time for the expected decision of the Council of the League of Nations approached. It was thought, however, that these stories might have been put about by the Poles in order to induce the *Selbstschutz* to take precipitate action, or to ascertain what attitude the British would assume.

ANNOUNCEMENT OF PARTITION

The decision of the League was promulgated by the Conference of Ambassadors on 21st October, on which day all troops were confined to barracks. It gave Germany most of the disputed territory, but only about a quarter of the coal fields, and to each of the contending nations a minority population of about a quarter of a million. A new duty for the soldiers arose: that of escort to the parties detailed by the International Mixed Commission to run the new boundary between Germany and Poland. A tiresome delay now occurred in the return of the troops owing to the long drawn-out negotiations of the German-Polish Committee at Geneva, appointed to settle details not dealt with in the League of Nations' award. During February, March and April, five new battalions, the 1/K.O.Y.L.I., 2/Cornwall L.I., 1/Gloucestershire, 2/K.R.R.C. and 1/Middlesex, arrived to relieve the 2/Leinster, 2/R. Inniskilling Fusiliers, 2/Connaught Rangers, 1/R. Munster Fusiliers and 1/R. Irish, and at first there was quiet.

[1] See Note at end of Chapter.
[2] Small detachments were constantly on the move, and soldiers, by order, had to walk out in parties of at least three, as assaults on single soldiers had occurred.

The peace was broken by the murder of a sergeant of the Intelligence Police at Antonienhütte, a mining village between Kattowitz and Gleiwitz, by a gang of Polish bandits. The 3/Middlesex, with two tanks, was despatched there from Beuthen, and in two night raids, in conjunction with the police, captured the leader with two more of the murderers and 35 of the gang, to the great satisfaction of the Polish population.

EVACUATION

On 25th May, 1922, the preliminary order for the evacuation of Upper Silesia and its transfer to the Poles and Germans was issued. The handing over was to be in six phases, taking 24 days. The cavalry, artillery, tanks and Headquarters Train Company, were to proceed direct to Cologne from their stations ; the rest of the British troops were to be concentrated in the Gross Strehlitz, Vassowska and Oppeln areas ; and those places were to be evacuated one by one in that sequence. From Oppeln the order of going would be 1/Middlesex, Divisional Troops and 1/K.O.Y.L.I.

The order of events in each district, on successive days, was to be the dissolution of the local police and the taking over by the German or Polish police, then the Allied troops would leave and the German or Polish troops arrive.

The 17th June was fixed as the first day, but by the beginning of the month considerable disturbances were occurring throughout the industrial area in anticipation of the partition being put into force. To quote the Intelligence Summary :

" The Germans have been compelling Poles to leave that part of the country which is to remain German ; and the Poles have likewise been ill-treating and driving out Germans in the districts which are to become Polish. Further, the Poles have formed bands who have been endeavouring to destroy mines and factories in the German portion of the country. In most places the *Gemeindewachen* have left their posts and in many of the areas political officers have also ceased to work."

A state of siege was therefore proclaimed in the districts affected. Detachments were sent to quell disturbances : two companies to Laband (two miles north of Gleiwitz) ; an international brigade of French-British-Italian battalions to the Rybnik district, where strong measures had to be taken ; and two companies of the 1/Gloucestershire and two tanks to Bobrek (a mile west of Beuthen). At the last-named place armed bands of Poles which were looting shops retired on the arrival of the British to villages near by, and opened fire ; but they showed no sign of fight when the villages were visited by tanks. In one village a garrison was left and the area became comparatively quiet. In other villages near-by trouble between Germans and Poles continued, and the 3/Middlesex was compelled to intervene to protect German mining officials. As murders were perpetrated by both contestants, more troops were moved to the industrial area, and many " caches " of arms and ammunition were seized by night. At one village where this was done some shots were fired and the crowd tried to rush the houses held by the troops and, being foiled, struck work in the mines next day. The officer commanding 1/Middlesex, who was in charge, convinced a deputation that they were only harming themselves by striking, and work was resumed. The expulsion of Germans and Poles from the opposing parts of the country continued ; but the impartial attitude of the Allied troops had an excellent effect and the situation gradually improved.

During the handing-over process, in order to reduce the possibility of any " incident," it was ordered that the troops must not walk about singly or late at night ; must not walk, cycle or ride far from their station, or frequent places where trouble might be expected ; and must avoid going near processions and demonstrations.

FINAL SCENES

The final handing-over ceremonies were simple : at eight selected towns the Allied flags were lowered to the accompaniment of the " General Salute," and the German or Polish flag hoisted ; the troops then marched away to entrain as soon as possible, having for the previous 24 hours been confined to barracks to make sure that no " incidents " happened. The last flags were hauled down at Gross Strehlitz on 8th July and at Oppeln on 9th July. At one place there was little " *panache* " about the ceremony, as the Polish general arrived in a peasant's cart drawn by oxen, sitting on a load of roots, with his kit in a straw-plaited bag.

The Allied troops were not able to leave by train without manifestation of the ill-feeling of the Germans towards the French. As a precaution, companies of British infantry were sent in lorries to Gleiwitz, Peiskretscham (on the railway to Gross Strehlitz) and Schimiscow (just west of Gross Strehlitz). At the first place they were to cover the departure of their Allies and in the two latter to stop them being fired on as they passed through by train. On 3rd July an order was issued : " you should not hesitate to shoot anyone who shoots at you or who shoots at or attempts to shoot at any of the Allied trains passing through." This nearly had unfortunate consequences ; for French troops, passing through Vassowska by train at night, opened fire on the 2nd Rhine Brigade, bivouacked near the junction : they had heard the sound of a horn, and, taking it to herald an attack, decided to anticipate it. The horn had been blown, as is German custom, by a pointsman engaged in shunting trucks.

The British carried off with them to Cologne, 35 prisoners (including the murderers of the Intelligence Police sergeant) who were under sentence for crimes against the Allied forces. As an attempt at rescue by some thousands of persons was expected in Gross Strehlitz prison, a special guard was mounted on the night before the departure, armed with machine guns and hand grenades. The prisoners were in charge of French gendarmes and British Military Police, and were taken from Gross Strehlitz prison to the station by a mixed escort, the route being piqueted, the station guarded and a cement works north of the station held. They were placed in wired carriages in the centre of the train, and the bolts and locks of the doors of the lavatories were removed. The train escort was two companies of French and two of British infantry, and a detachment of Italians. Further, an outer circle of defence of the station against attack from the neighbouring woods was formed by French and British troops, and an advanced dressing station opened. No precaution was omitted, and nothing untoward occurred.

Note

Instructions for Raiding Parties

Upper Silesia

29th August, 1921

1. All ranks must realize that, although bloodshed should be avoided if possible, they must protect themselves with all the means at their disposal if they are attacked, acting in every way as though they were in the presence of an enemy.

2. Should a patrol meet an armed party, the members of which can show no authority for carrying arms, it is the duty of the patrol to disarm them : should the order to disarm not be obeyed, resort must be had to fire action, if necessary, to enforce the order.

3. Every lorry patrol and raiding party will invariably include at least one Lewis-gun detachment.

4. Written orders will always be given to the commander of a raiding party stating the object of the raid, and the general course of action to be taken.

5. The officer ordering a raid will be responsible that all proper military precautions are taken : such as maintaining communication with the raiding party ; keeping himself informed of the progress of the raid and having an adequate reserve available should the raiding party require assistance.

6. When a civil official, such as a *Kreis* Controller, accompanies a raiding party or patrol, he has no military status whatever, even though he be a military officer in uniform.

The officer commanding the party, no matter what his rank, is the commander and is responsible for taking correct military action.

7. Should a case arise where the commander of a raiding party finds himself too weak to carry out his object, he should send back for reinforcements, whilst himself keeping in touch with the place he has been sent to raid, and endeavouring to prevent the escape of any of the inhabitants.

He should remember that modern weapons in well-trained hands give a very great power of defence even to a small party.

CHAPTER XV
LIEUT.-GENERAL SIR A. GODLEY'S COMMAND
25TH MARCH, 1922—16TH JUNE, 1924
1922
THE REPARATION CRISIS
(End Paper)
PEACE AND DRASTIC ECONOMY ON THE RHINE

The early months of Lieut.-General Sir Alexander Godley's command on the Rhine, like the last months of his predecessor's, were uneventful. So quiet were they that towards the end of the year, on 8th December, 1922, he proposed to the War Office that the rendering of a monthly war diary might cease. On the 22nd the Army Council approved of the discontinuance.

Except for the despatch of a party of Military Police in April to Knapsack to maintain order during a short strike, for ceremonial visits, and for small troop movements, nothing indeed is recorded in the General Staff war diary of the British Army of the Rhine from April to December, 1922. In June and July Major-General Heneker's division returned from Silesia, and three of the infantry battalions which had been longest in Germany—the 2/Black Watch, the 1/Durham L.I. and 3/Middlesex—were sent home and replaced by the 1/Northumberland Fusiliers, the 1/York & Lancaster and the 1/West Yorkshire.[1]

For economic reasons, Signals were cut down from a battalion organization to a company, and Lieut.-General Godley had a long correspondence with the War Office before he could obtain five wireless sets—he had asked for ten—for use in emergency should telegraphic and telephonic communication break down. His transport was reduced to two companies M.T. and two H.T., in each case instead of three, just sufficient for a small flying column. In July it was decided that all philanthropic institutions, with one or two exceptions, should cease work in barracks, as accommodation for them, paid out of Army funds, was very expensive. The only R.A.F. unit on the Rhine (No. 12 Squadron) was withdrawn early in 1923, and Bickendorf airfield was handed back to the Germans, who had to maintain it for use by Allied aircraft in case of emergency.

---

[1] The other five battalions in the Rhineland were now the 1/Middlesex, 1/K.O.Y.L.I., 2/Cornwall L.I., 1/Gloucestershire and 2/K.R.R.C.

As an outcome of economy discussions, the Army Council gave a decision that the rôle of the British Army of the Rhine was to be prepared to :

(1) participate in an Allied defence scheme ;

(2) participate in an Allied occupation of the Ruhr ; and

(3) provide a small column of a cavalry regiment, two battalions and a field battery, etc.

On Lieut.-General Godley's enquiry whether reinforcements would be sent out to mobilize his weak units, he was informed that, if necessary, complete units would be sent from home.

In May the British Consul-General at Cologne held a conference with the British High Commissioner and a staff officer of the B.A.R., in order to discover some means of regulating the entry of British subjects, who, attracted by the fall of the mark, swarmed into Occupied Territory. Many time-expired soldiers, too, had taken their discharge in Cologne, and the Army did not want any unemployed British in its zone. It was decided to exercise stricter supervision at the points of entry, to admit no one without a passport, to cancel the validity of passports issued to members of the B.A.R. when they ceased to belong to it, and to refuse to allow discharges to be taken in Cologne unless the soldier had a genuine offer of employment.

GERMAN RAILWAY CONSTRUCTION

German railway construction in the Rhineland first became a subject of discussion in 1922 when, on 19th January, the question was brought before the Allied Military Committee at Versailles by the French Section. In a memorandum laid before the Committee it was asserted that the majority of the railway improvements planned by the Germans would have a strategic rather than an economic value, and advised that the work should be stopped under Article 43 of the Peace Treaty, which forebade " the upkeep of all permanent works for mobilization " on the left bank of the Rhine and in the 50-km. Neutral Zone. The Military Committee reported to the Conference of Ambassadors that certain constructional work should be stopped and certain portions of the existing track destroyed. On 19th May a Note to that effect was sent to Berlin. Germany, of course, protested ; but in October the Conference of Ambassadors, ignoring the High Commission and the G.O.C. of the B.A.R., decided that the Inter-Allied Railway Commission should supervise the carrying out of the Allied demands. In the early part of 1923, after the occupation of the

Ruhr, to be related, the French doubled the Düren–Euskirchen line, and by using the material collected by the Germans, paralysed the new construction planned by them. The wrangle over the destruction of the existing track went on for years, the Foreign Office and the General Staff joining in, the one in 1927 laying down that the Locarno treaty made it impossible for the Allies to impose their own interpretation on Article 43, and the latter pointing out that no increased facilities could possibly be wanted for Germany's reduced Army of 100,000, as the existing lines were amply sufficient to deploy 21 divisions. Nothing was settled, and in October, 1928, Germany began to make applications for permission to enlarge certain stations, lengthen platforms, and construct three railway bridges over the Rhine ; in July, 1929, however, she agreed to " demilitarize " certain railways, the Allies then laying down that " all German railway improvements' were to " be considered solely from the point of view of the security of " the troops of occupation."

THE HIGH COMMISSION

The High Commission continued its activities in 1922. It obtained the removal of the Wiesbaden *Regierungspräsident*, Dr. Momm, and the sentencing of his *Regierungsassessor*, Dr. Prange, to five years' imprisonment for not preventing the Frankfort police from entering Occupied Territory and carrying off a German who was working in the French interests. It prohibited the German ex-officers' club (*Verein der ehemaligen Offiziere*), and forbade the celebration of the 50th Anniversary of the founding of the German Empire, the singing of the national anthem, and the carrying of flags by boy scouts (*Pfadfinder* and *Wandervögel*), and expelled certain officials and private persons. The High Commission also legislated for the ferries and railways, defined " school furniture," and ordered that applications for transport of arms, ammunition and war material should be in septuplicate.

The only new regulations which affected the Army, promulgated on 15th July, 1922, were :

" The High Commission has decided that a clock need only be provided in the dining room of officers' billets," and that members of the Army must not claim exemption from the tax on wine bought from *Verbraucherwirte*—which means " sellers of goods to be consumed on the premises " ; but canteens and other officially recognized organizations might claim exemption from the tax in respect of foreign tobacco, cigars and cigarettes bought by them in Germany for re-sale to the Armies of Occupation.

THE REPARATION PROBLEM

The interest of the year 1922 lay in the Reparation problem, and the manœuvres of the Germans to avoid payment, or at least to obtain an undated moratorium.

Seeing the Allied forces grow weaker, and knowing that their own military strength was now considerable and growing, the *Reichstag*, on 30th March, while refusing to increase taxation, passed a resolution of protest against the intolerable demands made of the German people by the latest, much reduced, proposals of the Reparation Commission. Significantly, on 24th June, Herr Walter Rathenau, the Minister of Foreign Affairs, head of the German delegation to the Reparations Commission, and to the Genoa Economic Congress, who was disposed to negotiate, was shot dead in front of his house by " Nationalists ". The general result of her manœuvres and the loss of Rathenau were disastrous to Germany's finances. On 1st August the mark was 2,850 to the £ ; on 5th September, 6,525 ; and at the end of the year, about 40,000. The confusion in the public finances was inextricable : official salaries and wages could not be raised quickly enough to keep pace with the rise in prices. It was a great time for the British Army of the Rhine, whose members could purchase for a few pence luxuries, ordinarily the privilege only of the very rich. The German Government proposed that reparation should be reduced definitely to " tolerable dimensions," that Germany should be released from all payments both in cash and kind for a period of several years, given a bank credit and restored to trade equality. Mr. Lloyd George's Coalition Government had gone out of office in October, and Mr. Bonar Law, who had succeeded him on the 24th, was equally anxious for a settlement. The forceful Monsieur Poincaré, however, since January, 1922, Prime Minister of France, now in control of the executive and no longer powerless as he had been when President, was against letting Germany off a *pfennig* or granting her a moratorium without "productive pledges". Yet by the fact of making no payments, except a proportion in kind, Germany did enjoy a moratorium in 1922.

With considerable effect, too, she still continued to resist disarmament, claiming that the Commission of Control was not competent in certain matters and at the same time requesting concessions : permission to retain supernumerary officers and n.c.os., mobile heavy artillery, equipment and transport.   The Commission having reported that the critical stage of disarmament had arrived, the Allied Governments on 29th September, 1922 by their Ambassadors in Berlin, handed another Note to the German Government.   This called for satisfaction on five points :

(1) The reorganization of the police ;

(2) the completion of the transformation of factories ;

(3) the delivery of non-authorized material ;

(4) the delivery of the accounts of the stocks of war material during the war and during the Armistice ;

(5) the promulgation of the laws placing German legislation in harmony with military clauses of the Peace Treaty.

RHINELAND OCCUPATION AREAS
JANUARY 1924

HOLLAND

BELGIUM

WESTPHALIA

Dortmund

ESSEN
Bochum
Duisburg
Krefeld
R. Ruhr

Neuss
DÜSSELDORF

BELGIAN

Solingen
Grevenbroich
Opladen
Bedburg
BRITISH
R. Erft
COLOGNE
Maastricht
Düren
Siegburg
AACHEN
BONN
LIEGE
Euskirchen

Marburg

HESSE

Giessen

COBLENCE

Homburg

R. Rhine
WIESBADEN
FRANKFORT
R. Moselle
MAYENCE
Bingen
Darmstadt
FRENCH

TREVES

LUXEMBURG
Mannheim

Thionville
Spires

METZ
Saarbrücken
Kaiserslautern

Karlsruhe

SCALE OF MILES.
10 5 0   10   20   30   40   50

Compiled in the Historical Section (Military Branch).

Ordnance Survey 1943.

CHAPTER XVI

LIEUT.-GENERAL SIR A. GODLEY'S COMMAND
(*Continued*)
1923

THE OCCUPATION OF THE RUHR AND ITS CONSEQUENCES
(End Paper and Sketch 5)

State of the British Army of the Rhine

The year 1923 was marked by the French and Belgian occupation of the Ruhr and its attendant troubles, by the culmination and failure of the Rhineland Separatist movement, and by the complete collapse of the mark. These great events in German history hardly affected the routine of the British troops on the Rhine, now all quartered in barracks and hutments in Cologne and its suburbs. Since the return of Heneker's division from Silesia, it numbered eight infantry battalions (organized in two brigades), a cavalry regiment, four batteries R.F.A., one battery R.G.A., a field company R.E., and a Tank company, with a minimum of services. The average strength for the year was 576 officers and 8,384 other ranks, with 1,500 horses, exclusive of one naval officer with a few ratings, and one flight R.A.F.

Manœuvres for the first time were held in the Eifel district in August. Extra guard duties became necessary whilst the French were in the Ruhr ; they included the stationing of a battalion on the edge of the bridgehead near Hilden. Some barricades were erected and other precautions taken in view of Separatist troubles in September. Officers' messes and additional married quarters, erected by the Germans under R.E. superintendence, contributed to the comfort of the garrison ; still more so did the continued fall of the mark, until the introduction in the winter of the *Rentenmark* brought inflation to an end, and put the advantage of the exchange on the German side.

French and Belgian Entry into the Ruhr

The anxieties of Lieut.-General Godley and his staff during the year were heavy. On 9th January French and Belgian troops entered the Ruhr, in spite of British efforts to dissuade their Governments from action which, it was considered, could bring no real advantage. Monsieur Poincaré was confident of Germany's capacity to pay for the damage she had done, and thought that Allied pressure would compel her to do so. Germany had made no money payment in 1922, and at the end of the year the Reparation Commission, which had a French president, formally declared her in default, and France decided to seize the Ruhr coal as a " productive pledge " and to occupy the Ruhr as " sanction " for the shortage in the delivery of the reparation quota of coal and wood in 1922. Belgium marched with her, sending a division to join the five French divisions ; Italy sent a party of civil engineers, but no troops. The British Empire remained passive ; the U.S.A. decided to withdraw her contingent, and by 19th February all the American troops—barely a thousand were then remaining[1] —had quitted the Rhineland, and their Zone had been taken over by the French. This left the small British Zone isolated in the midst of French and Belgian troops.[2]

Anticipating the early departure of the United States troops, Lieut.-General Godley had in April, 1922 raised the question of extending the British Zone to include the original Bonn area. The British High Commissioner was in favour of it ; but when Lord Cavan, the Chief of the Imperial General Staff, sounded Maréchal Foch personally, he found that the Frenchman was not only opposed to it, but anxious that the French should be in the possession of the whole Cologne *Bezirk*, to which belong Bonn, Siegburg and Euskirchen already in their hands. The value of Cologne to our Allies as a railway centre will be apparent as this chapter proceeds.

In January, 1923, when the immediate departure of the United States forces had been officially announced, the British Commander-in-Chief again raised the question, and suggested that the garrison should be increased to a division. The War Office, however, considered the matter of the extension of the area as settled ; as for more troops, none were available. As a result the French were placed in a stronger position than ever, without the fairminded and impartial American G.O.C. and his forces to humour and consider.[3]

---

[1] See Note II at end of Chapter IX.

[2] On 5th January President Harding had stated at a press conference that the Administration were in favour of withdrawing the American troops, but that Germany, Belgium, Great Britain and France all wanted them kept on the Rhine : " the Government had not wished to have them withdrawn at any time when the withdrawal might be considered a gesture on the part of the Government in relation to any European crisis." (Allen i., p. 281.)

On 6th January the Senate voted for withdrawal ; on the 11th the President, by cable, ordered the withdrawal. (Allen ii., p. 506, 573.)

[3] The French newspapers called him pro-German, and the German, francophile.

Late on 6th January General Degoutte, as Commander-in-Chief of the Allied Forces, had warned Lieut.-General Godley that French troops were to be concentrated by rail in the area east of Düsseldorf, beginning on 8th January, and suggested that the railways over which these troops would travel through the British Zone should be guarded in accordance with the scheme for the defence of railways already drawn up. Accordingly 6½ companies of British infantry were sent to guard the six lines in question. They remained in position until the 14th, and in the seven days 176 trains of French troops passed through towards the Ruhr.

Deliveries of reparation coal to the French ceased, and a cordon of French and Belgian customs officials and soldiers prevented other coal from being exported to unoccupied Germany ; the mines were soon at a standstill. Under the supervision of a *Mission Interalliée de Contrôle des Usines et Mines*, known as *Micum*, the invaders expelled or imprisoned the recalcitrant German officials and local magnates, removing inhabitants in order to find quarters for the labour which they proceeded to import.

On 19th January the High Commission issued three Ordinances, to take effect the next day ; they placed the coal companies in the Ruhr and in the remainder of the occupied territory, the financial and customs offices, and the forestry departments in the occupied territory, under the control of the Commission.

These Ordinances were bound to cause difficulty if applied in the British Zone. This was known in London, for on the same day Lieut.-General Godley received instructions from the War Office that he should co-operate with Lord Kilmarnock, the British High Commissioner, in carrying out any instructions issued to the latter by the Foreign Office. These instructions turned out to be to the effect that the British Government did not wish to be associated with the French and Belgian Governments in the action they were taking in the Ruhr, but obstacles were not to be placed in their way. On the 22nd, therefore, when by order of the High Commissioner, the French police in Cologne arrested the local head of the German Inland Revenue for refusing to produce his books, and the Director of the Brown Coal Syndicate for refusing to continue deliveries of reparation coal to France and Belgium, the British Military Police attended to prevent a disturbance, but did not otherwise assist and did not interfere.

The Question of Railway Facilities

The question of the railways caused considerable discussion. At 2 a.m. on the 24th, Lieut.-General Godley was informed that General Degoutte feared a general railway strike, and had put the Railway Defence Scheme into force in the French and Belgian areas. This scheme included the guarding and working of essential railway lines by French troops ; and General Payot, in command of the Lines of Communication, now asked that 750 French railway employees might be distributed along the railways in the British Zone, in order to ensure the continuance of traffic in the event of a strike. This request was refused. In the course of the day it was discovered that Herr Bosetter, the acting *Regierungsrat* of Cologne, had called on his employees to strike in the event of the Ruhr magnates, then before a Court Martial, being punished ; but his circular letter was addressed only to those outside the British Zone. He was told by Lieut.-General Godley that the strike, if begun, might nevertheless extend to the British Zone and result in the British Army being withdrawn, which was the last thing the Germans wanted, as it would have left them entirely in the hands of the French and Belgians. Acting on the instructions obtained from the Prussian Minister of the Interior, Bosetter then issued definite orders that the employees in the British Zone should not strike. In the Ruhr a general stand-still prevailed.

Two days later Lieut.-Colonel Ryan, the British Deputy High Commissioner in Coblence, returned from a visit to London where he had learnt the views of the Government. These were that they wished to retain the British Army on the Rhine and to maintain the Entente ; therefore, that it was of primary importance to avoid any incident in the British Zone which might lead to an outcry at home for the recall of the British troops. These views, he was told, were being made known to the French and German Governments, as it was understood that both of them desired the retention of the British Army in the Rhineland.

On the 25th a general strike of bargees took place ; but no disturbance occurred, and the British police boats were not molested. The Cologne newspapers had to be warned that unless they were more temperate in their tone they would be suspended, and the Police President was told that demonstrations in Cologne in support of the passive resisters would not be tolerated.

On the 25th, too, General Payot asked permission to be allowed to work the Mülheim (Cologne)–Opladen–Reisholz[1] line, as owing to the strike in Düsseldorf, the main line trains to Cologne and Paris were being diverted round that town. The request was not acceded to.

On the 27th, the German railwaymen, acting on orders from Berlin, refused to work the line from Coblence to Bonn for the passage of a French troop train, and the French representative on the Inter-Allied Railway Sub-Commission in Cologne, of which Lieut.-Colonel L. Manton, R.E., was president, took over control of all the lines in the Cologne Railway *Direktion* outside the British Zone.[2] General Payot once more asked permission to send his railway troops to the lines in that zone. It was again refused ; but Lieut.-Colonel Manton arranged with Herr von Guérard, the head of the Cologne *Direktion*, and with the leaders of the Railwaymen's Union, that the German railwaymen should take over French troop trains, but not reparation coal trains, at the boundary of the British Zone from the French technical troops, and work then across the zone. All French traffic for the north, however, was to be consigned, as far as possible, to Neuss (on the left bank in the Belgian area, opposite Düsseldorf), and exchange stations were established at Bruhl (9 miles south of Cologne) and Buir (15 miles W.S.W. of Cologne).

On the 29th, the British Commander-in-Chief had a conference with General Degoutte and high French authorities, the outcome of which was a proposal that the German railwaymen in the Cologne *Direktion* outside the British area, who were anxious to return to work, should be allowed to do so, on the understanding that they would not be asked to handle reparation coal trains without three days' notice. On these terms they resumed work on 2nd February.

Orders from Berlin not to assist the French in any way—in defiance of the Rhineland Agreement which had placed the rule of the Rhineland under the High Commission—upset this agreement, and led to the repudiation of the earlier one by which French troop trains were passed through the British Zone. The railwaymen ceased work at most stations, and, according to French reports, many cases of sabotage of the railway and the telegraph and telephone lines occurred. Consequently on 6th February the French and Belgians, with

---

[1] On the edge of the bridgehead, north-west of Hilden. See End Paper.
[2] This Sub-Commission, besides Lieut.-Colonel Manton, contained, of British officers alone, a D.A.D.G.T. and 11 Railway Traffic officers.

the authority of the Railway Sub-Commission, took over all the railways outside the British Zone and worked them for their own convenience with their own technical troops. The request of the G.O.C. of the British Army of the Rhine, that 600 railwaymen should be sent from home to work the essential lines in the British Zone was not approved in London, owing to the attitude of the Railwaymen's Union, which was opposed to lending men for what the executive regarded as strike-breaking. Lieut.-General Godley, therefore, set about having soldiers trained for the duty, and he suggested that the French might be allowed to work the portions of the Düren–Bedburg–Grevenbroich–Neuss line which ran through a corner of the British Zone. The matter was taken up by high authorities, Maréchal Foch requesting the Chief of the Imperial General Staff, who was in Paris, to grant facilities in the British Zone, and an important delegation went to London for the same purpose. After a conference at 10 Downing Street, the details of working the agreement were left to the French and British commanders on the spot. At 6 p.m. on 19th February, therefore, the line was handed over to the French, the broad principle being laid down that the French might send through the British Zone an amount of military traffic equal to the average amount so sent before the occupation of the Ruhr. Herr von Guérard offered no objection, but about a hundred British troops were sent to guard the vulnerable parts of the line against sabotage, until relieved by the French. The High Commission on 31st August belatedly sanctioned the transfer.

After some further discussion, without any interruption of the cordial relations which existed between the French and British officers, the small corner of the British Zone through which the Bedburg–Grevenbroich railway ran was transferred to the French. The Germans, after the intervention of the British Ambassador in Berlin, Lord d'Abernon (appointed in June, 1920), agreed, and consented to a maximum of 10 trains per day on one line on the left bank being run ; but no reparation coal might pass through the British Zone where, except for a protest that the French were using the telephone system, no disagreement of any kind occurred. The Germans were ever anxious to accentuate any small differences between the Allies ; but they were already beginning to lose heart. The occupation of the Ruhr was costing them large sums directly for the maintenance of the passive resistance, and even larger sums indirectly by the loss of the Ruhr supplies and manufactures. Although stirred to anger by the French seizing 12 milliards of marks sent to pay strike wages in the

Ruhr, falsely stated to be earmarked for the British Army of the Rhine, Berlin cancelled the instructions which had been given to cut off the electricity supply in the Ruhr.

In order to get control of the railway on the right bank of the Rhine leading to Siegburg, the French on the 25th proceeded to occupy the areas in the Neutral Zone between the Mayence and the Coblence bridgeheads and between the Coblence and the Cologne bridgeheads ; and on 1st March the High Commission issued Ordinance No. 149, to the effect that, both in the old and new occupied areas of the Rhineland, railways had been transferred to a French-Belgian Railway Administration (*Régie des chemins de fer des territoires occupés*), charged with the technical, commercial and financial exploitation of the railways in the interests of the Army, and " of the civil population in so far as the necessities of life are concerned."

On 2nd March the " *Régie*," as it was called, took over the railway from Coblence to Siegburg, ejecting the German personnel. It now controlled and worked all the railways leading into the British Zone except those running east and north-east from Cologne via Engelskirchen, Wermelskirchen, Solingen and Grafrath, and on these the Régie placed control posts where they left the British Zone. An agreement as to the working of the lines was reached ; but during 7th, 8th and 9th March, the French gradually encircled the British Zone on its eastern side,[1] by a belt of ground six to nine miles wide, and extended the customs posts into it, thus creating a trade barrier between the British Zone and Germany. On land, therefore, the British Army of the Rhine was cut off. The Rhine still remained an open fairway for the passage of supplies and leave-men. It had long been in use for the former purposes. Except, however, for occasional delays, the leave trains were not affected by the strikes.

In order to run as few French trains as possible through the British Zone, the Railway Commission, with the permission of the High Commission, set about doubling the Euskirchen–Düren line, as already noticed.

THE RÉGIE

The Régie operated all the railways in occupied territory except those on the British " island," where the Germans remained at work as before. By what is known as the " Godley-Payot Pact " of 3rd April, ten French transport trains and two supply trains were permitted to pass through the British Zone in both directions daily.

---

[1] See Sketch 5.

The Régie had to contend not only with passive resistance' but also with constant sabotage. This was dealt with, according to German precedent, by severe punishments, by placing hostages in the trains and by increasing the length of time for which the frontier between Germany and the occupied territory would be closed.[1] The German Government forbade its nationals to use the Régie lines, but with only partial success ; for the passenger traffic of 30,000 in May rose to over three million in August. The imported staff of French and Belgian engineers, guards and signalmen, numbering only 10,036, soon increased to over 15,000 by a call for volunteers, was quite insufficient to work a system which had employed 170,000 Germans ;[2] but, backed up by the High Commission and the French Commander-in-Chief, the Régie carried at least the reparation coal required, and the supplies and reinforcements for the Ruhr garrison, besides the civil traffic.

Seeing that passive resistance was a failure, in spite of the large cost of financing it ; terrified by the general unrest, due to the industrial confusion and the hardships brought about by the financial uncertainty and absence of coal supplies from the Ruhr ; and condemned by public opinion as favouring the capitalists and profiteers, the German Government in April and June tried to negotiate with Monsieur Poincaré ; but the payment it offered on reparation account, thirty million sterling, was wholly inadequate. On 13th August, therefore, the Ministry of Dr. Cuno, the " business " premier, gave place to a Coalition Government under Herr Gustav Stresemann, the manager of a chocolate combine, leader of the German People's Party, formerly a National Liberal.[3] But the fall of the mark continued, and living conditions, particularly in the middle classes, grew incredibly severe ; investments became mere paper ; previously well-to-do families were reduced to one

---

[1] A German youth named Schlageter was caught in the act of placing a charge in a bridge and shot. He at once became a German national hero, and has a memorial obelisk. Other saboteurs were sent to the penal settlement of Cayenne.

[2] Tirard, pp. 363–4.

[3] He is described in *Brockhaus* as " one of the astutest parliamentary speakers and tacticians of his time."

His so-called *Volkspartei* was the party of the great industrialists, while the *Deutsch-Nationalpartei* was that of the Prussian Junkers, the landed gentry, monarchists and militarists. During the 1914–18 war and before, he had been one of the most violent of the young pan-Germans and was, for Parliamentary purposes, at the disposal of the Great General Staff, so that he became known as " *Ludendorff's junger Mann.*" His fellow-countrymen mistrusted him, saying " *Stresemann der mal links kann und der mal rechts kann.*" (Stresemann sometimes inclines to the Right, sometimes to the Left.)

decent meal a week ; professional men were paid in kind.[1]
On 26th September, unable to obtain the reduction of Reparation to a " tolerable " figure, Stresemann called off passive resistance, and very soon about 70,000 railwaymen were working under French orders, and more French and Belgians, to a total of 32,000 of the former and 8,000 of the latter, were brought to supervise them.   The Régie system hardly paid its way, but the deficit was somewhat diminished by the putting into circulation of the Régie franc.

The occupation of the Ruhr, which still continued, as a " productive pledge " and the passive resistance as the countermove had proved costly experiments, neither of which had brought about the desired result.

THE RHINELAND SEPARATIST MOVEMENT

The calling off of passive resistance in occupied territory did nothing to improve the economic situation or quieten down unrest.   Spartacist and anti-Government risings took place in Saxony and Bavaria and Thuringia, and as far afield as Küstrin (50 miles east of Berlin).   They all, including the Ludendorff-Hitler putsch in Munich, quickly ended in failure. The only rising of interest to the British Army of the Rhine was the so-called " Separatist Movement," for the purpose of organizing a Rhineland republic, to which allusion has already been made.   According to the Military Governor " the possibility of the Rhineland's independence of Germany was present from the first days of the occupation".   It was mentioned in a Cologne newspaper in December, 1918[2] and as early as February, 1919, when the Military Governor sought instructions, he was informed that the inhabitants might be left to choose their own form of Government.   The French, as they had no Channel to guard their frontier, were eager to see a buffer State between themselves and their hereditary enemy.   They therefore decided to foster and support the

---

[1] At this period the fall of the mark was so rapid that farmers from outlying villages ceased bringing cattle, etc., to market in the towns of the occupied territory ; because by the time they had returned home with the price in paper money they found they had made a loss instead of a profit on the beasts.

A deputation of Germans, headed by a woman spokesman, came to G.H.Q. and demanded Army rations to feed the starving.   She was asked to show what her own countrymen were doing to help the poor, as that must be known before the case could be considered.   The deputation left and did not return.

[2] The *Kölnische Volkszeitung* of 4th December.

Brockhaus, in its article on " Separatisten," says the movement began in December, 1918.

Separatist movement. When in May, 1919 private enquiry was made of the Military Governor by a French emissary already well known to him, Major-General Clive told him, " We are here to keep order, and that is what we shall do " ; in the absence of General Robertson, he then decided to go to Paris to seek instructions of the Prime Minister, then in the French capital. Mr. Lloyd George spoke to him severely and at great length—although the Rhineland was in military occupation under the Armistice terms—on the impropriety of any soldier allowing himself to be mixed up in political matters, and said plainly that hard terms would be imposed on Germany, but he did not wish to see that country further weakened and should not at all like the Rhineland to break away. This was all the Military Governor wished to know. The day after his return to Cologne, 22nd May, he was rung up from General Degoutte's headquarters by his French friend, who then said, " the thing has started, at Wiesbaden. It is being run by a Dr. Dorten,[1] and it is going well." No more than " intellectual precautions " against disorder were taken in the British Zone, and the judgment exercised there proved right, as the Dorten putsch petered out in five days. A German warrant was issued for Dorten's arrest for high treason ; but it could not be executed in French occupied territory ; and when he was kidnapped by the Frankfort police, and carried into the *Reich*, French pressure exercised through the High Commission soon brought about his release.

Popular feeling in the British Zone for and against autonomy ran high, and both sides enquired of the British authorities how far they might go. On 21st August, 1919, therefore, the following proclamation, signed by the Military Governor, after approval by the Foreign and War Offices, was handed to the *Regierungspräsident* and the *Oberbürgermeister* of Cologne :

" It is hereby notified that, while the British military authorities remain in control of the area occupied by the British Army, no change in the German administration of that area will be permitted, and no new authority will be recognized without the previous sanction of the British military authorities.

" Any person who commits an act in disregard of this Notice, and any person who aids or abets in such action, will render himself liable to imprisonment or expulsion from the occupied zone, or to both penalties."

For nearly four years little more was heard of Separatism ; but concurrently with the French entry into the Ruhr, the agitation was openly renewed, propaganda meetings were held, local forces, called the *Rheinlandschutz*, organized, armbands of

---

[1] He was a young lawyer of Bonn.

Separatist colours—green, white, red—worn, arms procured
and drilling was carried out in the French and Belgian Zones.
The collapse of passive resistance in the Ruhr, where four
million people, with the men unemployed, were faced with the
prospect of starvation, and the general distress and unrest
elsewhere, seemed to bring the opportunity for the disintegra-
tion of the *Reich*. An independent Government was established
by Dorten and Matthes (a South German journalist) in Düsseldorf as *Das Rheinische Unabhängigkeitsbund Direktorium*, and
on the morning of 21st October, 1923 the Separatist bands
seized the Town Hall and other official buildings in Aachen,
prematurely, as it seems, and on the next day similar action
was taken in a number of Rhineland towns.

In Cologne nothing whatever occurred, and, in reply to a
War Office enquiry, Lieut.-General Godley telegraphed on the
23rd that there was no cause for anxiety in the British Zone,
and no reason why British troops should become engaged :
provided the rival factions were allowed to fight it out, the
German police were confident that they could crush any attempt
to proclaim a Republic. Later on the same day he telegraphed
that he conceived it to be his duty to allow the German police
to disarm or eject any armed body of Separatists which entered
the British Zone : he would give the German police such assistance as was necessary : the majority of the civil population of
Cologne were " all for a quiet life " : trouble was only likely
to come by armed bodies entering from outside—and barricades
had been erected and British troops were held in readiness
to deal with any such incursion. His action was approved.
Notice of these precautions was broadcast ; they were effective
in preventing any attempt at entry into the British area, and
killed any Separatist movement there.

In a written report dated the 23rd, and timed 7 p.m., the
G.O.C. of the B.A.R. stated that the Separatists were in control
at Treves, Wiesbaden, Ems, Düren, Bonn, Duisburg, and a
dozen small towns : at Mayence and Coblence the situation
was uncertain : at Aachen the movement was collapsing :
and all was quiet in Cologne and Düsseldorf (where a putsch
on 30th September, " Bloody Sunday," had failed). Separatism,
he thought, had not the sympathy of the " solid working man "
or of the Communist Party as a whole, and the Separatist
bands seemed to be composed mostly of " roughs." He ended
by saying that he did not expect any attempt by the Separatists
to seize Cologne by force ; if they had any success in the outlying districts it would not be of importance ; but if they
maintained control in the large towns where they had gained

it, they might bring pressure on Cologne to join them. From the military point of view, though the B.A.R. was sufficient to deal with local disorders, it would require reinforcement if the *Reich* moved against the new State should it be formed.

On the 25th the British High Commissioner reported to London that Britain was faced with the possible establishment, with French support and against the wishes of the majority, of an independent Rhineland State, and grave complications would then ensue. He asked if it was intended, in agreement with our Allies, to support the movement to establish a State within the framework of the *Reich*. He was instructed to give no encouragement to any movement.

The Separatist movement spread on 2nd November to the Palatinate ; but it received a heavy blow when, on 9th November, the Belgian Government decided to disarm the Separatists, on account of the murders, outrages and robberies committed. Want of funds, in spite of printing paper money to finance the unemployed, hampered the executive ; in the Rhineland the agitation petered out ; and on 26th November the temporary Government dissolved itself.

In the Palatinate the fight went on into February, 1924, even after its leader Heinz had been assassinated in a restaurant. The Rhineland leaders escaped to France, and there was no further talk of Separatism. Subsequently it was said to have failed because all decent Germans wanted to remain citizens of the *Reich*. According to Lieut.-General Godley, a factor which contributed to the lack of any enthusiasm for change was the prosperity of the Rhineland under occupation : cars were plentiful, expensive houses were being built, new municipal works were constantly being undertaken, the places of entertainment and refreshment were crowded : prices were high, but all classes had money to spend.

THE RENTENMARK

To remedy the financial situation in the *Reich*, on 15th November Herr Stresemann, on the advice of experts, introduced the *Rentenmark*, nominally the equivalent of a billion (1,000 million) ordinary marks. It was issued by a *Rentenbank*, formed for the purpose, with a capital of 3,200 million R.M., obtained by the issue of 500 gold mark interest-paying *Rentenbriefe*, secured on the agricultural industries and the banks of Germany. The mark was repudiated. This was calculated to stabilize the German currency and was not a deliberate attempt to rob the *Reich's* creditors. It incidentally reduced the soldiers of the British Army of the Rhine from being millionaires when the exchange was thousands of marks to the £, to extreme penury, as they did not even get 20 R.M. for the £, and with the introduction of the Rentenmark other marks had become valueless.[1] The Allied Governments did not interfere, as their experts informed them that, although stability would be attained for a few months, it was on a basis which, in the absence of other measures, could only be temporary.[2]

The general distress in Germany was not immediately removed, and on 22nd November, Stresemann's Ministry was defeated, and Dr. Marx, leader of the Centre, became Chancellor. Stresemann, however, remained as Foreign Secretary. The first act of the new Ministry was to renew diplomatic relations with France and Belgium and ask for a credit for food.

The Allies were disposed to be helpful, as they hoped that under the guidance of the new Ministry the scarcely disguised manœuvres of the military authorities to build up a large Army regardless of Treaty obligations would be discouraged. In the spring the Commission of Control had discovered and reported to the Conference of Ambassadors that reserves were being trained, and courses held, at least in Pomerania and Saxony, for the training of supernumerary officers. On 18th October the Premier of Saxony admitted in a speech that the military authorities were organizing an official " Black *Reichswehr*," as we should say a " Shadow Army," formed from the thousands of men available on the dissolution of the *Selbstchutz*. Far from the forbidden re-arming being discouraged, it had official support and increased in intensity, as will be seen, year by year.

ACTIVITIES OF THE HIGH COMMISSION

The Ordinances, Instructions and decisions of the High Commission had the force of law. Those issued in 1923 alone fill a volume of 996 pages. They vary in importance from Ordinances handing the railways, mines, etc., in occupied territory to the Régie down to petty domestic decisions such as, that the upkeep of gardens of new houses (officers') was " limited to brushing and weeding paths and cutting grass " ; that the following garden tools were to be issued free to each house : " 1 spade, 1 fork, 1 hoe, 1 rake and 1 trowel " ; and that " in

---

[1] Many mark notes were thrown fluttering down from the tower of the *Dom* or sent to London, where notes for millions of marks were sold as curios for a penny a piece by street hawkers.
[2] Dawes, p. 298.

regard to a billiard table in a requisitioned mess, old balls and cloth might be replaced by requisition orders under Article 6 of the [Rhineland] Agreement." By Ordinance No. 139, of thirteen Articles, the High Commission formed " The Inter-Allied Billeting and Quartering Committee for the Area of Coblence," in order to secure the best billets in the town for its staff.

Most of the legislation of the High Commission bore reference to the control of the Ruhr and the defeat one by one, as instances occurred, of new tricks invented by the Germans to circumvent, annoy and injure the occupiers.[1] A rumour ran round the British Army of the Rhine that throughout 1923 the British High Commissioner repeated the words " I abstain " at intervals, and that Monsieur Tirard and his Belgian colleague did as they pleased.[2]

The items of general application in the occupied territory, besides those already mentioned, were few.

The original Ordinance No. 2 was stiffened so that it was punishable to supply any members of the Armies of Occupation with any spirituous liquor, or intoxicating or stupefying drug, or supply wine or beer or any other alcoholic drink except in conformity with the regulations of the military authorities. The trade in absinthe and similar liquors was restricted. The surveillance of prostitution and " light women " was tightened up.

An Inter-Allied Coal Commission was set up to supervise the distribution of coal and brown coal to the Armies and other persons in occupied territory and apportion the allotment of coal to other persons.

Customs duties might not be paid in paper marks. Fines were increased as the mark fell ; later they were readjusted and had to be paid in gold marks. Banks were compelled to exhibit the rates of exchange. Shop windows might be requisitioned for the exhibition of the orders of the High Commission or the military commanders.

The military were charged with the execution of deportation orders. German police who entered occupied territory on duty were not permitted to carry firearms. The possession of asphyxiating-gas pistols was forbidden.

---

[1] As it may be useful to have a handy record, the headings are collected, roughly grouped, not in order of issue, in a Note at the end of the chapter.
[2] According to his American colleague, Lord Kilmarnock had instructions not to participate in any debate bearing on the Ruhr occupation. (Allen i., p. 287.)

An Industrial Restitution Service was empowered to sell, after giving public notice, goods on railway trucks of which it was impossible to ensure delivery. Similarly, the Customs might sell goods seized by its officers, legal ownership passing with the sale. The export tax on mineral waters was reduced from 10 to 4 per cent.

" School buildings attended by children of the Armies of Occupation " were to be considered as military buildings, and demands could be made on the German authorities to construct new buildings if the existing structures were considered inadequate or unsuitable. Bath houses, with light and heating, might be demanded, and water, fuel and other consumable articles, including soap, requisitioned. The installation of electric light for cinemas in soldiers' recreation rooms, both for lighting the room and for working the apparatus, might be demanded.

Platforms and 200 chairs, including transport and labour, might be requisitioned for fêtes. Racehorses sent by rail to Army race meetings would be considered Army horses in the matter of rates. The Armies of Occupation were exempted from dog tax, but *Kurtax* at watering-places had to be paid.

If articles belonging to the proprietor were stolen from a billet, the amount of the loss would be fixed, and contributory negligence, if any, established by a Local Assessment Commission. Claims for damage in a billet would be referred to the military authorities. Damage caused by fire in a billet or requisitioned building, except in cases of grave negligence, would be borne by the householder, who ought to have been insured, without prejudice to his right of recourse against the *Reich*. The return of requisitioned articles was provided for, a distinction being drawn between those requisitioned permanently and those, so to say, on hire without change of ownership. No occasion existed, it was ruled, to require the refund of turn-over tax on fees charged by a German doctor for attendance on the wife of a soldier.

NOTE

Ordinances, Instructions and Decisions of the Inter-Allied Rhineland High Commission Specially Affecting the Control of the Ruhr

The preamble of nearly every Ordinance contained the words that it was ordered, " as a result of the voluntary default on the part of Germany established by the Reparation Commission."

A series of Ordinances authorized the seizure and collection of the Coal Tax, the Customs receipts, the produce of the State forests and vineyards, all funds in banks, machinery and chattels, including animals, belonging to the German Government, the sequestration of stocks of coal and river craft ; and the formation of committees to manage these properties. Seized property, however, was to be taken charge of by a Liquidation Committee of the Restitution Department, and fines, and forfeitures and seizures of funds by a General Profitable Pledges Account.

The Inter-Allied Commission of Control of Mines and Factories (Micum), sitting at Essen, was substituted for the German Rhine-Westphalian Coal Syndicate, which had ruled over the industries of the Ruhr.

Powers were taken to protect German protegés and agents of the High Commission and of the French Commander-in-Chief in every possible way ; to prevent persons accused before, or convicted by a German Court being transferred to the *Reich* without permission ; to remove prisoners from German prisons ; to upset the sentences of German courts of law ; to deport German officials and others at will (for the purposes of deportation " family " was defined) ; to make use of the houses of deportees ; to have access to the records and documents of the German Administration ; to force banks to divulge information and newspapers to insert announcements ; to prohibit exports to Germany ; to prohibit meetings and to restrict movement by night ; to prevent German officials reseizing sequestrated goods, etc., which had been sold ; and to object to German legislation applying to occupied territories—a list of German laws " not applicable " was published monthly. The German representative on the High Commission was expelled and no ex-members of his staff were allowed to remain in occupied territories without a special permit.

A " Criminal Ordinance regarding Railways " was issued. It proved insufficient to prevent sabotage ; *Bürgermeistern* were therefore ordered to arrange for guarding the lines and level crossings, with penalties for neglect to do so ; persons, material and animals might be requisitioned to repair damage ; and the German police might be ordered to assist in the investigation of acts of sabotage, and in the removal of explosives. Thefts and pillage on the Régie railway could be very heavily punished. Another Ordinance gave to the railway personnel, including those of German nationality, the legal status of persons attached to the Armies of Occupation, and the benefit of the provisions of the Ordinances. Lorry traffic having greatly increased as a consequence of the " Edict of the German Government prohibiting the use of railways," lorries, and later all motors, were required to have a special permit issued by the Régie; later no vehicle carrying coal, coke or lignite originating in the occupied territories, might use the roads without a special pass. Tram-cars were not to carry more passengers than permitted in 1922. Authority was given to block roads ; and it was prohibited to move from one district to another any means of transport or any material which had been the subject of an earlier census. Night traffic between the occupied territories and the *Reich* was forbidden. On the other hand, penalties were fixed for the non-delivery of coal and coke and for crushing coke (which rendered it unfit for use in blast furnaces).

Water traffic was also legislated for. All barges required a licence. Night navigation within 500 metres of the Rhine bridges was forbidden, and no goods might be " deposited in proximity of the navigable waterways except at certain specified wharves or other places in use before 11th January 1923 ".

For movement between the occupied territory and Germany and countries adjacent, the stamp of the High Commission on the identity card was necessary.

The possession of prohibited publications could be presumed to be an act preparatory to the commission of an offence ; compensation for damage caused by civil disturbances was a charge against the *Reich* ; municipal police might not be employed outside their own district. The Committee and the branches of the *Ruhrhilfe*, a society founded after the French entry into the Ruhr to assist the necessitous there, were interdicted, and the veto was not escaped by the society changing its name to *Deutsche Volksopfer*. Similarly the *Deutscher Pfadfinderbund* was not able to evade the ban by changing its name to *Rheinischer Pfadfinderbund*. A new society, the *Bismarck Jugend*, was forbidden.

Heavy penalties were laid down for the offence of contesting the binding effect of any Ordinances or regulations made or orders given in pursuance of an Ordinance, either by means of the public press or by pamphlet, or by statements made orally or in writing either publicly or secretly ; or of resisting the Ordinances, regulations or orders ; or taking part in the distribution of funds or gifts intended to foster hostility against the Allied authorities, or to maintain disobedience, or active or passive resistance, or any act which tended to defeat the ends of the Ordinances or impede the normal workings of the bodies and departments created by the High Commission.

CHAPTER XVII

LIEUT.-GENERAL SIR A. GODLEY IS SUCCEEDED IN COMMAND BY LIEUT.-GENERAL SIR J. DU CANE

1924

THE DAWES PLAN AND ITS EFFECTS. DECLARATION OF GERMANY'S FAILURE TO DISARM

(End Paper)

EXPERT COMMITTEES ON REPARATION

On 16th June, 1924, Lieut.-General Sir Alexander Godley left the Rhineland to take over the Southern Command in England. He was succeeded at Cologne by Lieut.-General Sir John Du Cane. The last period of General Godley's command had been militarily uneventful : the only item of any interest was the disposal of some four thousand rounds of 4.5-in. howitzer gas shell. Objections were raised to the War Office proposal to dump them into the Rhine, and they were eventually fetched from Cologne by a W.D. vessel and dropped into the sea.

Owing to the fall in the rate of exchange brought about by the introduction of the *Rentenmark*, the cost of living in the British Army of the Rhine greatly increased. The Armies of Occupation were further affected adversely in the latter part of 1924 by readjustments consequent on the adoption of a new reparation scheme. The occupation of the Ruhr had been disastrous to Germany and had not helped France to the substantial benefits which she had expected. After the introduction of the *Rentenmark*, with a view to ascertaining the real financial position of Germany and what she could be expected to pay, the Reparation Commission, on 30th November, 1923, called into existence two committees of experts. The business of the first, of which Br.-General C. G. Dawes [1] was chairman, and Sir Josiah Stamp a member, was to ascertain facts and make suggestions as to the resources and capacity of Germany to provide reparation payments and at the same time balance her budget and stabilize her currency. The second committee, of which Mr. Reginald McKenna was chairman, was to consider the means of estimating the amount of exported German capital and of bringing it back to Germany.[2]

---

[1] He was a Chicago banker and financier, born 1865. Gazetted major of engineers in the National Army in 1917, he was appointed in January, 1918, Chairman of the General Purchasing Board and General Purchasing Agent of the American Expeditionary Force in Europe.

[2] The story of the Committees, with their report covering 200 pages, will be found in Br.-General Dawes's book, *A Journal of Reparations*.

The two committees reported in April, 1924, the outcome of their work being known to the world as the " Dawes Plan". By that date a Labour Ministry, under Mr. Ramsay MacDonald, was in power, having taken office on 22nd January, and very soon after, in May, Monsieur Herriot leader of the *Cartel des Gauches* succeeded Monsieur Poincaré. The two new Premiers accepted the " Dawes Plan", and at a conference in London which opened on 16th July, Germany also accepted the proposals, the Agreement being dated 30th August. Subsequently the *Reichstag* voted the laws necessary for the adoption of the Plan.

THE DAWES PLAN

It need only be said here that the Plan was much like the *Rentenmark* scheme, but it relied on a " Bank of Issue", supervised by an International General Board with a foreigner as chairman, instead of the *Rentenbank* (which was to be liquidated). The difference was that Germany was to be lent money to assist in setting her currency on a firm basis. To quote the words of the report : " an integral part of our scheme is the issue by Germany of a foreign loan of 800 million gold marks," in order to establish the bank and stabilize the currency. The capital of the Bank of Issue was to be 400 million gold marks, of which three-quarters would be provided from the foreign loan and the rest by the *Reichsbank*—which had a carefully-concealed gold reserve. The balance of the loan was to be allocated for the relief of unemployment.

The Reparation payments were to be made through the Bank of Issue to an " agent for reparation payments", the sums agreed being derived from foreign loans, mortgages on the German railways and industrial concerns, death duties, taxes on transport, alcohol, tobacco, sugar and beer, and the Customs.

The annual payments were to be as follows :—

First year ..	1,000,000,000 gold marks		Partly from foreign loans.
Second year..	1,220,000,000	,, ,,	500,000,000 from gold mark railway shares being put on the market.
Third year ..	1,200,000,000	,, ,,	} With a margin either way of 250,000,000.
Fourth year..	1,750,000,000	,, ,,	
Standard year	2,500,000,000	,, ,,	Plus a supplement computed on an " index of prosperity", the method of whose calculation was indicated.

Deliveries in kind were to be continued, and their value taken into account. Nothing was said about the total sums to be paid, or how long the annuities were to continue. Nor does reference seem to have been made to Article 233 of the Peace Treaty, which read that the schedule of reparation payments should be arranged for the discharge of " the entire obligation within a period of 30 years from 1st May, 1921." But, having their own plans for the future, the Germans did not bother about this point.

The report further contained these words :—

> " We refer below to the necessity of spending almost exclusively within Germany the sums available for Treaty payments in 1924–5 and 1925–6. In these circumstances, the Allied Governments will doubtless consider whether it is not advisable to continue the system whereby the costs of the Armies of Occupation were a first charge upon the proceeds of delivery in kind made to the Governments which maintain the Armies."

Another pregnant sentence in the report reads :

> " It is . . . our duty to point out clearly that our forecasts are based on the assumption that economic activity will be unhampered and unaffected by any foreign organization other than the controls herein provided. . . . We wish to add at once that if the economic system in operation in occupied territories is modified we are unanimously of the opinion that a settlement of reparation must be reinforced by adequate and productive securities. We propose for this purpose a system of control of the Bank of Issue, the railways, Mortgage and Budget accounts, by Commissioners, with a General Co-ordinator and such sub-commissioners as might be found necessary."

This meant that the Régie control of the railways in occupied territory and the Micum control of the mines and industries should cease, and supervised financial securities take the place of territorial pledges.

By the terms of the Agreement of 30th August Germany obtained not only capital, but the annulment of all French action in the Ruhr, except the retirement of the French troops. The German officials there were to be reinstated ; all railways, mines and other undertakings were to be restored to their proprietors ; and the special organizations established to exploit these undertakings (Régie and Micum) withdrawn ; all restrictions on the movement of persons, goods and vehicles—subject to the provisions of the Rhineland Agreement—were to be removed ; and, in general, the High Commission was to reverse its Ordinances in order to permit of the fiscal and economic unity of Germany. Thus a complete " as you were " was to take place.[1]

EFFECTS OF THE DAWES PLAN ON THE ARMIES OF OCCUPATION

One effect of the Plan was that Germany had no longer to pay the cost of the Armies of Occupation,[2] which became a first charge and was credited to Germany as part of the reparation payments. The more therefore the Armies spent the less reparation money would there be to divide. The effect on the British Army of the Rhine was that it came more under Treasury control, and that, by orders from home, expenditure was cut down in every direction. No longer could demands be made on the Germans to build offices, messes and better quarters, and provide airfields and ranges ; hotels and factories had to be given up ; billets, hitherto free, had to be paid for ; rentals for officers' quarters had to be referred to the War Office ; subsidies to institutions which provided entertainment and distraction were withdrawn ; the maintenance of football, cricket, tennis and athletic. grounds could still be charged to the public, but not facilities for squash racquets and golf. These curtailments, combined with the unfavourable rate of exchange, threw the troops almost entirely on their own resources for recreation.

GERMANY'S EVASION OF THE PEACE TERMS

Whilst the financiers were thus providing Germany with capital to pay reparation and enable her to resuscitate her industries and regain her old prosperity, for the benefit of the

---

[1] Finance being of interest here only as the arrangements affected the British Army of the Rhine, the subject may be closed by saying that in June, 1929, as Germany refused to tax herself even to a proportion of the extent to which the Allies were subjecting themselves, the Dawes Plan was superseded by " the Young Plan," drawn up by a committee of experts, of which Mr. Owen D. Young, President of the American General Electric Company and a member of the Dawes Committee, was chairman. This reduced the liabilities and fixed the total sum to be paid in 59 annuities, beginning on 1st September. That for the first half year was 676·9 million RM. ; and in the first full year, beginning on 1st April, 1,641·6, rising to 2,352·7. A fixed sum of 660 million was to be paid every year ; the balance was conditional, and payments might be suspended for two years by giving notice.

Germany continued, however, to protest her inability to pay, and in June, 1931, after the evacuation of the Rhineland, obtained the Hoover Moratorium ; in July, 1932, at Lausanne, the Young Plan came to an end, the Allies renouncing reparation in return for the promised payment of a substantial lump sum (£150,000,000). That promise was never kept.

[2] The Germans put the cost up to 1st September, 1924, at 5,500,000,000 gold marks, roughly 1,000,000,000 per annum (Wochendorf, p. 239).

world, as was hoped, the soldiers continued to make unpleasant discoveries about her secret rearming, and of an expenditure on her supposedly small force of a greater annual sum than the French spent on their much larger Army. On the entry of the Franco-Belgian troops into the Ruhr the operations of the Inter-Allied Military Commission of Control had been almost entirely suspended owing to the opposition to its work offered in every form, including intimidation, by the German Government and its officials ; even food and use of the telephone and telegraph were denied to its officers. On 6th March Herr Stresemann declared in the *Reichstag* that the disarmament of Germany was terminated. In June, however, the British and Italian delegations were allowed to resume their activities ; but the French and Belgians were prevented from doing so by direct order of the *Reichswehr* Minister ; so the other Allied officers decided to suspend work, pending instructions.

The Commission pointed out that the Peace Conditions had not been satisfied : not only was the disarmament of Germany unfinished, but there was no guarantee that the measure attained would be permanent. They had every reason to believe, they said, that Germany was trying to re-arm ; for instance, the debates in the *Reichstag* in February and March, 1923 revealed that the illicit manufacture of arms and munitions was going on unhindered, many depôts of arms had been discovered, and the existence of many more was suspected.[1] In violation of the Peace Treaty, serious efforts were being made to train reserves.

The Conference of Ambassadors, in consequence, invited the German Government to order the dissolution of military societies and discontinue the instruction of reserves, and to arrange that an immediate and complete resumption of control work might take place. They received the reply that, owing to the political crisis, this was impossible. Thereupon, on 21st November, the Conference ordered the Commission to resume control, and called the attention of the German Government to the serious consequences of another refusal. On 9th January, 1924 that Government informed the Commission that the necessary orders to permit the control officers to make visits had been given ; but, except for the settlement of a few outstanding questions, which could be done by correspondence,

---

[1] In 1926 it was discovered that the *Reichswehr* Ministry itself had collaborated in the formation of these depôts and provided the special personnel, called *Arbeitskommandos* (Labour Commandos), camouflaged as landworkers, under ex-officers, bound to secrecy, to look after them. See p. 214.

they regarded the work of the Commission as completed, and it was now the business of the League of Nations to make any investigation considered necessary under the Treaty. Members of the Commission made two visits of inspection on 10th and 12th January, 1924, without useful results as they were not allowed to see very much, and control was again suspended.[1]

After further delay and tergiversation on the part of the German Government, which admitted that stocks of ammunition judged inadequate were being completed, and spare guns manufactured, a " General Inspection " was agreed to on 22nd June ; but visits were not begun until 8th September. By request of the German authorities the inspecting officers wore civilian clothes, not uniform, for fear of incidents—which were encouraged instead of being forbidden by the police. But the inspections amounted to no more than verbal interrogations. It was at once discovered that the German officials had no intention of collaborating or of allowing the Commission to learn what had taken place in the twenty months during which inspection had been interrupted. On 25th January, 1925 even the General Inspection was brought to an end. The Commission managed, however, to arrive at a certain number of conclusions : that besides the munitions and guns whose existence was admitted by the Germans, they had manufactured arms, explosives and anti-gas apparatus (specifically forbidden) ; State munition factories had been extended and reconditioned ; the most important authorized factories (Krupp, Rheinmetall, Wasag, Dortmund Union) had systematically delayed reduction of plant ; non-authorized firms had manufactured munitions ; great quantities of machinery had not been broken up ; the *Reichswehr* and police were in possession of a greater number of arms than authorized ; and quantities of arms were concealed in secret hiding places. Further, the armament of the fortress of Konigsberg and of the coast fortifications was mobile instead of fixed ; the legislation regarding the import and export of war material had not been passed ; the sums allotted in the budget for replacement of weapons and for the payment and equipment of reserves were manifestly out of proportion to the size of the Army (for instance, the item, $4\frac{1}{2}$ million gold marks was put down for upkeep of machine guns, about £100 per authorized weapon) ; numbers above establishment were being trained by recruiting volunteers, by illegal enlistments and by creating

---

[1] Seeckt's biographer boasts (p. 447–8) that by his orders, " the keys were never or seldom available and the officials concerned uncommonly often not to be found " ; and that " things had an astonishing inclination to fall at the feet, on the head or strike the backs of the foreign control officers."

vacancies by allowing men to leave before they had completed 12 years' service. An air-arm was being developed. The police had 30,000 men over establishment ; and the Great General Staff had been re-created in another form.

To sum up, Germany had defaulted not only as regards reparation but also over the transformation] of war factories to peace production, over the disposal of war dumps, over the necessary legislation regarding recruiting and volunteers, over the import and export of war material, over coast defences and fortress guns, and over the reorganization of the police.

Determined to get the Allies out of the Cologne area and, if possible, separate Great Britain and France, the *Reich* Government borrowed an idea from the so-called " Geneva Protocol " of 2nd October (1924) " for the pacific settlement of International disputes," drawn up by the League of Nations experts, and on 5th February, 1925 suggested to the Allied Governments a pact of non-aggression combined with arbitration, offering to respect the Alsace-Lorraine frontier and submit other Franco-German disputes to arbitration. This was the step which was to lead to Locarno.[1]

EVACUATION OF THE COLOGNE AREA POSTPONED

Article 429 of the Peace Treaty had provided that if the conditions therein laid down were faithfully carried out by Germany there should be successive reductions of the occupied area : after 5 years, 10 years and 15 years, dating from the ratification of the Treaty. It read :

> " At the expiration of five years [that is on 10th January, 1925] there will be evacuated : the bridgehead of Cologne and the territories north of a line running along the Ruhr,[2] then along the railway Jülich, Düren, Euskirchen, Rheinbach, thence along the road Rheinbach to Sinzig, and reaching the Rhine at the confluence with the Ahr ; the roads, railways and places mentioned above are excluded from the area evacuated."

At the expiration of ten years the Coblence bridgehead was to be evacuated, also the territories north of a line starting from Bacharach (below Bingen, where the perimeter of this bridgehead struck the Rhine), and running roughly north-west to 2 miles south of Aachen, and thence to the southern end of the Limburg Appendix.

---

[1] The Allied reply will be found in the next chapter under date 4th June, 1925.

[2] See End Paper. This Ruhr (or Roer) flows through Düren into the Meuse (Maas) and is not the river near Essen.

At the expiration of fifteen years the bridgeheads of Mayence (containing Wiesbaden) and Kehl (opposite Strassburg) and the remainder of German territory in occupation, were to be given up.

In expectation that the first evacuation might be carried out, the War Office had approached the Foreign Office in July 1924 asking for notice of the Government's intentions. The letter pointed out that if the British Army of the Rhine were withdrawn altogether it would be difficult to provide accommodation for the troops at home, and therefore asked for four months' notice. On 2nd August, Lieut.-General Du Cane forwarded to London an appreciation of possible new zones, suggesting Coblence as the best on all counts. The Foreign Office was informed accordingly, and the request made for two months' notice should the move be to Coblence. The Foreign Office replied on 10th November to the effect that it was questionable whether Germany had fulfilled her Treaty obligations, and that if she had not done so the Cologne Zone would not be evacuated : in any case the allocation of a new zone was a matter for the military authorities : the notice asked for would be difficult to give : there was no reason to expect that a total withdrawal of British troops from Germany would be ordered.

In consequence of the evidence of the breaches of the Treaty produced by the Commission of Control and the subsequent agreements, the Allied Governments (Mr. Baldwin's Second Ministry had taken office on 7th November, 1924) decided not to evacuate the Cologne Zone and, on 5th January, 1925 by their Ambassadors in Berlin handed to the German Government a Collective Note in which the items of failure were recited and the remedying of them made a preliminary condition of the evacuation of the Cologne Zone.

The German Government made a paper protest, and, to use Herr Stresemann's words in the *Reichstag*, claimed that the *Reich* was in fact " completely disarmed and defenceless." In the formal protest the words used were

" Germany, by the conditions of the Peace Treaty, is disarmed to a degree that she is no more a military factor in European politics."

It spoke of the findings of the Commission of Control as petty details which could not form ground for retaliatory measures. In consonance with the new policy, therefore, by an order conveyed by Maréchal Foch, the Commission of Control ceased its operations almost completely, and did no more than carry on a small correspondence with the German Government.

ABANDONMENT OF THE " PRODUCTIVE PLEDGES " IN THE
RUHR

The measures to fulfil the conditions of the Dawes Plan as
they affected the Ruhr were implemented by order from Paris,
through Ordinances of the High Commission.   These gradually
withdrew, cancelled, or revised its special legislation, " as a
token of goodwill towards the population." Thus, on 9th
September 1924, the levying of customs duty on the frontier
between occupied and unoccupied Germany ceased, and on the
20th the posts were withdrawn. On 21st September the laws
and taxes of the *Reich* once more came into force in occupied
territory, though new legislation was still subject to examination
and veto by the High Commission. On the 28th all the Allied
services organized for the exploitation of the resources of the
Ruhr, including Micum, were suppressed, and the German
officials re-established in their old positions ; at midnight,
15th/16th November, the Régie handed back the management
of the railways ; but the military evacuation of the Ruhr was
not begun until the following July. Technical delegates were
appointed to settle the many financial and administrative
matters which required adjustment in the transitional period.
The pass system, motor permits, special barge licences and coal
tax were abolished ; restrictions on correspondence and postal
communication relaxed ; orders for the expulsion of and vetoes
on the appointment of German officials were now to be subject
to due notice and appeal.

Finally, the question of an amnesty, raised at the London
Conference in August, was considered. It was then found, as
regards the British Zone, where there had been a conspicuous
absence of political prosecution, that 134 Germans were in
custody on sentences by British Summary Courts, mostly for
cutting and stealing telegraph wire. The sentences were
allowed to stand ; but many Germans of the Ruhr convicted
of passive resistance, including Herr von Krupp und Bohlen,
were released. In the following year a general amnesty was
considered by a joint military conference. The German
representatives were unwilling, or unable, to give a categorical
assurance that there would be no reprisals against Germans
who had been of service to the Armies of Occupation, and no
agreement was come to until after " Locarno," as will be
narrated.[1]

On 11th December the corner of the British Zone through
which the Düren–Grevenbroich railway passed, which had been
transferred to the French earlier in the year, was handed back.

[1] See Chapter XVIII.

THE HIGH COMMISSION'S LEGISLATIVE CONCESSIONS

Many of the High Commission's new regulations concerned such routine details as parcels post rates, customs tariff, the alcohol trade, moneylending, cattle diseases, control of the currency, and permissions to municipalities to issue small paper currency (*Nothgeld*). It was ruled that whereas by a new German law the school fees for foreigners were fixed at five times those of native Germans, in the occupied territories they might not be more than twice as much.[1] The German authorities forbade the exportation by any person of more than 20,000 marks, or its equivalent in foreign currency ; the High Commission modified this to the extent that though the personnel of the British Army of the Rhine might not take more than 20,000 German marks, they could remove as much of their own currency as they liked.

A long Ordinance, No. 282, was issued defining the rights and duties of the Inter-Allied Rhineland Railway Commission, on which a German delegation represented the German railway companies. The Commission was

"alone empowered to transmit to the railway authorities of the Occupied Territories the orders of the Commander-in-Chief of the Allied Armies given for military purposes " ; and it was provided that when a state of siege was declared the Railway Commission might take over management of the railways.

Ordinance No. 245 was entitled " For the Suppression of the Activities of Associations Liable to Prejudice the Security of the Armies or to Disturb Public Order," and under this the *Kyffhäuser* Association of Unions of German Students[2] was suppressed, as one of its objects was the provision of military instruction for its members. It was, however, in the following year that the number of such societies became noticeable in occupied territory.

Some of the new legislation was of interest to the Armies of Occupation. For instance, transport to move furniture, fuel for laundries, and sewing machines to repair bedding might be requisitioned ; but all requisitions had now to be paid for, and in marks supplied by the German Government. The High

---

[1] In pre-War Germany there were three prices for most things : one for the local people, one for other Germans (*Fremden*) and one for foreigners (*Ausländer*).

[2] Kyffhäuser is the spot where, overlooking the Goldene Au, was erected in 1896 the war memorial which is known as the Kyffhäuser *Denkmal*. Before the 1914 war the Germans *Kriegervereine* (Veterans' Clubs) assumed the name of *Kyffhäuser Verband*.

Commission fixed in detail the responsibility for the " upkeep and cleaning of staircases, landings and corridors in houses or apartments occupied by members of the High Commission and of the Armies of Occupation," and gave the military authorities the right, later withdrawn, to requisition fishing permits, if an amicable arrangement could not be reached ; and Instruction No. 22 regulated the shooting rights of officers and of civilian persons graded as such.

Lieut.-General Du Cane objected to certain new proposals. For instance the relaxation of the regulations regarding the carrying of arms, the notification of indoor meetings and the censorship of letters ; the control of the flying of German flags ; the transfer of certain classes of offences from military to German civil courts ; and increased freedom of the Press. He thought the Army must retain the right to seize a newspaper, if necessary. He had no objection to the use of wireless sets, provided licensing and registration were subject to Allied supervision ; nor to the extension of civil flying rights, provided the Army could still name forbidden areas. The Germans were consulted, and much negotiation ensued, the French having a great deal to say, with the result that the codification of the new Ordinances had not been completed by September, 1927.

CHAPTER XVIII
GENERAL SIR J. DU CANE'S COMMAND
(continued)
1925
LOCARNO AND THE EVACUATION OF COLOGNE
(Sketch 5)

POSSIBILITY OF THE EVACUATION OF COLOGNE

The key to the events of 1925 is the determination of the Government of the *Reich* to recover the Cologne area and to get rid of the Commission of Control ; and to that end to obtain a declaration from the Allies that Germany had disarmed in accordance with the terms of the Peace Treaty. Among other pieces of propaganda, a general fête was ordered to celebrate " the 1,000 years' belonging of the Rhineland to the German *Reich*." [1]

On 29th January the Chief of the Imperial General Staff, Field-Marshal Lord Cavan, placed before the Committee of Imperial Defence a memorandum on the British strategic position as it would be after the 5-year or First Zone had been evacuated. [2] It may thus be summarized :

COLOGNE AREA : BRITISH STRATEGIC AREA
AFTER EVACUATION

1. When the five-year zone is evacuated, the position will be :

    (*a*) The Allies will still be occupying the 10-year and 15-year zones. The five-year zone and the Ruhr will have been restored to Germany, and the demilitarized zone laid down in the Peace Treaty will have been established in the five-year zone.

    (*b*) The Inter-Allied Military Commission of Control in Germany will have to be withdrawn or reduced to a small committee of verification.

    (*c*) Germany's adherence to the Treaty conditions (disarmament and demilitarized zone) will be subject only to investigation by the League of Nations (which will probably be ineffective).

---

[1] The year 925 A.D. is the date of the seizure of Lorraine (then comprising territory on both sides of the Rhine) by Henry the Fowler, King of the Germans, after the defeat of Charles the Simple by the Burgundians. According to German historians (and the Cambridge Medieval History III, p. 162), the Roman Empire, now claimed to be the First *Reich*, was established in 962 A.D. by Otto, son of Henry the Fowler.

[2] See p. 270. Cologne was included in this zone.

The French will probably want to secure a Resident Commission of Control in the demilitarized zone. This they are not entitled to—only to control by visits.

2. The position will thus be most dangerous and difficult should Germany choose to exploit it. When the evacuation of the five-year zone gives the Germans a crossing over the Rhine barrier, the main danger would be on the Allied left flank.

Plans for possible action by the Allied Armies must be evolved :

    (a) to meet German aggression ;

    (b) for counter-measures if German activities seem to threaten war.

3. The choice should be (b) rather than (a), that is, prevention rather than cure.

4. The first step in (b) would be the re-occupation of the Cologne area, probably followed by that of the Ruhr. The bridge-heads of Mayence and Coblence form pivots for such a movement. But the left flank, the Cologne area, would be the principal area of operations.

The Coblence area is separated from the approaches to the Cologne area by the difficult Eifel country.

5. It was originally considered that a position at Coblence between the French and Belgian Armies would be most suitable for the British ; but Coblence is of minor importance. Also, if action is taken, the British Army, being weak, must assume a secondary rôle until reinforced. In order to resume its traditional place on the French left and to use the line of communication Ostend–Aachen, it will have to move a considerable distance. It is immaterial whether it moves from Coblence or Wiesbaden.

6. There are no alternatives to Coblence or Wiesbaden. To go to Treves or to any back area would reduce our prestige and prevent our Intelligence service keeping in direct touch with unoccupied Germany.

The General Staff was prepared to consent to the choice between Coblence and Wiesbaden being settled on grounds of convenience of administration and economy—subject to the British Army of the Rhine's reconnaissance now proceeding.

In January, Lieut.-General Du Cane, looking ahead, discussed the selection of a new area with General Guillaumat, who had succeeded General Degoutte as French Commander-in-Chief on 25th November, 1924. General Guillaumat told him that even if the British did come to Coblence (in the 10-year zone of the Peace Treaty), which was the original suggestion, he could not entirely withdraw the French troops ; in fact, he would retain a regiment of field artillery and three battalions of infantry in order to keep in his hands the control of the Treves–Coblence railway. He would prefer the British to be at Wiesbaden (in the 15-year zone). Lieut.-General Du Cane then reconnoitred both Coblence and Wiesbaden, and reported the result to the War Office on 13th March. Both could furnish only inadequate accommodation. Coblence was a small town and a wine trade centre of about 60,000 inhabitants, at the junction of the Moselle with the Rhine, overlooked by the fortress of Ehrenbreitstein ; it had barracks for six battalions, six field batteries and two battalions of heavy artillery. Wiesbaden was the chief town of a *Bezirk* of that name, a tourist resort and a watering-place, with medicinal hot springs, situated at the base of the Taunus hills. It had 160,000 inhabitants and modern buildings, including barracks for five battalions. It is three miles from the Rhine ; in the town and near it a whole French division was accommodated, and it was a French corps headquarters. The move to Wiesbaden, being the longer and not possible by water farther than Bingen, 18 miles below Biebrich (the port of Wiesbaden) and thence by train, was the more expensive, but only £26,582 as against £18,166, and being in the 15-year zone, involved no further shift in another five years. Both the Army Council and the British High Commissioner were in favour of Coblence ; but the High Commission was entrenched in Coblence and refused to release accommodation by moving to Wiesbaden or elsewhere ; the French Government and the British Foreign Office were against the High Commission being moved, and the Treasury agreed with them. When it came to the point, the Army Council gave way.

Lieut.-General Du Cane asked for two months' notice of any move and that this move might not take place in mid-winter. It will be seen that neither condition was granted.

THE GERMAN ASSOCIATIONS

The year is remarkable for the emergence into prominence in the occupied territory of a large number of " associations ", most of them, by whatever name they were called, being for the purpose of secret training in arms and on account of their numbers a standing danger to the small Armies of Occupation. By far the most important, and remaining the most important until the advent of the Nazis, was the *Stahlhelm* (Steel Helmet), the *Bund der Frontsoldaten* (Union of Front Line Fighters), founded immediately after the signing of the Armistice.[1] It contained a very large number of ex-soldiers with a high percentage of officers ; its creed was monarchist and militarist, and its aim the military organization of the *Reich* in Prussian fashion, under Hohenzollern leadership. Meantime it formed a second line to the *Reichswehr*. By 1925 its members were said

---

[1] Brockhaus says, 13th November, 1918.

to number about a million, organized in first line, reserve and *Landsturm ;* its junior branch, known as *Junsta*, was nearly two million strong. It practised annual mobilization, and in 1932 assembled over 200,000 members on the Tempelhofer field outside Berlin.[1]   It was forbidden in occupied territory.[2] The most numerous society was the *Reichsbanner* (using the black-red-gold colours of the Republic) ; it was nominally political and its aim to defend the republican constitution and spread peace and understanding ; it was not proscribed in the occupied territory.

The first society to be detected in the British occupied area in giving military training, an important one because of its numerous branches, was the *Reiterverein* (Riding Club), which tried to carry on under pretence of providing instruction in horsemanship ; being banned, it nominally transformed itself into an agricultural society for the improvement of horse breeding.   A few societies, the *Kyffhäuserverband der Vereine deutscher Studenten*, which specialised in training students in arms ; the *Deutscher Pfadfinderverband* (German boy scout association), and the *Wehrverbände* (especially devoted to the military preparation of the young), were definitely prohibited by the High Commission.   But there were dozens of other similar unions disguised as art, literary, musical, naturalist, sport, games, rowing, swimming, ski-ing and gliding—even religious—clubs, besides regimental and the arms of the service (artillery, engineers, etc.) clubs, all devoted to physical training and military preparation or organized as mobilization centres.   Others were frankly military, e.g., the *Wehrwolf*, the *Jungdeutscher Orden* (*Jungdo*), the *Wikingbund*, the *Reichskriegsflagge*, the *Bund Oberland, Organization Consul, Organization Escherich*, etc.   Sometimes officially dissolved, they nevertheless continued to flourish, and to march, drill and exercise on Sundays.   Some 150 of them were

---

[1] Brockhaus.
[2] There were seven other military veterans' associations designed to form an official reserve of officers.   They were :
Deutsch Völkischer Offiziersbund (German National Officers' Union) : an active pan-German, anti-Semitic organization founded by General Ludendorff ;
Offiziersbund (German Officers Union) ;
Nationalverband deutscher Offiziere (National Society of German Officers) ;
Deutscher Reichskriegerbund Kyffhäuser (German *Reich's* Union of War Veterans Kyffhäuser) ;
Reichsoffizierbund (*Reich's* Officer Union) ;
Reichsbund ehemalige Kadetten (*Reich's* Union of ex-cadets) ; and *Bund der Asienkämpfer* (Union of Asia Warriors).
In the Spartacist camp was the *Roter Frontkämpfer Bund* (Red Front Fighters Union).

grouped into a single confederation, the *Vereinigte Vaterländische Verbände.* Lieut.-General Sir William Thwaites, when in command at Wiesbaden, had a collection of the badges of nearly a hundred of them. By May 1925 the local Germans, emboldened by the weakness of the Allies in letting them off the cost of occupation and lending them money, openly requested the High Commission that three " patriotic societies " might be permitted in the occupied territory. These were the banned *Kyffhäuserverband,* the *Rheinischer Pfadfinderverband* (the banned *Deutscher Pfadfinderverband* under a slightly altered name), and the *Hochschulring Deutscher Kunst* (High School Circle of German Art). The High Commission, including the British members were not in favour of granting the authorization. Lieut.-General Du Cane preferred to permit the societies, in which case, he said, their leaders would be personally responsible for their activities : no military training or anti-Allied propaganda would be allowed, nor uniforms, marching in formed bodies or bands : prohibition, he thought, merely drove movements underground and made control difficult. Nevertheless, the policy of prohibition was continued.

The partial training of the young, without the old discipline, led to collisions between the different political parties, and to demonstrations judged inopportune by the military rulers of Germany ; nevertheless the societies were encouraged. In April the Allied Military Committee at Versailles discovered the reason : the existence of the associations was a necessary element in General von Seeckt's scheme ; for he relied on them to provide reservists ; and the military instruction of their members was part of his plan for the reconstitution of the National Army.

COLLECTIVE NOTE ON GERMANY'S BREACHES OF FAITH

As the result of the general survey by the Versailles Allied Military Committee, on 10th April Maréchal Foch pointed out to the Conference of Ambassadors that Germany's behaviour amounted to a " *manquement général* " of the Treaty, rather than a failure to carry out the detail of a few Articles. On 4th June, therefore, the Allied Governments presented a Collective Note to Germany, which stated that the sum of her omissions, if not promptly remedied, would eventually permit her to reconstitute her Army based on a nation-in-arms, and this gave those omissions " a character too dangerous for the general peace ". To the note were attached the results of inspection and the demands of the Allies : the old five points less the fourth, with regard to handing over of the arms account books, which was abandoned.[1]

The Allied Governments, threatening that failure to comply would result in the Cologne Zone not being evacuated, specially demanded that suitable measures should be taken to put an end to the preparation of classes of reserves and to periods of instruction in the Army. This involved curbing both the military authorities and the associations. Article 177 of the Peace Treaty not only forbade associations of any description, including educational establishments, to occupy themselves with military matters, but also prohibited them from having any connection with the Ministry of War or any military authority. Yet, by Article 37 of the German Military Law of 23rd March, 1921, members and ex-members of the Army might be in relation with the associations, and be members of them, on the sole condition that they had no political character, the matter of military training being entirely ignored. In May and October, to satisfy the Allies, the Chief of the *Heeresleitung* decided that the *Wehrverbände* were political associations and therefore soldiers must have nothing to do with them ; but no action was taken on this decision.

Under pressure of the Conference of Ambassadors, the German President offered not indeed to cancel Article 37 of the Military Law above mentioned, but to issue a Decree forbidding the preparation of reserves by the Army, and the military instruction of volunteers not legally engaged in its establishments. This did not prevent officers and n.c.os. of the *Reichswehr* giving instruction to schools and associations. The Allied Governments nevertheless accepted the proposal, with the condition that if the Decree proved insufficient it was for the German Government to put it right. The Decree was not published until 30th December, 1926, more than eighteen months after the Note of the Allied Governments—and classes in the *Reichswehr*, for instruction of reserve officers at least, continued as before.

HINDENBURG BECOMES PRESIDENT

Meantime, on 28th February, President Ebert had died and, as a compromise between parties, on 26th April General Field-Marshal von Hindenburg had been elected in his place. At the end of July the military evacuation of the Ruhr was begun ; but the economic plight of Germany had become worse, and by the end of the year she had nearly a million-and-a-half unemployed.

[1] See p. 246.

The Locarno Conference

On 12th September, continuing the idea of the Geneva Protocol, and Herr Stresemann's January suggestion, but ignoring the evidence that the *Reich* was not only not disarmed, but rearming as fast as it could regardless of treaties, agreements and Allied Collective Notes, Germany was invited to an Allied conference on 5th October at Locarno on an equal footing. The object was to arrange a Security Pact.[1]

Shortly before the meeting the German Government, intent only on getting the Allies out of Germany, demanded that the 5-year zone should be evacuated forthwith before any Pact was concluded. This was naturally refused, and was a poor prelude to an amicable conference. The result of the meeting, however, was a general " Treaty of Mutual Guarantee " between the States represented, and four arbitration treaties between Germany on the one hand and France, Belgium, Poland and Czecho-Slovakia on the other. By the general treaty Great Britain, France, Germany, Belgium and Italy guaranteed to preserve the territorial *status quo* of the new German-Belgian and Franco-German frontier; that is, Germany abandoned any claim to Eupen–Malmédy and Alsace-Lorraine. The five principal nations also covenanted in no case to attack or invade each other, and to assist each other if attacked without provocation, and all agreed to submit any difference to the Council of the League of Nations or the Permanent Court of International Justice. For the Eastern Front, there was no Security Pact. Nothing was said about disarmament.

On the last point the German Ambassador in Paris, on 23rd October, wrote to the Conference of Ambassadors :—

> " Before the Collective Note was handed to the German Government, the latter had already carried out the disarmament of Germany in the most important parts. . . . The German Government are now in a position to inform the Ambassadors'

---

[1] Great Britain was represented by Mr. Austen Chamberlain, France by Monsieur Briand, Italy by Signor Benito Mussolini, and Germany by Herren Luther and Stresemann. Belgium, Poland and Czecho-Slovakia were also represented.

According to Viscount d'Abernon (ii., p. 154), about the middle of December, 1922, the German Ambassador at Washington informed the State Secretary that he had been instructed to propose the conclusion of an agreement under which Germany, Great Britain, France and Italy should pledge themselves not to make war against one another for a period of 30 years [the time that the German Great General Staff had calculated would be required to get ready for another attack] unless the matter had been decided by a popular vote [which would prevent Germany being taken by surprise]. Monsieur Poincaré called the German project "a clumsy manœuvre " and " dangerous hypocrisy."

Conference that a considerable number of the demands advanced have now been fulfilled, and that, moreover, as regards the great majority of the remaining demands, such progress has been made that their complete settlement can be safely expected by 15th November of this year."

The unfortunate Ambassador was, of course, only the mouthpiece for the lies of Berlin. In an enclosure 62 Allied demands were classified as :—

1. Demands fulfilled (14).

2. Demands which will be fulfilled by 15th November next (20)—" these include prohibition of training of reserve officers and illegal enlistments."

3. Demands the execution of which will be assured by the 15th November next (23)—" these included the abolition of the Great General Staff, the reduction of the police to 150,000, and the maintenance of " the effective strength of the *Reichsherr*."

4. " Demands, the execution of which involves special difficulties "—these (5) included the " Associations ".

In reply to this Note, the Conference of Ambassadors, on 14th November, informed the German Ambassador that they had decided to fix the beginning of the evacuation of the Cologne area for 1st December.

The German Army leaders and the National People's Party were by no means pleased at the idea of a permanent understanding with their conquerors, and at the thought, as the *Militär Wochenblatt* put it, of remaining underdog for ever. Perpetual peace, wrote that journal, was " all very well for the victors, but what about the vanquished ? " The pact, however, was ratified ; but on 5th December Luther and his Ministry were forced to resign. Fehrenbach, one of the delegates at Locarno, was unable to form a Ministry, and it was only after much negotiation that, on 19th January, 1926, Luther returned to power, and he kept Herr Stresemann as Foreign Minister.

" THE LOCARNO SPIRIT "

ECONOMIES EXPECTED

It was not the text of the Pact, signed on 16th October, but the so-called " spirit of Locarno ", which led to the British Army of the Rhine and other Armies of Occupation being adversely affected. On 16th November Lieut.-General Du Cane was told, what the Germans had already known for two days, that the evacuation of Cologne was to commence on 1st December, and that the Government had promised that it should be completed in two months from that date. The High Commission was to remain, but its representatives (responsible for dealing with the German civil administration) in every garrisoned town were to be abolished ; and the Ordinances were again to be softened down. Herr Stresemann had obtained his first point ; but he had still to gain his second, the suppression of the Inter-Allied Military Commissions of Control.

Although on 16th November the Conference of Ambassadors had further reduced the requirements of the four points, a press campaign, which increased in violence, was inaugurated on the pretext that control was incompatible with the " Locarno spirit." It was not, however, until after Germany had been admitted to the League of Nations on 8th September, 1926, that the Allied Ministers in conference at Geneva yielded to the request of the German Government, and the Commissions of Control were brought to an end on 31st January, 1927. The fact that General von Seeckt, the architect of rearmament, had just been removed from the headship of the army,[1] no doubt influenced the decision. From 4th June, 1923 until its dissolution, the Military Commission of Control had been practically impotent from want of effective support. The Naval and the Air Commissions had completed their work, respectively, four and two years earlier.

The first result of the " Locarno spirit " on the British Army of the Rhine was that, in spite of protest, it was compelled to remove itself and its establishments in the bitter cold of a Rhine valley winter ; and in order not to inconvenience the Germans by requiring billets for them, the War Office ordered home all married soldiers and families not on the married quarters list.

The British Treasury hoped for economies from the Locarno spirit. The reduction of the British Army of the Rhine was discussed, as the French and Belgians were withdrawing some of their much larger contingents, and the War Office agreed to the withdrawal of one battalion with the heavy battery and its ammunition column, though it had difficulty in finding accommodation for them at home. Lieut.-General Du Cane was also asked to say what else could be effected in the direction of economy. After thorough investigation, he reported that he was averse to recommending any reductions in the establishment of the fighting units, but, if urgently necessary, the transport of the field artillery brigade and of the infantry battalions might be reduced to home peace establishment, whereby, perhaps, £35,000 per annum would be saved. The

---

[1] See Chap. III, p. 6, footnote.

field ambulance column also might be abolished. Other economies could be made by reducing the personnel of the engineer, signals, supply and transport and other services, including the staffs of the Provost Marshal and of the Post Office, and by cutting down annual barrack estimates and the amount of hired labour. Soon after 1st April, at the turn of the Financial Year, the War Office ordered the reduction of the transport and the abolition of the ammunition column. On appeal, however, it consented to nothing being done until after the training season. In the following years transport had to be hired at exorbitant prices, and it was discovered that the German authorities in carrying out essential services, normally performed by the engineers, and chargeable against the Dawes annuities, were employing an unnecessarily large a personnel and paying them too highly.

ACTION OF THE HIGH COMMISSION

The legislation of the High Commission in 1925 was distinctly tinged by the Locarno spirit, the more so, perhaps, as a German representative was again admitted to its sittings ; but he proved only a channel for complaints and protests. The volume of decrees was very much less than in former years, and largely devoted to modifying and amending earlier Ordinances and reducing penalties. On 17th November, Ordinance 308 was promulgated, " to foster favourable relations between the German population and authorities and the forces of Occupation, and to collaborate in the work of peace among nations." It gave in 65 pages a number of revised regulations, and it cancelled others. Thus, municipal general regulations need not be submitted for approval ; the supervision of the appointment of officials was made less rigorous ; civilians from the *Reich*, if provided with identity cards, might move freely in the occupied territory ; the regulations regarding the possession of sporting guns were relaxed ; the police, customs and forestry officials might carry* arms and ammunition (20 rounds) on duty, but must have a permit, duly issued ; pigeons might, on licence, be kept. These concessions, naturally, led to the Germans asking for more. The rules, however, as regards " associations," including educational establishments, recruiting and military instruction, were tightened up, with penalties up to ten years' imprisonment and a fine of 10,000 R.M. ; no person residing in the occupied territory might belong to any organization for military instruction or training situated outside this territory, or take part in such instruction and training ; if anyone had already undertaken an obligation to serve in the new German Army, he might not re-enter the occupied territory without the special authorization of the High Commission.

THE AMNESTY

A special Amnesty Protocol in the spirit of Locarno was drafted in October, 1925, by Monsieur Briand and Herr Stresemann. It provoked much discussion and comment and led to much negotiation between the Conference of Ambassadors, the High Commission, the Foreign Office, the Army Council, the Armies of Occupation, and the *Reich* officials. Lieut.-General Du Cane objected to a clause which would enable the Germans after regaining the Cologne area to take action against individuals who had assisted the Army of Occupation, particularly its Intelligence. General Guillaumat doubted German good faith in this matter. The protocol was not issued until 21st August, 1926. Its provisions had the effect that the High Commission could no longer intervene in German judicial proceedings on behalf of Germans who had appealed on the ground that they had rendered services to the Allies ; but the Germans agreed to take no proceedings whatever against such individuals " unless such service constituted high treason ", leaving their punishment to private enterprise, and the Black *Reichswehr*, if no one else, saw to the matter.

The British Army of the Rhine, on appeal, won the point that 19 women imprisoned for breach of deportation orders should not benefit by the Amnesty, as their release would be a menace to the health of the troops.

CHAPTER XIX

LIEUT.-GENERAL SIR J. DU CANE'S COMMAND
(*concluded*)
1926

THE PRELIMINARIES OF THE MOVE TO WIESBADEN
(Sketch 6)

THE STRATEGIC POSITION

The position around Wiesbaden assigned to the British Army of the Rhine after the evacuation of Cologne was the northern half of the Mayence bridgehead, and it was strategically bad. The small British force was wedged in between French corps on the right and left, with the Neutral Zone, now called " The Demilitarized Zone," in front. It had three lines of communication from England :

> (i) for animals, by steamer from Harwich to Antwerp, and thence by rail through Belgium and Holland to Coblence and Wiesbaden ;

> (ii) for equipment, stores and ammunition, by War Department vessels from Woolwich to Rotterdam, by arrangement with the Dutch Government, and thence by barge up the Rhine to Bingen, where navigation ceased for the greater part of the year, and thence by lorry or rail to Wiesbaden ;

> (iii) for personnel, at first from Dover to Calais and by rail as in (i) ;[1] but in September a route to avoid traversing Holland and unoccupied Germany was proposed and adopted ; it was from Dover to Ostend, and thence by Brussels, Metz, Saarbrücken to Wiesbaden.

From the information acquired by the Committee of Control it was known that the *Reich* possessed an Army of at least 250,000 instead of the 100,000 of the Peace Treaty, with at least two million trained men available as reserves, with arms and equipment, ready to be summoned to join one or other " tradition " company, battery or squadron, by which all the former regiments were represented in the *Reichswehr*. Further, there were in the Demilitarized Zone 150,000 police, armed and trained as soldiers and under trained officers, ready to act as covering troops.

The general defence scheme devised by our Allies involved withdrawal to the French (Lorraine) frontier, 70 miles or more to the south-west, there to hold on until the main French

---

[1] With through trains. The British gave a subsidy of £15,000 per annum, and it was hoped that the service might pay ; but it did not, and in July the sleeping and dining cars were taken off.

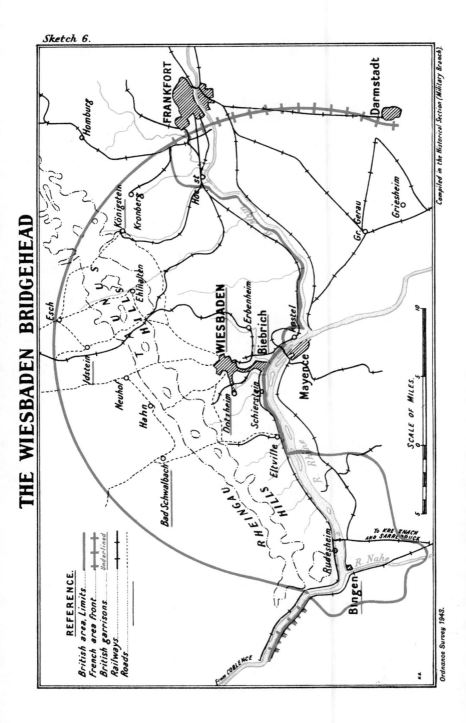

Sketch 6.

THE WIESBADEN BRIDGEHEAD

REFERENCE.

British area, Limits.
French area front.
British garrisons.
Railways.
Roads.
Under-lined

SCALE OF MILES.

Ordnance Survey 1943.

Compiled in the Historical Section (Military Branch).

Armies were ready to advance. The Mayence road-bridge, about six miles from the centre of Wiesbaden, was allotted to the British Army of the Rhine. The destruction of all the Rhine bridges was, however, an important feature of the scheme, and since the blowing up of the Mayence bridge was to be under French control—remembering that it was only by a few minutes that our Allies were stopped from destroying the bridges of the Marne behind the B.E.F. in the retreat from Mons in 1914—the situation was somewhat delicate. It was the more so because the first task of the British Army of the Rhine in the retirement was to safeguard the defile of the river Nahe at Kreuznach (nine miles south of Bingen) and this involved for the bulk of the force a diagonal march south-westwards after crossing at Mayence. The main force of the French Army of Occupation, with all its munition and supply depôts lay on the left bank, while on the right bank were only small infantry detachments at Ehrenbreitstein (opposite Coblence), Ems (blocking the valley of the Lahn, six miles east by south of Coblence), Höchst (five miles west of Frankfort) and Griesheim (south of the Main, west of Darmstadt). The tactical situation may be summed up by quoting a conversation on the subject in October, 1929, between Generals Weygand and Thwaites (who had succeeded Lieut.-General Du Cane). The former remarked " What an admirable advanced guard for us," and the answer came, " Much more like the forlorn hope of a rear guard."[1]

The nature of the ground in the bridgehead did not make for ease of withdrawal. The Rheingau and Taunus Hills, 1,500 to 1,600 feet high, which ran across the bridgehead from south-west to north-east, form the rim of a plateau, with slopes descending to the Rhine. Although covered with fir and beech woods, and furrowed by ravines which are generally marshy, they are everywhere traversable by cavalry and infantry, and many of the rides are passable for horsed artillery. The force available—the brigade of artillery with, it should be remembered, only sufficient animals to horse the guns, not the ammunition wagons, and the R.A.S.C. with only sufficient apparatus to supply the needs of a sedentary garrison or a small flying column—was far too small to block all the approaches to Wiesbaden, and cover the Hindenburg road-rail bridge east of Bingen. All that could be done was to guard the main roads. These were six in number, passing through Königstein,

---

[1] The point may be missed if it is not recalled that " forlorn hope " is a corruption of the German *Verlorene Haufe*, literally " the lost detachment ".

Ehlhalten, Idstein, Neuhof, Hahn and Bad Schwalbach, where the sixth bifurcated to Wiesbaden and Eltville. None, fortunately, ran through the Rheingau.

It had been deemed desirable by the French, therefore, to station battalions at Königstein, Idstein and Bad Schwalbach, and they had compelled the Germans to build barracks at these places. This distribution was followed by the British.

By special arrangement with the French, in order to secure communication from the bridgehead to the left bank, Bingen, a Rhine port on the left bank, with a small area around it, was transferred to the British, to form a small bridgehead on that bank, and to protect the Hindenburg Bridge, east of the town, the French retaining control of the Bingen–Mayence railway. This bridge, and the bridges of Mayence, 18 miles above it, were the only passages for retirement across the Rhine from the British part of the bridgehead. It will be seen from the distribution given later that the whole Army of the Rhine, with all its equipment, stores, ammunition and supplies, was on the right bank, with the exception of two infantry companies (one rifle and one machine-gun) with a battalion headquarters stationed at Bingen. No better arrangement could be made with the French, and the position, however much it was disliked, had to be accepted.

Königstein, Idstein (occupied by a Senegalese battalion and retaining a distinct " bouquet d'Afrique "), Bad Schwalbach (formerly Langenschwalbach) were all small summer resorts in the hills, and Schierstein was an orchard suburb of Wiesbaden. Its other suburbs and Bingen possessed barracks, constructed or adopted for the French during the occupation ; but Bingen was found to be so insanitary that it was judged advisable to send only 200 men instead of a whole battalion there. The French asked to be allowed to retain Kastel (on the Rhine, five miles S.S.E. of Wiesbaden, opposite Mayence, which was in French occupation), as the Marceau Barracks and a bridging school there could not be given up. In exchange, training facilities were offered to and accepted by the British, as was also the use of the excellent artillery practice ground at Bitche (Lorraine), after a nearer but inferior one had been suggested.

THE DIFFICULTIES OF THE WINTER MOVE

It may seem to some that a fortnight's notice was ample for the move of some 8,000 men a distance of slightly over a hundred miles. The move was, however, the migration of a sedentary garrison with its transport cut to a minimum but with all the apparatus of a much bigger force ; it was not the battle march of a fighting formation with full transport.

Before the area was finally vacated, as the Rhineland was to be demilitarized, it had been decided that certain demolitions should be carried out. Barracks were left intact, but the target apparatus on the rifle ranges were destroyed, and the 30-yard ranges rendered useless. The main ammunition depôt premises at Longerich, after some precautionary damage had been effected, were sold to civilians, as also were the Ordnance Depôt premises at Nippes. The Field Works School at Richt was destroyed by explosives ; buildings in the hutted camps were removed, and their telephone and electric light services put permanently out of gear. The fortifications had already been dealt with, and in the end no damage was done to the strategic railway lines.

In Cologne were over 150 establishments, including a polo ground, to be closed down or disposed of, and the German owners were out to spoil the now despised conquerors in the matter of " barrack damages," with a good percentage for " moral and intellectual damage " thrown in. An attempt was made to settle all claims by a lump sum ; but as the demands made were fantastic, this proved impossible and they were dealt with in detail. The claim of the Excelsior Hotel, when vacated by G.H.Q., was for £99,746, which was found to include a sum expended for advertising the re-opening of the hotel ! The *Bezirk* authorities had awarded heavy damages to its nationals for alleged damage to crops and billets during the training season ; these had been rejected by the Army as bogus, and the Germans now sought to recover the full amounts. The G.O.C. felt it necessary to report the " colossal impudence and mendacity of the Germans," and his successor who had to deal with final settlement wrote of their " frivolous and insolent claims." Matters were not expedited by the High Commission assessing damage for claims for which the Army had refused responsibility. In the circumstances, Burke's aphorism, that " magnanimity is often the truest wisdom," hardly applies.[1]

Owing to the inadequacy of the land transport required at both ends and the small number of barges for the river transport from Cologne to Bingen, it was obvious that many journeys

[1] The Foreign Office and the Treasury were inclined to accede in part to the German claims, and the Commission was empowered to open negotiations.

would have to be made. The French, too, it soon appeared, were in no hurry to clear out of the Wiesbaden area, and Maréchal Foch and General Guillaumat were rather ruffled when the Army Council appealed to the Foreign Office to intervene in order to hasten the vacating of quarters. Then the accommodation of which the French were in possession in the small area to be handed over was found to offer no room for the Engineer, Supply and Ordnance Services. This was not unexpected, as Wiesbaden had been used by our Allies only as a corps not an Army headquarters,[1] and in general was inadequate for British needs as the French had fewer married folk, and their officers were content with small quarters, regarding themselves on active service, not settled down in an overseas garrison.

In the end, owing to the severe weather, river traffic was much impeded by ice, so that only a small proportion of the stores were sent by water. A good deal of the transport went by road, by short stages, but all troop movements were made by rail, the trains arriving in Wiesbaden festooned with icicles a yard long, " looking as if they had come from the North Pole." The German authorities, delighted at recovering Cologne, gave every facility, providing sleeping cars for the greater part of the families, and arranging express timings for the trains.

Not only were the French slow and unwilling in vacating the quarters of which they were in occupation, but delay also occurred when they were taken over, as it was found that they badly required cleaning. The Hohenzollern Hotel, which was at once occupied as Advanced G.H.Q. had to be evacuated and gassed, as it was found to be " swarming with vermin." The hospital, most of the barracks and many private billets were in untenantable condition. A house was hired for the G.O.C., and quarters were similarly provided for married officers and other ranks married on the strength.

Premises in Wiesbaden and elsewhere additional to those which the French had used had to be requisitioned, as the troops could not well be asked to bivouac in the snow, and this brought protests from the *Reich* Government and the invocation of the spirit of Locarno. Few local protests were made at first,

---

[1] The Staff of the British Army of the Rhine in January, 1926, consisted of 62 officers, including R.A., R.E., Signals and services staffs, electrical and mechanical engineers, pathologist, liaison officers, Deputy Judge-Advocate General, Financial Advisers (2) ; while a British war corps staff contained only 32 and a French corps staff, 30. The number of clerks and orderlies was in proportion.

the proprietors being content with charging high rentals, £2,000 per annum being asked for a flat worth £250 ; but the municipality at Wiesbaden did object to the requisitioning of part of the civil hospital, though in this case there was no alternative ; and the authorities of Königstein proved rather difficult, alleging that the number of billets demanded was a great hardship on the inhabitants. On investigation it proved that Königstein was the summer resort of many of the wealthier families of Frankfort, the place, normally quite empty in winter, accommodating 10,000 visitors at a time ; it was they who would suffer, not the inhabitants. A question on this subject was asked in the House of Commons. Lieut.-General Du Cane, in replying to the War Office, said that no other distribution of the troops was possible unless the zone of occupation were extended, which General Guillaumat could not arrange ; and he gave the result of the investigation.

The New Garrisons

The first movement from Cologne was made on 30th November, 1925, and the transfer was completed, although at first there seemed no hope of it, in exactly the estimated two months.[1] The British flag on the Excelsior Hotel, where G.H.Q. had been housed, was hauled down at 3 p.m. on 30th January, 1926, with no more ceremony than the playing of " God Save the King," whilst a company of the 2/Shropshire L.I., the last troops remaining, presented arms. An enormous crowd filled the Domplatz ; no demonstration took place, but as the Shropshire L.I. marched to the station immense cheers greeted the hoisting of the Rhineland flag.

The location of the principal units in the new area was as follows :

G.H.Q.	Wiesbaden.
King's Dragoon Guards ..	Wiesbaden, Cavalry Barracks.
VIII. Field Brigade, R.F.A.	Biebrich, Shrapnel Barracks.
7th Field Company, R.E...	Wiesbaden, Ypres Barracks.
Elec. & Mech. Section.	
Printing Section.	
Staff for R.E. Services.	
Rhine Railway Company.	
Signals	Dotzheim (western suburb of Wiesbaden).

---

[1] The orders for the move are not available.

Headquarters, 1st Rhine Brigade. (Colonel-Commandant: W. J. Maxwell-Scott)	Wiesbaden.
1/ Cameron Highlanders	Wiesbaden, St. Andrew's Barracks.
2/Worcestershire.. ..	Biebrich, Gheluvelt Barracks.
2/R. Berkshire	Bingen (Marne and Victoria Barracks), and Schierstein (Kandahar Barracks, where also reserve ammunition and explosives were stored).
Headquarters, 2nd Rhine Brigade. (Colonel-Commandant: H. K. Bethell)	Wiesbaden
1/Oxfordshire & Buckinghamshire L.I.	Bad Schwalbach, Moore Barracks.
2/Shropshire L.I. ..	Wiesbaden, Ypres Barracks.
1/R. Ulster Rifles ..	Königstein (Givenchy Barracks) and Idstein (Senegalese Barracks).
1/Manchester	Königstein, Givenchy Barracks.
Tanks, B Company (personnel only).[1]	Biebrich.
R.A.S.C. (2 H.T. and 2 M.T. Companies), Supply Depôt and Workshops.	Wiesbaden, Buller Barracks.
Ordnance Ammunition Depôt.	Schierstein, Kandahar Barracks.
No. 8 Veterinary Hospital..	Wiesbaden, Cambrai Barracks.
Military Police	Wiesbaden, Connaught Barracks.

The total actual strength at the conclusion of the move was reported to be 7,843, establishment 9,197. The units were more scattered than they had been in the last years at Cologne.

Nine Germans convicted of criminal offences were taken from Cologne to Wiesbaden, as it was considered dangerous for them to be at large ; but they were handed over in September, 1926, to the local authorities to complete their sentences.

The Army Council, in congratulating the British Army of the Rhine and its commanders on the smoothness of the move, mentioned they had heard through the British Ambassador that the time and manner of the withdrawal from Cologne had provoked much favourable comment in Berlin official circles, and they assured Lieut.-General Du Cane that the Rhine Army had played its part to bring to success " the policy of appeasement and conciliation inaugurated at Locarno." The troops considered that this was hardly sufficient compensation for the discomforts inevitable in a move in a severe continental midwinter.

---

[1] Soon after replaced by a section of No. 12 Armoured Car Company from Northern Ireland. The tanks had been broken up as unserviceable after the training season, and it would have cost £3,000 to remove the repair workshop to Wiesbaden ; the unit was therefore sent home.

The pine-clad Taunus hill country of the Wiesbaden area was more picturesque and beautiful than that of Cologne with its mines, factories and workmen's quarters ; but it took some little time in the winter season before recreation could be organized, though Wiesbaden and its outlying localities, depending largely on visitors, had more facilities for it than had the Cologne area, and the venereal disease rate rose rather high in some units. This the principal medical officer attributed to the perfunctory examination of the " controlled " women in Wiesbaden by the German authorities.

The " Rhine Army Amusements " staff, however, soon got to work. From February, 1926, the Walhalla theatre in Wiesbaden, capable of seating nearly a thousand troops, was leased—as a charge against the Amusements Fund, not against public funds—and run as a cinema, and for dramatic and variety performances ; a book and newspaper shop added to the profits, the *Cologne Post* (now the *Cologne Post and Wiesbaden Times*) appearing only twice a week instead of daily. In each of the outlying stations, too, including Biebrich, but not the other suburbs of Wiesbaden, a cinema theatre was installed either in, or adjoining the barracks. Wiesbaden had its regulation opera season, and the troops were admitted to the house on the reduced terms usual in Germany. The football and hockey grounds were even harder than on the Rhine plain near Cologne, and the playing season in the Königstein and Bad Schwalbach areas in the hills was very short ; but the games flourished exceedingly. Cricket was played in the Stadium.[1] A derelict nine-hole golf course, three miles out to the north-west of Wiesbaden and 600 feet up, was discovered, taken over by private agreement with the German club and during 1926 considerably altered and improved. For polo 30 acres of level pastureland beyond Erbenheim were rented, two grounds laid out and a wooden pavilion erected, the N.A.A.F.I. providing tea and refreshments. For lawn tennis only a few scattered courts could be found, insufficient for the needs of the Army. Some Germans, however, were willing to build more, provided they were requisitioned. This was arranged, and sufficient hard courts obtained. An officers' club was organized in the basement annex of the Hohenzollern Hotel.

The ground for training was rather restricted until early in August, by which time the crops had been harvested ; it then

---

[1] This was a large sports ground attached to the German artillery and infantry barracks, west of Wiesbaden, called by the British the Cavalry, Ypres and St. Andrews Barracks.

became ideal, with the inestimable advantage that in bad weather shelter for the troops could be requisitioned under German law, in the villages. Unfortunately, owing to the necessary number of guards and other duties, the strength of units for training was very low. The machine-gunners shot their practice with the artillery at Bitche, where the French provided aircraft observation for the latter. For rifle practice, as there was no German *Übungsplatz* in the area, four 500-yard ranges were constructed by the engineers in the Taunus hills, and later some 30-yard ranges were organized in the barrack enclosures.

FURTHER REDUCTION OF THE BRITISH ARMY OF THE RHINE

When the move to Wiesbaden was nearing completion, the War Office again pressed for a reduction of the British Army of the Rhine, this time of the administrative services, " on account of financial stringency," but the mobility of the Army and its efficiency as a fighting force were not to be " seriously impaired." The services consisted of : engineer services (one electrical and mechanical officer, lieutenant, R.E.) ; supplies and transport (one colonel, one major R.A.S.C.) ; remounts (one major) ; medical (four officers, including one for hygiene and one for pathology) ; ordnance (three officers, including a mechanical engineer) ; veterinary (one major) ; and pay (one colonel); with four R.A.S.C. companies (for a mobile column) ; two R.A.O.C. companies, a veterinary hospital and a small R. Army Pay Corps detachment. No great reduction could be made in these essential services ; in April, therefore, the War Office decided, on Lieut.-General Du Cane's suggestion, to reduce the field brigade R.A. to peace establishment ; to abolish the Field Ambulance and Field Ammunition Column ; and to reduce the infantry transport to home establishment. At the G.O.C.'s request the reduction of the artillery was postponed until after the training at Bitche practice camp in June.

No troops were recalled to England on account of the General Strike in May, but a few changes in the units occurred during 1926 : the 8th Hussars relieved the 1st King's Dragoon Guards ; the XIX Brigade R.F.A., the VIII ; the 2/R. Welch Fusiliers, the 1/Camerons ; and the 2/Royal Fusiliers, the 1/R. Ulster Rifles.

CIVIL AFFAIRS BRANCH OF THE STAFF RECONSTITUTED

The representatives of the High Commission responsible for dealing with the German civil administration in every town garrisoned by the Allies having been abolished on the evacuation of Cologne, the military authorities were instructed by the High Commission to deal direct with the Germans, referring to it when necessary. The era of legislation and interference by the High Commission had come to an end. Lieut.-General Du Cane suggested to the War Office that an officer of the High Commission might be attached to his staff to deal with civil questions ; but it was learnt in London that the Germans had expressed a wish that none of the personnel of the hated civil High Commission should be employed with the Armies, and their views were deferred to. The British High Commissioner was allowed, however, to send a liaison officer (Lieut.-Colonel J. G. Birch) to G.H.Q. In consequence of the new duties imposed on him, Lieut.-General Du Cane asked for an extra staff officer and for authority to re-constitute a small branch of the General Staff (G.S. Civil Affairs), as in the days before the High Commission ; it would function under the supervision of the chief General Staff officer, instead of a staff officer called the Military Governor. This proposal was accepted on condition that the " I " Branch was correspondingly reduced in numbers. In its duties, in dealing with Germans at out-stations, the new branch was assisted by the Field Security Police. It had few difficulties : for, as the German officials said, they preferred to deal with soldiers rather than with civilians, and readily entered into a system of co-operation.

The British Summary Court, presided over by an officer barrister-at-law, began to sit in Wiesbaden on 12th January, 1926, with a permanent prosecutor, also a barrister. The Wiesbadeners took the greatest interest in its proceedings, and attended all sittings in large numbers in the accommodation allotted to the public. Many German lawyers visited the Court in order to study British procedure and methods.[1] The task of dealing with offences against the Ordinances was now effected in two ways :

> (a) Minor offences and purely technical breaches were left to the German authorities, with the condition that the record should be submitted to the Army commander ;

> (b) grave offences, and all cases in which politics played a part, were dealt with by the Summary Court.

---

[1] Major Fitzroy Gardner, of the Provost Police, in his " More Reminiscences of an Old Bohemian," p. 38, says :

" I have never been so conscious or proud of it [the British administration of justice] as when I heard Germans express their surprise at, and appreciation of, the strict impartiality with which their countrymen have been tried by the British Summary and Military Courts of the Army of Occupation on the Rhine."

Only two special Military Courts, to deal with serious cases (criminal assault and manslaughter, respectively) were assembled at Wiesbaden, and both found verdicts of not guilty.

The Ordinances of the High Commission still held good ; but now practically nothing was forbidden except the military associations, the singing of the German National Anthem and patriotic songs in the presence of the British, and plays and films about the war. In Bingen specially good relations were established with the inhabitants, as the town is in Hesse, not in Prussian territory, and memories of past brotherhood-in-arms still lingered. In the new area generally there was less objection to the members of the foreign " *Besatzung*," particularly when not in uniform, than in Cologne.

New Financial Procedure

A new procedure was adopted as regards Army payments to the Germans under the Dawes agreement. Instead of making monthly advances without final settlement, all bills had to be sent to the Command Paymaster, who distributed them to the heads of services and departments. If passed, or amended by agreement with the Germans, the bills were returned to the Paymaster ; if rejected totally, to the German authorities. The claims for rent of buildings, cost of special installations, etc., made by German owners were checked monthly by the Chief Engineer. Some reductions were obtained and some irregularities were detected ; when in doubt the Chief Engineer referred to the Financial Adviser to the British Army of the Rhine.

It was claimed by the Germans that the Allied Armies should pay the employer's insurance contribution, under German law, of Germans employed by them, and in February this was allowed.

Aviation Concessions

After Locarno, the future of aviation over the Occupied Territories had been discussed. In January, 1923, the High Commission had given the Instone Air Company (soon superseded by Imperial Airways) and a Belgian air company permission to fly over the occupied territory ; the former, in return, had to keep one aircraft always available for military purposes at Cologne. Other flights were subject to the authorization of the High Commission. It is now proposed that

German flights over the Rhineland should be permitted. The General Staff considered safeguards were essential, including the right to revoke any flying permit, to restrict flying over manœuvre areas and, in cases of emergency, to requisition airfields for military purposes. The German Government, being informed that flight over occupied territory would be allowed, at once pressed for acceptance of the principle of German sovereignty in the air over occupied territory, and also for permission to acquire four airfields in the Rhineland. In the result, the German requests for three airfields in the French Zone were granted, but it was left to the High Commission to give visas and issue permits for flights. The Germans continued to press for more concessions, including " *bandes de passage* ", but obtained none except that " period permissions " were issued to certain pilots, and that in May the *Deutsche Lufthansa* was allowed to co-operate in the development of a Paris—Berlin air route.

THE GERMANS AGITATE FOR FURTHER EVACUATIONS

Besides the evacuation of the Cologne area by the British, the Krefeld area had been given up by the Belgians on 2nd February, and the Bonn area by the French on 4th February— the simultaneous move of all three armies desired by Maréchal Foch had not quite been realized. In spite of these Locarno gestures, in July the Germans finding that even the " Locarno spirit " did not lead to the complete removal of the Armies of Occupation, pressed for big reductions of their strength, using the argument that the Allied garrison should be no larger than the German peace garrison of 50,000. By this time the French contingent was down to 59,613, the Belgian to 8,228 and the British to 8,118. The French offered to withdraw 6,000 men, and asked the British Government what they were prepared to do. A question was then put to the Army Council whether, " should occasion arise," they were prepared to reduce the British Army of the Rhine (*a*) by one half, (*b*) to a thousand of all ranks, or (*c*) to a single company to form a guard for the British High Commissioner ; but the Council would not agree to any reduction beyond that already mentioned. The discussion was continued into 1927.

In April the German Minister for Occupied Territory arrived in Wiesbaden, ostensibly for a cure. He was joined by the Prussian Minister of the Interior (Wiesbaden is in Prussian territory), and held a secret meeting with Press representatives and Trade Union leaders in Mayence. The French ignored the

matter but managed to learn that an agitation for an early
evacuation by the Allied Armies was discussed and planned. A
similar meeting was arranged to take place on 13th April in
Wiesbaden. The G.O.C. informed the *Regierungspräsident* that
he wished to be represented by an officer of his Civil Affairs
Staff. The German demurred, and as he continued to be
obstinate in objecting, he was informed that the meeting would
be regarded as political and therefore forbidden. In this the
British High Commissioner, who had been duly informed,
overruled the G.O.C. who at his wish had to be content
with a verbal protest. A report of the meeting was obtained
by the Security Staff. From this it appeared that the Minister
of the Interior said that he saw no signs that the British were
animated by the spirit of Locarno : he had already received
many complaints from the Wiesbaden population : he undertook to see the Foreign Minister on his return and hoped that
Herr Stresemann would be able to do something to hasten the
reduction of the garrison or its complete removal : the Press
should continue to agitate for the Allied evacuation. The
Regierungspräsident then became alarmed, and asked the Press
to say nothing about the alleged bad behaviour of British
soldiers, as it would have a detrimental effect on the number of
visitors to Wiesbaden—for whom there was plenty of room—
during the summer season. Actually, only two cases of improper
behaviour of the garrison, and these the acts of individual
soldiers, had been reported by the German officials, one in
Schierstein and one in Bingen ; none whatever had occurred
in Wiesbaden.

Otherwise the German Government did not give much
trouble, their attention for the moment being fully engaged on
home affairs, where the economic position was still deteriorating,
with numerous bankruptcies and over two million unemployed,
besides political controversies over the national flag, the
properties of the Hohenzollerns and other former ruling families,
tariffs, the Black *Reichswehr* murders, fears of putsches, and
ill-timed and clumsy interventions on the part of President
Hindenburg. Dr. Luther resigned in May, and was succeeded
by Herr Marx, who retained practically all the old Ministers,
including Herr Stresemann. The general political atmosphere
seemed to improve, as in September Germany was elected to a
permanent seat on the League of Nations Council. A week
later, Monsieur Briand (since July Foreign Minister in a Cabinet
formed by Monsieur Poincaré) and Herr Stresemann met at
Thoiry in Switzerland for more than a general good-will talk,
and promised each other, not with the President of the Council's

entire approval, to do all they could to promote a better understanding. Lord d'Abernon's comment was " the war spirit has been quelled, and the possibility of an era of peaceful development opens ".[1] This really seemed to have more than a chance when next month General von Seeckt was dismissed and was succeeded by General Heye, a less autocratic and more reasonable man ;[2] but on 16th December, Herr Scheidemann divulged in the *Reichstag* that the *Reichswehr* was giving military training to the patriotic associations.

During June, July and August Lieut.-General Du Cane gave permission for 29 festivals and processions, including a *Reichsbanner* 2-day festival, with torchlight processions and speeches, and a Social Democrat affair to celebrate the founding of the Weimar Republican Constitution—the others also had an internal political character. Under the new co-operation system the German police were responsible for all arrangements and good order, and although almost any of the German meetings might have provoked an anti-Allied demonstration, no incident occurred.

---

[1] D'Abernon iii., 267.
[2] He had been on the Great General Staff at O.H.L. in 1918, and later commanding a division of the *Reichswehr* at Königsberg.

CHAPTER XX

LIEUT.-GENERAL SIR W. THWAITES'S COMMAND 1927—1929 TO THE EVACUATION

(Sketch 6)

GERMAN EXTRAVAGANCE AND BRITISH ECONOMY

Lieut.-General Sir William Thwaites took over command from Sir John Du Cane on 30th April, 1927, and, owing no doubt in some degree to his thorough knowledge of German military and social customs, his tour of command was one of peace and understanding.[1] Yet the Germans were becoming impatient for the final evacuation and, having entirely got rid of the Inter-Allied Military Commission of Control at the beginning of the year—whose dissolution, the Berlin Government proclaimed, was admission by the Allies that Germany had fulfilled all her pledges as regards the reduction of her Army and disarmament in accordance with the Peace Treaty—she was now increasing her Army, training reserves, and rearming at speed. The Agent-General for Reparations under the Dawes Plan, indeed, drew attention in 1927 to the growth of her public expenditure, and called, in vain, for economy.

The efforts on the British side to reduce the cost of the Army of the Rhine to satisfy the Treasury, and to cut down its numbers to please the Germans, were continued, the War Office announcing on 1st September, 1927, that the establishment of the seven infantry battalions would be reduced from 4,144 to 3,720—the War Establishment in 1914 of this number had been 7,105. A few weeks later by taking away one complete battalion (the 1/Oxfordshire & Buckingham L.I. from the 2nd Rhine Brigade), and by cutting down the establishments of staffs and departments and of the remaining battalions the garrison was reduced by about 1,100 men, bringing its total down to 6,350. The station of Idstein was then evacuated.

On the other hand, avoidable expense was incurred in 1927 by sending from home the 2/Leicestershire and 2/Dorsetshire to relieve the 2/K. Shropshire L.I. and 1/Manchester of the 2nd Rhine Brigade, leaving only the 2/Royal Fusiliers of the

---

[1] He was the first Commander-in-Chief of the Rhine Army with an expert's knowledge of the German Army. He had been employed for an extended period as head of the Section of the Intelligence Branch, General Staff, War Office, which dealt with the German Army, and in 1918–1922 was Director of Military Intelligence, War Office, after commanding a brigade and a division on the Western Front. He had been at school in Germany and spoke German but never did so officially until the last day of the occupation.

original four ; and, similarly, in 1928 by sending the 2/Hampshire and 1/Prince of Wales's Volunteers (South Lancashire), to take the place of the 2/Worcestershire and 2/R. Berkshire.

The Saarbrücken Garrison

The duties, however, of the British Army of the Rhine were extended. The new British Commander-in-Chief found on his arrival that, by a decision of the League of Nations, the French force of between 2,000 and 3,000 men in the Saar Valley, through which the line of communication for both the French and the British Army ran, was to be replaced by 1st July, 1927, by an international contingent of 100 British, 100 Belgian and 600 French troops to be stationed at Saarbrücken (65 miles south-west of Bingen), under a French commander.[1] Early steps were taken to arrange for accommodation for the British detachment, much to the annoyance of our Allies. No orders were received by the Rhine Army to act on the decision until late in June ; and it was 12th July before the international force assembled in Saarbrücken. The French troops came from France, the other contingents were found by the small Armies of Occupation. This, on the British side, entailed sending a company—the companies of nominally 250 men were shrunken to little over a 100—every three months from one or other of the battalions. Its absence reduced the already inadequate number of men available for routine duties in the occupied territory and interfered considerably with the training of the infantry. The first unit to send a company was the Shropshire L.I., and it was played into Saarbrücken by the regimental band—but not by intent—to the tune of " Old Comrades ", which, being the same as the Prussian march of " Alte Kamaraden ", inclined the inhabitants to a favourable first impression of the British.

Education and Training

In June, 1928, the Commander-in-Chief had to bring to the notice of the War Office that many of the drafts sent to the Rhine did not contain even holders of 3rd Class Certificates of Education among them ; some sent to the Hampshire Regiment could not read or write : regimental n.c.o. instructors, too,

---

[1] By Articles 45–50 of the Peace Treaty, Germany had ceded the exploitation of the Saar (coal) Basin to France in part compensation for the destruction of coal mines in Northern France ; the League of Nations was made trustee for the territory ; at the end of 15 years the inhabitants were to vote which sovereignty they preferred.

did not yet appear to be as efficient as their predecessors either of the Army Education Corps or the old Corps of Army Schoolmasters. Yet the Army Education Corps officers in the Command were reduced in August from five to three, and the weak strength of battalions coupled with the heavy duties to be found made educational training difficult.

Military training, however, went on, and manœuvres were held each year, on one occasion in territory occupied by the French west of the Rhine, our Allies—or ex-Allies as they were then called—assisting every year with the co-operation of aircraft, of which the British Army of the Rhine had none. In 1927, the French and British engineers trained together in bridging operations on the Rhine ; and in 1928 the 8th Hussars, by invitation of General Guillaumat, the French Commander-in-Chief, and by authority of the War Office were brigaded with a French cavalry brigade at French cavalry manœuvres. The exercise took the form of a French advance into German territory covered by a cavalry corps, and at once the inspired German press set up a howl of rage and protest against Anglo-French co-operation.

In April and May, 1928, Brigadier O. E. Heathcote and Brigadier R. J. T. Hildyard, respectively, succeeded to the command of the two infantry brigades, the new rank of brigadier bearing the date of 1st June.

In June, 1929, Mr. Tom Shaw became Secretary of State for War in Mr. Ramsay MacDonald's Second Ministry. Soon afterwards it was ordered that collective training should be reduced in scope on grounds of economy, and in August the War Office informed the Commander-in-Chief that no billeting or concentrations should take place, that nothing in the nature of manœuvres should be held—even the use of the word was forbidden—and that the German population should be put to as little inconvenience as possible. Yet the British troops were always welcome and billeting was carried out according to a German law which was still in force.

A Severe Winter

The winter of 1928-9 was abnormally severe. The hard weather began in the second week of December and continued until the first week of March. The thermometer was often 32 degrees Fahrenheit below zero, and at one time as much as 52 degrees. The Rhine was completely frozen over, the ice at some points being more than three feet thick. As due precautions were taken, no casualties from frostbite occurred. Duty men, in particular the sentries, wore cap comforters under their ordinary caps, fur coats over regimental great coats and fur mitts ; lumps of sugar were issued to them, braziers provided, and tours of sentry duty reduced to one hour.

Much anxiety was caused at Bingen, where the barracks were situated at the confluence of the Nahe and the Rhine ; for should the ice on the former break up before that on the main stream, the safety of the buildings would be threatened by flooding. The German authorities persistently demanded permission to send for German technical troops, who, they said, having local knowledge, would understand better how to cope with the situation than foreigners. For political reasons, their request was refused, and the Royal Engineers stood by to do what was necessary. However, when the thaw came the Rhine opened first.

In April, 1928, some adjustment of the boundary of the British Zone was made in order to fit in with the German administrative areas. This added seven villages to the Wiesbaden area, among them Erbenheim, originally in the French Zone just beyond the British boundary, and included a racecourse which was being adapted for a temporary civil airfield.

RELATIONS WITH THE GERMANS

During the whole period of the Wiesbaden occupation the relations of the Army with the German officials, both Government and municipal, were, if not cordial, at least more friendly than at Cologne. In many cases, for instance, in the move between the two places, the German authorities helped to smooth out both actual and potential difficulties. Thanks to the sensible leadership of the *Bürgermeister* Dr. Travers, and Lieut.-General Thwaites's understanding of German mentality and official customs, no trouble whatever arose in Wiesbaden.

At Bingen one incident occurred. The *Kreisdirektor* categorically declined to attend a conference convened by the officer commanding the troops with regard to the singing of " *Deutschland über Alles* ' in public places, which was specifically forbidden by Ordinances, and sent a subordinate official to represent him. He eventually attended at the Commander-in-Chief's office and read out an apology.

One great difficulty in dealing with Germans was that they often behaved offensively because they were not sure of themselves. A good German wrote in 1931[1] that in the presence of

---

[1] *Germany and the Germans*, by E. Diesel (translated by W. Robson Scott).

foreigners " a German hovers between the desire to conceal the fact that he is a German, and the urge to manifest that fact as clearly as possible." One moment he will be sabre-rattling, and the next will be subservient to an absurd degree.

In respect of the singing of " *Deutschland über Alles* " in public, the Ordinance drew a distinction between a garrisoned town, where the song might be played or sung with the permission of the military authorities, and a non-garrisoned town, where it might be sung without permission, provided the ceremony was of an official nature. This left several loopholes, of which the Germans took advantage ; and they were not above employing trickery. In 1929, the director of the orchestra of the *Kurhaus* gardens in Wiesbaden submitted a programme which appeared unobjectionable, and it was approved. It contained, however, as one item a " Potpourri ", which, when this was played, turned out to include the forbidden air ; it was duly given an encore. The Acting *Bürgermeister* and the manager of the *Kurhaus* both appeared before the Commander-in-Chief to express their regret at the trick.

It was a point of honour with the troops, stimulated by addresses made on parade by the Commander-in-Chief to each new unit on arrival in the command, by weekly ceremonial guard-mounting parades at Headquarters and by an annual ceremonial parade of the whole garrison on the *Exerzierplatz* at Dotzheim, to maintain a high standard of turn-out, military bearing and behaviour. Thus all ranks commanded the respect and admiration of the Germans who came in thousands to watch the annual King's Birthday parade and other ceremonials mentioned above. The massed bands and the Royal Welch Fusiliers' goat were great attractions. The *Frankfurter Zeitung*, referring to the change of guard by that regiment preceded by the goat and nine pioneers, said that it was the practice of this unit to relieve guard headed by its ration sheep for the day, followed by the nine butchers ! The same journal boasted on another occasion, as regards the bearing of the British troops, that they had learnt much from the Prussians.

An offensive gesture came from the German Government in connection with Armistice Day, 1928. It happened to fall on a Sunday, and was celebrated by the British Army of the Rhine in the churches usually lent to the British. The German *Reichskommissar* of the High Commission was instructed to protest against the use of German churches at 11 a.m., as this deprived the civil population of their normal facilities of worship. Lieut.-General Thwaites in a personal interview informed him that this action on the part of the *Reich* Government was in the worst possible taste, and would not be forgotten by the British Army.

As regards the civil population, accustomed to make money out of foreign visitors, the question of financial advantage played a large part in determining their attitude, especially as elsewhere in Germany business was going from bad to worse with the national finances in an unsatisfactory condition and an adverse trade balance. The British Army of the Rhine spent annually a large sum of money, estimated at £300,000, in the occupied territory, and hotel-keepers, shop-keepers and public caterers reaped a good harvest. Some of the professional classes and their families, however, had little to live on except the rent of houses let to the British. A class difficult to be on good terms with was formed by the retired generals and government officials who resided in Wiesbaden ; their attitude was correct but unfriendly, and they usually affected to ignore the presence of foreign soldiers in uniform.

The attitude of the responsible German press in the British Zone was perfectly satisfactory. It was noticeable that, whereas in Cologne no reference was ever made to the British Army of the Rhine, except from time to time in the form of moderate anti-occupation propaganda, in Wiesbaden the local papers took a certain interest in its activities, and occasionally reported its doings. The press in the *Reich*, without let or hindrance from the authorities, so permeated was it with the Locarno spirit, took every opportunity to malign and insult the British Army, and even British justice ; certain journals were therefore excluded from occupied territory for periods varying up to three months.

First Appearance of " The Nazi "

A small but noisy party of the extreme right, then called the *National Sozialistische Deutsche Arbeiterpartei* (National Socialist German Workers' Party) for short *Nasdap*, which was to develop first into the *National Sozialistische Freiheitspartei* (Freedom Party) and then into the " *Nazi* ", occasioned trouble both to the occupation authorities and to their own Republican Government. Its avowed aims were the cancellation of the Peace Treaty, the overthrow of the Republic and the setting up of a dictator in Germany. Its literature, on account of bitter anti-Allied propaganda, was frequently excluded by the High Commission from the occupied territory. Being a recognized political party, in accordance with general policy it was not suppressed as long as the behaviour of the members was not prejudicial to the safety or insulting to the dignity of the troops. As a result, however, of street affrays with left wing organizations, the Party was suppressed for limited periods at places not only in occupied territory, but also in unoccupied territory by the German Government themselves. In 1929, owing to its attitude becoming more hostile and more noticeable, the High Commission, under pressure of Army Headquarters, forbade the wearing of the party uniform in all occupied zones. The *Reichskommissar*, as a matter of course, applied to have the order rescinded. No incident occurred between the *Nasdap* and the troops, but the Party had bloody affrays with the supporters of the Government.[1]

CO-OPERATION OF THE GERMAN POLICE

A very good liaison was created between the British Military Police and the German police. It was improved and stimulated by the close co-operation of the Deputy Provost-Marshal, Major F. S. Modera (Lancashire Fusiliers), and his successor Major J. A. T. Miller (14th/20th Hussars), with the Police President, Herr Otto Frotzheim, a well-known lawn tennis player. The year 1927 was quiet; in 1928 and 1929 the Germans became more self-assertive, and in the spring of 1928 considerable damage was done to Army motor cars by persons unknown. There were in all some 60 cases of assault and disturbance, mostly in *Bierhallen*, always favourite places for " scraps,"[2] committed by British soldiers, and some 40 similar cases committed by German nationals against members of the British Army of the Rhine. In the period of close on four years, from January, 1926, to December, 1929, 595 cases were tried by Summary Court, presided over by a barrister-at-law, Major H. Gatehouse, of which 54 resulted in acquittals ; most of the cases were charges against women in respect of violation of deportation orders made by the High Commission. The sentences ranged up to nine months' imprisonment served in German prisons.

In the American Area in the period from December, 1918, to 10th January, 1920, the " offences and convictions " of

---

[1] On his return home Lieut.-General Sir W. Thwaites, in an interview with Mr. T. Shaw, then Secretary of State for War, warned him that the *National Sozialistische Arbeiterpartei* was the most dangerous militant organization forming in Germany.

[2] They were an almost nightly occurrence in Munich in the pre-1914 days.

German civilians before Provost Courts amounted to no less than 9,702. In addition, three Germans were tried for murder before American Commissions.[1]

RELATIONS WITH THE FRENCH AND BELGIANS

The relations with the French Army were very good indeed during the Wiesbaden period. This was in some degree due to the two G.H.Qs., at Mayence and Wiesbaden, being barely four miles apart, while when the British Army of the Rhine was around Cologne they were over a hundred miles distant from one another. During the earlier period what the two Armies did see of each other they did not much like ; but in the later a new atmosphere prevailed. The excellent accord and good friendship between the British Commander-in-Chief and General Guillaumat, commanding the French Army of the Rhine, who had got to know the British whilst he was Commander-in-Chief at Salonika (December, 1917, to June, 1918) spread gradually to all ranks. By the end of the occupation the two staffs were well acquainted with each other and practised a close liaison. As each senior officer left and was replaced, the new arrival made a point of making the acquaintance of his opposite number on the other staff.

There were many tangible signs of the good relations. The combination of the two cavalries and of the two engineer corps at manœuvres and training, the loan of the Bitche artillery practice ground, and the co-operation of French aircraft have already been mentioned. In April, 1929, a tour was arranged for 40 British officers to visit Verdun and study the operations of the German attacks ; General Guillaumat, who had been in command there towards the close of the fighting, himself accompanied the party and gave his personal experiences, besides ensuring that hospitality was shown to the officers by the garrison and the Municipality.[2] On 14th July, the French National fête, it was the annual custom for General Guillaumat to invite the Commander-in-Chief of the British Army of the Rhine and a large number of officers to attend and for the British general to stand at his side during the march past. Similarly, the French Commander-in-Chief and his officers were invited to attend the King's Birthday Parade and other ceremonial occasions. In the course of time the playing

---

[1] American Occupation, p. 189.

[2] The local staff officer deputed to conduct the party was General de Gaulle, then a *Commandant.*

of National anthems at race meetings, athletic gatherings and football matches on the arrival of Allied Commanders-in-Chief was dropped by common consent as a formality unnecessary between friends, and the playing of these anthems reserved for official occasions only. As to "other ranks", relations, though cordial, could never become intimate on account of the language difficulty.

With the Belgian Army all the formal courtesies were maintained, the two generals exchanging visits every six months or so ; owing to distance, little else was possible. After the move to Wiesbaden, owing to the consequent reduction of staff, the appointment of liaison officers between the two Armies lapsed, and their duties were performed by the British and Belgian liaison officers at French headquarters. The official liaison with the French was always maintained.

RELATIONS WITH THE HIGH COMMISSION

Official relations between the High Commission and the command of the British Army of the Rhine were invariably most correct, and the personal relations between the High Commissioners and the Commander-in-Chief excellent. The British High Commissioner, the Earl of Erroll, was a charming personality, and his death on 20th February, 1928, was a great loss to the British Army, with which he was in close and sympathetic touch. The High Commission, under the presidency of Monsieur Tirard, was a sovereign body and, as such, it was said, was " a little inclined to be class conscious," and in its attitude to the Army to leave the impression that the troops were merely the instrument of its sovereign policy. On the other side, the Army of Occupation somewhat resented being under civilian control whilst in enemy country.

The funeral of Lord Erroll was carried out with international honours : French troops, under General Guillaumat, lined the route, over a mile long, from the church to the cemetery, the escort was formed by Belgian, British and French companies, with a British band, under arrangements made by the British Commander-in-Chief, and a British battery fired the salute.

EVENTS IN GERMANY. THE KELLOGG PACT

In the last years of the occupation, although Germany had paid (largely with borrowed money) the annuities of the Dawes Plan, owing to official extravagance,[1] there were large deficits

---

[1] Bavaria's expenditure, for example, was two and a half times her income.

in the German budget, with no prospect of balancing it. Foreign indebtedness too was on the increase ; bankruptcies in 1929 amounted to over 15,000, 4,000 more than in 1928 ; at the end of 1928 the total of unemployed was 1½ million and in March, 1929, over 2½ million. June, 1929, saw the birth of the " Young Plan," already mentioned, which scaled down the reparation payments. A somewhat disturbing event was that early in 1928, General Groener, a General Staff officer and successor of Ludendorff as First Quartermaster-General in October, 1918, took the place of Dr. Gessler as Minister of War, and though on 12th June, Dr. Marx resigned the Chancellorship, his successor, Herr Müller-Franken, maintained Groener in office as well as Stresemann.

German foreign policy was still wholly directed to securing an early evacuation of the Rhineland, and on 27th August, Stresemann, on behalf of Germany, signed—his being the first of the signatures—the Kellogg Pact for the " Renunciation of War " covenanting that—

> " the settlement or a solution of all disputes or conflicts, of whatever nature or of whatever origin they may be, which may arise among [the High Contracting Powers] shall never be sought except by pacific means."

That pacifism was not the belief of all Germany was obvious. In October, 1929, the German National and the National Socialist parties proposed a referendum to decide whether an official protest should not be made against Article 231 of the Peace Treaty, which read that the war was caused by " the aggression of Germany and her Allies " ; they demanded that the Young Plan should be rejected ; and that the whole policy of reparation and of striving for understanding should be abandoned. As the proposal for a referendum obtained the support of only about a quarter of the 50 per cent. of the voters required, the protest could not be proceeded with.

CHAPTER XXI

THE FINAL EVACUATION

(Sketch 6)

THE ARMY PREPARES AGAINST AN EVACUATION

The possibility of the evacuation of the Second (10-year) and Third (15-year) Zones defined in Article 429 of the Peace Treaty[1] before the agreed times, that is January, 1930, and January, 1935, respectively, had been discussed in both political and military circles in the early part of 1928 ; for on 30th January, 1928, Herr Stresemann had claimed the withdrawal of the Allied troops from the Rhineland as a consequence of Locarno. In order, therefore, not to be caught unprepared, Lieut.-General Thwaites, in October, set his administrative staff under Brigadier E. D. Young to work out in detail the evacuation of the British Army of the Rhine as a winter exercise.

The scheme provided not only for the movement of personnel, animals, military equipment, stores and baggage, but also for a careful handing over of all buildings and quarters with their equipment and fittings. This restitution, which was to be carried out under the Chief Engineer (Colonel L. C. Jackson) and the District Barrack Officer, was found to involve very lengthy proceedings that would require a minimum time of six months, if done thoroughly and so prevent the Germans from claiming exorbitant damages, as they had done at Cologne. The scheme was completed by the end of January, 1929. It was so drawn up that should the Germans accept a lump sum to meet all claims, or should a complete waiver of all claims be obtained, the period required for evacuation could be reduced to three months by alterations of the time table. A Rhineland Evacuation Committee was formed at the War Office consisting of Major-General E. Evans (Director of Movements and Quarterings), Major-General C. D. R. Watts (Director of Ordnance Services), Colonel B. L. Beddy (Assistant Director of Transport) and Mr. H. W. Moggridge (Director of Army Contracts).

The War Office Committee arrived in Wiesbaden on 17th February, and remained four days to discuss the scheme, with which they expressed their satisfaction. It was then forwarded

---

[1] See p. 270.

to London. In a subsequent report the Committee agreed that the minimum time required to carry out the scheme in full was six months. They stated that the actual cost of withdrawal would depend on the time of year, but that winter was unsuitable owing to the difficulty of co-ordinating sea passages, and the hardships, judging by the experiences in the move from Cologne to Wiesbaden, to which the troops might be exposed.

Meantime, Lieut.-General Thwaites had had a personal interview with Sir Laming Worthington-Evans, the Secretary of State for War, who informed him that, although the Army Council hoped for six months' notice, the Government were insistent that the evacuation should be completed in three months. The Commander-in-Chief impressed on him that this was not feasible unless a lump sum settlement were accepted. He further laid stress on the desirability of the three flags, Belgian, British and French, being hauled down together, so as to convince the Germans that a combined front still existed, in spite of the term " our ex-Allies " being used in London political circles. At a subsequent meeting in March, the Secretary of State informed Lieut.-General Thwaites that six months' notice could not be guaranteed. Political considerations, he said, were paramount and it was hardly likely that the troops would be kept in the Rhineland in order to give time for the settlement of claims, especially as the Government were pledged to evacuate " as rapidly as technical conditions permit ", which could not be held to cover a financial settlement. The Commander-in-Chief assured Sir Laming Worthington-Evans that all was ready to carry out the evacuation either on a 6-months' or 3-months' basis. The Chief of the Imperial General Staff (Field-Marshal Sir George Milne) was of opinion that the German acceptance of a lump sum agreement should be made a condition of an early evacuation.

On 8th June Mr. Ramsay MacDonald's Second Ministry took office, and information was soon received that no more than three months would be allowed for the evacuation. All preparations possible within the command were at once taken in hand, such as the evacuation or disposal of all animals and stores surplus to requirements, the making of packing cases, and the drafting of all letters and instructions which would be necessary, The High Commission formulated a basis of negotiations to settle outstanding German claims ; but, in view of the rapacity exhibited—the demands amounted to several millions—there seemed little chance of a deal.

THE HAGUE CONFERENCE OF AUGUST, 1929, AND ITS PROTOCOL

On 16th August a conference on reparation assembled at the Hague to consider the Young Plan, and negotiations with regard to early evacuation of the Rhineland were opened ; the French delegation being early informed that British public opinion was unanimous in its favour, and that it could not long be delayed. On 30th August, all being arranged satisfactorily, the Foreign Ministers of the three occupying Powers, Monsieur Paul Hymans, Monsieur Briand and Mr. Arthur Henderson, made known to Herr Stresemann in a formal letter that, subject to certain conditions given in attached Notes, the three Powers had agreed to begin the evacuation of the Rhineland during the month of September : the withdrawal of the Belgian and British forces would be completed within three months, the French forces evacuating the Second Zone within the same period : the evacuation by the French of the Third Zone would begin immediately after the Young Plan had been ratified by the French and German Parliaments and put into operation : the last movement would, at latest, be terminated by the end of June, 1930.

Mr. Henderson's Note,[1] in the drawing up of which he had received the assistance of a financial expert from the War Office, Major-General Evans and Brigadier E. D. Young from the Rhine Army, whose local knowledge was of the greatest value, went into considerable detail as regards the conditions. It descended even to a paragraph about " Engineer fittings such as stoves, baths, geysers, etc." which were to be taken over *in situ*. The gist of it was that unless a waiver of claims for services rendered and damages caused was accepted the evacuation could not be effected rapidly. Herr Stresemann formally accepted all the conditions on the same day, and the agreement was recorded in the protocol of the Conference and approved at its Plenary Session next day, with the addition that the costs of the Armies of Occupation would be paid from 1st September out of a fund to which all parties would contribute. Its terms in full were :

> " The Belgian, British, French and German Governments have agreed upon the following provisions :
>
> " 1. The costs of Armies of Occupation (including the Inter-Allied Rhineland High Commission) from the 1st September, 1929, will be provided out of a Reserve Fund fixed at 60 million *Reichsmarks*. To this sum the German Government will contribute a lump sum of 30 million once

---

[1] Given in full in Note I at the end of Chapter.

and for all. The Occupying Powers will contribute to the Fund on their side in the following proportions, viz. :

" France 35 per cent., Great Britain 12 per cent., Belgium 3 per cent.

" 2. The Occupying Powers and the German Government reciprocally abandon all their claims relating to damage under Article 6 of the Rhineland Agreement which shall not have been paid in cash on 1st September, 1929,[1] and also all present or future credits in regard to services and damages under Articles 8 to 12 of the Rhineland Agreement, whatever be their date. No claim of a pecuniary character on either side shall be raised on any ground in respect of a territory evacuated.

" The claims waived by the Government of the Occupying Powers are, in particular, the following :

" The claims to any balances outstanding in their favour in the ' special account ' of the Agent-General for Reparation Payments referred to in the Addition No. II. signed at Brussels ; the claims which arise out of advances made by the Agent-General in respect of Article 6 and Articles 8 to 12 of the Rhineland Agreement ; and any claims for the sale value of any buildings constructed by the German Government for the Occupying Armies and charged to the annuity.

" 3. The above provisions apply both to the occupying troops and to the Delegations on the Inter-Allied Rhineland High Commission and their staff.

" 4. In no case shall Germany be obliged to make any payments to the Creditor Governments over the above-mentioned sums either for the cost of Armies of Occupation or for the Inter-Allied Rhineland High Commission, or be entitled to claim any part of these sums."

A FORTNIGHT'S NOTICE

The 4th September was fixed by Mr. Henderson as the date of the commencement of the evacuation of the British Army of the Rhine, which allowed a precautionary period of a fortnight to enable the necessary train and barge arrangements to be completed. These were somewhat complicated, as three lines of communication, terminating in the ports of Ostend, Rotterdam and Antwerp, had to be used, respectively, for personnel, stores and animals, and this involved traversing the rail and waterway systems of four countries, Germany, France, Belgium and Holland, whose managements required due notice.[2] So much was already prepared by the A.Q.M.G.

---

[1] The Germans lost thereby an offer of £25,000 on account of the occupation of the Hotel Excelsior, Cologne, made some time before, which they had refused.

[2] See p. 286.

Movements of the Rhine Army, Colonel B. J. Lang, that, as will be seen, the units were able to leave to scheduled time.

The German Government at once appointed an Evacuation Committee, the local delegate for the Wiesbaden area being *Oberregierungsratspräsident* Kerp. The evacuation scheme was explained to him, and the British requirements stated. Further conferences were held to settle details of procedure. *Oberinspektor* Kammel was nominated to deal direct with the Chief Engineer in all matters connected with the inspection and handing over of lands, buildings, quarters and stores, and he undertook to carry out any urgent maintenance and repairs required during the transition period. Throughout the period of evacuation the German attitude was not only correct, but also willing and helpful.

The *Oberpräsident* of the Rhine Province issued a proclamation enjoining the population to refrain from demonstrations of any kind during the movements of evacuation ; for nothing must occur which might give the Allies an excuse for remaining.

A conference was held at the War Office on 3rd September to discuss the disposal of ordnance material. It had been intended to sell very little locally, otner than scrap, as German purchasers would have to pay import duty ; but under the recent agreement the tax had been waived. Mr. F. H. Bedford, a Deputy Assistant Director of Army Contracts, was therefore sent to Wiesbaden.

He found the evacuation programme complete even to the number of barges (twenty-one) required for the transport of stores. Tenders had already been invited for surplus and obsolete M.T. vehicles ; some ordnance stores were being despatched to Woolwich for sale there ; harness, saddlery and tools were being sent home as good prices were not obtainable locally ; local tenders were being invited for R.E. tools (axes, picks, spades, etc.) ; items from railway stores, including a van, wheels and axles and plate-laying lorries, were being included in an ordnance sale.

Horses and mules had been inspected by the Director of Remounts, War Office, in July and four decisions taken : that aged and worn-out animals should be destroyed at once ; that others found unfit for a year's service should be destroyed at a rate to suit the local market for horseflesh, when evacuation was ordered ; that no animals should be sold alive ; that the remainder should be taken home by the units holding them on charge, but that the Command Pool should be sent to the

Remount Depôt at Arborfield Cross. To ensure that the evacuation programme should not be upset by an outbreak of disease, a mallein test was carried out on all animals, and there were no reactions.

For packing stores, estimates were obtained by the R.A.O.C. from all units for cases, crates, packing material, and scotches and rope for making vehicles fast. There were approximately three thousand cases in stock, a thousand were purchased locally at a price considerably below " Vocabulary " rates, and about a thousand of special sizes (for hospital plant, motor bicycles, typewriters, etc.) were manufactured in the workshops from the stock of wood available, old racks, etc.

Roberts Barracks and certain minor buildings were handed over to the Germans before Zero Day to enable them to store furniture, etc., as it came again into their possession. Although claims for damage had been waived, the German Government had to settle with their own nationals ; in all privately owned quarters, therefore, it was arranged that as far as possible furniture and fittings should be checked and property handed over, and a note made of any damage not considered fair wear and tear.

THE SAAR DETACHMENT

The question of the Saar Detachment was put before the War Office Evacuation Committee, and it was decided, the maintenance of the isolated company being very expensive, that it should rejoin its battalion, a late one to leave, before evacuation began. The regimental band was sent to Saarbrücken, and the buildings, stores and furniture having been handed over to the Saar Commission, on 14th September the flag on the barracks was lowered with all due ceremony. The whole town turned out to witness the departure, and the local press printed very complimentary front page reports, with photographs. There had, in fact, been no incidents of any moment during the stay in the Saar.

The German Government however, took the opportunity to have a dig at the British Army, complaining to the British Ambassador in Berlin of insults offered to German women. The answer provided by G.H.Q., Wiesbaden, was that the British detachment consisted of one hundred men, while the number of amorous ladies on the German police registers of the area totalled over 7,000. So far from attacks having been made by the soldiers, the initiative had come from the other side, and it reflected great credit on the men that they had been able to extricate themselves from the unequal engagement without casualties.

THE SECRETARY OF STATE THANKS THE BRITISH ARMY OF THE RHINE : THE FAREWELL ORDER OF THE DAY

On the eve of the evacuation, on 12th September, the Secretary of State for War wrote the following letter to Lieut.-General Thwaites, which was issued as a Special Order of the Day on 14th :

" May I ask you to accept, and to convey to the officers and men under your command, my profound thanks for the way in which all of you have maintained the British reputation for chivalry, courtesy and fair play during the time the British troops have been occupying the Rhineland.

" It is a source of profound satisfaction to me, as indeed it must be to you, to feel that the British troops can come back from the Rhine with the respect of the people amongst whom they have been quartered so long.

Yours sincerely,
T. Shaw."

The Commander-in-Chief's own Farewell Order to the Troops was :

" For some eleven years, since the 12th December, 1918, the British Army has contributed varying numbers of troops of all arms to the Allied Armies of Occupation in Rhineland Territory. That occupation is about to come to an end and the units composing the present British Army of the Rhine will commence the evacuation of the British Zone on the 14th September, 1929. When the last unit has left, the British Army of the Rhine will have ceased to exist and my Command as its last General Officer Commanding-in-Chief will have come to an end.

" It has been the lot of many units of our Army in those eleven years gone by to assist in carrying out the duty laid upon the Allied Armies by the Treaty of Versailles. The watch on the Rhine could be inscribed in the annals of all such units as a phase in British military history, and will become in course of time a tradition of which all ranks may be justly proud, for during the whole course of the occupation the troops have gained a lasting prestige for themselves and the whole British Army in the eyes of all with whom they have come in contact on account of their soldierly bearing and efficiency, exemplary behaviour and consideration for and courtesy towards the people whose country they are now leaving. It is hardly necessary for me to say in full confidence and trust that I know that attitude will be maintained to the end.

" Before any units leave the Command I should like to thank with true sincerity all ranks for their unfailing and loyal support to myself since I have been here and for their ready response to all demands made upon them.

" It has been my great pride to have had the privilege of enjoying for two and a half years the comradeship and friendship of all members composing the existing British Army of the Rhine, both military and civil, and I wish all ranks God Speed and good luck in whatever part of the Empire they may be called upon to serve in the future.

William Thwaites,

Lieut.-General,

General Officer Commanding-in-Chief,

British Army of the Rhine."

THE EVACUATION ORDERS

The final orders embodying the Scheme of Evacuation in ninety days were issued on 31st August. The guiding principle for the move of the personnel was that each unit should travel in four portions : an advanced party, the families, the main body, and a rear party ; Staff officers, and officers and other ranks attached to the headquarters of formations, corps and departments received orders to entrain as they could be spared. By this time the garrison had so shrunk that it consisted of no more than 315 officers and 5,024 other ranks, with 787 horses and mules, and 4,187 tons of stores, 3,386 tons of baggage, 4,357 tons of vehicles ; the officers' wives numbered 161, officers' children, 181 ; other ranks' wives, 514, children, 915. Besides these there were a number of civilian employees with their wives and families.

The orders covered exactly one hundred typewritten pages, and comprised 47 headings, which dealt with every subject, including dental treatment to the last moment, cats and dogs, for which licences to land were required, and their quarantine, arrangements for which had been undertaken by the Royal Society for the Prevention of Cruelty to Animals, besides places of refreshment for the troops, reserve food for the journey, keys to enable the British Customs to open baggage, and the advice that personal luggage should be insured.[1] It is of note that a " Details Company " was formed on the ninth day, to which all personnel and animals remaining with the British Army of the Rhine after their units had been evacuated were to be attached, its staff being provided by the 2/Royal Fusiliers, the last battalion to leave : it had been selected for that honour as it had been one of the battalions which crossed the Rhine in December, 1918 and had performed two tours of duty on the Rhine in the 11 years of occupation. All the Services

---

[1] See Note II at end of Chapter.

gradually dwindled down, but were kept going to the last possible moment, the remaining members of their staffs moving into the G.H.Q. building.

To the orders there were four Appendices :

I. Giving a list of the quarters to be handed over, by whom and the date.

II. Train time-tables with unit, numbers (counting even children's nurses) and type of train (special, all third, etc.) .

III. Days of loading and departure of stores and baggage, winter clothing being left to the last in case it might be required ; and

IV. Days of loading of animals.

Fourteen " instructions " attached went into the specific duties of the staff and Services, e.g., of the Garrison Adjutant, Amusements Officer, the Command Education Officer, the Chief Engineer, the Signal Service and the Postal Service (maintenance of the service to the last, re-direction of letters, etc.).[1]

THE PROGRAMME OF MOVES

The moves of the advanced parties of two battalions began on Zero Day, 14th September, and those of the main bodies were carried out according to a March Table on the following days after Zero : 9th day, 2/Leicestershire ; 10th Day, 2/Dorsetshire ; 17th Day, Royal Artillery ; 20th Day, 8th Hussars and armoured cars ; 28th Day, 2/R. Welch Fusiliers ; 29th Day, 2/Prince of Wales's Volunteers ; 77th Day, R.E., Signals and R.A.S.C. ; 85th Day, 2/Hampshire ; 86th Day, 2/Royal Fusiliers. Then, on the 89th Day, the rear party of the 2/Hampshire entrained, and on the 90th Day (12th December) the rear party of the 2/Royal Fusiliers, together with the Commander-in-Chief and such of the headquarters Staff as remained.

The first barge for Rotterdam, and the first consignment of animals for Antwerp, also left on the evening of the 14th September. The flow of the Army homewards to Aldershot, Newcastle, Colchester, Lydd, Catterick, Tidworth, Sheffield and York continued steadily and without a hitch.

On 3rd November the final number of the *Cologne Post and Wiesbaden Times* was published.

On 15th November the High Commission moved from Coblence to Wiesbaden, bringing with it a French battalion to

---

[1] The Postal Service under Major E. E. Gawthorne, D.A.D. Postal Service, was maintained until the British flag was lowered on 12th December, the last letter in the last mail being addressed by him to Lieut.-General Sir W. Thwaites.

form its guard, and the guard supplied for the British High Commissioner rejoined its battalion.[1]

Progress reports were rendered daily, and a consolidated report every Monday morning. The Germans on several occasions expressed themselves as being entirely satisfied with the state in which the various barracks, etc., had been handed over. No effort had been spared by the units vacating them to leave them in as clean and satisfactory a state as possible. The only troubles reported were that one barge was delayed by fog and that at Schierstein, where ammunition was loaded into barges, only one 2½-ton steam crane was available. Trans-shipment at Rotterdam was supervised by an officer sent there for the purpose.

By 14th November all women and children had been evacuated and every billet handed over. This considerably facilitated the completion of the evacuation ; even the bulk of the three hundred cats and dogs had disappeared, also the goat of the R. Welch Fusiliers, which was to be let off with 28 days' detention on arrival at Tidworth, the new station of the battalion, while the lesser animals had to undergo the usual 3-months' quarantine.

One incident of the final period deserves mention as significant of the relations of the garrison with the civil population. The Commander-in-Chief had allotted to Sarrasini's travelling circus, for the erection of its tents, a portion of the Garrison Recreation Ground made by the British at the cost of several hundred pounds and subsequently handed to the municipality gratuitously. The proprietor of Sarrasini, whose real name was Baron von Stosch, to show his gratitude, allotted one evening to a free gala performance for the British garrison. On his arrival Lieut.-General Thwaites was received as a German *Kommandierender General* would have been. Addressed as *Excellenz*, he was met at the entrance by the entire staff of the circus, the band playing the General Salute, followed by the Royal Artillery Slow March—the general being a gunner—and the whole of the audience, several thousand in number, stood up until he was seated. But the Commander-in-Chief was under no illusion. In bidding farewell to the 2/Leicestershire at Königstein, he said :

> " You and I have lived among these people for some time and completely understand them. They have always been soldiers, they are soldiers at heart and will be soldiers again."

---

[1] The press correspondents were supplied with full information by the Civil Affairs Branch of the General Staff, but two of them sent reports home that the French were about to replace the British in the Wiesbaden area. They were warned and apologized.

The Final Scenes

The last week of the occupation was spent by the Commander-in-Chief and his staff in making farewell visits, and attending official dinners given in his honour. On 11th December he paid his official farewell to General Guillaumat, going by car to Mayence ; at the Rhine bridge he was met by a French cavalry escort and found a battalion as guard of honour drawn up at the French Commander-in-Chief's official residence. It was with deep regret at the end of their whole-hearted co-operation and at the break in their sincere and intimate friendship that he and General Guillaumat parted.[1] The same evening the British Commander-in-Chief attended the Wiesbaden Opera for the last time, Wagner's " *Der Fliegende Höllander* " being given at his request.

At 11 a.m. on 12th December, he paid an official visit of farewell to the municipal authorities of Wiesbaden, and was received by the *Regierungspräsident* and all the heads of departments, some twenty-five in number. Lieut.-General Thwaites made his speech in German, thanking them in particular for the pictures and furniture lent from the *Schloss* to help furnish his quarters, and for the facilities given to the troops at the Opera, the theatre and the concerts at the *Kurhaus*. He mentioned the good relations of the police of both nations, and the generally favourable attitude of the press. Dr. Ehrler replied in correct but friendly terms, saying that :

> " We are well aware that your visit means more than mere formal courtesy. . . . I feel that I ought to say that the correct and disciplined attitude of the British garrison on the one side, and the proper behaviour of the German population on the other, have combined to bring about that the period of the British Occupation has passed without serious incident and ended without any jars (*Erschütterungen*) ".

He added that members of the British Army of the Rhine who might elect to return to Wiesbaden would always be welcome.

The ceremony of hauling down the flag on the G.H.Q. was fixed for 2 p.m., an hour before the Commander-in-Chief's train left with what troops remained. The windows of British G.H.Q. were occupied by the three High Commissioners and their staffs, French officers, pressmen and others invited by Lieut.-General Thwaites. The public gardens opposite, and the *Kurhaus* gardens to the right, were packed with Germans, who climbed

---

[1] The Belgians had hauled down their flag in Aachen, in the Second Zone, on 30th November, and their troops left Germany for their own frontier, hardly five miles distant, by march route.

the precious trees and trespassed on the sacred grass, despite the efforts of the German Police aided by the British Military Police to prevent them, such action being " *strengst verboten* ". At 2.15 p.m. the company of the 2/Royal Fusiliers, with bayonets fixed and colours flying, headed by the full band, appeared and, breaking into slow time, formed up in the wide thoroughfare between the garden of the G.H.Q. building and the public gardens, facing the flagstaff at the main gate of the former. To emphasize the purely British nature of the ceremony, after the Commander-in-Chief had inspected the Royal Fusiliers, the British High Commissioner joined him by the flagstaff. Then came a long roll of the drums as warning, and the flag on the G.H.Q. building was slowly hauled down, the troops presenting arms as the regimental colours were lowered. The flag having been detached from the halyard, was presented to the Royal Fusiliers for safe-keeping.

The whole ceremony had lasted barely ten minutes. Proud though the British were at the bearing of their troops, many felt that they were leaving their old Allies in the lurch, and that it was not an occasion which stirred national pride. The Commander-in-Chief, who had refused the escort of a French cavalry squadron, as the asphalt was too slippery for horses to trot, drove to the station in a car, past the *Kurhaus* gardens and down the main street, lined by Germans on both sides, some of whom dressed in morning coats removed their tall hats as the Commander-in-Chief's car passed them, while others fell in and marched behind the troops in large numbers and in good order. When Lieut.-General Thwaites arrived at the station he inspected the 3rd Battalion of the French 21st Infantry Regiment which, with colours and band, was drawn up to pay farewell honours to the departing British troops, the regimental band playing the Royal Artillery Slow March. Then, with General Guillaumat and the three High Commissioners, he took up position to watch the final scene.

As the band and the company of the Royal Fusiliers reached the French battalion, they broke into slow time and, with eyes-right, marched past the French to the air of the *Marseillaise*, an honour never before rendered in. the interwoven history of the two nations. The troops filed into the station to entrain and the general and the High Commissioners were ushered into the former Imperial waiting room. Just before the train left at 3.20 p.m. General Guillaumat gave Lieut.-General Thwaites a final salute, and as the train moved off the band of the 21st Infantry Regiment on the platform struck up *Auld lang syne*.

The British Occupation of the Rhineland, which had lasted almost exactly 11 years, was over ; of the British Army of the Rhine nothing remained in Germany except one military policeman left behind in a hospital.

At Ostend, shortly before the departure of the boat at 9.30 a.m. on 13th December, General Galafay representing the Belgian Minister of War, accompanied by Colonel Daubeny, the British Military Attaché in Brussels, arrived to bid the British troops farewell. The officers and regimental band of the Belgian 3rd Infantry Regiment also appeared on the quay, and the band played British march tunes until the boat sailed, when it changed to " God Save the King ".

On arrival at Dover, the boat was met by Brigadier Sir Hereward Wake, commanding the 12th (Dover) Infantry Brigade, representing the General Officer Commanding-in-Chief, Eastern Command, with the band of the R. Sussex Regiment, and subsequently at Victoria Station the train was met by Major-General Evans of the Evacuation Committee, representing the Quarter-Master-General of the Forces.

This was the official end of the British Army of the Rhine, the Royal Fusiliers marching to Liverpool Street to take train to Colchester, and its late Commander-in-Chief and his staff dispersing in taxi-cabs towards their homes.

Six months later, according to plan, at 9.30 a.m. on 30th June, 1930, the British, Belgian and French flags on the Wilhelm Hotel, Wiesbaden, were hauled down in the presence of the High Commissioners, General Guillaumat and a small detachment of French troops. At 2 p.m. the flag on French G.H.Q. at Mayence was hauled down, and General Guillaumat and the remaining French troops there departed by special train at which stones were thrown as it left.

The Third, and last, Zone was clear of all foreign troops. Herr Stresemann had not lived to witness the success of his diplomacy ; he had died on 3rd October, 1929.

Letter from the Secretary of State for Foreign Affairs to the German Foreign Minister :

BRITISH DELEGATION,
THE HAGUE,
30th August, 1929.

Your Excellency,

It is the desire of His Majesty's Government in the United Kingdom to withdraw the British Forces at present in occupation of the Rhineland at an early date, but the speed with which such evacuation can be accomplished depends upon the nature of the Agreement which may be come to with the Government of the Reich.

This evacuation cannot be effected rapidly unless the German Government are prepared to give instructions to their authorities to facilitate in every way the withdrawal of the troops and will also agree to waive certain claims such as those under Article 6 and Articles 8–12 of the Rhineland Agreement.[1] Experience has shown that the assessment of claims under these Articles is a lengthy business. The British Government fears that the investigation of the facts in connection with such claims as may arise in future would necessitate the retention in the Rhineland of various elements of the Army of Occupation which might be withdrawn with the other troops if the claims are waived.

Among the services which the British authorities look to the German authorities to supply is the provision of :—

Rolling stock for the evacuation of personnel and animals, and the assistance of the railway authorities in arranging time-tables ;

barges and tugs on the Rhine, together with the necessary personnel ;

the personnel necessary for taking over, as and when required, barracks, buildings, lands and accommodation of all sorts as well as furniture and stores belonging to the Reich.

Engineer fittings such as stoves, baths, geysers, etc., will be taken over *in situ* as there will not be time to dismantle such fittings and hand them over unfixed.

I should be glad also to receive an assurance that :—

Any soldiers or members of families of soldiers who at the moment of evacuation are ill and unable to travel will be received into German civilian hospitals and kept there at the expense of His Majesty's Government until they can return home : sick animals and those suffering from contagious diseases will be received into German civilian veterinary hospitals ;

No objection will be raised to guards in uniform travelling on the barges for the protection of stores in the course of evacuation by the Rhine, and also that no customs dues will be imposed on British Government property which is disposed of locally in order to avoid evacuation.

The British authorities look to the German authorities to provide any labour which is required for assisting the evacuation.

---

[1] *See* Appendix XXIII.

The claims Your Excellency's Government are invited to waive are those claims under Articles 8–12 of the Rhineland Agreement, and those claims in respect of damages under Article 6, which will not have been finally settled before 1st September and included in the monthly returns already rendered to the Agent General or (as regards Article 6) paid in cash.

The waiver will thus include both claims for services rendered and damages caused before 1st September which have not been finally settled before that date and claims in respect of services rendered or damages caused after 31st August, including those in connection with the evacuation.

It is understood that the German Government will secure that the services to be rendered after 31st August, 1929, will be rendered as promptly and adequately as heretofore and His Majesty's Government undertake to exercise the same reasonable moderation in demanding services as hitherto, and to give instructions to this effect to the General Officer Commanding-in-Chief.

As regards requisitions under Article 6 of the Rhineland Agreement, His Majesty's Government will continue as heretofore to pay for them by means of German currency which will be obtained from the Reich and will be credited against the Dawes Annuities so long as these continue to be paid. Any other claims which have been or might be put forward by the German Government against His Majesty's Government under Article 6 will be waived.

The above provisions apply to the British Army of Occupation in the Rhineland and the British Section of the Rhineland High Commission.

The above waiver of claims is proposed and accepted in order to facilitate the early withdrawal of the British troops from the Rhineland and is agreed to independently of the putting into force of the Young Plan.

At the date when the special account of the Agent General for Reparation Payment was closed on November 30th, 1928, a credit balance was outstanding in favour of His Majesty's Government. This balance has gradually been diminished by debits which have been accepted against it. Should there be any balance on this account on 1st September, 1929, the payment of such balance will be waived by His Majesty's Government and it would accordingly be retained by the German Government.

The same arrangement will apply to any balances existing in favour of the British Government which arise out of advances previously made by the Agent General in respect of Article 6 and Articles 8–12 of the Rhineland Agreement. The British Government also waives any claim to the sale value of any buildings constructed by the German Government for the British Army and charged to the Annuity.

If the above arrangements are accepted by Your Excellency, it is the intention of His Majesty's Government to commence the evacuation about the middle of September and to complete it in a period of approximately three months.

I avail myself, etc.,

ARTHUR HENDERSON.

His Excellency,
   Dr. Stresemann.

EVACUATION ORDERS 325

42 Cemeteries.
43 Printing.
44 Flag Stations.
45 Military Identity Cards and Passports.
46 Dogs and Cats.
47 Maps.

APPENDICES

Appendix I   Quarters, Barracks and Buildings to be taken over.

Appendix II   Days of departure for married families, advance parties, main body, rear parties and detachments.

Appendix III

(a) Days for loading and departure of heavy baggage, stores and vehicles.

(b) Days for loading Ordnance Stores.

(c) Days on which M.T. is to be delivered at Bingen.

Appendix IV   Animals.

INSTRUCTIONS

Appendix V   General Staff Instructions.
Appendix VI   Engineer Services.
Appendix VII   Postal Services.
Appendix VIII   Signal Services.
Appendix IX   R.A.S.C. Services.
Appendix X   Barrack Services.
Appendix XI   Medical Services.
Appendix XII   Ordnance Services.
Appendix XIII   Veterinary Services.
Appendix XIV   Accounting Instructions (Pay).
Appendix XV   Military Police Instructions.
Appendix XVI   Garrison Adjutant's Instructions.
Appendix XVII   Movement Services.
Appendix XVIII   " A ".

NOTE

The following subjects are waiting for War Office decisions :—

  (i) Civilian Labour Policy.
 (ii) Establishment of a temporary H.Q. in the United Kingdom.
(iii) Disposal of Assessment Commissions.
 (iv) Disposal of Army Postal Services.
  (v) Disposal of Financial Adviser's Staff.
 (vi) Disposal of families separated from husbands.
(vii) Disbandment policy regarding units.

APPENDIX I

THE ARMISTICE CONVENTION WITH GERMANY OF 11TH NOVEMBER, 1918, AND ANNEXES

BETWEEN Marshal Foch, Commander-in-Chief of the Allied Armies, acting on behalf of the Allied and Associated Powers, in conjunction with Admiral Wemyss, First Sea Lord, of the one part ; and Secretary of State Erzberger, President of the German Delegation, Envoy Extraordinary and Minister Plenipotentiary Count von Oberndorff, Major-General von Winterfeldt, Captain Vanselow (German Navy), furnished with full powers in due form and acting with the approval of the German Chancellor, of the other part ;

An Armistice has been concluded on the following conditions :

CONDITIONS OF THE ARMISTICE CONCLUDED WITH GERMANY

(A) ON THE WESTERN FRONT

1. Cessation of hostilities on land and in the air six hours after the signature of the Armistice.

2. Immediate evacuation of the invaded countries : Belgium France, Luxemburg, as well as Alsace–Lorraine, so ordered as to be completed within 15 days from the signature of the Armistice. German troops which have not evacuated the above-mentioned territories within the period fixed will be made prisoners of war. Joint occupation by the Allied and United States forces shall keep pace with evacuation in these areas. All movements of evacuation or occupation shall be regulated in accordance with a Note (Annexe No. 1), drawn up at the time of signature of the Armistice.

3. Repatriation, beginning at once, to be completed within 15 days, of all inhabitants of the countries above enumerated (including hostages, persons under trial, or convicted).

4. Surrender in good condition by the German armies of the following war materials :

    5,000 guns (2,500 heavy, 2,500 field).

    25,000 machine guns.

    3,000 trench mortars.

    1,700 fighting and bombing aeroplanes—in the first place, all D 7's and all night-bombing aeroplanes.

The above to be delivered *in situ* to the Allied and United States troops in accordance with the detailed conditions laid down in Annexe No. 1, drawn up at the time of signature of the Armistice.

5. Evacuation by the German Armies of the territories on the left bank of the Rhine. These territories on the left bank of the Rhine shall be administered by the local authorities under the control of the Allied and United States Armies of Occupation. The occupation of these territories shall be carried out by Allied and United States garrisons holding the principal crossings of the Rhine (Mayence, Coblence, Cologne), together with bridgeheads, at these points of a 30-kilometre radius on the right bank, and by garrisons similarly holding the strategic points of each area. A Neutral Zone shall be reserved on the right bank of the

Rhine between the river and a line drawn parallel to the bridgeheads and to the river and at a distance of 10 kilometres, from the Dutch to the Swiss frontier. Evacuation by the enemy of the Rhineland (left and right banks) shall be so ordered as to be completed within a further period of 16 days—31 days in all after the signature of the Armistice. All movements of evacuation and occupation shall be regulated according to Annexe No. 1, drawn up at the time of signature of the Armistice.

6. In all the territories evacuated by the enemy there shall be no evacuation of inhabitants ; no damage or detriment shall be done to the persons or property of the inhabitants. No person shall be prosecuted for participation in military measures prior to the signature of the Armistice. No destruction of any kind to be committed. Military establishments of all kinds shall be handed over intact, as well as military stores, food, munitions and equipment not removed during the periods fixed for evacuation. Stores of food of all kinds for the civil population, cattle, etc., shall be left *in situ*. No measure of a general or official character shall be adopted which may result in a depreciation of industrial establishments or in a reduction of their personnel.

7. Roads and means of communication of every kind, railways, waterways, main roads, bridges, telegraphs and telephones shall be in no way damaged. All civil and military personnel at present employed on them shall be maintained. Five thousand locomotives and 150,000 wagons in good running order, and provided with all necessary spare parts and fittings, shall be delivered to the Associated Powers within the period fixed by Annexe No. 2, which shall not exceed 31 days. Five thousand motor lorries in good running order shall also be handed over within 36 days.

The railways of Alsace-Lorraine shall be handed over within 31 days, together with all personnel and material belonging directly to these lines. Further, material necessary for the working of railways in the territories on the left bank of the Rhine shall be left *in situ*. All stores of coal and material for upkeep of permanent way, signals, and repair-shops shall be left *in situ* and maintained by Germany as far as the working of these lines on the left bank of the Rhine is concerned. All barges taken from the Allies shall be restored to them. The Note appended as Annexe No. 1 regulates all details under this head.

8. The German Command shall be bound to disclose, within 48 hours after the signature of the Armistice, all mines or delay-action apparatus disposed on the territory evacuated by the German troops, and shall assist in their discovery and destruction. The German Command shall also disclose all harmful measures that may have been taken (such as poisoning or pollution of springs, wells, etc.). All the foregoing under penalty of reprisals.

9. The right of requisition shall be exercised by the Allied and United States Armies in all occupied territories, settlement of accounts with the persons concerned being provided for. The maintenance of the troops of occupation in the Rhineland (excluding Alsace-Lorraine) shall be defrayed by the German Government.

10. Immediate repatriation, without reciprocity, of all Allied and United States prisoners of war (including those under trial or convicted), according to detailed conditions which shall be fixed. The Allied Powers and the United States shall dispose of these prisoners as they

APPENDIX I

think fit. This condition cancels previous agreements on the subject of
the exchange of prisoners of war, including the agreement of July, 1918,
in course of ratification. The repatriation of German prisoners interned
in Holland and in Switzerland shall, however, continue as before.
The repatriation of German prisoners shall be settled upon the
conclusion of the peace preliminaries.

11. Sick and wounded who cannot be removed from territory
evacuated by the German armies shall be cared for by German
personnel, to be left on the spot with the material required.

(B) CLAUSES RELATING TO THE EASTERN FRONTIERS OF GERMANY

12. All German troops at present in any territory which before the
War belonged to Austria-Hungary, Rumania, or Turkey, must at once
withdraw within the frontiers of Germany as these existed on August 1,
1914. All German troops at present in territories which before the
War formed part of Russia shall likewise withdraw within the German
frontiers as above defined, as soon as the Allies shall consider this
desirable, having regard to the interior conditions of those territories.

13. Evacuation by German troops to begin at once, and all German
instructors, prisoners, and civilian or military agents now within
Russian territory (as defined on August 1, 1914), to be recalled.

14. German troops to cease at once all requisitions, seizures, or
coercive measures for obtaining supplies intended for Germany in
Rumania and Russia (according to frontiers existing on August 1, 1914).

15. Annulment of the Treaties of Bucharest and Brest-Litovsk and
of supplementary treaties.

16. The Allies shall have free access to the territories evacuated by
the Germans on their Eastern frontier, either via Danzig or by the
Vistula, in order to revictual the populations of those territories or to
maintain order.

(C) IN EAST AFRICA

17. Evacuation of all German forces operating in East Africa within
a period fixed by the Allies.

(D) GENERAL CLAUSES

18. Repatriation within a maximum period of one month, without
reciprocity, in accordance with detailed conditions hereafter to be
fixed, of all interned civilians, including hostages, and persons under
trial or convicted, who may be nationals of the Allied or Associated
States other than those mentioned in clause 3.

19. Financial Clauses.—With the reservation that any future claims
and demands of the Allies and United States shall remain unaffected,
the following financial conditions are required :

Reparation for damage done.

While the Armistice lasts, no public securities shall be removed by
the enemy which can serve as a guarantee to the Allies for the recovery
of reparation for war losses.

Immediate restitution of cash deposits in the National Bank of Belgium, and, in general, immediate return of all documents, specie, and securities of every kind (together with plant for the issue thereof) affecting public or private interests in the invaded countries.

Restitution of the Russian and Rumanian gold removed by the Germans or handed over to them. This gold to be delivered in trust to the Allies until the signature of peace.

(E) Naval Conditions

20. Immediate cessation of all hostilities at sea, and definite information to be given as to the location and movements of all German ships. Notification to be given to Neutrals that freedom of navigation in all territorial waters is given to the naval and mercantile marines of the Allied and Associated Powers, all questions of neutrality being waived.

21. Release, without reciprocity, of all prisoners of war in German hands belonging to the navies and mercantile marines of the Allied and Associated Powers.

22. Surrender to the Allies and the United States of all existing submarines (including all submarine cruisers and minelayers) with armament and equipment complete, in ports specified by the Allies and the United States. Those which cannot put to sea shall be paid off and disarmed, and shall remain under the supervision of the Allies and of the United States. Submarines which are ready to put to sea shall be prepared to leave German ports as soon as orders are received by wireless for them to proceed to the port of surrender, and the rest shall follow as soon as possible. The conditions of this clause shall be fulfilled within 14 days after the signature of the armistice.

23. The following German surface warships, which shall be designated by the Allies and the United States, shall forthwith be disarmed and thereafter interned in neutral ports, or, failing these, in Allied ports designated by the Allies and the United States, and there placed under the supervision of the Allies and the United States, only guards being left on board, namely :

> 6 battle cruisers
> 10 battleships
> 8 light cruisers, including two mine-layers
> 50 destroyers of the most modern types.

All other surface warships (including river craft) shall be concentrated in German naval bases to be designated by the Allies and the United States, completely disarmed, and there placed under the supervision of the Allies and the United States. All vessels of the auxiliary fleet shall be disarmed. All vessels selected for internment shall be ready to leave German ports seven days after the signature of the Armistice. Sailing orders shall be given by wireless.

24. The Allies and the United States shall have the right to sweep all minefields and destroy all obstructions laid by Germany outside German territorial waters. The position of such minefields and obstructions is to be indicated.

25. Freedom of access to and egress from the Baltic to be given to the naval and mercantile marines of the Allied and Associated Powers ; to secure this the Allies and the United States shall be empowered to

occupy all German forts, fortifications, batteries, and defence works of all kinds in all the channels from the Cattegat into the Baltic, and to sweep and destroy all mines and obstructions within and without German territorial waters. The plans and exact positions of the above shall be furnished by Germany, who may not raise any question of neutrality.

26. The existing blockade conditions set up by the Allied and Associated Powers shall remain unchanged, and all German merchant ships met at sea shall remain liable to capture. The Allies and the United States contemplate the provisioning of Germany, during the Armistice, to such extent as shall be found necessary.

27. All aircraft shall be concentrated and immobilised in German bases specified by the Allied Powers and the United States.

28. In evacuating the Belgian coast and ports, Germany shall leave *in situ* and intact all harbour material and materal for inland navigation, all merchant craft, tugs, and barges ; all naval aircraft, equipment, and stores, together with all armament, equipment, and stores of every description.

29. All Black Sea ports are to be evacuated by Germany ; Russian warships of all descriptions seized by Germany in the Black Sea are to be handed over to the Allies and the United States ; all neutral merchant ships seized are to be released ; war and other material of all kinds seized in those ports are to be returned, and German material as specified in clause 28 is to be abandoned.

30. All merchant ships now in German hands belonging to the Allied and Associated Powers shall be restored, without reciprocity, in ports specified by the Allies and the United States.

31. No destruction of ships or of material to be permitted before evacuation, surrender, or restoration.

32. The German Government shall formally notify all neutral Governments, and particularly the Governments of Norway, Sweden, Denmark and Holland, that all restrictions imposed on the trading of their vessels with the Allied and Associated countries, whether by the German Government or by private German interests, and whether in return for specific concessions, such as the export of shipbuilding materials or not, are immediately cancelled.

33. No transfers of German merchant shipping of any description to any neutral flag are to take place after the signature of the Armistice.

(F) Duration of the Armistice

34. The Duration of the Armistice shall be 36 days, with option to extend.

During such period the Armistice may, owing to non-execution of any of the above clauses, be denounced by one of the contracting parties, who shall give 48 hours' notice of its intention to that effect. It is agreed that the Armistice shall not be denounced owing to non-sufficient execution of the stipulations of clauses 3 and 18 within the time-limits specified, except in the case of intentional negligence in execution. To ensure the adequate fulfilment of the present agreement' the principle of a Permanent International Armistice Commission is admitted. This Commission shall work under the high authority of the military and naval Commander-in-Chief of the Allied forces.

This Armistice was signed on 11th November, 1918, at 5 a.m. (French time).

<table>
<tr><td>F. Foch</td><td>Erzberger</td></tr>
<tr><td>R. E. Wemyss</td><td>Oberndorff</td></tr>
<tr><td></td><td>Winterfeldt</td></tr>
<tr><td></td><td>Vanselow</td></tr>
</table>

ADDENDUM

The Allied Representatives declare that, owing to recent events, it appears necessary to them that the following condition should be added to the clauses of the Armistice :—

" In the event of the German vessels not being handed over within the periods specified, the Allied and United States Governments shall have the right to occupy Heligoland so as to ensure the surrender of the vessels."

R. E. Wemyss, Admiral   F. Foch

The German delegates state that they will transmit this declaration to the German Chancellor, with the recommendation that it should be accepted, together with the reasons upon which this demand on the part of the Allies is based.

Erzberger
Winterfeldt
Oberndorff
Vanselow

ANNEXE No. 1

I. THE EVACUATION OF THE INVADED TERRITORIES OF BELGIUM, FRANCE AND LUXEMBOURG, AS WELL AS OF ALSACE-LORRAINE

Shall be carried out in three successive stages under the following conditions :

First Stage. Evacuation of the territory situated between the present front and line No. 1 as shown on the attached map, [See Frontispiece] to be completed within five days after the signature of the Armistice.

Second Stage. Evacuation of the territory situated between line No. 1 and line No. 2, to be completed within four further days (nine days in all after the signature of the Armistice).

Third Stage. Evacuation of the territory situated between line No. 2 and line No. 3, to be completed within six further days (15 days in all after the signature of the Armistice).

Troops of the Allies and of the United States shall enter these different zones on the expiration of the periods allowed to the German troops for their evacuation. Thus the present German front line will be crossed by the Allied troops as from the sixth day following the signature of the Armistice, line No. 1 as from the tenth day, and line No. 2 as from the sixteenth day.

II. Evacuation of the Rhine Lands

This evacuation shall also be carried out in several successive stages, viz. :

First Stage. Evacuation of the territories situated between line 2, line 3 and line 4, to be completed within four further days (19 days in all after the signature of the Armistice).

Second Stage. Evacuation of the territory situated between line 4 and line 5 to be completed within four further days (23 days in all after the signature of the Armistice).

Third Stage. Evacuation of the territory situated between line 5 and line 6 (line of the Rhine) to be completed within four further days (27 days in all after the signature of the Armistice).

Fourth Stage. Evacuation of the bridgeheads and of the Neutral Zone on the right bank of the Rhine to be completed within four further days (31 days in all after the signature of the Armistice).

The Armies of Occupation of the Allies and the United States shall enter these different zones on the expiration of the period allowed to the German troops for the evacuation of each zone ; thus line No. 3 shall be crossed by them as from the twentieth day following the signature of the Armistice ; line No. 4 shall be crossed by them as from the twenty-fourth day following the signature of the Armistice ; line No. 5 as from the twenty-eighth day ; and line No. 6 (Rhine) as from the thirty-second day, for the occupation of the bridgeheads.

III. Surrender by the German Armies of the War Material Fixed by the Armistice Conditions

This war material shall be handed over in the following manner The first half before the tenth day, the second half before the twentieth day. This material shall be handed over to each Allied and United States Army by each tactical group of the German Army in proportions to be laid down by the Permanent Armistice Commission.

Annexe No. 2

Conditions relating to the Means of Communication (Railways, Waterways, Roads, River Harbours, Seaports, Telegraphs and Telephones)

1. All means of communication up to and including the Rhine, or included on the right bank of that river within the bridgeheads occupied by the Allied Armies, shall be placed under the full and complete control of the Commander-in-Chief of the Allied Armies, who shall have the right to take any steps which he may judge necessary in order to ensure their occupation and use. All documents relating to the means of communication shall be held in readiness to be delivered to him.

2. All the material and all civil and military personnel at present employed for the upkeep and use of the means of communication will be maintained *in toto* on these communications throughout the territory evacuated by the German troops.

Any additional material necessary for the maintenance of these lines of communication in the territories on the left bank of the Rhine shall be furnished by the German Government throughout the duration of the Armistice.

3. PERSONNEL. The French and Belgian personnel belonging to the communication services, whether interned or not, shall be returned to the French or Belgian Armies within 15 days of the signature of the Armistice. The personnel directly employed on the Alsace-Lorraine railway system shall be retained or shall return to their posts in order to keep these railways running.

The Commander-in-Chief of the Allied Armies shall have the right to change or replace any of the personnel of the communication services as he may think fit.

4. MATERIAL : (a) *Rolling-Stock.* The rolling-stock handed over to the Allied Armies in the zone between the front line and line No. 3 (not including Alsace-Lorraine) shall amount to at least 5,000 locomotives and 150,000 wagons. Delivery of this rolling-stock shall be carried out within the periods fixed by clause 7 of the Armistice, and under the detailed conditions to be settled by the Permanent International Armistice Commission.

All this rolling-stock shall be in a good state of repair and in running order, and provided with all usual spare parts or accessories. It shall be used (with its own or any other personnel) at any point of the railway system of the Allied Armies.

The rolling-stock directly employed on the railways of Alsace-Lorraine shall be retained *in situ* or returned to the French Army.

The material to be left *in situ* in the territories on the left bank of the Rhine, as well as within the bridgeheads, must allow of normal traffic being maintained on the lines in these areas.

(b) *Permanent-way, Signals and Workshop Plant.* The signalling apparatus, machinery and tools removed from the workshops and depôts of the French and Belgian railways shall be replaced in accordance with detailed conditions to be settled by the Permanent International Armistice Commission. The permanent-way material, rails, appurtenances, apparatus, bridging material, and timber necessary for repairing the destroyed lines beyond the present front shall be supplied to the Allied Armies.

(c) *Fuel and Materials for Upkeep.* During the period of the Armistice, fuel and materials for upkeep shall be supplied by the German Government to the depôts normally serving the traffic in the territories on the left bank of the Rhine.

5. TELEGRAPHIC AND TELEPHONIC COMMUNICATIONS. All telegraph and telephone lines and fixed wireless stations shall be surrendered to the Allied Armies with all the civil and military personnel and all equipment, including all stores existing on the left bank of the Rhine.

All additional stores necessary for the maintenance of traffic shall be supplied by the German Government during the period of the Armistice, as and when required.

The Commander-in-Chief of the Allied Armies shall assume military control of this system, guarantee its organisation, and replace or change any of the personnel as he may think fit.

He shall return to the German Army all the military personnel which he does not consider necessary for the working and maintenance of the system.

All plans of the German telegraph and telephone systems shall be handed over to the Commander-in-Chief of the Allied Armies.

APPENDIX II

NOTES ON SOME GERMAN ARMISTICES AND PEACE TREATIES

(1) PRUSSIA AND AUSTRIA, 1866

PEACE TREATIES AND ARMISTICE[1] 26TH JULY AND 23RD AUGUST

In 1866 the war for the hegemony of Germany was brought to an end by Austria accepting Prussia's terms of peace in the Preliminary Treaty of Nikolsburg on 26th July. Then, to quote from the Convention :

" The preliminaries of peace having been signed this day, hostilities cease between the Austrian and Saxon troops on one side and the Prussian troops on the other side, and an Armistice of four weeks begins on the 2nd of August."

That is, peace terms had to be accepted before an armistice was granted. The final Treaty of Peace was signed on 23rd August at Prague and ratified three days later.

The Preliminary Peace Treaty contained—omitting conventional matter—six short articles :

I. Austria gave up the Lombardo-Veneto Kingdom and Prussia agreed to withdraw her troops from Austrian territory as soon as peace was ratified, under reservation as regards guarantees for payment of her war indemnity.

II. Austria recognized her dissolution of the Germanic Confederation and consented to a new organization without her participation.

III. Austria transferred to Prussia all rights in the Duchies of Schleswig-Holstein.

IV. Austria undertook to pay a war indemnity of 40 million thalers.

V. Prussia permitted Austria's ally, the Kingdom of Saxony, to continue a separate entity.

VI. Prussia would recommend her ally, Italy, to conclude peace with Austria.

The Armistice Convention fixed lines of demarcation between the two armies. The Prussians, who were close to Vienna, were to withdraw a certain distance, the Austrians not following until the rear of the Prussians had passed the Thaya river, of which the latter were to give notice.

The sick and wounded in the evacuation area were to remain and be cared for, but no obstacle was to be placed in the way of their removal.

The maintenance of the Prussian troops was to be provided by the provinces they occupied.

---

[1] Extracted from *British and Foreign State Papers*, 1865–6.

M*

No more properties, stores and provisions of the State were to be seized.

Civil officials were to return to their posts and co-operate in providing for the Prussian Army.

From date of signature until 2nd August, when the Armistice came into force, the Prussians were not to cross a fixed line and the Austrians were to keep half a mile from it.

(2) FRANCE AND GERMANY 1871

ARMISTICE AND PEACE TREATY

The various diplomatic instruments which brought the Franco-German War of 1870–1 to an end number 19 and take up 110 pages in the 1871–2 volume of State Papers. The change of sovereignty in Alsace-Lorraine was the occasion for a number of protocols. The principal documents of general interest are :

The Armistice Convention, signed at Versailles, 28th January, 1871 ;

The Preliminary Treaty of Peace, signed at Versailles, 26th February, 1871 ;

The Convention concerning the return of French Prisoners of War signed at Ferrières, 11th March, 1871 ;

The Peace Treaty signed at Frankfort, 10th May, 1871 (ratifications exchanged on 20th May, 1871).

The gist of the terms of the Armistice, which in fact were the terms of surrender of Paris, is as follows :

Article I fixed the date—but not the hour—of the commencement : " for Paris to-day, for the Departments three days later." It was to terminate at noon on 19th February unless renewed. A line of demarcation was defined, but left its alignment vague in the area around Belfort, where operations were proceeding and were, including the siege of that fortress, to continue until further information was received.[1] " The two belligerent armies and their outposts will each keep at a distance of 10 kilometres at least from the line fixed to separate their positions. For the naval forces the Meridian of Dunkirk was selected as the line of demarcation. Prisoners and captures made after the conclusion and before the ratification of the Armistice were to be returned.

Article II stated that the Armistice was arranged in order to allow the Government of National Defence to summon an elected Assembly at Bordeaux, which would decide whether hostilities should be continued and if not on what conditions peace should be concluded.

Article III arranged for the immediate surrender of the outer forts of Paris and permitted the Germans to occupy the communes and houses outside the perimeter of the forts up to a fixed line. The ground between this line and the enceinte of Paris was forbidden to both parties. The procedure for handing over the forts and for fixing the line of demarcation was the subject of an annexed protocol.

---

[1] The Armistice in the named area was brought into effect by a Convention signed on 15th February. By this Belfort was surrendered, the undefeated garrison being accorded the honours of war.

Article IV settled that " the German Army shall not enter the City of Paris during the duration of the Armistice." It was superseded on 26th February by two Conventions for the prolongation of the Armistice and occupation of part of Paris, and the Germans were given the right to occupy part of Paris with a force of not more than 30,000 men, who would be lodged in public buildings as far as possible, but rationed by their own Army. A neutral zone was fixed ; but soldiers, without rifles and conducted by officers, were to be permitted to visit the galleries of the Louvre and the Hôtel des Invalides in the French area.

Article V provided that the enceinte of Paris should be disarmed of its guns, and that the gun carriages should be sent to the outer forts.

Article VI made the entire garrison prisoners of war, except 12,000 men whom the military authorities in Paris might retain for internal security.

Article VII gave the National Guard, the gendarmerie and similar municipal troops such as the Republican Guard, custom house officials and firemen the right to retain their arms for the security of Paris and the maintenance of order. The total of three categories was limited to 35,000 men. All the *francs-tireur* corps were to be disbanded.

Article VIII gave the immediate right to the French Government to send commissaries into the Departments and abroad to prepare for revictualling Paris and getting up merchandise intended for the city.

Article IX permitted the revictualling of Paris freely by land and water directly the handing over of the forts and the disarmament of the enceinte and the garrison had been completed.

Article X arranged for permits to leave Paris. They were granted without question to deputies and candidates for election to the National Assembly.

Article XI compelled the municipality to pay a " contribution " of 200 million francs before the fifteenth day of the Armistice.

Articles XII and XIII forbade the making away of public monetary securities and the importation into Paris of arms and material for their manufacture.

Article XIV arranged for an immediate exchange of prisoners. Lists of German prisoners in hands of the French were to be sent in to the German commanders in four places. " The German prisoners will be set at liberty at the nearest point to the frontier." The Germans would then exchange a similar number of French prisoners of similar ranks.

Article XV, the last, promised a postal service for unsealed letters between Paris and the provinces, via German headquarters in Versailles.

Besides the cession of Alsace-Lorraine the most important of the conditions of peace were : that France had to pay a large indemnity by instalments, the occupied territory being given up by the Germans belt by belt as the instalments were paid.

According to the Preliminary Treaty of Peace :—

"*Article II :* France will pay H.M. the Emperor of Germany (*sic*) the sum of 5 milliards of francs."

" The payment of at least one milliard of francs will take place in the course of the year 1871 and that of the balance of the debt within a period of three years beginning at the date of the ratification of the present treaty.

"*Article III.* The evacuation of French territory occupied by the German troops will commence after the ratification of the present treaty by the National Assembly sitting in Bordeaux. Immediately after the ratification the German troops will leave the inner part of the city also the forts situated on the left bank of the Seine, and will as quickly as possible—the time being fixed by agreement between the Military authorities of the two countries— entirely evacuate the Departments up to the left bank of the Seine. [Fourteen Departments are enumerated ; it meant that the Germans were to retire behind a line running south from Le Tréport nearly to the Seine and thence roughly south-eastward, north of Paris and Dijon.] At the same time the French troops will retire behind the Loire which they must not recross before a definite Treaty of Peace has been signed. The garrison of Paris is excepted from this retirement, but its numbers must not exceed 40,000 men and the necessary garrisons of the forts. [By the final Treaty, Article X, liberated prisoners who had completed their period of Military Service could be sent to their homes even if north of the Loire.]

" The evacuation of the Departments between the right bank of the Seine and the Eastern frontier will be carried out gradually after the ratification of the definite Treaty of Peace and the payment of the first half milliard of the contribution mentioned in Article II, beginning with the Departments nearest to Paris and continuing in proportion as the payments of the contribution are effected. After the first payment evacuation will take place in the following Departments. . . . Also the forts on the right bank of the Seine.

" After the payment of two milliards the Germans will hold only . . . [that is a second belt will be evacuated by them] which will serve as guarantee for the remaining 3 milliards and in which not more than 50,000 German troops will remain. [A clause then provided for the substitution of a financial for a territorial guarantee.] The 3 milliards of which the payment is postponed will bear interest at the rate of 5 per cent. from the ratification of the present Convention. [This was later amended so that any sum paid in advance on the final 3 milliards would cease to carry interest from the date of payment.]"

Article IV forbade requisition by the Germans either in money or kind in the occupied Departments, but laid down that the " alimentation " of the German occupying troops would be at the expense of the French Government. A Special Convention of the same date arranged by the Intendant Generals of the two Armies fixed the number of rations for man and horse which would be required for different periods and the monetary equivalent of such rations. The quota, originally 500,000 men and 150,000 horse rations on a scale laid down in appendices was to fall gradually and 15 days after the payment of the first 3 milliards to drop to 50,000 and 18,000 respectively. The regulation of deliveries in kind—by forming reserves—and their possible rejection, were legislated for.

Further " The French Government engage themselves to place at the disposal of the German Troops, in every town or village occupied by not less than a battalion, a squadron or a battery, all the military establishments they require, with the necessary furniture, heating and lighting in accordance with the Prussian regulations."

There follows a list of establishments. They included billets for officers and men, a guard room, a prison, workshops for regimental tradesmen, a clothing store, offices, schools, a hospital, a swimming bath if a stream was available, a covered or uncovered *manège*, rifle ranges, a training ground, ration and forage stores, space in a slaughter house, in a bakery and in a blacksmith's shop, and officers' messes. Troops would not be quartered on the inhabitants unless the public buildings or others rented for the purpose were insufficient. If billeted, fire and light had to be provided by the inhabitant. Married officers, if they preferred, might receive a money allowance in lieu of quarters. An annex laid down the number of rooms to which various ranks were entitled and the lodging allowances, which were much higher in the winter months than the summer.

Everything seems to have been minutely laid down, including assessment of damage, the rate of exchange, use of telegraph and postal service, and freedom from custom duties of military stores for the German army.

Special Conventions provided for railway facilities for the occupying army, and for the return of French prisoners of war by three fixed railway routes to fixed destinations, and by sea from Hamburg and Bremerhafen to French ports.

In the definite Treaty of Peace the two signatories accepted the conditions of the Preliminary Treaty with certain modifications. The first six and the ninth articles referred to details of handing over Alsace-Lorraine, the seventh article to the method of payment of the indemnity :

" The payment may be made only in the principal business towns of Germany, and will be effected in bar metal or coin, in notes of the Bank of England, the Bank of Prussia, the Royal Bank of the Netherlands or the National Bank of Belgium, or in bills to order and letters of exchange of the first order payable on demand."

The French Government was to inform the German Government three months in advance of any projected payment.

Interpolated in this article was the paragraph " In the interest of the security of the German troops, they will have at their service (*disposition*) the neutral zone situated between the German line of demarcation and the enceinte of Paris on the right bank of the Seine."

Article VIII gave the Germans the right to requisition or raise money by taxation if the French Government failed in their obligations to feed and lodge the troops in occupied territory.

Article XI dealt with the renewal of commercial and navigation (railway) treaties.

Article XII read : " All Germans who have been expelled retain the full and complete enjoyment of all property acquired in France ", and were restored any rights of domicile they might have obtained.

Article XII left as prize any German ships condemned before 2nd March, 1871 ; ships and cargoes condemned after that date were to be restored.

The only other article of general interest is No. XVI by which the two Governments mutually engaged to respect and keep up military cemeteries in their territory.

Some " Additional Articles " arranged for the release to the French Government of any rolling stock and its accessories in German possession, and for the purchase by the German Government for 325 million francs, of the property of the Eastern Railway Company in the ceded territory of Alsace-Lorraine. This sum could be deducted from the Indemnity.

(3) (a) ARMISTICE TERMS BETWEEN THE CENTRAL POWERS AND RUSSIA, 1917

SIGNED AT BREST LITOVSK, 15TH DECEMBER

Article I fixed the commencement and termination, adding " the contracting parties have the right on the twenty-first day of the Armistice to give seven days' notice of its termination ; if this is not done, the Armistice remains in force automatically until one of the parties gives seven days' notice of its termination."

Article II was concerned with the land and air forces on the land fronts between the Black Sea and the Baltic and in the Russo-Turkish theatres in Asia. Certain movements behind the fronts were forbidden :

" The contracting parties undertake during the duration of the Armistice neither to increase the number of troop units on the above-named fronts nor on the islands of Moon Sound—this applies also to their order of battle and establishments—nor to take in hand any regrouping in preparation for an offensive.

" Further the contracting parties bind themselves not to carry out any strategic transfers of troops on the front between the Black Sea and the Baltic, unless such transfers had been already begun at the moment of the signing of the Armistice.

" Finally the contracting parties bind themselves not to assemble any troops in the ports of the Baltic east of the 15° Greenwich Meridian, nor in the ports of the Black Sea during the duration of the Armistice."

Article III laid down the lines of demarcation : where obstacles had been constructed, the foremost of these were, on the European front, to be the respective limits. Where no obstacles existed a straight line was to be drawn between the foremost occupied posts. Navigable rivers separating the two positions were to be neutral water and closed to navigation, except in the case of agreed merchant shipping. When the two positions were far apart an Armistice Commission was to fix and mark lines of demarcation. (Article VII.) The conditions for crossing the neutral zone are enumerated in Article IV.

In the Russo-Turkish theatre in Asia-Minor the lines of demarcation, as well as the control of traffic through them, were to be settled by the Senior Commanders in the theatre.

Article IV was peculiar. Besides arranging as is normal for the passage of parlementaries and members of the Armistice Commission, and for the burial of the dead in the neutral zone, it permitted organized intercourse between the troops under the following conditions :—

" In each section of a Russian division organized intercourse is permitted at two or three places."

Centres were to be established in the neutral zone and marked by white flags.

Intercourse might take place only by day between sunrise and sunset.

No more than 25 persons from each side were to be present at a centre at one time.

Exchange of news and newspapers, the handing over of open letters for despatch, and sale and exchange of goods of everyday use were to be permitted at the centres.

Article V dealt with the naval and air forces and arranged for lanes for unrestricted trade and passage of merchant shipping in the sea areas.

Article VI forbade musketry practice nearer than 5 kilometres, and artillery practice nearer than 15 kilometres behind the fronts.

Mine warfare was to cease entirely. Aeroplanes and balloons were not to come within 10 kilometres of the front.

Article VII provided for a number of local Armistice Commissions. " Direct and uncontrolled telegraph lines to their home countries will be placed at the disposal of these commissioners," each side building lines to midway in the neutral zones.

A Supplement to the Armistice Convention arranged for a settlement as quickly as possible of the exchange, directly through the front, of civilian prisoners and prisoners of war unfit for military service. " The repatriation of women and children under 14 years detained by either side in the course of the war shall receive first consideration."

The greatest feasible amelioration of the condition of the prisoners of war of both sides was to be one of the principal tasks of the Governments engaged.

(3) (b) TREATY OF PEACE BETWEEN THE CENTRAL POWERS AND THE UKRAINIAN REPUBLIC, 1918

Signed at Brest Litovsk, 9th February

This treaty left the Austro-Hungarian Russian frontier unchanged, but the German-Ukrainian frontier was made a line on the eastern side of Poland, a little west of the later Polish-Ukrainian frontier. It arranged for the evacuation of Ukraine by the Germans and for prisoners of war of both parties " to return home " if they so wished, and renounced indemnities. The rest of the articles dealt with economic and commercial matters, even trade-marks and copyright.

(3) (c) THE PEACE TREATY BETWEEN THE CENTRAL POWERS AND RUSSIA, 1918

SIGNED AT BREST LITOVSK, 3RD MARCH

The principal feature of these peace terms was that Germany took from Russia a huge strip of territory—most of Poland and Courland—the new frontier running from Ukraine, east of Wilna, thence north-east to the Duna river, along this river and down the middle of the Gulf of Riga, but inclusive of Riga city and of the islands of Oesel and Dagö. There was to be no compensation nor indemnity and " no obligations whatever towards Russia shall devolve upon the territories in question because they formerly belonged to Russia."

The contracting parties agreed to refrain from any agitation or propaganda against the Government or the political and military institutions of the other party : " this holds good as regards Russia in respect of the territories occupied by the Central Powers."

(4) (a) RUMANIA AND CENTRAL POWERS, 5TH MARCH, 1918 PRELIMINARY TREATY OF PEACE [1]

SIGNED AT BUFTEA (NEAR BUKAREST)

This treaty settled the basis of the final peace terms :—
The important items were :

(1) Rumania relinquishes the Dobrudja and accepts rectification of the frontier (that is for its whole length from Turn-Severin on the Danube to Czernowitz on the Pruth, a strip averaging about ten miles was to be handed over, placing all the passes of the mountains in the hands of her enemies) ; (2) accepts such economic measures as are judged adequate ; (3) agrees to demobilize at least eight divisions forthwith and the rest as soon as peace between Rumania and Russia is re-established, except such troops as are required for the maintenance of order along the Russo-Rumanian frontier.

(4) (b) RUMANIA AND CENTRAL POWERS, 7TH MAY, 1918 THE PEACE TREATY OF BUKAREST [1]

The important articles were :—

III. After signature the demobilization of the Rumanian Army under way will be carried out immediately.

IV. Two divisions and two cavalry divisions remain on a war footing until, as a result of the Central Powers' operations in Ukraine, there is no longer any danger for the frontiers of Rumania. Eight divisions remain on a reduced peace footing ; the total to be retained shall not exceed 20,000 in the divisions and 3,200 cavalry.

V. Surplus ordnance, machine guns, rifles. wagons and munitions will be handed over, the ammunition being limited to 250 rounds per rifle, 2,500 per machine gun, and 150 rounds per gun.

---

[1] Translated from German newspapers.

X. In this article the new frontiers are minutely described.

XII. State properties within the ceded territory pass without indemnity and without encumbrances to the victors.

XIII. War indemnities are renounced ; special agreements as to war damage are reserved.

XIV. The evacuation of occupied territory will be determined later.

XV. The present administration of the occupied territory will continue.

XVI. On ratification of the peace treaty the civil administration of the occupied territories will be transferred to the Rumanian authorities.

XVII. The Rumanian authorities in the occupied territories will conform to any regulations the commanders of the army of occupation may issue, and all means of communication, especially railways, posts and telegraphs, will remain under military control ; the High Command will co-operate in all financial and monetary operations, in particular those of the Rumanian National Bank.

XVIII. Acts committed against the army of occupation and infractions of the regulations and ordinances of the army of occupation will be dealt with by military courts.

XIX. The High Command of the army of occupation will regulate the relations between the occupied and non-occupied territories.

XX. After ratification of the peace treaty, the army of occupation will no longer requisition either money or produce except grains, fodder, wool, cattle and meat of the year 1918, timber, mineral oil and oil products. For orderly distribution the High Command will devise a plan which will take into consideration Rumanian domestic needs.

XXI. From the date of the ratification of the peace treaty the maintenance of the army of occupation, inclusive of requisitions, is at the expense of Rumania.

XXII. No claim for damage on account of the ordinances issued may be submitted.

XXIII. Expenses incurred by the Allied Powers within the occupied territory for public works, inclusive of industrial enterprises, will be refunded on transfer of the territories ; until then they will remain under administration of the Central Powers.

XXIV–XXVI. These Articles deal with the regulation of the Danube Navigation, settle that delegates only of States situated on the Danube or on the European shore of the Black Sea shall be members of the Danube Commission, thus abolishing the freedom of navigation under a European Commission on which Great Britain, France and Italy were represented, assured by the Treaty of Paris of 1856. Further, they give to the Central Powers the right to keep an unlimited number of warships on the Danube.

On the same day as the above treaty was signed a Trade Treaty (in German) also was signed between the Central Powers and Rumania. It included a petroleum agreement, an economic agreement and a navigation agreement, and practically handed over to Germany the control of the oilfields, agricultural products and the trade of Rumania, and gave her as complete economic hold over the country as she had military.

For a term of 30 years, extensible to 55, a German company (*Oelländereien-Pachtgesellschaft*) was given the exclusive rights to to exploit all the Rumanian Crown Lands, including those let on long lease, for the extraction and manufacture of mineral oils, natural gas, mineral wax, asphalt, etc. ; the Company was entitled to build and use, without paying any taxes whatever, roads, railways, pipe lines, power-transmission lines, etc., and make use of anything it required by paying " an equitable fee " ; the Rumanian State was compelled to put at the disposal of the Company at the appointed places any timber it might require, and if the demand was not completed within six weeks, it might produce the timber by other means and charge the Rumanian Government.

All rights and privileges of existing corporations were by forced liquidation to be handed over to a German Petroleum Industries Development Company (*Erdöl-Industrieanlagengesellschaft*).

A State commercial monopoly for mineral oils was to be established and transferred to a German-Austro-Hungarian finance group, a Commercial Monopoly Company (*Handelsmonopolgesellschaft*), which was to have the exclusive right without interference of any kind, to export mineral oil and its products.

The Economic Agreement compelled Rumania to sell to Germany and Austria-Hungary the surplus—or what proportion of it they chose to take—of grains of all kinds, inclusive of oil seeds, fodder, poultry, cattle and meat, textile plants and wool ; other agricultural products such as fruit and wine were reserved for special agreement. The surplus available was to be determined on averages by the Rumanian Government in co-operation with representatives of Germany and Austria-Hungary. The prices were to be fixed by a mixed commission, and the business generally managed by a German-Austrian office, which was to be kept informed of all exportation. Further, Rumania was to promote trade with Germany-Austria by means of favourable tariffs and railway rates.

The Navigation Agreement gave Germany-Austria equal rights with Rumania in Rumanian Danube waters, docks and ports, and forced Rumania to take over on payment the installations, grain elevators, etc., erected by Germany in her territory during the war.

The above treaties took up 50 pages in the copies available ; minor treaties and agreements, covering another 100 pages, legislated with regard to details, e.g. railways, freights, new docks, posts and telegraphs, including new constructions, customs, redemption of paper currency, German parishes and schools in Rumania, re-establishment of private rights, debts, copyright, exchange of prisoners and interned civilians, restitution of stolen art treasures, the forbidding and prevention of any activities of societies and individuals of an irredentist nature ; school books and other means of instruction were to be kept free from any matter of this kind, and penalties for breaches of this agreement were to be introduced.

APPENDIX III

ORDER OF BATTLE FOR THE MARCH TO THE GERMAN FRONTIER AND TO THE RHINE[1]

SECOND ARMY

Cavalry Corps ..	Lieut.-Gen. Sir C. T. McM. Kavanagh.	
1st Cavalry Div...	Major-Gen. R. L. Mullens.	
3rd Cavalry Div.	Major-Gen. A. E. W. Harman.	
II. Corps	Lieut.-Gen. Sir Claud Jacob	Already in the Second Army.
9th Div.	Major-Gen. H. H. Tudor ..	Already in the Second Army.
29th Div... ..	Major-Gen. D. E. Cayley ..	Already in the Second Army.
34th Div. ..	Major-Gen. C. L. Nicholson..	Already in the Second Army.
41st Div... ..	Major-Gen. S. T. B. Lawford	Already in the Second Army.
New Zealand Div.	Major-Gen. Sir Andrew Russell	From IV. Corps, Fourth Army
III. Corps	Lieut.-Gen. Sir Richard Butler.	From Fifth Army.
8th Div.	Major-Gen. W. C. G. Heneker	From First Army.
15th Div. ..	Major-Gen. H. L. Reed ..	From Fifth Army.
55th Div. ..	Major-Gen. H. S. Jeudwine..	Already in the III. Corps.
74th Div. ..	Major-Gen. E. S. Girdwood..	Already in the III. Corps.
Canadian Corps ..	Lieut.-Gen. Sir Arthur Currie	From First Army.
1st Canadian Div.	Major-Gen. A. C. Macdonald	Already in the Canadian Corps.
2nd Canadian Div.	Major-Gen. Sir Henry Burstall	Already in the Canadian Corps.
30th Div. ..	Major-Gen. W. de L. Williams	Already in the Second Army (X. Corps).
40th Div. ..	Major-Gen. Sir William Peyton	Already in the Second Army (XV. Corps).
XXII. Corps ..	Lieut.-Gen. Sir Alexander Godley.	From the First Army.
4th Div.	Major-Gen. C. H. T. Lucas..	Already in the XXII. Corps.
51st Div... ..	Major-Gen. G. T. C. Carter-Campbell.	Already in the XXII. Corps.
52nd Div. ..	Major-Gen. F. J. Marshall ..	From the First Army.
56th Div. ..	Major-Gen. Sir Amyatt Hull	From the First Army.

Army Troops and an R.A.F. Brigade of 19 Squadrons.

---

[1] Only those corps and divisions in *italics* marched into Germany, and then in the Second Army.

FOURTH ARMY [1]

2nd Cavalry Div...	Major-Gen. T. T. Pitman.	
VI. Corps ..	Lieut.-Gen. Sir Aylmer Haldane.	
Guards Div.	Major-Gen. T. G. Matheson.	
2nd Div. ..	Major-Gen. C. E. Pereira.	
3rd Div. ..	Major-Gen. C. J. Deverell.	
62nd Div.	Major-Gen. Sir Robert Whigham.	Transferred to IX. Corps.
IV. Corps	Lieut.-Gen. Sir Montague Harper.	
5th Div. ..	Major-Gen. J. Ponsonby.	
37th Div.	Major-Gen. H. Bruce Williams.	
42nd Div.	Major-Gen. A. Solly Flood.	
Australian Corps ..	Lieut.-Gen. Sir John Monash.	
1st Australian Div.	Major-Gen. T. W. Glasgow.	
2nd Australian Div.	Major-Gen. C. Rosenthal	
4th Australian Div.	Major-Gen. E. G. Sinclair-Maclagan.	
5th Australian Div.	Major-Gen. Sir John Talbot-Hobbs.	
IX. Corps ..	Lieut.-Gen. Sir Walter Braithwaite.	
1st Div. ..	Major-Gen. E. P. Strickland.	
6th Div. ..	Major-Gen. T. O. Marden.	
32nd Div.	Major-Gen. T. S. Lambert.	
66th Div.	Major-Gen. H. K. Bethell ..	From XIII. Corps.
62nd Div.		From VI. Corps.

Army Troops and an R.A.F. Brigade of 18 Squadrons.

APPENDIX IV

Q.M.G.'s ORDERS OF THE 13TH NOVEMBER, 1918

(Frontispiece)

First Army
Second Army
Third Army
Fourth Army
Fifth Army

(Unless otherwise stated, paragraphs refer to Second and Fourth Armies only.)

With reference to G.H.Q. letter O.A.D. 953/2, dated 12th November, 1918[2] :

1. *Railways.*—Railway construction work will be concentrated on completing the lines Tournai–Ath, Valenciennes–Mons and Aulnoye–Maubeuge. Every effort will be made to concentrate work first on that

---

[1] The divisions assigned to the Fourth Army already belonged to the Corps named except the 66th Division transferred from the XIII. to the IX. Corps.

[2] See p. 18.

line which it is estimated will give through communication earliest. Until this railway communication has been completed the Second and Fourth Armies will be dependent on the railheads given below :—

Second Army	Courtrai	Baisieux [between Lille and Tournai]
	Deerlyck	
	Vichte }[East of	Fretin [between Lille and Valenciennes]
	Swereghem } Courtrai]	
	Ascq [between Lille and Tournai]	Bruay [2 miles north of Valenciennes]
		Fresnes [north of Valenciennes]
		Valenciennes
		Templeuve [between Lille and Valenciennes]
Fourth Army	St. Vaast [south-west of Valenciennes]	Vaux Andigny [south-east of Busigny]
	Solesmes [10 miles east of Cambrai]	Busigny
	Bertry }[north of	Bohain [south of Busigny]
	Honnechy } Busigny]	and possibly St. Souplet [east of Busigny]

2. *Roads.*—Second and Fourth Armies will be responsible for the repair and upkeep of roads from railheads required for their maintenance during the advance. In principle roads will be limited to two main routes per army. Further information will be sent as soon as obtained regarding the conditions of roads forward of our present line, the stone available, and the labour which will be required.

3. *Transport.*—The following transport will be allotted to each of the Second and Fourth Armies and will be detailed separately by G.H.Q. :

Six G.H.Q. Reserve M.T. Companies for supplies, winter clothing, etc.

Any G.H.Q. Reserve M.T. Companies now allotted to the above Armies above this scale will be withdrawn into G.H.Q. reserve under separate instructions which will be issued later.

One Auxiliary Bus Company, seating capacity approximately 2,000 (subject to the approval of the General Staff).

One M.T. Pontoon Park (less pontoon equipment).

For the Cavalry Corps, to be divided between the Second and Fourth Armies :

Two G.H.Q. Reserve M.T. Companies.

All lorries which are in such a condition as render them liable to evacuation will be collected by armies and disposed of under instructions to be issued by the Director of Transport.

4. *Supplies.*—One day's reserve of rations will be taken forward and will be held on wheels (transport being provided from Army resources). Arrangements will be made to send two trucks of supplies per corps pack train, including Cavalry Corps pack train, for distribution at *need* to civil inhabitants. If not off-loaded these trucks will be sent back daily with the returning supply train.

5. *Remounts.*—Artillery will remain as at present organised on the four-horse team basis. Arrangements will be made by the Director of Remounts to bring units as far as possible up to strength in horses before the commencement of the move, by re-distribution among the Armies if they cannot be obtained from base in time.

6. *Ammunition.*—The following ammunition will be earmarked at existing dumps in Army Areas for the use of the Second and Fourth Armies and will be kept ready for issue at short notice. It will be in addition to the ammunition carried on horsed echelons and units. Details as regards the situation of this ammunition, etc., will be fixed mutually between the Second and Fourth Armies and the First, Third and Fifth Armies :—

Per 15-pdr. (R.H.A.)	500 rounds
Per 18-pdr. gun	500 rounds
Per 4·5-in. howitzer	450 rounds
Per 60-pdr. gun	300 rounds
Per 6-in. howitzer	300 rounds
Per 6-in. gun	150 rounds
Per 8-in. howitzer	200 rounds
Per 9·2-in. howitzer	200 rounds

and in addition small arms ammunition at the rate of 1,000 boxes per division (including cavalry divisions).

7. *Veterinary.*—Second and Fourth Armies will arrange to evacuate as many sick or debilitated animals as possible before the commencement of the move. Any sick or debilitated animals which cannot thus be evacuated will be handed over to First, Third or Fifth Armies as may be most convenient by mutual agreement.

8. *Surplus Stores.*—Units will move with their Mobilization Store Table equipment and in addition winter clothing and blankets. Surplus stores above that scale and all R.E. stores, huts, etc., on charge of the Second and Fourth Armies will be handed over by mutual agreement to the First, Third and Fifth Armies. Receipts will be obtained for the more valuable stores.

9. *Ordnance Stores.*—As it will not be possible during the advance to ensure the distribution of ordnance stores to units, Second and Fourth Armies will arrange with the Director of Ordnance Services the nature and quantities of stores, and the dates on which they will be in a position to deal with them at railheads. This does not apply to the two Corps in each Army mentioned in paragraph 7 of O.A.D. 953/2, which will continue to be maintained in the normal manner.

10. *Ordnance Mobile Workshops.*—At the discretion of Army commanders, up to two mobile and one medium ordnance mobile workshops per corps may accompany the Second and Fourth Armies. The selection of these units will be arranged between the Director of Ordnance Services and the Armies concerned. Only such equipment and stores as can be carried by the present establishment of transport will be taken forward.

11. *Army Gun Parks.*—Army gun parks will not be established forward by the Second and Fourth Armies. Parks now established will be handed over to the First, Third and Fifth Armies as may be most convenient by mutual arrangement.

12. *Expeditionary Force Canteen Stores.*—Arrangements will be made to forward E.F.C. stores by supply trains. Trucks for the Fourth Army will be loaded as now at Romescamps, and those for the Second Army will be loaded at Boulogne or Calais.

13. *British Prisoners of War.*—If any released British prisoners of war are met with, every care is to be taken to supply their immediate needs, to give them priority over other troops as regards providing them with blankets and clothing, and to send them to Calais by the most expeditious means available, number despatched daily to be wired to A.G., G.H.Q., and repeated Base Commandant, Calais.

14. *Captured Material.*—It is understood that details regarding the captured material to be handed over according to the Armistice by the Germans will be arranged by an International Commission. Further instructions as regards this material will be issued at a later date.

15. *Cars for Divisional Trains.*—Arrangements will be made by the Director of Transport to bring the divisional trains of the divisions other than those in paragraph 7 of O.A.D. 953/2 to a strength of three cars, by re-distribution of cars on the strength of divisional trains in the First, Third and Fifth Armies.

16. *Administrative Units.*—A separate communication will be issued later as regards administrative units to be taken forward and those to be transferred from Second and Fourth Armies to First, Third and Fifth Armies.

G.H.Q.   TRAVERS CLARKE, Lieut.-Gen.
                                     Quarter-Master-General.

APPENDIX V

INSTRUCTIONS RELATIVE TO THE GENERAL ORGANIZATION OF THE LINES OF COMMUNICATION (RAILWAYS, ROADS, NAVIGABLE WATERWAYS, RIVER PORTS, TELEGRAPHS AND TELEPHONES)

INSTRUCTIONS ISSUED BY THE COMMANDER-IN-CHIEF OF THE ALLIED ARMIES RELATIVE TO THE PROVISIONS OF ANNEX No. 2 OF THE ARMISTICE CONVENTION

Under Article I of Annex No. 2 of the Armistice Convention all lines of communication as far as the Rhine inclusive, and including the territory on the right bank of this river inside the bridgeheads occupied by the Allied Armies will be placed absolutely and completely under the authority of the Commander-in-Chief of the Allied Armies, who will have the right to take such measures as he may consider necessary to ensure their occupation and exploitation.

The principles given below will govern the organization of the lines of communication :

I. *Railways*

(a) The operation of the reoccupied lines of the Nord and Est systems even if allotted to the British or to the Americans will remain under the control of the *Commissions de Reseaux*.

(b) The operation of the lines of the Belgian System will be carried out, under the authority of the Calais Commission (*Commission Internationale de Calais*), by the military railway organizations of the Belgian, British and French Armies. As and when it becomes possible these organizations will be replaced by Belgian civil railway personnel under the authority of the *Commission de Reseau Belge*.

(c) The operation of the lines in the system of the Alsace-Lorraine Railways will be carried out by a Commission of the French Field Railways to be called that of Alsace-Lorraine.

(d) The operation of the Luxembourg lines (excepting those normally operated by the Alsace-Lorraine Railways), and those of the German System west of the Rhine, will be carried out by an Inter-Allied Commission of Field Railways which will have at its disposal the military railway organizations of the Armies concerned, and certain sub-commissions.

The principle will be adopted of forming one sub-commission in each Allied Army which will direct the exploitation of the lines comprised within the zone allotted to that Army.

The Commission of Field Railways shall include a military member for each Allied Army who shall be assisted by such technical members as he may consider necessary. The president shall be the Director of Military Transport on the staff of the Maréchal Commanding-in-Chief the Allied Armies.

The Commission will be located at a place to be decided by the Maréchal Commanding-in-Chief the Allied Armies, to whom recommendations for the location and the number of sub-commissions will be addressed.

The Commission of the Alsace-Lorraine Railways and the Field Railway Commission will be placed under the orders of the Maréchal Commanding-in-Chief the Allied Armies, on whom the additional duty will fall of co-ordinating all railway operating organizations for the general satisfaction of the needs of the Allied Armies.

II. *Navigable Waterways and River Ports*

(a) The operation of navigable waterways in Belgium shall be carried out by the Calais International Commission of Navigable Waterways with the co-operation of the military inland water transport services of the Belgian, British and French Armies.

As and when it becomes possible these services shall be replaced by Belgian civil personnel, under the authority of a Belgian Military Navigation Commission (*Commission Militaire de Navigation Belge*).

(b) The operation of navigable waterways in Alsace-Lorraine shall be carried out by the French Field Navigation Commission, which will also exercise the control of the navigation on the Rhine in its zone of operation.

(c) The control of the navigation on the Rhine between the Dutch frontier and Alsace-Lorraine shall be exercised by a field navigation commission, which will include a representative of each Allied Army, assisted by such technical personnel as he may consider necessary.

The President will be the Director of Transport on the Staff of the Maréchal Commanding-in-Chief the Allied Armies. The authority of the Commission shall extend also to the Moselle from the point where it leaves Alsace-Lorraine to its junction with the Rhine, and to the Saar from the point where it leaves Alsace-Lorraine to its junction with the Moselle.

The Navigation Commission of Alsace-Lorraine and the Inter-Allied Field Navigation Commission are placed under the orders of the Maréchal Commanding-in-Chief the Allied Armies, on whom the additional duty will fall of co-ordinating all the organizations for the operation of navigable waterways for the satisfaction of the general needs of the Allied Armies.

III. *Road Communications*

(a) As far as Lines 2 and 3 the roads required shall be maintained by the Road Services of the Allied Armies with the assistance of the departmental services under the same conditions as are now in operation by agreement between the Armies concerned.

(b) Between Line 3 and the Rhine all road work shall be carried out by the Allied Armies, each in its allotted zone, making full use of all resources in personnel and material left *in situ* or replaced, and also of the local resources of the country.

(c) An inter-Allied road commission shall be formed under the presidency of the Director of Transport on the Staff of the Maréchal Commanding-in-Chief the Allied Armies, and composed of one military member from each of the Allied Armies, assisted by such technical members as he may consider necessary.

The duty of this Commission will be as follows :

(i) To decide upon the main routes of common interest necessary to ensure adequate lateral road communication behind the front.

(ii) To decide upon the quarries situated in the territory between Line 3 and the left bank of the Rhine, the output of which can be divided between the various Armies to compensate for any insufficiency of stone in the resources available in a particular Army Zone.

This Commission will be placed under the orders of the Maréchal Commanding-in-Chief the Allied Armies.

IV. *Telegraph and Telephone Systems*

(a) In France and in Belgium each Allied Army shall re-establish the telegraph and telephone systems not only with a view to purely military requirements, but also to assist in the revival of the economic life of the country and for the use of the civil administrative services.

(b) *In Belgian Territory.*—The operation of the telegraph and telephone services will be carried out by the Belgian authorities, it being understood that all circuits required by the Allied Armies for their own use shall be put at their disposal.

(c) *In Alsace-Lorraine.*—The organization will be analogous to that in reoccupied French territory.

(d) *Between Line 3 and the Rhine.*—The operation of the system will be under the direction of an Inter-Allied commission which will include a military member, assisted by such technical personnel as he may consider necessary for each of the Allied Armies. The location of the Commission will be decided by the Maréchal Commanding-in-Chief the Allied Armies, who will also nominate the president.

The Maréchal Commanding-in-Chief will decide, in agreement with the Allied Armies, as to which lines shall be specially reserved as main arteries for the common use.

APPENDIX VI

CAVALRY CORPS ADMINISTRATIVE ORDERS REGARDING THE FORWARD MOVE TO THE RHINE

Cavalry Corps Q/4600
15th November, 1918.

1. Discipline :

Discipline will on no account be relaxed.
All breaches of discipline will be severely dealt with.
Swords will be drawn through villages.
Ceremonial parades will be held during the march.
Divisional, brigade and regimental guards will be formed.
Trumpet calls will be sounded.

2. Dress :

Uniformity in officers' dress will be aimed at.
All ranks riding on the line of march will wear marching order with steel helmets.
Wallets will not be carried.
Lancer regiments may carry pennons.
Officers' horses may be clipped all over. Men's horses will be clipped trace high.

3. Welfare :

Every effort must be made to provide recreation for the men, under the following headings :

concert parties ; football leagues ; visits to places of interest and provision of transport ; demonstrations ; competitions ; recreation rooms ; canteens ; 30-yard ranges ; lectures on after the war problems and demobilization.

Brigade amusement committees will be formed.
Regimental and battery officers' messes will be formed as far as possible.
G.H.Q. hope to be able to provide funds for games, if not available in units.

4. Schools :

Cavalry Corps School, Dieppe, will be closed down at end of present course.

Cavalry Corps Hotchkiss School, Le Touquet, will close down at once.

Cavalry Corps Equitation School, Cayeux, will continue. Only officers and n.c.os. who are likely to remain in the Service after the war will be sent to the school.

Cavalry Corps Signal School, Prouvelle, will continue.

5. Reinforcement Camp :

Up to 50 men per regiment have been despatched from the reinforcement camp to divisions.

All remaining details have been sent down to Rouen base, and the camp is being closed down.

6. Prisoners of War :

All British prisoners of war encountered during the advance will be re-clothed and well cared for, and despatched to the base with the least possible delay. Numbers to be reported daily to Cavalry Corps "A" by wire.

Instructions with regard to the treatment of Allied prisoners of war other than British will be issued later.

7. Mechanical Transport :

M.T. personnel will be made up to strength as soon as possible.

Nos. 2 and 10 G.H.Q Reserve M.T. Companies are allotted to Cavalry Corps. Of these, 3 sections (48 lorries) will be handed over to each division ; the remainder being held at corps headquarters.

These lorries will be used as a third echelon for supplies when required and must always be available for that purpose.

Ammunition lorries of divisional M.T. Companies will also be at disposal of divisions, as no ammunition will be carried on M.T.

A.D. S. & T. Cavalry Corps will arrange that all broken-down and worn-out vehicles will be handed over to the nearest Army, and replacement obtained.

A.D. S. & T. will arrange that each lorry carries reserve supply of 32 gallons of petrol. No additional arrangements will be made by divisions.

A section of a water tank company is being allotted to Cavalry Corps.

8. Horse Transport :

Light Section Reserve Park will carry 10 lbs. oats per horse and one hard ration per man.

One G.S. wagon from Heavy Section Reserve Park will accompany H.Q. and Light Section as " B " Echelon.

A. H. Company will accompany and be split up amongst units to carry horse rugs.

Any deficiencies in G.S. wagons of units or A.H. Company will be made up from the Heavy Section Reserve Park.

Divisions will render to Cavalry Corps "Q" by 6 p.m. on the 17th instant a list showing all units which are being left behind by them and the position of any portions of those units which are detached. This especially refers to Heavy Section Reserve Park of which any undetached portions will be handed over to Fifth Army.

The G.S. water tank wagons allotted to divisions for dismounted men will be disposed of under order of Cavalry Corps Q.

9. Supplies :

Iron rations will be carried on A.2 Echelon and not on the man.

Oats in second nosebag will be consumed. The second nosebag will still be carried on the horse and used for carrying cleaning kit, etc.

Coal and wood will be sent up daily on packs if ordered by S.S.Os.

Two truck loads of iron rations will be sent up on the Cavalry Corps H.Q. pack for the feeding of civilians. These rations will be carried on the lorries of the G.H.Q. Reserve M.T. companies retained with Corps H.Q. rations will be distributed at the rate of one iron ration to four civilians per day.

All rationing of civilian population in Belgium will be done in consultation with officials of the Belgian Mission who have already been posted to 1st and 3rd Cavalry Divisions (one officer and six interpreters per division).

Railheads :

Railheads from 18th instant inclusive.

Cavalry Corps Troops	..	.. ..	Valenciennes
1st Cavalry Division	..	.. ..	Valenciennes
3rd Cavalry Division	..	.. ..	Audenarde

10. Medical :

(a) Six C.C.Ss. will accompany the Second Army.

(b) Sick will be collected by divisional ambulance wagons and cars to a main divisional collecting post. Six M.A.C. cars will be attached to each division and three to Cavalry Corps H.Q. for the evacuation of sick from the main divisional collecting post to the nearest casualty clearing station.

Casualty clearing stations will be established along the lines of railway :

(1) Valenciennes–Maubeuge–Charleroi–Namur.

(2) Tournai–Brussels.

There will be some delay as regards (2), and in the meantime casualty clearing stations will be located in the intermediate area Leuze–Enghien.

Locations of casualty clearing stations will be notified later.

(c) Divisional rest stations will be formed at each halting place to avoid men being evacuated.

(d) Divisions will detach one lorry for C.R.A. for dismounted men and will also arrange for transport of sanitary sections.

Sanitation on the Line of March.—The strictest attention must be given to sanitary arrangements on the line of march. *It must be borne in mind that all billets vacated by cavalry will be occupied the following day by infantry units.*

The following points will be observed :

(1) Shallow trench latrines will be dug in sufficient numbers at all resting billets and filled in on leaving. During the march, excreta must invariably be covered with earth.

(2) All refuse will be collected and burnt or buried before leaving billeting areas.

(3) All sources of water supply will be tested, and labelled accordingly. A.Ds. M.S. cavalry divisions will forward to D.D.M.S. Cavalry Corps a list of all tested and labelled water supplies as soon as completed and before leaving each area.

Every unit will leave behind a clearing-up party under an officer to ensure that horse-lines and billets are left in a thoroughly clean and sanitary condition and all rubbish burnt or buried.

11. Ordnance :

A.D.O.S. Cavalry Corps will arrange for the handing over of all surplus ordnance stores of all natures to Fifth Army. Nothing will be returned to the base by units of Second Army.

Second Army will have priority regarding supply of ordnance stores to railheads.

No. 43 Light Ordnance Mobile Workshop is allotted to Cavalry Corps.

As it is possible that no ordnance stores will be available for a considerable period, divisions will carry spare boots and underclothing.

Frost cogs will be issued and divisions will carry a small reserve supply.

Respirators :

No reserve of box respirators will be carried.

The one respirator per man formerly carried on the man will be carried as directed by divisions in such a way that they become available if required at short notice.

All horse respirators will be evacuated to the base.

All reserves of respirators will be evacuated to the base.

Dumps :

Any Government stores that are not required at present but may be of use later will be dumped in Tournai. Site to be selected by Cavalry Corps Q. and notified to divisions, who will be responsible for guarding and dumping. Cavalry Corps Q. will arrange *re* rationing the guards.

Any private kits stored will be at owner's risk.

Stores :

The following should be dumped : tents, trench shelters, tables and chairs, bathing suits.

Armstrong huts will be handed over to Town Major, Tournai, and receipts forwarded to Cavalry Corps Q.

Field forges will accompany units.

Ammunition :

Reserve of ammunition at the rate of 500 rounds per gun and 1,000 boxes s.a.a. per cavalry division to be formed :

1st and 3rd Cavalry Divisions at A.S.C. Q. under Cavalry Corps arrangements :

2nd Cavalry Division at Honnechy under 2nd Cavalry Division arrangements.

Ammunition in horse bandoliers will be withdrawn and returned to railhead. Bandoliers will be carried empty in the usual manner.

12. Veterinary :

No. 2 Veterinary Evacuating Station will be established at Audenarde and the 1st Canadian V.E.S. at Valenciennes.

13. Canteen Stores :

It is proposed to send up canteen stores from the base on divisional pack trains.

Beer and soda-water, when available, will be included.

14. Various :

Postal

Mails will be sent up by supply train at first, and later by special train.

Billeting

Certificates will be given as usual.

H. Medlicott,
Lieut.-Colonel for Br.-General
D.A. & Q.M.G., Cavalry Corps.

APPENDIX VII

CONVENTION OF 16TH JANUARY, 1919, PROLONGING THE ARMISTICE WITH GERMANY FOR THE SECOND TIME

The undersigned plenipotentiaries (Admiral Browning taking the place of Admiral Wemyss) vested with the powers in virtue of which the Armistice Agreement of 11th November, 1918, was signed, have concluded the following supplementary Agreement :—

1. The Armistice of 11th November, 1918, which was prolonged until 17th January, 1919, by the Agreement of 13th December, 1918, shall be again prolonged for one month, that is to say, until 17th February, 1919, at 5 a.m.

This prolongation of one month shall be extended until the conclusion of the Peace preliminaries, subject to the approval of the Allied Governments.

2. The execution of those clauses of the Agreement of 11th November which have not been entirely carried out shall be proceeded with and completed during the prolongation of the Armistice, in accordance with the detailed conditions fixed by the Permanent International Armistice Commission on the instructions of the Allied High Command.

3. In substitution of the supplementary railway material[1] specified by Tables 1 and 2 of the Spa Protocol of 17th December, i.e. 500 locomotives and 19,000 wagons, the German Government shall supply the following agricultural machinery and instruments :—

400 two-engined steam plough outfits, complete, with suitable ploughs ; 6,500 drills ; 6,500 manure distributors ; 6,500 ploughs ; 6,500 Brabant ploughs ; 12,500 harrows ; 6,500 scarifiers ; 2,500 steel rollers ; 2,500 Groskill rollers ; 2,500 mowing machines ; 2,500 hay-making machines ; 3,000 reapers and binders ; or equivalent implements, according to the scale of interchangeability of various kinds of implements considered permissible by the Permanent International Armistice Commission. All this material, which shall be either new, or in very good condition, shall be delivered together with all accessories belonging to each implement, and with the spare parts required for 18 months' use.

The German Armistice Commission shall, between the present date and 23rd January, supply the Allied Armistice Commission with a list of the material that can be delivered by 1st March, which must, in principle, constitute not less than one-third of the total quantity. The International Armistice Commission shall, between now and 23rd January, fix the latest dates of delivery, which shall, in principle, not extend beyond 1st June.

4. The officers in Germany delegated by the Allied and Associated Powers to organize the evacuation of the prisoners of war belonging to the Armies of the Entente, together with representatives of the Relief Associations of the United States, France, Great Britain and Italy, shall form a Commission charged with the care of Russian prisoners of war in Germany.

This Commission, the headquarters of which shall be in Berlin, shall be empowered to deal with the German Government direct, upon instructions from the Allied Governments, regarding all questions relating to Russian prisoners of war.

The German Government shall accord the Commission all travelling facilities necessary for the purpose of investigating the housing conditions and food supply of such prisoners.

The Allied Governments reserve the right to arrange for the repatriation of Russian prisoners of war to any region which they may consider most suitable.

5. *Naval Clauses.*—Article XXII of the Armistice Agreement of 11th November, 1918, shall be supplemented as follows :—

" In order to ensure the execution of such clause, the German authorities shall be bound to carry out the following conditions, viz. :—

" All submarines capable of putting to sea, or of being towed, shall be handed over immediately and shall make for Allied ports. Such vessels shall include submarine cruisers, minelayers, relief

---

[1] No copy of this has been found. From German sources, it appears it was laid down that—

From 17th to 27th December	110 locomotives and 2,400 wagons should be delivered daily ;	
From 27th December to 16th January	180 locomotives and 350 wagons should be delivered daily	

divided among the reception stations.

ships and submarine docks. All submarines which cannot be surrendered shall be completely destroyed or dismantled, under the supervision of the Allied Commissioners. Submarine construction shall cease immediately, and all submarines in course of construction shall be destroyed or dismantled, under the supervision of the Allied Commissioners."

Article XXIII of the Armistice Agreement of 11th November, 1918, shall be supplemented as follows :—

" In order to ensure the execution of such clause, the German Commission shall furnish the Inter-Allied Naval Armistice Commission with a complete list of all surface vessels constructed or in course of construction (launched or on the stocks), specifying probable dates of completion."

Article XXX of the Armistice Agreement of 11th November, 1918, shall be supplemented as follows :—

" In order to ensure the execution of such clause, the Allied High Command informs the German High Command that all possible measures must be taken immediately for delivery, in Allied ports, of all Allied merchantmen still detained in German ports."

6. *Restitution of Material carried off from Belgian and French Territories.*—As restitution of material carried off from French and Belgian territory is indispensable for setting factories once more into working order, the following measures shall be carried out, viz. :—

(*a*) All machinery, machinery parts, industrial or agricultural plant, accessories of all kinds and, generally, all industrial or agricultural articles carried off by German military or civilian authorities or individuals, under any pretext whatever, from territories formerly occupied by the German Armies on the Western Front, shall be placed at the disposal of the Allies for the purpose of being returned to their places or origin, should the French and Belgian Governments so desire.

These articles shall be returned without further alteration and undamaged.

(*b*) In view of such restitution, the German Government shall immediately furnish the Armistice Commission with all official or private accounts, agreements for sale or hire, or correspondence relating to such articles, together with all necessary declarations or information regarding their existence, origin, adaptation, present condition and locality.

(*c*) The delegates of the French or Belgian Government shall cause inventories or examinations of such articles to be made on the spot in Germany, should they think fit.

(*d*) The return of such articles shall be effected in accordance with special instructions to be given as required by the French or Belgian authorities.

(*e*) With a view to immediate restitution, declarations shall more particularly be made of all stocks of driving belts, electric motors, and parts thereof, or plant removed from France or Belgium and existing in depôt parks, railways, ships and factories.

(*f*) The furnishing of the particulars referred to in Articles 3 and 6 hereof shall commence within eight clear days from 20th January, 1919, and shall be completed in principle before 1st April, 1919.

7. As a further guarantee, the Supreme Allied Command reserves to itself the right to occupy, whenever it shall consider this desirable, the sector of the fortress of Strassburg formed by the fortifications on the right bank of the Rhine, with a strip of territory extending from 5 to 10 kilometres in front of such fortifications, within the boundaries defined on the map appended hereto.[1]

The Supreme Allied Command shall give six days' notice prior to such occupation, which shall not be preceded by any destruction of material or of buildings.

The limits of the Neutral Zone will, therefore, be advanced by 10 kilometres.

8. In order to secure the provisioning of Germany and of the rest of Europe, the German Government shall take all necessary steps to place the German Fleet, for the duration of the Armistice, under the control and flags of the Allied Powers and the United States, who shall be assisted by a German delegate.

This arrangement shall in no wise affect the final disposal of such vessels. The Allies and the United States shall, if they consider this necessary, replace the crews either entirely or in part, and the officers and crews so replaced shall be repatriated to Germany. Suitable compensation, to be fixed by the Allied Governments, shall be made for the use of such vessels.

All questions of detail, as also any exceptions to be made in the case of certain types of vessel, shall be settled by a special agreement to be concluded immediately.

Trèves.	Foch Browning	Erzberger Oberndorff
16th January, 1919.		von Winterfeldt Vanselow

APPENDIX VIII

CONVENTION OF 16TH FEBRUARY, 1919, PROLONGING THE ARMISTICE WITH GERMANY FOR THE THIRD TIME

The Plenipotentiaries who have signed below (Admiral Wemyss being replaced by Admiral Browning ; Major-General von Winterfeldt by Major-General von Hammerstein ; and the Minister Plenipotentiary Count von Oberndorff by the Minister Plenipotentiary von Haniel) who have been duly furnished with the powers by virtue of which the Armistice Convention of 11th November, 1918, was signed, have concluded the following additional convention :

I. The Germans must immediately abandon all offensive operations against the Poles in the region of Posen, or in any other region. To ensure this they are forbidden to send their troops across the line : former frontier of East Prussia and of West Prussia with Russia, as far as Luisenfelde, from that point, west of Luisenfelde, west of Gr. Neudorff, south of Brzoze, north of

---

[1] Not reproduced.

Schubin, north of Exin, sóuth of Samoczin, south of Chodzienzen, north of Czarnikow, west of Mialla, west of Birnbaum, west of Bentschen, west of Wollstein, north of Lissa, north of Rawicz, south of Krotoszyn, west of Adelnau, west of Schildberg, north of Vieruchov, then the Silesian frontier. (Green lines on the attached map.)[1]

II. The Armistice of 11th November prolonged by the Conventions of 13th December, 1918, and 16th January, 1919, to 17th February, 1919, is again prolonged for a short period, without, however, any date for its expiration, the Allied and associated Powers reserving to themselves the right of terminating it by giving three days' notice.

III. The execution of the clauses of the Convention of 11th November, 1918, and of the additional Conventions of 13th December, 1918, and 16th January, 1919, not fully accomplished will be proceeded with and brought to a conclusion during the prolongation of the Armistice under the conditions as regards details laid down by the Permanent Armistice Commission, in accordance with the instructions laid down by the Allied Supreme Command.

F. Foch	Erzberger
M. E. Browning	Freiherr von Hammerstein
	von Haniel
	Vanselow

APPENDIX IX

THE HAGUE RULES WITH REGARD TO OCCUPIED TERRITORY

Article 42 :

Territory is considered occupied when actually placed under the authority of the hostile army.

The occupation extends only to the territories where such authority has been established and is in a position to assert itself.

Article 43 :

The authority of the power of the State having passed *de facto* into the hands of the occupant, the latter shall do all in his power to restore, and ensure, as far as possible, public order and safety, respecting at the same time, unless absolutely prevented, the laws in force in the country.

Article 44[2] :

A belligerent is forbidden to compel the inhabitants of territory occupied by it to furnish information about the army of the other belligerent, or about its means of defence.

---

[1] Not reproduced.
[2] This article has not been accepted by Germany and Russia.

Article 45 :

It is forbidden to force the inhabitants of occupied territory to swear allegiance to the hostile Power.

Article 46 :

Family honour and rights, individual life, and private property, as well as religious convictions and worship must be respected.

Private property may not be confiscated.

Article 47 :

Pillage is expressly forbidden.

Article 48 :

If, in the territory occupied, the occupant collects the taxes, dues and tolls payable to the State, he shall do so, as far as is possible, in accordance with the legal basis and assessment in force at the time, and shall in consequence be bound to defray the expenses of the administration of the occupied territory to the same extent as the national Government had been so bound.

Article 49 :

If, in addition to the taxes mentioned in the above Article, the occupant levies other money contributions in the occupied territory, they shall only be applied to the needs of the army or of the administration of the territory in question.

Article 50 :

No collective penalty, pecuniary or otherwise, shall be inflicted upon the population on account of the acts of individuals for which it cannot be regarded as collectively responsible.

Article 51 :

No contribution shall be collected except under a written order, and on the responsibility of a General in command.

The collection of the said contribution shall only be effected in accordance, as far as is possible, with the legal basis and assessment of taxes in force at the time.

For every contribution a receipt shall be given to the contributories.

Article 52 :

Requisitions in kind and services shall not be demanded from local authorities or inhabitants except for the needs of the army of occupation. They shall be in proportion to the resources of the country, and of such a nature as not to involve the inhabitants in the obligation of taking part in military operations against their own country.

Such requisitions and services shall only be demanded on the authority of the commander in the locality occupied.

Contributions in kind shall as far as possible be paid for in ready money ; if not, a receipt shall be given and the payment of the amount due shall be made as soon as possible.

Article 53 :

An army of occupation shall only take possession of cash, funds and realizable securities which are strictly the property of the State, depôts of arms, means of transport, stores and supplies, and, generally, all movable property belonging to the State which may be used for military operations.

Except in cases governed by naval law, all appliances adapted for the transmission of news, or for the transmission of persons or goods, whether on land, at sea, or in the air, depôts of arms, and, in general, all kinds of war material may be seized, even if they belong to private individuals, but they must be restored at the conclusion of peace, and indemnities must be paid for them.

Article 54 :

Submarine cables connecting an occupied territory with a neutral territory shall not be seized or destroyed except in the case of absolute necessity. They also must be restored at the conclusion of peace, and indemnities paid for them.

Article 55 :

The occupying State shall be regarded as administrator and usufructuary of public buildings, landed property, forests and agricultural undertakings belonging to the hostile State and situated in the occupied country. It must safeguard the capital of such properties, and administer them in accordance with the rules of usufruct.

Article 56 :

The property of local authorities, as well as that of institutions dedicated to public worship, charity, education, and to science and art, even when State property, shall be treated as private property.

Any seizure or destruction of, or wilful damage to, institutions of this character, historic monuments and works of science and art, is forbidden, and should be made the subject of legal proceedings.

APPENDIX X

MARÉCHAL FOCH'S INSTRUCTIONS FOR THE ADMINISTRATION OF THE OCCUPIED TERRITORIES

[Official Translation[1]]

The Commander-in-Chief
Allied Armies

General Staff

*Direction Générale des
Communications et des
Ravitaillements aux
Armées.*

No. 561/C.R.   15th November, 1918

To : The Commanders-in-Chief, Allied Armies.

I have the honour to give you hereunder the guiding principles to govern the administration of the Rhine territories which the Allied Armies are to occupy under the terms of the Armistice.

I. PRINCIPLES

The Allied Armies should adhere to the principles laid down with regard to cases of occupation by the Hague convention.

The control of the German Administrations still functioning will be carried out by the Cs.-in-C., Allied Armies, under the authority of the Generalissimo.

II. ORGANIZATION

The following Services will be established :

A. In order to ensure the unity of control with the Generalissimo (D.G.C.R.A.), a delegate, head of the branch, together with a staff, to be charged with the examination and drawing up of the instructions *de principe.*

B. In order to ensure this control with the Cs.-in-C., the Belgian, British, American and French Armies, a technical adviser specialized in administrative matters.

C. With each Army commander, an adviser possessing the same technical abilities, who will act as chief of the staff for civilian matters.

D. The service will operate at echelons of army corps and infantry divisions under the seal and with the co-operation of the 2nd Bureau (civilian matters).

III. The same principles should be applied, to the greatest possible extent, by the Allied Armies to their relations with the local authorities and the enemy populations (requisitions, civil and penal legislation, relations with the local authorities, control of administrations, etc . . .)

---

[1] As the original French of these instructions was not available for collation, the English version has been left as it was found in the G.H.Q. files.

To that effect :

(1) The three Allied delegates should, as a matter of principle, meet every week at the Inter-Allied Committee, at the H.Q. of the Generalissimo with his delegate, (D.G.C.R.A.), for the purpose of examining the common instructions which will be submitted to the Generalissimo, for his approval.

(2) The following documents are attached to the present Note :

A. For necessary action : An instruction relative to the administration of the enemy territories occupied by the Allied Armies, drawn up in accordance with the principles laid down by the Hague Convention, together with a proclamation for the purpose of bringing these principles to the notice of the population.

B. For the information of the Armies administering the districts : various annexes specifying the conditions of application of the instruction referred to above in the territories occupied by the French Armies. These annexes are liable to amendment as demanded by circumstances.

INSTRUCTION REGARDING THE CIVIL ADMINISTRATION OF THE OCCUPIED TERRITORIES UNDER THE CLAUSES OF THE ARMISTICE OF 11th NOVEMBER, 1918

[Official Translation]

G.H.Q.A., November 15th, 1918.

The Commander-in-Chief
Allied Armies

General Staff

Direction Générale des Communications et des Ravitaillements aux Armées.

No. 562/C.R.

I. PRINCIPLE

In accordance with the principles laid down by the Hague Convention, the control of the German Administrations will be entrusted to the General Cs.-in-C., Allied Armies, under the supreme command of the Generalissimo.

II. CIVIL ADMINISTRATION OF THE OCCUPIED TERRITORIES

The German officials will continue to perform the functions entrusted to them and they are to carry out the administration of the occupied territories under the direction and control of the military authorities.

For this purpose, interpreters and officers specially qualified will be placed in due course at the disposal of the Army commanders.

The Army commanders will, within all the area under their authority, act as the higher authorities of the district with regard to administrative decisions ; it will be for them to issue the *arrêtés* to be enforced throughout the said territory.

They will nominate the officers who, in each of the territorial districts of the occupied territories, will be entrusted with the control of the civil administrations, apart from the military functions which they may have to perform in addition, as the result of their functions. These officers will be named *officiers chargés de l'Administration.* Besides their proper military subordination based upon the Administrative Division of the Territory, they will be under the local military commandants (army corps or division commanders, governors of *places, Commandants d'Armes*) to whom the Army commanders may have delegated part of their personal authority.

These officers will control, throughout the administrative districts allotted to them, the administration of the German officials.

All *arrêtés* relative to police, public order or safety of the Armies will be issued by the Allied commandants, or signed by them, if emanating from the German authorities.

Any measure which should have formed the subject of a decree or an act will be submitted to the Maréchal, C-in-C., Allied Armies.

The principles to be followed by the Officers i/c of the Administration in the carrying out of their duties are indicated in No. 1 Annexe attached, which comprises specimens of a standard *arrêté* and proclamation.

III. Carrying Out of Occupation

The occupation of districts will necessarily be progressive.

In order to carry out the general plan of occupation, the troops charged with this will therefore have to march through and be stationed in enemy territories over which the Allied Command has not yet been able to establish authority. So long as they have not reached the zone allotted to them under the general plan, these troops will not have the time required for enforcing, throughout the district through which they will merely pass, the preparatory measures for the control of all the administrative services of the country by the Allied military authorities. As it is of the greatest necessity that these preparatory measures should be adopted as soon as possible after the arrival of the first Allied troops, the following dispositions will be enforced :

(1) Within the period preceding the occupation, the G.O.C the Groups of Armies and the Armies concerned, will proceed with the appointment of the officers placed at their disposal in view of the administration of the various Administrative Districts to be occupied.[1]

(2) As soon as the final plan of occupation and the military measures foreseen for its execution (composition, itineraries and successive staging areas of columns) have been laid down, the officers designated to carry out the administration of the districts situated on the itinerary or itineraries of each infantry division of first line, will temporarily be attached to this infantry division, along with the subordinate personnel, the formations[2] and the means of communication which they will require as soon as they commence their duties.

---

[1] In the event of these officers failing to arrive in time or should their number be insufficient, the G.O. concerned should appoint for that purpose temporary administrator officers drawn from the formations under his command.

[2] These formations should be selected amongst those which according to final plan, are to occupy the districts concerned.

(3) As the first line divisions advance in the interior of the country to be occupied, the officers in charge of the administration will establish themselves in the districts allotted to them and will immediately take such urgent steps as may be required for the occupation. Being relieved of this duty, the O.C. units will merely make the necessary arrangements for ensuring the safety of their troops and maintaining order in the localities temporarily used for their billeting. If required, they will lend assistance to the administrators and help them in the fulfilment of their duties.

The attached annexes specify the steps which, during the first stage of the occupation, will concern, on the one hand, the passing troops and, on the other hand, the officers in charge of the administration.

STANDARD *ARRÊTÉ* TO BE ATTACHED, FOR INFORMATION, TO ANNEXE I

[Official Translation]

The Commander-in-Chief
Allied Armies

General Staff

D.G.C.R.A.

ARRÊTÉ

Art. 1. The present *Arrêté* is applicable to the area limited by..................

DECLARATION OF RESIDENCE

Art 2. All persons over 12 (twelve) years of age residing in the area specified in *Art. 1* since 1st August, 1914, but who are not usually domiciled there, are under the obligation to report at the *Mairie* within two days, viz. : no later than the........................at ....o'clock, being in possession of identification papers and of any such documents as may justify their presence in the District.

Art. 3. Within a period of........................ (longer than the previous one), viz. : before the.................at............, all inhabitants over 12 (twelve) years of age who were domiciled in the area defined by *Art. 1*, prior to 1st August, 1914, must make to the *Mairie* a declaration of residence for themselves, the children in their charge, their servants, relatives or any other persons living in the same house.

Art. 4. All persons over 12 (twelve) years of age must be in possession of an identification card. The signature of the Burgomaster countersigned by the military authorities concerned, will be affixed to the identification cards or the *permis de séjour* of which the inhabitants might already be in possession, after their identity has been verified and their capacity of inhabitant of the District proved.

Those persons who are not in possession of an identification card will have to furnish such particulars as are required to enable one of these cards to be delivered to them at an early date.

The identification cards of the persons specified in *Art. 2* will only be signed after enquiries have been made for each individual and special decisions given by the military authorities concerned.

Art. 5. The lists of inhabitants will be completed, if required, by the Burgomaster under his own responsibility, by means of the information which he personally possesses and will be held at the disposal of the military authorities.

Art. 6. All persons domiciled in the area defined in *Art. 1* and residing there at the time of the occupation, are under the obligation to remain at their residence. All changes of residence are prohibited, save with the permission of the *Commandant d'Armes* or *Directeur des Etapes* recorded on the identification card issued or by a *sauf conduit* referring to the identification card.

Art. 7. All inhabitants have to report immediately to the military authorities, whether they obtain this information direct or by hearsay :

(1) Those persons who have failed to comply with the stipulations of *Arts. 2 and 3*.

(2) The soldiers in hiding, also the wounded or sick soldiers who have remained in the area defined in Art. 1.

CIRCULATION

Art. 8. No one is allowed to enter or leave the area defined in *Art. 1* without being in possession of an authorization from the Army commander or the *Directeur des Etapes* concerned.

Art. 9. No one is allowed to travel by railway, motor-car, bicycle, horse or cart, without being bearer of a special permit issued by the Army commander or *Directeur des Etapes* who signed the identification card.

Art. 10. Pedestrian traffic is permitted within the boundaries of the District by day, viz. : from................to....................
It is prohibited outside roads, except in the case of agricultural work. Night traffic is prohibited without a special and written authorization from the local military authorities.

In order to travel between their district and the neighbouring ones, all inhabitants must be in possession of a *sauf-conduit* issued by the local military authorities who signed the identification card.

Inhabitants must return to their home at night no later than ....and are not allowed to go out in the morning before .... a.m.

MEETINGS

Art. 11. All gatherings of people are prohibited.

Art. 12. No meeting, performance or assembly of any description is to take place without the authorization of the military authorities and without the programme having first been approved.

N*

PUBLICATIONS

Art. 13. No newspaper, book, pamphlet, bill, placard, sketch, notice will be allowed to be printed, published or distributed without the authorization of the military authorities. A specimen of all publications as stated above will have to be handed to the local military authorities at time of publication.

Art. 14. Only persons in possession of a written authorization issued by the military authorities will be allowed to carry out the trade of vendor or distributor of newspapers, books, pamphlets, sketches, notices. This authorization is always liable to be cancelled.

Art. 15. Any act of spreading news either false or likely to disturb public order will be severely dealt with.

Art. 16. The carriage or use of photographic apparatus is prohibited without a written authorization from the Army commander or the *Directeur des Etapes.*

POSTAL SERVICES (Telegraph, Telephone)

Art. 17. Until further notice, all letters, correspondence, messages, telegrams must be deposited at........................for delivery to the military authorities.

The forwarding of letters and messages by civilians and soldiers is strictly prohibited.

Art. 18. The use of telephone is prohibited.

Art. 19. All telephone, telegraph, also underground or overhead wireless installations, underground cables, etc., not belonging to the public postal services must be reported.

All existing apparatuses must be deposited with the local military authorities not later than.....................

PIGEONS

Art. 20. All owners of carrier pigeons must immediately report their loft to the military authorities and furnish a descriptive statement of their pigeons.

Pigeon lofts must be kept open day and night ; no pigeons whatever may be kept in a cage or in a closed place.

The transportation of live carrier or ordinary pigeons is prohibited.

All secret pigeon lofts or depôts must be reported.

ARMS AND AMMUNITION

Art. 21. The carriage of arms and ammunition is prohibited. All arms, including side-arms, also arms of collection fit for use, together with ammunition, must be deposited with the military authorities by the.....................at.....................

Any person who is aware either through his own experience or by hearsay of the existence of dumps of arms, ammunition, equipment or any other military material, must immediately report it to the local military authorities.

REQUISITIONS

Art. 22. Requisitions will be made in accordance with the French Law.

Very heavy penalties will be inflicted on any person trying to evade a requisition of articles or services.

SPIRITS—PUBLIC HOUSES

Art. 23. The sale, transportation or offer of alcohol or alcoholic drinks is prohibited. This prohibition applies equally to dealers in spirits and to private people.

No authorization for the opening of a new public house will be granted.

This prohibition does not apply to alcohol for chemists, hospitals, or for industrial purposes.

Art. 24. Access to public houses, cafés and restaurants is prohibited to the civilian population

Between.................and....................

From 8 p.m. to..........

Public houses, cafés and restaurants will be open to soldiers of all ranks during the following hours :—

From 10.30 a.m. to 1 p.m.
From 5.31 p.m. to 9 p.m.
From 10.30 a.m. to 1 p.m.
From 5 p.m. to 8 p.m.

Art. 25. Pealing of bells and use of sirens will be regulated by the local military authorities.

Art. 26. Depôts of abandoned records or documents, also wells or fountains either polluted or poisoned, and, generally, any action in the interest of public order and good administration of the country, must be reported to the local military authorities.

Any persons found guilty of having failed to reveal the existence of a fact (*fait*) which they should have brought to the notice of the military authorities will severely be dealt with.

Art. 27. All applications for authorization, permit, safe-conduct, are to be addressed to the local authorities, whoever the authorities competent to decide in the matter may be.

PENALTIES

Art. 28. In cases where it is presumed that acts deemed to be crimes or offences have been committed, the culprit will be put under arrest and tried by court martial.

In all cases the military authorities will be qualified to pass sentences up to one year's imprisonment and 1,000 francs fine, also the evacuation of offenders, the closing down of commercial or industrial establishments.

It will be permissible to lodge an appeal, within 48 hours after notification of the sentence, with the authorities who passed the verdict.

The military authorities will be allowed to take any such steps as may be required to ensure the carrying out of the above-mentioned sentences.

Art. 29. The present Decree will come into force immediately it has been published.

the....................191

APPENDIX XI

FRENCH DRAFT REGULATIONS FOR DISCUSSION

POLICE AND ADMINISTRATION OF THE OCCUPIED GERMAN TERRITORIES

DUTIES OF OFFICERS IN CHARGE OF ADMINISTRATION

[OFFICIAL TRANSLATION]

RULES AND REGULATIONS. The rules and regulations in force at the time of the occupation will be respected inasmuch as they do not prejudice the rights of the occupant and do not endanger his security. *Requisitions will, however, be made in accordance with the rules and regulations of the Allied Armies concerned.*

Pending new orders, the municipal authorities will only be given receipts for these requisitions ; the conditions of payment will be laid down later.

All commodities necessary for the population will be left at their disposal. It is absolutely necessary that this rule should strictly be adhered to in order to avoid agitation in the population, on the one hand, and, on the other, save the Allies from being under the obligation to supply the population.

The officers in charge of administration should not fail, whenever they deem it advisable, to demand from the leading people and qualified German officials all information regarding legal and administrative matters which they might be in need of ; moreover, they will find in the libraries of administrations and tribunals all necessary documents.

SERVICES.—The organization of public services will be maintained under the close control of the Allied military authorities. The latter should endeavour to ensure the resumption of local life ; they will authorize and promote as early as possible the normal working of schools, churches, tribunals, charity institutions, hospitals, asylums, infants' homes, also the meeting of administrative councils, chambers of commerce, boards of administrators, etc. . . .

Instructions will be given later with regard to the conditions under which the financial services will be allowed to operate, the rate of exchange, collection of taxes, premiums, contributions, salaries of officials, seizure of money deposits, postage stamps, issues of paper money and municipal money notes.

As a matter of principle, all officials and employees, particularly those belonging to administrative services, justice, finance, religion, public schools, health service, will be left in their situation.

It will be preferable not to compel officials to carry on their duties against their wish. However, in cases of emergency, it will be advisable to resort to the requisition of some special personal services.

The replacement of officials, either absent or dismissed, should be demanded from the local administrations. In the event of the latter refusing to do so, the service will be performed by an officer appointed for the purpose.

The officers in charge of the administration should summon at the earliest possible date the leading officials still in charge, the mayors, municipal councillors, presidents of chambers of commerce, to ratify them in their functions and warn them that they have to hold themselves constantly at the disposal of the Allied authorities. These officials should be notified that the services will have to work under their responsibility and that they will be liable to punishment in the event of destruction or concealment of documents, books or money, also of means of communication (telephone, wireless telegraph, carrier pigeons). Heavy penalties should be inflicted on those who might fail to carry out conscientiously the duties inherent to their employment.

Administrative assemblies, boards of administrators, committees called upon to operate, should meet in accordance with the order or authorization of the Allied authorities. Deliberations will have to apply exclusively to the questions specified in the order or authorization given.

PROCLAMATION. The G.O.C. an army or group of armies should address a proclamation for the purpose of notifying to the population the occupation of the country by the Allied military authorities, warning them at the same time that they have duties and obligations to carry out and that they have to comply with same.

POLICE REGULATIONS. The officers in charge of the administration should issue as soon as possible an order worded in both languages, laying down the police regulations with regard to cantonment, circulation, public houses, meetings, publications, photographs, carriage and sale of arms and ammunition, etc. The attached specimen of proclamation is forwarded as an indication. It can be altered in its details as circumstances may require.[1]

PENALTIES. Whenever the breach of a decision or the refusal to obey an order given by the Allied authorities is deemed to be a crime or offence under the Penal Code of the Allied Nations, the offenders will be tried by court martial.

Any breach of orders issued by the G.O.C. a group of armies or an army, or by the officers in charge of administration, will be punished by a condemnation which may amount to one year's imprisonment and 1,000 francs fine. The authorities mentioned above have the power to evacuate the offenders or defaulters or temporarily or permanently to close commercial or industrial establishments.

Appeal against decisions inflicting a penalty can be lodged within 48 hours from the time when the verdict has been notified ; appeal against the decisions of the officers in charge of the administration should be forwarded to the Army Commander[2] for his decision : appeal against decisions of Army Commanders should be forwarded to the C.-in-C., for his decision.

A specimen of an *arrêté* is attached.

---

[1] Not reproduced as the British proclamations are given in this volume.
[2] Or a general *Directeur des Etapes* in their area, in the case of Allied Armies having a *Direction des Etapes*.

A. Measures to be taken by Os.C. Units passing through Enemy Localities which have not been Occupied yet

(1) To place sentry posts at entrances to cantonments. These sentries are to prohibit inhabitants from leaving or entering the locality until they have been notified of any orders issued by the officer in charge of cantonment. The latter officer will maintain this prohibition, if he considers this course necessary and will be allowed to order inhabitants to stay within their premises from a specified hour.

(2) To place posts and sentries with a view to ensuring the protection of public buildings and services, official records, barracks, army staff offices, military buildings of all kinds, factories and all machinery of a military or general nature.

(3) To put under arrest and question all suspicious individuals. To evacuate to the divisional H.Q. all those who are to be considered as suspect.

(4) To issue immediately any such police orders as circumstances may require (traffic, closing of public houses, etc. . . .).

B. Measures to be taken by Officers in Charge of the Administration from the time they Commence their Duties in the District

Measures of First Urgency

Military buildings :

(1) Staff offices, barracks, forts, recruiting offices, arsenals and, generally, all military buildings should immediately be occupied by a small detachment who will be responsible for their guarding. No one will be permitted to enter any of those buildings until a Staff Officer of the nearest unit has inspected them and has had all documents or material of importance seized. The premises will afterwards be placed again at the disposal of the military authorities.

All documents should be forwarded to the 2nd Bureau [Intelligence], at the Army H.Q.

(2) To search for enemy soldiers, stragglers, wounded, etc.

(3) To summon the burgomaster or, in his absence, one or several leading people offering guarantees, and to question them as to the position of telephone exchanges, civilian or military telegraph or wireless stations, aerial or underground lines, private lines, pigeon lofts. To detail at once some officers or n.c.os. to reconnoitre and ascertain the organizations or establishments stated above.

(4) To ensure the protection of those public buildings and services which might not yet have been provided for by passing troops, viz. : finance offices, income tax offices, contribution offices, octroi offices, savings-banks, tribunals, notary offices, solicitor offices, bailiff offices, police stations, gendarmerie and generally all establishments or places where public funds are likely to have been deposited.

To post sentries there without delay.

To affix seals to offices and services to be preserved as well as to lockers containing public records, to safes containing public money or to private safes in public establishments.

To place notice boards prohibiting troops from tampering with any of the things stored therein.

To question officials and employees as to the working of their service, request them to carry on their functions and hold them responsible for same as well as for any act of concealment or destruction : to entrust them with the preservation of seals, public records and cash and, if necessary to appoint some civilian watchmen for the protection of buildings.

Nothing should be destroyed.

(5) In the case of postal services (telegraph, telephone), railways, railway stations, offices of the administration in charge of bridges and roads, forestry and water offices, light and power supply companies, hospitals and chemists' shops, banks and public treasury offices, to arrange for the guarding of all apparatuses, documents and cash pending instructions from the military authorities concerned.

(6) At the *Mairie* (*Rathaus*) and at the *Kreisdirection*, to seize :

The plan of the locality, also directories, latest billeting returns and military documents ;

The records of special police and espionage.

At the Justice of Peace :

To keep a very strict watch over the property record book which is kept in the premises of the justice of peace and the disappearance of which might prove of interest to some people.

MEASURES OF SECOND URGENCY

The urgent measures referred to above should be completed as soon as possible by the following :

(1) To sort out the suspects and to evacuate them ; to continue to put under arrest all suspicious individuals ; to arrange for the protection of abandoned premises ; to have a guard kept at the prisons and to have a census made of the inmates ; the jail-book will make it possible for political prisoners to be distinguished from those of common law.

(2) To ask the burgomaster, or the official provisionally in charge of the municipal functions, for the list of men from 17 up to 48 years of age who are not with the Colours ; and the list of horses and vehicles of all description available for use.

(3) To search for mines and connecting wires in barracks, public buildings and sewers.

(4) To reconnoitre and arrange for the guarding of armourers' stocks, dumps of arms and explosives, depôts of paraffin, petrol, timber, building materials ; to draw up an inventory of all above items. To keep watch over pigeon lofts (pigeon lofts must be kept open day and night : the owners must make a declaration and hand a descriptive list of their pigeons).

(5) To regulate in agreement with the military administration the duties of civilian doctors and veterinary surgeons. To prescribe all necessary measures for hygiene and sanitation (analysis of water).

(6) To have a census made of all means of transportation, carriages, motor vehicles, bicycles and articles required for the aforesaid vehicles (tyres, spare parts, oil, petrol).

APPENDIX XII

REMOBILIZATION SCHEME[1]

A. General :

Remobilization may take place during any stage of demobilization, the numbers and situation of troops to be remobilized depending on stage of demobilization reached.

Each Command is to prepare a remobilization scheme. In the case of a general remobilization units in a Command would be remobilized as follows :

    (i) Regular units.

    (ii) Units whose regimental equipment is stored in the command :

        (a) Expeditionary Forces from overseas ;
        (b) Home Defence units.

    (iii) Reserve units and those for Home Service as required.

B. Personnel :

Calling out will be done by notices in the press, posters, etc. Certain personnel will be called out by " Special Instructions " issued by letter.

Personnel of annual classes (except those belonging to cadres) will be called out separately or in groups (possibly sub-divided into medical categories). Special Reserve and Territorial may be called out separately. Soldiers on 28 days' demobilization furlough (maximum of 1,120,000) can be recalled.

Provided there were a considerable number of the last they would be the first lot called up, being in receipt of pay, having clothing, and being serving soldiers. As officers do not get demobilization furlough, the War Office will make arrangements for calling out necessary proportion of officers.

Calling out will probably be as follows :

    (a) Demobilization will be stopped and men will rejoin on completion of furlough.

    (b) Men on demobilization furlough will be ordered by notices in the press to rejoin by groups of annual classes.

    (c) Army reserve will be called out by annual classes as required.

Personnel will come out at " rejoining places," from which personnel will be sent to either " Cadre Assembling Places," to form units, or to a " Draft Collection Station " to proceed as drafts overseas or to another Command.

Soldiers rejoining will be armed and equipped at rejoining places. Personnel will be posted if possible to the corps in which they served previously.

C. Cadres and Units :

Cadres formed for demobilization will form cadre personnel for remobilization. A disbanded or disembodied unit whose cadre has come from overseas will be remobilized in the area allotted to it in the Command which it is in or to which it belongs.

---

[1] Summary of the printed War Office " Remobilization Scheme," dated 30th January, 1919, and 22nd February, 1919.

As a general rule, units still existing in the United Kingdom or overseas will be remobilized wherever they are situated at the time of the issue of the remobilization order. Units overseas will be brought up to War Establishment by drafts from the United Kingdom. Reconstruction of " Formations " will be carried out by the G.O.C. in command of the Expeditionary Forces.

Existing staffs of the Schools of Instruction (in United Kingdom) will be expanded by personnel called up by means of special instructions.

OFFICERS :

R.A.M.C. officers will be called up under special instructions ; also officers forming part of cadre personnel.

All other officers liable for military service will be called up under the same general rules as for " personnel ".

On remobilization, officers required for Expeditionary Forces for extra regimental or staff appointments will be called out by special instructions by the War Office.

Officers of Indian and Colonial Establishments on leaving United Kingdom would report in writing to War Office.

Officers on leave from a unit in United Kingdom or France, when remobilization is ordered would rejoin their appointment or unit at once without waiting for orders.

Points directly affecting B.E.F. marked thus ‖

APPENDIX XIII

PRINCIPLES OF DEFENCE OF COLOGNE BRIDGEHEAD IN CANADIAN CORPS AREA
19TH DECEMBER, 1918

The following outline gives the tactical principles to be observed in the establishment of that portion of the Cologne Bridgehead allotted to the Canadian Corps :—

POLICY

1. In accordance with instructions from Second Army, the tactical organization of the area will be drawn up with a view to offensive rather than defensive action.

It will, therefore, be necessary to make such preparations as will permit of :—

(a) The rapid concentration of the corps preparatory to a further advance eastwards ;

(b) the defence of the present bridgehead against hostile attack for a period of time, say, three days, during which formations in rear could be brought up to reinforce troops occupying the bridgehead.

Organization

2. For these purposes each divisional area will be organized into :—

(a) An Outpost Line to control all approaches and exits to and from the perimeter ;

(b) a Line of Resistance composed of defended localities, sited on the main tactical features in the area ;

in this connection it is to be noted that in certain instances the Outpost and Resistance Lines will be practically coincident ;

(c) a Support Line to the Line of Main Resistance also composed of defended localities.

Map

3. Map[1] is attached showing a proposed Outpost Line, Line of Main Resistance and Support Line, together with the corps area subdivided into divisional areas.

Divisional Schemes

4. In conformity with the above, each division will prepare a detailed scheme whereby the complete mobilization of the troops in the area, both for offensive and defence can be effected with the least possible delay. These schemes will include plans for the seizure of all ground of tactical importance in the Neutral Zone which it would be desirable to hold in the event of open hostilities.

Defended Localities

5. Each defended locality will be organized for all-round defence, and sited at once in consultation with the Chief Engineer, Canadian Corps. The localities will be stocked with reserve ammunition supply and reserve rations, under divisional arrangements.

Artillery

6. The Artillery policy will be drawn up under the supervision of the G.O.C. R.A., in accordance with the principles herein outlined. No guns will be placed in position ; but emplacements will be sited and inconspicuously marked, and the guns and personnel located so as to be available to take up their positions at short notice.

Machine Guns

7. The G.O.C., Canadian Machine Gun Corps, will prepare a similar scheme as regards the machine gun defences.

Roads

8. The Chief Engineer Canadian Corps will consult with the D.A. & Q.M.G., and division concerned as to the desirability of either improving existing roads or constructing new roads so as to give the fullest communication, both frontal and lateral.

Signals

9. The A.D. Signals, Canadian Corps, will prepare a scheme of communication between corps and divisional headquarters. Corps Battle Headquarters will be at Wahn.

Accommodation

10. Finally, it is to be understood that although every preparation is to be made for the resumption of offensive hostilities at short notice, yet the comfort of the troops is to be a primary consideration. It is

---

[1] See Sketch 2.

therefore to be impressed on all commanders that outpost troops are to be reduced to the minimum necessary to the correct carrying out of the duty imposed on them, and that the best available accommodation is placed at the disposal of the remainder.

ADMINISTRATION

11. (a) For general purposes of the military administration of the area, divisions will arrange for brigade areas to coincide as far as possible, with the civil boundaries of districts. These are given on Map attached[1].

(b) The D.A. & Q.M.G. will issue administrative instructions dealing with the treatment of civilians and the degree of intercourse to be allowed between the outpost and Neutral Zones.

APPENDIX XIV

THE MILITARY GOVERNOR'S INSTRUCTIONS FOR GERMAN CIVIL OFFICIALS WITHIN THE BRITISH OCCUPIED AREA WHO ARE DEPUTED TO EXAMINE AND CERTIFY LETTERS ADDRESSED TO UNOCCUPIED GERMANY AND NEUTRAL COUNTRIES

(1) You should have for guidance a copy of the published *Regulations for Civil Postal Service in German Territory Occupied by British Army.*

(2) You will examine every letter which is brought to you for unoccupied Germany or neutral countries and see that the regulations and conditions as published are strictly complied with, more especially that the letters refer solely to important business or to urgent private affairs. You will satisfy yourself of the identity of the sender whose name appears on the back of the envelope.

(3) You will return to the senders, either direct or through the civil post office, any letter which does not comply with the conditions and regulations, and you will endorse it with the reason for return. The postage prepaid will not be refunded.

(4) All letters which in your judgment comply with the regulations and fulfil the conditions you will endorse " *Geprüft* " followed by your initials and your official stamp. You will then transfer without delay all such letters to the civil post office, which will be responsible for transmitting them to the British censors at Cologne.

(5) You are forbidden to hand back to the sender for posting any letter which has been certified by you for transmission.

(6) Any breaches of the conditions and regulations in letters which bear your certificate will be dealt with by the British Military Governor.

(7) You may send to the British censor at Cologne without certificate any letter written in a language that you do not understand.

Charles Fergusson,
Lieut.-General ;
British Military Governor of
Occupied German Territory.

Cologne.
8th January, 1919.

---

[1] Not reproduced.

APPENDIX XV

THE MILITARY GOVERNOR'S INSTRUCTIONS TO THE *OBERPOSTDIREKTOR* AND THE POSTAL PERSONNEL UNDER HIS CONTROL IN GERMAN TERRITORY OCCUPIED BY THE BRITISH ARMY

The following instructions are issued for attention supplementary to the Regulations for the Civil Postal Service dated 4th January, 1919 :

(1) POSTING OF LETTERS AND PARCELS WITHIN THE BRITISH OCCUPIED AREA

(a) *You will refuse to accept over the counter at post offices :*

(i) Letters or parcels for registration, except letters or parcels containing coin or paper money sent by persons who produce a licence from the Military Governor authorizing them to send such letters or parcels ;

(ii) letters or parcels for express delivery ;

(iii) letters or parcels from British soldiers ;

(iv) letters not open for inspection or parcels not made up in such a manner as to permit of ready examination by the censors ;

(v) letters or parcels addressed to Allied countries, except for prisoners of war ;

(vi) parcels, printed papers, or newspapers for places outside the British occupied area, except newspapers or official publications tendered by publishers who have the written permission of the Military Governor to send them by post.

(b) *If collected from posting boxes or otherwise received :*

You will return to the senders :

(i) Letters, etc., not open for inspection (except those posted by the British Army) ;

(ii) letters, etc., addressed to the Allied countries (except for prisoners of war) ;

(iii) letters, etc., rejected by the British censors or by the civil certifying official and handed back to the Post Office marked for return to senders.

You will transfer to the Burgomaster or other Local Civil Official deputed to deal with them :

All letters for unoccupied Germany and neutral countries which do not bear the certificate *Geprüft* and the stamp and initials of the civil official appointed to examine and certify them.

You will send to the Head Post Office at Cologne :

(i) Letters for unoccupied Germany and neutral countries which bear the certificate, stamp and initials of the appointed civil official, but do not bear the British censor's stamp ;

(ii) Letters and parcels for prisoners of war.

You will send to a British Censor Office :

(i) Letters, etc., which do not bear the name and address of the sender ;

(ii) Letters, etc., which appear to have been posted by British soldiers (unless they bear two censor stamp impressions). See para. (5) (c) ;

(iii) letters, etc., addressed to British soldiers ;

(iv) letters for the Belgian, American and French-occupied areas except local letters from offices which make up direct " short distance " mails as described in para. (3) (c) ;

(v) All letters, etc.—additional to the foregoing—which the British military censors may from time to time demand to have transferred to them for examination.

You will despatch by ordinary course of post all letters, etc., which are not included in the foregoing instructions.

(2) PRIMARY SORTING OF LETTERS AND PARCELS

To facilitate compliance with the British censors' demands, all letters, etc., posted will, on reaching the Post Office, be divided according to destination as follows :

(i) local delivery ;
(ii) provincial delivery (British occupied area) ;
(iii) French, Belgian and American occupied areas ;
(iv) unoccupied Germany and neutral countries—not certified ;
(v) unoccupied Germany and neutral countries—certified ;
(vi) prisoners of war ;
(vii) British Army ;
(viii) closed before posting ;
(ix) without name and address of sender ; ⎫
(x) for Allied countries (except prisoners of war) ; ⎬ Irregularly posted
(xi) posted by British soldiers. ⎭

(3) CIRCULATION OF LETTERS FROM THE BRITISH OCCUPIED AREA TO OTHER OCCUPIED AREAS AND TO OTHER COUNTRIES

(a) No postal communications will be allowed to pass the boundary of the British occupied area except in sealed bags, which will be made up only for specially authorized destinations. A list of the despatches authorized will be issued separately.

(b) Sealed bags for destinations outside the British occupied area must bear a British censor seal and label in addition to the civil post office seal and label, and with the exception of the " short distance " direct mails referred to in the following paragraph (c), no bag should be despatched without the British censor seal and label.

(c) To the German territory occupied by the Belgian, American and French Armies the main despatches permitted will be made up at Bonn, Cologne, Düren, Montjoie and Solingen. Certain Post Offices near the boundary will make up direct " short distance " mails in accordance with an approved list.

(d) To unoccupied Germany and to neutral countries the only despatches permitted will be made up at Cologne.

(e) For prisoners of war in Allied and neutral countries letters and parcels will also be centralized at Cologne and no despatches will leave the occupied area except from Cologne.

(4) Circulation of Letters to the British Occupied Area from other Occupied Areas and from other Countries

(a) Letters from outside the British occupied area for delivery within the occupied area will be received only in sealed bags for specially authorized destinations. A list of the authorized closed mails will be issued separately.

(b) From the Belgian, American and French occupied areas such mails may, in the absence of special instructions from the British censors, be delivered without examination.

(c) From unoccupied Germany and neutral countries all mails will be examined by the British censors before they are passed to the civil post office for delivery. It is forbidden to the civil post office to open any such closed mail without the approval of the British censors.

(d) From prisoners of war all letters for the occupied area will arrive via Cologne. If received from the Allied countries such mails may be distributed on arrival unless specially asked for by the censors. If received from neutral countries via unoccupied Germany such mails should not be opened until they have been passed by the British censors.

(5) Letters, etc., from the British Army to the German Population of the Occupied Area, and Vice Versa

(a) Intercommunication by post between the British Army and German civilians will be permitted only through the British censorship centres, viz. Bonn, Cologne, Düren, Montjoie, Solingen.

(b) All letters and other postal communications received by the German Post Office addressed to British soldiers should be transferred to the British Censor Office, from whence, if passed by the censors, they will be handed over to the British Army Post Office for delivery. No letters or parcels should be accepted from British soldiers for despatch or delivery ; if any such letters are collected from the posting boxes they should be sent to the British Censor Office.

(c) Letters, etc., for the German population, which may be transferred from the British censors or from the British Army Post Office to the German Post Office for delivery, will bear the impression of two censor stamps and should not be delivered unless so stamped.

(d) Letters, etc., from the British Army will be closed. They will not be prepaid and should be delivered free of charge.

(e) Exception to the foregoing rules will be made in the case of official letters for and from the British Military Authorities, which should not be sent to the censors but should be transmitted through the post without delay. Official letters *from* the British Military Authorities will be enclosed in envelopes headed " On His Majesty's Service " and will bear the signature or stamp of the sender. Official letters *for* the British military authorities will be addressed to staff officers or departments.

(6) GENERAL

All postal services including rural deliveries which now work across the boundaries of the British occupied area must be cut at the boundary on and from the date these regulations are applied, with the exception of any which may be specially authorized by the Military Governor. The *Oberpostdirektor* is charged with the execution of this order and with making such arrangements as will ensure the observance of the regulations.

Cologne.

8th January, 1919

Charles Fergusson,

Lieut.-General,

British Military Governor of
Occupied German Territory.

APPENDIX XVI

THE DUTIES OF ECONOMIC SECTIONS

The Inter-Allied Economic Committee met at Luxembourg on 12th January, 1919, and came to the following agreement :

The District Sub-Commissions previously contemplated will be replaced by " Economic Sections " placed under the orders of the military commander of the territory.

1. *Composition of the Economic Sections*

These sections will consist of :

   (i) The offices already formed by the Armies for dealing with economic questions ;
   (ii) the representatives of my staff and eventually those of the Allied Armies ;
   (iii) delegates from the *sous-commissions* of the Field Railway and Field Navigation Commissions.

2. *Powers of the Economic Sections*

The Economic Sections are responsible for keeping general records and more especially those required by the Economic Committee for the distribution of raw materials and manufactured goods.

Until further orders, the Inter-Allied Economic Committee will delegate to the Economic Sections the power to sanction exportation to that part of Germany which is not occupied by the Allies, under conditions that have been decided conjointly. Authority to export into Alsace-Lorraine and into Allied and neutral countries will, until further orders, be referred by the sections with their recommendations to the Economic Committee for decision.

3. Supervision of production, reception of produce and keeping of records.

Officers of the Allied Armies will be sent into various zones by the Inter-Allied Committee to keep an eye on the manufactures and to verify receipts. These officers will be placed under the orders of their corresponding Economic Sections which will give them all the necessary facilities for carrying out their duties.

15th January, 1919

Weygand.

INSTRUCTION NO. 1 REGARDING TRANSPORTATION EMANATING FROM
OR DESTINED TO THE OCCUPIED RHINE TERRITORIES

1. Introduction

The Commander-in-Chief, Allied Armies, notified in his letter
No. 2808/CR, dated 8th January, 1919, that he could not contemplate,
as the German Government was trying to obtain, the complete uncontrolled restoration of commercial relations between the occupied territories and the remainder of Germany.

In fact, it is important, not to allow stocks of manufactured goods
to dwindle, which constitute for the Allies an appreciable security
and are also partly required for the restoration of the devastated areas.

A state of war perfectly justifies a certain slowing down of the
economic life in the occupied territories. At the same time, there
would be a certain amount of serious inconvenience if the industries
of these regions were completely shut down, and it is *solely in order to
avoid complete stoppage* that the authority may be given for the transportation of goods to and from the occupied Rhine territories.

2. Forwarding goods from the occupied Rhine territories to the
remainder of Germany

The forwarding of manufactured goods from the occupied territories
to the rest of Germany should be strictly confined by the Economic
Sections to the daily output of the factories, and the application for
this should contain a special statement that the delivery of the goods
will leave intact the stock existing on 15th January. These statements
will be verified.

Authority to send goods out, within the limits above indicated,
cannot be given for the materials and goods quoted in the previously
mentioned letter of the C.-in-C. of which a copy is attached.[1] If
important reason arise for an Economic Section to approve the export
of certain goods or materials mentioned in the list referred to, the
requests of the firms concerned will be sent to the Inter-Allied
Economic Committee. No requests will, however, be forwarded as
regards railway engines or wagons (either complete or in parts).

3. Forwarding goods from the interior of Germany to the occupied
Rhine territories

The following are authorized without special formality :

(i) Supplies of foodstuffs, including drinks, forage and grain for
feeding animals, agricultural seeds.
(ii) Raw materials and implements required for industrial purposes.

As regards (ii) above, the *sous-commissions* of the Navigation
Commission will forward to the Inter-Allied Committee on the 1st and
15th of each month a statement of the tonnage admitted of each kind.
From the statement the Committee can decide as regards prohibitions.

This authority being for the benefit of the manufacturers themselves,
the export of no manufactured goods is allowed which are destined for
wholesale firms or retailers within the occupied territories. Economic
sections will ensure by enquiries that the goods brought in for industrial
purposes are not wholly or partly supplied to merchants before
transformation.

---

[1] Not found.

4. Forwarding into Alsace-Lorraine, neutral and Allied countries

Until further orders all applications for forwarding goods to the Allied and neutral countries will be sent to the Luxembourg Committee with the recommendations of the Economic Sections.

The applications regarding Alsace and Lorraine will be addressed to the Committee of Derogation at Strassburg.

5. The working of this service

Applications by the interested parties for authority to forward goods will be sent to the Economic Sections in quadruplicate.

As regards applications whose approval lies within the jurisdiction of the Economic Section, one copy will be returned after approval to the firm concerned, a second copy will be sent to the *Sous-Commission de Réseau*, who will arrange for the transportation authorized by the railway authorities according to the available traffic facilities, and finally deciding the order of importance in agreement with the Economic Sections, a third copy being reserved by the Inter-Allied Economic Section.

As regards applications that lie within the powers of the Inter-Allied Economic Committee, the four copies will be forwarded to the Committee which will retain one and return three to the Economic Section ; the latter will keep one and send the other two to the *Sous-Commission de Réseau*.

The following details should be stated in the applications :

(1) Name of senders ; (2) destination of the goods ; (3) number and approximate weight of the packages ; (4) station of departure ; (5) station of arrival ; (6) the approval or refusal of the Economic Section ; (7) date of the above decision ; (8) registered number of the above decision.

(6), (7) and (8) to be filled in by the Economic Section or the Economic Committee.

The copies destined for the *Sous-Commission de Réseau* should bear the stamp of the section or committee giving the approval, and an authoritative signature.

The copies returned to the applicants will only bear the office stamp.

The above will come into operation on 25th January, 1919.

18th January, 1919   Weygand

PROVISIONAL LIST OF MATERIALS AND PRODUCE WHOSE EXPORT
FROM THE OCCUPIED TERRITORIES IS FORBIDDEN
UNTIL FURTHER ORDERS

1. Coal and fuel : Special regulations.
2. Metal products :
>   Sheet iron and small iron bars, rails.
>   Large iron bars and angle irons.
>   Iron of various commercial sections.
>   Tubing.
>   Wire.
>   Special steel.
3. Various metals :
>   Zinc, lead, aluminium, copper, etc.

4. Mechanical tools, etc.

> Various motors, engines and wagons.
> Machine tools.
> Electrical material.
> Spinning and weaving machinery.

5. Cement :

> Glass, window and roofing.
> Tiles (not bricks).
> Fireproof material.

6. Carpentering wood :

> Mining timber.
> Sleepers.

7. Leather :

> Hides.

8. Sugar :

9. Chemicals :

> Colouring matters (not medicinal).

10. Paper

APPENDIX XVII

THE MILITARY GOVERNOR'S INSTRUCTIONS GOVERNING THE CIRCULATION OF CIVILIANS AND THE ISSUE OF PASSES

(Cancels and replaces previous Instructions)

1. Within British Occupied Territory :

Inhabitants may circulate freely within the British Occupied Territory provided they are in possession of their identity cards.

2. Between British Occupied and Belgian or American Occupied Territory

(a) Authority for the issue of passes (brown and green)[1] is delegated to Area Commandants. Passes will be stamped by the D.A.P.M. or A/D.A.P.M. with the square stamp.

British passes giving permission to cross the frontier into the American or Belgian zones will be valid in the American and Belgian zones respectively.

The destination of the bearer will be clearly marked on all such passes.

(b) Persons holding passes approved and stamped by the American, Belgian or French military authorities with the round stamp will be permitted to enter British occupied territory.

The destination of the bearer will be clearly marked on all such passes.

---

[1] A list of passes is given at the end.

(c) In the case of individuals who live inside the British area and work in the American or Belgian area or vice versa, Area Commandants and Sub-Area Commandants are authorized to issue special workers' passes (blue). The number of these passes issued will be as limited as possible. These passes will be valid up to a period of three months from the date of issue at the discretion of the issuing officer.

3. From the British Occupied Territory into Unoccupied German Territory

(a) Authority is delegated to Area Commandants to issue passes (brown and green) without return. These passes will be issued at the discretion of Area Commandants. As a general principle there is no objection to people leaving the area.

(b) Applications for passes with return, if approved by Area Commandants, will be endorsed and forwarded direct to the Permit Office, D.P.M., Second Army.

(c) In the case of individuals who live inside the British area and work in the unoccupied area, or in the Neutral Zone, Area and Sub-Area Commandants are authorized to issue special workers' passes (blue). Passes issued under this heading should be limited to local journeys. The number of these passes issued will be as limited as possible. These passes will be valid up to a period of three months from the date of issue at the discretion of the issuing officer.

(d) Passes issued according to (a), (b) and (c) will be stamped by the D.A.P.M. or A/D.A.P.M. with the square stamp.

(e) Persons travelling from the American area through the British area into the unoccupied German area will be allowed to proceed if bearing an American pass bearing the British square stamp. These passes will be stamped by the British Mission with the American Army.

4. From British Occupied Territory to Neutral or Allied Countries

These applications will include :

(a) Repatriation of Allied and neutral subjects, living in British occupied territory.

(b) Repatriation to the land of their birth of persons of German nationality but of Allied or neutral birth.

(c) Passes for urgent private and business affairs.

Applications, if approved by Area Commandants, will be endorsed and forwarded direct to the Permit Office, D.P.M., Second Army.

As a general principle passes (brown and green) for return will not be issued except in the case of accredited neutral agents.

5. From Unoccupied German Territory into British Occupied Territory

Procedure to be adopted in the case of any person in unoccupied German territory who wishes to enter British occupied territory, and who is not already in possession of the requisite pass.

The application, endorsed and stamped by the local civil authorities (*Bürgermeister* or *Landrat*) will be forwarded by post to the civil authorities of the town to which the applicant wishes to travel.

The application must contain :

(i) Photograph of the applicant (duly stamped and verified by the civil authorities) ;

(ii) certified copy of applicant's signature ;

(iii) reason for the journey ;

(iv) address of a person in British occupied territory to whom reference can be made regarding the object of the journey ;

(v) duration of stay.

The applications, if approved by the civil authorities in the British occupied territory, will be endorsed, stamped and forwarded direct to the Branch Permit Office, D.P.M., Second Army, Blaubach 1, Cologne. If the application is approved by the British military authorities, a telegram will be sent to the local civil authority who originally endorsed the application as follows :—

" Authority granted to Herr ....,...... to proceed to Cologne by passenger train, on or before the.................. (one week after date of wire).

" Report on arrival to British Military Authorities at Cologne station for pass."

The production of this telegram will pass bearer through frontier to Cologne station.

6. From the Neutral Zone into British Occupied Territory

(a) In the case of individuals, who live in the Neutral Zone and work inside the British area, applying for workers' passes.

Applications will be forwarded to the local civil authorities (*Landrat* or *Bürgermeister*) who will endorse the application, if approved, and forward it with the identity card or photograph of the applicant to the nearest Sub-Area Commandant either by post or through the British piquet line. Passes will be returned through the piquet line to the local civil authorities for delivery to the applicant.

Passes (blue) issued under this heading should be limited to local journeys.

Authority is delegated as in 3 (c).

(b) In the case of individuals who live in the Neutral Zone and wish to enter the British area for urgent private or business affairs.

Applications made out in accordance with the instructions in paragraph 5 may be forwarded as follows :

(i) By post ;

(ii) by the local civil authorities to the British piquet post on the Wermelskirchen–Bonn road or by such other posts as may be established for the purpose, for transmission to the lcoal Sub-Area Commandant.

Passes (green and brown) will be returned as in 6 (a) above.

Authority is delegated to Area Commandants to issue passes to persons residing in the neutral zone wishing to enter their own area.

(c) Passes issued according to (a) and (b) will be stamped by the D.A.P.M. or A/D.A.P.M. with the square stamp. The destination of the bearer will be clearly marked on all such passes.

A special clause will be inserted in the recommendation of the local civil authority that the applicant was previously domiciled in the Neutral Zone.

7. From Neutral and Allied Countries to British Occupied Territory

(*a*) Persons of German nationality living in neutral or Allied countries, who wish to be repatriated to or enter British occupied territory.

(*b*) Persons of neutral or Allied nationality who wish to return to or enter British occupied territory.

Applications will be forwarded to the Permit Office, D.P.M., Second Army, as described in paragraph 5.

In cases of repatriation it is essential that such individuals should have been previously domiciled in British occupied territory.

8. Entry into British Occupied Area

All other applications for entry into British Occupied Territory, not specifically mentioned in this memorandum, will be made in the manner described in paragraph 5.

9. Circulation by Night between the Hours of 2100 and 0500

Authority to issue passes for circulation within British occupied territory between these hours is delegated to Area and Sub-Area Commandants.

A special night pass (white pass with a horizontal red band across the face), valid up to a period of three months from date of issue, will be issued and will be stamped by the D.A.P.M. or A/D.A.P.M. with the round stamp.

The blue workers' pass will be valid for night circulation when endorsed to that effect, and will replace the special white pass mentioned above.

10. Circulation by Motor and Bicycle

(*a*) Authority to issue these passes is delegated down to Sub-Area Commandants.

A special pink coloured pass, valid up to a period of three months from date of issue will be issued. This pass will be stamped by the D.A.P.M. or A/D.A.P.M. with the round stamp.

(*b*) In addition to clergymen, doctors and midwives, the right of circulation by motor car may be granted to :—

(i) *Bürgermeistern, Landräte,* postal and other government officials whose duties necessitate the use of a car.

(ii) Managers and high officials of works of public importance, such as electric and water works, banks, etc.

(*c*) A yellow pass for circulation by pedal bicycle may be granted to workmen who reside at a distance from their place of work to whom the use of a bicycle is considered essential to enable them to maintain their livelihood.

(d) The right of use of lorries may be granted to factories and other industrial installations to which lorry transport is considered essential. Each lorry must be in possession of the pink motor pass. The word " car " must be altered to " lorry ".

11. Passes

The following procedure will be adopted by all applicants for passes, subject to such modifications as may be necessary to suit local requirements.

Written application must be made, even when delivered personally, to the local civil authorities, who will stamp and endorse the application, if approved, and forward the original application with a short *précis* of the case to the local military authorities, sufficient information being contained in the *précis* to enable the military authorities to give a decision.

German clerks may be employed where necessary for the purpose of filling in the pass-forms.

All applications for passes made by persons living in the British occupied territory or neutral zone will, if recommended by the local civil authorities, be investigated as far as possible by Sub-Area Commandants, who, if not competent to deal with the application, will forward it with their recommendations to the Area Commandant.

Similarly the latter, if not competent to deal with the application, will forward it with his recommendation, direct to the Permit Office, D.P.M., Second Army.

Only such cases will be referred to I (b) as are considered to require investigation from I (b) point of view. In these cases the application will be returned by the local I (b), after investigation, to the Area Commandant and all papers will be forwarded by the Area Commandant as above, direct to the Permit Office, D.P.M., Second Army.

Applications approved by the Permit Office, D.P.M., Second Army, will be returned, with the necessary pass, through Area Commandants concerned, for distribution to the individual.

Area Commandants will arrange for weekly lists of all passes issued under paragraphs 3 (b) and 4 in their area to be furnished to their local I (b) made up to Thursday, 6 p.m.

Similar weekly lists of all passes issued under paragraphs 5 and 7 will be furnished by Permit Office, D.P.M., Second Army, to I (b), Military Governor.

12. Mode of Conveyance

(a) *Within Occupied British Territory or from British to American or Belgian Occupied Territory*

Identity cards within British occupied territory and passes from British to American or Belgian occupied territory will be valid for circulation by tram, train, boat, horse-drawn vehicle, or on foot.

Persons travelling by motor car, bicycle or lorry must also be in possession of the special passes (yellow and pink) laid down in paragraph 10 (a) above.

(b) *Between Occupied and Unoccupied German Territory*

(1) General passes will be valid for circulation by foot, tram (if running), passenger trains mentioned below, and by boat.

(2) The following passenger trains across the frontier have been authorised :—

(a) Spa–Berlin Express.   Three corridor carriages (160 seats) and one sleeping car (20 seats) will be reserved on this train for inward and outward journeys.   Passengers must join this train at Cologne.

(b) Certain workmen's trains.

(3) All railway officials will be in possession of white passes (in three languages) signed by Lieut.-Colonel Ditmas, President, Sub-Commission, Inter-Allied Railway Commission, Cologne.

This pass entitles holders to travel at any time of the day or night on and off duty within or through British occupied territory.

(4) Crews of boats plying on the Rhine will be in possession of passes (white), in three languages, issued by the President of the *Commission Interalliée de Navigation de Campagne.*

All passengers on board these boats must be in possession of the requisite pass according to destination.

(5) Persons travelling by motor car or bicycle will be allowed to proceed if in possession of the special pass as laid down in paragraph 10 (a) above.

13. Definition of the term " Worker "

Industrial and factory hands, etc., including managers and clerical staff.

Representatives of industrial concerns, whose work necessitates constant travelling.

Managers, secretaries and high officials of works of public importance, such as electric and waterworks, banks, insurance companies, etc.

Government and postal officials on duty.

Doctors, veterinary surgeons, clergymen, midwives, etc.

14. Considerable latitude will be allowed with regard to the interpretation of the term " urgent private or business affairs ".

Cases such as the following should receive due consideration :
    Serious illness or accidents to near relatives.
    Winding up of business matters.
    Questions of inheritance.
    Cases where personal attendance of applicant is essential.
    Care of children and invalids, etc.

15. Persons in possession of the Adjutant-General's white passes, unless such are marked " Not valid for Germany " will be permitted to enter British Occupied Territory, according to destination.

6th January, 1919

APPENDIX XVII

LIST OF PASSES FOR CIVILIANS IN USE BY THE BRITISH SECOND ARMY

	Available	*Remarks*
1. Identity card ..	For circulation as in paragraph 1.	Identity card must be produced with all passes including 7 and 8.
2. Brown—Male .. Green—Female	For circulation. When stamped with square stamp as in paragraphs 2(*a*), 3(*a*), (*b*), 4, 5, 6(*b*).	
3. Blue worker's pass.	For circulation when stamped with round stamp as in paragraphs 9 and 10(*c*). When stamped with square stamp as in paragraphs 2(*c*), 3(*c*), 6(*a*), 9, 10(*c*).	Can be made available for circulation by bicycle and also for circulating after 21 hours instead of extra passes being issued.
4. Pink (motor car, or lorry) pass.	For circulation as in paragraph 10(*a*).	Available as an ordinary pass when holder is not travelling by motor car.
5. Yellow bicycle pass.	For circulation as in paragraph 10(*c*).	Ditto by bicycle.
6. White with horizontal bar, night pass.	For night circulation as in paragraph 9.	
7. Railway officials' pass. (White)	For circulation as in paragraph 12(*b*) 3.	Available either on or off duty at any time or anywhere in British area.
8. Navigation pass. (White)	For every permanent member of the crews of all vessels on the river.	Ditto Also available without identity card up to midnight, Jan 31st, 1919.

Note 1.—In the case of persons arriving from unoccupied territory (of paragraph 5), on the pass, which will be handed to them at Cologne station, the words " Identity Card No......." will be erased and the word " Photograph " substituted. The photograph will be pasted on the back of the pass. The words " The bearer of Identity Card No......." will also be erased.

2.—Instructions are being issued that all persons in possession of passes 7 and 8 must be provided with identity cards by midnight, January 31st, 1919.

[A later instruction stated that American and other passes would not be valid without a British *visé*.]

APPENDIX XVIII

INSTRUCTIONS FOR OFFICERS PROCEEDING TO GERMANY TO ASCERTAIN THE ECONOMIC CONDITION AS REGARDS FOOD SUPPLY

1. You will ascertain the localities and class of inhabitants where food is most required, and what type of food is most urgently wanted, namely meat or bread.

2. You will find out what system is adopted in the locality for the distribution of food and whether it is likely to reach the persons who are in most urgent need of it, if handed over to the local authorities in bulk, or whether it will be necessary to establish Allied distribution missions.

3. You will report on the local facilities for the distribution of food and whether these facilities are sufficient to enable the food to be issued by the Allies in bulk in certain localities. That is to say, whether a very large depot of food can be established to serve a large area, or whether many small depots are required.

4. You will ascertain the staple food of the local inhabitants and the scale they have been subsisting on up to the time when the Armistice was signed.

5. You will report on the present condition of winter crops and winter sowing, the prospects of next year's harvest and the steps that are being taken locally to secure an adequate food supply. That is to say, whether the agricultural portion of the inhabitants are actually working or prepared to work in the fields.

6. You will report on the resources of the country as regards stocks of cattle and pigs, vegetables (especially potatoes), corn and flour or any other staple article of food.

7. You will observe the present condition of the inhabitants, especially the children, and study and report upon the local milk supply.

8. You will ascertain details of local food substitutes and their nutritive powers, both for human consumption and for cattle.

9. You will report on the clothing situation, including extra garments for winter weather, and the nature and condition of footwear.

10. You will endeavour to ascertain whether the reported shortage of food in Germany is a real menace to the country and like to lead to starvation, and whether it is having any effect on the political feelings of the inhabitants especially as regards a tendency to increase bolshevism.

11. You will report on the general behaviour of the inhabitants as regards the higher authority because on this will depend a good deal the possibility of getting food without risk of looting to the people who require it most.

12. You will endeavour to ascertain whether work is going on in factories and on farms and whether the scale of wages is abnormal.

13. You will ascertain the local price of ordinary food as compared with luxuries and whether it is true that those who can afford it can get as much food as they want whilst others may be starving.

14. You will carefully study the whole questions of the supply of food to Germany by the Allies in its smaller details, as outlined above, and forward any suggestions that occur to you which would facilitate and economise the supplies that are absolutely necessary to send into the country so that the inhabitants can carry on their economic life without fear of actual starvation.

You will understand that it is no part of the Allied plan to feed the poorer classes so as to release more food for the wealthy class.

Spa.
3rd January, 1919

R. Haking, Lieut.-Gen.,
Chief of British Armistice Commission.

APPENDIX XIX

BRITISH ARMY OF THE RHINE
ORDER OF BATTLE
1st JANUARY 1920
HEADQUARTER TROOPS

ARTILLERY :

Brigade, R.G.A.—

29th (Mobile) .. ⎰ 121st Heavy Battery (six 60-pdr. guns)[1]
128th Heavy Battery (six 60-pdr. guns)[1]
195th Siege Battery (six 6-in. howitzers)
303rd Siege Battery (six 6-in. howitzers).

ENGINEERS :

No. 2 Advanced R.E. Park.
145th Army Troops Company, R.E.
354th Electrical and Mechanical Company, R.E.
Detachment of 4th Field Survey Battalion.
1 Section No. 24 Base Park Company, R.E.

SIGNAL SERVICE :

Rhine Signal Battalion. (Will eventually become Rhine Garrison Signal Company.)

PROVOST MARSHAL :

Infantry : 51st Hampshire (for duty on L. of C.).
Military Police :

No. 1 Traffic Control Squadron.
No. 3 Traffic Control Squadron.
No. 1 Traffic Control Company.
No. 3 Traffic Control Company.
Military Police Pool, 1,062 men.
Military Prison.

---

[1] One battery for Rhine Garrison eventually.

CYCLISTS :
6th Cyclist Battalion.

R.A.S.C. :
No. 20 Motor Ambulance Convoy (No. 638 Coy., R.A.S.C.).
Army Troops M.T. Company (No. 585 Coy., R.A.S.C.).
No. 18 Army Auxiliary (Horse) Company (No. 165 Coy., R.A.S.C.)
R.A.S.C. attached X Corps Heavy Artillery M.T. Column to form
Mobile Bde. M.T. Company (No. 594 Coy., R.A.S.C.).
Detachment of No. 2 Water Tank Company (No. 718 Coy., R.A.S.C.)
H.Q. and two-thirds of No. 2 L. of C. Supply Company.
Nos. 2, 3, 8, 41 and 46 Railhead Supply Detachments.
No. 3 Field Bakery (with reduced establishment—120 O.Rs.)

MEDICAL :
General hospitals—
No. 25 (Venereal) and No. 3 at 500 beds each.
Casualty clearing stations :
No. 29 at Bonn and Nos. 36, 37 and 44 at Cologne, at 200 beds each
No. 8 Ambulance Train
No. 2 Mobile Dental Unit
No. 25 Sanitary Section
No. 2 Advanced Depôt of Medical Stores
No. 1 Mobile Bacteriological Laboratory
No. 4 Mobile X-ray Unit

REMOUNTS :
No. 35 Remount Squadron.

VETERINARY :
No. 8 Veterinary Hospital

R.A.O.C. :
Base Depôt :—
Nos. 8, 13, 14 Ordnance Coys. (including Base Ordnance Workshop
and Transit Depôt at Antwerp)
Half of No. 50 Boot Repairing Company.
Officers' Clothing Depôt.
Nos. 51 and 82 Ordnance Ammunition Sections.
Nos. 10 and 20 Ordnance Mobile Workshops (Light).
Rhine Army Clothing Exchange

LABOUR CORPS :
No. 31 Labour Group Headquarters
Nos. 49 and 180 Labour Companies
No. 257 (H.Q.) Employment Company

ARMY PRINTING AND STATIONERY SERVICES

ARMY POSTAL SERVICES :
Base Post Office, 1 } On reduced establishment
Auxiliary Postal Company, 1 }

TRANSPORTATION :
Three-quarters of No. 1 Railway Traffic Section

ROYAL AIR FORCE :
No. 12 Squadron

RHINE GARRISON

1st Rhine Brigade	*2nd Rhine Brigade*
Headquarters :	Headquarters :
10/ Queen's	51/ Northumberland Fusiliers
11/ Queen's	51/ Rifle Brigade
23/ Royal Fusiliers	52/ Rifle Brigade
Light Trench Mortar Battery	Light Trench Mortar Battery

RHINE GARRISON TROOPS

Headquarters, Rhine Garrison
Cavalry, 6th (Inniskilling) Dragoons
187th Bde., R.F.A. (four batteries, 12 18-pdrs., 4 4·5-in. howitzers)
Bde. ammunition column
121st Heavy Battery, R.G.A. (six 60-pdr. guns) and ammunition column
231st Field Company, R.E.
19/ Middlesex (Pioneers)
No. 41 Bn. Machine Gun Corps
Rhine Garrison Train (three companies)
Rhine Garrison M.T. Company
Detachment 25 M.M.P.
No. 52 Mobile Veterinary Section
No. 238 Divisional Employment Company
No. 140 and 142 Field Ambulances

INDEPENDENT DIVISION

Southern Brigade	*Northern Brigade*
Headquarters :	Headquarters :
51/ R. Warwickshire	52/ King's
52/ R. Warwickshire	52/ Manchester
52/ Devonshire	52/ Durham L.I.
Light Trench Mortar Battery	Light Trench Mortar Battery

Light Brigade

Headquarters :
13/ K.R.R.C.   20/ K.R.R.C.
18/ K.R.R.C.   Light Trench Mortar Battery

DIVISIONAL TROOPS

Headquarters, Independent Division
113th Bde., R.F.A. (four batteries, 12 18-pdrs., 4 4·5-in. howitzers)
Independent Division Ammunition Column
H.Q., Independent Division Engineers
  206th Field Coy., R.E.
  218th Field Coy., R.E.
  219th Field Coy., R.E.
Independent Division Signal Company
20/ Durham L.I. (Pioneers)
51/ Hampshire
No. 29 Bn. Machine Gun Corps
Independent Division Train
Independent Division, M.T. Company
Nos. 5, 6 and 7 Field Ambulances
No. 61 Sanitary Section
No. 18 Mobile Veterinary Section
No. 226 Divisional Employment Coy.
Detachment 25 M.M.P.

APPENDIX XX

BRITISH ARMY OF THE RHINE
ORDERS IN EVENT OF CIVIL DISTURBANCES
13TH DECEMBER, 1919

1. According to information received, a considerable propaganda is being carried out among the unruly elements of the German population, especially in the unoccupied area, with a view to the overthrow of the existing Government and the introduction of a Communist regime. Exactly how much truth there may be in these reports it is difficult to say, but in any case it is necessary that we should be prepared for a hostile rising involving the whole of our area, as well as for civil disturbances on a smaller scale.

2. It is improbable that such a rising would take place without previous warning ; and perhaps the most likely course of events would be a series of minor outbreaks culminating in general disorder. In either case the precautions laid down in corps and division defence schemes would be adopted in the first instance.

3. The following instructions are issued for guidance in regard to the additional measures which might have to be taken to ensure the preservation of law and order :—

(*a*) It is not intended, unless compelled by superior force, to vacate any of the localities held in strength by our troops in accordance with the defence schemes.

(*b*) Isolated detachments (such as at Engelskirchen), which are distant from support and liable to be surrounded, and guards on vulnerable points other than those given in the attached appendix[1], may be withdrawn at the discretion of the commanders of the VI. Corps and Independent Division respectively.

(*c*) The guards on the vulnerable points shown on the attached appendix, if threatened by attack, will be reinforced to ensure that they do not fall into the hands of the revolutionaries.

The passages of the Rhine at the five bridges in the British occupied area (vide appendix) will be maintained, and the guards if necessary reinforced. Crossings by the main ferries of Rheindorf-Mondorf and Wesseling-Porz will be controlled by the Rhine Flotilla.

(*d*) The battalions earmarked in the VI. Corps and Independent Division areas for reinforcing the adjoining area will not be employed except in the case of real emergency without reference to G.H.Q., and will be regarded as G.H.Q. reserve. Should it be found necessary to employ them, the fact will be notified immediately to G.H.Q.

(*e*) The action taken to restore order should include the following :—

(i) Assemblages of any considerable number of persons will be prohibited, and if necessary dispersed by force.

---

[1] Not reproduced.

(ii) Civilians without special passes issued by the local commander will be required to remain indoors between sunset and sunrise, or between such hours as may be fixed by the local commander.

(iii) Civilians found in possession of arms will be arrested.

(*f*) Motor transport for use by G.H.Q. will be held in readiness by the D.D.S. & T. to enable troops to be transported rapidly to any threatened locality.

(*g*) The 12th Squadron R.A.F. will come under the orders of G.H.Q. and will send a liaison officer immediately to the Headquarters office.

(*h*) The above instructions will come into force on the receipt of the code word " Madrid," which will be issued from these headquarters.

APPENDIX XXI

PEACE TREATY OF VERSAILLES
MILITARY CLAUSES

CHAPTER I

EFFECTIVES AND CADRES OF THE GERMAN ARMY

Article 159

The German military forces shall be demobilized and reduced as prescribed hereinafter.

Article 160

(1) By a date which must not be later than March 31st, 1920, the German Army must not comprise more than seven divisions of infantry and three divisions of cavalry.

After that date the total number of effectives in the Army of the States constituting Germany must not exceed one hundred thousand men, including officers and establishments of depots. The Army shall be devoted exclusively to the maintenance of order within the territory and to the control of the frontiers.

The total effective strength of officers, including the personnel of staffs, whatever their composition, must not exceed four thousand.

(2) Divisions and Army Corps headquarters staffs shall be organized in accordance with Table No. 1 annexed to this section[1].

The number and strengths of the units of infantry, artillery, engineers, technical services and troops laid down in the aforesaid table constitute maxima which must not be exceeded.

---

[1] Tables of Army Corps Headquarters Staffs, establishments of an infantry division and a cavalry division, armament establishment and maximum stocks which followed are not reproduced.

The following units may each have their own depot :

An infantry regiment ; a cavalry regiment ; a regiment of field artillery ; a battalion of pioneers.

(3) The divisions must not be grouped under more than two army corps headquarters staffs.

The maintenance or formation of forces differently grouped or of other organizations for the command of troops or for preparation for war is forbidden.

The Great German General Staff and all similar organizations shall be dissolved and may not be reconstituted in any form.

The officers, or persons in the position of officers, in the Ministries of War in the different States in Germany and in the administrations attached to them, must not exceed three hundred in number and are included in the maximum strength of four thousand laid down in the third sub-paragraph of paragraph (1) of this Article.

Article 161

Army administrative services consisting of civilian personnel not included in the number of effectives prescribed by the present Treaty will have such personnel reduced in each class to one-tenth of that laid down in the Budget of 1913.

Article 162

The number of employees or officials of the German States, such as customs officers, forest guards and coastguards, shall not exceed that of the employees or officials functioning in these capacities in 1913.

The number of gendarmes and employees or officials of the local or municipal police may only be increased to an extent corresponding to the increase of population since 1913 in the districts or municipalities in which they are employed.

These employees and officials may not be assembled for military training.

Article 163

The reduction of the strength of the German military forces as provided for in Article 160 may be effected gradually in the following manner :

Within three months from the coming into force of the present Treaty the total number of effectives must be reduced to 200,000 and the number of units must not exceed twice the number of those laid down in Article 160.

At the expiration of this period, and at the end of each subsequent period of three months, a Conference of military experts of the Principal Allied and Associated Powers will fix the reductions to be made in the ensuing three months, so that by March 31st, 1920, at the latest, the total number of German effectives does not exceed the maximum number of 100,000 men laid down in Article 160. In these successive reductions the same ratio between the number of officers and of men, and between the various kinds of units, shall be maintained as is laid down in that Article.

APPENDIX XXI

CHAPTER II

ARMAMENT, MUNITIONS AND MATERIAL

Article 164

Up till the time at which Germany is admitted as a member of the League of Nations the German Army must not possess an armament greater than the amounts fixed in Table No. II annexed to this Section, with the exception of an optional increase not exceeding one twenty-fifth part for small arms and one-fiftieth part for guns, which shall be exclusively used to provide for such eventual replacements as may be necessary.

Germany agrees that after she has become a member of the League of Nations the armaments fixed in the said Table shall remain in force until they are modified by the Council of the League. Furthermore she hereby agrees strictly to observe the decisions of the Council of the League on this subject.

Article 165

The maximum number of guns, machine guns, trench-mortars, rifles and the amount of ammunition and equipment which Germany is allowed to maintain during the period between the coming into force of the present Treaty and the date of March 31st, 1920, referred to in Article 160, shall bear the same proportion to the amount authorized in Table No. III annexed to this Section as the strength of the German Army as reduced from time to time in accordance with Article 163 bears to the strength permitted under Article 160.

Article 166

At the date of March 31st, 1920, the stock of munitions which the German Army may have at its disposal shall not exceed the amounts fixed in Table No. III annexed to this Section.

Within the same period the German Government will store these stocks at points to be notified to the Governments of the Principal Allied and Associated Powers. The German Government is forbidden to establish any other stocks, depots or reserves of munitions.

Article 167

The number and calibre of the guns constituting at the date of the coming into force of the present Treaty the armament of the fortified works, fortresses, and any land or coast forts which Germany is allowed to retain must be notified immediately by the German Government to the Governments of the Principal Allied and Associated Powers, and will constitute maximum amounts which may not be exceeded.

Within two months from the coming into force of the present Treaty, the maximum stock of ammunition for these guns will be reduced to, and maintained at, the following uniform rates : fifteen hundred rounds per piece for those the calibre of which is 10·5 cm. and under ; five hundred rounds per piece for those of higher calibre.

Article 168

The manufacture of arms, munitions, or any war material, shall only be carried out in factories or works the location of which shall be communicated to and approved by the Governments of the Principal Allied and Associated Powers, and the number of which they retain the right to restrict.

Within three months from the coming into force of the present Treaty, all other establishments for the manufacture, preparation, storage or design of arms, munitions, or any war material whatever shall be closed down. The same applies to all arsenals except those used as depots for the authorized stocks of munitions. Within the same period the personnel of these arsenals will be dismissed.

Article 169

Within two months from the coming into force of the present Treaty German arms, munitions and war material, including anti-aircraft material, existing in Germany in excess of the quantities allowed, must be surrendered to the Governments of the Principal Allied and Associated Powers to be destroyed or rendered useless. This will also apply to any special plant intended for the manufacture of military material, except such as may be recognized as necessary for equipping the authorized strength of the German Army.

The surrender in question will be effected at such points in German territory as may be selected by the said Governments.

Within the same period arms, munitions and war material, including anti-aircraft material, of origin other than German, in whatever state they may be, will be delivered to the said Governments, who will decide as to their disposal.

Arms and munitions which on account of the successive reductions in the strength of the German Army become in excess of the amounts authorized by Tables II and III annexed to this Section must be handed over in the manner laid down above within such periods as may be decided by the Conferences referred to in Article 163.

Article 170

Importation into Germany of arms, munitions and war material of every kind shall be strictly prohibited.

The same applies to the manufacture for, and export to, foreign countries of arms, munitions and war material of every kind.

Article 171

The use of asphyxiating, poisonous or other gases and all analogous liquids, materials or devices being prohibited, their manufacture and importation are strictly forbidden in Germany.

The same applies to materials specially intended for the manufacture, storage and use of the said products or devices.

The manufacture and the importation into Germany of armoured cars, tanks and all similar constructions suitable for use in war are also prohibited.

Article 172

Within a period of three months from the coming into force of the present Treaty, the German Government will disclose to the Governments of the principal Allied and Associated Powers the nature and mode of manufacture of all explosives, toxic substances or other like chemical preparations used by them in the war or prepared by them for the purpose of being so used.

CHAPTER III

RECRUITING AND MILITARY TRAINING

Article 173

Universal compulsory military service shall be abolished in Germany.

The German Army may only be constituted and recruited by means of voluntary enlistment.

Article 174

The period of enlistment for non-commissioned officers and privates must be twelve consecutive years.

The number of men discharged for any reason before the expiration of their term of enlistment must not exceed in any year five per cent. of the total effectives fixed by the second sub-paragraph of paragraph (1) of Article 160 of the present Treaty.

Article 175

The officers who are retained in the Army must undertake the obligation to serve in it up to the age of forty-five years at least.

Officers newly appointed must undertake to serve on the active list for twenty-five consecutive years at least.

Officers who have previously belonged to any formations whatever of the Army, and who are not retained in the units allowed to be maintained, must not take part in any military exercise whether theoretical or practical, and will not be under any military obligations whatever.

The number of officers discharged for any reason before the expiration of their term of service must not exceed in any year five per cent. of the total effectives of officers provided for in the third sub-paragraph of paragraph (1) of Article 160 of the present Treaty.

Article 176

On the expiration of two months from the coming into force of the present Treaty there must only exist in Germany the number of military schools which is absolutely indispensable for the recruitment of the officers of the units allowed. These schools will be exclusively intended for the recruitment of officers of each arm, in the proportion of one school per arm.

The number of students admitted to attend the courses of the said schools will be strictly in proportion to the vacancies to be filled in the cadres of officers. The students and the cadres will be reckoned in the effectives fixed by the second and third sub-paragraphs of paragraph (1) of Article 160 of the present Treaty.

Consequently, and during the period fixed above, all military academies or similar institutions in Germany, as well as the different military schools for officers, student officers (*Aspiranten*), cadets, non-commissioned officers or student non-commissioned officers (*Aspiranten*), other than the schools above provided for, will be abolished.

Article 177

Educational establishments, the universities, societies of discharged soldiers, shooting or touring clubs and, generally speaking, associations of every description, whatever be the age of their members, must not occupy themselves with any military matters.

In particular they will be forbidden to instruct or exercise their members, or to allow them to be instructed or exercised, in the profession or use of arms.

These societies, associations, educational establishments and universities must have no connection with the Ministries of War or any other military authority.

Article 178

All measures of mobilization or appertaining to mobilization are forbidden.

In no case must formations, administrative services or General Staffs include supplementary cadres.

Article 179

Germany agrees, from the coming into force of the present Treaty, not to accredit nor to send to any foreign country any military, naval or air mission, nor to allow any such mission to leave her territory, and Germany further agrees to take appropriate measures to prevent German nationals from leaving her territory to become enrolled in the Army, Navy or Air Service of any foreign Power, or to be attached to such Army, Navy or Air Service for the purpose of assisting in the military, naval or air training thereof, or otherwise for the purpose of giving military, naval or air instruction in any foreign country.

The Allied and Associated Powers agree, so far as they are concerned, from the coming into force of the present Treaty, not to enrol in nor to attach to their armies or naval or air forces any German national for the purpose of assisting in the military training of such armies, or naval or air forces, or otherwise to employ any such German national as military, naval or aeronautic instructor.

The present provision does not, however, affect the right of France to recruit for the Foreign Legion in accordance with French military laws and regulations.

CHAPTER IV

FORTIFICATIONS

Article 180

All fortified works, fortresses and field works situated in German territory to the west of a line drawn fifty kilometres to the east of the Rhine shall be disarmed and dismantled.

Within a period of two months from the coming into force of the present Treaty such of the above fortified works, fortresses and field works as are situated in territory not occupied by Allied and associated troops shall be disarmed, and within a further period of four months they shall be dismantled. Those which are situated in territory occupied by Allied and Associated troops shall be disarmed and dismantled within such periods as may be fixed by the Allied High Command.

The construction of any new fortification, whatever its nature and importance, is forbidden in the zone referred to in the first paragraph above.

The system of fortified works of the southern and eastern areas of Germany shall be maintained in its existing state.

APPENDIX XXII

DECLARATION BY THE GOVERNMENTS OF THE UNITED STATES OF AMERICA, GREAT BRITAIN AND FRANCE IN REGARD TO THE OCCUPATION OF THE RHINE PROVINCES

The Allied and Associated Powers did not insist on making the period of occupation last until the reparation clauses were completely executed, because they assumed that Germany would be obliged to give every proof of her goodwill and every necessary guarantee before the end of the fifteen years' time.

As the cost of occupation involves an equivalent reduction of the amount available for reparations, the Allied and Associated Powers stipulated, by Article 431 of the Treaty, that if before the end of the fifteen years' period Germany had fulfilled all her obligations under the Treaty, the troops of occupation should be immediately withdrawn.

If Germany, at an earlier date, has given proofs of her goodwill and satisfactory guarantees to assure the fulfilment of her obligations the Allied and Associated Powers concerned will be ready to come to an agreement between themselves for the earlier termination of the period of occupation.

Now and henceforward, in order to alleviate the burden of the Reparations Bill, they agree that as soon as the Allied and Associated Powers concerned are convinced that the conditions of disarmament by Germany are being satisfactorily fulfilled, the annual amount of the sums to be paid by Germany to cover the cost of occupation shall not exceed 240 million marks (gold). This provision can be modified if the Allied and Associated Powers agree as to the necessity of such modification.

16th June 1919

Woodrow Wilson
G. Clemenceau
D. Lloyd George

APPENDIX XXIII

THE RHINELAND AGREEMENT

between the UNITED STATES OF AMERICA, BELGIUM, the BRITISH EMPIRE and FRANCE, of the one part, and GERMANY, of the other part, with regard to the military occupation of the territories of the Rhine[1]

Article 1

In accordance with Article 428 and the following Articles of the Treaty of even date, the armed forces of the Allied and Associated Powers will continue in occupation of German territory (as such occupation is defined by Article 5 of the Armistice Convention of 11th November, 1918, as extended by Article 7 of the Additional Convention of 16th January, 1919), as a guarantee of the execution by Germany of the Treaty.

---

[1] Not ratified by the U.S.A.

No German troops, except prisoners of war in process of repatriation, shall be admitted to the occupied territories, even in transit ; but police forces of a strength to be determined by the Allied and Associated Powers may be maintained in these territories for the purpose of ensuring order.

Article 2

There shall be constituted a civilian body styled the Inter-Allied Rhineland High Commission, and hereinafter called the High Commission, which, except in so far as the Treaty may otherwise provide, shall be the supreme representative of the Allied and Associated Powers within the occupied territory. It shall consist of four members representing Belgium, France, Great Britain and the United States.

Article 3

(a) The High Commission shall have the power to issue ordinances so far as may be necessary for securing the maintenance, safety and requirements of the Allied and Associated forces. Such ordinances shall be published under the authority of the High Commission, and copies thereof shall be sent to each of the Allied and Associated Governments and also to the German Government.

When so published they shall have the force of law and shall be recognised as such by all the Allied and Associated military authorities and by the German civil authorities.

(b) The members of the High Commission shall enjoy diplomatic privileges and immunities.

(c) The German courts shall continue to exercise civil and criminal jurisdiction subject to the exceptions contained in paragraphs (d) and (e) below.

(d) The armed forces of the Allied and Associated Powers and the persons accompanying them, to whom the General Officers Commanding the Armies of Occupation shall have issued a revocable pass, and any persons employed by or in the service of such troops, shall be exclusively subject to the military law and jurisdiction of such forces.

(e) Any person who commits any offence against the persons or property of the armed forces of the Allied and Associated Powers may be made amenable to the military jurisdiction of the said forces.

Article 4

The German authorities, both in the occupied and in the unoccupied territories, shall, on the demand of any duly authorised military officer of the occupying forces, arrest and hand over to the nearest commander of the Allied or Associated troops any person charged with an offence who is amenable under paragraph (d) or paragraph (e) of Article 3 above to the military jurisdiction of the Allied or Associated Forces.

Article 5

The civil administration of the provinces (*Provinzen*), Government departments (*Regierungsbezirke*), Urban Circles (*Stadtkreise*), Rural Circles (*Landkreise*), and Communes (*Gemeinde*), shall remain in the hands of the German authorities, and the civil administration of these areas shall continue under German law and under the authority of the Central German Government, except in so far as it may be necessary for the High Commission by Ordinance under Article 3 to adapt that administration to the needs and circumstances of military occupation. It is understood that the German authorities shall be obliged, under penalty of removal, to conform to the ordinances issued in virtue of Article 3 above.

Article 6

The right to requisition in kind and to demand services in the manner laid down in the Hague Convention, 1907, shall be exercised by the Allied and Associated Armies of Occupation.

The charges for the requisitions effected in the zone of each Allied and Associated Army and the estimate of damage caused by the troops of occupation shall be determined by local Commissions composed in equal representation of German civilians appointed by the German civil authorities and Allied or Associated military officers, and presided over by some person appointed by the High Commission.

The German Government shall continue to be responsible for the cost of maintenance of the troops of occupation under the conditions fixed by the Treaty. The German Government shall also be responsible for the costs and expenses of the High Commission, and for its housing. Suitable premises for the housing of the High Commission shall be selected after consultation with the German Government.

Article 7

The Allied and Associated troops shall continue undisturbed in possession of any premises at present occupied by them, subject to the provision of Article 8 (b) below.

Article 8

(a) The German Government shall undertake, moreover, to place at the disposal of the Allied and Associated troops and to maintain in good state of repair all the military establishments required for the said troops, with the necessary furniture, heating and lighting, in accordance with the regulations concerning these matters in force in the various armies concerned. These shall include accommodation for officers and men, guard-rooms, offices, administrative, regimental and staff headquarters, workshops, store-rooms, hospitals, laundries, regimental schools, riding schools, stables, training grounds and rifle and artillery ranges, aviation grounds, grazing grounds, warehouses for supplies and grounds for military manoeuvres, also theatre and cinema premises, and reasonable facilities for sport and for recreation grounds for the troops.

(b) Private soldiers and non-commissioned officers shall be accommodated in barracks, and shall not be billeted on the inhabitants, except in cases of exceptional emergency.

In the event of the existing military establishments being insufficient or not being considered suitable, the Allied and Associated troops may take possession of any other public or private establishment with its personnel, suitable for those purposes, or, if there are no such suitable premises, they may require the construction of new barracks.

Civilian and military officers and their families may be billeted on the inhabitants in accordance with the billeting regulations in force in each army.

Article 9

No German direct taxes or duties will be payable by the High Commission, the Allied and Associated Armies or their personnel.

Food supplies, arms, clothing, equipment and provisions of all kind for the use of the Allied and Associated Armies, or addressed to the military authorities, or to the High Commission, or to canteens and officers' messes, shall be transported free of charge and free of all import duties of any kind.

Article 10

The personnel employed on all means of communication (railways, railroads and tramways of all kinds, waterways (including the Rhine), roads and rivers), shall obey any orders given by, or on behalf of, the Commander-in-Chief of the Allied and Associated Armies for military purposes.

All the material and all the civil personnel necessary for the maintenance and working of all means of communication must be kept intact on all such means of communication in the occupied territory.

The transport on the railways of troops or individual soldiers or officers, on duty or furnished with a warrant, will be effected without payment.

Article 11

The Armies of Occupation may continue to use for military purposes all existing telegraphic and telephonic installations.

The Armies of Occupation shall also have the right to continue to install and use military telegraph and telephone lines, wireless stations and all other similar means of communication which may appear to them expedient. For this purpose, subject to the approval of the High Commission, they may enter upon and occupy any land, whether public or private.

The personnel of the public telegraph and telephone services shall continue to obey the orders of the Commander-in-Chief of the Allied and Associated Armies given for military purposes.

Telegrams and messages to or from the Allied and Associated authorities and the High Commission and of an official nature shall be entitled to priority over all other communications and shall be despatched free of charge. The Allied and Associated military authorities shall have the right to supervise the order in which such communications are transmitted.

No wireless telegraphy installations shall be allowed to be erected by the authorities or by the inhabitants of the occupied territory without previous authorisation by the Allied and Associated military authorities.

Article 12

The personnel of the postal services shall obey any orders given by or on behalf of the Commander-in-Chief of the Allied and Associated Armies for military purposes. The public postal service shall continue to be carried out by the German authorities, but this shall not in any way affect the retention of the military postal services organised by the Armies of Occupation, who shall have the right to use all existing postal routes for military requirements.

The said Armies shall have the right to run postal wagons with all necessary personnel on all existing postal routes.

The German Government shall transmit free of charge and without examination letters and parcels which may be entrusted to its post offices by or for the Armies of Occupation or by or for the High Commission ; and shall be responsible for the value of any letters or parcels lost.

Article 13

The High Commission shall have the power, whenever they think it necessary, to declare a state of siege in any part of the territory or in the whole of it. Upon such declaration the military authorities shall have the powers provided in the German Imperial Law of May 30th, 1892.

In case of emergency, where public order is disturbed or threatened in any district, the local military authorities shall have the power to take such temporary measures as may be necessary for restoring order. In such case the military authorities shall report the facts to the High Commission.

Done at Versailles, the twenty-eighth day of June, One thousand nine hundred and nineteen.

APPENDIX XXIV

ORDINANCES OF THE INTER-ALLIED RHINELAND HIGH COMMISSION

ORDINANCE No. 1

ORDINANCE OF THE INTER-ALLIED RHINELAND HIGH COMMISSION REGARDING THE LEGISLATIVE POWER OF THE HIGH COMMISSION, THE ORDERS OF THE MILITARY AUTHORITIES, AND THE OPERATION OF GERMAN LAWS AND REGULATIONS IN THE OCCUPIED TERRITORIES

Whereas by virtue of the Agreement, dated June 28th, 1919, annexed to the Treaty of Peace, it is the duty of the Inter-Allied High Commission to secure the maintenance, safety and requirements of the Armies of Occupation, and the consequent preservation of public order, and that the Ordinances issued by it for this end are respected by all ;

And whereas the Agreement annexed to the Treaty of Peace has been ratified by the Parliaments or Governments of the Allied States and by the German Parliament :

The Inter-Allied High Commission hereby orders as follows :

PART I.—THE ORDINANCES OF THE HIGH COMMISSION

Article 1

The Ordinances of the High Commission shall have the force of law, and on publication shall be recognised as such by the Allied Authorities and by the German Authorities.

Article 2

The Ordinances of the High Commission shall be published in an official gazette of the Inter-Allied High Commission.

Article 3

An Ordinance of the High Commission shall come into effect on the day of its publication, unless it is otherwise expressly provided.

Article 4

The Inter-Allied High Commission, the Inter-Allied High Command, the Army Commands, and the competent German Authorities shall be responsible, in so far as they are severally concerned, for the execution of the Ordinances of the High Commission.

Article 5

Any German Authority disobeying any Ordinance of the High Commission may, in addition to being liable to the penalties provided for an offence against an Ordinance of the High Commission, be suspended or deprived of his office or expelled by decision of the High Commission.

PART II.—ORDERS OF THE MILITARY AUTHORITIES

Article 6

(i) It is the duty of all German Authorities and of all persons within the Occupied Territories to obey all orders, including orders of requisition, given by or on behalf of the Allied Military Authorities of the said territories, in pursuance of their lawful power, subject to the provisions of the Agreement annexed to the Treaty of Peace.

(ii) Any German Authority disobeying such orders may, in addition to being liable to the penalties provided for an offence against an Ordinance of the High Commission, be suspended or deprived of his office by decision of the High Commission.

PART III.—THE OPERATION OF GERMAN LAWS AND REGULATIONS IN THE OCCUPIED TERRITORIES

Article 7

German Imperial and State Laws or General Regulations not already actually in force throughout the Occupied Territories shall, previously to their coming into force in the Occupied Territories, be transmitted by the competent Authorities to the High Commission, who will examine them in order to ensure that no provision is contained therein of a nature likely to prejudice the maintenance, safety or requirements of the troops of occupation.

Article 8

The said Laws and Regulations shall come into force in the Occupied Territories ten days after they have been duly registered with the High Commission, provided always that no provisional or final veto has been pronounced against them by the High Commission.

The High Commission may subsequently order the suspension of any of the said Laws and Regulations.

The High Commission may, at the request of the German Government, order immediate application of any Law or Regulation as soon as it is published.

Article 9

The High Commission, when necessary, and after consultation with the competent German Authorities, shall examine the methods by which the said Laws and Regulations may be made to conform with the conditions set out in Article 7 above.

When necessary, the High Commission shall issue an Ordinance to modify, temporarily to suspend, or to prohibit the said Laws and Regulations.

Done at Coblence, this tenth day of January, 1920.

THE INTER-ALLIED HIGH COMMISSION.

ORDINANCE No. 2

ORDINANCE OF THE INTER-ALLIED RHINELAND HIGH COMMISSION REGARDING CRIMINAL AND CIVIL LAW

Whereas in virtue of the Agreement, dated June 28th, 1919, annexed to the Treaty of Peace, it is the duty of the Inter-Allied High Commission to secure the maintenance, safety and requirements of the Armies of Occupation and the consequent preservation of public order and that the Ordinances issued by it for this end are respected by all ;

And whereas the Agreement annexed to the Treaty of Peace has been ratified by the Parliaments or Governments of the Allied States and by the German Parliament.

The Inter-Allied High Commission hereby orders as follows :

PART I.—CRIMINAL JURISDICTION

Article 1

The armed forces of the Allies and the persons accompanying them, to whom the General Officers Commanding the Armies of Occupation shall have issued a pass revocable at their pleasure, and any persons employed by or in the service of such troops, shall be exclusively subject to the military law and jurisdiction of such forces.

Article 2

(1) Any person, other than those specified in Article 1, who contravenes any Ordinance of the High Commission, or commits any offence against the persons or property of the armed forces of the Allies may be made amenable to the military jurisdiction of the said forces.

(2) The High Commission reserves to itself the right to establish such Courts as may be considered necessary for the exercise of the jurisdiction given by the provisions of the Agreement annexed to the Treaty of Peace.

(3) The rules of procedure followed and the penalties awarded by the Military Courts shall be those provided by the laws of the Army concerned or by the Ordinances of the High Commission.

(4) In the case of German nationals and Allied nationals being jointly concerned in the commission of an offence, the competent tribunal shall always be that which would have been competent if the offence had been committed by Allied nationals alone.

(5) Nothing contained in this Ordinance shall be deemed to give Allied Military Courts or German Courts criminal jurisdiction over members of the High Commission or any person employed under the members of the High Commission or the families of such members or persons, unless such jurisdiction is expressly given by a specific order of the High Commission.

Article 3

The German Authorities, both in the Occupied and in Unoccupied Territories, shall, on the demand of any duly authorised military officer of the occupying forces, arrest and hand over to the nearest Commander of Allied troops any person charged with an offence, who is amenable under Article 1 or Article 2 above to the military jurisdiction of the Allied forces.

Article 4

(1) When the German Authorities have taken cognisance of the commission of an offence, or arrested an accused person, they shall immediately forward the papers in the case to the Allied Military Authorities who are competent to bring the matter before a Military Court.

If the Military Authorities decide to bring the case before a military court, they will inform the High Commission and will later acquaint it with the judgment pronounced.

If the Military Authorities decide to leave the case to the German judicial authorities, they will transmit the papers in the case to them. The German Court which takes cognisance of the case must within eight days of the notification of the return of the papers inform the Representative of the High Commission in the *Kreis* concerned of the judgment pronounced, or of the stage which the proceedings have reached.

A monthly return shall be made by the German judicial authorities to the High Commission showing the stages which all current cases have reached.

(2) The Military Authorities may also leave to the German Courts the trial of offences concerning which information has been lodged by the Allied police.

(3) The High Commission reserves to itself the right to decide as to the classes of such cases which may be sent to the Allied Military Courts.

It also reserves the right at any stage of a case to make any order transferring any such case to any other court.

Article 5

It is the duty of all members of the police force, whether Allied or German, to ensure the execution of the Ordinances of the High Commission. They shall collect evidence, present charges and arrest accused persons for offences against the Ordinances of the High Commission, according to the forms and conditions prescribed by their respective laws.

Article 6

Whenever persons are caught in the act, or in cases of urgency, or when proceedings are being taken before the Allied Military Courts, the Allied police shall have the powers of arrest and of search given in conformity with the forms and conditions laid down by their respective laws.

Article 7

In cases where under Article 4 above proceedings have been left to the German Courts, German procedure shall be followed.

Article 8

Notwithstanding any provisions to the contrary contained in German law, any Allied Court may cause any administrative or other documents, the production of which it deems necessary for the purpose of any enquiry or trial before it, to be produced before it.

Article 9

Unless it is forbidden by the national laws of the Military Court concerned, the amount of the fines imposed by, and the court fees paid into, the Military Courts and the Courts established by the High Commission, shall be placed to the credit of the Reparation account and shall be deducted from the payment due by the German Government.

Article 10

The High Commission may pardon any offender who has been sentenced, or commute or reduce any sentence which has been passed, by a German Court in exercise of jurisdiction conferred on it by an Ordinance of the High Commission.

Article 11

In respect of sentences which have been pronounced by a Military Court, the power of pardon, commutation or reduction shall be exercised in conformity with the laws and regulations of the nation concerned.

Article 12

All sentences of imprisonment passed by Allied Courts and all such sentences passed by German Courts for offences against the Ordinances of the High Commission shall be served in German prisons of the Occupied Territories, except as may be otherwise prescribed by the High Commission.

Article 13

The High Commission reserves to itself the right of supervision over German prisons for the purpose of ascertaining that the sentences, executed in conformity with Article 12, are being carried out in accordance with the judgment passed.

Article 14

The High Commission may, in special cases, or classes of cases, decide in which prison of the Occupied Territories the sentence shall be served.

PART II.—CIVIL JURISDICTION

Article 15

(1) German Courts shall continue to exercise their civil jurisdiction, except over the persons mentioned in Article 1 and in Clause 5 of Article 2 above.

(2) Notwithstanding anything contained in the Clause (1) above, civil actions brought by or against any of the persons referred to therein in their private capacity shall be tried before the German Courts according to German law ;

Provided that the High Commission may decide that any case or classes of cases covered by this clause shall, by reason of their character or the status of the persons named as parties, not be heard before the German Courts, but be tried by the Courts of the High Commission mentioned below, or disposed of in such other way as the High Commission may direct.

Article 16

(1) Every writ, summons or notice shall be accompanied by a certified translation in the language of the party served.

(2) Every writ shall be transmitted for service either to the High Commissioner of the nation concerned for the members of his staff or to their superior officer for members of the Allied forces, for Allied officials or for the families of either, or to the authority designated on this behalf by the High Commission in the *Kreis*.

Article 17

Any party to a suit brought in a German Court by virtue of the jurisdiction conferred by Clause 2 of Article 15 above who contends that his case is not covered by the provisions of the said clause may, by an application to the High Commission, object to the jurisdiction of the German Court, and the High Commission or any authority empowered by it on its behalf may hear and pass orders on such objection, and such order shall be binding on the German Court.

On being informed that such an application has been made to the High Commission, the German Court shall suspend proceedings until orders have been passed on the application.

Article 18

(1) There shall be set up in each zone of occupation one or more civil Courts which shall be entitled " High Commission Courts." Each such Court shall be composed of three members ; two shall be Allied nationals, one of whom shall be president of the Court ; the third shall be a German. All shall be learned in the law.

(2) The procedure of the High Commission Courts shall be as the Court may direct, subject to revision by the High Commission. If several Courts exist in the same zone the procedure shall be the same for all such Courts.

(3) It shall be the duty of these Courts to decide any civil cases referred to them under the provisions of the proviso to clause 2 of Article 15 above. Their jurisdiction within the area of the zone in which they shall have been established shall extend to the nationals of any occupying nation.

Article 19

(1) Any person referred to in Clause 2 of Article 15 above, who is a party to a civil proceeding in a German Court may, if he considers he has suffered injury from a miscarriage of justice on the part of the German Court, appeal from it to the High Commission Court specified in the immediately foregoing Article.

(2) The High Commission Court may either confirm the judgment which has been referred to it or remit the case for rehearing or pass final judgment itself.

(3) If the High Commission Court considers that the circumstances of the case justify it in so doing, it may inflict a fine not exceeding 10,000 marks upon any party who has frivolously or improperly appealed against the decision of the German Court.

Article 20

The High Commission reserves to itself the right at any stage of proceedings to make an order to transfer any case from one Court to another notwithstanding any previous decision given, and to decide questions of conflicting jurisdiction.

Article 21

When final judgment has been given by a German Court and execution has issued against the Allied party, a certified duplicate copy of the judgment shall be transmitted for execution to the High Commissioner of the nation concerned for the members of his staff, or to the appropriate Army Commander for members of the Allied forces, Allied officials or the families of either.

PART III.—OFFENCES RELATING TO THE OCCUPATION

Article 22

Except as otherwise provided any person committing an offence against an Ordinance of the High Commission shall, on conviction, be liable to a fine of not more than 10,000 marks and to imprisonment for not more than one year, or both.

Article 23

Any person, who, singly or in combination with others, shall attempt to commit, or who shall be accessory to the committing of an offence against an Ordinance of the High Commission shall, on conviction, be liable, except as may otherwise be provided, to the same penalties as the principal offender.

Article 24

Any person who :—

(a) Does violence to or assaults or wilfully obstructs in the execution of his duty any of the personnel of the Allied Armies or of the High Commission ;

(b) Wilfully damages, in a manner likely to prejudice the security of the troops of occupation, any building, road, railway, canal, bridge, telegraph or telephone line, water supplies or works or other work ;

shall, on conviction, be liable to the same penalties as are provided for such offences under the Military Law of the several Allied Armies in their respective zones.

Article 25

(1) No person shall by word, act or gesture conduct himself in a manner insulting to the members of the High Commission or to the persons attached thereto, or to the forces of occupation or to any member of such forces, or to the Military Colours or Insignia of the Allied Powers.

(2) All Germans of the Armed Military Forces, Police, Fire Brigades, Customs and Forestry Services shall, when in uniform, salute the Colours and Officers of the Allied Powers.

Article 26

Any person who commits or abets the commission of any act calculated to promote bad feeling, dissatisfaction, indiscipline or mutiny amongst the troops of occupation shall, on conviction, be liable to imprisonment for not more than five years.

Article 27

No person may acquire, sell or be in possession of war material, equipment or stores (including any article belonging to military canteens, clothing stores and regimental institutions) or any military property whatsoever, belonging to or intended for the troops of occupation, or to a member of such troops, except such as may be shown to have been lawfully obtained by him.

The burden of proving his title to the ownership of possession shall rest upon the person in possession of the property in question.

Article 28

No person shall supply by sale, gift or otherwise any alcoholic beverage or intoxicating or stupefying drug to members of the troops of occupation in contravention of regulations issued by the armies.

Upon a second conviction in such a case the Court, in addition to the ordinary penalties provided, may order the closing of the establishment in which the offence was committed for a period of not more than three months, provided that the responsibility of the owner has been established.

Article 29

All merchants, manufacturers and retailers, and, in general, all persons trading with the public, are forbidden to sell to any member of the Allied forces or to any Allied Official any commodity, merchandise or article of any sort whatsoever at a higher price than that which is usually paid by the German public.

Article 30

No person who is not a member of the Allied forces or employed under the High Commission shall wear a uniform or badge of the Allied Armies or of the High Commission or any colourable imitation thereof.

PART IV.—IMMUNITY AND CONTINUATION PROVISIONS

Article 31

(1) No judicial proceedings shall be instituted or continued and no punitive measures shall be taken against any person, firm or company in the Occupied Territories for any commercial, financial or banking operation which he or they may have carried out during the period of the Armistice with the expressed or implied permission of the Allied Authorities. The decision of the High Commission that any operation was carried out with such expressed or implied permission shall be final and conclusive upon all parties.

(2) No judicial proceedings shall be instituted or continued, and no punitive measures shall be taken, against any Allied banking firm or company, or against any member thereof, on the ground that such banking firm or company has not obtained registration, licence or authority in accordance with German laws and regulations. Provided that the above shall not apply to any such person, firm or company unless it shall have carried on business in the Occupied Territories during the period of the Armistice and shall have applied for registration, licence or authority before the expiry of two months from the date of the coming into force of the Treaty of Peace.

(3) Without the consent of the High Commission no judicial proceedings shall be instituted or continue and no punitive measures shall be taken against any person in the Occupied Territories for any administrative or political act done during the period of the Armistice. The decision of the High Commission that any act was of an administrative or political nature shall be final and conclusive upon all parties.

Article 32

No person deported by the Allied Military Authorities from the Occupied Territories during the period of the Armistice shall re-enter the Occupied Territories without permission of the High Commission granted after consultation with the Military Authorities of the Power in whose name the order of deportation has been made.

Article 33

Officials suspended or dismissed from their positions during the period of the Armistice by the Allied Military Authorities may not again take up their duties in the Occupied Territories without permission of the High Commission granted after consultation with the Military Authorities of the Power in whose name the order of suspension or dismissal has been made.

Article 34

All proceedings instituted by the occupying Military Authorities before the entry into force of the Treaty of Peace and of the Agreement annexed thereto, may be continued before the Courts seized therewith, notwithstanding the entry into force of the Treaty of Peace and the Agreement.

Article 35

Judgments and Orders made by the Military Courts before the entry into force of the Treaty of Peace, or in consequence of proceedings instituted as laid down above, shall be carried out, notwithstanding the entry into force of the Treaty of Peace and of the Agreement thereto annexed.

Done at Coblence, this tenth day of January, 1920.

THE INTER-ALLIED HIGH COMMISSION.

ORDINANCE No. 3

ORDINANCE OF THE INTER-ALLIED RHINELAND HIGH COMMISSION REGARDING THE MOVEMENT OF PERSONS; POSTAL, TELEGRAPHIC AND TELEPHONIC COMMUNICATION; THE PRESS; MEETINGS; THE POSSESSION OF AND TRADE IN ARMS AND AMMUNITION; AND SPORT

Whereas by virtue of the Agreement, dated June 28th, 1919, annexed to the Treaty of Peace, it is the duty of the Inter-Allied High Commission to secure the maintenance, safety and requirements of the Armies of Occupation and the consequent preservation of public order and that the Ordinances issued by it for this end are respected by all;

And whereas the Agreement annexed to the Treaty of Peace has been ratified by the Parliaments or Governments of the Allied States and by the German Parliament:

The Inter-Allied High Commission hereby orders as follows:

PART I.—THE MOVEMENT OF PERSONS
Article 1

Nothing in this part shall apply to the persons referred to in Article 1 and Clause 5 of Article 2 of the Ordinance regarding criminal and civil law.

Article 2

Every person over 14 years of age, of whatsoever nationality, having his legal domicile in the Occupied Rhineland Territories, shall provide himself with an identity card with a photograph attached, and endorsed under their responsibility by the competent German Authorities.

Article 3

Any person domiciled in Non-Occupied Germany may enter the Occupied Territories if he is provided with a similar identity card.

The identity cards must be produced whenever demanded by the Allied Authorities.

Article 4

Any person furnished with an identity card may move freely in and about any part of the Occupied Territories and between the Occupied Territories and Non-Occupied Germany.

Article 5

The entry into the Occupied Territories of persons other than those referred to in the immediately foregoing Article is subject to the following conditions:

(a) Any person of the nationality of the troops of occupation shall be free to enter the Occupied Territories if he holds a passport or safe conduct given or endorsed by his national authorities.

(b) German nationals coming from countries other than Germany and nationals of countries other than those of the troops of occupation who desire to enter the Occupied Territories shall provide themselves with passports given or endorsed by their national authorities. Such passports must, within two days after the arrival of the holder in the Occupied Territories, be submitted for endorsement to the competent German Authorities who will immediately inform the Representative of the High Commission in the *Kreis*. Such passports must be produced whenever demanded by the Allied Authorities.

Article 6

Departure from the Occupied Territories is unrestricted save for the regulations imposed by each country on the entry of persons within its limits.

Article 7

Every person travelling within the Occupied Territories shall obey the provisions of the German law on travellers. The responsible German Authorities shall, whenever required, produce the police registers for the inspection of the Allied Authorities.

Article 8

Any person who wishes to take up his residence in the Occupied Territories shall make an application in writing to the German Authorities of the locality in which he wishes to reside. Such Authorities may give the required permission and shall within three days communicate the decision reached to the Representative of the High Commission in the *Kreis*.

Article 9

No members of the German Military forces on the active list shall enter the Occupied Territories except upon special authorisation given by the Military Authorities of the zone where he wishes to stay. The permit shall state the number of days for which it is available. Such persons shall report within twenty-four hours of their arrival to the Representative of the High Commission in the *Kreis* in order to obtain an endorsement of their permit.

Article 10

If it appears to the High Commission that the presence of any person in the Occupied Territories is dangerous to the maintenance, safety or requirements of the troops of occupation, or to the interests of public order, the High Commission may make an order for the deportation of such person from the Occupied Territories, subject to such terms and conditions as may be contained in the order.

Any person who disobeys an order of deportation shall be liable on conviction to the penalties provided for an offence against an Ordinance of the High Commission.

PART II.—CONTROL OF TELEGRAPHIC AND TELEPHONIC COMMUNICATIONS

Article 11

(1) If such a course is necessary in the interests of public order or to secure the safety of the troops of occupation, the High Commission or any officer specially authorised in this behalf by the High Commission may, by order in writing, direct that any postal article or class or description of postal article in course of transmission shall be intercepted or detained and shall be disposed of in such manner as the High Commission may direct.

(2) A similar control may be exercised in respect to telegraphic or telephonic communications, or to any class or description of such messages.

Article 12

Telegraphic and telephonic communications between the Occupied Territories and Unoccupied Germany shall be effected only through offices or exchanges of which a list has been drawn up and communicated to the High Commission by the German Government.

PART III.—THE PRESS

Article 13

All newspapers, pamphlets or publications, all printed matter, all productions obtained by mechanical or chemical methods, intended for public distribution, all pictures with or without words, all music with words or explanations, and all cinematograph films of a nature to prejudice public order or endanger the security or the dignity of the High Commission or of the troops of occupation, are forbidden, and if published may be seized by order of the High Commission or, in case of emergency, by order of the Representative of the High Commission in the *Kreis*. In the case of a daily publication the Representative of the High Commission in the *Kreis* may order its suspension or exclusion from the Occupied Territories for three days.

The action taken will be reported immediately to the High Commission, who will pass orders on it. The High Commission may order that a journal be suspended or excluded from the Occupied Territories for a period not exceeding three months.

Article 14

In addition to such administrative action, proceedings may be taken against the authors, proprietors, editors or publishers of offending publications before the competent judicial authorities.

Article 15

No person shall sell, exhibit, hawk, or otherwise distribute forbidden publications or films. In addition to persons so offending being liable to the penalties provided for an offence against an Ordinance of the High Commission, copies of such publications and films found in the possession of such persons shall be immediately seized, and the High Commission may order the closing of any premises concerned for a period not exceeding three months.

PART IV.—MEETINGS

Article 16

No political meeting shall be held unless the organiser or organisers thereof shall have given notice in writing forty-eight hours before the day of the meeting to the Representative of the High Commission in the *Kreis*. The notice shall set out the object of the meeting and shall give the names of the organisers.

Article 17

(1) The Representative of the High Commission in the *Kreis* may be present in person or by representative.

(2) In cases where the discussion touches on subjects not in the notice submitted, or where disturbances endangering the public order may arise, the meeting may be dissolved by the Allied Representative present, and judicial proceedings may be taken against the organisers.

Article 18

The High Commission may prohibit the holding of political meetings or of any other meeting which it considers may endanger the security of the Allied Armies.

PART V.—THE POSSESSION OF AND TRADE IN ARMS AND AMMUNITION

Article 19

Nothing in this part shall apply to persons referred to in Article 1 and Clause 5 of Article 2 of the Ordinance regarding criminal and civil law.

Article 20

The possession of and traffic in arms of any nature (whether firearms or otherwise) and ammunition are strictly forbidden except as provided in the following Articles.

Any person contravening the terms of the above Clause shall on conviction be liable to the penalties provided for an offence against an Ordinance of the High Commission, and further to imprisonment for not more than two years.

In all such cases the arms and ammunition shall be confiscated.

Article 21

All members of the police force and customs and forestry services, lawfully appointed by the German Authorities, are authorised, when on duty, to carry arms and ammunition, subject to the conditions laid down by the High Commission. Certain classes of persons, such as private guards and watchmen of isolated buildings, who, by reason of the special duties they have to perform, should be armed, may be authorised by special decision of the High Commission to carry arms and ammunition, subject to the conditions laid down by the High Commission.

Article 22

(1) The possession and carrying of sporting arms and ammunition shall be authorised, subject to the conditions laid down in Part VI below.

(2) Traffic in sporting arms and ammunition shall be authorised subject to the following conditions :

Any person wishing to trade in sporting arms or to manufacture or sell ammunition shall make a declaration stating the class of arms and ammunition which he desires to deal in or manufacture, to the Representative of the High Commission in the *Kreis* in which he wishes to trade or manufacture. He shall make a classified return of the stocks of arms and ammunition he holds and shall keep a register of the goods he manufactures, buys and sells.

These registers shall be always open to inspection by the Representative of the High Commission in the *Kreis* and by the Allied Military Authorities who may determine if the size of the stock is justified by the sales and purchase detailed in the register.

Any person trading in arms and ammunition may be called upon to furnish to the High Commission a return detailing his sales and stock.

(3) Sporting arms shall only be sold to persons in possession of a gun licence, as laid down by Part VI below. Ammunition shall only be supplied to persons in possession of an ammunition card issued as laid down by Part VI below, and subject to the conditions specified on the said card.

(4) All registers and documents which are required to be maintained by the German law on the subject of the manufacture, sale or possession of explosives shall be always open to inspection by the Representatives of the High Commission and the Allied Military Authorities.

PART VI.—SPORT

Article 23

Nothing in this part shall apply to persons referred to in Article 1 and Clause 5 of Article 2 of the Ordinance regarding criminal and civil law.

Article 24

In addition to the game licences required by German law, any person desiring to shoot for sporting purposes shall obtain from the German Authorities a gun licence which specifies the number and class of weapons which he is authorised to carry.

Article 25

Any person desiring to shoot for sporting purposes shall apply for an ammunition card, which may be supplied him by the German Authorities on receipt of a statement showing the number of hectares over which he intends to shoot and the nature of the game to be shot. The card shall show the amount and nature of ammunition to which the holder is entitled, having regard to the importance of the shooting and the nature of the game.

Article 26

A duplicate of the gun licence and of the ammunition card shall be forwarded immediately to the Representative of the High Commission in the *Kreis*, who, in cases of abuse, may cancel the licence and card or may limit the number and quantity to be issued, and who may also order that arms in the possession of persons from whom gun licences have been withdrawn be confiscated.

Article 27

The gun licence and ammunition card shall be withdrawn from any person who has been deprived by German law of his game licence.

Done at Coblence, this tenth day of January, 1920.

THE INTER-ALLIED HIGH COMMISSION.

ORDINANCE No. 4

ORDINANCE OF THE INTER-ALLIED RHINELAND HIGH COMMISSION REGARDING THE ADMINISTRATION OF THE KEHL BRIDGEHEAD

The Inter-Allied High Commission hereby orders as follows :

Article 1

(1) The Ordinances of the High Commission shall not be in force in the Bridgehead of Kehl until they are applied thereto by a special order of the High Commission in this behalf.

(2) The High Commission reserves to itself the right to adopt any modifications in its Ordinance regarding the administration of this territory.

Done at Coblence, this tenth day of January, 1920.

THE INTER-ALLIED HIGH COMMISSION.

ORDINANCE No. 5

ORDINANCE OF THE INTER-ALLIED RHINELAND HIGH COMMISSION REGARDING THE SAFETY AND REQUIRE-MENTS OF THE ALLIED FORCES IN CASES OF INDUSTRIAL DISPUTES

Whereas by virtue of the Agreement, dated June 28, 1919, annexed to the Treaty of Peace, it is the duty of the Inter-Allied High Com-mission to secure the maintenance, safety and requirements of the Armies of Occupation and the consequent preservation of public order and that the Ordinances issued by it for this end are respected by all ;

And whereas the Agreement annexed to the Treaty of Peace has been ratified by the Parliaments or Governments of the Allied States and by the German Parliament ;

The Inter-Allied High Commission hereby orders as follows :

Article 1

(1) The provisions contained in this Ordinance shall apply only to strikes of persons employed in or about any steam railways, railway workshops, telegraphic, telephonic and postal services, coal mines, navigation, gas, electricity works and water works ; but the High Commission may at any time, by an order duly published, apply this Ordinance to any other undertaking which is necessary for the main-tenance, safety or requirements of the Armies of Occupation.

(2) In case of doubt whether any undertaking comes within the scope of Clause (1), a decision of the High Commission that it is of the nature mentioned in that clause shall be conclusive.

Article 2

(1) In the cases mentioned in the foregoing article no strike shall take place until the matter in dispute shall have been submitted for decision to the authorities prescribed by the German law on the subject of conciliation in industrial disputes.

(2) The Award of the Court of Conciliation shall be given within a period of one week, calculated from the date on which the demand for conciliation was received by the prescribed authority, and shall be submitted to the Representative of the High Commission of the district (*Bezirk*) in which the dispute arose, who shall transmit it immediately to the High Commission.

(3) Any party to an award made by the German Court of Conciliation may, within one week from the date of the award, appeal to the High Commission. Every such appeal must be heard by a Board of Conciliation appointed by the High Commission, consisting of a president and two members with four Germans as assessors, two of whom will represent the employers and two the employees. The decision of this Board of Conciliation shall be given within a period not exceeding one week from the date on which the Board was fully constituted.

(4) No strike may take place after conclusion of the conciliation proceedings prescribed in Clauses (1), (2) and (3) above, unless a formal written notice of the intention to strike has been given to the Representative of the High Commission mentioned in Clause (2), nor until the expiry of one week from the date of the receipt of such notice by the said Representative.

Article 3

The provisions of Article 2 shall apply equally to any lock-out by the employers of workmen employed in any undertaking of the nature described in Article 1.

Article 4

Where any strike has occurred in an undertaking to which this Ordinance does not apply, but to which it may be applied under the provisions of Article 1, the High Commission may forbid the continuance of such strike and direct all persons concerned to take the action prescribed in this Ordinance.

Article 5

Notwithstanding any provision of any existing German law, no German authority within the occupied territories shall have the power to declare that any conciliation award given under such law shall be final.

Done at Coblence, this tenth day of January, 1920.

THE INTER-ALLIED HIGH COMMISSION.

APPENDIX XXIV

INSTRUCTION No. 1

INSTRUCTION OF THE INTER-ALLIED RHINELAND HIGH COMMISSION REGARDING THE USE OF THE ALLIED FORCES IN THE OCCUPIED TERRITORIES FOR THE MAINTENANCE OF PUBLIC ORDER

In exercise of the powers under the Agreement annexed to the Treaty of Peace (Articles 1 and 13), and Whereas the maintenance of public order is the first duty of the German Police Authorities ;

The Inter-Allied High Commission hereby orders as follows :

1

In the first instance the German Authorities and the German Police Force are responsible for the maintenance of public order.

2

The use of the Allied Military Forces for the re-establishment of public order may, as a rule, only be ordered by the High Commission under the powers given the Military Authorities by Article 13 of the Agreement annexed to the Treaty of Peace.

3

Whenever the means of the German Police are insufficient to re-establish order, the chief of such Police or the responsible authority shall make application to the representative of the High Commission in the *Kreis* for the use of the Allied Military Forces in order to re-establish order. This request shall be in writing, dated and signed, and shall contain the reason for making the request.

4

The Representative of the High Commission shall forward this request with his opinion to the Military Authorities in charge of the Allied troops concerned.

5

The Commander of the Allied Forces responsible for the employment of his troops shall comply with the request made to him, subject to his right of referring the matter to his superior authorities and to the provisions of Clause 7 below.

6

When the Military Authorities agree to the request made to them, they will take over the entire maintenance of order, and all the German police forces in the district put under military authority will be under the exclusive orders of that authority.

7

(1) In case of emergency, where public order is disturbed or threatened in a district, the local Military Authorities shall have the power to take such temporary measures as may be necessary for restoring order. In such cases the Military Authorities shall report the facts to the High Commission.

(2) The Military Authorities shall decide whether at any time circumstances have arisen which render it desirable to request the High Commission to declare a general or local state of siege.

Done at Coblence, this tenth day of January, 1920.

THE INTER-ALLIED HIGH COMMISSION.

INSTRUCTION No. 2

INSTRUCTION REGARDING THE DUTIES OF GERMAN AUTHORITIES IN MATTERS OF SECURITY AND OF POLICE

Whereas, according to the terms of the Agreement annexed to the Treaty of Peace, the German Authorities are in control of the Administration of the Occupied Territories, and, further ;

Whereas it may be the duty of the Allied Troops to intervene in order to secure the maintenance of public order ;

And, whereas, in consequence, they are finally responsible for the actions of the German Administration ;

The Inter-Allied High Commission hereby directs as follows :

1

It shall be the duty of the German Administrative and Judicial Authorities of the *Gemeinde*, *Kreis*, *Bezirk* and *Provinz*, to report immediately to the Representative of the High Commission in the *Kreis*, *Bezirk* and *Provinz*, respectively, any information brought to their knowledge concerning public order, such as serious disturbances, strikes, industrial unrest, the state of the food supply, public meetings, popular feeling, political movements, elections, and any other matters which affect public order.

They shall report in good time to the above-mentioned Representatives the administrative acts, decisions or legal proceedings or arrests which are likely to affect public order.

Apart from the supply of information of an urgent nature, as laid down in paragraph 1 of this Instruction, the German Authorities shall supply on the 1st and 15th day of each month to the Representatives of the High Commission reports upon the foregoing subjects.

Done at Coblence, this tenth day of January, 1920.

The Inter-Allied High Commission.

INSTRUCTION No. 3

INSTRUCTION OF THE INTER-ALLIED RHINELAND HIGH COMMISSION REGARDING GERMAN PUBLIC OFFICIALS IN THE OCCUPIED TERRITORIES

The Inter-Allied High Commission hereby directs as follows :

1

The competent German Authorities shall forward to the local Representative of the High Commission, within 15 days of the promulgation of this Instruction, a classified return of the officials of all ranks who were on duty in the Occupied Territories at the date of the entry into force of the Treaty of Peace.

2

Whenever an official dies, resigns, goes on leave for a period of more than one month, or is dismissed or transferred, the fact shall be reported forthwith by the competent German Authority to the local Representative of the High Commission.

3

Whenever a new appointment, whether temporary or permanent, is made to an office, the fact shall be reported to the local Representative of the High Commission 15 days before the order of appointment takes effect. Provided that, in cases of urgency, provisional effect may, with the consent of the local Representative of the High Commission, be allowed to the order of appointment.

4

The " local competent Representative of the High Commission " is the Representative for the *Kreis*, in the case of reports relating to officials whose authority does not extend beyond the *Kreis*, and the Representative for the *Bezirk* in the case of reports relating to officials whose authority extends beyond the *Kreis* but not beyond the *Bezirk*. Reports relating to officials whose authority extends beyond the *Bezirk* shall be made to the Representative of the High Commission in the *Provinz*. Reports relating to officials whose authority extends to the area of a State or the whole of the Occupied Territories must be sent to the High Commission itself.

Done at Coblence, this tenth day of January, 1920.

THE INTER-ALLIED HIGH COMMISSION.

INSTRUCTION No. 4

INSTRUCTION REGARDING THE NOTIFICATION OF DISEASE IN THE OCCUPIED TERRITORIES

In exercise of the Powers under the Agreement annexed to the Treaty of Peace, and Whereas measures of sanitation greatly affect the security of the Troops of Occupation, and Whereas, consequently, it is important to supervise a strict exercise of the regulations in force ;

The Inter-Allied High Commission hereby directs as follows :

1

Every case of contagious or infectious disease shall be immediately reported by the German local authorities to the Representative of the High Commission in the *Kreis*, and, where one exists, to the Military Authority stationed in the locality.

2

The High Commission may appoint special officers to supervise the execution by the competent German Authorities of the German Sanitary Police Regulations, including those relating to prostitution and the prevention of venereal disease. These officers shall also see that the measures taken by the German Authorities are not designed to prejudice, and do not in practice affect, the dignity or the safety of the troops of occupation.

Done at Coblence, this tenth day of January, 1920.

THE INTER-ALLIED HIGH COMMISSION.

INSTRUCTION No. 5

INSTRUCTION REGARDING EXEMPTIONS FROM JURISDICTION OF COURTS

The Inter-Allied High Commission hereby directs as follows :

1

Pursuant to the proviso in Paragraph 2 of Article 15 of the Ordinance of the High Commission relating to Civil Jurisdiction, the High Commission announces its decision that, by reason of their character and status, the following shall be exempt from the jurisdiction of all Courts in Occupied German territory :

1. Four High Commissioners,
2. Four Deputy High Commissioners,
3. The General Officers of the Armies of Occupation.

Done at Coblence, this tenth day of January, 1920.

THE INTER-ALLIED HIGH COMMISSION.

APPENDIX XXV

ADMINISTRATIVE INSTRUCTIONS FOR THE MOVE OF A BRITISH FORCE TO UPPER SILESIA

1. The Force will leave Cologne for Upper Silesia (regulating station, Oppeln) during the first week in March ; probable date of departure of first train is the 3rd March.

2. The staff captain, an R.T.O., a supply officer, and an intelligence officer proceeded to Oppeln on 24th February to make arrangements for the reception, quartering, etc., of the troops. The detachment on arrival in Silesia will probably be distributed at Beuthen, Tarnowitz, Lublinitz, Rosenberg, Kreutzburg, with headquarters at Lublinitz.

TRANSPORTATION

3. All arrangements for provision of the necessary rolling stock and despatch of trains will be made by the A.D.G.T., who will issue time tables, information re the route, *haltes repas*, and instructions to be observed by the troops on the journey to all concerned. The actual details as to composition and loads on each train will be worked out by traffic in conjunction with Colonel Wauchope and his staff and directorates concerned. Attention is to be directed to the proper and efficient lighting and heating of rolling stock.

MAINTENANCE

4. The Force will be maintained in personnel, stores, supplies, etc., by means of maintenance trains which run ONCE weekly via Mayence (Bischoffshein) to Oppeln.

The O.C. Force will therefore forward his demands to G.H.Q. (" Q " Branch), British Army of the Rhine, who will co-ordinate and pass them at once to the necessary heads of departments and services for action.

SUPPLIES

5. A British supply depôt with 30 days' supplies will be established at Lublinitz.

Fresh meat can be purchased once a week locally, and frozen meat can be stored at Konigshutte.

Contracts for baking can be made at the towns mentioned in paragraph 2. Fuel is obtainable locally.

6. The following amount of rations will be loaded on each train, including forage :

(*a*) Five days' consumption for journey for every man and animal on the train (including one complete day loaded in the supply wagons of the train, for consumption on day after detrainment).

These rations will contain two days' fresh meat and three days fresh bread, and fuel for five days.

Note.—The journey Cologne to Oppeln is approximately three days.

(*b*) Ten days' rations in addition to (*a*).

7. Thirty days' bulk rations will be despatched to Lublinitz either with the troops or independently under a special guard. On arrival at destination they will be handed over by the O.C. Train to the Officer i/c Supply Depôt, who will receive instructions from the A.D.S. & T. as to issue and accounting.

8. Units will be responsible for drawing and loading the one day's rations to be conveyed on the supply wagons, vide paragraph 6 (*a*).

The A.D.S. & T. will be responsible for loading all the other rations mentioned in paragraphs 6 and 7, but at the loading at Eiffel Tor of the five days' journey rations (less the one on the supply wagons) and the ten days' rations mentioned in paragraph 6 (*b*) representatives of each unit will be present and will sign for these rations after completion of loading. The A.D.S. & T. will be responsible for sacking of the coal for the journey—25 cwts. per train.

9. The daily forage ration for the journey will contain a larger proportion of hay than the normal ration and will be made up as follows :—

			H.D.	*L.D.*	*Mules*
Hay	..	..	16½ lbs.	12½ lbs.	11¾ lbs.
Oats	..	..	5½ lbs.	3 lbs.	3 lbs.
Bran	..	..	4 lbs.	4 lbs.	2 lbs.

10. The man's daily ration including that for the journey will, until 31st March inclusive, be augmented by 4 oz. bread, ½ oz. milk and ¼ oz. cocoa.

A daily issue of rum for bona-fide rum-drinkers may be issued at the discretion of O.C. Force.

ORDNANCE

11. The scale of clothing and necessaries to accompany the troops will be the same as that on the Rhine, with the following additional articles :

Public Clothing

Two extra blankets, making a total of six per man.
One jerkin, leather, per man.
One pair gloves, lined, fingerless, per man, except M.T. drivers.
One pair shields, hand, per motor-cyclist.
Coats, sheepskin lined, 10 per cent. of strength, for use of sentries.
One cap, balaclava, per man.

Personal Clothing

An initial issue of one muffler and two vests, woollen, may be made to each man, and will be maintained out of the clothing allowance.

One month's reserve expendable stores will accompany each unit.

All articles of public clothing taken will be kept and accounted for distinct from those forming part of the personal issue.

ANIMALS

14. [1]Accommodation on the train for saddlery and horse gear, except nose-bags and water buckets, is to be found in trucks other than those provided for animals.

15. No oats will be fed for first 12 hours of journey.

16. Animals are to be tied up short in the trucks.

17. The A.D.G.T. will arrange to place ashes or sand in horse trucks to give foothold.

18. Particular attention is to be given to the efficient ventilation of horse trucks.

19. The door on side of running way of truck is to be kept locked.

20. Every facility for watering is to be taken advantage of.

21. Cooking, fires, naked lights and smoking in horse trucks is forbidden.

22. Sick or injured animals incapable of completing the journey will be removed from the train and handed over to the local authorities and receipt obtained. The D.A.D.V.S., Rhine Army, is to be notified of such handing over, with nature of complaint. He will then arrange for disposal.

23. Each horse truck is to be provided with a lantern to be supplied by the unit concerned.

24. Animals are to be tied to a break-rope to be furnished by the unit concerned ; spare breast-rope and head-ropes are also to be provided.

25. All animals are to be provided with horse-rugs.

---

[1] Paras. 12 and 13 are missing on the original.

REQUISITIONING

26. Requisitioning in the Plebiscite Area is only to take place in case of real emergency and then only to be resorted to under instructions from the High Commissioner.

In any event, the command of the Force will have no power to requisition.

CANTEENS

27. The N.A.A.F.I. will arrange with O.C. Force for the despatch of canteen stores with the Force and replenishment of same. The question of accounting for these stores and whether the actual sale of articles is carried out by N.A.A.F.I. or military personnel will also be mutually arranged.

LAUNDRY

28. Laundry and disinfecting arrangements will be made locally by O.C. Force.

MEDICAL

29. A Red Cross van to accommodate eight sick men is being provided on each train.

The D.D.M.S. will be responsible for seeing that these trucks are fitted out with essential stores and stoves and will arrange direct with the Chief Engineer and Traffic thereon.

30. Medical personnel with necessary medical equipment will travel on each train containing personnel.

31. Men who in the opinion of the medical authorities or C.O. of train are too sick to complete the railway journey will be sent to a German hospital, whence they will be returned to Cologne when fit to travel ; all cases of admission to German hospitals will be reported by wire to the D.D.M.S., Rhine Army, the report to include number, rank, name, unit, nature of case and designation of hospital receiving the patient or patients.

KITCHEN VAN

32. A kitchen van will be provided on each personnel train. Notes on train cooking are available and will be issued without demand by the D.A.D.A.P. & S.S. to each unit or part of unit proceeding to Silesia.

The equipment of these vans with cooking utensils, *vide* paragraph 2 of the Notes, and with water will be undertaken as follows :—

For trains conveying units provided by ⎱ Colonel-Commandant,
   the 1st Rhine Infantry Brigade. ⎰ 1st Rhine Infantry Bde.

For trains conveying all other units .. Colonel-Commandant,
                                       2nd Rhine Infantry Bde.

ENTRAINMENT

33. Except where otherwise stated above, the preparation of the Force for despatch to Silesia, together with their entrainment, will be undertaken by the O.C. formations, units and heads of administration services concerned. The responsibility of the O.C. Force, except as specially defined in the preceding paragraphs, commences after he or his representative is satisfied after taking over on entrainment.

POSTAL ARRANGEMENTS

34. A Field Post Office No. S.120 will be established at the Headquarters of the Force. The staff will consist of one N.C.O. and two men.

POSTAL COMMUNICATIONS

35. A daily service can be provided if the existing courier service between Oppeln and Berlin is run daily instead of weekly as at present. The present courier is provided by the Plebiscite Commission. It is suggested that the O.C. British Troops arrange with the British Commissioner to send a courier daily to Army Courier Office S.5 at Berlin. The courier should reach Berlin before 18·00 hours in time to connect the service leaving for Cologne the same night ; he should leave Berlin for Oppeln in the morning after the arrival of the mail from Cologne. All official letters and private correspondence could be sent by this route. Parcels will be sent by the route used for supplies.

ADDRESS

36. No change is necessary in the form of address used for correspondence for complete units. Detachments and individuals should have correspondence addressed as follows :—

> Name, rank and appointment........................
> Field Post Office S.120,
> British Forces in Germany.

Detachments and individuals will forward nominal rolls of personnel leaving for Silesia to the A.D.P.S., in order that correspondence may be re-directed from Cologne.

PERSONNEL

37. (i) The strength of details left behind in barracks will not exceed two officers and 30 other ranks.

(ii) Families of officers and other ranks will not proceed and may remain in their present billets.

(iii) Soldiers at present detached on army postal work in Cologne will not be relieved.

(iv) Chaplains will proceed under instructions to be issued by principal chaplains.

LEAVE

38. (i) Leave for the Plebiscite Force will cease on 1st March, 1921. Personnel may proceed on leave up to and including the ordinary leave train leaving Cologne midnight, 28th February/1st March, 1921.

(ii) No personnel need be recalled from leave unless the commanding officer considers their presence essential.

MILITARY POLICE

39. (i) One officer and 25 other ranks of the M.M.P. will accompany the Force. These will be detailed by the D.P.M.

COURT MARTIAL OFFICER

40. (i) A Court Martial Officer, to be detailed by D.J.A.G., will be attached to the Force Headquarters.

(ii) A warrant is being prepared to enable the Officer Commanding the British Forces in Silesia to convene General Courts Martial.

(iii) Soldiers sentenced to not less than 21 days' detention will be despatched under escort to the Bonner Wall Detention Barracks, Cologne.

RETURNS

41. (i) Battalions will forward to G.H.Q. "A" by 10.00 hours on Saturday, 26th February, 1921, a return showing the number of each battalion which are left behind in Cologne giving the reason in each case. This will take the place of the return called for under C.R., B.A.R. No. 5751/A, dated 23rd February, 1921.

(ii) As each unit leaves an entraining state will be forwarded to G.H.Q. "A" by brigade commanders and heads of directorates.

(iii) All personnel of the four battalions proceeding to Upper Silesia who return to Cologne from leave, hospital, etc., after departure of these battalions will rejoin their details. Officer i/c Details will report by wire daily at 09.00 hours to "A" Branch G.H.Q., repeating to brigade headquarters the numbers of officers and other ranks showing numbers in excess of the permanent details mentioned in paragraph 37 (ii).

Arrangements will then be made to send the temporary details by maintenance train to rejoin their units in Upper Silesia.

G.H.Q.,
British Army of the Rhine.
25.2.1921.
A.G.S.

APPENDIX XXVI
ORDINANCE
No. 71

REGARDING ESPIONAGE AND SIMILAR MATTERS

THE INTER-ALLIED RHINELAND HIGH COMMISSION
Pursuant to Article 5 of the Agreement annexed to the Treaty of Peace
HEREBY ORDERS AS FOLLOWS :
Article 1

If any person for any purpose prejudicial to the safety of the Armies of Occupation

(*a*) approaches, inspects, passes over or enters any place the access to which shall, by order duly published, be specially prohibited with a view to the security of the Armies of Occupation by a General Officer Commanding-in-Chief an Army of Occupation ; or

(*b*) makes any photograph, sketch, plan, model, map, or note or other document ; or

(*c*) obtains, collects, records, has in his possession, publishes or communicates to any other person any photograph, sketch, plan, model, map or note, or other document or information ; or

(*d*) engages in a conspiracy or holds communication with Powers other than those participating in the Occupation :

he shall be liable to imprisonment for life or for such term as the Court may determine.

Article 2

No person shall without the written permission of the Commander-in-Chief of the Zone take any photographic apparatus into any place the access to which shall be prohibited within the meaning of Article 1 (*a*).

Article 3

No person shall without the written permission of the Commander-in-Chief of the Zone erect or operate any wireless telegraph or wireless telephone apparatus or make, buy, sell or have in his possession or under his control any such apparatus or any apparatus intended to be used as a component part of such apparatus; and no person shall sell or dispose of any such apparatus to any person in the Occupied Territories who has not obtained such permission.

The foregoing provision shall in no case be deemed to exempt any person from compliance with the German laws and regulations on this subject.

Article 4

No person who is not a member of the Allied Forces or employed under the High Commission shall wear a uniform or badge of the Allied Armies or of the High Commission or any colourable imitation thereof.

Article 5

If any person

(*a*) forges, alters or tampers with any passport or any naval, military, air-force or other official pass, permit, certificate, licence or other document, or uses or has in his possession any such forged, altered or irregular document; or

(*b*) with intent to obtain any such passport, pass, permit, certificate, licence or other document, knowingly makes any false statement; or

(*c*) uses, or has in his possession or under his control, without lawful authority, any die, seal or stamp of any of the Allied and Associated Governments or of any diplomatic, civil, naval, military or air-force authority of any of the Allied and Associated States or of the High Commission, or any die, seal or stamp so nearly resembling any such die, seal or stamp as to be calculated to deceive; or counterfeits, manufactures or sells any such die, seal or stamp, or uses, or has in his possession or under his control, any such counterfeited die, seal or stamp:

he shall be guilty of an offence under this Ordinance and shall be liable to imprisonment for life or such other term as the Court may determine, or to a fine not exceeding 100,000 marks, or to both imprisonment and fine.

Article 6

Article 30 of Ordinance No. 2 is hereby cancelled.

Article 7

This Ordinance shall apply to the Kehl Bridgehead.

Article 8

This Ordinance shall become immediately operative.

Coblence, this twenty-sixth day of January, 1921.

THE INTER-ALLIED HIGH COMMISSION.

GENERAL INDEX

A

Abrahamson, Mr. (British Red Cross), 48

Acheson, Commr. Hon. P. G. E. C., R.N. (Rhine Flotilla), 102

Addison, Lieut.-Col. G. H. (Armistice Com.), 34, 41

Administrator, British, 194

Advance into Germany, direction, 11 ; orders, 12 ; Q.M.G's. instructions, 14 ; difficulties, 15 ; Foch's procedure order, 24 ; dispositions, 25 ; delays, 26 ; incidents, 27–29 ; crossing the frontier, 86–91

Adye, Major-Gen. Sir John (Armistice Com.), 34, 41

Agreement, Rhineland, 402

Aircraft, Sub-Commission at Spa, 41, 43

Airfield, 208, 242, 297

Air strength, 147, 208, 221, 242, 296

Albert, H.M. King of the Belgians, 7, 27

Alcohol, sale, 65, 68, 77, 260

Allen, Major-Gen. H. T. (C.-in-C. American Army of Occupation), 162, 168, 169, 183, 190, 191, 248

Allenstein plebiscite, 178–80

Ambassadors, Conference of, 199, 201, 212, 215, 243, 259, 268, 280, 283

American troops, return by British, 13, 27 ; Civil affairs officer, 113 ; army of occupation, 161–2 ; quit, 248 ; legal affairs, 306–7

Amnesty, 272, 285

Amusements, 118, 293

Anordnungen, 68, 76, 113, 136

Arbeitskommandos, 214, 216

Arbitration Courts, 133, 139

Armament, surrender of, 4, 10, 11 ; Sub-Commission at Spa, 41, 46. *See also* Control

Armies of occupation. *See* Occupation

Armistice, terms, 1–5, 327–34 ; Commission, *see* Commission, Armistice; standfast order, 9 ; training during, 13 ; first prolongation, 42, 56–9 ; second and third prolongations, 42-3, 356–9 ; infractions, 29, 30, 42, 56

Ashby, Mrs. Corbett, 209

Asser, Lieut.-Gen. Sir John (Commanding Clearing Up Army), 150, 154, 155, 157

Associations, German, 273, 277–9, 280, 296

Australian repatriation, 107–8

Aviation, concessions, 296

B

Baltic campaign, 214

Baring-Gould, Captain E. A. (Armistice Com.), 34

Bauer, Col. (German G.S.), 35

Beddy, Col. B. L. (B.A.R.), 310

Bedford, F. H., 314

Belfield, Gen. Sir Herbert (Prisoners of War), 48

Belgian Army, strength, 181, 227, 297 ; relations with, 308

Bellhouse, Lieut. S. (Armistice Com.), 34

Bethell, Major-Gen. H. K. (66th Div.), 9, 346 ; Col.-Comdt. 2nd Rhine Bde., 292

Bingen, incidents at, 303

Bingham, Major-Gen. Hon. F. R. (Mil. Cttee. of Control), 195 ; *quoted,* 199

Birch, Lieut.-Col. J. G. (Rhineland High Com.), 295

Birdwood, Gen. Sir William (Fifth Army), 9

Black *Reichswehr,* 214, 216, 259, 298

Blockade, 127, 129

Bonn, 91, 92

Bourdillon, Mr. F. B. (Foreign Office), 220

Boyd, Major-Gen. G. F. (Midland Div.), 146

Braithwaite, Lieut.-Gen. Sir Walter (IX. Corps), 86, 113, 146, 346

Briand, Monsieur A., 281, 285, 298, 312

Bridgeheads, Rhine, 1, 92 ; occupation, 94 ; instructions, 94–7 ; reconnoitring parties, 96 ; defence scheme, 100–1 ; alterations, 101–2 ; trains, 115

British Army of the Rhine. *See* Rhine, Army of

Brothels, 66, 75, 81, 120

Browne, Lieut.-Col. J. G. (14th Hrs.), 221, 224

Bruce, Br.-Gen. C. D., 48

Bruce-Williams, Major-Gen. H. (37th Div. and Fourth Army Area), 150, 154, 346

Buckland, Major-Gen. Sir Reginald (C.E., B.A.R.), 147

Buckle, Major-Gen. C. R. (C.R.A., B.A.R.), 147

Burstall, Major-Gen. Sir Henry (1st Cdn. Div.), 345

Butler, Lieut.-Gen. Sir Richard (III Corps), 345

Byng, Gen. Hon. Sir Julian (Third Army), 9

433

INDEX TO ARMS, FORMATIONS AND UNITS

441

Printed in the United Kingdom for Her Majesty's Stationery Office
Dd238894 C16 9/87 G3379 10170

BRITISH OCCUPIED AREA OF THE RHINELAND

DEC. 1918

BELGIAN AREA

NEUTRAL ZONE

II CORPS

CON. CORPS

VI CORPS

1st Cav. Div.

Witten

Essen · Bochum

Mülheim

Ruhrort · Duisburg

R. Ruhr

Ratingen

Düsseldorf

Retsholz

Grefrath

Wald

Hilden

Benrath Ohligs

Barmen

Eberfeld

Remscheid

Solingen

R. Wupper

Opladen

Wermelskirchen

Engelskirchen

Bensburg

Rösrath

Siegburg

Wahn

Mülheim

COLOGNE

Rieh · Kalk

Deutz

Brekendorf

Ehrenfeld · Frechen

Mabbelrath · Wödrath

Bruh

Knapsack

Niblar

R. Dhün

Grevenbroich

Bedburg

Bergheim · R. Erft

Buir

Blatzhem

Gymnich

Lechenich

Jülich

R. Rur (Roer)

To ROERMUND